Fodor's First Edition

Belgium and Luxembourg

The complete guide, thoroughly up-to-date

Packed with details that will make your trip

The must-see sights, off and on the beaten path

What to see, what to skip

Mix-and-match vacation itineraries

City strolls, countryside adventures

Smart lodging and dining options

Essential local do's and taboos

Transportation tips, distances, and directions

Key contacts, savvy travel tips

When to go, what to pack

Clear, accurate, easy-to-use maps

Fodor's Travel Publications • New York, Toronto, London, Sydney, Auckland
www.fodors.com

Fodor's Belgium and Luxembourg

EDITORS: Matt Lombardi, Holly S. Smith

Editorial Contributors: Jennifer Abramsohn, Leslie Adler, Nancy Coons, Matthew Davis, Eric Drosin, Ursula Fahy, Barbara Jacobs, Lea Lane, Katharine Mill, Stephen Roth, Michael Schiffer, Clare Thomson, Emily Wasserman, Wendy Wasserman, Sarah Wolff
Maps: David Lindroth Inc., Mapping Specialists, *cartographers*; Rebecca Baer, Robert Blake, *map editors*
Design: Fabrizio La Rocca, *creative director*; Guido Caroti, *art director*; Jolie Novak, *senior picture editor*; Melanie Marin, *photo researcher*
Cover Design: Pentagram
Production/Manufacturing: Robert B. Shields
Cover Photograph: Bob Krist

Copyright

First Edition

ISBN 0–679–00770–9

ISSN 1533–2225

Special Sales

Fodor's Travel Publications are available at special discounts for bulk purchases for sales promotions or premiums. Special editions, including personalized covers, excerpts of existing guides, and corporate imprints, can be created in large quantities for special needs. For more information, contact your local bookseller or write to Special Markets, Fodor's Travel Publications, 280 Park Avenue, New York, NY 10017. Inquiries from Canada should be directed to your local Canadian bookseller or sent to Random House of Canada, Ltd., Marketing Department, 2775 Matheson Boulevard East, Mississauga, Ontario L4W 4P7. Inquiries from the United Kingdom should be sent to Fodor's Travel Publications, 20 Vauxhall Bridge Road, London SW1V 2SA, England.

PRINTED IN THE UNITED STATES OF AMERICA

10 9 8 7 6 5 4 3 2 1

Important Tip

Although all prices, opening times, and other details in this book are based on information supplied to us at press time, changes occur all the time in the travel world, and Fodor's cannot accept responsibility for facts that become outdated or for inadvertent errors or omissions. So **always confirm information when it matters,** especially if you're making a detour to visit a specific place.

CONTENTS

ON THE ROAD WITH FODOR'S

EVERY TRIP is a significant trip. Acutely aware of that fact, we've pulled out all stops in preparing *Fodor's Belgium and Luxembourg*. To guide you in putting together your experience, we've created multiday itineraries and neighborhood walks. And to direct you to the places that are truly worth your time and money, we've rallied the team of endearingly picky know-it-alls we're pleased to call our writers. Having seen all corners of the regions they cover for us, they're real experts. If you knew them, you'd poll them for tips yourself.

Leslie Adler is a Brussels-based journalist with an international news organization. After living on both the East and West coasts and the Midwest of America, she moved to London in 1995, and to Brussels in 1998. She's written extensively about Belgium and the long-standing divide between the Dutch-speaking Flemish and French-speaking Walloons. "I love traveling and exploring new places, and living in Europe has allowed me to indulge that passion. As a journalist in Brussels, I continually find new challenges in trying to understand the Belgian mentality." For this book she contributed to the Brussels and Antwerp chapters.

Brussels native **Eric R. Drosin** has traveled throughout Europe, the United States, and Africa, but Belgium's appeal has never flagged. He worked as a copy editor at *The Wall Street Journal Europe* for five years before joining the Dow Jones Newswires Brussels bureau as a journalist covering E.U. agriculture, environment, and health and consumer safety issues. He lent his expertise to the Northeast Belgium chapter here.

After living for nearly 24 years in New York, **Ursula Fahy** moved to Belgium to be an editor at *The Wall Street Journal Europe*, all the time assuming that she'd soon return to the bright lights and hot dogs of her hometown. This certainty melted away as soon as she laid foot on the cobblestone streets of Antwerp (whose dining, lodging, and nightlife she covers for this book). First, she caught sight of Flemish femmes wrapped fashionably, strutting in and out of Rubens's house. Then she became hypnotized by the deafeningly different music ofAntwerp nightlife. Such youthful energy, in such a culturally rich city! Now the smell of sugar and dough wafting through the Grote Markt is enough to make her weep.

Barbara Jacobs, a Philadelphia native, first visited Belgium—her first taste of continental Europe—as a girl in 1967. She vowed to return, and 10 years later accepted a two-year assignment as a translator at the U.S. Embassy in Brussels. Before the two years had ended, Belgium had become her home, and she has lived there ever since. Through her Belgian husband, she has gained insight to the understated richness of the region's culture and humor. She shares her knowledge and appreciation of the heart of Europe in Smart Travel Tips A to Z.

London-born **Katharine Mill** moved to Belgium in 1998, having previously taught English at Bordeaux University, France, and completed her studies at Bristol University, England. A keen cyclist (and former coeditor of the official guide to the Tour de France), she was drawn by the country's reputation in the two-wheeled world. Now deputy editor of Brussels's English-language weekly magazine, *The Bulletin,* she thinks the capital of Europe has everything a city needs—yet remarkably few of the drawbacks. For this book she reviews the high points of its dining, lodging, and nightlife.

Lea Lane has been traveling to Belgium since the 1960s and marvels at how its historic charms have been preserved, despite increasing tourism. She enjoys not only Brugge and Gent—which she covers in this book, along with the rest of Flanders and the North Coast—but also Antwerp, and Brussels's lyrical art-nouveau architecture and great museums. Lea is a valued contributor to other Fodor's Gold Guides, including *Greece* and *Naples and the Amalfi Coast,* and has been a forum host at Fodors.com. She is currently a travel columnist and a TV travel correspondent, as well as an author of books on bed-and-breakfasts in New England and New York City. And all that fantasy travel has inspired her to coauthor a romance novel—set on a cruise ship far from Belgium.

Stephen Roth has always been restless: first with his feet, then with his pen. So, fresh out of college, he began travels that, over the last 25 years, have taken him all over Europe and into Asia. To stay alive, he used his one natural resource—the English language. Besides teaching English, he has regularly contributed to tourism and trade magazines. Like many people, he once thought that all you needed to know about Belgium came out of a beer bottle or a box of chocolates. Now, after three years in Brussels working in one of those many European institutions, and after countless weekend trips into the countryside, he has discovered a discreet richness that is as much atmospheric as monumental or natural. He shares his experiences in our Hainaut chapter.

Despite his fear of flying, **Michael Schiffer** has been traveling since he was in utero. He has lived in Geneva, Paris, London, Tokyo, New York, Los Angeles, Vermont, and Hawaii, and has traveled extensively throughout Asia, the Middle East, and Europe, including Luxembourg, which he covers here with Wendy Wasserman. He now lives in Washington, D.C., where he is a member of the legislative staff of U.S. Senator Dianne Feinstein (D-CA).

Emily Wasserman, an attorney, freelance travel writer specializing in Belgium, and former jazz club owner, lives with two cats, a dog, and a mammoth fig tree in Brooklyn, New York. She offers a "grand merci" to everyone who made her work on the Meuse and Ardennes chapter of this book so pleasurable.

Among other things, **Wendy Wasserman** has been a ranger for the National Park Service in Virginia, an educational consultant for the Smithsonian Institution in Washington, D.C., and manager of a bed-and-breakfast in Hawaii. Her passport took her to Belgium, Luxembourg, Vietnam, Cambodia, Thailand, Singapore, France, Italy, and Slovenia, before it was lost in Cuba. She contributed to the Luxembourg chapter with her husband, Michael Schiffer, and the Meuse and the Ardennes chapter with her sister, Emily Wasserman.

Don't Forget to Write

Keeping a travel guide fresh and up-to-date is a big job. So we love your feedback—positive and negative—and follow up on all suggestions. Contact the Belgium and Luxembourg editor at editors@fodors.com or c/o Fodor's, 280 Park Avenue, New York, NY 10017. And have a wonderful trip!

Karen Cure
Editorial Director

Belgium and Luxembourg

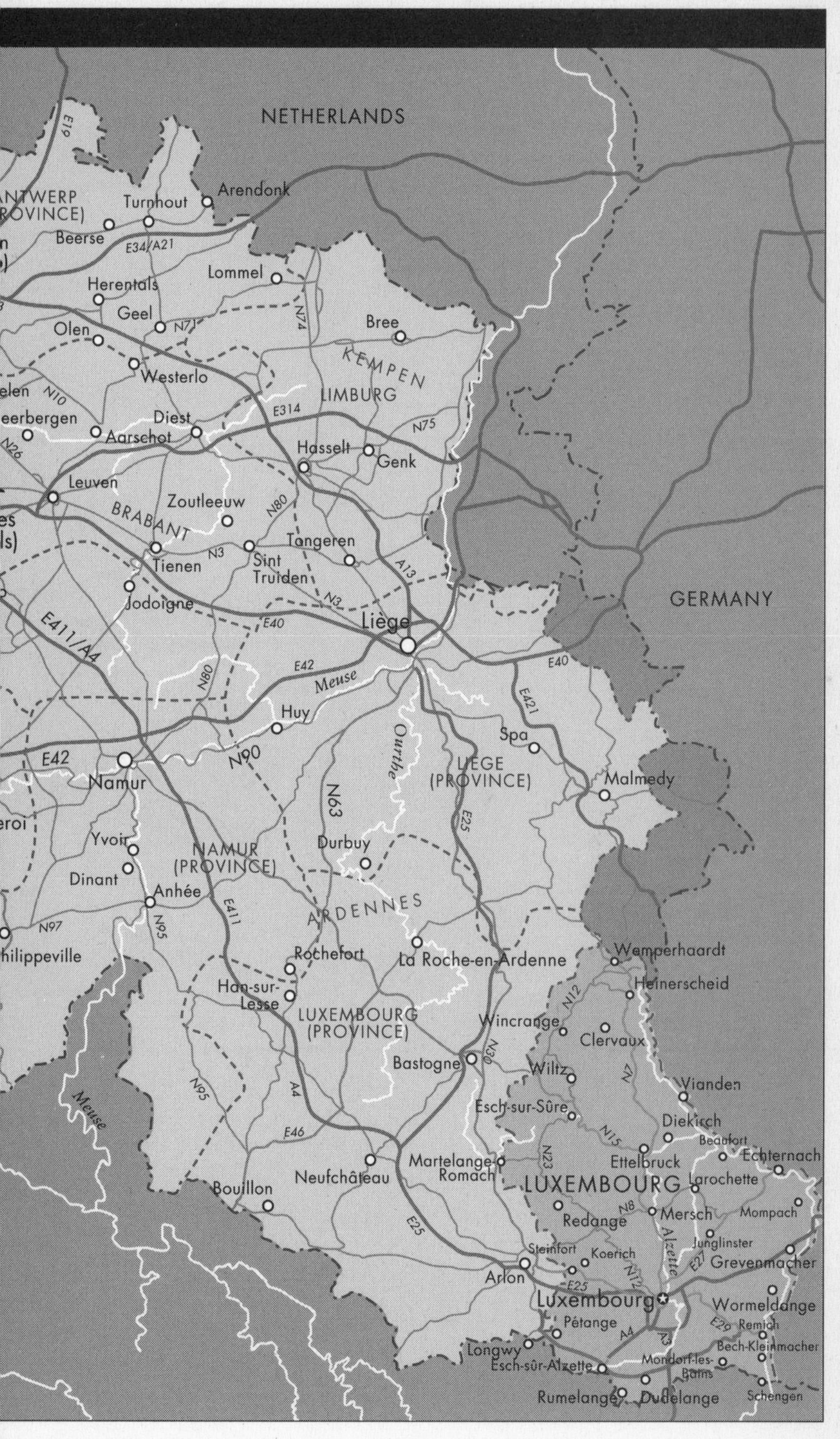

NETHERLANDS
GERMANY
NTWERP
OVINCE)
Turnhout
Arendonk
Beerse
E34/A21
E19
Lommel
Herentals
Geel
N71
N74
Bree
Olen
Westerlo
KEMPEN
LIMBURG
elen
N10
eerbergen
Diest
Aarschot
E314
N75
N26
Hasselt
Genk
Leuven
BRABANT
Zoutleeuw
N80
es
ls)
Tienen
N3
Sint
Truiden
Tongeren
A13
Jodoigne
E40
N3
Liège
E411/A4
E42
Meuse
N80
Huy
Ourthe
E421
Spa
E42
Namur
N90
N63
LIÈGE
(PROVINCE)
Malmedy
eroi
E25
Yvoir
NAMUR
(PROVINCE)
Durbuy
Dinant
Anhée
ARDENNES
N97
N95
E411
hilippeville
Rochefort
La Roche-en-Ardenne
Wemperhaardt
Heinerscheid
Han-sur-
Lesse
LUXEMBOURG
(PROVINCE)
Wincrange
N12
Clervaux
Bastogne
N30
Wiltz
N7
Meuse
N95
A4
Vianden
Esch-sur-Sûre
N15
Diekirch
Beaufort
E46
Ettelbruck
Echternach
Neufchâteau
Martelange
Romach
N23
LUXEMBOURG
Larochette
Bouillon
Redange
N8
Mersch
Mompach
E25
Alzette
Junglinster
Steinfort
Koerich
N12
E27
Grevenmacher
Arlon
E25
Luxembourg
Wormeldange
Pétange
A4
A3
E29
Remich
Longwy
Bech-Kleinmacher
Esch-sûr-Alzette
Mondorf-les-
Bains
Rumelange
Dudelange
Schengen

Europe

Reykjavík
ICELAND
NORWAY
Bergen
SCOTLAND
NORTHERN IRELAND
Edinburgh
Skagerrak
North Sea
Belfast
IRELAND
Irish Sea
DENMARK
Dublin
UNITED KINGDOM
WALES
Hamburg
ENGLAND
NETHERLANDS
Cardiff
Amsterdam
The Hague
London
Rotterdam
ATLANTIC OCEAN
English Channel
GERM
Brussels
Bonn
BELGIUM
Frankfurt
Paris
LUXEMBOURG
FRANCE
Zürich
Munich
Bern
SWITZERLAND
Lyon
LIECHTENSTEIN
Milan
Venice
Monte Carlo
Nice
Marseille
MONACO
PORTUGAL
ANDORRA
Florence
Madrid
Lisbon
Barcelona
Corsica
SPAIN
Sardinia
Seville
Granada
Balearic Islands
Tyrrhenian
Gibraltar
Mediterranean Sea
MOROCCO
ALGERIA
0
400 miles
TUNISIA
0
600 km

FINLAND
Gulf of Bothnia
Oslo
SWEDEN
Helsinki
Gulf of Finland
St. Petersburg
Tallinn
Stockholm
ESTONIA
Göteborg
Kattegat
Riga
LATVIA
Moscow
Copenhagen
LITHUANIA
Baltic Sea
Kaunas
RUSSIA
Vilnius
RUSSIA
Kaliningrad
Minsk
Berlin
POLAND
BELARUS
Warsaw
MANY
Kraków
Kiev
Prague
CZECH REPUBLIC
UKRAINE
SLOVAKIA
Vienna
Bratislava
Salzburg
Budapest
MOLDOVA
AUSTRIA
HUNGARY
Chişinău
SLOVENIA
Ljubljana
Zagreb
ROMANIA
CROATIA
Novi Sad
Bucharest
BOSNIA AND HERZEGOVINA
Belgrade
SERBIA
Black Sea
Adriatic Sea
Sarajevo
BULGARIA
Priština
Sofia
MONTENEGRO
Rome
Skopje
Podgorica
F.Y.R. of MACEDONIA
Istanbul
ITALY
Tiranë
Naples
ALBANIA
Ankara
TURKEY
GREECE
an Sea
Aegean Sea
Ionian Sea
Athens
Sicily
CYPRUS
MALTA
Crete
Mediterranean Sea

SMART TRAVEL TIPS A TO Z

Basic Information on Traveling in Belgium and Luxembourg, Savvy Tips to Make Your Trip a Breeze, and Companies and Organizations to Contact

AIR TRAVEL

BOOKING

When you book **look for nonstop flights** and **remember that "direct" flights stop at least once.** Try to avoid connecting flights, which require a change of plane.

CARRIERS

When flying internationally, you must usually choose between a domestic carrier, the national flag carrier of the country, such as Sabena Airlines for Belgium, and a foreign carrier from a third country. There are no long-haul flights to Luxembourg, but there are flights from the United States to Luxembourg via London, Frankfurt, and Paris with British Airways, Lufthansa, and Air France, respectively. Smaller carriers are usually inexpensive, but do not fly daily and often do not fly year-round.

Sabena airlines has flights between Brussels and Luxembourg. Neither Belgium nor Luxembourg has domestic flights.

➤ MAJOR AIRLINES: **Air France** (☎ 800/237–2724). **American** (☎ 800/433–7300). **British Airways** (☎ 800/247–99297). **Continental** (☎ 800/344–6888). **Delta** (☎ 800/221–1212). **Sabena** (☎ 800/221–4750). **United** (☎ 800/241–6522).

➤ SMALLER AIRLINES: **City Bird** (☎ 888/248–9247). **Canada 3000** (☎ 888/226–3000). **Virgin Express** (☎ 0207/744–0004 in the U.K.; 02/752–0505 in Belgium).

CHECK-IN & BOARDING

Check-in for long-haul flights to and from Brussels two hours prior to departure. If you are flying within Europe, check-in time is one hour prior to departure. There is no curbside check-in at airports in Belgium or Luxembourg.

While in the check-in line, travelers flying from Brussels to the United States on U.S. carriers are asked a series of security questions regarding who packed the baggage, where it has been since it was packed, and if any third party has given you something to carry.

Assuming that not everyone with a ticket will show up, airlines routinely overbook planes. When everyone does, airlines ask for volunteers to give up their seats. In return these volunteers usually get a certificate for a free flight and are rebooked on the next flight out. If there are not enough volunteers, the airline must choose who will be denied boarding. The first to get bumped are passengers who checked in late and those flying on discounted tickets, so **get to the gate and check in as early as possible,** especially during peak periods.

Always **bring a government-issued photo I.D. to the airport.** You may be asked to show it before you are allowed to check in.

CUTTING COSTS

The least expensive airfares to Belgium and Luxembourg must usually be purchased in advance and are nonrefundable. It's smart to **call a number of airlines, and when you are quoted a good price, book it on the spot**—the same fare may not be available the next day. Always **check different routings** and look into using different airports. Travel agents, especially low-fare specialists (☞ Discounts & Deals, *below*), are helpful.

Consolidators are another good source. They buy tickets for scheduled international flights at reduced rates from the airlines, then sell them at prices that beat the best fare available directly from the airlines, usually without restrictions. Sometimes you can even get your money back if you need to return the ticket. Carefully read the fine print detailing penalties for changes and cancellations, and **confirm your consolidator reservation with the airline.**

If you wish to travel by air from Brussels to other European destinations, **ask about flights within Europe when you book your trans-Atlantic flight.** It is often less expensive to use the same carrier used for the transatlantic portion of your trip.

➤ CONSOLIDATORS: **Cheap Tickets** (☎ 800/377–1000). **Discount Airline Ticket Service** (☎ 800/576–1600). **Unitravel** (☎ 800/325–2222). **Up & Away Travel** (☎ 212/889–2345). **World Travel Network** (☎ 800/409–6753).

ENJOYING THE FLIGHT

For more legroom, **request an emergency-aisle seat.** Don't sit in the row in front of the emergency aisle or in front of a bulkhead, where seats may not recline. If you have dietary concerns, **ask for special meals when booking or at least 48 hours prior to your flight.** These can be vegetarian, low-cholesterol, or kosher, for example. On long flights, try to maintain a normal routine, to help fight jetlag. At night **get some sleep.** By day **eat light meals, drink water** (not alcohol), and **move around the cabin** to stretch your legs.

Smoking is not permitted on long-haul flights to Brussels or other western European gateway cities. It is also banned on flights between Brussels and Luxembourg.

FLYING TIMES

Flying time to Belgium is about 7 hours from New York and 8½ hours from Chicago. Depending upon your routing and transit time, flights from Dallas last approximately 13 hours; flights from Los Angeles, approximately 17 hours; and flights from Sydney, approximately 24 hours. There are no nonstop flights to Luxembourg from the United States or Canada.

HOW TO COMPLAIN

If your baggage goes astray or your flight goes awry, complain right away. Most carriers require that you **file a claim immediately, at your arrival airport.**

➤ AIRLINE COMPLAINTS: U.S. Department of Transportation **Aviation Consumer Protection Division** (✉ C-75, Room 4107, Washington, DC 20590, ☎ 202/366–2220, airconsumer@ost.dot.gov, www.dot.gov/airconsumer). **Federal Aviation Administration Consumer Hotline** (☎ 800/322–7873).

RECONFIRMING

You are not required to reconfirm flights from Brussels or Luxembourg, but you should **reconfirm departure time by telephone if you have made your reservation considerably in advance,** as flight schedules are subject to change without notice.

AIRPORTS

The major airports serving Belgium and Luxembourg are **Brussels National Airport** at Zaventem and **Findel Airport** in Luxembourg-Ville. Brussels National Airport is far larger than Findel Airport and has nonstop flights from the United States and Canada. It also has a wider range of amenities such as airport hotels, rental car agencies, and travel agencies.

➤ AIRPORT INFORMATION: **Brussels National Airport** (☎ 02/753–3913). **Findel Airport** (☎ 352/47981).

DUTY-FREE SHOPPING

Brussels National Airport has a good selection of duty-free shops, including high-quality shoes and clothing, watches, cameras and electronics, perfume, alcohol, cigarettes, lace, and chocolates. The choice in chocolates is particularly extensive. In addition to the main duty-free shops, closer to the gates there are satellite shops with smaller selections of duty-free items. Savings on such luxury items are about 22%. Findel Airport does not have duty-free shopping.

BIKE TRAVEL

Travel by bicycle is popular and easy in Belgium and Luxembourg. Bike paths border Belgium's scenic canals and seaside roads. Many towns provide special lanes parallel to main streets for bicycles, and bicycle racks are available to the public.

Cycling in cities is less pleasant, as traffic is dense, bicycle paths are scarce, and city drivers are generally not as hospitable about sharing the road with cyclists.

You can **rent bicycles at Belgium's seaside resorts by the hour, half-day, or day,** with daily prices usually ranging from $15 to $20. If you are traveling in a group, consider another popular seaside rental option, a bicycle built for six peddlers.

You can also **rent bicycles as part of a train/bike package** at approximately 30 train stations in the country's most popular tourist destinations. The package includes one round-trip one-day ticket and bike rental at your destination station, with a total cost running from $10 to $20. Four stations also offer mountain bikes for $20–$25. You are required to make a deposit, which is reimbursed when you return your bicycle. A booklet called *B-Excursions,* available at major train stations, lists participating stations.

From April through October, youth hostels (☞ Hostels *under* Lodging *below*) in Luxembourg rent bicycles in conjunction with your hostel stay. You can also rent bicycles in Luxembourg for about $10 per day at rural inns and campsites.

Géocarte map makers produce bicycle guides with maps for nine Belgian regions. They are for sale in bookstores such as La Route de Jade, for about $10 per region. You can also pick up bicycle maps from national and local tourist information centers (☞ Visitor Information *below*).

➤ BIKE MAPS: **La Route de Jade** (✉ 116 rue de Stassart, Brussels, ☎ 02/ 512–9654).

➤ BIKE RENTALS: In Luxembourg, contact: **Auberge Eisléker Stuff** (✉ Derenbach, ☎ 99–45–73). **Auberge Zeimen** (✉ Kaundorf, ☎ 83–91–72). **Camping de la Sûre** (✉ Diekirch, ☎ 80–94–05). **Hotel de la Sûre** (✉ Esch-sur-Sûre, ☎ 83–91–10). **Luxembourg-Ville** (✉ Bisserwee 8, Luxembourg-Grund, ☎ 4796–2383). **Outdoor Center** (✉ 10 rue de la Sûre, Dillingen, ☎ 86–91–35). **Syndicat d'Initiative** (✉ 26-28 av. des Bains, Mondorf-les-Bains, ☎ 66–75–75). **Trisport** (✉ 31 route de Luxembourg, Echternach, ☎ 72–00–86). **Viandan** (✉ Train station, ☎ 84–93–87).

BIKES IN FLIGHT

Most airlines accommodate bikes as luggage, provided they are dismantled and boxed. For bike boxes, often free at bike shops, you'll pay about $5 from airlines (at least $100 for bike bags). International travelers can sometimes substitute a bike for a piece of checked luggage at no charge; otherwise, the cost is about $100. Domestic and Canadian airlines charge $25–$50.

BOAT & FERRY TRAVEL

FARES & SCHEDULES

Travel agencies in the United Kingdom and in Belgium sell ferry tickets and provide exact fares and schedules. Five-day excursion fares are significantly less expensive than last-minute bookings. They must be booked at least seven days in advance and must include a weekend.

➤ FROM THE U.K.: **Hoverspeed LTD** (☎ 08705/240–241) has services between Dover and Oostende, with up to eight daily round-trips. **P & O North Sea Ferries** (✉ King George Dock, Hedon Rd., Hull HU9 5QA, England, ☎ 01482/377–177) operates overnight ferry services once daily from Hull to Zeebrugge.

BUS TRAVEL

Bus service between Belgium and Luxembourg is minimal. *See* regional chapters for specific availability.

CLASSES

There is only one class on buses and smoking is prohibited.

CUTTING COSTS

If you're planning to travel extensively in Europe, it may make sense to invest in a **Eurolines Pass** for unlimited travel between 48 cities including Brussels.

FARES & SCHEDULES

Fares and schedules are available at the Eurolines sales office or at local travel agencies. As of spring 2000, a

30-day Eurolines Pass cost $350 ($280 if you're under 26).

➤ CARRIERS: **Eurolines** (✉ 52 Grosvenor Gardens, London SW1W 0AU, U.K., ☎ 0171/730–8235, FAX 0171/730–8721).

BUSINESS HOURS

BANKS & OFFICES

Banks in Belgium and Luxembourg are open from 9 until 4, Monday through Friday. Small local banks close between 12:30 and 2. Office hours are generally from 9 until 6. Most offices close for lunch between 12:30 and 2, although post offices do not close for lunch. Government offices are open from 9 until 5.

GAS STATIONS

Gas stations are generally open from 7 AM until 7 PM. In small villages, gas stations often close on Sunday and for lunch from 12:30 until 2. Gas stations on highways do not close for lunch and are usually open until midnight.

MUSEUMS & SIGHTS

Most museums in Belgium and Luxembourg are closed on Monday, Christmas Day, New Years Day, All Saints Day, and Armistice Day. Museum hours are generally from 10 until 5. National museums stay open during lunchtime. Smaller private museums may close between 12:30 and 2.

PHARMACIES

Most pharmacies are open until 7 on weekdays and are closed on weekends. For urgent prescriptions, closed pharmacies post signs indicating the nearest open pharmacies (*pharmaciens de guarde* in French or *dienstdoend apotekers* in Flemish). In cities where security is a problem, rather than keep the entire shop open, pharmacists use a small window for fulfilling prescriptions at night.

SHOPS

Except for souvenir shops in tourist areas, bakeries, and some delicatessens and flower shops, all shops are closed on Sunday. The rest of the week, shops are open from 10 until 6. Small neighborhood shops often close for lunch between 1 and 2. Bakeries, delicatessens, and other small grocery stores remain open until 7. Supermarkets are open from 9 until 8, and the larger ones remain open until 9 on Friday. Duty-free shops at Brussels National Airport are open daily from 6 AM until 9 PM.

CAMERAS & PHOTOGRAPHY

Interesting subjects to photograph include the art nouveau architecture in Brussels, Luxembourg's fortress, Brugge's lace makers, and the many castles throughout the region. For natural daylight photography, **remember that sunny days are rare in the winter** and that, even on a sunny day, daylight hours are very limited in December and January. In the summer, sunsets last long and are late in the day.

To be polite, **ask local people for permission** before taking their photos. They are usually honored to oblige and are also likely to volunteer as photographer for your group shot.

➤ PHOTO HELP: **Kodak Information Center** (☎ 800/242–2424). ***Kodak Guide to Shooting Great Travel Pictures,*** available in bookstores or from Fodor's Travel Publications (☎ 800/533–6478; $16.50 plus $5.50 shipping).

EQUIPMENT PRECAUTIONS

Always **keep your film and tape out of the sun.** Carry an extra supply of batteries, and **be prepared to turn on your camera or camcorder** to prove to security personnel that the device is real. Always **ask for hand inspection of film,** which becomes clouded after repeated exposure to airport X-ray machines, and **keep videotapes away from metal detectors.**

FILM & DEVELOPING

Film is available in photo shops, supermarkets, and souvenir shops. The most common brands found in Belgium and Luxembourg are Kodak, Agfa, and Fuji. A 36-exposure roll of film costs approximately $7. Some photo shops offer 24-hour development.

VIDEOS

The PAL system is standard in Belgium and Luxembourg. The cost of an hour-long video tape ranges from $8 to $15.

CAR RENTAL

The major car rental firms have booths at the airports. This is convenient, but the airports charge rental companies a fee that is passed on to customers, so you may want to rent from the downtown locations of rental firms. Consider also whether you want to get off a transatlantic flight and into an unfamiliar car in an unfamiliar city. Rental agencies are also at the Midi train station in Brussels.

Rental cars are European brands and range from economy, such as an Opel Corsa, to luxury, such as a Mercedes. It is also possible to rent minivans. Rates in Belgium and Luxembourg vary from company to company; daily rates for budget companies start at approximately $40 for an economy car including collision insurance. This does not include mileage, airport fee, and 17½% VAT tax. Weekly rates often include unlimited mileage.

➤ MAJOR AGENCIES: **Alamo** (☎ 800/522–9696; 020/8759–6200 in the U.K.). **Avis** (☎ 800/331–1084; 800/331–1084 in Canada; 02/9353–9000 in Australia; 09/525–1982 in New Zealand). **Budget** (☎ 800/527–0700; 0870/607–5000 in the U.K., through affiliate Europcar). **Dollar** (☎ 800/800–6000; 0124/622–0111 in the U.K., through affiliate Sixt Kenning; 02/9223–1444 in Australia). **Hertz** (☎ 800/654–3001; 800/263–0600 in Canada; 020/8897–2072 in the U.K.; 02/9669–2444 in Australia; 09/256–8690 in New Zealand). **National Car Rental** (☎ 800/227–7368; 020/8680–4800 in the U.K., where it is known as National Europe).

CUTTING COSTS

If you are traveling to Belgium and Luxembourg, **consider renting your car in Luxembourg,** which is far less expensive than in Belgium. It is usually less expensive to reserve your car before your departure, through your local travel agent. To get the best deal, **book through a travel agent who will shop around.**

Do **look into wholesalers,** companies that do not own fleets but rent in bulk from those that do and often offer better rates than traditional car-rental operations. Payment must be made before you leave home.

➤ WHOLESALERS: **Auto Europe** (☎ 207/842–2000 or 800/223–5555, FAX 800–235–6321, www.autoeurope.com). **Europe by Car** (☎ 212/581–3040 or 800/223–1516, FAX 212/246–1458, www.europebycar.com). **DER Travel Services** (✉ 9501 W. Devon Ave., Rosemont, IL 60018, ☎ 800/782–2424, FAX 800/282–7474 for information; 800/860–9944 for brochures, www.dertravel.com). **Kemwel Holiday Autos** (☎ 800/678–0678, FAX 914/825–3160, www.kemwel.com).

INSURANCE

When driving a rented car you are generally responsible for any damage to or loss of the vehicle. Before you rent see what coverage your personal auto-insurance policy and credit cards already provide.

Collision policies that car-rental companies sell for European rentals usually do not include stolen-vehicle coverage. Before you buy, check your existing policies—you may already be covered.

REQUIREMENTS & RESTRICTIONS

In Belgium and Luxembourg your own driver's license is acceptable. Your driver's license should be valid for at least one year. An International Driver's Permit is a good idea; it's available from the American or Canadian automobile association, and, in the United Kingdom, from the Automobile Association or Royal Automobile Club. These international permits are universally recognized, and having one in your wallet may save you a problem with the local authorities. You must also produce a national identity card or passport.

You must be at least 21 years old to rent cars from most agencies. Some agencies require renters to be 25.

SURCHARGES

Before you pick up a car in one city and leave it in another, **ask about drop-off charges or one-way service fees,** which can be substantial. Note, too, that some rental agencies charge extra if you return the car before the time specified in your contract. To avoid a hefty refueling fee, **fill the tank just before you turn in the car,** but be aware that gas stations near the rental outlet may overcharge.

CAR TRAVEL

Highway travel is easy in Belgium and Luxembourg. Highways are well lit and well maintained, and there are no tolls. Under good conditions, you should be able to travel on highways at an average of about 70 mi per hour.

AUTO CLUBS

➤ IN AUSTRALIA: **Australian Automobile Association** (☎ 02/6247–7311).

➤ IN CANADA: **Canadian Automobile Association** (CAA, ☎ 613/247–0117).

➤ IN NEW ZEALAND: **New Zealand Automobile Association** (☎ 09/377–4660).

➤ IN THE U.K.: **Automobile Association** (AA, ☎ 0990/500–600). **Royal Automobile Club** (RAC, ☎ 0990/722–722 for membership; 0345/121–345 for insurance).

➤ IN THE U.S.: **American Automobile Association** (☎ 800/564–6222).

FROM THE U.K.

From Calais, you can choose to drive along the coast via Lille and Tournai toward Gent and Antwerp; or toward Mons and Brussels; or toward Namur and Luxembourg.

EMERGENCY SERVICES

If you break down on the highway, **look for emergency telephones** located at regular intervals. The emergency telephones are connected to an emergency control room that can send a tow truck. It is also possible to take out an emergency automobile insurance that covers all of your expenses in case of a breakdown on the road.

➤ CONTACTS: **Europ Assistance** (☎ 02/533–7575). **Touring Secours** (☎ 02/233–2211).

GASOLINE

Gasoline stations are plentiful throughout Belgium and Luxembourg. Major credit cards are widely accepted. If you pay with cash and need a receipt, ask for a *reçu*. Leaded and unleaded gas and deisel fuel are available at all stations. Costs vary between 75¢ per liter for deisel fuel and $1 per liter for unleaded gas. Drivers normally pump their own gas, but full service is available at many stations. If your bank card is part of the EC network, you can pay with the Bancontact or Mister Cash machine 24 hours a day, seven days a week. For all other payments, including credit card payments, you must **pay an attendant during open hours.**

ROAD CONDITIONS

A network of well-maintained, well-lit superhighways and other roads covers Belgium and Luxembourg, making car travel convenient. There are no border controls between Belgium and Luxembourg.

Directions to superhighways are indicated on green signs that include the number of the highway and the direction in terms of destination city rather than "north," "south," "east," or "west."

If you are traveling in Belgium outside of Brussels, **be prepared to see city names in either French or Flemish,** depending upon whether you are in the south or the north of the country, respectively. So, you need to know that Antwerp is Antwerpen in Dutch and Anvers in French; likewise, Brugge is Bruges in French, and Brussels is Bruxelles in French and Brussel in Dutch; Gent is Gand in French. Even more confusing, Liège and Luik are the same place, as are Louvain and Leuven, and Namur and Namen. Yet more difficult is Mons (French) and Bergen (Dutch), or Tournai (French) and Doornik (Dutch). On the Brussels-Liège/Luik motorway, signs change language with alarming frequency as you crisscross the Wallonia-Flanders border. *Uitrit* is Dutch for exit.

Traffic can be heavy around the major cities, especially on the roads to southern Europe in late June and late July, when many Belgians begin their vacations, and on roads approaching the North Sea beaches on summer weekends. Summer road repair can also cause some traffic jams on highways and in town.

Rush hour traffic is worst from September until June. Peak rush hour traffic is from 7 AM to 9:30 AM and from 4 PM to 7:30 PM, Monday through Friday. You are most likely to encounter traffic jams as you travel into cities in the morning, out of cities in the afternoon, and on ring roads around major cities in the morning and in the afternoon.

City driving is challenging because of chronic double parking and lack of street-side parking. Beware of slick cobblestone streets in rainy weather.

ROAD MAPS

Michelin maps are regularly updated and are the best countrywide maps; they offer the advantage of being consistent with Michelin maps of other countries you may visit. They are available at news dealers and book shops. Free city maps are generally available at tourist offices, and more complete city guides can be bought in bookstores. Gas stations near borders generally sell a variety of more detailed maps.

RULES OF THE ROAD

Be sure to **observe speed limits.** On highways in Belgium and Luxembourg, the speed limit is 120 kph (74 mph), though the cruising speed is mostly about 140 kph (about 87 mph). The speed limits on other rural roads is 90 kph (55 mph) and 50 kph (30 mph) in urban areas. Speed limits are enforced, sometimes with hidden cameras, and speeding penalties are a hefty $100–$200.

For safe highway driving, go with the flow, stay in the right-hand lane unless you want to pass, and **make way for faster cars wanting to pass you.** Drivers in Belgium and Luxembourg can be impatient with slower drivers using the left lanes, which are considered strictly for passing. If you forget this rule of the road, drivers will remind you by flashing their high beams.

Fog can be a danger on highways, particularly in the south of Belgium and in Luxembourg. In such cases, it is obligatory to **use your fog lights.**

Use of seatbelts is compulsory in Belgium and Luxembourg, both in front and rear seats, and there are fines for disobeying. Turning right on a red light is not permitted.

Drinking and driving is prohibited. The maximum permissible alcohol level is 0.5 grams per liter. Breathalyzer controls are routine on highways on weekend nights and very common throughout Belgium and Luxembourg over holiday weekends, Christmas, and New Year's Eve. Drunk drivers are fined at least $100 and their cars are confiscated until the following day.

In cities and towns, **approach crossings with care.** Stop signs are few and far between. Instead, small triangles are painted on the road of the driver who must yield. Otherwise, priority is given to the driver coming from the right, and drivers in Belgium and Luxembourg exercise that priority fervently.

Illegally parked cars are ticketed, and the fine is approximately $25. If you park in a tow-away zone, you risk having your car towed, paying a fee of about $100, and receiving a traffic ticket.

THE CHANNEL TUNNEL

Short of flying, the "Chunnel" is the fastest way to cross the English Channel: 35 minutes from Folkestone to Calais, 60 minutes from motorway to motorway, or 3 hours from London's Waterloo Station to Paris's Gare du Nord.

➤ CAR TRANSPORT: **Le Shuttle** (☎ 0990/353–535 in the U.K.).

➤ PASSENGER SERVICE: In the U.K.: **Eurostar** (☎ 0990/186–186), **Inter-City Europe** (✉ Victoria Station, London, ☎ 0990/848–848 for credit-card bookings). In the U.S.: **BritRail Travel** (☎ 800/677–8585), **Rail Europe** (☎ 800/942–4866).

CHILDREN IN BELGIUM & LUXEMBOURG

Summer, when the days are long and the weather is pleasant, is the best time to visit Belgium and Luxembourg with children. Attractions range from beaches and zoos to castles and amusement parks. The text of this book identifies sights and attractions of special interest to children with a duckie .

The Belgian railway (☞ Train Travel, *below*) offers family excursions that include train travel and entrance to attractions throughout Belgium. Its booklet featuring such excursions, *B-Excursions,* is available at major train stations in Belgium.

If you are planning a stay of at least one week in one location, consider renting an apartment (☞ Apartment & Villa Rentals under Lodging, *below*) or staying in one of Belgium's Vacation Parks, which offer entertainment and themed activities for families with children.

If you are renting a car, don't forget to **arrange for a car seat** when you reserve.

In Belgium and Luxembourg, the National Tourist Offices (☞ Visitor Information, *below*) publish a free pamphlet listing vacation parks, holiday apartments, and houses. There is also a brochure for "rural holidays," in which you spend a few days on a farm and participate in the daily activities with your family.

FLYING

If your children are two or older, **ask about children's airfares.** Discounts are usually available for children under 12. As a general rule, infants under two not occupying a seat fly at greatly reduced fares or even for free. When booking, **confirm carry-on allowances** if you're traveling with infants. In general, for babies charged 10% of the adult fare you are allowed one carry-on bag and a collapsible stroller; if the flight is full, the stroller may have to be checked or you may be limited to less.

Experts agree that it's a good idea to use safety seats aloft for children weighing less than 40 pounds. Airlines set their own policies: U.S. carriers usually require that the child be ticketed, even if he or she is young enough to ride free, since the seats must be strapped into regular seats. Do **check your airline's policy about using safety seats during takeoff and landing.** And since safety seats are not allowed just everywhere in the plane, get your seat assignments early.

When reserving, **request children's meals or a freestanding bassinet** if you need them. But note that bulkhead seats, where you must sit to use the bassinet, may lack an overhead bin or storage space on the floor.

FOOD

Snack bars, cafeterias, and fast food restaurants are plentiful at tourist destinations, on the highway, and at train stations. **McDonald's** and **Pizza Hut** chains, as well as a local chain, **Quick,** which serves fare similar to McDonald's, can be found in cities, near highways, and at shopping malls. Throughout Belgium, roadside french fry stands (*Friterie* in French or *Frituur* in Flemish) offer servings of french fries with a selection of condiments. Another favorite snack is the famous Belgian waffle (*gaufres* in French, *waffels* in Flemish), which you can buy at waffle stands in cities. Waffles are considered an afternoon snack, so waffle stands do not generally open until noon.

Children are welcome at restaurants in tourist areas and roadside establishments. In cities, however, it is not very common for families with children to dine out in the evening, and restaurants are often not equipped with high chairs, children's menus, or activities to keep children occupied.

LODGING

Most hotels in Belgium and Luxembourg allow children under a certain age to stay in their parents' room at no extra charge, but others charge for them as extra adults; be sure to **find out the cutoff age for children's discounts.** Smaller hotels and inns have only a limited amount of rooms accommodating three people, and very few can accommodate four people in one room. Chain motels along highways usually provide cribs and cots, but most small downtown hotels do not. Hotels in Belgium and Luxembourg generally do not provide baby-sitters or children's programs.

At the Best Western hotels (☎ 800/528–1234) in Brussels, Oostende, and Brugge in Belgium and Luxembourg-

Ville, children under 12 may stay free when sharing a room with two paying adults. A maximum of five persons is allowed per room. Hilton hotels in Antwerp and Brussels allow one child of any age to stay free in his or her parents' room. In Luxembourg, the Inter-Continental hotel allows one child of any age to stay free in his or her parents' room.

➤ BEST CHOICES: **Best Western** (☎ 800/528–1234). **Hilton** (☎ 800/445–8667). **Inter-Continental** (☎ 800/327–0200).

SUPPLIES & EQUIPMENT

You can find a wide range of disposable diapers (*leiur* in Flemish, *lange* in French) in supermarkets throughout Belgium and Luxembourg in boxes of 12 to 36. Baby formula in powder form is sold at pharmacies only. Distilled water is sold in the households section of hypermarkets and supermarkets. Premixed liquid formula is not commonly used. The most common brands are Nestlè and Nutricia. It is difficult to find American brands, so **if you are traveling for a short period of time, buy your formula at home and take it with you.** The price of disposable diapers is about the same as in the United States. Formula is slightly more expensive.

TRANSPORTATION

You can obtain discounted train travel for children under 12. Children under six ride free in Belgium, and children under four ride free between Belgium and Luxembourg. Children do not have to sit on the lap of an adult.

Car seats and bassinets are not available on trains. Local trains do not have dining cars, and international trains do not provide special meals for children.

Car seats are obligatory for children under four years. If you rent a car with a car seat, **reserve your car seat in advance.**

COMPUTERS ON THE ROAD

If you're traveling with a laptop, **take a spare battery and an electrical-plug adapter with you,** as new batteries and replacement adapters are expensive and not all brands are available in Belgium and Luxembourg. Business hotels are equipped with jacks for computers. You can find cyber cafés in major cities.

CONSUMER PROTECTION

If you have purchased something you wish to return, **be prepared to show your receipt.** You must also provide a valid reason for the return.

Whenever shopping or buying travel services in Belgium or Luxembourg, **pay with a major credit card** so you can cancel payment or get reimbursed if there's a problem. If you're doing business with a particular company for the first time, **contact your local Better Business Bureau and the attorney generals' offices** in your own state and the company's home state, as well. Have any complaints been filed? Finally, if you're buying a package or tour, always **consider travel insurance** that includes default coverage (☞ Insurance, *below*).

➤ BBBS: **Council of Better Business Bureaus** (✉ 4200 Wilson Blvd., Suite 800, Arlington, VA 22203, ☎ 703/276–0100, FAX 703/525–8277 www.bbb.org).

CRUISE TRAVEL

Belgium's rivers and canals provide an interesting perspective for sightseeing. A variety of half-day and full-day cruises are available from May to September. Reservations are required.

➤ CRUISE LINES: **Brussels by Water** (✉ 2bis, quai des Péniches, 1000, Brussels, ☎ 322/203–6404). **Centraal Boekingskantoor Bootochten (CBB)** (✉ Heilig Hartlaan 30, 9300, Aalst, ☎ 3253/729–440).

CUSTOMS & DUTIES

When shopping, **keep receipts** for all purchases. Upon reentering the country, **be ready to show customs officials what you've bought.** If you feel a duty is incorrect or object to the way your clearance was handled, note the inspector's badge number and ask to see a supervisor. If the problem isn't resolved, write to the appropriate authorities, beginning with the port director at your point of entry.

IN AUSTRALIA

Australian residents who are 18 or older may bring home $A400 worth of souvenirs and gifts (including jewelry), 250 cigarettes or 250 grams of tobacco, and 1,125 ml of alcohol (including wine, beer, and spirits). Residents under 18 may bring back $A200 worth of goods. Prohibited items include meat products. Seeds, plants, and fruits need to be declared upon arrival.

➤ INFORMATION: **Australian Customs Service** (Regional Director, ✉ Box 8, Sydney, NSW 2001, ☎ 02/9213–2000, FAX 02/9213–4000).

IN BELGIUM & LUXEMBOURG

Americans and other non-EU members are allowed to bring in no more than 200 cigarettes, 50 cigars, 1 liter of spirits, 2 liters of wine or sparkling wine, 50 grams of perfume, and 25 liters of toilet water. **EU members** may bring in 800 cigarettes; 200 cigars; 10 liters of spirits; 90 liters of wine, of which 60 liters may be sparkling wine; 50 grams of perfume; and 25 liters of toilet water.

IN CANADA

Canadian residents who have been out of Canada for at least 7 days may bring home C$500 worth of goods duty-free. If you've been away less than 7 days but more than 48 hours, the duty-free allowance drops to C$200; if your trip lasts 24–48 hours, the allowance is C$50. You may not pool allowances with family members. Goods claimed under the C$500 exemption may follow you by mail; those claimed under the lesser exemptions must accompany you. Alcohol and tobacco products may be included in the 7-day and 48-hour exemptions but not in the 24-hour exemption. If you meet the age requirements of the province or territory through which you reenter Canada, you may bring in, duty-free, 1.14 liters (40 imperial ounces) of wine or liquor *or* 24 12-ounce cans or bottles of beer or ale. If you are 16 or older you may bring in, duty-free, 200 cigarettes and 50 cigars. Check ahead of time with Revenue Canada or the Department of Agriculture for policies regarding meat products, seeds, plants, and fruits.

You may send an unlimited number of gifts worth up to C$60 each duty-free to Canada. Label the package UNSOLICITED GIFT—VALUE UNDER $60. Alcohol and tobacco are excluded.

➤ INFORMATION: **Revenue Canada** (✉ 2265 St. Laurent Blvd. S, Ottawa, Ontario K1G 4K3, ☎ 613/993–0534; 800/461–9999 in Canada, FAX 613/957–8911, www.ccra-adrc.gc.ca).

IN NEW ZEALAND

Homeward-bound residents 17 or older may bring back $700 worth of souvenirs and gifts. Your duty-free allowance also includes 4.5 liters of wine or beer; one 1,125-ml bottle of spirits; and either 200 cigarettes, 250 grams of tobacco, 50 cigars, or a combination of the three up to 250 grams. Prohibited items include meat products, seeds, plants, and fruits.

➤ INFORMATION: **New Zealand Customs** (Custom House, ✉ 50 Anzac Ave., Box 29, Auckland, ☎ 09/359–6655, FAX 09/359–6732).

IN THE U.K.

If you are a U.K. resident and your journey was wholly within the European Union (EU), you won't have to pass through customs when you return to the United Kingdom. If you plan to bring back large quantities of alcohol or tobacco, check EU limits beforehand.

➤ INFORMATION: **HM Customs and Excise** (✉ Dorset House, Stamford St., Bromley, Kent BR1 1XX, ☎ 0171/202–4227).

IN THE U.S.

U.S. residents who have been out of the country for at least 48 hours (and who have not used the $400 allowance or any part of it in the past 30 days) may bring home $400 worth of foreign goods duty-free.

U.S. residents 21 and older may bring back 1 liter of alcohol duty-free. In addition, regardless of your age, you are allowed 200 cigarettes and 100 non-Cuban cigars. Antiques, which the U.S. Customs Service defines as objects more than 100 years old, enter duty-free, as do original works of art done entirely by hand, including paintings, drawings, and sculptures.

You may also send packages home duty-free: up to $200 worth of goods for personal use, with a limit of one parcel per addressee per day (except alcohol or tobacco products or perfume worth more than $5); label the package PERSONAL USE and attach a list of its contents and their retail value. Do not label the package UNSOLICITED GIFT or your duty-free exemption will drop to $100. Mailed items do not affect your duty-free allowance on your return.

➤ INFORMATION: **U.S. Customs Service** (✉ 1300 Pennsylvania Ave. NW, Washington, DC 20229, www.customs.gov; inquiries ☎ 202/354–1000; complaints c/o ✉ Office of Regulations and Rulings; registration of equipment c/o ✉ Resource Management, ☎ 202/927–0540).

DINING

Belgium and Luxembourg offer a wide variety of restaurants ranging from snack stands, cafés, and pubs to top-rated restaurants serving gourmet cuisine. The better restaurants are on a par with the most renowned in the world. Prices ranges are similar to those in France and in Great Britain. The restaurants we list throughout this book are the cream of the crop in each price category.

Most restaurants are open for lunch and dinner only. Restaurants and hotel pension packages serve hot three-course meals including a starter or soup, a main course, and dessert. A set-price, three-course menu for lunch (*déjeuner* in French, *middagmaal* in Flemish) is offered in many restaurants. Dinner (*dîner* in French, *avondmaal* in Flemish) menus are very similar to lunch menus. Diners are not commonly given a choice of vegetables or salad dressing.

Some large hotels serve buffet breakfast (*petit déjeuner* in French, *ontbijt* in Flemish) with cooked American fare. Smaller hotels and bed-and-breakfasts serve bread, rolls, butter, jam, and cheese with juice and coffee or tea and occasionally a soft-boiled egg.

Cafés and snack bars are open in the morning and serve coffee, tea, juice, and rolls, but they do not serve a full American-style breakfast. You can also order a quick sandwich lunch or light one-course meal at cafés, pubs, cafeterias, and snack bars.

MEALS & SPECIALTIES

Most of Belgium's and Luxembourg's restaurants feature Continental cuisine similar to that of France. Many restaurants, particularly those in the countryside, also offer hearty traditional fare. During hunting season, restaurants and country inns often feature a special hunter's menu including *sanglier* (wild boar) and *faisan* (pheasant).

If you enjoy tasting local specialities of Belgium, try *waterzooi,* which is a creamy chicken stew, or *carbonnades,* a beef stew cooked in beer. *Stoemp* is a filling mixture of mashed potatoes and vegetables. Belgian endive (*chicons* in French, *witloof* in Flemish) is usually cooked with ham, braised, and topped with a cheese gratin. A popular first course is tomato filled with tiny gray shrimp (*crevettes* in French, *garnaal* in Flemish), fresh from Belgium's North Sea. Complete your Belgian meal with *frites* (french fries), which Belgians proudly claim to have been invented not in France but in Belgium.

Luxembourg's local farms produce fresh pork, and its restaurants often feature pork products such as *jambon d'Ardennes* (cold ham with pickles and onions) or *choucroute* (pork with sauerkraut). *Truite* (fresh trout) fished from Luxembourg's rivers is a favorite at country inns and restaurants.

MEALTIMES

Breakfast is served in hotels from about 7 to 10. Lunch is served in restaurants from noon until 2, and dinner from 7 to 9. Pubs and cafés serve snacks until midnight. Many restaurants are closed on Sunday for dinner, and restaurants in cities often close on Saturday for lunch.

Unless otherwise noted, the restaurants listed in this guide are open daily for lunch and dinner.

PAYING

Major credit cards are accepted in most restaurants in Belgium and Luxembourg. Visa is the most widely accepted credit card. Smaller establishments occasionally do not accept American Express or Diners Club. Credit cards usually cannot be used for purchasing snacks at pubs and cafés. Do not rely on travelers checks for paying restaurant bills.

A 15% service charge is usually included in the cost of a meal. Nonetheless, it is customary to **round off the total,** adding a small amount for good service.

RESERVATIONS & DRESS

Reservations are always a good idea: we mention them only when they're essential or not accepted. Book as far ahead as you can, and confirm as soon as you arrive. We mention dress only when men are required to wear a jacket or a jacket and tie.

WINE, BEER, & SPIRITS

Belgium is a beer-lover's paradise. Artisanal breweries produce more than 400 types of beer, many of which are offered in Belgian pubs and cafés. Kriek, a fruit-flavored beer, is popular among Belgians. Duvel, a very strong dark beer, is another favorite. Some of Belgium's trappist monastaries still produce their own brews, such as Orval, Leffe, and Chimay. Popular mass-produced brands are Stella Artois and Maes.

Luxembourg's Moselle Valley produces inexpensive *Rivaner* and *Elbling* white wines. These and the more expensive *Auxerrois* can be tasted and bought at wineries. Luxembourg distilleries produce *quetsch* (plum liqueur) and *kirsch* (cherry liqueur).

Licenses are not required for sale of beer or wine in dining establishments. As a result, beer is served at virtually all restaurants, snack bars, pubs, and cafés, and wine is served at all restaurants and most other establishments. There is no legal minimum age for consumption of beer or wine. Sale of hard liquor does require a license, and the legal age for consumption of liquor is 18. The cost of beer and wine in dining establishments is very reasonable. Liquor and mixed cocktails are considerably more expensive.

DISABILITIES & ACCESSIBILITY

In Belgium and Luxembourg, hotels with facilities to accommodate guests with disabilities are identified in guides published by national and local tourist offices. Awareness of the sensitivities of people with disabilities is generally high but has not yet impacted on the language; the words *handicapé* (French) and *gehandicapt* (Dutch) are still commonly used. Visitors with disabilities should be aware that many streets in Belgium Luxembourg are cobblestone.

For information on facilities in Belgium, contact **Vlaamse Federatie voor Gehandicapten**. The **Luxembourg Ministry of Health** handles provisions for people with disabilities. Most trains and buses have special seats for riders with disabilities, and parking lots have spaces reserved for people with disabilities. Contact **Info–Handicap.**

➤ LOCAL RESOURCES: **Info–Handicap** (✉ Box 33, 5801, Hesperange, Luxembourg, ☎ 0352/366466). **Vlaamse Federatie voor Gehandicapten** (✉ 66 Grensstraat 1210, Brussels, ☎ 02/219–8800).

LODGING

The following hotels in Brussels (listed from most expensive to least) have rooms for guests with disabilities: Conrad, Hilton, Jolly Hotel Grand Sablon, Meridien, Radisson SAS, Renaissance, Sodehotel La Woluwe, Bristol Stephanie, Sheraton Brussels, Sheraton Brussels Airport, Arctia, Four Points, Métropole, Holiday Inn Brussels Airport, Jolly Atlanta, Mercure, Novotel Brussels (off Grand'Place), Novotel Airport, Aris, Atlas, Palace, Albert Premier, Astrid, Capital, Green Park, Fimotel Airport, Fimotel Expo, Ibis (Brussels Centre, Sainte-Catherine, and Airport), Balladins, Orion, Campanile, Comfort Inn, Gerfaut, France.

The same applies for a number of hotels outside Brussels, including the Ramada Inn in Liège, the Switel and Hilton hotels in Antwerp, Hotel Pullman in Brugge, and Hotel des Ardennes in Spa-Balmoral.

RESERVATIONS

When discussing accessibility with an operator or reservations agent, **ask hard questions.** Are there any stairs, inside *or* out? Are there grab bars next to the toilet *and* in the shower/tub? How wide is the doorway to the room? To the bathroom? For the most extensive facilities meeting the latest legal specifications, **opt for newer accommodations.**

SIGHTS & ATTRACTIONS

Many, but not all, of Belgium's and Luxembourg's tourist attractions are wheelchair accessible. Belgium's tourism office (☞ Visitor Information, *below*) publishes a brochure that lists all of its attractions and museums, indicating with a wheelchair icon the attractions that are wheelchair accessible.

TRANSPORTATION

Public transportation and trains provide priority seating for travelers with disabilities. However, although many trains are equipped with platforms for wheelchairs, buses are not. Very few train stations have elevators. Smaller train stations do not have escalators. For detailed information about specific train stations, *see* Train Travel, *below.*

For the visually impaired, intersections in large cities are equipped with sound signals indicating when it is safe to cross.

➤ COMPLAINTS: **Disability Rights Section** for general complaints (✉ U.S. Department of Justice, Civil Rights Division, Box 66738, Washington, DC 20035-6738, ☎ 202/514–0301 or 800/514–0301; TTY 202/514–0301 or 800/514–0301, FAX 202/307–1198). **Aviation Consumer Protection Division** for airline-related problems (☞ Air Travel, *above*). **Civil Rights Office** for problems with surface transportation (✉ U.S. Department of Transportation, Departmental Office of Civil Rights, S-30, 400 7th St. SW, Room 10215, Washington, DC 20590, ☎ 202/366–4648, FAX 202/366–9371).

TRAVEL AGENCIES

In the United States, the Americans with Disabilities Act requires that travel firms serve the needs of all travelers. Some agencies specialize in working with people with disabilities.

➤ TRAVELERS WITH MOBILITY PROBLEMS: **Access Adventures** (✉ 206 Chestnut Ridge Rd., Rochester, NY 14624, ☎ 716/889–9096, dltravel@prodigy.net), run by a former physical-rehabilitation counselor. **CareVacations** (✉ 5-5110 50th Ave., Leduc, Alberta T9E 6V4, ☎ 780/986–6404 or 877/478–7827, FAX 780/986–8332, www.carevacations.com), for group tours and cruise vacations. **Flying Wheels Travel** (✉ 143 W. Bridge St., Box 382, Owatonna, MN 55060, ☎ 507/451–5005 or 800/535–6790, FAX 507/451–1685, thq@ll.net, www.flyingwheels.com).

DISCOUNTS & DEALS

Be a smart shopper and **compare all your options** before making decisions. A plane ticket bought with a promotional coupon from travel clubs, coupon books, and direct-mail offers may not be cheaper than the least expensive fare from a discount ticket agency. And always keep in mind that what you get is just as important as what you save.

Many discounts are available to those traveling by rail. The Belgian railway offers packages including rail travel and entrance to almost 50 attractions as well as to temporary exhibits. (☞ Train Travel, *below*).

Discounts for children under 12, students under 26, and those over 65 are granted for museum entrances, public transportation, and other public facilities.

DISCOUNT RESERVATIONS

To save money, **look into discount reservations services** with toll-free numbers, which use their buying power to get a better price on hotels, airline tickets, even car rentals. When booking a room, always **call the hotel's local toll-free number** (if one is available) rather than the central reservations number—you'll often get a better price. Always ask about special packages or corporate rates.

When shopping for the best deal on hotels and car rentals, **look for guaranteed exchange rates,** which protect you against a falling dollar. With your rate locked in, you won't pay more, even if the price goes up in the local currency.

➤ AIRLINE TICKETS: ☎ **800/FLY-4-LESS.** ☎ **800/FLY-ASAP.**

➤ HOTEL ROOMS: **International Marketing & Travel Concepts** (☎ 800/790-4682, imtc@mindspring.com). **Steigenberger Reservation Service** (☎ 800/223-5652, www.srs-worldhotels.com). **Travel Interlink** (☎ 800/888-5898, www.travelinterlink.com).

PACKAGE DEALS

Don't confuse packages and guided tours. When you buy a package, you travel on your own, just as though you had planned the trip yourself. Fly/drive packages, which combine airfare and car rental, are often a good deal. If you **buy a rail/drive pass,** you may save on train tickets and car rentals. All Eurail- and Europass holders get a discount on Eurostar fares through the Channel Tunnel.

ELECTRICITY

To use your U.S.-purchased electric-powered equipment, **bring a converter and adapter.** The electrical current in Belgium and Luxembourg is 220 volts, 50 cycles alternating current (AC); wall outlets take Continental-type plugs, with two round prongs.

If your appliances are dual-voltage, you'll need only an adapter. Don't use 110-volt outlets marked FOR SHAVERS ONLY for high-wattage appliances such as blow-dryers. Most laptops operate equally well on 110 and 220 volts and so require only an adapter.

EMBASSIES

➤ AUSTRALIA: **Australian Embassy to Belgium and Luxembourg** (✉ Rue Guimard 6 8, 1000, Brussels, ☎ 02/286-0500).

➤ CANADA: **Canadian Embassy to Belgium and Luxembourg** (✉ Av. Tervueren 2, 1040, Brussels, ☎ 02/741-0611).

➤ NEW ZEALAND: **New Zealand Embassy to Belgium** (✉ Boulevard du Régent 47, 1000, Brussels, ☎ 02/512-1040).

➤ UNITED KINGDOM: **United Kingdom Embassy to Belgium** (✉ Rue Arlon 85, 1040, Brussels, ☎ 02/287-6232).

➤ UNITED STATES: **United States Embassy to Belgium** (✉ Boulevard du Régent 27, 1000, Brussels, ☎ 32/2-508-2111). **United States Embassy to Luxembourg** (✉ 22, Boulevard Emmanuel Servais L2535, Luxembourg City, ☎ 352/46-01-23).

EMERGENCIES

In case of medical emergencies, call an ambulance, which will take you to the nearest hospital or clinic's emergency center. Ambulance personnel and police in Belgium and Luxembourg are very cooperative and can speak some English.

➤ CONTACTS: In Belgium: **Police** (☎ 101). **Medical emergencies, fire, accidents, ambulance** (☎ 100). **Poison control** (☎ 070/245-245). **English-speaking help line** (☎ 02/648-4014).

In Luxembourg: **Police** (☎ 113). **Ambulance, doctor, dentist** (☎ 112).

ENGLISH-LANGUAGE MEDIA

Because of the cosmopolitan character of Belgium and Luxembourg and their proximity to Great Britain, a wide selection of English-language media is available.

BOOKS

English-language books are sold in specialized English-language book stores in Brussels or in the English-language section of book stores in major cities in Belgium and Luxembourg. Because of shipping and duties, the cost of an English-language paperback book in Belgium or Luxembourg is a bit more expensive than in the United States or Great Britain.

➤ BOOKSTORES: **Reading Room** (✉ 502, av. Georges Henri, 1200, Woluwe St-Lambert, ☎ 02/734-7917). **Sterling Books** (✉ 38, rue du Fossé-aux-Loups, 100, Brussels, ☎ 02/223-6223). **Waterstone's** (✉ 71, boulevard Adolphe Max, 1000, Brussels, ☎ 02/219-2708).

NEWSPAPERS & MAGAZINES

Bookstores and newspaper shops in major cities carry English press, such as *The Times* and *Financial Times* and English-language international press, such as *International Herald Tribune* and *Wall Street Journal Europe*. You can find current English and American magazines such as *Time* and *Newsweek* in the international section of larger magazine and newspaper shops throughout cities in Belgium and Luxembourg. *The Bulletin*, an English-language weekly covering Belgian current events and culture, is sold in most larger magazine shops.

RADIO & TELEVISION

English-language news is aired on the BBC World Service, on 648 AM. Radio 4, on 198 kHz LW from Britain, features music and news. The Flemish radio station VRT has an English-language program called "Brussels Calling" on 1512 kHz MW.

Belgium and Luxembourg offer a vast choice international television channels, including programs in English. British television channels BBC1 and BBC2 are available in most large cities and throughout the north of Belgium. CNN news service is available in most hotels, and MTV music channel is widely available. In the evening hours, throughout northern Belgium and in Brussels, Flemish public channel VRT and private channels VTM, KA2, and VT4 often air American films and programs that are subtitled, not dubbed, in Flemish. (French-language channels do dub American and British movies and sitcoms.)

ETIQUETTE & BEHAVIOR

Belgians and Luxembourgers are warm and cordial people who delight in welcoming visitors from abroad. Despite their reserved demeanor, they are very willing to help and do their utmost to speak English and understand others' customs.

Belgians greet friends and family with three superficial kisses—right cheek, left cheek, right cheek. Less intimate greetings are made with a handshake.

If you are invited to a home in Belgium or Luxembourg, **bring a gift**; a bouquet of flowers and a box of pralines or a bottle of wine are appropriate gifts to present to your host. If the host has young children, offer a small toy, a book, or sweets. You should **arrive about 10 minutes late,** to allow your host time for last-minute preparations. With before-dinner drinks, **allow your host to serve you** olives, chips, and crackers rather than helping yourself. During the meal, **keep both hands above the table.**

BUSINESS ETIQUETTE

It is acceptable to arrive up to 10 minutes late for business appointments. Even so, expect a short wait once you have been announced. Exchange business cards as introductions are made. The pace of business meetings is more relaxed than in the United States, so **don't rush into business too promptly**; instead spend a few minutes chatting about weather or travel. If you have met your associate's family previously, ask about them before beginning business.

Breakfast meetings are not popular in Belgium and Luxembourg, as most business people take a light breakfast at home. Business lunches are far more popular.

If you initiate the luncheon engagement, you are expected to **select the wine and pay for the meal.** If you are unfamiliar with restaurants, menus, or wines, **ask your guest to make suggestions.** Allow yourself and your guest to order and enjoy the meal, conversing about neutral topics such as vacations or the food itself before engaging in business. **Leave your props and handouts in your briefcase until after the meal.**

If you are invited to a business outing, unless your spouse or your business associates are expressly invited, assume that the invitation is for you alone.

GAY & LESBIAN TRAVEL

Social attitudes in Belgium are tolerant toward gays, especially in bigger cities. There are several gay and lesbian organizations in Brussels. Luxembourg is more conservative, but in Luxembourg City attitudes similar to Belgium apply.

➤ LOCAL RESOURCES: **English-Speaking Gay Group** (EGG; ✉ B.P. 198, 1060 Brussels, 100522.30@compuserve.com). For Jewish gays and lesbians, **Shalhomo** (✉ Av. Besme 127, 1190 Brussels, Belgium).

➤ GAY- & LESBIAN-FRIENDLY TRAVEL AGENCIES: **Different Roads Travel** (✉ 8383 Wilshire Blvd., Suite 902, Beverly Hills, CA 90211, ☎ 323/ 651–5557 or 800/429–8747, FAX 323/ 651–3678, leigh@west.tzell.com). **Kennedy Travel** (✉ 314 Jericho Turnpike, Floral Park, NY 11001, ☎ 516/352–4888 or 800/237–7433, FAX 516/354–8849, main@kennedytravel.com, www.kennedytravel.com). **Now Voyager** (✉ 4406 18th St., San Francisco, CA 94114, ☎ 415/626–1169 or 800/255–6951, FAX 415/626–8626, www.nowvoyager.com). **Skylink Travel and Tour** (✉ 1006 Mendocino Ave., Santa Rosa, CA 95401, ☎ 707/ 546–9888 or 800/225–5759, FAX 707/ 546–9891, skylinktvl@aol.com, www.skylinktravel.com), serving lesbian travelers.

HEALTH

English-speaking medical help is easy to find in Belgium and Luxembourg. Most doctors have a basic English vocabulary and are familiar with English medical terms.

Pharmacies (*apotheek* in Flemish, *pharmacie* in French) are clearly identified by a green cross displayed over the storefront.

OVER-THE-COUNTER REMEDIES

For diarrhea or intestinal problems, *Ercéfuryl* is very effective and is sold in capsules or liquid without prescription in pharmacies. For indigestion, *Rennie* tablets are also sold without prescription in pharmacies. Aspirin and vitamins are sold only in pharmacies.

PESTS & OTHER HAZARDS

Belgium and Luxembourg are relatively insect-free. Nonetheless, country rivers and canals attract mosquitoes in the summertime. Air-conditioning is rare and screens are not used, so **if you sleep with open windows, turn off lights,** which attract mosquitoes.

Belgians are not disciplined in curbing their dogs, so **beware of droppings,** particularly if you are walking in a residential area or near a park or a cemetery. Dogs are permitted in restaurants. They are not permitted in supermarkets.

HOLIDAYS

All government and post offices, banks, and most shops are closed in Belgium on Belgium's national day, July 21, and in Luxembourg on its national day, June 23. Businesses are also closed on Easter Monday, Labor Day (May 1), the Ascension (May), Pentecost (June), the Assumption (August), All Saints Day (early November), Armistice Day (November 11), Christmas Day (December 25), and New Years Day (January 1). If a holiday falls on a weekend, offices close the preceding Friday or following Monday.

INSURANCE

The most useful travel insurance plan is a comprehensive policy that includes coverage for trip cancelation and interruption, default, trip delay, and medical expenses (with a waiver for preexisting conditions).

Without insurance you will lose all or most of your money if you cancel your trip, regardless of the reason. Default insurance covers you if your tour operator, airline, or cruise line goes out of business. Trip-delay covers expenses that arise because of bad weather or mechanical delays. Study the fine print when comparing policies.

If you're traveling internationally, a key component of travel insurance is coverage for medical bills incurred if you get sick on the road. Such expenses are not generally covered by Medicare or private policies. U.K. residents can buy a travel insurance policy valid for most vacations taken during the year in which it's purchased (but check preexisting-condition coverage). British and Australian citizens need extra medical coverage when traveling overseas.

Always **buy travel policies directly from the insurance company**; if you buy them from a cruise line, airline, or tour operator that goes out of business you probably will not be covered for the agency or operator's default, a major risk. Before making any purchase, **review your existing health and home-owner's policies** to find what they cover away from home.

➤ TRAVEL INSURERS: In the U.S.: **Access America** (✉ 6600 W. Broad St., Richmond, VA 23230, ☏ 804/ 285–3300 or 800/284–8300, FAX 804/ 673–1583, www.previewtravel.com), **Travel Guard International** (✉ 1145 Clark St., Stevens Point, WI 54481, ☏ 715/345–0505 or 800/826–1300, FAX 800/955–8785, www.noelgroup.com). In Canada: **Voyager Insurance** (✉ 44 Peel Center Dr., Brampton, Ontario L6T 4M8, ☏ 905/791–8700; 800/668–4342 in Canada).

➤ INSURANCE INFORMATION: In the U.K.: **Association of British Insurers** (✉ 51–55 Gresham St., London EC2V 7HQ, ☏ 0171/600–3333, FAX 0171/696–8999, info@abi.org.uk, www.abi.org.uk). In Australia: **Insurance Council of Australia** (☏ 03/ 9614–1077, FAX 03/9614–7924).

LANGUAGE

Belgium has three official languages: Flemish, French, and German (spoken by a small minority). Many Flemish-speaking Belgians understand French and vice versa. Nonetheless, Belgians are often uncomfortable using the other region's language, and many are capable and more than willing to speak English, especially to anglophones. So, **speak the language of the region if you know it, or use English.**

In Luxembourg, the official language is French, but German is a compulsory subject in schools, and everyone speaks Luxembourgish, the native tongue (a language descended from an ancient dialect of the Franks); most people also know a fair amount of English.

LANGUAGES FOR TRAVELERS

A phrase book and language-tape set can help get you started.

➤ PHRASE BOOKS & LANGUAGE-TAPE SETS: *Fodor's French for Travelers*, *Fodor's German for Travelers* (☏ 800/733–3000 in the U.S.; 800/668–4247 in Canada; $7 for phrasebook, $16.95 for audio set).

LODGING

Belgium and Luxembourg offer a range of lodging, from the major international hotel chains and small, modern local hotels to family-run restored inns and historic houses to elegant country châteaux and resorts. Prices in metropolitan areas are significantly higher than those in outlying towns and the countryside.

Most hotels that cater to business travelers will grant substantial weekend rebates. These discounted rates are often available during the week as well as in July and early August, when business travelers are thin on the ground. Moreover, you can often qualify for a "corporate rate" when hotel occupancy is low. The moral is, always ask what's the best rate a hotel can offer before you book. No hotelier was ever born who will give a lower rate unless you ask for it.

The lodgings we list are the cream of the crop in each price category. We always list the facilities that are available—but we don't specify whether they cost extra: when pricing accommodations, always ask what's included and what costs extra.

Assume that hotels operate on the **European Plan** (with no meals) unless we specify that they use the **Continental Plan** (CP, with a Continental breakfast), **Modified American Plan** (MAP, with breakfast and dinner), or the **Full American Plan** (FAP, with all meals).

➤ RESERVATIONS: For hotel reservations in Belgium (a free service): **Belgian Tourist Reservations** (BTR; ✉ Bd. Anspach 111, 1000 Brussels, ☏ 02/513–7484, FAX 02/513–9277). For self-catering accommodations and B&Bs in Wallonia: **Belsud Réservation** (✉ R. Marché-aux-Herbes 61, 1000 Brussels, ☏ 02/504–0280, FAX 02/514–5335). For hotel and B&B reservations in Antwerp: **Toerisme Stad Antwerpen** (✉ Grote Markt 15, 2000 Antwerp, ☏ 03/232–0103, FAX 03/231–1937).

APARTMENT & VILLA RENTALS

If you want a home base that's roomy enough for a family and comes with cooking facilities, **consider a furnished rental.** These can save you money, especially if you're traveling with a group. Home-exchange directories sometimes list rentals as well as exchanges.

Apartment and villa rentals and *gites* (farmhouse rentals) are easy to find in popular vacation areas, such as the Belgian coast and the Ardennes countryside. Rentals from private individuals are usually for a one or two-week minimum. Sheets and towels are not provided.

You can also rent vacation villas within Belgium's vacation parks. These self-contained parks, in rural or seaside settings, consist of residences and facilities such as swimming pools, hiking and bicycling trails, restaurants, and activities for children. There is usually a one-week minimum, although it is often possible to rent for less than one week during the winter months.

Listings with photos and details of local vacation parks and vacation villa rentals are available from the national tourism office of Belgium. The national tourism office of Luxembourg publishes a brochures with villa and apartment listings, including photos, details, and a reservation form. (☞ Visitor Information, *below.*) Listings of local rental agents are also available at local tourist information centers at seaside towns along the Belgian coast. Local rentals by individuals in Belgium can be found in the classified section of French-language *Le Soir* and Flemish *De Morgen* daily newspapers or in *Vlan* weekly.

➤ INTERNATIONAL AGENTS: **Interhome** (✉ 1990 N.E. 163rd St., Suite 110, N. Miami Beach, FL 33162, ☎ 305/940–2299 or 800/882–6864, FAX 305/940–2911, interhomeu@aol.com, www.interhome.com).

➤ LOCAL AGENTS: **Fédération Flamande pour le Tourisme Rural et à la Ferme** (✉ Minderbroedersstraat 8, 3000 Leuven, ☎ 016/242–158, FAX 016/242–187). **Tourisme à la Ferme** (✉ Ave. Prince de Liège 1, 5100 Namur, ☎ 081/311–800, FAX 081/310–200).

B&BS

Bed & Breakfast accommodations (*Chambres d'Hôtes* in French or *Gastenkamers* in Flemish) are far less common in Belgium and in Luxembourg than in Great Britain; the ones you do find usually need to be reserved in advance. Most are in rural or residential areas. Although clean, B&Bs are very simple and inexpensive, often without private bathrooms.

Listings are available at local tourist information centers, however you must make your own reservations directly with the proprietor. *Taxistop* sells a Bed & Breakfast guide to Belgium and Luxembourg and makes reservations.

➤ RESERVATION SERVICES: **Fédération de Gîtes de Wallonie** (✉ Ave. Prince de Liège 1, 5100 Namur, ☎ 081/311–800). **Gîtes d'Etape du Centre Belge du Tourisme des Jeunes** (✉ Rue van Orley 4, 1000 Brussels, ☎ 02/209–0300). **Taxistop** (✉ 28 rue Fossé aux Loups, 1000 Brussels, ☎ 02/223–2310).

CAMPING

Campsites are plentiful in Belgium and Luxembourg, especially at the Belgian coast, in the Ardennes area of Belgium and Luxembourg, and in Luxembourg's Moselle Valley. Camping is popular among Belgians and even more so among the neighboring Dutch, who are fervent campers, so sites fill up quickly. They are clean but may seem cramped by American standards, as space is at a premium. Fellow campers are likely to be Dutch, Belgian, and German families on a budget holiday. Virtually all sites have running water, although some do not have hot water. Belgian campsites are rated with stars, one being the most rustic and five the most sumptuous, with indoor pool, restaurant, and spa. Campsites range from about $8 to $20 per night.

Luxembourg's well organized camping facilities are rated according to a strictly monitored 1-to-3 numbering system. "Three" is the the most primitive (no showers) and "one" the most fully equipped.

Sleeping overnight in cars or vans at public rest spots is strictly forbidden in Belgium and in Luxembourg.

HOME EXCHANGES

If you would like to exchange your home for someone else's, **join a home-**

exchange organization, which will send you its updated listings of available exchanges for a year and will include your own listing in at least one of them. It's up to you to make specific arrangements.

➤ EXCHANGE CLUBS: **HomeLink International** (✉ Box 650, Key West, FL 33041, ☎ 305/294–7766 or 800/638–3841, FAX 305/294–1448, usa@homelink.org, www.homelink.org; $98 per year). **Intervac U.S.** (✉ Box 590504, San Francisco, CA 94159, ☎ 800/756–4663, FAX 415/435–7440, www.intervac.com; $89 per year includes two catalogues).

HOSTELS

No matter what your age, you can **save on lodging costs by staying at hostels.** Hostels in Belgium and Luxembourg are well organized and clean. Rooms with 1–10 beds are available and hostels are suitable for family stays. Many are conveniently located near train stations.

In some 5,000 locations in more than 70 countries around the world, Hostelling International (HI), the umbrella group for a number of national youth-hostel associations, offers single-sex, dorm-style beds and, at many hostels, rooms for couples and family accommodations. Membership in any HI national hostel association, open to travelers of all ages, allows you to stay in HI-affiliated hostels at member rates; one-year membership is about $25 for adults (C$26.75 in Canada, £9.30 in the U.K., $30 in Australia, and $30 in New Zealand); hostels run about $10–$25 per night. Members have priority if the hostel is full; they're also eligible for discounts around the world, even on rail and bus travel in some countries.

➤ BEST OPTIONS: **Auberges de Jeunesse de la Belgique Francophone** (✉ Rue de la Sablonnière 28, 1000 Brussels, ☎ 02/219–5676, FAX 02/219–1451). **Central des Auberges de Jeunesse Luxembourgeoises** (✉ 2, rue du Fort Olisy, Luxembourg, ☎ 352/22–55–88, FAX 352/46–39–87). **Vlaamse Jeugdherbergen** (✉ Van Stralenstraat 40, Antwerp, ☎ 03/232–7213, FAX 03/231–8126).

➤ ORGANIZATIONS: **Hostelling International—American Youth Hostels** (✉ 733 15th St. NW, Suite 840, Washington, DC 20005, ☎ 202/783–6161, FAX 202/783–6171, www.hiayh.org). **Hostelling International—Canada** (✉ 400–205 Catherine St., Ottawa, Ontario K2P 1C3, ☎ 613/237–7884, FAX 613/237–7868, www.hostellingintl.ca). **Youth Hostel Association of England and Wales** (✉ Trevelyan House, 8 St. Stephen's Hill, St. Albans, Hertfordshire AL1 2DY, ☎ 01727/855215 or 01727/845047, FAX 01727/844126, www.yha.uk). **Australian Youth Hostel Association** (✉ 10 Mallett St., Camperdown, NSW 2050, ☎ 02/9565–1699, FAX 02/9565–1325, www.yha.com.au). **Youth Hostels Association of New Zealand** (✉ Box 436, Christchurch, New Zealand, ☎ 03/379–9970, FAX 03/365–4476, www.yha.org.nz).

HOTELS

Hotels in Belgium and Luxembourg are rated with stars, one star indicating the most basic and five stars indicating the most luxurious. Rooms in one-star hotels are likely not to have a telephone or television, and two-star hotels may not have carpeting, air-conditioning, or elevators. Four- and five-star hotels have conference facilities and offer amenities such as pools, tennis courts, saunas, private parking, and room service.

Three-, four-, and five-star hotels are usually equipped with hair dryers and coffeemakers. Hotels in Belgium and Luxembourg do not provide irons, although four- and five-star hotels offer dry-cleaning service. Most hotels have at least one restaurant.

All hotels listed in this book have private bath unless otherwise noted. Single rooms in one- to three-star hotels often have a shower (*douche* in French, *stortbui* in Flemish) rather than a bathtub (*bain* in French, *badkuip* in Flemish). A double room includes either one double bed (*lit double* in French, *tweepersoonsbed* in Flemish) or two single beds. A single room includes one single bed (*lit simple* in French or *eenpersoonsbed* in Flemish). Three people who wish to room together should **ask about the possibility of adding a small bed**

in a double room. Rooms that accommodate four people are rare, except in five-star hotels.

Taking meals at the hotel restaurant usually provides you with a discount. Some restaurants, especially country inns, require that guests take half-board (*demi-pension*in French, *half-pension* in Flemish), at least lunch or dinner, at the hotel. Full pension (*Pension complet* in French, *volledig pension* in Flemish) entitles guests to both lunch and dinner. Guests taking either half or full board also receive breakfast. If you take a *pension,* you pay per person, regardless of the number of rooms. If you are not taking half or full pension, **ask if breakfast is included in the price of the room.**

It is wise to **reserve your hotel in advance.** Rooms fill up quickly at the Belgian coast, in the Ardennes, and in the Luxembourg countryside in July and August, during the period around Easter, and on May 1. Throughout the year conventions can fill up business hotels in Brussels.

RESERVING A ROOM

You may **reserve your room by telephoning or writing in English,** as all hoteliers and reservations services in Belgium and Luxembourg understand the language. If you reserve a double room, be sure to **specify whether you want two single beds or one double bed.** Inquire about possibilities for more than two people in one room. **Specify if you want a room with a bathtub,** shower, or both. Ask if breakfast is included and **specify if you wish to take half or full board.** If you are traveling in the summer, **ask if the property is air-conditioned.** If you are traveling by car, **inquire about parking facilities.** If the hotel is in a city, **consider asking for a high floor** or a room that is not above the street.

Hotels prefer that you **confirm your reservation by fax.** If you are having an extended stay, the property commonly asks for a deposit either in the local currency or billed to your credit card.

➤ Toll-Free Numbers: **Best Western** (☎ 800/528–1234, www.bestwestern.com). **Choice** (☎ 800/221–2222, www.hotelchoice.com). **Holiday Inn** (☎ 800/465–4329, www.holiday-inn.com). **Inter-Continental** (☎ 800/327–0200, www.interconti.com). **Sheraton** (☎ 800/325–3535, www.sheraton.com).

MAIL & SHIPPING

From Belgium, first-class (airmail) letters and postcards to the United States cost BF34 (84¢), second-class (surface) BF23 (55¢). Airmail letters and postcards to the United Kingdom cost BF21 (50¢), second-class BF19 (47¢). All international first-class mail must be marked with a blue A-PRIOR sticker (available in post offices). The **central post office** (✉ Av. Frosny 1, 1060 Brussels) is open 24 hours a day, seven days a week.

From Luxembourg, airmail postcards and letters weighing less than 20 grams cost Flux 25 (60) to the United States. Letters and postcards to the United Kingdom cost Flux 16 (40).

OVERNIGHT SERVICES

Express delivery services are available in major cities throughout Belgium and Luxembourg. Deliveries can be made to the United Kingdom in one day, to the United States in one or two days, and to Australia and New Zealand in two to three days. There are no drop-off boxes; however, pickup service from major cities is prompt and efficient. Cost for sending a document express to the United States is about $70.

➤ Major Services: **DHL** (☎ 02/715–5050). **Federal Express** (☎ 0800/153–55).

RECEIVING MAIL

Your hotel is the best address to use for having shipments sent to you. The address should include your name and the date of your arrival at the hotel. Be sure that customs formalities are in order. Advise your hotel in advance if you expect to receive mail or deliveries that require a signature upon receipt.

SHIPPING PARCELS

For your convenience, **ask shops about shipping purchases back home.** Godiva and Neuhaus chocolate shops, for example, often provide this service for a minimal surcharge.

MONEY MATTERS

Prices throughout this guide are given for adults. Substantially reduced fees are almost always available for children, students, and senior citizens. For information on taxes, *see* Taxes, *below*.

ATMS

ATMs (*distributeur automatique* in French, *automatisch uitdeler* in Flemish) are located at banks throughout Belgium and Luxembourg, either inside the bank itself or on the facade of the bank building. They are accessible 24 hours a day, seven days per week, but are occasionally guarded and inaccessible, usually for about an hour, when cash is being transferred from the machines. The distributors themselves determine with which networks they work. For example, **BBL** works with Maestro, **General Bank** also works with Maestro and Cirrus, and **CGER-ASLK** works with Maestro, Cirrus, and Plus. To be sure, **inquire at your home bank** about use of its network in Belgium or Luxembourg.

CREDIT CARDS

Major credit cards are accepted in most hotels, gas stations, and restaurants in Belgium and Luxembourg. Smaller establishments, shops, and supermarkets often accept Visa cards only.

Throughout this guide, the following abbreviations are used: **AE**, American Express; **DC**, Diners Club; **MC**, Master Card; and **V**, Visa.

➤ REPORTING LOST CARDS: To report lost or stolen credit cards, call the following toll-free numbers: **American Express** (☎ 800/327–2177); **Diner's Club** (☎ 800/234–6377); **Master Card** (☎ 800/307–7309); and **Visa** (☎ 800/847–2911).

In Belgium and in Luxembourg, use the following numbers: **American Express** (☎ 02/676-2626). **Diner's Club** (☎ 02/206–9800). **Master Card/Visa** (☎ 070/344–344).

CURRENCY

The monetary unit in Belgium is the Belgian franc (BF); in Luxembourg, it is the Luxembourg franc (Flux), which is interchangeable with the Belgian franc. The currency exchange rates fluctuate daily, so check them at the time of your departure.

As members of the European Union, Belgium and Luxembourg adopted the European currency, the **euro,** in January 1999. As of that date, it has been possible to make banking transactions in euros as well as in the local currency, and many invoices and receipts are stated in both currencies. As of January 1, 2002, all bank transactions must be made in euros, and euro coins and banknotes will replace the coins and notes of the local currency.

CURRENCY EXCHANGE

Currency exchange booths are widely available throughout the large cities in Belgium and Luxembourg, at major train stations, and at major tourist destinations. There is a surcharge for each transaction, regardless of the amount exchanged.

For the most favorable rates, **change money through banks.** Although ATM transaction fees may be higher abroad than at home, ATM rates are excellent because they are based on wholesale rates offered only by major banks. You won't do as well at exchange booths in airports or rail and bus stations, in hotels, in restaurants, or in stores. To avoid lines at airport exchange booths, **get a bit of local currency before you leave home.**

➤ EXCHANGE SERVICES: **International Currency Express** (☎ 888/278–6628 for orders, www.foreignmoney.com). **Thomas Cook Currency Services** (☎ 800/287–7362 for telephone orders and retail locations, www.us.thomascook.com).

TRAVELER'S CHECKS

Do you need traveler's checks? It depends on where you're headed. If you're going to rural areas and small towns, go with cash; traveler's checks are best used in cities. Lost or stolen checks can usually be replaced within 24 hours. To ensure a speedy refund, buy your own traveler's checks—don't let someone else pay for them: irregularities like this can cause delays. The person who bought the checks should make the call to request a refund.

OUTDOORS & SPORTS

CROSS-COUNTRY SKIING

The gently rolling hills of Belgium and Luxembourg lend themselves nicely to cross-country skiing. You can rent equipment from country hotels and inns and from ski equipment shops in major cities. Because winters in Belgium and Luxembourg can be mild, you can't always depend on a good snow base.

CYCLING

Belgians are proud of their native cycling champion, multiple Tour de France winner Eddie Merckx, and are avid spectators of bicycle races. Cycling lends itself well to the relatively flat countryside of northern Belgium. The Belgian Ardennes and Luxembourg present more challenging terrain (☞ Bike Travel, *above*).

GOLF

Until recently, golfing in Belgium and Luxembourg required a club membership. It is becoming more democratic and, although there are no public golf courses, there are locations near major cities where nonmembers can golf. Contact **Fédération Royale Belge de Golf** (✉ Chaussée de La Hulpe 110, 1000 Brussels, ☎ 02/672–2389).

The Luxembourg National Tourism Office (☞ Visitor Information, *below*) offers golf packages, detailed in the brochure *Pouponné au Grand-Duché*.

MOUNTAINEERING

The Meuse Valley of southern Belgium and the Mullerthal and Wanterbaach regions of Luxembourg are good spots for cliff-climbing. If you climb in Luxembourg, you must obtain authorization from **Eaux et Forêts de Diekirch** (✉ B.P. 50, 9201, Diekirch).

➤ MOUNTAINEERING CLUBS: **Club Alpin Belge** (✉ Ave. Albert I, 129, Namur, Belgium, ☎ 081/224–085). **Mondorf Le Club** (✉ B.P. 52, 5601 Mondorf-les-Bains, Luxembourg, ☎ 661–212).

TENNIS

Many hotels and campsites in the countryside of Belgium and Luxembourg have outdoor tennis courts. Although there are few public tennis courts in Belgium and Luxembourg, there are many clubs with indoor and outdoor courts that accept nonmembers.

➤ TENNIS ASSOCIATIONS: In Belgium: **Fédération Royal Belge de Tennis** (✉ Galerie Porte Louise 203, 1050, Brussels, ☎ 02/513–2920). In Luxembourg: **Fédération Luxemourgeoise de Tennis** (✉ bv. Hubert Clément, 4064, Esch-sur-Alzette, ☎ 574–470).

WATER SPORTS

Windsurfing and sailing are popular along Belgium's coast and in the lakes of Belgium and Luxembourg. Waterskiing and windsurfing require authorization on some lakes. In the summer, kayaking and white-water rafting trips are organized along Belgium's Lesse River and Luxembourg's Sûre River.

➤ WATER SPORTS ASSOCIATIONS: **Vlaamse Watersportvereiningen** (Flemish Water Sport Association; ✉ Beatrijslaan 25, Antwerp, ☎ 03/216–6967). **Fédération Luxembourgeoise de Voile** (FLV, Luxembourg Sailing Association; ☎ 36–83–23). **Union Luxembourgeoise de Ski Nautique** (Luxembourg Water Skiing Association; ✉ 14, ave. de la Gare, 1610 Luxembourg City, ☎ 48–56–42). **Fédération Luxembourgeoise de Canoë-Kayak** (Luxembourg Canoeing and Kayaking Association; ✉ 6, rue de Pulvermuhl, 2356 Luxembourg City).

PACKING

The best advice for a trip to Belgium and Luxembourg in any season is to pack light, be flexible, bring an umbrella (and trench coat with a liner in winter), and always have a sweater or jacket available. For daytime wear and casual evenings, turtlenecks and flannel shirts are ideal for winter, alone or under a sweater, and cotton shirts with sleeves are perfect in summer. Blue jeans are popular and are even sometimes worn to the office; sweat suits, however, are never seen outside fitness centers. For women, high heels are nothing but trouble on the cobblestone streets of Brussels and other old cities, and sneakers or running shoes are a dead giveaway that you are an American tourist; a better choice is a pair of dark-color walking shoes or low-heeled pumps.

Women here wear skirts more frequently than do women in the United States, especially those over 35. Men would be wise to include a jacket and tie, especially if you're planning to visit one of the upper-echelon restaurants.

In your carry-on luggage, **pack an extra pair of eyeglasses or contact lenses** and **enough of any medication you take** to last the entire trip. You may also ask your doctor to write a spare prescription using the drug's generic name, since brand names may vary from country to country. In luggage to be checked, **never pack prescription drugs or valuables.** To avoid customs delays, carry medications in their original packaging. And don't forget to carry with you the addresses of offices that handle refunds of lost traveler's checks.

CHECKING LUGGAGE

How many carry-on bags you can bring with you is up to the airline. Most allow two, but not always, so make sure that everything you carry aboard will fit under your seat or in the overhead bin, and get to the gate early. Note that if you have a seat at the back of the plane, you'll probably board first, while the overhead bins are still empty.

If you are flying internationally, note that baggage allowances may be determined not by piece but by weight—generally 88 pounds (40 kilograms) in first class, 66 pounds (30 kilograms) in business class, and 44 pounds (20 kilograms) in economy.

Airline liability for baggage is limited to $1,250 per person on flights within the United States. On international flights it amounts to $9.07 per pound or $20 per kilogram for checked baggage (roughly $640 per 70-pound bag) and $400 per passenger for unchecked baggage. You can buy additional coverage at check-in for about $10 per $1,000 of coverage, but it excludes a rather extensive list of items, shown on your airline ticket.

Before departure, **itemize your bags' contents** and their worth, and label the bags with your name, address, and phone number. (If you use your home address, cover it so potential thieves can't see it readily.) Inside each bag, **pack a copy of your itinerary.** At check-in, **make sure that each bag is correctly tagged** with the destination airport's three-letter code. If your bags arrive damaged or fail to arrive at all, file a written report with the airline before leaving the airport.

PASSPORTS & VISAS

When traveling internationally, **carry your passport even if you don't need one** (it's always the best form of I.D.) and **make two photocopies of the data page** (one for someone at home and another for you, carried separately from your passport). If you lose your passport, promptly call the nearest embassy or consulate and the local police.

ENTERING BELGIUM & LUXEMBOURG

All Australian, Canadian, New Zealand, U.K., and U.S. citizens, even infants, need a valid passport to enter Belgium and Luxembourg for stays of up to 90 days.

PASSPORT OFFICES

The best time to apply for a passport or to renew is in fall and winter. Before any trip, check your passport's expiration date, and, if necessary, renew it as soon as possible.

➤ AUSTRALIAN CITIZENS: **Australian Passport Office** (☎ 131–232, www.dfat.gov.au/passports).

➤ CANADIAN CITIZENS: **Passport Office** (☎ 819/994–3500 or 800/567–6868, www.dfait-maeci.gc.ca/passport).

➤ NEW ZEALAND CITIZENS: **New Zealand Passport Office** (☎ 04/494–0700, www.passports.govt.nz).

➤ U.K. CITIZENS: **London Passport Office** (☎ 0990/210–410) for fees and documentation requirements and to request an emergency passport.

➤ U.S. CITIZENS: **National Passport Information Center** (☎ 900/225–5674; calls are 35¢ per minute for automated service, $1.05 per minute for operator service).

REST ROOMS

Public rest rooms (*Toilettes* in French, *Toiletten* in Flemish) are also referred to as *WC*. There are no free public rest rooms in cities or at rest stops on highways. Train stations, tourist spots, beaches, and highway restaurants have rest rooms manned by attendants who charge about 15 francs per visit. Payment is made on the way out. Thanks to the attendant, these rest rooms are clean and equipped with toilet paper. Similarly, restaurants in cities often hire attendants who charge per visit. **Expect to pay, even if you are a patron of the restaurant.**

Rest rooms in cafés and pubs are not manned by attendants and are free to patrons. Therefore, even if your visit to a café is expressly to use the rest room, **you are expected to buy a drink.** If you do not have the time or inclination to drink, ask first before using the rest room in cafés. Offering the bartender 15 francs for the hospitality is a fair gesture.

Gas stations along highways usually have a unisex rest room. For access you need not buy gas, just **ask the gas station attendant for the key.** Rest rooms in cafés, bars, and gas stations are often not up to the same standards as those manned by attendants, so **take tissues with you.**

SAFETY

Belgium and Luxembourg are relatively safe, even at night. Nontheless, it is wise to **avoid highway rest stops and sparsely populated metro stations at night.** Although they are not likely to assault, tramps and derelicts tend to make train stations unsavory at night.

Beware of pickpockets, especially around tourist attractions, in public transportation, and in the airport. Even in restaurants, particularly those in tourist areas, keep an eye on your handbag or wallet. **Lock your car.** Do not expect a great deal of sympathy if you have been pickpocketed or burglarized. Local police make reports but usually investigate no further.

LOCAL SCAMS

As in other destinations around the world, avoid buying "leather" goods, or "wool" carpets from vendors selling out of car trunks, in metro stations or other makeshift stores.

In popular tourist areas, **beware of restaurant personnel beckoning tourists on the street** and luring prospective diners with a complimentary glass of champagne. At the end of the meal, the "compliments" are reflected in the tab.

Although begging is against the law in Belgium and in Luxembourg, it is common to encounter beggars, often using children as props, in busy shopping areas and on metros. Because Belgium and Luxembourg provide social assistance to the truly destitute, consider beggars' tales of woe with scepticism.

WOMEN IN BELGIUM & LUXEMBOURG

Belgium and Luxembourg enjoy equality of sexes. Women can travel, check in at hotels, and relax at cafés and restaurants with virtually the same ease as men.

Women traveling alone should nonetheless **avoid lingering around neighborhoods near train stations,** as these neighborhoods are traditionally where prostitutes operate.

SENIOR-CITIZEN TRAVEL

Senior citizens over 60 years old are granted discounts on public transportation, for many cultural events, and for entrance to many museums. **Be prepared to document your age** in order to receive such deals.

To qualify for age-related discounts, **mention your senior-citizen status up front** when booking hotel reservations (not when checking out) and before you're seated in restaurants (not when paying the bill). When renting a car, ask about promotional car-rental discounts, which can be cheaper than senior-citizen rates.

The Radisson SAS Hotel in Brussels offers a 25% reduction off the rack rate to senior citizens over 65. For other hotels, check on the availability of senior rates when you book.

➤ EDUCATIONAL PROGRAMS: **Elderhostel** (✉ 75 Federal St., 3rd floor, Boston, MA 02110, ☎ 877/426–8056, FAX 877/426–2166, www.elderhostel.org). **Interhostel** (✉ University of New Hampshire, 6 Garrison Ave., Durham, NH 03824, ☎ 603/862–1147 or 800/733–9753, FAX 603/862–1113, www.learn.unh.edu).

SHOPPING

Shopping in Belgium and Luxembourg can be expensive, but goods are of the finest quality. You can find lace, tapestries, linen, chocolate, crystal, and porcelain near the Grand'Place in Brussels, in Antwerp's Meir district, in Brugge, in Luxembourg City, and at the airport. If you make a significant purchase, **ask about a discount.**

Discounts are also commonly given at factory shops. If you are interested in Val St-Lambert crystal, you can visit the factory shop at **Cristalleries du Val St-Lambert** (✉ Rue du Val 245, Seraing, ☎ 04/337–0960). For bargains on **Villeroy & Bosche** porcelain, visit its factory outlet shop (✉ Rue de Rollingergrund 330, bus 2, Luxembourg City, ☎ 4682–1278).

Art galleries and antiques shops are plentiful in Brussels, Gent, Brugge, Antwerp, and Luxembourg City. *Antiquaire* shops deal with bonafide antiques. If you are simply looking for interesting, older "vintage" items, visit a *brocante* or look for street sales organized, usually in May and September, by villages and neighborhoods.

Bargaining is expected at antiques shops, brocantes, and street sales. Depending on the volume of your purchase, you can usually trim your price by 10% to 35%. If you are not satisfied with the price quoted and wish to be taken seriously, **walk away and then visit the vendor later for another chance to bargain.**

Visiting local weekly markets is an interesting way to get the flavor of a village or neighborhood. Local markets sell everything from fresh produce and cheeses to household goods, flowers, clothes, and shoes. Market prices are not less expensive than prices in shops, but market produce is often much fresher. If you buy in quantity, you can usually strike a small bargain with market vendors.

Belgium's largest department store, INNO, found in major cities and shopping centers, stocks a wide variety of quality clothing and housewares. Less expensive are hypermarkets GB-Maxi and Cora, located on the cities' outskirts. In January and July these shops and most others put their goods on sale, often with reductions of 50%.

Exchanging items is possible but not as simple as in the United States, so **keep your receipts.** You will also need an excuse such as an obvious flaw in the goods. If you exchange for fit, you may not receive your money back but be asked instead to purchase another item of the same value. There is usually a 30-day period in which you may exchange items, but it is better to act as soon as possible. Sale items are usually not exchangeable.

KEY DESTINATIONS

Although you can find many lace shops in Brussels, the greatest selection is in Brugge. If you are lucky enough to be shopping for diamonds, visit Antwerp's diamond district. The largest selection of crystal is in Liège, and best bargains for Villeroy & Bosche porcelain are in Luxembourg. If you like browsing secondhand book shops, when you are in the Belgian Ardennes visit Redu, an entire village full of small secondhand book and record stores.

Most book shops or newspaper shops carry books of Belgium's comic book hero, Tin-Tin. English versions and Tin-Tin-theme items are sold in Brussels near the Grand'Place at **Boutique Tin-Tin** (✉ 13, rue de la Colline, ☎ 02/514–4550).

SMART SOUVENIRS

Lace is lightweight and takes up little space in your suitcase. Tapestry cushion covers are also conveniently compact. Both are sold at the Brussels airport duty-free shop. Brussels's Fine Arts Museum shop sells stationery, T-shirts, and other items emblazoned with the surreal art of Belgian René Magritte.

WATCH OUT

Because of different technical standards, European videotapes and equipment are not compatible and generally do not work in the United States.

Although bed linens are beautiful, dimensions of Belgian beds are different from American beds, so **beware if you buy fitted sheets.**

SIGHTSEEING GUIDES

English-language sightseeing tours are routinely organized in tourist cities such as Brussels, Brugge, and Luxembourg City. You can find information about reliable tours, guides, and schedules through national tourism offices (☞ Visitor Information, *below*). Museums and special exhibits often offer English-language guides or headphones with explanations in English.

STUDENTS IN BELGIUM & LUXEMBOURG

Students or young people under 26 can benefit from many discounts, including public transportation, museum entrances, cultural events, and even discount haircuts at some stylists. Be sure to **take your student ID and government identification** with your date of birth.

➤ I.D.S & SERVICES: **Council Travel** (CIEE; ✉ 205 E. 42nd St., 14th floor, New York, NY 10017, ☎ 212/822–2700 or 888/268–6245, FAX 212/822–2699, info@councilexchanges.org, www.councilexchanges.org) for mail orders only, in the U.S. **Travel Cuts** (✉ 187 College St., Toronto, Ontario M5T 1P7, ☎ 416/979–2406 or 800/667–2887, www.travelcuts.com) in Canada. **Carte Jeunes** (✉ Rue des Mineurs 16, Liège Belgium, ☎ 04/221–3355, FAX 04/221–0621).

TAXES

AIRPORT

The Brussels National Airport tax is BF525/€13.00, levied on all tickets and payable with your ticket purchase.

HOTELS

All hotels in Belgium charge a 6% Value Added Tax (TVA), included in the room rate; in Brussels, there is also a 9% city tax.

Hotels in Luxembourg charge a visitor's tax of 5%, included in the room rate.

VALUE-ADDED TAX

In Belgium, VAT ranges from 6% on food and clothing to 33% on luxury goods. Restaurants are in between; 21% VAT is included in quoted prices.

To get a VAT refund you need to reside outside the European Union and to have spent 5,001 Belgian or Luxembourg francs (€125) or more in the same shop on the same day. Provided that you personally carry the goods out of the country within 30 days, you may claim a refund. Systems for doing this vary. Most leading stores will issue you a "VAT cheque" as proof of purchase (and charge a commission for the service). Then have these tax-refund forms stamped at customs as you leave the final European Union country on your itinerary; send the stamped form back to the store. Alternatively, if you shop at a store that is part of the Global Refund program, you can simplify the process.

Global Refund is a VAT refund service that makes getting your money back hassle-free. The service is available Europe-wide at 130,000 affiliated stores. In participating stores, **ask for the Global Refund form** (called a Shopping Cheque). Have it stamped like any customs form by customs officials when you leave the European Union. Then take the form to one of the more than 700 Global Refund counters—conveniently located at every major airport and border crossing—and your money will be refunded on the spot in the form of cash, check, or a refund to your credit-card account (minus a small percentage for processing).

➤ VAT REFUNDS: **Global Refund** (✉ 707 Summer St., Stamford, CT 06901, ☎ 800/566–9828, FAX 203/674–8709, taxfree@us.globalrefund.com, www.globalrefund.com).

TELEPHONES

Telephone lines in Belgium and Luxembourg are modern and efficient, and direct dialing is possible throughout both countries. The dial tone is a constant flute-like sound.

In Belgium, phone numbers have nine digits: either a six-digit local number preceded by a three-digit area code, or a seven-digit local number preceded by a two-digit area code.

In Luxembourg, all telephone numbers are six digits, except in Luxembourg City, where they are eight digits. There are no area codes.

Cell phones are called GSMs. British cell phones work in Belgium and Luxembourg, but American and Canadian cells phones do not. Cell phone telephone numbers are preceded by 075, 077, 095, or 097, followed by six digits.

AREA & COUNTRY CODES

The country code (used when calling from abroad) for Belgium is 32 and for Luxembourg is 352. In Belgium, the two- or three-digit area code (called a city code when applied to metropolitan areas) will always begin with zero; the zero is dropped when calling Belgium from abroad. The city code for Brussels is 02; for Antwerp, 03; and for Liège, 04.

Luxembourg does not use area codes.

The country code for the United States and Canada is 1. The country code is 61 for Australia, 64 for New Zealand, 44 for the United Kingdom, and 353 for Ireland.

Toll-free numbers begin with 0800. Premium rate calls begin with 0900.

DIRECTORY & OPERATOR ASSISTANCE

For English-language telephone assistance, dial 1405.

INTERNATIONAL CALLS

For international calls, dial 00, followed by the country code, followed by the area code and telephone number.

LOCAL CALLS

In Belgium, local calls are made using the six- or seven-digit local number, except in Brussels. **Use the city code (02) for all calls within Brussels,** followed by the seven-digit local number. In Luxembourg, where there are no city or area codes, simply dial the six- or eight-digit number for all calls.

Unlike in the United States, the cost of local calls in Belgium and Luxembourg increases depending upon the duration of the call.

LONG-DISTANCE CALLS

If your are making a call from city to city within Belgium, the number you dial will have a total of nine digits, either a two-digit area code and a seven-digit local number or a three-digit area code and a six-digit local number.

Within Luxembourg, the procedure for dialing long-distance calls is the same as that for local calls.

LONG-DISTANCE SERVICES

Avoid making lengthy long-distance telephone calls directly from your hotel room, as hefty surplus charges are added. Instead use a phone card (☞ *below*) or use a long-distance provider.

AT&T, MCI, and Sprint access codes make calling long distance relatively convenient, but you may find the local access number blocked in many hotel rooms. First ask the hotel operator to connect you. If the hotel operator balks, ask for an international operator, or dial the international operator yourself. One way to improve your odds of getting connected to your long-distance carrier is to travel with more than one company's calling card (a hotel may block Sprint, for example, but not MCI). If all else fails, call from a pay phone.

However, if you plan to travel to Belgium and Luxembourg only, study your long-distance service options carefully and **avoid paying for unnecessary options promoted by long-distance providers.** Good service and English-speaking assistance available from local providers make such options redundant.

➤ ACCESS CODES: AT&T Direct (☎ 080010010 Belgium; 08000111 Luxembourg; 800/435–0812 other areas). MCI WorldPhone (☎ 080010012 Belgium; 08000112 Luxembourg; 800/444–4141 other areas). Sprint International Access (☎ 080010014 Belgium; 08000115 Luxembourg; 800/877–7746 other areas).

PHONE CARDS

Most coin-operated public telephones in Belgium and Luxembourg have been replaced by card-operated phones. Telephone cards are sold at post offices, newspaper stands, and many train stations. The minimum card costs 200 Belgian or Luxembourg francs (€4.95).

PUBLIC PHONES

Public pay phones are easy to find in densely populated Belgium and Luxembourg. Most require a telephone card (☞ Phone Cards, *above*). Those that still accept coins require BF20 or Flux 20 for a three-minute call. After the dial tone, pay with either your telephone card or with coins, then dial your number.

TIME

Belgium and Luxembourg are in the same time zone as France, Germany, Italy, and Spain and are one hour ahead of England, Ireland, and Portugal. They are six hours ahead of New York, seven hours ahead of Chicago, nine hours ahead of Los Angeles, and nine hours behind Sydney.

TIPPING

In Belgium, a tip (*service compris* or *service inclusief*) is always included in restaurant and hotel bills and in taxi fares. Railway porters expect BF30/€0.75 per item on weekdays and BF40/€1.00 per item on weekends. For bellhops and doormen, BF100/€2.50 is adequate. Give movie ushers BF20/€0.50 per person in your party, whether or not they show you to your seat. And tip doormen at bars, nightclubs, or discos at least BF50/€1.25 if you're planning to go back.

In Luxembourg, service charges of 15% are included in restaurant bills; for a modest meal, most people leave the small change. At a grander restaurant, you will be expected to leave a larger tip—up to 10% extra when a large staff is involved. For porters, a tip of Flux 50/€1.25 per bag is adequate. Cab drivers expect a tip of about 10%.

TOURS & PACKAGES

Because everything is prearranged on a prepackaged tour or independent vacation, you'll spend less time planning—and often get it all at a good price.

BOOKING WITH AN AGENT

Travel agents are excellent resources. But it's a good idea to collect brochures from several agencies as some agents' suggestions may be influenced by relationships with tour and package firms that reward them for volume sales. If you have a special interest, **find an agent with expertise in that area**; ASTA (☞ Travel Agencies, *below*) has a database of specialists worldwide.

Make sure your travel agent knows the accommodations and other services of the place they're recommending. Ask about the hotel's location, room size, beds, and whether it has a pool, room service, or programs for children, if you care about these. Has your agent been there in person or sent others whom you can contact?

Do some homework on your own, too: local tourism boards can provide information about lesser-known and small-niche operators, some of which may sell only direct.

BUYER BEWARE

Each year consumers are stranded or lose their money when tour operators—even large ones with excellent reputations—go out of business. So **check out the operator.** Ask several travel agents about its reputation, and try to **book with a company that has a consumer-protection program.** (Look for information in the company's brochure.) In the United States, members of the National Tour Association and the United States Tour Operators Association are required to set aside funds to cover your payments and travel arrangements in the event that the company defaults. It's also a good idea to choose a company that participates in the American Society of Travel Agents' Tour Operator Program

(TOP); ASTA will act as mediator in any disputes between you and your tour operator.

Remember that the more your package or tour includes the better you can predict the ultimate cost of your vacation. Make sure you know exactly what is covered, and **beware of hidden costs.** Are taxes, tips, and transfers included? Entertainment and excursions? These can add up.

➤ TOUR-OPERATOR RECOMMENDATIONS: **American Society of Travel Agents** (☞ Travel Agencies, *below*). **National Tour Association** (NTA; ✉ 546 E. Main St., Lexington, KY 40508, ☎ 606/226–4444 or 800/682–8886, www.ntaonline.com). **United States Tour Operators Association** (USTOA; ✉ 342 Madison Ave., Suite 1522, New York, NY 10173, ☎ 212/599–6599 or 800/468–7862, FAX 212/599–6744, ustoa@aol.com, www.ustoa.com).

GROUP TOURS

Among companies that sell tours to Belgium and Luxembourg, the following are nationally known, have a proven reputation, and offer plenty of options. The classifications used below represent different price categories, and you'll probably encounter these terms when talking to a travel agent or tour operator. The key difference is usually in accommodations, which run from budget to better, and better-yet to best.

➤ SUPER-DELUXE: **Abercrombie & Kent** (✉ 1520 Kensington Rd., Oak Brook, IL 60521-2141, ☎ 630/954–2944 or 800/323–7308, FAX 630/954–3324). **Travcoa** (✉ Box 2630, 2350 S.E. Bristol St., Newport Beach, CA 92660, ☎ 714/476–2800 or 800/992–2003, FAX 714/476–2538).

➤ DELUXE: **Globus** (✉ 5301 S. Federal Circle, Littleton, CO 80123-2980, ☎ 303/797–2800 or 800/221–0090, FAX 303/347–2080). **Maupintour** (✉ 1515 St. Andrews Dr., Lawrence, KS 66047, ☎ 785/843–1211 or 800/255–4266, FAX 785/843–8351). **Tauck Tours** (✉ Box 5027, 276 Post Rd. W, Westport, CT 06881-5027, ☎ 203/226–6911 or 800/468–2825, FAX 203/221–6866).

➤ FIRST-CLASS: **Brendan Tours** (✉ 15137 Califa St., Van Nuys, CA 91411, ☎ 818/785–9696 or 800/421–8446, FAX 818/902–9876). **Caravan Tours** (✉ 401 N. Michigan Ave., Chicago, IL 60611, ☎ 312/321–9800 or 800/227–2826, FAX 312/321–9845). **Central Holidays** (✉ 206 Central Ave., Jersey City, NJ 07307, ☎ 201/798–5777 or 800/935–5000). **Insight International Tours** (✉ 745 Atlantic Ave., #720, Boston, MA 02111, ☎ 617/482–2000 or 800/582–8380, FAX 617/482–2884 or 800/622–5015). **Trafalgar Tours** (✉ 11 E. 26th St., New York, NY 10010, ☎ 212/689–8977 or 800/854–0103, FAX 800/457–6644).

➤ BUDGET: **Cosmos** (☞ Globus, *above*). **Trafalgar Tours** (☞ *above*).

PACKAGES

Independent vacation packages are available from major tour operators and airlines. The companies listed below offer vacation packages.

➤ AIR/HOTEL: **Central Holidays** (☞ Group Tours, *above*). **Delta Vacations** (☎ 800/872–7786). **DER Travel Services** (✉ 9501 W. Devon St., Rosemont, IL 60018, ☎ 800/937–1235, FAX 847/692–4141; 800/282–7474; 800/860–9944 for brochures). **TWA Getaway Vacations** (☎ 800/438–2929). **US Airways Vacations** (☎ 800/455–0123).

➤ FROM THE U.K.: **British Airways Holidays** (✉ Astral Towers, Betts Way, London Rd., Crawley, West Sussex RH10 2XA, ☎ 01293/722–727, FAX 01293/722–624). **Cosmos** (✉ Tourama House, 17 Homesdale Rd., Bromley, Kent BR2 9LX, England, ☎ 0181/464–3444 or 0161/480–5799). **Travelscene** (✉ Travelscene House, 11–15 St. Ann's Rd., Harrow, Middlesex HA1 1AS, England, ☎ 0181/427–8800).

THEME TRIPS

➤ ART & ARCHITECTURE: **Endless Beginnings Tours** (✉ 9825 Dowdy Dr., #105, San Diego, CA 92126, ☎ 619/566–4166 or 800/822–7855, FAX 619/549–9655).

➤ BARGE/RIVER CRUISES: **Etoile de Champagne** (✉ 88 Broad St., Boston, MA 02110, ☎ 800/280–1492,

FAX 617/426–4689). **European Waterways** (✉ 140 E. 56th St., Suite 4C, New York, NY 10022, ☎ 212/688–9489 or 800/217–4447, FAX 212/688–3778 or 800/296–4554). **KD River Cruises of Europe** (✉ 2500 Westchester Ave., Purchase, NY 10577, ☎ 914/696–3600 or 800/346–6525, FAX 914/696–0833). **Kemwel's Premier Selections** (✉ 106 Calvert St., Harrison, NY 10528, ☎ 914/835–5555 or 800/234–4000, FAX 914/835–5449). **Le Boat** (✉ 10 S. Franklin Turnpike, #204B, Ramsey, NJ 07446, ☎ 201/236–2333 or 800/922–0291).

➤ BEER: **MIR Corporation** (✉ 85 S. Washington St., #210, Seattle, WA 98104, ☎ 206/624–7289 or 800/424–7289, FAX 206/624–7360).

➤ BICYCLING: **Euro-Bike Tours** (✉ Box 990, De Kalb, IL 60115, ☎ 800/321–6060, FAX 815/758–8851). **Uniquely Europe** (✉ 2819 1st Ave., Suite 280, Seattle, WA 98121-1113, ☎ 206/441–8682 or 800/426–3615, FAX 206/441–8862). **Vermont Bicycle Touring** (✉ Box 711, Bristol, VT, 05443-0711, ☎ 802/453–4811 or 800/245–3868, FAX 802/453–4806).

➤ GARDENS: **Coopersmith's England** (✉ Box 900, Inverness, CA 94937, ☎ 415/669–1914, FAX 415/669–1942). **Expo Garden Tours** (✉ 70 Great Oak, Redding, CT 06896, ☎ 203/938–0410 or 800/448–2685, FAX 203/938–0427).

➤ MOTORCYCLE: **Edelweiss Bike Travel** (✉ Hartford Holidays Travel, 129 Hillside Ave., Williston Park, NY 11596, ☎ 516/746–6761 or 800/877–2784, FAX 516/746–6690).

TRAIN TRAVEL

Rail travel in Europe, even first-class including supplements, is consistently cheaper than the lowest available one-way airline fare.

Eurostar operates high-speed passenger-only trains, which whisk riders between new stations in London and Brussels (Midi) in 3¼ hours. At press time, fares were $230 for a one-way, first-class ticket and $111 for an economy fare. A number of promotional return fares are available.

On the new Thalys high-speed trains, a one-way ticket from Brussels to Paris costs about $90 in first class and $60 in economy. The trip lasts 1⅓ hours. Reserved seats are obligatory for both Eurostar and Thalys trains.

An extensive network makes train travel within Belgium and Luxembourg and between the two countries the easiest mode of transportation. Service is prompt and frequent.

CLASSES

Train travel is available in first or second class. First-class seats are slightly more spacious and are upholstered. First-class passengers on Thalys trips to Paris are served a light meal and beverage.

High-speed trains, intercity trains, and local trains alike offer smoking or no-smoking sections.

CUTTING COSTS

To save money, **look into rail passes.** But be aware that if you don't plan to cover many miles you may come out ahead by buying individual tickets.

One program, B-Tourrail, allows you travel throughout Belgium for any five days in one month. If you are traveling in a group of two to five people, the Belgian railway offers discounted fixed prices for two one-way trips or one return trip. If you are under 26 years old, a discount train pass entitles you to 10 one-way train trips to any destination in Belgium. For those over 60, the Belgian railway offers a reduced-fare non-nominative pass for six one-way trips. There are reduced fares for weekend trips to the Belgian seaside or the Ardennes. You can **pick up a booklet of Belgian railway package excursions,** B-Excursions, available at Belgium's major train stations.

For travel between Belgium and Luxembourg, consider the *Billet Benelux Week-end* and *Carte Benelux Tourrail,* which offer significant discounts for weekend travel and travel within one month.

Belgium and Luxembourg are among the 17 countries in which you can **use EurailPasses,** which provide unlimited first-class rail travel, in all of the participating countries, for the duration of the pass. If you plan to rack up the miles, get a standard pass.

These are available for 15 days ($538), 21 days ($698), one month ($864), two months ($1,224), and three months ($1,512). If your plans call for only limited train travel, **look into a Europass,** which costs less than a EurailPass. Unlike with EurailPasses, however, you get a limited number of travel days, in a limited number of countries, during a specified time period. For example, a two-month pass ($386) that includes the Netherlands, Belgium, and Luxembourg allows between 5 and 15 days of rail travel but costs $150 less than the least expensive EurailPass. Keep in mind, however, that the Europass is also good only in France, Germany, Italy, Spain, and Switzerland.

In addition to standard EurailPasses, **ask about special rail-pass plans.** Among these are the Eurail Youthpass (for people under age 26), the Eurail Saverpass (which gives a discount for two or more people traveling together), a Eurail Flexipass (which allows a certain number of travel days within a set period), the Euraildrive Pass, and the Europass Drive (which combines travel by train and rental car). Whichever pass you choose, remember that you must **purchase your pass before you leave** for Europe.

Many travelers assume that rail passes guarantee them seats on the trains they wish to ride. Not so. You need to **book seats ahead even if you are using a rail pass**; seat reservations are required on some European trains, particularly high-speed trains, and are a good idea on trains that may be crowded—particularly in summer on popular routes. You will also need a reservation if you purchase sleeping accommodations.

➤ INFORMATION & PASSES: **CIT Tours Corp** (✉ 15 W. 44th St., 10th Floor, New York, NY 10036, ☎ 212/730–2400 or 800/248–7245 in the U.S.; 800/387–0711 or 800/361–7799 in Canada). **DER Travel Services** (✉ 9501 W. Devon Ave., Rosemont, IL 60018, ☎ 800/782–2424, FAX 800/282–7474 for information; 800/860–9944 for brochures). **Rail Europe** (✉ 500 Mamaroneck Ave., Harrison, NY 10528, ☎ 914/682–5172 or 800/438–7245, FAX 800/432–1329; ✉ 2087 Dundas E, Suite 106, Mississauga, Ontario L4X 1M2, ☎ 800/361–7245, FAX 905/602–4198).

FARES & SCHEDULES

Major train stations have an information office for information about fares and schedules. All train stations post complete listings, by time, of arrivals and departures, including the track number.

To avoid crowds, don't travel by train to the Belgian coast on Saturday morning or return from there on Sunday afternoon in the summer. Belgium's national holiday, July 21, also draws train travelers from Brussels to the seaside and the Ardennes.

➤ TRAIN INFORMATION: Train station telephone numbers: **Antwerp Central** (☎ 03/204–2040). **Brugge** (☎ 050/382–382). **Brussels** (☎ 02/555–2555). **Namur** (☎ 081/252–222). **Ostende** (☎ 059/701–517). **Luxembourg City** (☎ 4990–4990).

PAYING

Train tickets bought in Belgium and Luxembourg can be paid for using currency or a major credit card—American Express, Diners Club, Master Card, or Visa. You cannot pay for train tickets with traveler's checks, but currency exchange booths in the stations can cash your checks. For international travel, you may pay and reserve with a credit card by telephone, at the train station itself, or through a local travel agency.

RESERVATIONS

Reservations are obligatory on the Eurostar train to London and on the Thalys train to Paris. Reservations are not required for domestic trains or for trains between Brussels and Luxembourg City. For further information contact the Brussels or Luxembourg City train station (☞ Fares and Schedules, *above*).

➤ CONTACTS: **Eurostar** (☎ 0900/10–366). **Thalys** (☎ 0900–10–177).

TRANSPORTATION AROUND BELGIUM & LUXEMBOURG

If you are traveling between cities and are able to manage your luggage, train travel is your best option. If you prefer to enjoy the countryside and make stops along the way, consider renting a car. Local buses are not as frequent as trains and make more stops.

In cities, public transportation by tram, metro, and bus is not as frequent or easy to master as in London or Paris. Taxis are available at major train stations, and fares within the city are reasonable. Fares increase dramatically once you travel outside city limits.

TRAVEL AGENCIES

A good travel agent puts your needs first. Look for an agency that has been in business at least five years, emphasizes customer service, and has someone on staff who specializes in your destination. In addition, **make sure the agency belongs to a professional trade organization.** The American Society of Travel Agents (ASTA), with 27,000 agents in some 170 countries, is the largest and most influential in the field. Operating under the motto "Integrity in Travel," it maintains and enforces a strict code of ethics and will step in to help mediate any agent-client disputes if necessary. ASTA also maintains a Web site that includes a directory of agents. (If a travel agency is also acting as your tour operator, *see* Buyer Beware *in* Tours & Packages, *above.*)

➤ LOCAL AGENT REFERRALS: **American Society of Travel Agents** (ASTA; ☏ 800/965–2782 24-hr hot line, FAX 703/684–8319, www.astanet.com). **Association of British Travel Agents** (✉ 68–71 Newman St., London W1P 4AH, ☏ 0171/637–2444, FAX 0171/637–0713, abta.co.uk, www.abtanet.com). **Association of Canadian Travel Agents** (✉ 1729 Bank St., Suite 201, Ottawa, Ontario K1V 7Z5, ☏ 613/521–0474, FAX 613/521–0805, acta.ntl@sympatico.ca). **Australian Federation of Travel Agents** (✉ Level 3, 309 Pitt St., Sydney 2000, ☏ 02/9264–3299, FAX 02/9264–1085, www.afta.com.au). **Travel Agents' Association of New Zealand** (✉ Box 1888, Wellington 10033, ☏ 04/499–0104, FAX 04/499–0827, taanz@tiasnet.co.nz).

VISITOR INFORMATION

➤ BELGIAN NATIONAL TOURIST OFFICE: **In the U.S.:** ✉ 780 3rd Ave., New York, NY 10017, ☏ 212/758–8130, FAX 212/355–7675. **In Canada:** ✉ Box 760 NDG, Montréal, Québec H4A 3S2, ☏ 514/484–3594, FAX 514/489–8965. **In the U.K.:** ✉ 29 Princes St., London W1R 7RG, ☏ 0171/629–0230, FAX 0171/629–0454.

➤ LUXEMBOURG NATIONAL TOURIST OFFICE: **In the U.S.:** ✉ 17 Beekman Pl., New York, NY 10022, ☏ 212/935–8888, FAX 212/935–5896. **In the U.K.:** ✉ 122 Regent St., London W1R 5FE, ☏ 0171/434–2800.

➤ WITHIN BELGIUM & LUXEMBOURG: **Belgian Office of Tourism** (✉ 61-63, rue Marché aux Herbes, 1000 Brussels, ☏ 02/513–6950, FAX 02/513–8803). **Luxembourg Office of Tourism** (✉ B.P. 1001, 1010 Luxembourg City, ☏ 4282–8220, FAX 4282–8238).

➤ U.S. GOVERNMENT ADVISORIES: **U.S. Department of State** (✉ Overseas Citizens Services Office, Room 4811 N.S., 2201 C St. NW, Washington, DC 20520, ☏ 202/647–5225 for interactive hot line; 301/946–4400 for computer bulletin board; FAX 202/647–3000 for interactive hot line); enclose a self-addressed, stamped, business-size envelope.

WEB SITES

Do check out the World Wide Web when you're planning. You'll find everything from current weather forecasts to virtual tours of famous cities. Fodor's Web site, www.fodors.com, is a great place to start your online travels. When you see a 🖱 in this book, go to www.fodors.com/urls for an up-to-date link to that destination's site.

For more information specifically on Belgium and Luxembourg, visit www.Belgium.fgov.be, www.toervl.be, www.opt.be, www.hotels-belgium.com, www.belgium-tourism.net, and www.ont.lu.

Railway Web sites are as follows: Belgian Railway, www.b-rail.be; Luxembourg Railway, www.CFL.lu; Thalys, www.thalys.com; Eurostar, www.sncb.be

WHEN TO GO

The best times to visit these two countries are in the late spring—when the northern European days are long and the summer crowds have not yet filled the beaches, the highways, or the museums—and in fall.

Because **Belgians** take vacations in July and August, these months are not ideal for visiting the coast or the Ardennes, but summer is a very good time to be in Brussels, Antwerp, or Liège. In summer you will also be able to get a break on hotel prices; on the other hand, this is also vacation time for many restaurants. For touring the country and visiting much-frequented tourist attractions such as Brugge, the best times are April–June and September–October.

Luxembourg (like Belgium) is a northern country—parallel in latitude to Newfoundland and Canada—with the same seasonal extremes in the amount of daylight. In late spring, summer, and early fall, you have daylight until 10 PM; in winter, however, be prepared for dusk closing in before 4 PM. There's rarely a long spell of heavy snow, but winters tend to be dank and rainy. Many attractions, especially outside the city, maintain shortened visiting hours (or close altogether) from late fall to Pentecost (late spring), except for a brief time around Easter. Summer is the principal tourist season, when Luxembourg polishes up its sightseeing train and restaurants set out terrace tables under the sycamores; gardens are in full bloom and weather can be comfortably warm. Spring and early fall are attractive as well.

CLIMATE

What follows are average daily maximum and minimum temperatures in Brussels and Luxembourg City.

➤ FORECASTS: **Weather Channel Connection** (☎ 900/932–8437), 95¢ per minute from a Touch-Tone phone.

BRUSSELS

Jan.	40F	4C	May	65F	18C	Sept.	70F	21C
	31	–1		47	8		52	11
Feb.	45F	7C	June	72F	22C	Oct.	59F	15C
	32	0		52	11		45	7
Mar.	50F	10C	July	74F	23C	Nov.	49F	9C
	36	2		54	12		38	3
Apr.	58F	14C	Aug.	72F	22C	Dec.	43F	6C
	41	5		54	12		34	1

LUXEMBOURG CITY

Jan.	38F	3C	May	65F	18C	Sept.	67F	19C
	31	– 1		47	8		50	10
Feb.	40F	4C	June	70F	21C	Oct.	56F	13C
	31	– 1		52	11		43	6
Mar.	50F	10C	July	74F	23C	Nov.	45F	7C
	34	1		56	13		38	3
Apr.	58F	14C	Aug.	72F	22C	Dec.	40F	4C

1 DESTINATION: BELGIUM AND LUXEMBOURG

REFLECTIONS IN A PEWTER BOWL

SLATE-COLOR SKIES CURVE like a pewter bowl over an undulating landscape, the long, low horizon punctuated by blunt steeples and a scattering of deep-roofed farmhouses that seem to enfold the land like a mother goose spreading wings over her brood. Inky crows wheel over spindle-fingered pollards; jackdaws pepper the ocher grainfields; and a magpie, flashing black and white, drags a long, iridescent tail through the damp air. These are the 16th-century landscapes of Pieter Bruegel the Elder—stained-glass planes in sepia tones, leaded by black branches, crooked spires, dark-frozen streams.

And these, too, are the 20th-century landscapes of Belgium and Luxembourg—a wedge of northern Europe squeezed between the massive and ancient kingdoms of France and Germany, bounded by the harsh North Sea to the northwest, defined by the rough, high forests of the Ardennes to the southeast. No wonder so much of their appeal, past and present, is interior—their weather-beaten cultures have turned inward over the centuries, toward the hearth. Indoors, Bruegel's otherwise sepia scenes warm subtly with color—earthy browns, berry reds, loden greens, muted indigos, coral cheeks. So it is today: the Flemish nurse goblets of mahogany beer by candlelight in dark-beamed halls, a scarlet splash of paisley runner thrown over the pine tabletop; red-vested Walloons—French-speaking Belgians—read the newspaper in high-back oak banquettes polished blue-black by generations of rough tweed. In Luxembourg, the glass of light beer and *drüp* of eau-de-vie go down behind the candy-color leaded glass of spare, brightly lit *stuff*, or pubs, where village life finds its social focus, day in, day out. In these small northern lands, so often lashed by winter rain, soaked by drizzle, wrapped in fog, the people live out the rich-hued interior scenes of the Old Masters.

Yet the skies do clear, come spring. Then the real pleasure begins—an intense appreciation that residents of more moderate climates would be hard-put to understand. As if the people's gratitude took physical form, it manifests itself in flowers, a frenzy of color spilling from every windowsill, over rose trellises, through wisteria-woven archways. Fruit trees explode like fireworks, and whole orchards shimmer pink. Chestnut branches sag under the weight of their leaves and the heavy, grapelike clusters of blossom that thrust upward, defying gravity. In the midst of this orgy of scent and color, Flemish farmers in blue overalls open their half-doors and bask, and the international bankers of Luxembourg swing their Versace suit coats over their shoulders and head for the benches in the green Pétrusse Valley.

Then café society, and home life with it, moves outdoors to bask in the warmth. Terrace cafés on the Grote Markts and Grand'Places rival any piazza in Italy. And when there's no café around, the family simply sets out a cluster of folding chairs, perhaps a checkered-cloth-covered card table, whether smack on the sidewalk or behind the barn door, to make the most of fine weather. A suntan remains (as it does in sun-starved North Germany) the most sought-after of status symbols—doubly prestigious if flaunted in midwinter, as northerners, once pale and prune-skinned, return from the ski slopes of the Alps or the beaches of the Canary Islands. The shared climate, from inexorable gray to luxurious sun, may form a common bond, but Belgium and Luxembourg sustain distinct identities.

Belgium is a country torn in half, split by two tongues and two cultures. The division between Wallonia and Flanders traces back to Merov ingian times, and the Walloon patois and Belgian French represent the last northward wave of the Roman empire and its lingual residue. Twice in this century Flemish citizens (and possibly a king) were known to collaborate with German invaders, allying themselves against what they saw as French-speaking domination. In turn, francophone Belgians, made powerful by their region's blossoming heavy industry, looked down upon their Flemish countrymen: the country's constitution was not translated into Dutch until 1961. Today the bickering over bilingual rights—which leaves Brussels a no-man's-land, with extra-wide enamel signs naming every street and alley in two tongues—is especially acute. Many intellectuals believe politicians on both sides are whipping up national sentiment, when they should be looking at urgent matters like reform of the police and justice system.

The cultures are as different as their languages: the Flemish are proud and tidy, their homes filled with the exterior light that pours in through tall, multipaned windows; a spare, avant-garde current in fashion, film, and literature shows their Dutch leanings. The Walloons, on the other hand, remain more laissez-faire, their homes often dark, cozy, and cluttered with knickknacks and lace. A women's clothing shop in Gent is likely to include progressive, trendy, severe clothing, while the equivalent in Liège will show cardigans, A-line skirts, and fussy floral prints. These two separate worlds share a Catholic culture that, beyond the spiritual realm, finds expression in a shared appreciation of the good things in life, such as the pleasures of the table.

While Belgium is a picture of inner conflict, the natives of little Luxembourg present a solid front to the outside, interacting in French, German, or English, but maintaining their private world in their own native *Lëtzebuergesch* (Luxembourgish). Thus, having survived centuries of conquest and occupation, they can open their country to European Union "Eurocrats" and more than a hundred international banks, and still keep to themselves. Luxembourg sustains two parallel cultures, with some cafés catering to trendy, international, or tourist crowds and others reserved for the loden-coated locals, who may greet an aberrant visitor with stunned silence as thick as the cigarette smoke that fills the air.

Belgium and Luxembourg, having been conquered and economically dwarfed for generations by their larger neighbors, felt compelled in 1958 to join with the Netherlands in an economic alliance that served as a foundation for the European Union. Since then, "Benelux" has become a convenient abbreviation for a small, independent wedge of northern Europe where even fruit juice is labeled in French and in Dutch.

But Belgium and Luxembourg are considerably more than two thirds of an arbitrary economic unit—they make up a rich, varied region with strong (and conflicting) cultural identities. In their cities, burnished with age, museums display the masterpieces of Bruegel, Van Eyck, Memlings, and Rubens, while their inspiration—the magnificent, brooding countryside and time-polished interiors—remains much unchanged.

— Nancy Coons

WHAT'S WHERE

Belgium

Belgium has visitor attractions out of all proportion to its diminutive size. Old World charm, a great cuisine, golden beaches, and the scenic forest of the Ardennes: these are but a few. The rest is art, to which Belgium, at the cultural crossroads of Europe, has been one of the supreme contributors. Jan van Eyck, said to have invented oil painting, heads a distinguished list of Flemish artists that includes Rogier Van der Weyden, Dirck Bouts, Hugo Van der Goes, Hans Memling, Quentin Matsys, the Pieters Bruegel (elder and younger), Pieter Paul Rubens, and Anthony Van Dyck. Their work still shines with themystic aura of the 15th century, the rich humanism of the Renaissance, the decorative exuberance of the Baroque. You can still find the people and the landscapes of Flanders almost unchanged since Pieter Bruegel the Elder brought his extraordinary powers of observation to focus on scenes of Flemish peasant life.

The two largest, most cosmopolitan cities are Brussels (Bruxelles, Brussel)—a lively capital, a great shopping center, and the site of several fine museums—and Antwerp, a bustling port that is also a notable museum city. The so-called picture-book towns, Gent (Gand) and Brugge (Bruges), are gems of medieval reminiscence. If you are interested in military history, or appalled by the suffering that war has caused, Belgium offers you a chance to marvel and remember: from Kortrijk (Courtrai), where

Flemish peasant soldiers defeated French horsemen in 1302; to Waterloo, where Wellington confronted Napoléon; to Ieper (Ypres), site of the bloodiest stalemates of World War I; and Bastogne, where Hitler's armies fought their rearguard. Among the numerous other cities of historic and artistic interest are Liège, Leuven (Louvain), Namur (Namen), Mechelen (Malines), and Tournai (Doornik). The ancestor of all health resorts is Spa. On the seacoast, Oostende and Knokke-Heist are the two main lures. Away from the busy life of Belgium's cities lie the rolling hills, dark woods, and green fields of the Ardennes and Belgium's greatest natural curiosity, the grottoes of Han-sur-Lesse and of neighboring Rochefort. Artisanal breweries dot the landscape, with monasteries such as Orval, Rochefort, and Mardesous producing some of the best beers in this country of beer connoisseurs.

Brussels

In Belgium, all roads lead to Brussels—and this goes for the railroads and airlines, too. Brussels is now the capital of the European Union, the boomtown home of international businesspeople, Eurocrats, and lobbyists with their legendary expense accounts. However, side by side with the European institutions lies the old traditional capital, the ancient heart of the Brabant. In many respects, it is a thoroughly modern city, with shining steel-and-glass office blocks jostling Gothic spires and Art Nouveau town houses.

Victor Hugo once called the city's **Grand'-Place** "the most beautiful square in the world." Flanked by flamboyantly decorated 17th-century guild houses, many of whose ground floors harbor superb cafés, it's dominated by the resplendent **Hôtel de Ville** (town hall), which is in regal Brabant Gothic style. In summertime, the square is spectacularly floodlit at night. Three blocks behind the town hall stands Belgium's "oldest inhabitant," the charming *Manneken Pis*—many amusing legends surround this statue of a peeing boy. The city's superlatives include: magnificent Rubenses and Bruegels at the **Musée d'Art Ancien,** the grand **Cathédrale de St. Michel et Ste. Gudule,** the delightful museum devoted to the art of comic strips, the fashionable square of the **Grand Sablon** (great antiques, pastry shops, and restaurants), the opulent **Théâtre de la Monnaie** for the best concerts and ballet, and the haunting Magritte and Delvaux paintings on view at the **Musée d'Art Moderne.** The **Victor Horta house,** the finest Art Nouveau building on the continent, is now a museum, and other treasures of both Art Nouveau and Art Deco lie in the residential areas to the south and southeast of the city center. Brussels also serves some of Europe's finest cuisine: from *biftec et frites* (steak and fries) in a bistro to *waterzooi* (an elegant chicken stew) in a brasserie to *gaufres* (waffles) or death-by-chocolate pralines on the sidewalk.

Gent, Brugge, and the Coast

"The Art Cities of Flanders" is a phrase that conjures up images of proud Gent, now calm but in the past often torn by civil strife, and medieval Brugge (Bruges), contemplating its weathered beauty in the dark mirror of its peaceful canals. In the 15th century, these were among the richest cities in Europe, and the aura of that golden age still seems to emanate from their cloth halls, opulent merchants' homes, and cathedrals. **Gent** is a city—one of Belgium's largest—not an inanimate museum, as is often said of Brugge. While much is medieval in this city, every stone is, in fact, part of 20th-century life. On a summer evening, viewed from Sint-Michielsbrug (St. Michael's Bridge), Gent's noble medieval buildings assume a fairy-tale quality under the floodlights. One of the three great medieval spires is that of **St. Bavo's Cathedral,** home of that world-wonder, the 15th-century *Adoration of the Mystic Lamb* altarpiece, which Jan van Eyck must have painted with a magnifying glass, so miraculous is its detail. Among the town's other sights are the Gravensteen, the grand castle of the counts of Flanders; the imposing Town Hall; the proud Belfort (Belfry); and many fine centuries-old buildings.

If it were not for people in modern clothes (and the fact that outlying portions of the city are modern business districts), it would be difficult to realize you are living in the 20th century in **Brugge.** Scarcely a facade on any street or canal fails to conjure up visions of the past. Like a northern Venice—and just as evocative—it is laced with tranquil canals and quaint bridges (Brugge, indeed, means bridges). Famed as the birthplace of Flemish painting, it has in the **Groeninge Museum** on the Dijver some of the finest masterpieces of Jan van Eyck (his magnificent *Madonna with Canon Van der Paele*), Van der Goes, Memling, Gerard David, and Hieronymus Bosch. Nearby stands the **Memling Museum** (with just six paintings—but they are six of the greatest Memlings in the world) within the walls of the 12th-century St. John's Hospice. Nothing remains of the castle that gave the **Burg** its name, but even so this is an extraordinary square, with its Gothic town hall and Romanesque chapel. The highways south from Brugge and Gent point to Flanders Fields—there are countless military cemeteries in the area surrounding **Ieper** (Ypres), risen from the ashes of World War I. The beach-fringed **North Sea Coast** has more than 20 resorts, the James Ensor Museum in **Oostende,** and some of the best seafood in the country.

Antwerp

If you like to combine atmosphere and history with urban energy, trendy Antwerp may fit the bill even better than Brussels. While the city has grown and modernized apace—today it is a mighty port and diamond mecca (handling 70% of the world's diamonds)—it preserves a great deal of yesterday's glories. In Antwerp's greatest period, the late 17th century, three painters—Pieter Paul Rubens, Jacob Jordaens, and Anthony van Dyck—made the city into a standard bearer of style second only to Rome. At the **Cathedral,** three great Rubens altarpieces dazzle the eye. Off the Meir, **Rubenshuis,** the house occupied by the artist from 1610 for the last quarter century of his life, is a truly patrician palace, marked by a large Flamboyant Baroque portico and a lovely garden. Nearby is the **Mayer van den Bergh Museum,** a connoisseur's delight, with several masterpieces on view, including Bruegel's unforgettable *Dulle Griet* (Mad Meg). Two other august houses are a few blocks away: the **Rockoxhuis,** home of Rubens's patron, and the **Plantin-Moretus Museum,** once the home and print shop of Europe's most noted 17th-century publisher. Here too are a **Diamond District,** opulent churches, Renaissance guildhalls, and the **Koninklijk Museum voor Schone Kunsten,** with its noted Rubens masterworks and four centuries of Dutch and Flemish art on view.

The Northeast

The eastern portion of Flemish Belgium is dominated to the north by the Kempen, a moorland alternating with sandy plains that makes up the bulk of the provinces of Antwerp and Limburg. Here outdoor enthusiasts will enjoy **Bokrijk,** the largest open-air museum and nature reserve in Europe, and **Kalmthout,** a vast park teeming with wildlife. In addition to the city of Antwerp, several smaller towns are of note: **Leuven,** east of Brussels, is the home of the country's most prestigious university (Erasmus taught here) and carries a strong sense of its Flemish identity. Midway between Brussels and Antwerp is **Mechelen,** a well-preserved medieval gem valued both as a place of the spirit (it is the residence of Belgium's Roman Catholic Primate) and the earth (for here you'll find the country's best asparagus and endive). To the east, **Hasselt,** Limburg's principal city, is a leading distiller of *jenever,* Belgium's national spirit, and a burgeoning fashion center. South from there is **Sint-Truiden,** set amid the orchards of the fertile Haspengouw region.

Hainaut and Wallonian Brabant

The region to the south and east of Brussels has a delightful atmosphere of historic interest and rural calm. Wellington's Headquarters stand near the battlefield at **Waterloo,** most of which remains as it was that fateful day in 1815. In **Gaasbeek** one of Belgium's most beautiful châteaux is set within a landscape that inspired the great Bruegel.

Tucked into the gentle hills of the French-speaking region of Hainaut are the three principal cities of **Charleroi, Mons,** and **Tournai,** which trace their origins back to the Romans. While little remains of that era, the architecture and the artifacts preserved in the numerous museums bear witness to the varied political, religious, and cultural influences that have held sway in Hainaut over the last 2000 years. In particular, the region abounds in châteaux and castles, of special note being those at **Antoing, Beloeil,** and **Ecaussines,** and the five-tower **Cathedral of Notre Dame** in Tournai. Further southwest, toward France, the rolling plains give way to more pronounced hills and thicker forests where national parks have been set aside.

The Meuse Valley and the Ardennes

Perhaps more than any other part of historic Belgium, the **Meuse Valley** is marked by humans' centuries of efforts to survive and protect themselves. Here, side by side, are the graves of Stone Age hunters and neatly lined crosses for the countless casualties of the 20th century's wars. Next to each town is a hilltop fort intended to repel invaders, French as well as German. Signs of the great Belgian craft of metalwork are everywhere, especially in **Dinant,** squeezed between the river and the cliff side, and in 17th-century **Namur,** at the confluence of the Meuse and the Sambre. The symbol of Walloon independence and pride is **Liège,** hard hit by the international steel crisis but still an important industrial center. (Val-St-Lambert crystal is made here.) Its old city is riddled with secret courtyards, narrow medieval lanes, steeply stepped streets, and *cafés chantants,* where everyone bursts into song.

The Ardennes is a rolling forest region, full of fast-flowing streams and wooded glens, one of Belgium's most favored vacationlands. The enchanted Forest of Arden of Shakespeare's *As You Like It* offers the double charm of quaint villages and a beautiful landscape. The Ardennes forms an arc through the Belgian provinces of Namur, Liège, and Luxembourg, and on to the neighboring Grand Duchy. It remains one of the finest places in Europe to fill your lungs with fresh mountain air.

Luxembourg

When you try to locate Luxembourg on a map, look for "Lux." at the heart of Western Europe. Even abbreviated, the name runs over—west into Belgium, east into Germany, south into France—as the country's influence has done for centuries. The Grand Duchy of Luxembourg is a thriving, Rhode Island–size land that offers surprising variety and contrasts. On its northern borders and down along the Our and Súre rivers is a rugged, wildly beautiful highland country studded with castles, rich in history. To the south, farmlands lie in the broad, central river valleys, giving way to lush vineyards along the southeastern frontier down the Wine Route through the Moselle valley. A 20-minute drive north from the French border stands the capital, its ancient fortress towering above the south central plain. Seen through early morning mists, it revives the magic of Camelot. It is the nerve center of a thousand-year-old seat of government, a functional working element of the European Union, a spot where the past still speaks, the present interprets, and the future listens.

There is an old saying that describes the life of the Luxembourgers—or *Luxembourgeois,* if you prefer the more elegant French term: "One Luxembourger, a rose garden; two Luxembourgers, a kaffeeklatsch; three Luxembourgers, a band." This is a country of parades and processions, good cheer, and a hearty capacity for beer and Moselle wine. Everybody here speaks French and German, and English is widely understood, which is fortunate because the official language, Lëtzeburgesch, is like nothing else you ever heard before.

Luxembourg City

The capital of the country looks just like a setting for Franz Lehar's operetta, *The Count of Luxembourg*; yet, despite its medieval aura, this city is a major European Union center. All periods exist together in a kind of helter-skelter harmony, but the place seems ageless: centuries-old bridges, watchtowers, and ramparts reassert themselves to the exclusion of all incongruities. The city itself is small, a perfect place to explore on foot, re-creating the past when this was one of the impregnable citadels of Europe.

Luxembourg's appellation as the "Gibraltar of the North" is due to the thousand-year-old fortress known as the **Bock.** Nearby is the 17th-century **Citadelle du St-Esprit** (Citadel of the Holy Spirit). The historic military **Casemates** (tunnels) run under parts of the city. The **Place d'Armes** is the most welcoming corner of town. Other attractions are the **Grand Ducal Palace,** the **Musée National,** and the **Grand'rue,** the city's leading shopping street, which overflows with luxury boutiques. The beautiful scenic ramparts of **the Corniche** offer magnificent views over the deep valley below.

The Luxembourg Ardennes

The northern part of the country, called the Luxembourg Ardennes, is similar in many ways to its Belgian namesake. Romantic winding valleys of fast rivers, ideal for angling, cut into the plateau of high hills. Here and there are magnificent medieval castles—such as those at **Vianden, Bourscheid, Wiltz,** and **Clervaux.** The last was virtually reduced to rubble (but now amazingly restored) by an event that shook the world just over 50 years ago—the devastating Battle of the Ardennes, or Bulge. In **Diekirch** and **Wiltz** are museums devoted to this heroic battle.

The Petite Suisse and the Moselle

In the region that Luxembourgers regard as their own Switzerland, **Müllerthal** is not exactly the Alps but still a hiker's paradise, with leafy hills, flowering fields, and rushing streams. At **Echternach,** a major center of pilgrimage and the arts, the town's exquisite abbey was once famed for its fine medieval school of illumination. To the south, in the **Moselle valley,** vines cover every exposed slope. The method of making sparkling Moselle wine is illustrated by local vintners in the most refreshing way—by offering you several glasses of the bubbly stuff.

The Redlands

Once a center of industry, the southernmost region of Luxembourg is being redeveloped as a tourist destination. Factory towns such as **Esch Sur Alzette** and **Dudelange** are sprouting museums and rediscovering their Roman and medieval heritage. Lush parks and hiking trails crisscross the same landscape that was once dominated by iron mines. There are also lots of activities down for kids, including amusement parks and tourist trains.

NEW AND NOTEWORTHY

Belgium

Brussels gleams anew in 2001, benefiting from major face-lifts to public parks and buildings. A thorough renovation of the **Parc de Bruxelles** overlooking the Palais du Roi has restored it to grace. Nearby, the **Eglise Notre-Dame du Sablon** at the eastern end of the elegant Place du Grand Sablon is luminously white even on wintry days as a result of laborious cleaning that stripped away years of grime from its facade. Music lovers should head to Brussels's recently opened **Musée des Instruments de Musique** (Museum of Musical Instruments) to see a world-class collection of instruments that span both the centuries and the globe. In addition to preserving its heritage, Brussels continues to add to its skyline. The European Commission's **Berlaymont** building is taking shape as a shining new skyscraper after years under wraps due to asbestos contamination.

The year 2001 is celebrated as "Mode 2001" in **Antwerp,** a tribute to the city's continued success as a center for fashion design. Throughout the year Antwerp museums will be hosting special fashion exhibitions. The biggest extravaganza takes place in late spring, when the Modenatie, a classic 19th-century building, will open in its new incarnation as the **Modemuseum** (Momu the Provincial Fashion Museum), with Walter Van Beirendonck as curator.

In the eastern town of **Stavelot** in the Ardennes, the 18th-century abbey in the middle of town houses a new, sophisticated cultural complex featuring an interpretive center, a race-car museum, and a museum devoted to the provocative poet Apollinaire.

Luxembourg

Since the mid-1980s, Luxembourg has invested heavily in its cultural centers, underwriting museums, music halls, and theaters across the country. Several more venues make their debut in the first years of the 21st century. In 2000, the town of Ettlebruck became home to the **Centre des Artes Pluriels,** a music center featuring a conservatory, a concert hall, and a theater. In Luxembourg City, the I. M. Pei–designed **Musée Grand Duc Jean,** opening in 2001, will provide the Grand Duchy a world-class venue for contemporary art. The **Musée de Fortifications,** due to open in 2001 in the renovated women's prison in the Grund, will delve into Luxembourg City's history.

In addition to the new construction, several of Luxembourg's old favorites are completing renovations. In **Esch Sur Alzette,** the **Musée National de la Résistance** will reopen in 2001 with state-of-the-art exhibitions about Luxembourg's experience during World War II. There will also be galleries specifically devoted to Luxembourg's lost Jewish communities. In **Vian-**

den, the house where Victor Hugo spent his voluntary exile will reopen with great fanfare as the **Victor Hugo Museum** on the writer's 200th birthday in 2002.

Luxembourg City's **Grund** is quickly becoming the trendy quarter for hanging out. Once a squalid neighborhood, its streets are now lined with fashionable restaurants, cafés, and bars. At the base of the city's fortifications, the Grund is best reached via the elevator at the Place de St-Espirit.

One of the newest things in the Grand Duchy is the Grand Duke himself. The handsome Grand Duc Henri was invested in September 2000, after the decision of his father, the Grand Duc Jean, to surrender the role to a new generation.

FODOR'S CHOICE

No two people will agree on what makes a perfect vacation, but it's fun and helpful to know what others think. We hope you'll have a chance to experience some of Fodor's Choices yourself while visiting Belgium and Luxembourg. For detailed information about each entry, refer to the appropriate chapters within this guidebook.

Belgium

Quintessential Belgium

★ **The canals of Brugge.** If you wake up at dawn to view the canals before the masses of tourists who arrive after breakfast and through the day, they appear like three-dimensional Hans Memling paintings. At night, they transform into a fairytale light show. Although the open boats gliding under humpbacked bridges and past quayside merchant's homes are usually packed with sightseers, they offer a swan's-eye glimpse of this waterside city.

★ **Grand'Place, Brussels.** This jewel box of a square ranks among Europe's great treasures. The soaring lines of the Gothic Town Hall dominate one side, in contrast with the elaborately decorated Baroque guildhalls that surround it.

★ **Sint-Michielsbrug, Gent.** From this vantage point, the spiritual, mercantile, and military glory that was Gent is spread out before you. To the east are the three great medieval spires of the gray St. Nicholas Church, the honey-color St. Bavo's Cathedral, and the gilt-encrusted Belfry. To the north, on either side of the River Leie, note the grand old quays of Korenlei and Graslei, now revitalized with restaurants, cafés, and shops in recycled old warehouses along the cobbled lanes. And in the background looms the ancient, hulking fortress of Gravensteen.

★ **Les Hautes Fagnes.** These "High Fens" in easternmost Liège Province are mossy, waterlogged moors—a windswept, desolate landscape punctuated by bushes and copses of beech and oak trees, rich in bird life and mountain vegetation. The frequent mist adds to the mystery, and hikers are urged not to stray from the well-marked paths.

★ **L'Abbeye de Mardesous, Mardesous.** Meuse valley visitors in the know drive from Dinant up the winding road to this peaceful retreat. Settle in for an afternoon picnic of Mardesous beer and cheese, stroll the graceful grounds, or take a horseback ride through the lush surrounding forest. End the day in the acoustically magical cathedral during evening vespers, and watch the dramatic sunset blanket the valley in regal shades of red and orange.

★ **Namur.** The history of Belgium is alive and well in this handsome and friendly city at the confluence of the Sambre and Meuse rivers. You'll find evidence of Belgian's earliest inhabitants, of a visit by Caesar, and of the bloody battles between Europe's rival ruling families from the Middle Ages through the 19th century. Wandering the narrow streets lined with historical and architectural gems is a lovely way to spend the day. Watching sunset from the Citadelle, perched above the river valleys, is the perfect way to end it.

★ **Abbeye d'Orval, Orval.** When Mathilde, the Duchess of Lorraine (Godfrey de Bouillon's aunt), lost her wedding ring in a spring, a trout leapt out of the water and presented it back to her in its mouth. An abbey celebrating the miracle was built on the site, and it has been routinely destroyed and rebuilt over the centuries. The latest version is a working monastery that supports itself by making some of Belgium's finest beer and cheese. The ruins of the old abbeys are spiritually moving, and you can stand over Mathilde's spring, where Belgian women still pray for love and luck.

★ **La Roche-en-Ardenne, Ourthe River Valley.** This is the vacationland Belgians dream about. Deep down between wooded hills, the lively river winds a meandering course, carrying kayaks that seem to move now toward you, now away. Families camp by the river while children splash in the chilly water. A small village clings to the hillside, its farms and church built of stone and slate. From above, look out over an undulating vista of green hills.

★ **The North Sea Coast.** One long, wide beach, the North Sea Coast often looks like a scene from an Impressionist painting: couples strolling arm-in-arm, riders galloping along the water's edge, kites flying high above, tiny tots digging sand castles that will be swallowed by the tide. Out at sea: pleasure craft and fishing vessels. Behind the dike: vacation apartment houses, sand dunes, nature preserves, and cafés serving glistening seafood along with ubiquitous Belgian pancakes and waffles.

Where Art Comes First

★ **Museum Mayer Van den Bergh, Antwerp.** If you think of Pieter Bruegel as a painter of jolly village scenes, you're in for a surprise. His *Dulle Griet* (badly translated to "Mad Meg," as if she were some 16th-century bag lady) strides angrily across a landscape of surrealist horrors, a sword in one hand and a cooking pot in the other. Many interpretations have been advanced, but it certainly can be read as a prophetic antiwar statement, as pertinent to the wars of the 20th century as to the Thirty Years' War, which in Bruegel's day was just around the corner.

★ **Château of Beloeil, Beloeil.** This 17th-century château is undoubtedly one of the finest in Belgium and is every bit the equal of some of the most beautiful in the French Loire Valley. Its gardens are reputed to be the best outside of Versailles. Although the château is a delight to visit at any moment, it takes on a magical atmosphere during the Nocturne de Beloeil in the summer when a classical music concert is coupled with a light show and period costumes for an unforgettable evening, crowned at midnight with fireworks.

★ **St. John's Hospital, Brugge.** The small Memling Museum is installed in this vast hospital, which served Brugge's sick and poor for 800 years. This is the most important collection of the few works by Memling to have survived. The realism of the so-called Flemish Primitives is present in all meticulously rendered details, but just as some of his women's faces are covered by delicately painted veils, so in his work a gossamer veil of mysticism points up the spirituality of the subject.

★ **Modern Art Museum, Brussels.** In conception and structure, the museum is among Europe's most unusual. Snaking into the ground like an upended Guggenheim, its winding passages offer surprises at every turn—the disturbingly altered reality of René Magritte and Giorgio Di Chirico, the naive eroticism of Paul Delvaux, and the caustic polemics of James Ensor. Wilder modern creations by Pierre Alechinksy and sculptor Pol Bury round out a superb collection.

★ **Musée des Instruments de Musique, Brussels.** Newly opened in mid-2000, this museum combines a loving restoration of one of Brussels's finest Art Deco buildings with a dazzling collection of musical instruments from every corner of the world. An ingenious system of infrared headphones allows visitors to enjoy a miniconcert of many of the instruments on display while touring the collection.

★ **St. Bavo's Cathedral, Gent.** Van Eyck's *Adoration of the Mystic Lamb,* completed in 1432, inspires all the awe that its creator could have hoped for. This mother of all oil paintings was executed with brilliant, miniaturist realism. Though the brush strokes are microscopic, they are brilliantly held together by a unifying view of the redemption of mankind.

★ **St. Bartholomew's Church, Liège.** Under the prince-bishops of Liège in the 11th and 12th centuries there flourished *L'Art Mosan*—one of the most distinctive of all medieval styles. The leader of the school was Renier de Huy, and here you will find his masterpiece, a huge baptismal bronze font decorated with sculpted reliefs. Note, in particular, the high-relief scenes of St. John the Baptist and of the baptism of Christ—sculptures of extraordinary plasticity and emotion.

★ **James Ensorhuis, Oostende.** The house and studio of this great early 20th-century artist display copies of his paintings and scads of the objects he painted in them. Ensor's macabre carnival themes are rendered in satirical style and wild colors.

★ **Cathedral of Notre Dame, Tournai.** This 12th-century edifice, with its unique five towers, is easily the most impressive cathedral in the entire region and has influenced the architecture throughout Belgium, marking the passage from Roman to Gothic style. It alone justifies a side trip to Tournai.

Lodging and Dining Gems

★ **Villa Gracia, Weipon.** To describe this splendid mansion, a few kilometers outside of Namur, as "gracious" is an understatement—its few rooms are all glorious. Sipping an aperitif on the plant-filled terrace, overlooking the river, is a delight. *$$$$*

★ **Château du Pont D'oye, Habay la Neuve.** This splendid château is a countryside oasis. Its halls link spacious, classically decorated guest rooms, libraries filled with literary treasures, and private chapels. Outside, the formal gardens surround a pond, and a rose garden leads to secluded hiking trails. The château also has an outstanding restaurant, giving guests little reason to leave. *$$$*

★ **Firean, Antwerp.** Every detail is authentic Art Deco at this small hotel. It is family-owned with family service and wonderful attention to details, including its own brand of toiletries. Just inside the Ring Road, it is well located if you'd rather not negotiate Antwerp's one-way maze, but you have to hop a tram to get to the Old Town from here. *$$$*

★ **Die Swaene, Brugge.** Chandeliers, Louis XV furniture, four-poster beds, burgundy wallpaper, ancient tapestries, candlelit dinners, open fireplaces, marble nymphs, canal-side setting: if romance is what you crave, you'll find it here. The cuisine keeps getting better and now ranks among the best in Brugge. *$$$* (hotel), *$$$$* (restaurant)

★ **Amigo, Brussels.** Even diplomats feel at home here thanks to personalized service (and even bankers appreciate that a junior suite costs no more than a double in the top price category). Althougha mere 50 years old, the Amigo blends perfectly into its Old Town surroundings. *$$$*

★ **Moulin de Lisogne, Lisogne.** This old stone mill was renovated into a gorgeous, secluded inn. Handsome rooms look out to full vegetable gardens, a babbling brook and the surrounding woods. The restaurant serves lamb and veal from the neighboring farm, trout from the garden stream, and bread from an on-site bakery. *$$$*

★ **Welcome/Truite d'Argent, Brussels.** The smallest hotel in Brussels is one of its most charming. It owes its double name to the fact that taxi drivers are more familiar with the name of its 100-year-old restaurant, the Truite d'Argent ($$$). The good news: Michel and Sophie Smeesters are working on expanding from 6 to 10 rooms. Wearing his chef's hat, Michel prepares great seafood specialties, with Sophie in charge of the dining room. *$*

Taste Treats

★ **De Karmeliet, Brugge.** One of Europe's most honored restaurants offers labor-intensive culinary creations, choreographed in hushed 18th-century rooms usually packed with gourmands from around the world. Starters are savored in the garden area, and the following courses (with seemingly endless silver, china, and crystal) are served in the high-ceilinged house. Reserve far ahead, and prepare to spend the evening and to pay the price for great food and wine. *$$$$*

★ **Ogenblik, Brussels.** Slap in the historic center, in the Galeries St-Hubert, this rough-and-ready bistro has been packing them in for more than 20 years. Marble-top tables, green-shade lamps, and superior grub all add up to a delightful experience. *$$$*

★ **Le Pressoir, Tournai.** This restaurant takes its name from its location in a former wine press dating from the 17th century and sits in a choice spot at the foot of the Cathedral of Notre Dame. You'll find a sophisticated menu and unpretentious service in memorable surroundings. *$$$*

★ **Neuze Neuze, Antwerp.** The ever-present, mustachioed Domien Sels has transformed several small 16th-century houses in the shadow of the cathedral into one stylish restaurant that seems to consist exclusively of nooks and crannies. His is a cuisine of surprises: goose liver meunière with caramelized pineapple, sole with a purée of shrimp. He pulls it all off impressively. *$$*

★ **Chez Léon de Bruxelles, Brussels.** Léon has celebrated its first century by changing its name from plain old Chez Léon; prices have started to edge upward but little else has changed. Most diners opt for the specialty, a heaping bowl of blue-shelled mussels accompanied by lots of super fries, but Léon does a mean *filet américain* (steak tartare) as well. $

★ **Maison Bouillon & Fils, La Roche-en-Ardenne.** Some of the best *jambon d'Ardennes* (Ardennes ham) is found at this family-owned charcuterie. Phillipe Bouillon, a true craftsman, pampers his meats, slowly smoking and drying them with local herbs for up to four months. The result is earthy, aromatic, and crisp, each morsel imbued with the Ardennes. $

Special Memories

★ **Vlaeykensgang, Antwerp.** Linger in the alley that progress forgot—where small whitewashed houses stand shoulder to shoulder along a narrow cobblestone alleyway—and listen to the Monday evening carillon concert from the great cathedral. As you emerge into Pelgrimstraat, you're rewarded by the best possible view of the white cathedral spire, whose Gothic lines sweep upward to an incomparable, openwork summit.

★ **Minnewater at Dawn, Brugge.** It's worth the loss of sleep to sit by the willows on this little lake by the Begijnhof, watching the swans and their cygnets gliding in and out of pink-tinged mist. Then stroll to breakfast along the quiet canals—Brugge at its most magical.

★ **The Ommegang, Brussels.** Once a year, in July, the noble ladies and gentlemen of Belgium revert to the pomp and circumstance of yore, as they reenact the stately procession, with standards flying, that greeted the Holy Roman Emperor Charles V on the self-same Grand'Place in 1549. Horsemen, acrobats, fire-eaters, and stilt-walkers participate with gusto.

★ **The Grottes de Han, Han-sur-Lesse.** As you wander through the dark, cool caves, where Neolithic people found shelter and later generations found a hiding place from marauding armies, you come upon a vast hall under a domelike rock roof 400 ft high. Suddenly, on the guided tour, a single torch-carrier appears, running a slalom-like course down the steeply slanting wall: you feel transported thousands—not hundreds—of years back in time.

★ **Bird-watching, Het Zwin.** In spring, this 375-acre bird sanctuary on the North Coast teems with migratory birds, and an aviary is home to nesting storks and numerous feathery delights. Midsummer finds a carpet of purple sea lavender along the dunes. When you tire of peering through binoculars and trudging along the marshy dikes, take respite in the Chalet du Zwin for lunch.

★ **The Last Post, Ieper.** Every night at 8, buglers sound the Last Post at the Menin Gate in memory of the 300,000 British soldiers who passed through here to their death in the trenches of "Flanders Fields." For one poignant moment, traffic is stopped, as Ieper remembers.

★ **La Batte, Liège.** Every Sunday morning, Liège's quai erupts into one of Europe's oldest and biggest outdoor markets. Here is the perfect place to experience the colorful spirit of Belgium. Hawkers sell everything from cheap watches to fine antiques, and shoppers come from surrounding provinces (and countries) to bargain their way along the strip. The market holds culinary pleasures as well—treats like fresh sausage and fruit-stuffed waffles abound.

Luxembourg

Quintessential Luxembourg

★ **Luxembourg City.** The 1,000-year-old fortress city, classified as a World Heritage Monument by the United Nations, was once thought so formidable a stronghold that its mere presence was considered a threat to international peace. Today the vast panorama of medieval stonework and fortified towers guards Luxembourg's considerable wealth as one of the world's leading financial centers and its political clout within the European Union as home to the European Court of Justice.

★ **The Château of Vianden.** This grand castle looms dramatically from the top of a hill as you approach Vianden. It has a special significance to Luxembourgers: it was the ancestral home of the ruling Orange-Nassau dynasty and was the last part of Luxembourg to be liberated by U.S. troops in World War II.

★ **National Museum of Military History, Diekirch.** World War II's gruesome Battle of the Bulge ravaged Luxembourg and made a permanent imprint on the country's psyche. This museum is the best place to comprehend the war's impact on the Grand Duchy. What began as a passionate corps of volunteers curating a moving collection of war paraphernalia has now become a national treasure. Even if the war doesn't hold any interest for you, visit this museum for its extraordinary insight into Luxembourg's national identity.

Dining and Lodging Gems

★ **La Bergerie, Geyershof.** A soufflé of brill, flavored with basil, may not be what you expect in the middle of the Luxembourg forest, but that's what father-and-son team Claude and Thierry Phal have in mind for you in this pastoral hideaway. *$$$$*

★ **Clairefontaine, Luxembourg City.** Tony and Margot Tintinger have served one pope, several presidents, and many prime ministers in their swank restaurant, decorated with restrained opulence. It stands on the handsomest square in town, a stone's throw from the ministries that supply much of the clientele, and on fine days tables spill out over the square. The menu begins with five different preparations of *foie gras d'oie* (goose liver), which suggests that this is far from your garden-variety bar-and-grill. *$$$$*

★ **Iwwert de Steiler, Luxembourg City.** Luxembourg City's first café had a glorious view over the Alzette river valley. The view from the original windows is the same, but now the café has been transformed into a colorful, chic restaurant with multiple grand dining rooms. Feast on fish from the area's rivers, accompanied by a delicious Moselle wine. *$$$$*

★ **Vieux Moulin, Asselborn.** Tucked deep in the Ardennes, this romantic country inn is in a restored 10th-century mill. Spend the day hiking or biking through the forest and then enjoy a meal that combines traditional Luxembourg game with modern gourmet delights. Let the sound of the nearby brook lull you to sleep, and wake up the next day to do it all over again. Lodging *$$*; Restaurant *$$$*

Special Memories

★ **Le Bock, Luxembourg City.** This is Sigefroid's 1,000-year-old castle, protected in its heyday by three rings of defense and 53 forts. As you wander through the casemates—underground corridors tunneled through the rock—stop at an aperture to look out over the valley below, and imagine the thousands of banner-topped tents and campfires of an army laying siege to the impenetrable fortress.

★ **The Moselle Valley.** No trip to Luxembourg is complete without spending at least a day exploring the Moselle river valley. Travel the *Route du Vin* by car, on foot, by bicycle, or along the river itself by boat. Stop at any of the caves along the way to taste the flavorful still white wine and bubbling *cremant* (similar to champagne) that are characteristic of the region.

★ **Müllerthal.** Spread your picnic of dark bread, pink Ardennes ham, and smoky sausage alongside a twisting brook in Luxembourg's "Little Switzerland." Butterflies flutter over the meadow, swallows dart about in the sky, and the only sounds are the drone of the bees and the gurgle of the stream rushing between high bluffs.

★ **Springprozession, Echternach.** Every year on Whit Tuesday (the eighth Tuesday after Easter) Echternach explodes in a celebration of religious fervor. One of the last of its kind in Western Europe, this festival dating from the 15th century features up to 10,000 pilgrims dancing through the streets in historic costumes. Almost as many onlookers join the crowd.

GREAT ITINERARIES

Haute Cuisine and Country Air

The peripatetic gourmet chooses overnight stops to ensure that each evening meal is a feast. It is a bonus that many of the finest small hotels with outstanding restaurants are in out-of-the-way places that you might not otherwise visit. This kind of travel obviously does not come cheap.

➤DURATION: 13 days.

➤GETTING AROUND: **By Car.** In Belgium, highways link Antwerp and Noirefontaine, by way of the coast, for an arc of some 600 kilometers (360 miles). To travel from meal to meal in Luxembourg, a car is indispensable.

By Train. Trains in Belgium connect, through Brussels, with the main towns on the route; a car is necessary in the Ardennes. In Luxembourg, only Luxembourg City is easily reached by direct rail lines.

➤THE MAIN ROUTE: **9 Nights: Belgium.** Start your trip in **Antwerp,** where 't Fornuis is the top restaurant. The 10 exquisite rooms of De Witte Lelie are only minutes away. Make your next stop **Brugge,** to eat at the revered De Karmeliet or the young, imaginative Den Gouden Harynk, both within easy walking distance of the aristocratic rooms of De Tuilerieën. From Brugge, head for the coast and **Oostende,** where you can stay and dine at the sumptuous Oostendse Compagnie, overlooking the sea. At the west end of the coast, dine and stay in **De Panne** at the exquisite Le Fox. As you head inland, stop first at Eddy Vandekerckhove's Gastronomic Village just outside **Kortrijk,** where the rooms have views of a tropical garden or the Flemish countryside, and the cuisine will delight you. **Brussels** would be an obvious stop, with its Comme Chez Soi and other renowned restaurants. For something more unusual, stop instead at **Genval,** near Brussels, where the Château du Lac's restaurant, Le Trèfle à Quatre, offers lake views and superb food. Farther east, just west of **Hasselt,** the world-class Scholteshof restaurant provides extraordinary dining and superb accommodations. The Clos St-Denis in nearby **Tongeren** runs a close second but offers no lodging. Head south to **Bouillon** in Belgian Luxembourg and treat yourself to an overnight stay at the nearby Aubergedu Moulin Hideux, where you can savor fine, leisurely meals and work off the calories by taking enchanting walks in the woods.

3 Nights: Luxembourg. In **Luxembourg City,** settle for the night in either the traditional Hotel Cravat or the modern luxury of Le Royal. You'll dine in the splendid Clairefontaine on the charming square of the same name. The next day, head south toward the French border for **Frisange,** where Lea Linster will serve a world-class lunch, and dine at the converted farmhouse of A la Table des Guilloux, south of the city. Next day, explore the castle country of the Ardennes, lunching at the idyllic La Bergerie, in the middle of the woods near **Echternach,** where Claude and Thierry Phal's cooking reaches new heights. Spend your final night at the hotel Oranienburg in **Vianden** and take dinner at its posh restaurant, Le Châtelain.

Ancient Crafts of the Low Countries

The extraordinary flourishing of decorative crafts in the Low Countries during the Middle Ages was the result of the rulers' insatiable appetite for ornamentation, an appetite shared by local gentry and wealthy burghers. The clothing and jewelry lovingly depicted in 15th-century Flemish paintings indicate the high standards of the artisans of the era, whose traditions continue.

➤DURATION: 8 days.

➤GETTING AROUND: **By Car.** Luxembourg City is easy to reach by car. The Villeroy & Boch complex lies just outside the center, on the northwest edge, toward Wiltz. The itinerary (Luxembourg City to Antwerp) covers about 780 kilometers (468 miles), some 10 hours' driving time.

By Train. If you're visiting Luxembourg by train, use city buses to reach the Villeroy & Boch outlet. All Belgian cities on this itinerary are accessible by train, but you'll have to double back from Brugge to Brussels to get to Antwerp.

➤THE MAIN ROUTE: **1 Night: Luxembourg.** A weekday stop in Luxembourg will give you a chance to visit the on-site factory outlet store of Villeroy & Boch, whose popular vitro-porcelain sells here at discount prices. Watch for specials on patterns being phased out, and be sure to dig through the bargain bin. The factory does not ship, so be prepared to schlep. If you can round up a group of 20 visitors, you can take a guided tour of the factory.

1 Night: Liège. Arriving from Luxembourg, start your Belgian crafts tour in Liège. The Val Saint-Lambert glassworks in Seraing, on the outskirts of the city, is one of the finest in the world; you can visit the showroom and watch glassblowers in action. The factory outlet offers great values.

3 Nights: Brussels. Halfway between Brussels and Antwerp, **Mechelen** has the only workshops in Belgium where traditional tapestry weaving is still practiced; Gaspard De Wit's Royal Tapestry Factory (open for visits Saturday morning only) is at the Refuge van Tongerlo. In **Brussels,** some of the finest examples of Belgian tapestry, from the 14th to 16th centuries, are on view in the Musées Royaux d'Art et d'Histoire (Royal Museums of Art and History), and lace and needlework are on view in the Musée du Costume et de la Dentelle (Costume and Lace Museum). **Tournai** (southwest of Brussels) is one of the old centers of tapestry; at the Musée da la Tapisserie (Museum of Tapestry) you can see how it is done.

1 Night: Brugge. Brugge is intimately associated with lace-making, and there are shops selling everything from lace souvenirs to works of art. The best place to get a real understanding of the craft is the Kantencentrum (Lace Center), incorporating a museum and a lace-making school.

1 Night: Antwerp. Diamonds are big business in Antwerp, where the origins and history of diamond cutting are shown at the Provincial Diamond Museum. Diamondland, where you can also see diamond-cutting demonstrations, is probably the most spectacular diamond showroom in the world.

The Ardennes

To experience the Ardennes fully, you must take your time. Explore the hamlets and river valleys off the highway. Stop in the small towns along the way for a meal of hearty Ardennaise fare—smoked ham, cheese, and farm bread, and crayfish and trout from the rushing streams. Enjoy the inns, and visit the churches and castles. You'll be amply rewarded.

➤DURATION: 9 days.

➤GETTING AROUND: **By Car.** The Belgian portions of the trip add up to about 430 kilometers (258 miles). Much of this is on secondary routes, so expect driving time of about eight hours. To see the best of the Luxembourg Ardennes, you'll need a car for the *routes nationales* and secondary roads that snake through the forests.

By Train. The cities on the itinerary are accessible by train, but not necessarily in the same sequence as they are listed below. Rail connections in Luxembourg are minimal, though a train does run from Luxembourg City to Clervaux, in the north.

➤THE MAIN ROUTE: **2 Nights: Liège and Malmédy.** From **Liège,** go by way of Eupen toward Malmédy, stopping to explore the high moorland known as the **Hautes Fagnes.**

1 Night: La-Roche-en-Ardenne. Passing Stavelot, continue to La-Roche-en-Ardenne in the heart of the Belgian mountain range. Here, in the valley of the River Ourthe, you will see the finest scenery the Ardennes offers.

2 Nights: Luxembourg. Enter the Grand Duchy of Luxembourg from the north, stopping to visit **Clervaux**'s castle museum before winding through rolling countryside toward **Vianden,** where the spectacular castle dominates the hill village. Then, though it falls just below the Ardennes plateau, drive into **Luxembourg City** for the medieval fortifications, cathedral, and Old Town streets.

3 Nights: Belgium. Driving west from Luxembourg City, follow the Semois River, with a stop to see the romantic ruins of Orval Abbey, and then to **Bouillon** with its mountaintop fort. Through dense woods you reach **St-Hubert,** going on to **Rochefort** and neighboring Han-sur-Lesse, with its remarkable caves and nature reserve. Follow the Lesse to **Dinant**—part of the way by kayak, if you wish—spectacularly situated on the River Meuse. As you drive along the Meuse, notice the sheer cliffs lining the riverbank on the opposite side. Continuing along the river, with stops in **Huy** and **Modave,** you return to **Liège.**

FESTIVALS AND SEASONAL EVENTS

The top seasonal events of Belgium and Luxembourg are listed below; any one of them could provide the stuff of lasting memories. Contact the relevant country's tourist office for complete information, or call the contact numbers below (Belgium's country code is 32 and Luxembourg's is 352; drop the initial 0 if calling from outside the country).

Belgium

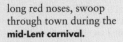

WINTER

END JAN.➢ Brussels's **International Film Festival,** which is forcing its way onto the international agenda, takes place across the capital.

EARLY FEB.➢ **Carnival** is celebrated with great gusto, especially at Binche with its extravagantly costumed Gilles, and at Tournai and Charleroi, each of which has its own style and verve. Mardi Gras (Shrove Tuesday) and the preceding Sunday are the high points.

1ST SUN. OF LENT➢ **The Great Bonfire**—actually seven of them—burn around Namur's hills, as music plays, games ensue, and much merriment is made.

VALENTINE'S DAY➢ **The International Festival of Films d'Amour** is held in Mons during the week of Valentine's Day.

4TH SUN. OF LENT➢ In Stavelot, the hilarious Blancs Moussis, with their long red noses, swoop through town during the **mid-Lent carnival.**

FEB.➢ The small town of Andenne was once menaced by a ferocious bear. The bear was slaughtered, and the townspeople remember the liberation by throwing stuffed bears into the streets.

MAR.➢ For a weekend in March, chocolatiers fill Durbuy with their tasty morsels.

SPRING

EARLY APR.➢ The fishing season gets underway at Bouillon's annual **Trout Festival.**

EASTER➢ On **Easter Monday,** the **Cavalcade de Jenmappes,** a traditional costumed procession, is held in Mons.

LATE APR.➢ One of the world's leading flower shows, the **Floralies** (☎ 09/222–7336), is held every five years in the Flanders Expo Hall in Gent. Plan ahead: the next is in 2005.

LATE APR.–EARLY MAY➢ The **Royal Greenhouses** (☎ 02/513–0770), at Laeken Palace near Brussels, with superb flower and plant arrangements, are open to the public for a limited period.

EARLY MAY➢ On Ascension Day, the **Procession of the Holy Blood** (☎ 050/44–86–64) in Brugge is one of the oldest and most elaborate religious and historical processions in Europe. Early seat reservations are recommended.

MAY➢ The **Queen Elisabeth International Music Competition** (☎ 02/513–0099) is one of the most demanding events of its kind. In 2001, the 50th anniversary of the competition will put the focus on violinists. Returning to its regular four-year cycle, there will be no competition in 2002, with the next competition in 2003 focusing on pianists.

MAY➢ Laughter abounds at Rochefort's annual **Comedy Festival,** attracting comedians from across the continent.

MAY➢ The **KunstenFESTIVALdesArts** (☎ 02/219–0707) in Brussels is a monthlong international celebration of contemporary drama, dance, and music.

LATE MAY➢ The **Brussels Jazz Marathon** (☎ 0900/00606) encompasses gigs and informal sessions in more than 50 clubs and pubs, plus outdoor concerts in the Grand'Place and Grand Sablon headlining leading jazz musicians. One ticket pays for admission to all events, plus free shuttle between venues and public transport.

LATE MAY➢ The **Brussels 20 Kilometer Race** ☎ 02/511–9000), held every year on the last Sunday in May, begins and ends at the Parc du Cinquantenaire. It attracts both serious runners and casual enthusiasts.

LATE MAY➢ The **Ducasse** held in Mons on the first Saturday and Sunday following Whit Sunday is the continuation of a citywide festival dating back to the 14th century. It has a procession of the Golden Carriage, an enactment of St. George's battle with the dragon, and hordes of fun-loving people.

SUMMER

LAST WEEKEND IN JUNE➢ The **Folklore and Shrimp Festival** (☎ 058/511189) in Oostduinkerke features shrimp fishermen on horseback, brass bands, floats, and folklore ensembles.

LAST WEEKEND IN JUNE➢ The **Brocante sur les Quais** (the Street Market on the Quais) in Charleroi offers 24 hours of nonstop, open-air wheeling and dealing along the quais of the Sabre River, which flows through the city center. It's usually organized to coincide with the **Festival of Music.**

1ST TUES. AND THURS. IN JULY➢ The **Ommegang** (☎ 02/512–1961) takes over Brussels's Grand'-Place. It's a sumptuous and stately pageant reenacting a procession that honored Emperor Charles V in 1549. Book early if you want a room in town during the festivities.

MID-JULY➢ The **Gentse Feesten** (☎ 091/24–15–55), originally intended to curb summer drinking by workers in Gent, is a 10-day celebration of indulgence, with music-making, entertainment, and assorted happenings in the streets of the city and a world-class dance music festival that lasts until the early hours.

JULY 21➢ **Belgium's National Day** is celebrated in Brussels with a military march, followed by a popular feast in the Parc de Bruxelles and brilliant fireworks.

Spa celebrates Belgium's National Day at the **Francofolie Music Festival,** where French music of all styles swells through the streets.

END OF JULY➢ Might is right at the annual **Arm Wrestling Competition** in Rochefort, which draws an international field.

END OF JULY➢ The **Marche of the Madeleine,** a traditional parade that takes place in Jumet, a small town near Charleroi, involves multitudes of costumes and the participation of several thousand parading troops.

LAST WEEKEND IN JULY➢ Bouillon takes a step back in time during the **Medieval Village Fair,** featuring markets, parades, and tournaments.

JULY–AUG.➢ Among Belgium's most important rock festivals, attracting international acts, are: **Torhout/Werchter,** held in two separate Flemish towns; **Axion Beach Rock,** in the sweltering seaside heat of Zeebrugge; and **Dour,** a cutting-edge event in the heart of rural Wallonia.

AUG.➢ Dinant honors its native son, Adolphe Sax, with the annual **Saxophone Festival.**

MID-AUG.➢ A **Flower Carpet,** painstakingly laid out, transforms the entire Grand'Place of Brussels for two days. It's done even years only; the next will be in 2002.

AUG. 15➢ The **Outremeuse Festival** in Liège combines religious and folkloric elements in a joyous tide that sweeps through the Outremeuse section of town.

AUG. 15➢ Bathtubs of all shapes and sizes float through Dinant during the annual **Bathtub Regatta.**

LATE AUG.➢ : In the **Canal Festival** (☎ 050/44–86–86) in Brugge, events from the city's past are recreated alongside the romantic canals. It is celebrated every third year; the next takes place in 2001.

LAST WEEKEND IN AUG.➢ Durbuy's town square is blanketed in flowers during the yearly **Flower Market.**

AUTUMN

SEPT.➢ Stuff yourself silly with tasty cheese and egg *flamiche* tarts during Dinant's **Flamiche Eating Contest.**

SEPT.➢ Tournai's **Grande Procession** dates to the 11th century. It thanks the Virgin Mary for delivering the city from the Black Plague.

END OF SEPT.➢ The **Annual Meeting of Hot Air Balloons** takes place just outside of Tournai, attracting thousands of visitors.

SEPT.–MID-OCT.➢ The **Festival of Flanders** (✉ Eugeen Flageyplein 18, 1050 Brussels, ☎ 02/640–1525) brings hundreds of concerts to all the old Flemish cities.

SEPT.–DEC.➢ Every year, **Europalia** (☎ 02/507–8550) honors a different country with exhibitions, concerts, and other events amounting to a thorough inventory of its cultural heritage. In 2001, Brussels itself will be the theme as "Brussels: Crossroads for Cultures" takes center stage in Brussels and in other cities.

2ND WEEKEND IN SEPT.➢ On **National Heritage Day** (☎ 02/511–1840) buildings of architectural or historical interest throughout Belgium that are not normally accessible to the public open their doors to all.

EARLY OCT.➢ The **Flanders International Film Festival,** the most important in the country, screens new Belgian talent as well as important international directors.

NOV.➢ The **European Community Challenge** (☎ 03/326–1010) in Antwerp is a major event on the international tennis circuit, with a diamond-studded racquet worth $1 million available to anyone who wins the event three times in five years.

NOV. 3➢ Animals are lead from far and wide to St-Hubert to be blessed on **St. Hubert's Feast Day.**

2ND WEEKEND IN DEC.➢ The **European Christmas Market** in the Grand'Place in Brussels presents the traditions and products of many different European countries.

Luxembourg

WINTER

EARLY FEB.➢ During **Carnival** processions and masked balls are especially festive in Vianden, Echternach, Diekirch, and Wormeldange.

EARLY MAR.➢ On Laetare Sunday, the festival of **Bretzelsonndeg** is dedicated to lovers, and the banks of the Moselle are decorated with folk art displays.

MAR.➢ The **Celtic Celebration** in Dudelange combines music, dance, and food of Celtic origin.

MAR.–MAY➢ The performing arts are alive and well throughout Luxembourg City during the **Printemps Musical-Festival de Luxembourg.**

SPRING

EASTER MON.➢ At the **E'maischen** fair at Nospelt in old Luxembourg, lovers give each other "whistling" clay birds (*Peckvillchen*) to usher in spring.

3RD SUN. AFTER EASTER➢ In Luxembourg City and in Diekirch, since the 17th century, for two weeks beginning on this Sunday, grateful villagers have walked in the **Octave** procession from their local church to the cathedral, accompanied by chants, incense, and often the community band. The procession commemorates the Holy Mother's rescue of the devout from a raging plague. During Octave, a **fair** holds forth in the Place Guillaume, with arcade games, crafts, and food stands selling the traditional batter-fried *merlan* (whiting). On the final Sunday the royal family participates in a solemn procession.

MAY➢ Rollerbladers and skateboarders from across Europe flock to Dudelange to compete in the annual **Rollerblade Festival.**

MAY–JUNE➢ The **Echternach Music Festival** presents classical music concerts by renowned soloists and groups in the city's basilica.

WHIT TUES. (LATE MAY)➢ During Echternach's **Spring Procession** (Dance-Procession), Luxembourg's most famous spring pageant, pilgrims and townspeople dance through the streets, leaping from one foot to the other and chanting prayers to St. Willibrord, each group accompanied by musicians who all play the same haunting melody.

SUMMER

JUNE 23➢ **Luxembourg's National Day** honors the country's beloved Grand Duke with parades, ceremonies, and gun salutes; the night before, there's a torchlight military exercise and spectacular fireworks.

EARLY JULY➢ Dudelange invites craftspeople and crafts cooperatives from around the world to sell their wares at the **Third World Market.**

JULY➢ The international **Festival of Open-Air Theater and Music** in Wiltz always attracts thousands.

LATE JULY➢ For two days, Dudelange becomes a rock music mecca during the **Open Air Rock Festival.**

JULY–AUG.➢ Music swells through streets of Luxembourg City during the **Summer in the City** music festival.

LATE AUG.➢ The **Schueberfouer** (a former shepherds' market begun in 1340) has become the capital's giant funfair, interspersed with a procession of sheep with colorful ribbons being herded through the city streets.

AUTUMN

2ND WEEKEND IN SEPT.➢ The three-day **Wine and Grape Festival** in Grevenmacher is a popular September event.

OCT. AND NOV.➢ **Live at Vauban** is held in Luxembourg City during the fall to showcase musicians and their art.

2ND SUN. IN OCT.➢ **Walnut Market** is held in Vianden: an outdoor sale of fresh walnuts, walnut cake, walnut candy, and walnut liqueur, accompanied by the music of popular bands.

2 BRUSSELS

From the gilded splendor of the city's medieval Grand'Place to the sinuous curves of its art nouveau buildings, Brussels is a jewel box of architectural and historical surprises. An efficient tunnel system makes it possible to cross the city by car in a matter of minutes—better yet, explore on foot to discover its graceful homes and vibrant neighborhoods. Cafés and restaurants, serving local specialties and international cuisine, beckon at every turn, and the staples of beer, chocolates, and lace abound in the shops. However, standing side-by-side with these hallmarks of Belgian tradition are the gleaming, international headquarters of the European Union and NATO, which make Brussels a cosmopolitan hub for world affairs.

Updated by Leslie Adler and Katharine Mill

BRUSSELS (Bruxelles in French, Brussel in Flemish) is a provincial city at heart, even after it assumed a new identity as capital of the European Union (EU) in 1958. Within Belgium, Brussels has equal status with Flanders and Wallonia as an autonomous region. It is a bilingual enclave just north of the language border that divides the country into Flemish- and French-speaking parts. Historically, it is also the capital of Flanders.

At the end of the 19th century, Brussels was one of the liveliest cities in Europe, known for its splendid cafés and graceful art nouveau architecture. That gaiety, however, was stamped out by German occupation during the First and Second World Wars. Still, the city made a comeback little more than a decade later, its reemergence on the international scene heralded by the World's Fair and the Universal Exposition of 1958.

As a by-product of Europe's increasing integration, international business has invaded the city in a big way since the 1960s. The result: city blocks of steel-and-glass office buildings set only a few steps from cobbled-street neighborhoods featuring hallmarks of the city's eventful past. Over the centuries, Brussels has been shaped by the different cultures of the foreign powers that have ruled it. It has learned the art of accommodating them and, in the process, prepared itself for its role as the political capital of Europe.

Pleasures and Pastimes

Architecture

Brussels ranks as one of Europe's greatest art nouveau capitals. The works of Victor Horta, probably Belgium's best-known architect, grace many quarters of the city, as do buildings by many of his disciples. The flowing lines of the art nouveau buildings, along with their trademark stained-glass windows and lavishly decorative mosaics, make many streets living museums. The art deco style adopted by Horta later in his career is also in evidence, including in the Palais des Beaux Arts concert hall and main train station.

Art

The city's museums embrace a diversity of styles and celebrate its native artists. Traditional Flemish artists, including Pieter Bruegel the Elder, are well represented, as are the works of Belgian surrealist René Magritte and other 20th century artists such as Paul Delvaux. In addition to the main modern and ancient art museums, there are a handful of unusual, small museums.

Béguinages

Key historic sights of the city are its cathedrals and béguinages, which highlight the region's religious history and architectural innovations. Beautiful stained-glass windows and gleaming white towers are the hallmarks of the renovated, 13th-century Cathédrale St-Michel et Ste-Gudule in the heart of town. In the same neighborhood, visit the attractive, Flemish Baroque Eglise St-Jean-du-Béguinage and the 1,000-year-old Eglise St-Nicolas for a glimpse into lives of the Beguines. West of the center, the Anderlecht Béguinage is also open to the public.

Dining

It would be hard to hungry in Brussels. Eating is a popular pastime and good food is available everywhere—from the humblest corner cafés to the most luxurious international restaurants.

As a European crossroads, the Belgian capital has places to suit all tastes, occasions, and budgets, and the settings are as eclectic as the people who live, work, and play here. Restaurants can be located in everything from grand town houses to former factories. Inside, the decor might be anything from baroque glam to minimalist chic.

Whatever else changes, though, the quality of food is one dependable constant. Whether the restaurant is Belgian or Portuguese, Indian or Japanese, you can count on a satisfying experience. Indeed, most visitors to Brussels note there dining memories as among the best elements of there stays in the city.

Lodging

With the arrival of the European institutions in recent decades, Brussels has evolved into a capital city buzzing with social and political action—and visitors who expect a range of top-quality accommodations. It's also a key meeting point for those on the international business circut, resulting in high rates and full hotel bookings during the week. However, the low occupancy and fiercely competitive rates on the weekends make this one of the most cost-effective times for leisure travelers to stay. Rates in the middle to upper price bracket are particularly worth negotiating.

Although there are a range of lodgings, don't look for charming, family-run hostelries or designer-lable lodgings; these are almost nonexistent. The range here is Belle Epoque hostels, which were occupied during the war, abandoned mid-century, and have fought their way back to the center stage. Such hotels offer dual attractions: the charms of a bygone era alongside amenities for the information age. In addition, a range of quirky, old-world places promise an authentic, Belgium-style atmosphere that's rare in a world of growing uniformity.

Except for the top-class hotels, service is sometimes criticized for falling short of what you'd expect in the U.S. However, if you come with an open mind and a smile, you're unlikely to be disappointed.

Markets

Bring good walking shoes for exploring the city, because you'll spend hours strolling through the open-air markets. What's for sale? Everything—at the separate Flower Market, Bird Market, Antiques and Books Market, and Vieux Marché flea market, among others. Sunday morning brings the Boitsfort market and the exotic Marché du Midi, a bazaar of North African spices and goods. Place du Châtelaine and Place Ste-Cathérine have enormous markets where fish, fruit and vegetables, and other produce are sold.

Museums

Brussels is steeped in centuries of cross-European history, and its many museums help tell the stories of the city's many sectors and interests. The majority of museums are located in the area around the Cinquantenaire and the Ronde-Point Schuman; look for those specializing in military history, art history, and central African history. Here, you'll also find a museum of Belgian folk history; Autoworld, which houses one of the world's best collections of vintage cars; and—of course—a brewery museum. The museums of fine art and modern art are found in Upper Town, as is the musical instruments museum. South of the center are the children's museum and those featuring art deco and art nouveau collections by Belgian artists.

Squares

The way to tour Brussels is by way of its plazas, which you can connect to make a thorough circle of the city's most popular tourist stops.

These busy squares not only function as landmarks for walking tours, but also as rest stops between sights, and as shopping hubs for those who are short on time for souvenirs. Some, like the Place Ste-Catherine, have bustling markets; others, like the Place de la Monnaie, the Place des Martyrs, and the Place Royale, feature historic landmarks. The most famous is the Place du Grand Sablon, an elegant, shop- and café-surrounded hill that's the most popular see-and-be-seen address in town. The Place Louise is another place of posh boutiques and bistros.

EXPLORING BRUSSELS

Around the 1,000-year-old historic center of Brussels, a group of ring roads form concentric circles. Crossing them is like traveling back and forth across the centuries. Brussels once had a river, the Senne, but it was buried in the 19th century after becoming clogged with sewage; the absence of left and right river banks can make orientation in the city a bit difficult.

The center, sitting in a bowl, is sometimes known as the Pentagon, from the shape of the oldest ring road, which roughly follows the ancient ramparts. The remains of the ruins include one of the gates, the Porte de Hal, the Tour Noire (Black Tower) on Place Ste-Catherine, and a small patch of wall next to a bowling alley near Place de la Chapelle. On either side of the 19th-century ring road you can see the cupolas of the Palais de Justice and the Basilique. In the center, the slender belfry of the Hôtel de Ville rises like a beacon.

Brussels is small enough that you can get a superficial impression of it from a car window in a single day. For a more substantial appreciation, however, you need one day for the historic city heart, another for the uptown squares and museums, and additional days for museums outside the center and excursions to the periphery. There are many attractive nooks and crannies to explore.

Great Itineraries

IF YOU HAVE 1 DAY

Head for the Grand'Place to drink in the gilded splendor of its medieval buildings. Wander the narrow, cobbled lanes surrounding the square and visit the graceful, arcaded Galeries St-Hubert, an elegant 19th-century shopping gallery. Head down Rue de l'Étuve to see the Mannekin Pis, the statue of the little boy whom according to legend saved Brussels by urinating to extinguish a fire. Continue by foot to the Place du Grand Sablon to window-shop at its many fine antiques stores and galleries. If it's a weekend, enjoy the outdoor antiques market. Have lunch in one of the cafés lining the square, perhaps trying a Belgian specialty such as *carbonnades à la flamandes* (a Flemish beef stew simmered in beer). Don't forget to buy chocolates at one of the top chocolatiers on the square. Then cross over Rue de la Réence to see the Place du Petit Sablon before walking down the street to the Musée d'Art Moderne and the Musée d'Art Ancien to view collections ranging from the surrealism of Belgian artist René Magritte to the delicately wrought details of Pieter Bruegel the Elder's *The Fall of Icarus.* Pick out a restaurant on the fashionable Rue Antoine Dansaert for dinner. Finally, return to the Grand'Place to cap off the evening with a drink at one of the cafés in order to see the shimmer of the golden facades under the glow of lights.

IF YOU HAVE 3 DAYS

On your second day, start at the Parc de Bruxelles, a formal urban park that originated as a game park. Note the austere Palais du Roi on the park's south side, now used only for state occasions. Cross the street to the elegant Place Royale and the adjoining square, La Place du Musée, graced with a Calder sculpture. Take time to visit the nearby Musée des Instruments de Musique, which houses one of Europe's finest collections of musical instruments. Hop a tram to Avenue Louise to Ixelles, one of Brussels' liveliest neighborhoods. Walk down Rue Paul-Emile Janson, stopping to look at No. 6, considered one of architect Victor Horta's finest art nouveau works. Check out the shops on Rue Bailli, an eclectic mixture of trendy boutiques, old-fashioned bakeries and antiques shops, before continuing on to Place du Chatelain for lunch.

After lunch, visit architect Horta's own house, now the Horta Museum, on Rue Américaine. If you crave more art and architecture, go to the Musée David-et-Alice-Van-Buuren, a 1930s art deco masterpiece that also features a fine collection of Old Masters paintings, including one of three versions of Bruegel's *Fall of Icarus*. If you're in the mood for lighter entertainment, head towards the Gare du Midi and visit the Gueuze Museum to see how Lambic beer is brewed the old-fashioned way. Enjoy a tasting at the museum, and maybe go on to a café to compare the taste to that of the commercially brewed versions. For dinner head to St. Catherine's Place for a feast of Belgian seafood specialties. Later, check out the many cafés and bars that crowd the narrow streets around the Bourse.

On day three, take the Metro to Schuman, walk past the cluster of modern buildings that house various functions of the European Union as you head up through Parc Cinquantenaire, which is easy to spot courtesy of the massive arch constructed in 1880 to celebrate Belgium's 50th anniversary as an independent state. Visit the Autoworld museum, housing a fantastic collection of vintage cars. Head up Avenue Tervuren to catch a tram to Tervuren and the Musée Royal de l'Afrique Centrale, a legacy of Belgium's role as a colonist in the Congo, including objects and memorabilia from explorers. Relax in the surrounding park before heading back into town for another fine dinner.

IF YOU HAVE 7 DAYS

A week is more than enough time to explore the city, which gives you the opportunity to add ventures into the surrounding countryside to your itinerary. To get your bearings and adjust to the city when you arrive, follow the three-day tour above. On days four through seven, however, consider driving to or taking a day tour of some of the famous sights and towns on the border of Brussels. First on the list is **Waterloo** (☞ Side Trip, *below*), the battlefield that changed the course of European history, where you can explore the Musée Wellington, the Butte de Lion, and the Champ de Bataille field. On day five, head for Gaasbeek, where you'll find the Gaasbeek Château and scenery straight out of a Bruegel painting. Make a visit to **Nivelles** (☞ Chapter 6) on day six, where you can tour the reconstructed La Collégiale Ste-Gertrude, which along with more than 500 of the town's buildings was destroyed during World War II. On day seven, you could tour Villers-la-Ville and its **Abbaye de Villers-la-Ville** (☞ Chapter 6), which dates from 1147; open-air concerts and drama performances are scheduled in the summer months. Alternatively, if you'd like to spend several consecutive days outside the city, you could follow the Good Tour of Hainaut in Chapter 6.

Lower Town: The Heart of Brussels

During the latter half of the 10th century, a village began to emerge on the site of present-day Brussels. A population of craftspeople and traders settled gradually around the castle of the counts of Leuven, who were later succeeded by the dukes of Brabant.

In 1430 Philip the Good, Duke of Burgundy, took possession of Brussels, then known as Brabant. During this era, Brussels became a center for the production of tapestry, lace, and other luxury goods. By 1555, when Charles V abdicated in favor of his son, Philip II of Spain, the Protestant Reformation was spreading through the Low Countries. Philip, a devout Catholic, dealt ruthlessly with advocates of the Reformation. His governor, the Duke of Alva, had the leaders of the revolt, the Counts of Egmont and Hoorn, executed on the Grand'Place. A monument to them stands in the square of the Petit Sablon.

In 1695, on the orders of French King Louis XIV, Marshal Villeroy bombarded the city with red-hot cannonballs. The ensuing fires destroyed 4,000 houses, 16 churches, and all of the Grand'Place, with the exception of the Town Hall. The buildings around the square were immediately rebuilt, in the splendor that we see today.

In 1713, the Spanish Netherlands came under the rule of the Austrian Habsburgs. Despite the influence of Enlightenment theories on the province's governors, nationalist feeling had set in among large sections of the populace. These sentiments were quashed by neither the repressive armies of Napoléon nor the post-Waterloo incorporation of Belgium into a new Kingdom of the Netherlands. On August 25, 1830, a rousing duet from an Auber opera being performed at La Monnaie inflamed patriots in the audience, who burst onto the streets and raised the flag of Brabant. With support from Britain and France, independence came swiftly.

Since then, Brussels has undergone image upheavals almost as significant as the impact of this century's two world wars. At the turn of the 20th century, the wide boulevards and sumptuous art nouveau buildings symbolized a city as bustling and metropolitan as Paris. However, from the 1950s onward, Brussels became a byword for boring: a gray, faceless city of bureaucrats where cavalier neglect of urban planning created a new word—bruxellization—for the destruction of architectural heritage. Now the pace of European integration (and the wonders of the city's food and drink) has helped to restore the city's international reputation—but internal tensions between Flemings and French-speakers still threaten to tear it apart.

Numbers in the text correspond to numbers in the margin and on the Central Brussels map.

A Good Walk

Start at Rues de l'Etuve and du Chêne at **Manneken Pis** ①, a bronze statue of a small boy urinating that symbolizes the insouciant spirit of the Bruxellois. Thousands of copies are on sale in the souvenir shops along the three blocks of Rue de l'Etuve leading to the **Grand'Place** ②, the magnificent square surrounded by the Hôtel de Ville (Town Hall) and ornate guild houses. The alley next to the Maison du Roi (opposite the Town Hall) leads into the restaurant-lined Petite Rue des Bouchers with the highly original puppet theater, **Théâtre Toone** ③, in the **Quartier de l'Ilôt Sacré** ④. Turn right at the top of the street to reach the **Galeries St-Hubert** ⑤, an impressively engineered and decorated shopping gallery from 1847.

At the exit from the gallery, turn right on Rue d'Arenberg and cross the uninspiring Boulevard de Berlaymont, heading for the twin Gothic towers of the **Cathédrale St-Michel et Ste-Gudule** ⑥, a 13th-century edifice with outstanding stained-glass windows. Walk back down the hill and turn right on Boulevard de Berlaymont. Take the second flight of stairs on the left, with a large statue of the cartoon character Gaston Lagaffe at the top of the stairs, down to the Rue des Sables and the

Centre Belge de la Bande Dessinée ⑦, or Belgian Comic Strip Center, which is as engrossing to adults as it is enchanting to kids. A left and a right take you into Rue du Persil and the **Place des Martyrs** ⑧. Half a block away, the pedestrian shopping street of Rue Neuve is filled with bargain-seeking shoppers in the daytime. This street leads to the Place de la Monnaie and its **Théâtre de la Monnaie** ⑨, one of Europe's leading opera stages.

As you cross the busy Boulevard Anspach onto the Rue des Augustins, the remnants of the **Tour Noire** ⑩ are on your left. To the right, the short Rue des Cyprès leads to the Flemish Baroque **Eglise St-Jean-du-Béguinage** ⑪. Walk down the Rue du Peuplier and you're in the old Fish Market area—although the canal has been replaced by ponds, and every house is now a seafood restaurant. Turn left toward the blackened church of Ste-Catherine and you'll find a busy market in front of it on the **Place Ste-Catherine** ⑫. Take the first right, Rue de Flandre. Halfway up the block is the gateway to the **Maison de la Bellonne** ⑬, now a theater museum. Returning to the Place Ste-Catherine, cross the square and take the second street on the right. This is **Rue Antoine Dansaert** ⑭, the heart of the city's fashionable quarter. You are now facing the grandiose stock exchange, the **Bourse** ⑮. Next to it is Bruxella 1238, an in situ archaeological museum, and the small **Eglise St-Nicolas** ⑯, hemmed in by tiny houses. From where you now stand on Rue au Beurre it's just half a block back to the Grand'Place.

TIMING

Walking the route will take you about two hours—and note that you will need good walking shoes for the cobblestone streets. The Grand'-Place requires half an hour, more if you linger in one of its cafés. Stops in churches and museums may add another hour and a half. With a break for lunch, this is a comfortable, one-day program any day of the week, especially Monday, when museums are closed. (Most of the city's must-see museums are in the Upper Town or farther outside the center.)

Sights to See

⓯ **Bourse.** At the Stock Exchange, the decorative frieze of allegorical statues in various stages of nudity—some of them by Rodin—forms a sort of idealization of the common man. Trading here, as at most European stock exchanges, is via electronic computer screens, meaning that there is no longer a trading floor. Next door lies **Bruxella 1238**, an in situ archaeological museum where you can inspect the excavation of a 13th-century church. ✉ *R. de la Bourse,* ☎ *02/279–4355.* 🎫 *BF100/€2.50.* ⏲ *Guided visits from Town Hall, Wed. 10:15, 11:15, 1:45, 2:30, 3:15.*

❻ **Cathédrale St-Michel et Ste-Gudule.** Next to nothing is known about St. Gudule, the daughter of a 7th-century Carolingian nobleman, but this is where her relics have been preserved for the past 1,000 years. Construction of the cathedral began in 1226. Its twin Gothic towers are gleaming white again after the removal of centuries of grime. The interior was recently renovated, and the remains of an earlier, 11th-century Romanesque church that was on the site can be glimpsed through glass apertures set into the floor. Among the windows in the cathedral, designed by various artists, those by Bernard van Orley, a 16th-century court painter, are outstanding. The window of *The Last Judgment,* at the bottom of the nave, is illuminated from within in the evening. ✉ *Parvis Ste-Gudule,* ☎ *02/217–8345.* ⏲ *Daily 7:30–6.*

★ ❼ **Centre Belge de la Bande Dessinée.** It fell to the land of Tintin, a cherished cartoon character, to create the Belgian Comic Strip Center, the world's first museum dedicated to this type of art. Despite its primary

Central Brussels

Bourse	15
Cathédrale St-Michel et Ste-Gudule	6
Centre Belge de la Bande Dessinée	7
Eglise St-Jean-du-Béguinage	11
Eglise St-Nicholas	16
Galeries St-Hubert	5
Grand'Place	2
Kermesse du Midi	27
Maison de la Bellone	13
Manneken Pis	1
Les Marolles	26
Musée d'Art Ancien	19
Musée d'Art Moderne	20
Musée des Instruments de Musique	22
Palais de Justice	25
Parc de Bruxelles	23
Place des Martyrs	8
Place du Grand Sablon	17
Place du Petit Sablon	18
Place Louise	24
Place Royale	21
Place Ste-Catherine	12
Quartier de l'Ilôt Sacré	4
Rue Antoine Dansaert	14
Théâtre de la Monnaie	9
Théâtre Toone	3
Tour Noire	10

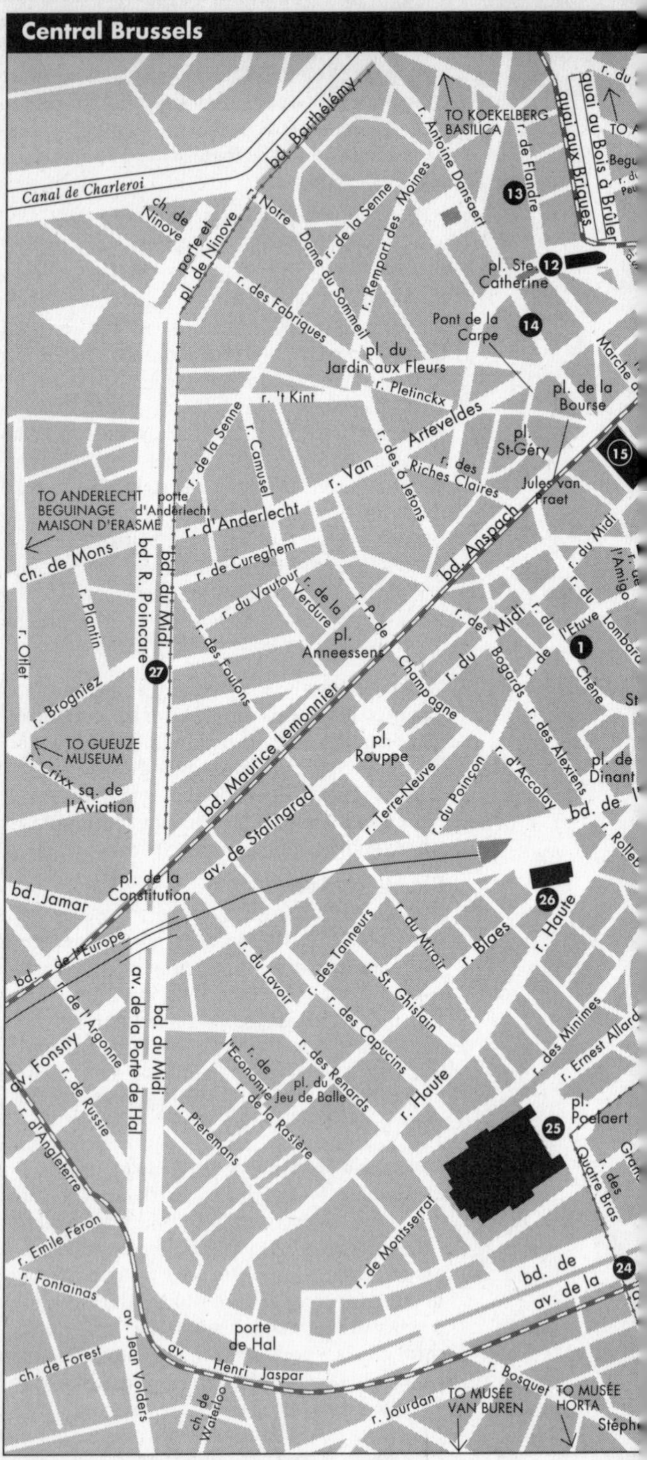

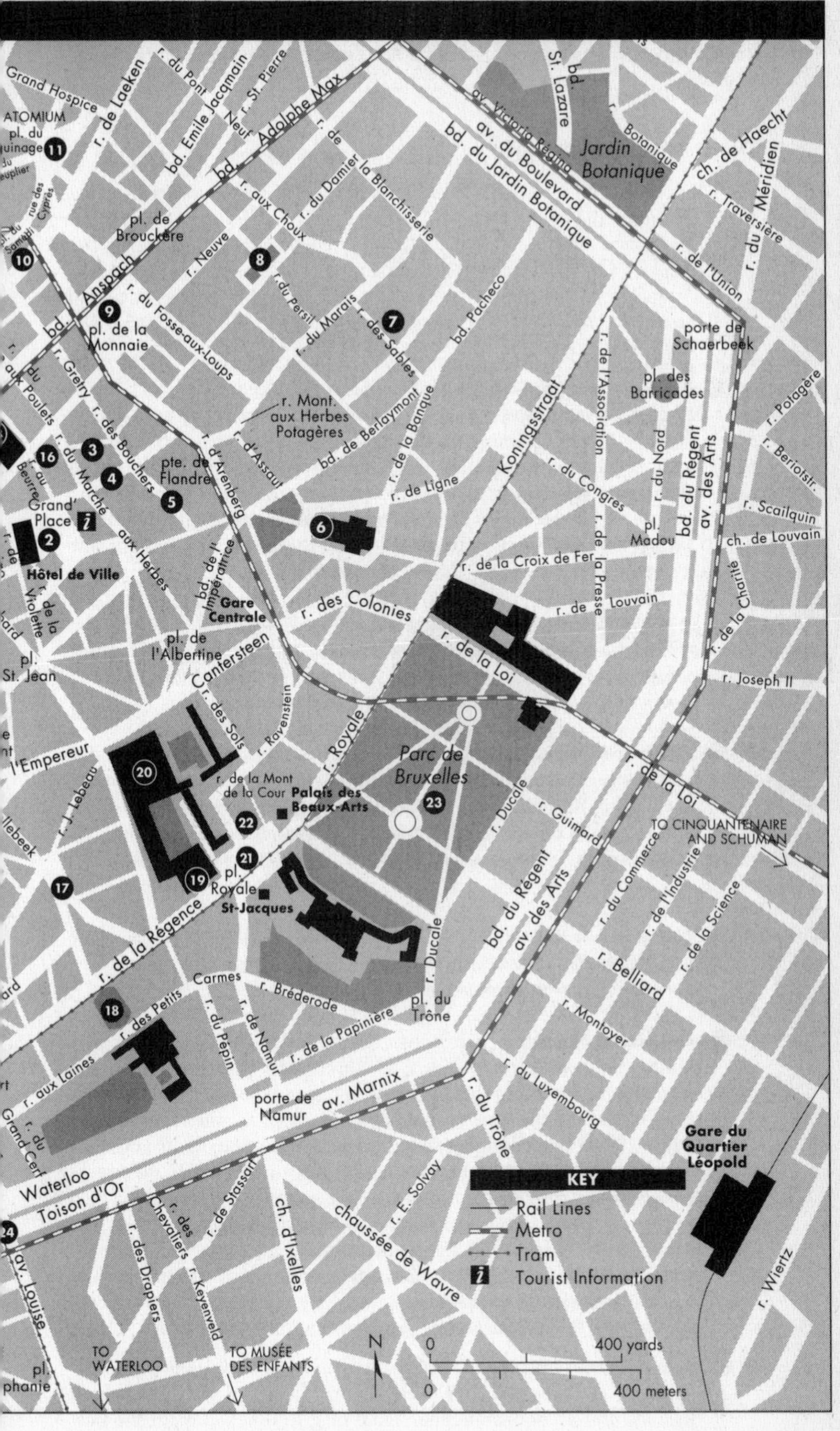
KEY
Rail Lines
Metro
Tram
Tourist Information
Jardin Botanique
Parc de Bruxelles
Gare Centrale
Hôtel de Ville
Grand' Place
Palais des Beaux-Arts
St-Jacques
Gare du Quartier Léopold
TO CINQUANTENAIRE AND SCHUMAN
TO WATERLOO
TO MUSÉE DES ENFANTS
400 yards
400 meters
bd. Adolphe Max
bd. Anspach
bd. du Jardin Botanique
av. du Boulevard
Koningsstraat
bd. de Berlaymont
r. des Colonies
r. de la Loi
r. Royale
r. de la Régence
av. Marnix
porte de Namur
chaussée de Wavre
ch. d'Ixelles
av. Louise
bd. du Régent
av. des Arts
r. Belliard
r. du Luxembourg
r. du Trône
pl. du Trône
porte de Schaerbeek
pl. des Barricades
pl. Madou
ch. de Louvain
ch. de Haecht
pl. de Brouckère
pl. de la Monnaie
pl. Royale
pl. de l'Albertine
pl. St. Jean
Toison d'Or
Waterloo

appeal to children, comic strip art has been taken seriously in Belgium for many years, and in this museum it is wedded to another strongly Belgian art form: art nouveau. The building was designed by Victor Horta in 1903 for a textile wholesaler, and the lighting and stairs, always important to Horta, are impressive. They serve the purposes of the new owner equally well. Tintin, the creation of the late, great Hergé, became a worldwide favorite cartoon character, and his albums have sold an estimated 80 million copies. But many other artists have followed in Hergé's footsteps, some of them even more innovative. The collection includes more than 400 original plates by Hergé and his successors and 25,000 cartoon works; those not exhibited can be viewed in the archive. There's also a large comic strip shop, a library, and an attractive art nouveau brasserie. ✉ *R. des Sables 20,* ☎ *02/219–1980.* *BF250/€6.20.* ⏲ *Tues.–Sun. 10–6.*

11 **Eglise St-Jean-du-Béguinage.** Originally this elegant Flemish baroque church served as the center for the *béguines* (lay sisters) who lived in houses clustered around it. The interior has preserved its Gothic elements, with soaring vaults. The surprisingly different architectural styles combine to make this one of the most attractive churches in Brussels. A number of streets converge on the small, serene, circular square, which is surrounded by buildings that help create a harmonious architectural whole. ✉ *Pl. du Béguinage.* ⏲ *Tues.–Fri. 10–5.*

NEED A BREAK?

A la Mort Subite (✉ R. Montagne-aux-Herbes-Potagères 7, ☎ 02/513–1318) is a Brussels institution named after a card game called "Sudden Death." This café, unaltered for 75 years, serves Mort Subite lambic beers on tap, in a wide range of fruit flavors.

16 **Eglise St-Nicolas.** This small church, surrounded by tiny houses that seem to huddle under it, is almost 1,000 years old. Little remains of the original structure, but a cannonball fired by the French in 1695 is still lodged in one of the pillars. ✉ *R. au Beurre 1,* ☎ *02/513–8022.* ⏲ *Weekdays 7:45–6:30, Sat. 9–6, Sun. 9–7:30; mass in English, Sun. at 10 AM.*

NEED A BREAK?

Cirio (✉ R. de la Bourse 18–20, ☎ 02/512–1395) is a peaceful café with outstanding art nouveau decor that hasn't changed for generations—nor, apparently, has some of the clientele.

5 **Galeries St-Hubert.** A visit to this arcade is like going shopping with your great-grandparents. There are three parts to it: *de la Reine, du Roi,* and *du Prince* (of the queen, the king, and the prince). They were built in 1847 as the world's first covered shopping galleries, thanks to new engineering techniques that allowed architects to use iron girders to design soaring constructions of glass. Neoclassical gods and heroes look down from their sculpted niches on the crowded scene below; flags of many nations billow ever so slightly; and the buskers play classical music, while diffused daylight penetrates the gallery from the glassed arches. The shops, which are generally open Monday to Saturday 10–6, are interspersed with cafés, restaurants, a theater, and a cinema. ✉ *Access from R. des Bouchers or Carrefour de l'Europe,* ☎ *02/512–2116.*

★ 2 **Grand'Place.** This jewel box of a square is arguably Europe's most ornate and most theatrical. It is close to the hearts of all the people of the city, and all ages come here from time to time. At night the burnished facades of the guild houses and their gilded statuary look especially dramatic: from April to September, the square is floodlit after sundown with waves of changing colors, accompanied by music. Try to be here for the *Ommegang,* a magnificent historical pageant re-creating Emperor Charles V's reception in the city in 1549 (the first Tuesday and Thursday in July). You'll find here a daily flower market, frequent jazz and classical concerts, and in December, under the majestic Christmas tree, a life-size crèche with sheep grazing around it. ✉ *Intersection of R. des Chapeliers, R. Buls, R. de la Tête d'Or, R. au Beurre, R. Chair et Pain, R. des Harengs, and R. de la Colline.*

Guild Houses of the Grand'Place. Built in ornate baroque style soon after the 1695 bombardment, the guild houses have a striking architectural coherence. Among the buildings on the north side of the square, No. 1–2, **Le Roy d'Espagne**, belonged to the bakers' guild. It is surmounted by a cupola on which the figure of Fame is perched. **Le Sac**, No. 4, commissioned by the guild of joiners and coopers, and No. 6, **Le Cornet**, built for the boatmen, were both designed by Antoon Pastorana, a gifted furniture maker. **Le Renard**, No. 7, was designed for the guild of haberdashers and peddlers; a sculpture of St. Christopher, their patron, stands on top of the gable. **Le Cygne**, No. 9, was formerly a butchers' guild. Today, it is an elegant restaurant (☞ Maison du Cygne *in* Dining, *below*), but before that it was a popular tavern often frequented by Karl Marx. ✉ *Grand'Place.*

Hôtel de Ville. The Gothic Town Hall, which dates from the early 15th century, dominates the Grand'Place (☞ *above*). Nearly 300 years older than the guild houses, which were rebuilt after the French bombardment of 1695, it was renovated most recently in 1997. The left wing was begun in 1402 but was soon found to be too small. Charles the Bold laid the first stone for the extension in 1444, and it was completed four years later. The extension left the slender belfry off center; it has now been fully restored. The belfry is topped by a bronze statue of St. Michael crushing the devil beneath his feet. Over the gateway are statues of the prophets, female figures representing lofty virtues, and effigies of long-gone dukes and duchesses. Inside the Town Hall are a number of excellent Brussels and Mechelen tapestries, some of them in the Gothic Hall, where recitals and chamber-music concerts are frequently held. ✉ *Grand'Place,* ☎ *02/279–4365.* 🎟 *BF100/€2.50.* ⏲ *Guided tours only, Tues. and Wed.: Dutch: 1:45, French 2:30, English 3:15.*

NEED A BREAK? There are plenty of cafés to choose from on Grand'Place. On the ground floor of No. 1, the vast and popular **Le Roy d'Espagne** (☎ 02/513–0807) has an open fire and solid wooden furniture.

⓭ **Maison de la Bellonne.** This patrician 18th-century building was named for the Roman goddess of war, whose effigy decorates the baroque facade. It often hosts concerts and dance performances. ✉ *R. de Flandre 46,* ☎ *02/513–3333.* 🎟 *Free.* ⏲ *Tues.–Fri. 10–6.*

Maison de la Brasserie. On the same side of the Grand'Place (☞ *above*) as the Town Hall, this was once the brewers' guild. Today it houses a modest **Brewery Museum,** appropriate enough in a country that still brews 400 different beers. ✉ *Grand'Place 10,* ☎ *02/511–4987.* 🎟 *BF100/€2.50.* ⏲ *Daily 10–5.*

Musée du Cacao et du Chocolat. The Museum of Cacao and Chocolate is another modest museum giving an inside look at one of Belgium's prize products. The museum explains how the cacao beans are grown and processed and takes viewers through the entire stage of chocolate production. Visitors even get a small tasting. ✉ *Grand'Place 13,* ☎ *02/514–2048.* 🎟 *BF200/€4.95.* ⏲ *Tues.–Sat. 10–5.*

Maison du Roi. No ruler ever lived in this House of the King; rather, it was named for its grandeur. Today, it houses the **Musée Communal,**

a Municipal Museum that has some fine tapestries, altarpieces, and paintings, notably the *Marriage Procession,* by Pieter Bruegel the Elder. On the top floor you can see the extravagant wardrobe of costumes donated to clothe the little statue of *Manneken Pis* (☞ *below*) on festive occasions. ✉ *Grand'Place,* ☎ *02/279–4355.* 🎫 *BF100/€2.50 for House and Museum.* ⏲ *Tues.–Fri. 10–5, weekends 10–1.*

1 Manneken Pis. For centuries, the small bronze statue of a chubby boy urinating into a fountain has drawn visitors from near and far. (A rarely remarked-upon fact is that he is left-handed.) The first mention of him dates from 1377. Sometimes called "Brussels's Oldest Citizen," he has also been said to symbolize what Belgians think of the authorities, especially those of occupying forces. The present version was commissioned from sculptor Jerome Duquesnoy in 1619. It is a copy; the original was seized by French soldiers in 1747. In restitution, King Louis XV of France was the first to present *Manneken Pis* with a gold-embroidered suit. The statue now has 517 other costumes for ceremonial occasions, an ever-increasing collection whose recent benefactors include John Malkovich and Dennis Hopper. Thousands of copies, in various materials and sizes, are sold as souvenirs every year. A female version, the Jeanneke Pis, can be found at the Petit Sablon (☞ *below*). ✉ *Corner R. de l'Etuve and R. du Chêne.*

8 Place des Martyrs. This square is dedicated to the 445 patriots who died in the brief 1830 war of independence against the Dutch. The shrine to the patriots is underneath the square. The square itself is a neoclassical architectural ensemble built in 1795 in the cool style favored by the Austrian Habsburgs. This noble square has also been a martyr to local political and real estate interests, notably squabbling between the two linguistic administrations, which has hampered much-needed renovations. ✉ *R. du Persil.*

12 Place Ste-Catherine. If you find the Grand'Place overrun by tourists, come to this square, a favorite of locals. It's a working market every weekday from 7 to 5, where people come to shop for necessities and banter with fishmongers. There's a stall where you can down a few oysters, accompanied by a glass of ice-cold muscadet. In the evening the action moves to the old **Vismet** (Fish Market), which branches off from the Eglise de Ste-Catherine. All that remains of the old canal is a couple of elongated ponds, but both sides are lined with seafood restaurants, some excellent, many overpriced. In good weather, there's outdoor waterside dining. ✉ *Intersection of R. Ste-Catherine, R. du Vieux Marché aux Grains, R. de Flandre, Quai aux Briques, Quai au Bois à Bruler, Pl. du Samedi, R. Plateau, and R. Melsens.*

★ **4 Quartier de l'Ilôt Sacré.** Pickpockets, flimflam artists, and jewelry vendors mingle with the crowds in the narrow Rue des Bouchers and even narrower Petite Rue des Bouchers. Still, except for the pickpockets, it's all good-natured fun in the liveliest area in Brussels, where restaurants and cafés stand cheek by jowl, their tables spilling out onto the sidewalks. One local street person makes a specialty of picking up a heaped plate and emptying it into his bag. The waiters laugh and bring another plate. The restaurants make strenuous efforts to pull you in with huge displays of seafood and game. The quality, alas, is a different matter. (For some outstanding exceptions, *see* Dining, *below.*)

14 Rue Antoine Dansaert. Bordering the city center and the run-down "little Chicago" district, this is the flagship street of Brussels's fashionable quarter, which extends south to the Place St-Géry. Avant-garde boutiques sell Belgian-designed men's and women's fashions along with more familiar high-fashion names. There are also inexpensive restaurants, cozy bars and cafés, avant-garde galleries, and stylish furniture shops.

9 **Théâtre de la Monnaie.** It was here, during a performance of Auber's *La Muette de Portici* on August 25, 1830, that some members of the audience became so inflamed by the duet "Amour sacré de la patrie" that they stormed out and started a riot that led to independence. The pleasing hall, on the **Place de la Monnaie**, is among Europe's leading opera stages. ✉ *Between De Brouckere and Fossé aux Loups at R. Neuve and R. des Fripiers,* ☎ *02/218–1202.*

3 **Théâtre Toone.** An old puppet theater, now run by José Geal—a seventh-generation member of the Toone family who's thus known as Toone VII—this theater has a repertory of 33 plays, including some by Shakespeare. You won't understand a word, as performances are given in the local *vloms* dialect, but it's fun anyway. There's a puppet museum (only accessible during the shows) and a bar with great, old-fashioned ambience. ✉ *Impasse Schuddeveld, off Petite R. des Bouchers,* ☎ *02/511–7137 or 02/513–7486.* *Performance BF400/€9.95; entrance to museum free with show.* ⏲ *Performance most evenings at 8:30.*

10 **Tour Noire.** Part of the 12th-century fortifications, the Black Tower is now regrettably being assimilated into the structure of a chain hotel. ✉ *Pl. Ste-Catherine.*

OFF THE BEATEN PATH

CHÂTEAU ROYAL DE LAEKEN– Home to the Belgian royal family, the Royal Castle of Laeken was built in 1784 in a 160-hectare park north of central Brussels. The extensive royal greenhouses, built in 1902 and home to a lush collection of exotic plants, are open to the public for two weeks in April and May. The castle and park are only open to visitors during greenhouse tours; dates are set each year in February. Contact the Brussels Tourist Office (☞ Visitor Information *in* Smart Travel Tips) for more information. ✉ *Av. Jules Van Praet 44,* ☎ *no phone.*

LA TOUR JAPONAISE– King Leopold II was so impressed by a Japanese structure constructed for the 1900 Paris Exhibition that he bought the plans for the 125-ft Japanese Tower and had a replica built on the edge of royal estate at Laeken. The wood doors and sculpted panels are the work of Japanese craftsmen, and the building houses temporary exhibits related to Japan. ✉ *Av. Jules Van Praet 44,* ☎ *02/268–1608.* *BF80/€2.00.* ⏲ *Tues.–Sun 10–4:30 Laeken, or trams 52, 92.*

PAVILLON CHINOIS– Adjacent to the Japanese Tower, King Leopold had constructed the Chinese Pavillion, originally intended to house a deluxe restaurant. The kiosk and most exterior woodwork were made in Shanghai. The building is home to a collection of 17th- and 18th-century Chinese porcelain and furniture. ☎ *02/268–2538.* *BF80/€2.00; combined Tower and Pavillion tickets BF120/€2.95.* ⏲ *Tues.–Sun. 10–4:30.*

Upper Town: Royal Brussels

Uptown Brussels bears the hallmarks of two rulers, Austrian Charles of Lorraine and Leopold II, Belgium's empire builder. The 1713 Treaty of Utrecht, which distributed bits of Europe like pieces in a jigsaw puzzle at the end of one of the continent's many wars, handed the Low Countries to Austria. Fortunately for the Belgians, the man Austria sent here as governor was a tolerant visionary who oversaw the construction of a new palace, the neoclassical Place Royale, and other buildings that transformed the Upper Town.

The next large-scale rebuilding of Brussels was initiated by Leopold II, the second king of independent Belgium, in the latter part of the 19th century. Cousin of Queen Victoria and the Kaiser, he annexed the Congo for Belgium and applied some of the profits to grand urban projects. Present-day Brussels is indebted to him for its wide avenues and thoroughfares.

Numbers in the text correspond to numbers in the margin and on the Central Brussels map.

A Good Walk

Start at the **Place du Grand Sablon** ⑰, window-shopping at its overpriced antiques stores and often unadventurous galleries. Cross the Rue de la Régence into its sister square, the peaceful **Place du Petit Sablon** ⑱, whose formal garden is filled with, and surrounded by, statuary. Turn right on the Rue de la Régence to the **Musée d'Art Ancien** ⑲, which holds many Old Masters, and the spectacular **Musée d'Art Moderne** ⑳, which burrows underground for space to show its modern and contemporary art.

You're now on the gleaming white **Place Royale** ㉑, a pearl of 18th-century neoclassicism, with the Eglise de St-Jacques. Walk down the Rue de la Montagne du Cour; on the left is the elegant courtyard of the Palace of Charles de Lorraine. On the right is the new **Musée des Instruments de Musique** ㉒, housed in the art nouveau building that was originally home to the Old England department store. Continue along the Rue Ravenstein around Victor Horta's **Palais des Beaux-Arts,** the city's principal concert venue, and up the handsome steps to the formal **Parc de Bruxelles** ㉓. At its end, on the right, stands Leopold II's vast, hulking **Palais du Roi.**

Returning to Place Royale, pass through the gateway on the corner next to the church, and up the Rue de Namur to the Porte de Namur. You have now reached the city's most expensive shopping area. As you walk right on the Boulevard de Waterloo, you'll pass the same high-fashion names that you find in Paris, London, and New York. The focus of the shopping district is the **Place Louise** ㉔, with the avenue and gallery of the same name.

For a fitting finale, walk down the short Rue des Quatre Bras toward the looming, oppressive **Palais de Justice** ㉕. The balustrade facing the old town has a panoramic view of the city, from the cupola of the Koekelberg Basilica, the world's fifth-largest church, to the Atomium, the replica of a vastly enlarged molecule. Walk down the steps to explore the colorful neighborhood of **Les Marolles** ㉖, where many of Brussels's immigrants have settled. Less than 1 km (½ mi) northwest along Boulevard du Midi is where the colorful **Kermesse du Midi** ㉗ carnival is held in summer.

TIMING

Walking time, without stopping, is about an hour and a half. For stops in the art museums (closed Monday) add another two to three hours, plus one hour for window shopping in the Grand Sablon and Place Louise areas.

Sights to See

㉗ **Kermesse du Midi.** From mid-July until the end of August, all of Belgium's carnival barkers and showmen and their carousels, ghost trains, Ferris wheels, shooting galleries, rides, swings, and merry-go-rounds congregate along the Boulevard du Midi for this giant and hugely popular funfair. It extends for blocks and blocks. ✉ *Both sides of Bd. du Midi, from Pl. de la Constitution to Porte d'Anderlecht.* 🎫 *Attractions separately priced.* ⏲ *10 AM–midnight.*

26 **Les Marolles.** If the Grand'Place stands for old money, the Marolles neighborhood stands for old—and current—poverty. Walk down the steps in front of the Palais de Justice and you have arrived. This was home to the workers who produced the luxury goods for which Brussels was famous. There may not be many left who still speak the old Brussels dialect, mixing French and Flemish with a bit of Spanish thrown in, but the area still has raffish charm, although gentrification is in progress. The Marolles has welcomed many waves of immigrants, the most recent from Spain, North Africa, and Turkey. Many come to the daily **Flea Market** at the Place du Jeu de Balle, where old clothes are sold along with every kind of bric-a-brac, plain junk, and the occasional gem. ✉ *Center: R. Haute and R. Blaes. Bordered by Bd. du Midi, Bd. de Waterloo heading southwest from Palais de Justice, and imaginary line running west from Pl. de la Chapelle to Bd. Maurice Lemonnier.*

★ 19 **Musée d'Art Ancien.** In the first of the interconnected art museums, the Fine Arts Museum pays special attention to the great, so-called Flemish Primitives of the 15th century, who invented the art of painting with oil. The Spanish and the Austrians pilfered some of the finest works, but there's plenty left by the likes of Memling, Petrus Christus, and Rogier Van der Weyden. The collection of works by Pieter Bruegel the Elder is outstanding; it includes *The Fall of Icarus,* in which the figure of the mythological hero disappearing in the sea is but one detail of a scene in which people continue to go about their business. A century later Rubens, Van Dyck, and Jordaens dominated the art scene; their works are on the floor above. The 19th-century collection on the ground floor includes the melodramatic *Death of Marat* by Jacques-Louis David, who, like many other French artists and writers, spent years of exile in Belgium. ✉ *R. de la Régence 3,* ☎ *02/508–3211.* 🎫 *BF150/€3.70.* ⏲ *Tues.–Sun. 10–5.*

★ 20 **Musée d'Art Moderne.** Rather like New York's Guggenheim Museum in reverse, the Modern Art Museum burrows underground and circles downward eight floors. You can reach it by an underground passage from the Fine Arts Museum or you can enter it from the house on Place Royale where Alexandre Dumas (*père*) once lived and wrote. The collection is strong on Belgian and French art of the past 100 years, including Belgian artists who have acquired international prominence, such as the Expressionist James Ensor and the Surrealists Paul Delvaux and René Magritte, as well as Pierre Alechinsky and sculptor Pol Bury. Note that lunch hours at this and the Musée d'Ancien (☞ *above*) are staggered so as not to inconvenience visitors. ✉ *Pl. Royale 1,* ☎ *02/508–3211.* 🎫 *BF150/€3.70.* ⏲ *Tues.–Sun. 10–5.*

Musée de la Dynastie. The Dynasty Museum traces the relatively short history of the Belgian royal family, since the country's independence from the Netherlands in 1830. ✉ *Place Palais 7,* ☎ *02/511–5578.* 🎫 *Free.* ⏲ *Tues.–Sun. 10–6.*

22 **Musée des Instruments de Musique.** The first-rate Museum of Musical Instruments opened in 1999, bringing together under one roof a collection of more than 7,000 international musical instruments from the past five centuries. The site combines the former Old England department store, designed by architect Paul Saintenoy in 1899 and one of the city's most beautiful art nouveau buildings, and the adjoining neoclassical Barré-Guimard building from 1913. A third building in the adjoining Rue Villa Hermosa houses the instrument reserve. The four-story museum includes about 1,500 instruments and features a complete 17th-century orchestra, a precious 1619 spinet-harpsichord (only two such instruments exist), a rare Chedeville bagpipe, and about

100 Indian instruments given to King Leopold II by the Rajah Sourindro Mohun Tagore. In addition to seeing the instruments, visitors may actually listen to them via infrared headphones, which play about 200 extracts ranging from ancient Greek times to the mid-20th century. In the basement, the Garden of Orpheus is set up for children to discover musical instruments. In addition, the museum's 200-seat concert hall hosts regular performances that feature harpsichords, virginals, and pianos from the collection. The tearoom and restaurant on the sixth floor offer panoramic views of Brussels. ✉ *R. Montagne de la Cour 2,* ☎ *02/545–0130.* 🎫 *BF150/€3.70.* ⏲ *Tues., Wed., and Fri. 9:30–5, Thurs. 9:30–8, weekends 10–5. Concerts Thursdays at 8.*

25 **Palais de Justice.** Many a nasty comment—"the ugliest building in Europe," for instance—has been made about Leopold II's giant late-19th-century Law Courts on the site of the old Gallows Hill. However, unlike the country's famously inept law enforcers, the pompous edifice actually strikes fear into the heart of the malefactor. Much of the Marolles district was pulled down to make way for the monstrosity, leaving thousands homeless. ✉ *Pl. Poelaert,* ☎ *02/508–6111.* 🎫 *Entrance hall free.* ⏲ *Weekdays 9–5.*

23 **Parc de Bruxelles.** This was once a game park, but in the late 18th century it was tamed into rigid symmetry and laid out in the design of Masonic symbols. The huge **Palais du Roi** occupies the entire south side of the park. It was built by Leopold II at the beginning of this century on a scale corresponding to his megalomaniacal ambitions. The present monarch, King Albert II, comes here for state occasions, although he lives at the more private Laeken Palace on the outskirts of Brussels. ✉ *Pl. des Palais, R. Royale, adjacent to Pl. Royale.* 🎫 *Palais du Roi free.* ⏲ *July 22–early Sept., Tues.–Sun. 10–4.*

★ 17 **Place du Grand Sablon.** The Large Sand Place is where the people of Brussels come to see and be seen. Once, as the name implies, it was nothing more than a sandy hill. Today, it is an elegant square, surrounded by numerous restaurants, cafés, and antiques shops, some in intriguing alleys and arcades. Every Saturday and Sunday morning a lively antiques market of more than 100 stands takes over the upper end of the square. It's not for bargain hunters, however. Downhill from the square stands the **Eglise de la Chapelle**, dating from 1134. Inside, there's a memorial to Pieter Bruegel the Elder, who was married in this church and buried here just a few years later. At the eastern end of the square stands the **Eglise Notre-Dame du Sablon**, a Flamboyant-Gothic church founded in 1304 by the guild of crossbowmen (the original purpose of the square was crossbow practice) and rebuilt in the 15th century. It's one of Brussels's most beautiful churches, and at night the stained-glass windows are illuminated from within. ✉ *Intersection of R. de Rollebeek, R. Lebeau, R. de la Paille, R. Ste-Anne, R. Boedenbroeck, R. des Sablons, Petite Rue des Minimes, R. des Minimes, and R. Joseph Stevens.*

NEED A BREAK?

Wittamer, the best of Brussels's many excellent pastry shops (✉ Pl. du Grand Sablon 12, ☎ 02/512–3742), has an attractive upstairs tearoom, which also serves breakfast and light lunches, featuring by Wittamer's unbeatable pastries.

18 **Place du Petit Sablon.** Opposite the Grand Sablon (☞ *above*), this square is surrounded by a magnificent wrought-iron fence, topped by 48 small bronze statues representing the city's guilds. Inside the peaceful garden stands a double statue of the Flemish patriots Counts Egmont and Hoorn on their way to the Spaniards' scaffold in 1568.

(24) **Place Louise.** There's a certain type of young Belgian matron—tall, blond, bejeweled, and freshly tanned whatever the season—whose natural urban habitat is around Place Louise. The most expensive shops are along Boulevard Waterloo. Prices are somewhat lower on the other side of the street, on Avenue de la Toison d'Or, which means the Golden Fleece. Additional shops and boutiques line both sides of Avenue Louise and the Galerie Louise, which burrows through the block to link Avenue de la Toison d'Or with Place Stéphanie. This is an area for browsing, window-shopping, movie-going, and café-sitting, but don't go expecting a bargain. ✉ *Av. Louise and Bd. de Waterloo.*

NEED A BREAK?

Nemrod (✉ Bd. de Waterloo 61, ☎ 02/511–1127) is an expensive but handily placed café-pub garishly dressed up as a hunting lodge with a blazing fire. It's very popular for a shopping break or before a show.

★ (21) **Place Royale.** Although the Royal Square was built in the French style by Austrian overlords, it is distinctly Belgian. White and elegantly proportioned, it is the centerpiece of the Upper Town, which became the center of power during the 18th century. The equestrian statue in its center, representing Godefroid de Bouillon, crusader and King of Jerusalem, is a romantic afterthought. The buildings are being restored one by one, leaving the facades intact. Place Royale was built on the ruins of the Palace of the Dukes of Brabant, which had burned down. The site has been excavated, and it is possible to see the underground digs and the main hall, Aula Magna, where Charles V was crowned Holy Roman Emperor in 1519 and where, 37 years later, he abdicated to retire to a monastery. The church on the square, **St-Jacques-sur-Coudenberg**, was originally designed to look like a Greek temple. After the French Revolution reached Belgium, it briefly served as a "Temple of Reason." The art nouveau building on the northwest corner is the former Old England department store, home of the Musée des Instruments de Musique (☞ *above*).

On or near Place Royale are the neoclassical courtyard of the **Palace of Charles of Lorraine** (✉ Coudenberg); the **Hôtel Ravenstein** (✉ 3 R. Ravenstein), built in the 15th century and the only surviving aristocratic house from that period; and the **Palais des Beaux-Arts** (✉ 23 R. Ravenstein), an art deco concert hall, designed in the 1920s by Victor Horta and remarkable more for the ingenuity with which he overcame its tricky location than for its aesthetic appeal.

OFF THE BEATEN PATH

ATOMIUM – Built for the 1958 World's Fair, the model of an iron molecule enlarged 165 billion times is one of Brussels's landmarks. Take an express elevator to the top, 400 ft up, for panoramic views of Brussels. ✉ *Bd. du Centenaire,* ☎ *02/474–8904.* *BF200/€4.95.* *Apr.–Oct., daily 9–7; May–Sept., daily 10–5:30. Metro: Heysel.*

MINI-EUROPE – In a 5-acre park next to the Atomium (☞ *above*) stands an impressive collection of 1:25 scale models of more than 300 famous buildings from the 15 European Union countries. ✉ *Bd. du Centenaire 20,* ☎ *02/478–0550.* *BF420/€10.50.* *Daily 9:30–5 (July–Aug. until 7).*

OCEADE – Attractions at this water park include water slides, a Jacuzzi, and a wave pool. ✉ *Bruparck, near Atomium and next to Mini-Europe,* ☎ *02/478–4944.* *BF480/€11.95.* *Tues.–Thurs. 10–6; Fri., weekends, and holidays 10–10.*

Museums and the EU: Cinquantenaire and Schuman

East of the center at the end of Rue de la Loi, Ronde-Point Robert Schuman is the focus of the buildings that house the European institutions. A number of vast museums flank Brussels's version of the Arc de Triomphe, known as Cinquantenaire, planned by Leopold II for the 50th anniversary of Belgian independence in 1880. Leopold's inability to coax funding from a reluctant government meant it was not completed until 25 years later.

Numbers in the text correspond to numbers in the margin and on the Cinquantenaire and Schuman map.

A Good Walk

Start at Rond-Point Schuman, where among the buildings of the **European Institutions** ㉘–㉚ you can see the Justus Lipsius Building, named for the Renaissance humanist and friend of Rubens and home to the secretive Council of Ministers. You can also see the Berlaymont, a star-shape building that is normally home to the European Commission. After having been closed due to an asbestos scare and spending eight years wrapped in plastic sheeting, it is due to reopen in October 2001 following a thorough environmental cleanup and complete rebuilding. Walk down Rue Archimede, with the Berlaymont building on your left, and continue until the street joins Square Ambiorix. The heavy presence of the European Union community is evident in the English- and Irish-style pubs. Turn left onto the square and continue in a counter-clockwise direction on the square until it joins Avenue Palmerston. Take another left onto Palmerston until you reach Square Marie Louise, with its pond and false grotto—one of only three ponds left in Brussels from the approximately 60 that had existed in the 15th century. Continue on Palmerston. The Hotel Van Eetvelde at No. 44 was designed by art nouveau architect Victor Horta between 1895–1901. (here, *hotel* refers to a large, private house). After Palmerston rejoins Square Ambiorix, continue to No. 11, a curvaceous art nouveau treasure designed in 1900 by Gustave Strauven for painter Georges de St.-Cyr. Walk back across the square and turn left, then head right at Rue Michel Ange and continue until it ends at Avenue Cortenbergh. The Parc du Cinquantenaire is across the street. Continue east through the park until you reach the Cinquantenaire Musée, which houses the **Musée Royal de l'Armée et de l'Histoire Militaire** ㉛ and the **Musées Royaux d'Art et de l'Histoire** ㉜, and **Autoworld** ㉝. Walk down Avenue de Tervuren, a broad, straight road created by Leopold II at the end of the 19th century, to link the Cinquantenaire arch with Tervuren. When you reach Place Montgomery, take a 44 tram to Tervuren and the **Koninklijk Museum voor Midden Afrika/Musée Royal de l'Afrique Centrale.** ㉞

TIMING

From Ronde-Point Schuman, it's about 50 minutes to the Cinquantenaire Museum and Autoworld. To walk to Square Montgomery, allow around 30 minutes. The tram to Tervuren takes about 20 minutes.

Sights to See

33 **Autoworld.** Here, under the high glass roof of the south hall in the Parc de Cinquantenaire, is arrayed one of the best collections of vintage cars in the world. More than 450 are in the stellar collection. ✉ *Parc du Cinquantenaire 11,* ☎ *02/736–4165.* *BF200/€4.95.* ⊙ *Apr. 1–Sept. 30, daily 10–6; Oct. 1–Mar. 31, daily 10–5. Subway: Mérode.*

European Institutions. The European Commission and related institutions have had a significant impact on Brussels. Entire neighborhoods east of the center have been razed to make room for steel-and-glass

Cinquantenaire and Schuman

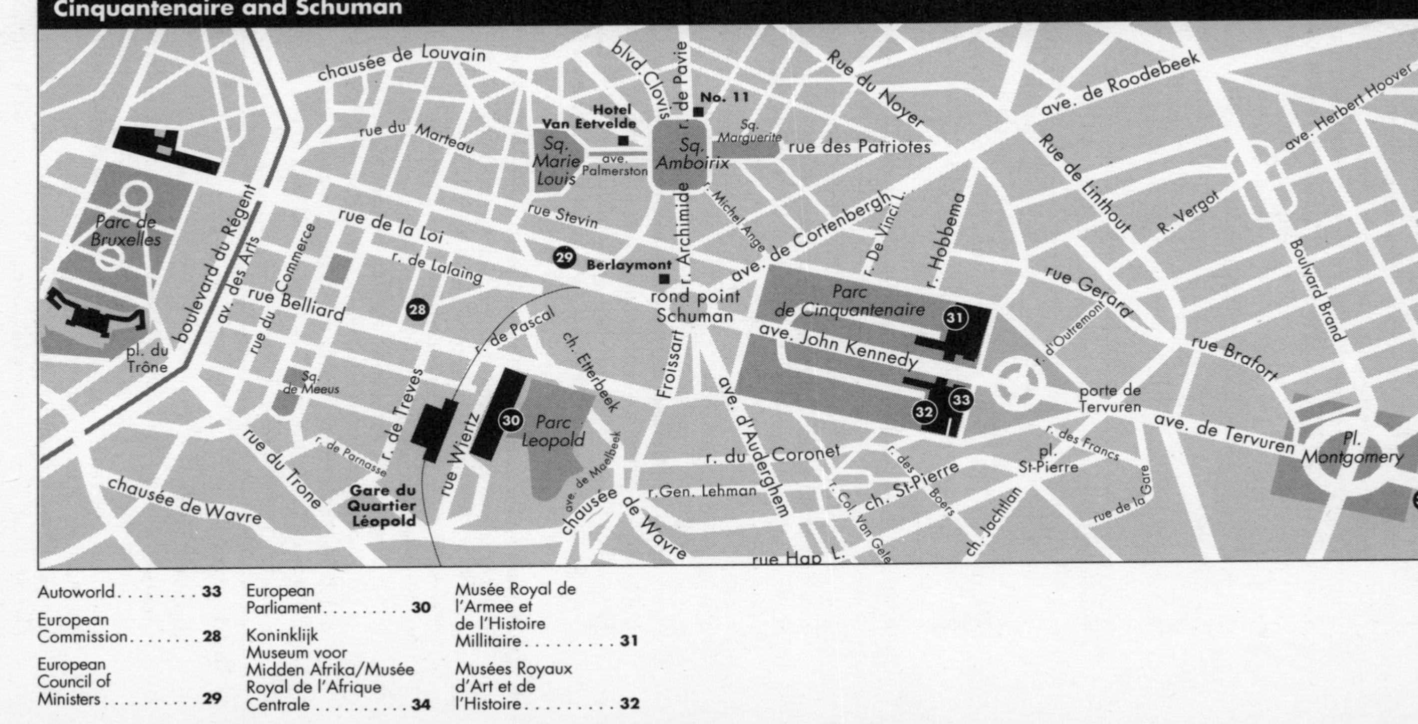

Autoworld **33**
European Commission **28**
European Council of Ministers **29**
European Parliament **30**
Koninklijk Museum voor Midden Afrika/Musée Royal de l'Afrique Centrale **34**
Musée Royal de l'Armee et de l'Histoire Millitaire **31**
Musées Royaux d'Art et de l'Histoire **32**

buildings. What remains of the old blocks has also seen an influx of ethnic restaurants catering to the tastes of lower-level Eurocrats; the grandees eat in splendid isolation in their own dining rooms. The landmark, star-shape Berlaymont building was closed in 1991 for asbestos removal. Following a full environmental cleanup and restora-
28 tion it is to reopen in October 2001. During the work, the **European**
29 **Commission** (✉ R. de Trèves 120) and the **European Council of Ministers** (✉ R. de la Loi 170) are occupying temporary headquarters. The
30 controversial **European Parliament** building (✉ R. Wiertz 43)—France still insists on regular Parliament meetings in Strasbourg—is named Les Caprices des Dieux, or Folly of the Gods. Its central element, a rounded glass summit, looms behind the Gare de Luxembourg. ✉ *Rond-Point R. Schuman. Subway: from Ste-Cathérine via De Brouckère to Schuman.*

Musée des Transports Urbains Bruxellois. The Museum of Brussels Urban Transport houses historic trams and buses—rides are offered as well. The museum also organizes tourist visits on historic trams on Sunday mornings from April to October for BF400/€9.95, including a beverage, or for BF700/€17.50 including a meal. ✉ *Avenue du Tervuren 364b,* ☎ *02/515–3108.* *BF50/€1.25 or BF150/€3.70 including a tram ride.* ⏲ *Apr.–Oct., weekends 1:30–7.*

34 **Koninklijk Museum voor Midden Afrika/Musée Royal de l'Afrique Centrale.** The Africa Museum is part of King Leopold II's legacy to Belgium, an incredible collection of 250,000 objects, including masks, sculpture, and memorabilia of the journeys of the explorers of Africa. The museum stands in the middle of a beautifully landscaped park. ✉ *Leuvensesteenweg 13,* ☎ *02/767–5401.* *BF50/€1.25.* ⏲ *Tues.–Fri. 10–5, weekends 10–6. Subway: to Pl. Montgomery, then Tram 44 to Tervuren.*

31 **Musée Royal de l'Armée et de l'Histoire Militaire.** The highlight of this vast collection of the Royal Museum of Arms and Military History, part of the Cinquantenaire Museum, is the hall filled with 130 aircraft from World War I to the Gulf War. ✉ *Parc du Cinquantenaire 3,* ☎ *02/733–4493.* *Free.* ⏲ *Tues.–Sun. 9–noon and 1–4:30.*

★ 32 **Musées Royaux d'Art et de l'Histoire.** The 140 rooms at the Royal Museums of Art and History contain important antiquities and ethnographic collections. The most significant sections are devoted to Belgian archaeology and to the immense tapestries for which Brussels once was famous. Renovations in the late 1990s have brought to the museum a new treasure room, plenty of temporary exhibitions, and a more dynamic approach, as well as a new name, joining it with the Musée Royal de l'Armée et de l'Histoire Militaire as the Cinquantenaire Museum. ✉ *Parc du Cinquantenaire 10,* ☎ *02/741–7211.* *BF100.* ⏲ *Tues.–Fri. 9:30–5, weekends 10–5.*

East of the Center

A Good Walk

Begin at the **Musée des Sciences Naturelles** on Rue Vautier, where the hulking sculpture of a dinosaur outside is a precursor to the museum's collection. Continue on Rue Vautier to the **Musée Wiertz,** housed in the studio of 19th-century classical artist Antoine Wiertz. Turn right from Rue Vautier onto Rue Wiertz, taking you through the **European Parliament,** a 13-story behemoth. From Rue Wiertz walk through **Parc Leopold** to enjoy a respite from the city. Turn right onto Rue Beillard and then left on Rue Froissart to head to the Schuman metro station. From Schuman it's a short metro ride to the Arts-Loi station, handy for a visit to the **Musée Charlier,** the former residence of sculptor Guillaume Charlier.

TIMING

It's about a 10-minute walk from the Natural Science Museum to the European Parliament. Allow another 20 minutes to walk to the Schuman metro station and another five minutes on the Metro to Arts-Loi. Including museums, the visit should take about an hour and a half.

Sights to See

Musée Charlier. The former home of 19th-century sculptor Guillaume Charlier is now a museum housing both his own work and his collection of paintings, sculpture, tapestry, and furniture from the 15th through 19th centuries. ✉ *Av. des Arts 16,* ☎ *02/218–5382.* 🎫 *BF200/€4.95.* ⏲ *Tues.–Sun. 10–6.*

Musée des Sciences Naturel. The highlights of the Natural Sciences Museum are the skeletons of 14 iguanodons found in 1878 in the coal mines of Bernissart—these are believed to be about 120 million years old. There are also displays on mammals, insects, and tropical shells, as well as a whale gallery. ✉ *R. Vautier 29,* ☎ *02/627–4211.* 🎫 *BF120/€2.95.* ⏲ *Tues.–Sat. 9:30–4:45, Sun. 9:30–6.*

Musée Wiertz. Antoine Wiertz was an early 19th-century artist who once won the Grand Prize of Rome for a classical painting. He later adopted the style of Flemish grand master Pieter Paul Rubens, but failing to find success turned to portrait painting. The Belgian government in 1850 gave him a studio in exchange for some of his works, and he later lived in an adjoining house. The museum is housed in the studio. ✉ *R. Vautier 62,* ☎ *02/648–1718.* 🎫 *Free.* ⏲ *Tues.–Fri. 10–noon and 1–5, every other weekend 10–noon and 1–5.*

West of the Center

A Good Walk

Start with a walk westward from Boulevard du Midi to the **Gueuze Museum.** Take Rue Crickx or Rue Brogniez to Rue Gheude, then walk north to the end of the street. Or, take a short detour before heading to the Gueuze by turning right onto Avenue de Stalingrad to visit the **Musée Juif de Belgique.** From the Gueuze, take a taxi or the 47 tram on Chaussée de Mons to Place de la Vaillance. Rue du Chapître, with the **Anderlecht Béguinage** and the **Maison d'Erasme,** is on your right.

TIMING

It's a 5- to 10-minute walk from the Kermesse to Gueuze. The tram ride takes about 10 minutes.

Sights to See

Anderlecht Béguinage. The Béguines, lay sisters and mostly widows of Crusaders, lived here in a collection of small houses, built between 1252 and the 17th century, grouped around a garden. Now it's open to the public, sharing a common administrative office with the Erasmushuis (☞ Maison d'Erasme, *below*). ✉ *R. du Chapître 8.*

Gueuze Museum. At this living museum of the noble art of brewing you can see Lambic being produced the old way, and also enjoy a tasting. The quintessential Brussels beer, created through spontaneous fermentation, is brewed nowhere else and is the basic ingredient in other popular Belgian beers, such as Gueuze, cherry-flavored Kriek, and raspberry-flavored Framboise. Sadly, many of the commercially brewed Lambics bear scant resemblance to the real thing. ✉ *R. Gheude 56,* ☎ *02/521–4928.* 🎫 *BF100/€2.50.* ⏲ *Weekdays 8:30–5, Sat. 10–5 (mid-Oct.–May, until 6). Metro: Gare du Midi.*

Musée Juif de Belgique. The Jewish Museum of Belgium's houses a collection of religious objects dating from the 16th century, as well as documents and books that illustrate traditional Jewish life. In addition to objects that illustrate Jewish customs throughout Europe are a number of pieces, including textiles and silver, made in Belgium. ✉ *Avenue de Stalingrad,* ☎ *02/512–1963.* *BF100/€2.50.* ⊙ *Mon.–Thurs. noon–5, Sun. 10–1. Metro: Lemonnier.*

Maison d'Erasme/Erasmushuis. In the middle of a commonplace neighborhood in the commune of Anderlecht stands the remarkable redbrick Erasmus House, which has been restored to its condition in 1521, the year the great humanist came to Brussels for the fresh air. First editions of *In Praise of Folly,* and other books by Erasmus can be inspected, and there are some extraordinary works of art: prints by Albrecht Dürer and oils by Holbein and Hieronymus Bosch. Erasmus was out of tune with the ecclesiastical authorities of his day, and some of the pages on view show where the censors stepped in to protect the faithful. ✉ *R. du Chapître 31,* ☎ *02/521–1383.* *BF50.* ⊙ *Wed.–Thurs. and Sat.–Mon. 10–noon and 2–5. Subway: Ste-Catherine to St-Guidon station in Anderlecht commune.*

South of the Center: Art Deco and Art Nouveau

A Good Walk

Start at the art deco **Musée David-et-Alice-Van-Buuren** ㉟, off the commune of Uccle's Rond-Point Churchill; then return to the circle and head left along the affluent Avenue Winston Churchill until you reach Place Vanderkindere. From here, turn right and head down Avenue Brugmann, past a remarkable assortment of art nouveau houses. Look particularly for Brunfaut's Hôtel Hannon, at the intersection of Brugmann and Avenue de la Jonction, and the charming redbrick Les Hiboux next door. Cross Chaussée de Waterloo and head up Chaussée de Charleroi, then head right onto Rue Américaine to the **Musée Horta** ㊱. Continue on Rue Américaine, then turn left on Rue du Page, crossing Place du Chatelain and turning left on Rue Simonis. Take a right on Rue du Bailli, then turn left onto Rue du Livourne. Turn right on Rue Paul-Émile Janson, stopping at No. 6 to see the Tassel house, also designed by Victor Horta. At Avenue Louise turn right, keeping your eye open for the Hotel Solvay at No. 224, which is generally considered Horta's finest work. Continue on Avenue Louise to the roundabout and turn left onto Rue de la Monastère. Pick up Avenue Bernier, cross Avenue de la Hippodrome, and you're on Rue du Bourmestre. The **Musée des Enfants** ㊲ is on the left. If you like, circle back east past the Abbaye de la Czmbre to the Musée Constantin Neunier ㊳.

TIMING

Allow two or three hours for this walk, including time in the museums, the 20-minute walk from the Van Buuren to the Horta Museum, and the 15 or so minutes to the Musée des Enfants.

Sights to See

㊳ **Musée Constantin Meunier.** Nineteenth-century painter and sculptor Constantin Meunier made his mark capturing the hardships of Belgian workers in a distinctive and realistic style. Both his paintings and sculptures are displayed in his former house and studio. ✉ *Rue de l'Abbaye 59,* ☎ *02/648–4449.* *Free.* ⊙ *Tues.–Sun. 10–noon and 1–5.*

㉟ **Musée David-et-Alice-Van-Buuren.** A perfect art deco interior from the 1930s is preserved in this museum. The made-to-order carpets and furnishings are supplemented by paintings by the Van Buurens, as well as Old Masters including a Bruegel, *Fall of Icarus,* one of the three ver-

Musée Constantin Meunier 38

Musée David-et-Alice-Van-Buuren . . 35

Musée des Enfants 37

Musée Horta. 36

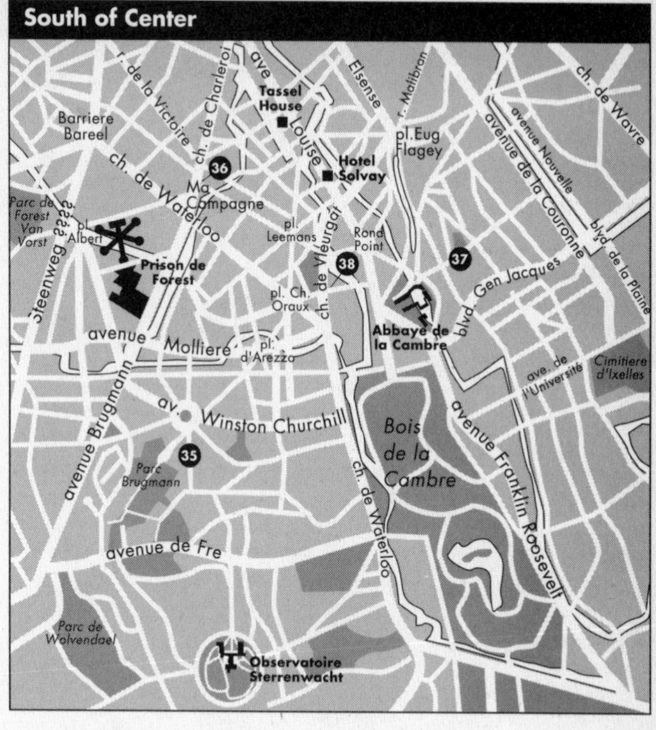

sions he painted. The house is surrounded by lush formal gardens. ✉ *Av. Leo Errera 41,* ☎ *02/343–4851.* 🎫 *BF300/€7.40, BF500/€12.40 for house and gardens.* 🕓 *Sun. 1–6, Mon. 2–6, Tues.–Sat. by appointment for groups of up to 20. Trams 23 and 90.*

37 **Musée des Enfants** (Children's Museum). At this museum for 2- to 12-year-olds, the purpose may be educational—learning to handle objects and emotions—but the results are fun. Kids get to plunge their arms into sticky goo, dress up in eccentric costumes, walk through a hall of mirrors, crawl through tunnels, and take photographs with an oversize camera. ✉ *R. du Bourgmestre 15,* ☎ *02/640–0107.* 🎫 *BF200.* 🕓 *Sept.–July, Wed. and weekends 2:30–5. Trams 93 and 94.*

★ 36 **Musée Horta.** The house where Victor Horta (1861–1947), the creator of art nouveau, lived and worked until 1919 is the best place to see his joyful interiors and furniture. Horta's genius lay in his ability to create a sense of opulence, light, and spaciousness where little light or space existed. Lamps hang from the ceilings like tendrils, and mirrored skylights evoke giant butterflies with multicolor wings of glass and steel. For examples of how Horta and his colleagues transformed the face of Brussels in little more than 10 years, ride down Avenue Louise to Vleurgat and walk along Rue Vilain XIIII to the area surrounding the **ponds of Ixelles.** ✉ *R. Américaine 25,* ☎ *02/543–0490.* 🎫 *BF150/€3.70 (weekends BF200/€4.95).* 🕓 *Tues.–Sun. 2–5:30. To house: Tram 91 or 92 to Ma Campagne. To Ixelles: Tram 93 or 94.*

DINING

The star-studded Brussels restaurant scene is a boon to visitors and natives alike. Some suggest that the European Commission chose Brussels for its headquarters because of the excellence of its restaurants.

Dining

Adrienne **60**
Alban Chambon **8**
Au Stekerlapatte **65**
Au Vieux Saint Martin **50**
Aux Armes de Bruxelles **25**
Aux Marches de la Chapelle **49**
Bazaar **66**
Bij Den Boer. **13**
Bonsoir Clara. **5**
Bruneau. **1**
Castello Banfi. **54**
Chez Jean **38**
Chez Léon de Bruxelles **26**
Comme Chez Soi . . . **45**
Falstaff **22**
Gallery **63**
In 't Spinnekopke . . . **19**
Jacques **14**
La Clef des Champs . **51**
La Grande Porte **46**
La Joueur de Flûte . . . **67**
La Manufacture. **18**
La Roue d'Or **37**
L'Ecailler du Palais Royal **55**
L'Epicerie. **35**
Le Saint-Boniface . . . **58**
Les Capucines **64**
Les Petits Oignons . . . **47**
L'Idiot du Village. . . . **48**
Maison du Cygne . . . **40**
Ogenblik **28**
Sea Grill **29**
Strofilia **12**
Taverne du Passage . **31**
't Kelderke **39**
Vincent **27**

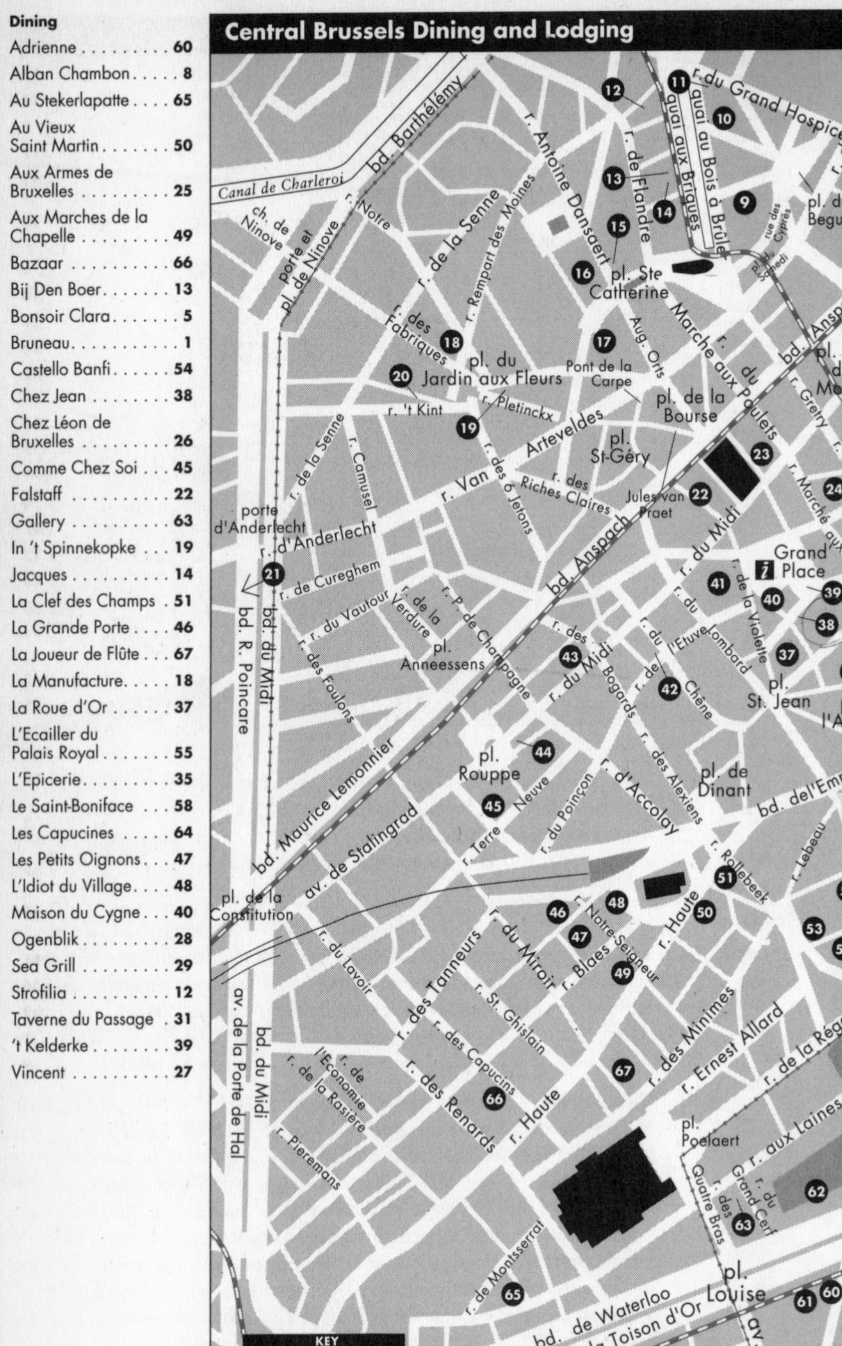

Central Brussels Dining and Lodging

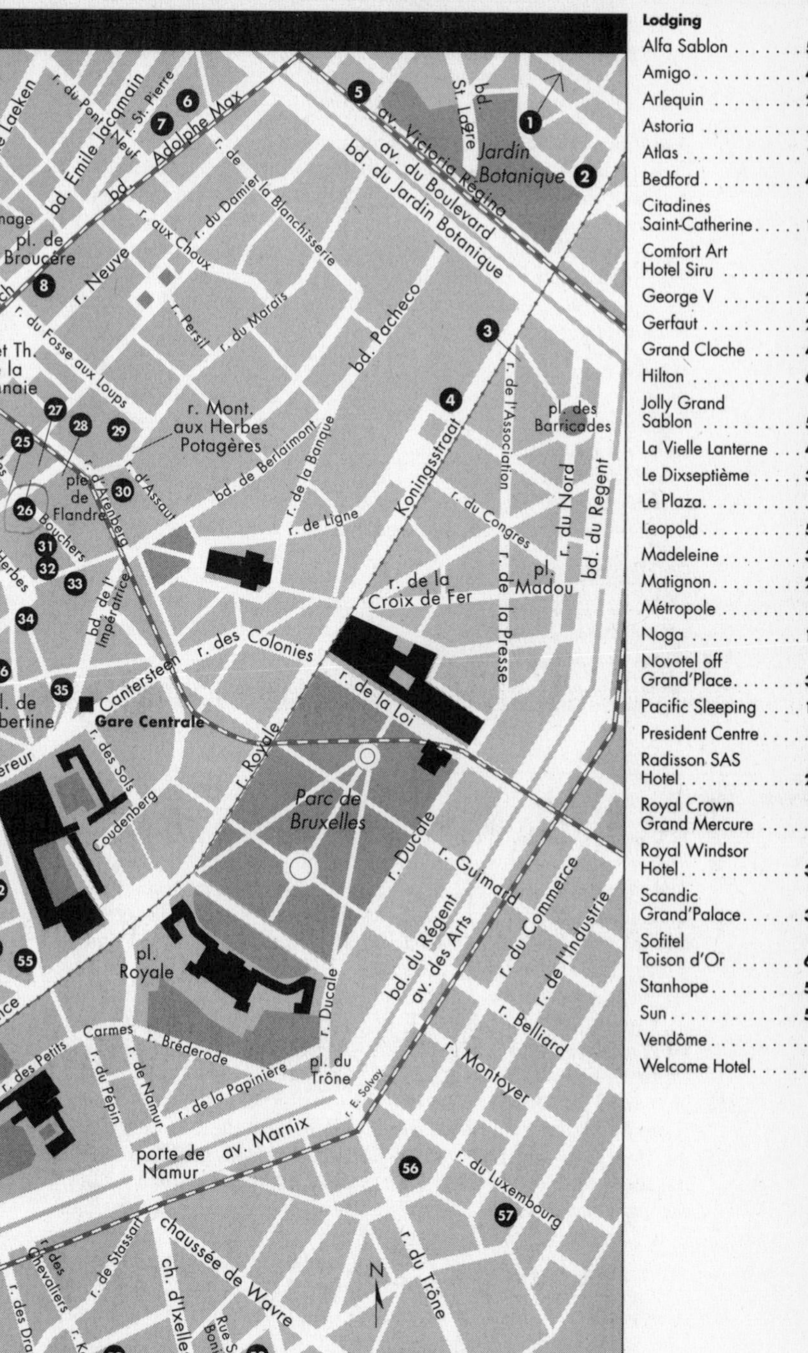

Lodging

- Alfa Sablon **52**
- Amigo **41**
- Arlequin **24**
- Astoria **3**
- Atlas **17**
- Bedford **43**
- Citadines Saint-Catherine **10**
- Comfort Art Hotel Siru **5**
- George V **20**
- Gerfaut **21**
- Grand Cloche **44**
- Hilton **62**
- Jolly Grand Sablon **53**
- La Vielle Lanterne . . . **42**
- Le Dixseptième **34**
- Le Plaza **6**
- Leopold **57**
- Madeleine **32**
- Matignon **23**
- Métropole **8**
- Noga **11**
- Novotel off Grand'Place **33**
- Pacific Sleeping **15**
- President Centre **4**
- Radisson SAS Hotel **29**
- Royal Crown Grand Mercure **2**
- Royal Windsor Hotel **36**
- Scandic Grand'Palace **30**
- Sofitel Toison d'Or **61**
- Stanhope **56**
- Sun **59**
- Vendôme **7**
- Welcome Hotel **9**

Although this may not be wholly true, the top Brussels restaurants rival the best Parisian restaurants; so, alas, do the prices. Most Belgians, however, value haute cuisine as a work of art and are prepared to part with a substantial sum for a special occasion.

A number of neighborhood restaurants have risen to the challenge of making dining out affordable. The choice of dishes may be more limited, and the ingredients less costly, but an animated ambience more than makes up for it. The tab is likely to be a quarter of what a dinner would cost you in one of the grand restaurants, and the uniformly high quality puts Paris to shame. The city is also richly endowed with good and mostly inexpensive Vietnamese, Italian, and Portuguese restaurants.

You can reduce the check almost by half by choosing a set menu. Fixed-price luncheon menus are often an especially good bargain. Menus and prices are always posted outside restaurants. Don't feel that you're under an obligation to eat a three-course meal; many people order just a main course. If you don't want two full restaurant meals a day, there are plenty of snack bars for a light midday meal, and most cafés serve sandwiches and light hot meals both noon and night.

CATEGORY	COST*
$$$$	over BF3,500/€85
$$$	BF2,500–BF3,500/€60–€85
$$	BF1,500–BF2,500/€35–€60
$	under BF1,500/€35

**per person for a three-course meal, including service, taxes, but not beverages*

Lower Town

$$$$ ★ ✕ **Comme Chez Soi.** Pierre Wynants, the perfectionist owner-chef, has decorated his bistro-size restaurant in sumptuous art nouveau style. The superb cuisine, excellent wines, and attentive service complement the warm decor. Wynants is ceaselessly inventive, and earlier creations are quickly relegated to the back page of the menu. One all-time favorite, fillet of sole with a white wine mousseline and shrimp, is, however, always available. One minus: ventilation is poor and it can get very smoky. ✉ *Pl. Rouppe 23,* ☎ *02/512–2921. Reservations essential. Jacket and tie. AE, DC, MC, V. Closed Sun.–Mon., July, Dec. 25–Jan. 1.*

$$$$ ✕ **Maison du Cygne.** With decor to match its classic cuisine, this restaurant is set in a 17th-century guildhall on the Grand'Place. It's the place to go for power dining. The paneled walls of the formal dining room upstairs are hung with Old Masters, and a small room on the mezzanine contains two priceless Bruegels. Service is flawless in the grand manner of old. Typical French-Belgian dishes include *cocotte d'écrévisses et petits gris de Namur* (shrimp and crayfish), and *agneau pavillac à Cygne* (lamb). ✉ *R. Charles Buyls 2,* ☎ *02/511–8244. Reservations essential. Jacket and tie. AE, DC, MC, V. No lunch Sat. Closed Sun. and 3 wks in Aug.*

$$$ ✕ **Alban Chambon.** The eatery of the splendid Belle Epoque Mètropole Hotel (☞ Lodging, *below*) lives up to the style of its surroundings. Named after its architect, the gastronomic restaurant sparkles with light from chandeliers reflected in the mirrors all round, while piano music filters in from the bar next door. The cuisine, wine list, and service are all one would expect in such grandiose surroundings: diners can munch on large raviolis of langoustine with wild mushrooms and white sauce, or fried fillet of lamb with vegetable and mint tabbouleh and new pota-

South of Center/Schuman Dining and Lodging

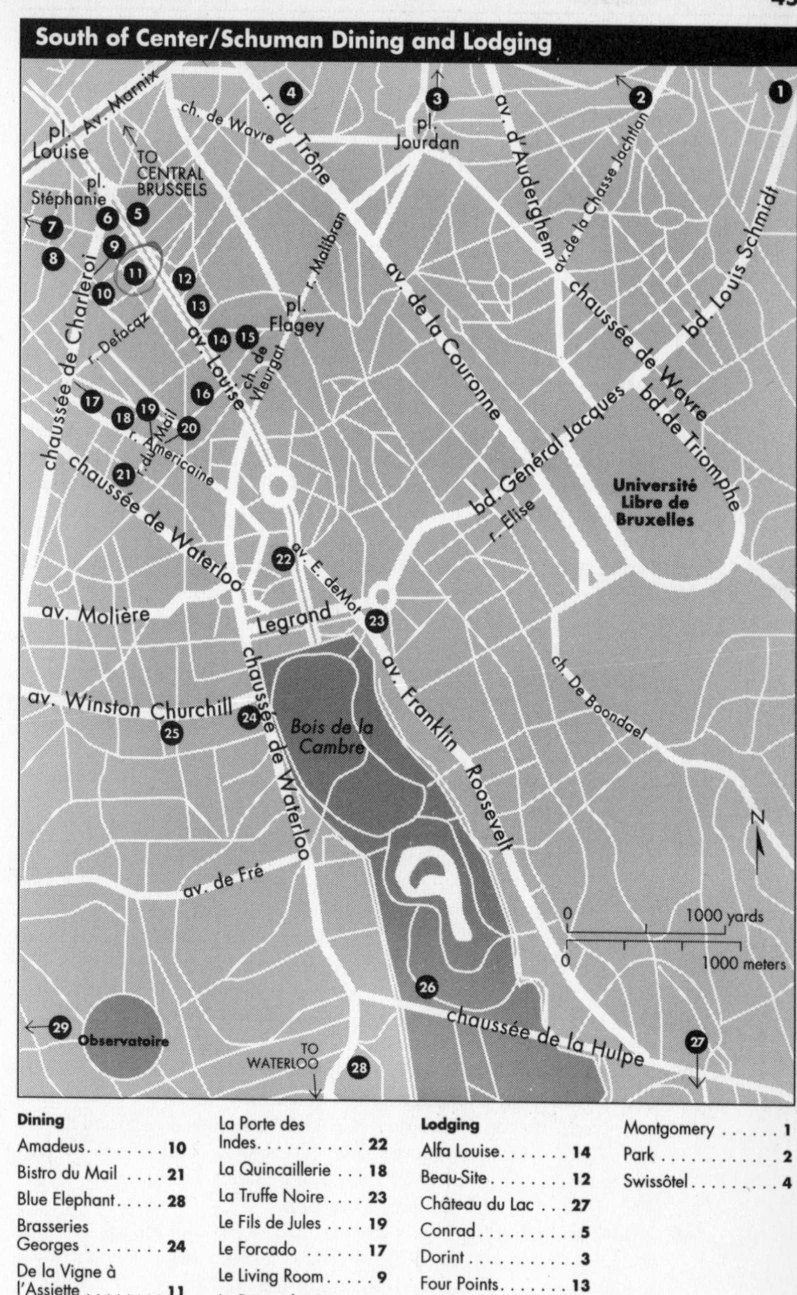

Dining

Amadeus **10**
Bistro du Mail **21**
Blue Elephant **28**
Brasseries Georges **24**
De la Vigne à l'Assiette **11**
Inada **8**
Kushi-tei of Tokyo . . **15**
La Duchesse **1**
La Porte des Indes **22**
La Quincaillerie . . . **18**
La Truffe Noire **23**
Le Fils de Jules **19**
Le Forcado **17**
Le Living Room **9**
Le Pain et le Vin . . . **29**
Majestic **16**
Thoumieux **20**
Villa Lorraine **26**

Lodging

Alfa Louise **14**
Beau-Site **12**
Château du Lac . . . **27**
Conrad **5**
Dorint **3**
Four Points **13**
Les Bluets **7**
Les Tourelles **25**
Manos Stéphanie **6**
Montgomery **1**
Park **2**
Swissôtel **4**

toes. ✉ *Mètropole Hotel, Place de Broucère,* ☎ *02/217–2300. AE, DC, MC, V. Closed weekends.*

$$$ ✕ **L'Epicerie.** Highly acclaimed young chef David Martin blends the traditional with the exotic in this, the restaurant of the Meridien Hotel, opposite the Gare Centrale. The results are daring adventures in international flavors. In an elegant, Mediterranean-style setting, diners feast on sea bass with cocoa and thyme-flavored caramelized salsify; or hare in a sauce of dates, chestnuts, and oranges. On Sundays, a self-service brunch is served in place of the usual menu. A pianist tinkles away in the background every evening except Sunday. ✉ *Meridien Hotel, Carrefour de l'Europe 3,* ☎ *02/548–4716. AE, DC, MC, V. No lunch Sat.*

$$$ ★ ✕ **Ogenblik.** This small, split-level restaurant, in a side alley off the Galeries St-Hubert, has all the trappings of an old-time bistro: green-shaded lamps over marble-top tables, sawdust on the floor, and laid-back waiters. There's nothing casual about the French-style cuisine, however: grilled sweetbreads with courgette gratin, millefeuille of lobster and salmon with a coulis of langoustines, saddle of lamb with spring vegetables and potato gratin. The selection of Beaujolais is particularly good. ✉ *Galerie des Princes 1,* ☎ *02/511–6151. AE, DC, MC, V. Closed Sun.*

$$$ ★ ✕ **Sea Grill.** Dashing superstar chef Yves Mattagne presides in the kitchen of this, arguably the best seafood place in town and one of the restaurants in the Radisson SAS Hotel (☞ Lodging, *below*). Gastronomes rub shoulders here with tycoons and aristocrats, as they tuck into king crab from the Barents Sea, Brittany lobster in lobster press sauce, and line-caught sea bass prepared in crusted sea salt. Inevitably, because of its hotel situation, the restaurant has a rather corporate feel, but it is spacious and elegant, and service is impeccable. ✉ *Radisson SAS Hotel, R. du Fossè aux loups,* ☎ *02/227–3120. AE, DC, MC, V. No lunch Sat. Closed Sun.*

$$ ✕ **Aux Armes de Bruxelles.** Hidden among the tourist traps of the Ilôt Sacré, this child-friendly restaurant attracts a largely local clientele with its slightly tarnished middle-class elegance and its Belgian classics: turbot waterzooi, eels in green sauce, a variety of steaks, mussels prepared every which way, and *frites* (french fries), which the Belgians believe, with some justification, they prepare better than anyone else. The place is cheerful and light, and service is friendly if frequently overstretched. ✉ *R. des Bouchers 13,* ☎ *02/511–5550. AE, DC, MC, V. Closed Mon.*

$$ ✕ **Bij Den Boer.** This old-fashioned Brussels bistro with wooden benches and mirrors does good, honest fish and seafood in an informal atmosphere near the old fish market. It serves classic Belgian seafood dishes, such as grey shrimp croquettes, eels in green sauce, and mussels, as well as the southern French bouillabaisse. ✉ *Quai aux Briques 60,* ☎ *02/512–6122. AE, DC, MC, V. Closed Sun.*

$$ ✕ **In 't Spinnekopke.** This is where true Brussels cooking has survived and continues to flourish. The low ceilings and benches around the walls remain from its days as a coach inn during the 18th century. You can choose from among 100 artisanal beers, and many dishes are made with beer. ✉ *Pl. du Jardin aux Fleurs 1,* ☎ *02/511–8695. AE, DC, MC, V. No lunch Sat. Closed Sun.*

$$ ✕ **Jacques.** Quality and simplicity are the watchwords in this busy fish restaurant, which serves its speciality unadorned, with just boiled potatoes or frites and a simple green salad. Eels in green sauce, tomatoes stuffed with tiny grey shrimps, and scampi with garlic are typical of the Belgian specialities dished up in a bistro setting. Lobster must be ordered in advance and sauces are available as extras. A note of warning: it's noisy and smoky, and service is on the surly side. ✉ *Quai aux Briques 44,* ☎ *02/513–2762. No credit cards. Closed Sun. and July.*

$$ ✕ **La Manufacture.** A former leather goods factory (for Belgian handbag brand Delvaux) converted into a restaurant of modern, industrial design, this place attracts a fashionable crowd that spills over into a quiet, sheltered courtyard. The cuisine mixes Mediterranean and Asian influences and the wine list is good, but people mostly come here for the superb setting. ✉ *R. Notre Dame du Sommeil,* ☎ *02/502–2525. AE, DC, MC, V. No lunch Sat. Closed Sun.*

$$ ✕ **La Roue d'Or.** This art nouveau brasserie has bright orange and yellow murals that pay humorous homage to Surrealist René Magritte. Bowler-hatted gentlemen ascend serenely to the ceiling, a blue sky inhabited by tropical birds. The good cuisine includes traditional Belgian fare—a generous fish waterzooi and homemade frites—as well as such staples of the French brasserie repertory as lamb's tongue vinaigrette with shallots, veal kidneys with tarragon and watercress cream, and foie gras. ✉ *R. des Chapeliers 26,* ☎ *02/514–2554. AE, DC, MC, V. Closed approximately July 15–Aug. 15.*

$$ ✕ **Taverne du Passage.** This art deco brasserie in the famous shopping arcade has been here since 1928 and remains a classic of its kind, serving chicken waterzooi, sauerkraut, and lobster from noon to midnight nonstop. Most fun of all, however, are the roasts, which are carved in front of you. The waiters are multilingual and jolly and the wine list is exceptional—not surprising in a restaurant owned by the president of the Belgian guild of wine waiters. Reserve a table outside if you like to watch the world go by. ✉ *Gal. de la Reine 30,* ☎ *02/512–3731. AE, DC, MC, V. Closed Wed. and Thurs. in June and July.*

$$ ✕ **Vincent.** In a town where most of the fashionable places now concentrate on seafood, Vincent unapologetically remains a red-meat stronghold. Sides of beef and big slabs of butter in the window announce what awaits you. You pass through the kitchen on your way to the dining room, which is decorated with hand-painted tiles. ✉ *R. des Dominicains 8–10,* ☎ *02/511–2303. AE, DC, MC, V. Closed 1st two wks Aug.*

$ ✕ **Bonsoir Clara.** On downtown's trendy Rue Dansaert, this is the jewel in the crown of young restaurateur Frédéric Nicolay, who runs half a dozen fashionable cafés and eateries in the capital, including the Kasbah next door. An upbeat, refined brasserie serving excellent caramelized duck as well as fish and red-meat dishes, it's best-known for eye-catching decor, especially a back wall entirely composed of large colored squares, as if you were in a Rubik's Cube factory. ✉ *R. Dansaert 22,* ☎ *02/502–0990. AE, MC, V. No lunch weekends.*

$ ★ ✕ **Chez Jean.** Jean Cambien runs a reliable, unpretentious restaurant, unchanged since 1931. Oak benches sit against the walls, which are backed by mirrors upon which the dishes of the day are written in whitewash. Waitresses in black and white serve poached cod, mussels cooked in white wine, chicken waterzooi (with free seconds and thirds), chicken in *kriek* (cherry-flavored lambic beer) with cherries, and other quintessentially Belgian fare. ✉ *R. des Chapeliers 6,* ☎ *02/511–9815. AE, DC, MC, V. Closed Sun. and June.*

$ ★ ✕ **Chez Léon de Bruxelles.** More than a century old, this cheerful restaurant has over the years expanded into a row of eight old houses, while its franchises can now be found across Belgium and even in Paris. Heaped plates of mussels and other Belgian specialties, such as eels in a green sauce and fish soup, are continually served, accompanied by arguably the best french fries in town. ✉ *R. des Bouchers 18,* ☎ *02/511–1415. AE, DC, MC, V.*

$ ★ ✕ **Falstaff.** After a surprise bankruptcy that kept it closed for several months in 1999, this huge Brussels tavern with the wonderful art nouveau interior was bought and renovated by a Paris investor. Fears that it would lose its character seem unfounded, however; apart from an extensive menu of cocktails and some Cuban sounds, it still dishes up the straightforward Belgian cuisine that makes it popular with everyone from students to pensioners. Customers are welcome well into the early hours (5 AM on weekends). The Latin-flavored Montecristo Café next door is owned by the same group and gets louder and fuller the later it gets. ✉ *R. Henri Maus 19,* ☎ *02/511–9877. AE, DC, MC, V.*

$ ✕ **Strofilia.** Set in a restored 17th-century warehouse with exposed brick walls and a magnificent vaulted wine cellar, this restaurant does a good selection of hot and cold meze to mix and match, as well as salads for vegetarians. Eggplant purée with pine nuts and minced lamb kebabs are among the choices. It's open until 1 AM on Friday and Saturday. ✉ *R. du Marché aux Porcs 11–13,* ☎ *02/512–3293. AE, DC, MC, V. No lunch. Closed Sun.*

$ ✕ **'t Kelderke.** This beautiful, 17th-century vaulted cellar restaurant features traditional Belgian cuisine served at plain wooden tables. Portions are generous and mussels are the house specialty. It's a popular place with locals, open from noon to 2 AM; even the house cat is friendly. Beware of the low door frame when entering. ✉ *Grand'Place 15,* ☎ *02/513–7344. AE, DC, MC, V.*

South of Center

$$$$ ★ ✕ **La Truffe Noire.** Luigi Ciciriello's "Black Truffle" attracts a sophisticated clientele with its modern design, well-spaced tables, and cuisine that draws on classic Italian and modern French cooking. Carpaccio is prepared at the table and served with long strips of truffle and Parmesan. Entrées may include Vendé pigeon with truffles, steamed John Dory with truffles and leeks, and leg of Pauillac lamb in pie crust. The restaurant also has a garden. ✉ *Bd. de la Cambre 12,* ☎ *02/640–4422. Reservations essential. Jacket and tie. AE, DC, MC, V. No lunch Sat. Closed Sun., Jan. 1–10, last wk July, 1st 2 wks Aug.*

$$$$ ✕ **Villa Lorraine.** Generations of American business travelers have been introduced to the three-hour Belgian lunch at the opulent Villa, on the edge of the Bois de la Cambre. The green terrace room is light, elegant, and airy, and there's alfresco dining under the spreading chestnut tree. Feast on emincé of lobster with tomatoes, mozzarella and pesto, fried sweetbreads *forestière* (garnished with morels, bacon, and sautéed potatoes), or quails and duckling with peaches and green pepper. ✉ *Chaussée de la Hulpe 28,* ☎ *02/374–3163. Jacket and tie. AE, DC, MC, V. Closed Sun. and 1st 3 wks July.*

$$$ ✕ **La Porte des Indes.** This is the city's foremost Indian restaurant—the creation of Karl Steppe, a Belgian antiques dealer turned restaurateur, who also owns the global Blue Elephant chain (☞ *below*). The gracious staff wears traditional Indian attire. The plant-filled lobby, wood carvings, and rich red and mauve decor provide a luxuriant backdrop. The cuisine ranges from a mild pilaf to a spicy vindaloo. The "brass tray" offers an assortment of specialties. A vegetarian menu is also available. ✉ *Av. Louise 455,* ☎ *02/647–8651. AE, DC, MC, V. No lunch Sun.*

$$ ✕ **Bistro du Mail.** By no means a bistro in the fast-food sense, this popular Ixelles restaurant does sophisticated modern French food: roast Landaise chicken with rosemary and olives, and poached foie gras with chanterelle mushrooms and baby leeks are two of the succulent choices. The elegant setting has trendy terra-cotta walls and jazz playing in the background. ✉ *R. du Mail 81,* ☎ *02/539–0697. AE, DC, MC, V. No lunch Sat. Closed Sun.*

$$ ✕ **Blue Elephant.** In the suburb of Uccle, this excellent Thai restaurant is owned by Karl Steppe, the antiquarian behind the city's top Indian restaurant, La Porte des Indes (☞ *above*). Opened in 1975, this is the cornerstone of the Blue Elephant empire, which now extends to London, Paris, Copenhagen, New Delhi, Dubai, and Beirut. Inside, it's like a tropical garden scattered with southeast Asian antiques; daylight floods in from above and filters through the splendid greenery and exotic flower arrangements. The food is just as impressive: curries seasoned with lemongrass, coconut milk, and aromatic spices. The set lunch is a good value. ✉ *Ch. de Waterloo 1120,* ☎ *02/374–4962. AE, DC, MC, V. No lunch Sat.*

$$ ★ ✕ **Brasseries Georges.** This brash, hugely successful brasserie was the first in Brussels and is still the best. Efficient service and quality food is guaranteed. Past the splendid display of shellfish at the entrance, an art deco interior with a tile floor and potted palms awaits. Fast, efficient service is the hallmark of waitresses in black-and-white uniforms. Traditional dishes include sauerkraut, poached cod, and potted duck, while among the more adventurous dishes are salmon tartare and swordfish chop with a light chicory curry. Shellfish is the speciality. Twenty-five different wines are sold by the glass. ✉ *Av. Winston Churchill 259,* ☎ *02/347–2100. AE, DC, MC, V.*

$$ ✕ **Le Fils de Jules.** Vivid, colorful Basque cuisine from southwest France is served with wines to match within the candlelit, art deco–inspired setting. A well-heeled, local crowd flocks here to sup on warm foie gras with grapes, and tartare of tuna with tapenade. ✉ *R. du Page 37,* ☎ *02/534–0057. AE, DC, MC, V. No lunch weekends.*

$$ ✕ **Le Forcado.** Not a knob of butter can be found in this Portuguese restaurant where olive oil reigns supreme. Decorated in beautiful, blue and white antique tiles, it's the stylish eatery of choice for the capital's large Portuguese community. The speciality is the national dish of *baccalhau* (salt cod), which can be prepared every which way: try it simply grilled with garlic and olive oil. For a final treat, sample the pastries—made on the premises—with eggs, almonds, and oranges. The patisserie just round the corner on R. Américaine sells these, too. ✉ *Ch. de Charleroi 192,* ☎ *02/537–9220. AE, DC, MC, V. Closed Sun., Mon., and Aug.*

$$ ✕ **Majestic.** Grandiose, plush decor makes this town house restaurant and bar a fashionable hangout for an upwardly mobile crowd. Even the bathroom taps are a design statement. The cuisine, French with Asian influences, is equally trendy; however, it doesn't compromise on quality as might be expected. Baby lobster roasted in sauternes and flavored with curry, and duck's liver with roast figs in port are two of the dishes on offer. ✉ *R. du Magistrat 33,* ☎ *02/639–1330. AE, MC, V. No lunch.*

$$ ★ ✕ **Le Pain et le Vin.** Good taste reigns supreme in this suburban temple to quality food and drink. Reopened in 2000, renovations added a contemporary, minimalist decor of dazzling white, with dark wood seating. The restaurant is co-owned by acclaimed sommelier Eric Boschman; hence, the cellar is excellent, and wines can be ordered by the glass to accompany different courses of the pared-down cuisine. The large, paved garden surrounded by greenery is a plus in fine weather. ✉ *Ch. d'Alsemberg 812A,* ☎ *02/332–3774. AE, MC, V. No lunch Sat. Closed Sun.*

$$ ✕ **La Quincaillerie.** The name means "The Hardware Store," and that's precisely what this place used to be. It still looks the part, except now there are tables perched on the narrow balcony, and there's an oyster bar downstairs. It attracts a youngish, upwardly mobile clientele and offers good deals on business lunches. The menu consists mostly of brasserie grub, such as baked ham knuckle, but it's enlivened by such selections as honey-baked Barbary duck with lime, and a glorious seafood platter. Regional and international specialties are often featured. ✉ *R. du Page 45,* ☎ *02/538–2553. AE, DC, MC, V. No lunch weekends.*

$$ ✕ **Thoumieux.** One of the best-known brasseries in Paris brought a flavor of the French capital to a corner site in Ixelles, down the road from the Horta Museum. The traditional setting includes mirrors, cushioned benches, crisp white tablecloths, and waiters in long, starched aprons. On the menu are such French regional specialities as cassoulet, a bean and meat stew from the southwest, as well as typical brasserie staples: a seafood platter with lobster, and sweetbreads with egg, shallot, and herb dressing. ✉ *R. Américaine 124,* ☎ *02/538–9909. AE, MC, V. Closed Sun.*

$ ✕ **Kushi-tei of Tokyo.** This restaurant offers an authentic Japanese experience that is sushi-free. It specializes in *kushiyaki* (wooden skewers of meat and vegetables grilled over charcoal), including chicken teriyaki. The chef works in sight of diners behind a counter. Wine, sake, and Japanese beer are available. ✉ *R. Lesbroussart 118,* ☎ *02/646–4815. AE, DC, MC, V. No lunch Sat. Closed Sun.*

Upper Town

$$$$ ✕ **L'Ecailler du Palais Royal.** This excellent seafood-only restaurant, just off the Grand Sablon, feels like a comfortable club; many of the clients seem to have known one another and the staff for years. The menu changes twice annually, but such delicacies as risotto of prawns in champagne, lobster ravioli, and top-quality turbot were among the recent choices. ✉ *R. Bodenbroek 18,* ☎ *02/512–8751. Reservations essential. Jacket and tie. AE, DC, MC, V. Closed Sun., Easter wk, Aug.*

$$$ ✕ **Les Capucines.** This pleasant restaurant stands out amid the mediocre eateries in the Place Louise shopping area. The dining room is inviting, decorated in shades of green, with huge flower arrangements. Chef Pierre Burtonboy prepares such delicate dishes as grilled fillet of sea bream, set on a bed of shredded leek and dressed with nut oil; lamb interleaved with goose liver, rolled and encased in pastry, with rosemary and thinly sliced potatoes; bitter chocolate mousse with crème anglaise; and iced peach soup with mint. ✉ *R. Jourdan 22,* ☎ *02/538–6924. AE, DC, MC, V. No dinner Mon. Closed Sun., Easter, and 2nd ½ of Aug.*

$$$ ✕ **Castello Banfi.** On the Grand Sablon in beige-and-brown postmodern surroundings, you can enjoy classic French and Italian dishes with added refinements, such as toasted pine nuts with pesto. There's excellent carpaccio with Parmesan and celery, red mullet with ratatouille, and unbelievable mascarpone. The quality of the ingredients (sublime olive oil, milk-fed veal imported from France) is very high. The wine list is strong on fine Chianti aged in wood. ✉ *R. Bodenbroek 12,* ☎ *02/512–8794. Jacket and tie. AE, DC, MC, V. No dinner Sun. Closed Mon., Easter wk, Christmas wk, and last 3 wks Aug.*

$$$ ✕ **Inada.** This restaurant on a residential street near the Porte de Hal does exceptional French cuisine courtesy of Japanese chef and owner, Saburo Inada, who reportedly gets his poultry from the same supplier as French President Jacques Chirac. The approach is low-key, but the linen-covered tables are well-spaced and the food and wine are excellent. The dishes incorporate subtle Asian references, such as the young caramelized pigeon in an Oriental sauce, and Japanese-style grilled-eel salad. ✉ *R. de la Source 73,* ☎ *02/538–0113. AE, MC, V. No lunch Sat. Closed Sun., Mon., last 2 wks July, and 1st wk Aug.*

$$ ✕ **Au Stekerlapatte.** In the shadow of the Palais de Justice, this efficient, down-to-earth bistro serves Belgian specialties that include cassoulet, sauerkraut, grilled pig's trotters, spare ribs, and black pudding with caramelized apples. ✉ *R. des Prêtres 4,* ☎ *02/512–8681. MC, V. No lunch. Closed Mon.*

$$ ★ ✕ **Au Vieux Saint Martin.** Even when neighboring restaurants on Grand Sablon are empty, this one is full. A rack of glossy magazines is a thoughtful touch for lone diners, and you're equally welcome whether you order a cup of coffee or a full meal. The short menu emphasizes Brussels specialties, and portions are generous. The owner, a wine importer, serves unusually good wine for the price, by the glass or by the bottle. The red walls are hung with large, contemporary paintings, including works by Pierre Alechinsky, and picture windows overlook the pleasant square. A brass plaque marks the table where President Bill Clinton relaxed during a Brussels walkabout. ✉ *Grand Sablon 38,* ☎ *02/512–6476. Reservations not accepted. MC, V.*

$$ ★ ✕ **Aux Marches de la Chapelle.** This very attractive restaurant, opposite the Eglise de la Chapelle near the Grand Sablon, offers brasserie fare of the highest quality, including traditional sauerkraut. One of the Belle Epoque rooms is dominated by a splendid old bar, the other by an enormous open fireplace. ✉ *Pl. de la Chapelle 5,* ☎ *02/512–6891. AE, DC, MC, V. No lunch Sat. Closed Sun. and 3rd wk July–3rd wk Aug.*

$$ ✕ **La Clef des Champs.** Enter this restaurant and discover a corner of Provence on a cobbled street off the Place du Grand Sablon. The blue and yellow decor is set off by watercolors, photographs, and poems of the multitalented chef and owner. His welcoming wife, who sets the stage in the dining room, is a former dentist—the pair met when he went to have a tooth pulled! The cooking is regional French, with dishes including Mediterranean bass in olive oil; lobster gratin; and duck confit. With the charming service and the golden walls, this has to be one of the sunniest places in the city center. ✉ *R. de Rollebeek 23,* ☎ *02/512–1193. AE, DC, MC, V. Closed Sun. and Mon.*

$$ ✕ **L'Idiot du Village.** Don't believe the modest name of this restaurant in the Marolles; it serves excellent food and attracts a loyal clientele. The emphasis is on quality dining in a relaxed atmosphere rather than attracting the "in" crowd, and the decor is kitschy and warmly intimate. Sample dishes include grilled tuna with artichokes and Parmesan, and warm escalope of foie gras with pepper and vanilla. ✉ *R. Notre-Seigneur 19,* ☎ *02/502–5582. AE, DC, MC, V. Closed weekends.*

$$ ✕ **Le Joueur de Flûte.** There's only space for 16 diners in this one-man-show restaurant, which offers a single menu each evening. Philippe Van Cappelen named his place after a drawing he picked up at the flea market, and the walls are decorated with musical manuscripts. It's an intimate, candlelit setting near the hulking Palais de Justice, and because of the formula it's only open for one service each evening. For an idea of what the day's menu is, think fillet of bass with mixed vegetables in olive oil, or Mechelen chicken with licorice. ✉ *R. de l'Epée 26,* ☎ *02/513–4311. Reservations essential. MC, V. No lunch. Closed weekends.*

$$ ✕ **Le Living Room.** A modish restaurant that lives up to much of the hype, this place gets busy late on weekend evenings as night owls arrive to cluster around the bar. A fashionable, uptown crowd haunts the restaurant-cum-club, which is set in an attractive town house with dining on two floors and in the garden. The bar area bustles, while dining rooms at the front are more refined, with plush, modern decor and armchairs in bright-colored velvets. The menu is international, from Japan (sushi) and France (chicken breast with morels) by way of Thailand (sautéed beef); the wine list is equally diverse. ✉ *Ch. de Charleroi 50,* ☎ *02/534–4434. AE, DC, MC, V. No lunch.*

$$ ✕ **Les Petits Oignons.** This airy 17th-century restaurant, in the heart of the Marolles, has been furnished with plants and bright, modern paintings. It places no demands on your palate, but the ambience is enticing, and you are well looked after. The menu changes every cou-

ple of weeks, but staples include fried goose liver with caramelized onions, roast pigeon with carrots and cumin, and leg of lamb with potatoes au gratin. ✉ *R. Notre-Seigneur 13,* ☎ *02/512–4738. AE, DC, MC, V. Closed Sun. and Aug.*

$$ ✕ **Le Saint-Boniface.** Near the church of the same name in Ixelles, this defiantly untrendy restaurant serves wholesome, traditional fare from southern France. The intricacies of duck confit and *andouillette* (sausage made from pig's intestines) will be patiently explained by the friendly wife of the chef. Portions are generous and the setting is classic French bistro, with red-and-white check tablecloths, posters on the walls, and classical music or jazz in the background. ✉ *R. St-Boniface 9,* ☎ *02/511–5366. AE, DC, MC, V. No lunch Sat. Closed Sun.*

$–$$ ✕ **Amadeus.** It is not so much the food (goat cheese with honey, spare ribs, tagliatelle with salmon) as the decor that makes this converted artist's studio near the Place Stéphanie a must. Ultra-romantic, not to say kitschy, its dining rooms have an abundance of mirrors, candles, and intimate alcoves, creating a trysty, almost conspiratorial baroque feel. ✉ *R. Veydt 13,* ☎ *02/538–3427. AE, DC, MC, V. No lunch. Closed mid-July–mid-Aug.*

$ ✕ **Adrienne.** The huge buffet draws crowds year after year at this upstairs restaurant, just around the corner from Avenue Toison d'Or. The look is rustic, with red-and-white check tablecloths; you can eat on the terrace in summer. The location is great for uptown shopping and movies as well as Sunday brunch, and it's also fun for kids. The Atomium branch, which is under different management, is cheaper but of equally good quality. ✉ *R. Capitaine Crespel 1A,* ☎ *02/511–9339;* ✉ *Atomium du Heysel, near Atomium,* ☎ *02/478–3000. AE, DC, MC, V. No dinner Sun.*

$ ✕ **Bazaar.** An taste of exoticism along a side street in the Marolles, this building has an interesting history—it was once a convent—and a tendency to catch fire. That doesn't stop the candles burning in the cavernous dining room, where a beautiful air balloon is suspended over the bar and Moroccan lamps and sofas create intimacy in a bric-a-brac setting. It's young and fashionable, there's a disco on the lower floor at weekends, and monthly concerts of world music are performed here. The eclectic, inexpensive menu includes such choices as chicken *tajine* (slow-cooked with gravy in a deep, glazed earthenware dish) with olives and lemon and ostrich carpaccio. ✉ *R. des Capucins 63,* ☎ *02/511–2600. AE, DC, MC, V. No lunch. Closed Sun. and Mon.*

$ ★ ✕ **De la Vigne à l'Assiette.** This homely, no-frills bistro off Avenue Louise opened in early 2000 and offers a food and wine formula that's an exceptionally good value. The modern French cuisine is embellished with such exotic flourishes as star anise sauce with Asian spicing, and grilled salmon topped with crisp angel-hair pastry. Menus, which change with the seasons, include interesting choices like hop shoots topped with a poached egg, and frothy mousseline sauce. The excellent wine list, chosen by co-owner Eddy Dandrimont, a former best sommelier of Belgium, is free of the usual hefty markup. ✉ *R. de la Longue Haie,* ☎ *02/647–6803. AE, DC, MC, V. No lunch Sat. Closed Sun. and Mon.*

$ ✕ **Gallery.** This Vietnamese restaurant looks like a minimalist art gallery, with contemporary black chairs and tables, artfully suspended spotlights, and temporary exhibitions of black-and-white photographs. The kitchen holds no surprises, but the food is well prepared and the helpings of dishes such as Vietnamese pancakes, hot-and-sour soup, and beef with chilis and peppers are substantial. ✉ *R. du Grand Cerf 7,* ☎ *02/511–8035. AE, DC, MC, V. No lunch Sun. Closed 1 wk in Aug.*

$ ✕ **La Grande Porte.** A longtime favorite in the Marolles area that makes no concession to fashion or style, this old place has a player piano and offhand but jovial waiters. It serves copious portions of popular

Brussels specialties, such as *ballekes à la marollienne* (spicy meatballs) and *carbonnade à la flamande* (beef and onions stewed in beer). The later in the evening it becomes, the livelier the atmosphere and the greater the demand for the restaurant's famous onion soup. ✉ *R. Notre-Seigneur 9,* ☎ *02/512–8998. MC, V. No lunch Sat. Closed Sun.*

Cinquantenaire and Schuman

$$$ ✕ **La Duchesse.** The eatery within the homely Montgomery Hotel offers more than the average hotel restaurant. Chef Yves Defontaine specializes in fish but is extremely creative with vegetables, which he incorporates into inventive, modern French cuisine. Roast fillet of bass with tarragon and fresh-grilled bacon with Guinea pepper is one of the specialities. ✉ *Av. de Tervuren 134,* ☎ *02/741–8511. AE, DC, MC, V. Closed weekends.*

West of Center

$$$$ ✕ **Bruneau.** Although it's outside the city center, this quarter-century-old restaurant is famous with gourmets in Belgium and beyond. They come for top-notch food served in a lavishly decorated town house, or in the garden during summer. The food is complex and ornate, the wine list excellent. Jean-Pierre Bruneau works in the open kitchen and is a master of gastronomic art. His fans swear by his cooking and flex their plastic to prove it. ✉ *Av. Broustin 75,* ☎ *02/427–6978. AE, DC, MC, V. No dinner Tues. Closed Wed., Aug., and 1st wk Feb.*

LODGING

As the capital of Europe, Brussels attracts a large number of high-powered visitors—one in two travelers are here on business—hence, a disproportionate number of very attractive luxury hotels have been built to accommodate them. Their prices are higher than what most tourists would like to pay, but on weekends and during July and August, when there aren't many business travelers, prices can drop to below BF5,000 for a double room. As a rule though, always negotiate a price: the listed rate is rarely applied in practice in the larger hotels.

Happily, new hotels catering to cost-conscious travelers, priced at less than BF3,000 for a double, have also been constructed over the last few years. They may be less ostentatious, but they're squeaky-clean and offer as much attention to your comfort as the palatial five-star hotels.

CATEGORY	COST*
$$$$	over BF9,000/€225
$$$	BF6,500–BF9,000/€160–€225
$$	BF3,500–BF6,500/€85–€160
$	under BF3,500/€85

**for two persons sharing double room, including service and tax*

🖱 following the text of a review is your signal that the property has a Web site, where you will find details and, usually, images; for a link, visit www.fodors.com/urls.

Lower Town

$$$$ ★ 🏨 **Amigo.** Just a block from the Grand'Place and decorated in Spanish Renaissance style with touches of Louis XV, the Amigo looks more turn-of-the-20th-century than 1950s, when it was built. Rooms vary in furnishings, size, and price; those on higher floors, with views over the surrounding rooftops, are more expensive. The Presidential Suite has a large terrace overlooking the Grand'Place. Taken over in 2000 by Sir Rocco Forte, the hotel is known for its understated luxury and is popular with celebrities. The service is excellent. ✉ *R. d'Amigo 1–3, B1000,* ☎ *02/547–4747,* FAX *02/502–2805. 178 rooms, 7 suites. Restaurant, bar, meeting rooms, parking (fee). AE, DC, MC, V.*

$$$$ **Bedford.** This hotel has been rebuilt and modified since the current owners took over in 1955. It stands on the site of a hotel that, according to legend, was frequented by Luftwaffe and RAF pilots in Brussels for romantic trysts during and after World War II. A family-run place, it has a grand, wide lobby with marble pillars, thick pink carpeting in corridors, and rooms with pink decor and carpets and cherry-wood furniture. All have telephone, TV, and minibar. Bathrooms are small but sparkling in cream marble; 10 rooms have only showers. ✉ *R. du Midi 135, B1000,* ☎ *02/512–7840,* FAX *02/514–1759. 321 rooms. Restaurant, bar, meeting rooms, parking (fee). AE, DC, MC, V.*

$$$$ ★ **Le Plaza.** Inspired by the George V in Paris, the Plaza opened in 1930 and has maintained a grandiose reputation. Pillaged by the Germans at the end of World War II, it closed in 1976, reopening 20 years later after exceptional refurbishment. The hotel has fittings of outstanding quality, from the new corridor carpet made using the pattern of the original, to rooms decorated with the greatest attention to taste and detail: elegant wide sinks in the bathrooms, framed illustrations, cream standard lamps. All have private fax lines, modem connection, and bathrobes. Deluxe rooms and suites have free access to the neighboring Fitness Factory. The bar-restaurant is in a grand, high-ceilinged room with a domed roof; the breakfast room is in a palatial room done in apricot and red. But the real treasure is the hotel's historic theater, a former cinema that is now used for conferences, banquets, and presentations. ✉ *Bd. Adolphe Max 118-126, B1000,* ☎ *02/227–6736,* FAX *02/223–7929. 176 rooms, 17 suites. Bar, restaurant, in-room data ports, in-room safes, exercise room, meeting rooms, parking (fee). AE, DC, MC, V.*

$$$$ **Métropole.** Stepping into this classic hotel, you would think you were boarding the *Orient Express*. The hotel, built in 1895, has been restored to the palace it was during the Belle Epoque. The lobby sets the tone, with its enormously high coffered ceiling, chandeliers, marble, Oriental rugs, and old-fashioned wood-paneled elevator. The theme is carried through in the bar, with potted palms, deep leather sofas, and Corinthian columns; in the café, which opens onto the sidewalk of Place de Brouckère; and in the Alban Chambon restaurant (named for the architect) (☞ Dining, *above*). The rooms are understated modern in varying shades of pastel (some with trompe l'oeil murals), with furniture upholstered in the same material as the bedspreads. ✉ *Pl. de Brouckère 31, B1000,* ☎ *02/217–2300,* FAX *02/218–0220. 400 rooms, 10 suites. Restaurant, bar, café, health club, convention center, free parking. AE, DC, MC, V.*

$$$$ ★ **Radisson SAS Hotel.** Near the northern end of the Galeries St-Hubert, this hotel is decorated in a variety of styles—Asian (wicker furniture and Asian art), Italian (art deco fixtures and furnishings), and Scandinavian (light-wood furniture and parquet flooring). The greenery-filled atrium incorporates a 10-ft-high section of the 12th-century city wall. The Sea Grill is a first-rate seafood restaurant (☞ Dining, *above*), and Danish open-face sandwiches are served in the atrium's café. A copious buffet breakfast is included. There's no extra charge for children under 15. ✉ *R. du Fossé-aux-Loups 47, B1000,* ☎ *02/219–2828,* FAX *02/219–6262. 261 rooms, 20 suites. 2 restaurants, bar, sauna, health club, business services, convention center, parking (fee). AE, DC, MC, V.*

$$$$ **Royal Windsor Hotel.** Near the Grand'Place and favored by visiting dignitaries, this hotel has survived for more than a quarter century. All rooms have blond-wood paneling, and although the bathrooms are small they're done in Portuguese marble and are among the most beautiful in Brussels. The lobby is businesslike, with leafy plants, comfortable sofas and chairs placed around marble-top tables, and music wafting in from the adjacent piano bar. The elegant dining room, Les Quatre Saisons, serves light, imaginative, and expensive French cuisine; the Windsor Arms is an English-style pub. ✉ *R. Duquesnoy 5, B1000,* ☎ *02/505–5555,* FAX *02/505–5500. 223 rooms, 43 suites. Restaurant, bar, sauna, health club, dance club, convention center, parking (fee). AE, DC, MC, V.*

$$–$$$ **Novotel off Grand'Place.** A stone's throw from the Grand'Place, this 1989 hotel was built with an old-style, gabled facade. Some French lodging chains mass-produce hotels that are functional but motel-like inside, and this is no exception. The rooms have white walls, russet carpets, and a sofa bed (extra guests BF500 per night). Twenty executive rooms are also available. There's no extra charge for up to two children under 16. ✉ *R. du Marché-aux-Herbes 120, B1000,* ☎ *02/514–3333,* FAX *02/511–7723. 136 rooms. Restaurant, bar, meeting rooms, parking (fee). AE, DC, MC, V.*

$$ **Arlequin.** This pleasant, unpretentious hotel in the heart of the Ilot Sacré tourist area has undergone a renovation of all its rooms and common areas. Well-lighted rooms have large TVs, cream-color bamboo fittings, and Impressionist prints; some bathrooms have only showers. Buffet breakfasts are served in the panoramic Septième Ciel (Seventh Heaven) restaurant, which has views over the rooftops to the spires of the Town Hall and Cathedral. The basement bar is '70s chic, all curved walls, red velvet benches, and club chairs, with a wood-and-brushed-steel bar. A jazz band plays several nights a week. The Actors Studio cinema in the same arcade shows second-run and art-house movies. ✉ *R. de la Fourche, 17–19, B1000,* ☎ *02/514–1614,* FAX *02/514–2202. 92 rooms. Bar, breakfast room, in-room data ports (some), in-room VCRs, meeting rooms. AE, DC, MC, V.*

$$ **Atlas.** This hotel offers comfort and unpretentious surroundings in a building dating from the 18th century. Rooms have cream walls, grey carpets, and blue-and-white furniture. Suites, on two floors, each have a kitchenette in the lounge area. Buffet breakfasts are served in the blue-and-white basement with abstract art and the exposed brick of an ancient city wall. There's no bar, but all rooms have minibars and drinks are served on weekday evenings. Cheaper weekend rates are offered for internet bookings, subject to availability. ✉ *R. du Vieux Marché aux Grains 30, B1000,* ☎ *02/502–6006,* FAX *02/502–6935. 83 rooms, 5 suites. Breakfast room, minibars, meeting room, parking (fee). AE, DC, MC, V.*

$$ **Citadines Sainte-Catherine.** This residential apartment hotel also accepts guests staying for a single night. The whitewashed surfaces are offset by bright red details. Rooms, which are more studios and apartments than classic hotel rooms, have pull-out twin beds; junior suites sleep four. All have fully equipped kitchenettes. Rooms on the courtyard are the quietest. ✉ *Quai au Bois-à-Brûler 51, B1000,* ☎ *02/221–1411,* FAX *02/221–1599. 169 rooms. Kitchenettes, meeting rooms, parking (fee). AE, DC, MC, V.*

$$ **Comfort Art Hotel Siru.** All rooms and corridors in this chain hotel contain original work by a Belgian artist. Numbering 130, the works vary from enormous wall murals to fake granite blocks hanging from the ceiling above the bed. The effect runs from refined to truly kitsch but makes for a fun stay. In contrast to the unique embellishments, furnishings are functional and bathrooms are plainly white-tiled. Rooms

at the back are quieter but only have a view on higher floors. The art deco building is on a square at the end of pedestrian shopping mecca Rue Neuve. Breakfast is served in the adjoining but independent brasserie. ✉ *Pl. Rogier 1, B1210,* ☎ *02/203–3580,* FAX *02/203–3303. 101 rooms. Minibars, 2 no-smoking floors, parking (fee). AE, DC, MC, V.*

$$ ★ **Le Dixseptième.** This hotel between the Grand'Place and Gare Centrale (Central Station) occupies the stylishly restored 17th-century residence of the Spanish ambassador. Rooms surround a pleasant interior courtyard, and suites are up a splendid Louis XVI staircase. Named after Belgian artists, rooms have whitewashed walls, plain floorboards, exposed beams, suede sofas, colorful draperies, desks, blow-dryers, and second telephones. Suites have decorative fireplaces. ✉ *R. de la Madeleine 25, B1000,* ☎ *02/502–5744,* FAX *02/502–6424. 24 rooms. Bar, kitchenettes, in-room data ports, in-room safes, meeting room. AE, DC, MC, V.*

$$ **Vendôme.** Opposite Waterstone's bookshop and a stone's throw from the capital's main pedestrian shopping street is this unpretentious hotel. It's owned by the same Belgian chain as the Madeleine, and the bright rooms have similar fittings: table lamps, green bamboo furniture, and white-tiled bathrooms. All have a bathroom, telephone, minibar, small TV, and desk. Those in the "business category" also have air-conditioning and in-room data ports, and are slightly larger. Rooms at the back are quieter. A hot and cold buffet breakfast is taken in the glass-roofed Veranda room. The restaurant serves brasserie fare. Sightseeing tours can be booked at reception. ✉ *Bd. Adolphe Max 98, B1000,* ☎ *02/227–0300,* FAX *02/218–0683. 99 rooms, 7 suites. Restaurant, bar, in-room data ports, minibars, meeting rooms, parking (fee). AE, DC, MC, V.*

$–$$ **Madeleine.** A brick facade is the public exterior of this modest but friendly hotel that is part of the small, Belgian, Belhotel chain. Between the Central Station and the Grand'Place, it sits just off the bustling Place Agora with its crafts market, buskers, and pavement cafés. Rooms have pale yellow walls, green carpets, and green bamboo furniture. Those at the back have no view but are quieter. The white-tiled bathrooms are compact; small baths have shower attachments. The green and white breakfast room looks out to the square. ✉ *R. de la Montagne 20-22, B1000,* ☎ *02/513–2973,* FAX *02/502–1350. 52 rooms. Breakfast room. AE, DC, MC, V.*

$ **George V.** Located in a central, residential area, this ivy-bedecked hotel is a quiet, English-style hotel in a large house dating from 1859. Rooms, which accommodate up to four people, are simple but spacious, bright, and clean. All have telephones, TVs, and private bathrooms—though some have a deep shower tub rather than a bath. The homey breakfast room has checkered tablecloths, wicker chairs, and a dark pink carpet. ✉ *R. t' Kint 23, B1000,* ☎ *02/513–5093,* FAX *02/513–4493. 16 rooms. Bar, breakfast room, parking (fee). AE, MC, V.*

$ **Grande Cloche.** This well-appointed family hotel occupies a south-facing corner on a square between the Gare du Midi and the Grand'-Place. The green and white facade and yellow entrance hall are fresh and welcoming. Some rooms have a shower but no toilet, others have a full bathroom with separate toilet, and there's a shared hair dryer in the corridor for those who don't have one in their room. Carpets and bedspreads are green, and the walls are beige above a carpeted lower half. The back rooms are particularly peaceful. The ground-floor breakfast room is decorated in springlike green and yellow and has lead-light windows. ✉ *Pl. Rouppe 10, B1000,* ☎ *02/512–6140,* FAX *02/512–6591. 37 rooms. Breakfast room, parking (fee). AE, MC, V.*

$ **Matignon.** Only the facade was preserved in the conversion of this Belle Epoque building to a hotel in 1993. The lobby is no more than a corridor, making room for the large café-brasserie that is part of the family-owned operation. Rooms are small but have generous beds, hair dryers, and large-screen TVs, a welcome change from the dinky TVs you find in most other European budget hotels. Recently added rooms are decorated in salmon and with floral prints. Windows are double-glazed, vital in this busy spot across the street from the Bourse and two blocks from the Grand'Place. ✉ *R. de la Bourse 10, B1000,* ☎ *02/511–0888,* FAX *02/513–6927. 37 rooms. Restaurant, bar. AE, DC, MC, V.*

$ ★ **Noga.** This little hotel has a popular address in the charming Béguinage quarter near the Ste-Catherine fish market. Opened in 1958, the exceptionally well-maintained Noga has earthenware tubs of greenery along the facade, while ornaments and pictures inside evoke the Jazz Age, from table lamps to the black-and-white photographs of the period. Easy chairs in warm yellows and reds adorn the cluttered but cozy lobby area. There are rooms on four floors for two, three, or four people—larger rooms have sofas—and all have bathrooms with shower only. Natural light floods the breakfast room–bar. ✉ *R. du Béguinage 38, B1000,* ☎ *02/218–6763,* FAX *02/218–1603. 19 rooms. Bar, breakfast room, recreation room, parking (fee). AE, DC, MC, V.*

$ **Pacific Sleeping.** A noteworthy budget option on the most fashionable street in town, the quirky Pacific is run by the elderly Monsieur Powells. The 1892 building is a treasure trove of early 20th-century style—the breakfast-room decor hasn't changed since his forebears opened the place in 1901. Belgium's colonial past is evoked by the zebra skin that hangs behind the counter of the wood-paneled room with chandeliers and a wallpapered ceiling; an eclectic assortment of artwork clutters the walls here and throughout the hotel. Rooms have old furniture and no bathrooms, but all boast antique china sinks, some double. The shared toilet facilities are spotless; use of the shower costs extra, and there's a midnight curfew. A substantial Belgian breakfast of omelets and cheese is included in the room price. A courteous and informative welcome is guaranteed. ✉ *R. Dansaert 57, B1000,* ☎ *02/511–8459. 15 rooms. Breakfast room. No credit cards.*

$ **La Vieille Lanterne.** More bed-and-breakfast than hotel, this tiny, old place of six rooms is run by the family that owns the gift shops on the ground floor. All rooms look out onto the street and the crowds that cluster round the famous Manneken Pis fountain opposite; each has a bathroom with shower only. Fresh and clean with solid-wood, cottagey furniture and lead-light windows in tints of pink, green, and yellow, they are bright and have linoleum floors. Breakfast is served in the rooms. ✉ *R. des Grands Carmes 29, B1000,* ☎ *02/512–7494,* FAX *02/512–1397. 6 rooms. Shop. AE, DC, MC, V.*

$ **Welcome Hotel.** Among the charms of the smallest hotel in Brussels are the young owners, Michel and Sophie Smeesters. The six rooms, divided into economy, business, and first class and with king- or queen-size beds, are as comfortable as those in far more expensive establishments. This little hotel, located in the center of Brussels near the fish market, is much in demand, so book early. There's a charming breakfast room and around the corner on the fish market, Michel doubles as chef of the excellent seafood restaurant La Truite d'Argent ($$$), where hotel guests get a special rate. ✉ *R. du Peuplier 5, B1000,* ☎ *02/219–9546,* FAX *02/217–1887. 6 rooms. 2 restaurants, meeting room, free parking. AE, DC, MC, V.*

Upper Town

$$$$ **Astoria.** Built a year before the Brussels World Fair in 1910, the Astoria is a grand hotel in Belle Epoque style. Its checkered history has seen glittering banquets and illustrious guests (Winston Churchill, Sal-

vador Dali, and the wife of the Aga Khan, whose bath was filled with ass's milk), as well as occupation by German forces in both World Wars. Now in the hands of the Sofitel chain, its traditions are still respected, with modernizing touches such as air-conditioning achieved without visible effect. The vast, imposing entrance hall and wide, elegant staircase are noteworthy, as is the Pullman Bar, modeled on the Orient Express, and the Waldorf Room, where classical concerts are held each Sunday at lunchtime. The original bedrooms are much more spacious than those in modern hotels and have high ceilings, period furniture, and chandeliers. Breakfast is in the Palais Royal restaurant. ✉ *R. Royale 103, B1000,* ☎ *02/227–0505,* FAX *02/217–1150. 125 rooms, 14 suites. Restaurant, bar, in-room data ports, exercise room, concert hall, meeting rooms, parking (fee). AE, DC, MC, V.*

$$$$ **Conrad.** The classic facade of an 1865 mansion was combined with a sleek, deluxe American interior in this hotel on the elegant Avenue Louise. Rooms come in many different shapes, but all are spacious and have three telephones, a desk, bathrobes, and in-room checkout. The intimate, gourmet Maison de Maître restaurant is well respected, while Café Wiltcher's offers all-day brasserie dining. The large piano bar is pleasantly chummy. A branch of the exclusive English health club Champneys located in the basement offers all manner of beauty treatments as well as the usual gym facilities. ✉ *Av. Louise 71, B1050,* ☎ *02/542–4242,* FAX *02/542–4300. 269 rooms, 15 suites. 2 restaurants, 2 bars, health club, shops, convention center, parking (fee). AE, DC, MC, V.*

$$$$ **Hilton.** One of the first high-rises in Brussels back in the 1960s, this one outclasses most other Hiltons in Europe and is continuously being refurbished floor by floor. The four stories of executive rooms have a separate check-in area; there are nine floors of business rooms. The location is great for upscale shopping, and the building has a fine panoramic view over the capital. The first-floor restaurant, the Maison du Boeuf, is one of the best in town; the ground-floor Café d'Egmont stays open around the clock. ✉ *Bd. de Waterloo 38, B1000,* ☎ *02/504–1111,* FAX *02/504–2111. 431 rooms, 39 suites. 2 restaurants, bar, sauna, exercise room, shops, convention center, parking (fee). AE, DC, MC, V.*

$$$$ **Sofitel Toison d'Or.** The six-floor Sofitel has a great location opposite the Hilton. There's a chic shopping arcade on the ground floor, and you reach the lobby on an escalator. Public and guest rooms have been refreshed with green and russet colors. Bathroom telephones and bathrobes are standard. The restaurant, at the back of the lobby, has been downgraded to a buffet breakfast room, but there is good room service and the bar serves light snacks and light meals. ✉ *Av. de la Toison d'Or 40, B1000,* ☎ *02/514–2200,* FAX *02/514–5744. 160 rooms, 10 suites. Bar, room service, exercise room, meeting rooms. AE, DC, MC, V.*

$$$$ ★ **Stanhope.** This small, exclusive hotel was created out of three adjoining town houses. All the rooms and suites have high ceilings, marble bathrooms, and luxurious furniture, but each has its own name, and no two are alike. The Linley, for example, has furniture handmade by Viscount Linley, nephew of the Queen of England. You can have English-style afternoon tea (on request) in the ground-floor salon; the gastronomic Brighton restaurant, a copy of the banqueting room of the Royal Palace, serves French specialties. The bar is open to the public. ✉ *R. du Commerce 9, B1000,* ☎ *02/506–9111,* FAX *02/512–1708. 25 rooms, 25 suites. Restaurant, bar, sauna, health club, meeting rooms, parking (fee). AE, DC, MC, V.*

$$$ **Beau-Site.** Gleaming white and with flower boxes suspended from the windowsills, this former office building makes a smart impression.

The location, a block from the city-center end of Avenue Louise, and the attentive staff are big pluses. The good-size rooms come in shapes other than the standard cube, and bathrooms have hair dryers and bidets. ✉ *R. de la Longue Haie 76, B1000,* ☎ *02/640–8889,* FAX *02/640–1611. 38 rooms. In-room safes, minibars, parking (fee). AE, DC, MC, V.*

$$$ **Jolly Grand Sablon.** With an enviable position among the Sablon antiques and fine art shops, pavement cafés, and chocolate makers, the Jolly offers discreet luxury behind an elegant white facade. Its reception area, set within a hushed arcade of private art galleries, is decorated in warm russet and apricot marble. The restaurant serves Italian specialties and Sunday brunch, and looks out over a narrow alley and a pretty interior cobbled courtyard surrounded by lovingly restored red-brick houses. Rooms are decorated in pink and grey and, though some bathrooms only have showers, all include bathrobes. Suites are on the opulent side, with peach taffeta upholstery and a wall mirror that swivels round to reveal the TV. Ask for a room at the back, as the square outside is often clogged with traffic and the weekend antiques market gets going at 6 AM. ✉ *R. Bodenbroeck 2-4, B1000,* ☎ *02/512–8800,* FAX *02/512–6766. 201 rooms, 13 suites. Restaurant, bar, meeting rooms, parking (fee). AE, DC, MC, V.*

$$$ **President Centre.** One of three President hotels in Brussels, the Centre offers a friendly welcome in an eight-story block along the road from the Parc de Bruxelles and near the Jardin Botanique. There's a small bar at the front of the hotel and breakfast is served is a long, bright room with greenery and white tablecloths. Room service provides snacks and light meals. Furnishings are not the most modern (squashy beige plastic sofas, flowery wallpaper in bathrooms), but are in good order. Clients can use the gym and swimming pool at the President hotel near the Gare du Nord. ✉ *R. Royale 160, B1000,* ☎ *02/219–0065,* FAX *02/218–0910. 73 rooms, 5 suites. Bar, breakfast room, room service, parking (fee). AE, DC, MC, V.*

$$$ **Royal Crown Grand Mercure.** With all the services of a luxury hotel, this lodging has a friendly reception staff that promises to fulfill your wishes. Rooms in the modern, eight-story building are spacious and fully air-conditioned; all are done in smart honey, green, or pink shades. Rooms on the side overlook the Jardin Botanique. ✉ *R. Royale 250, B1000,* ☎ *02/220–6611,* FAX *02/217–8444. 315 rooms, 2 suites. Bar, restaurant, no-smoking floor, exercise room, sauna, solarium, meeting rooms, parking (fee). AE, DC, MC, V.*

$$$ **Scandic Grand'Place.** As its name implies, this Swedish-owned hotel near the chic Galeries St-Hubert shopping arcade is Scandinavian in inspiration and bright and efficient in manner. The reception area and bar-restaurant sit beneath a lofty atrium, and some rooms look out onto this, their window boxes filled with imitation ivy. Rooms are a little pokey and some beds are small for doubles, but there are glossy wood fittings throughout and modem connections in each. One room is specially designed for wheelchair access, several have parquet flooring to suit allergy sufferers, and some have balconies overlooking the street. The tinted windows give the impression that the weather's even greyer than it usually is outside, but their soundproofing qualities are welcome. ✉ *R. d'Arenberg, 18, B1000,* ☎ *02/548–1811,* FAX *02/548–1820. 100 rooms. Bar, restaurant, in-room data ports, 2 saunas, 6 meeting rooms. AE, DC, MC, V.*

$$ **Alfa Sablon.** On a quiet street between the Sablon and the Grand'-Place, this hotel offers spacious rooms at an attractive price and is free of the corporate feel common to many Brussels hotels. Some rooms are on the dark side, though all have bathrooms, TV, a trouser press, and a minibar. Suites arranged in duplex style favor comfort over corporate entertainment, with a gingham-covered sofa, a spiral staircase leading up to a tiny landing and a modern classic-style bedroom in cherry wood and cream. Top-floor rooms have sloping ceilings. The basement breakfast room is rustic Mediterranean in shades of blue and yellow. ✉ *R. de la Paille, B1000,* ☎ *02/513–6040,* FAX *02/511–8141. 32 rooms, 4 suites. Bar, minibars, sauna. AE, DC, MC, V.*

$$ ★ **Manos Stéphanie.** The marble lobby, antiques, and Louis XV furniture set a standard of elegance seldom encountered in a hotel in this price category. The rooms have rust-color carpets, green bedspreads, and good-size sitting areas. The hotel occupies a grand town house, so the rooms are not rigidly standardized. The hotel's older brother (**Manos**, Chaussée de Charleroi 100-104, ☎ 02/537–9682, FAX 02/539–3655) is due to reopen in 2001 with a pool and restaurant. ✉ *Chaussée de Charleroi 28, B1060,* ☎ *02/539–0250,* FAX *02/537–5729. 48 rooms, 7 suites. Bar, room service, meeting rooms, parking (fee). AE, DC, MC, V.*

$ ★ **Les Bluets.** The floral-bedecked facade gives you an idea of what to expect inside. The family that runs this no-smoking hotel has filled their town house with all sorts of antiques and curios, including an English grandfather clock, an ecclesiastical tile mural from Colombia, and a screeching exotic bird. Every room is different—styles range from tastefully old-world to cluttered and kitschy—but all make you feel like a visitor in a much-loved house. The mother can be fearsome, especially if you don't respect the silence rule, but an authentic stay is guaranteed. There's tea and coffee in each room; some have bathrooms, some small shower units. A copious breakfast is served. ✉ *R. Berckmans 124, B1060,* ☎ *02/534–3983,* FAX *02/543–0970. 10 rooms, 1 suite. Breakfast room. AE, MC, V.*

$ **Sun.** Rooms are on the small side and the bathrooms are cramped, but the beds have firm mattresses and decor is a pleasant pastel green. The attractive breakfast room has a striking glass mural; snacks are served around the clock. The hotel is on a quiet but slightly dilapidated side street off the busy Chaussée d'Ixelles. ✉ *R. du Berger 38, B1050,* ☎ *02/511–2119,* FAX *02/512–3271. 22 rooms with bath or shower. Parking (fee). AE, DC, MC, V.*

Cinquantenaire and Schuman

$$$$ **Dorint.** About as close as Brussels gets to a designer hotel, the Dorint is inspired by contemporary photography. Each room is decorated with works of a different photographer, and the navy, black, and dark-wood furnishings are sober and smart. Attention to perspective and style are evident in the chrome, black marble, and spotlights around the hotel: the circular reception area looks along a gangway to the circular restaurant, where traditional Mediterranean fare is served, but arresting artwork and greenery save it from appearing over-clinical. The green mosaic-tiled sauna, hammam, spa, and fitness center are inviting, but admission isn't included in the price. Neither is breakfast, but there's a café on site. ✉ *Bd. Charlemagne 11-19, B1000,* ☎ *02/231–0909,* FAX *02/230–3371. 210 rooms, 2 suites. Restaurant, bar, in-room data ports, in-room safes, sauna, spa, health club, meeting rooms, parking (fee). AE, DC, MC, V.*

$$$$ **Montgomery.** The owners of this hotel set out to create new standards of service for the business traveler—and, for the most part, they have succeeded. Fax machines, three telephones (with a private line for incoming calls), good working desks, safes, triple-glazed windows, and bathrobes are standard. Rooms are decorated in Chinese; English cozy; or cool, clean colonial style. There's a library and a bar-restaurant with a wood-burning fireplace. The small meeting rooms are well appointed. The location is conveniently close to the European Com-

mission. ✉ *Av. de Tervuren 134, B1150, ☎ 02/741–8511, FAX 02/741–8500. 61 rooms, 2 penthouses, 1 suite. Restaurant, bar, in-room data ports, in-room safes, health club, library, meeting rooms, parking (fee). AE, DC, MC, V.*

$$$$ **Swissôtel.** Contemporary luxury in classic style is the flavor of this addition to the Brussels hotel scene. Completely renovated on its 1997 acquisition by Swissair, it is close to the European Parliament and is a bustling hub for international lobbyists, businesspeople, and politicians. Rooms, half of which are no-smoking, are divided into standard and business; the latter have large desk, espresso machines, free access to a business center with boardroom and a club lounge, and a superior breakfast menu. The independently run health club has a pool, Jacuzzi, children's play area, extensive gym, aerobics classes, and beauty treatments. Rooms at the back overlook a shared garden; all have two phone lines and voice mail, and ISDN on demand. Apartments, including two duplexes, can be rented for a week or more. The hotel's Nico Central restaurant is the Brussels outpost of Britain's gastronomic chain and offers contemporary cuisine in a comfortable setting with yellow and blue armchairs. ✉ *R. du Parnasse 19, B1050, ☎ 02/505–2929, FAX 02/505–2555. 244 rooms, 19 suites, 57 apartments. Bar, restaurant, in-room safes, no-smoking floors, pool, beauty salon, aerobics, health club, playground, business services, meeting rooms, parking (fee). AE, DC, MC, V.*

$$$ **Park.** Opposite the tall trees of the Cinquantenaire Park and with a view over their tops to the museum's glass roof, the Park Hotel offers a rare patch of green in the city's hotel spectrum. As well as the view, the grand old house has a large garden where guests can hold barbecues during the summer. The lobby with tiny bar at the end of the reception desk is colonial in style, with pillars, potted palms, and a bust of Henry Morton Stanley, who was dispatched by King Leopold II to explore the Congo. Rooms vary in size from enormous to standard; the breakfast room, which serves an English buffet breakfast, extends under a glass roof conservatory-style and overlooks the garden. The fitness center at the back of the house is small but inviting. ✉ *Av. de l'Yser 21, B1040, ☎ 02/735–7400, FAX 02/735–1967. 51 rooms, 1 suite. Bar, exercise room, sauna, spa, meeting rooms. AE, DC, MC, V.*

$$ **Leopold.** A discreet establishment near the European Parliament, the 10-year-old, privately owned Leopold has smallish rooms decorated in pink and grey. Bathrooms have either bath or shower. The honey-colored gastronomic restaurant has high, corniced ceilings; this is where the annual Silver Whisk competition of European hotel schools is held. There is also a pasta bar and a lunchtime brasserie; the interior courtyard is used by all three restaurants in fine weather. The solarium is a pleasant place to relax after a meal. ✉ *R. du Luxembourg 35, B1050, ☎ 02/511–1828, FAX 02/514–1939. 82 rooms, 4 suites, 6 apartments. 3 restaurants, bar, sauna, parking (fee). AE, DC, MC, V.*

South of Center

$$$$ ★ ✕ **Château du Lac.** Half an hour from the city center and a good choice as a peaceful base from which to visit the capital and the provinces, this mock-Florentine castle is a former Schweppes bottling plant. In the late 1990s the hotel expanded to make room for more luxurious green-and-white rooms. The older, light-beige rooms are equally well furnished; the decor in the public rooms is contemporary, mostly green and wine red. The splendid gastronomic restaurant, Le Trèfle à Quatre, serves classic French cuisine and is itself worth a visit, not only for its superb fish and game, but also for the views over the lake. ✉ *Av. du Lac 87, B1332 Genval, ☎ 02/654–1122, FAX 02/655–7444. 119* *rooms, 2 suites. Restaurant, bar, pool, sauna, health club, convention center. AE, DC, MC, V.*

$$$ **Alfa Louise.** Located on the prestigious Avenue Louise, this hotel is distinguished by its large rooms with sitting areas and office-size desks, making it an excellent choice for budget-minded business travelers. Bathrobes and room safes are additional conveniences. ✉ *Av. Louise 212, B1000,* ☎ *02/644–2929,* FAX *02/644–1878. 43 rooms. Bar, meeting rooms. AE, DC, MC, V.*

$$$ **Four Points.** The concept of this Sheraton property is to offer superior rooms with limited services at moderate rates. Large rooms feature blond-wood furniture, a reclining chair, and good work space. There is a beige-and-green atrium bar, and the restaurant serves generous breakfasts and a limited selection of specialties for lunch and dinner. The basement restaurant has a separate entrance. ✉ *R. Paul Spaak 15, B1000,* ☎ *02/645–6111,* FAX *02/646–6344. 128 rooms. 2 restaurants, bar, sauna, health club, meeting rooms, parking (fee). AE, DC, MC, V.*

$$ **Les Tourelles.** This cheerful, family-run hotel is south of central Brussels but well connected by tram and street networks. The mock-medieval turreted facade and traditional wood decor suggest an antique hunting lodge, with comfortable rooms and friendly service. Try to get a back-facing room as the front looks out over a main road. ✉ *Av. Winston Churchill 135, B1180,* ☎ *02/344–9573,* FAX *02/346–4270. 22 rooms. 2 conference rooms, parking. AE, MC, V.*

West of Center

$$ **Gerfaut.** Reasonably sized rooms in this cheerful hotel are done in light beige with colorful spreads. Those with three and four beds are available at modest supplements. Breakfast is served in the bright and friendly Winter Garden room. The location in Anderlecht near the Gare du Midi (South Station), though not choice, provides an opportunity to see a part of Brussels most visitors ignore. ✉ *Chaussée de Mons 115–117, B1070,* ☎ *02/524–2044,* FAX *02/524–3044. 48 rooms. Bar, breakfast room, free parking. AE, DC, MC, V.*

NIGHTLIFE AND THE ARTS

The Arts

The arts in Brussels are thriving in the wake of the capital's stint as the year 2000 European city of culture. Although the linguistic division drives a wedge through the cultural landscape, the advantage is that funds are injected by both Flemish- and French-language authorities eager to promote their separate contributions. A glance at the "What's On" supplement of weekly English-language newsmagazine *The Bulletin* reveals the breadth of the offerings in all categories of cultural life. Tickets for major events can be purchased by calling **Fnac Ticket Line** (☎ 0900/00600).

Film

First-run English-language and French movies predominate: the Belgian film industry is small but of high quality. At the 1999 Cannes Film Festival, director brothers Luc and Jean-Pierre Dardenne won the Palme d'Or for "Rosetta," a deadbeat tale set in Líge; directors Jaco Van Dormael, Alain Berliner, Gérard Corbiau, and Stijn Coninx have also achieved international acclaim. In summer, the excellent cinema **Arenberg/Galeries** (✉ Galeries St-Hubert, ☎ 0900/29550) hosts the Ecran Total (Total Cinema) festival, which screens classic Hollywood and French movies alongside new talent from around the world. The most convenient movie theater complexes are **UGC/Acropole** (✉ Av.

de la Toison d'Or, ☎ 0900/29930) and **UGC/De Brouckère** (✉ Pl. de Brouckère, ☎ 0900/29930). Art-house films show at the **Vendôme** (✉ Chaussée de Wavre 18, ☎ 0900/29909), which also puts on regular themed festivals (e.g., Latin American or Jewish cinema). The small **Actor's Studio** (✉ Petite rue des Bouchers 16, ☎ 0900/27854) shows second-run and art-house films. The avant-garde **Nova** (✉ R. d'Arenberg 3, ☎ 02/511–2774) shows a quirky, uncommercial selection of animation, shorts, and sound installations despite its shoestring budget and uncertain tenancy. The biggest, with 26 theaters, is the futuristic **Kinepolis** (✉ Av. du Centenaire 1, Heysel, ☎ 02/474–2604). The **Musée du Cinéma** (✉ R. Baron Horta 9, ☎ 02/507–8370) shows classic and silent movies, the latter accompanied live by an improvising pianist. It is one of the only places in the world that shows silent movies daily. Buying a ticket to see a film also gains entry to the small but fascinating museum (BF60 24 hours in advance; BF90 at door). In March, the International Festival of Fantasy Film takes over **Auditorium Passage 44** (✉ Bld. du Jardin Botanique 44, ☎ 02/201–1495) and other venues for a packed program of thrillers and chillers, culminating in a Vampires Ball.

Classical Music

The principal venue for classical music concerts is the Horta-designed **Palais des Beaux-Arts** (✉ R. Ravenstein 23, ☎ 02/507–8200). The complex, which also houses the Film Museum, an art gallery, and a theater, was the first multipurpose arts complex in Europe when it opened in 1928. Its Henry Le Boeuf concert hall has been restored to world-class acoustic standards since recent renovations corrected some earlier misguided alterations. Chamber music concerts and recitals are held in the more intimate **Royal Conservatory** (✉ R. de la Régence 30, ☎ 02/507–8200). Many concerts are held in churches, especially the **Chapelle Protestante** (✉ Pl. du Musée) and the **Eglise des Minimes** (✉ R. des Minimes 62).

Belgium is particularly renowned in the fields of early and Baroque music—look out for conductors René Jacobs and Philippe Herreweghe and the Sablon Baroque Spring festival in April/May. Also in spring, the grueling **Queen Elisabeth Music Competition** (the penultimate round is at the Royal Conservatory, the final week at the Palais des Beaux-Arts), a prestigious competition for young pianists, violinists, and singers, takes place in Brussels. The monthlong **Ars Musica** (☎ 02/512–1717) festival of contemporary music in March and April attracts new music ensembles from around the world. The best new music group in Belgium is the Ictus Ensemble, which pops up all over the place, especially in collaboration with dance troupes.

Opera and Dance

The national opera house is the excellent **La Monnaie/De Munt** (✉ Pl. de la Monnaie, ☎ 02/218–1211). This is where the 1830 revolution started: inflamed by the aria starting "Amour sacré de la patrie" (Sacred love of your country) in Auber's *La Muette de Portici*, members of the audience rushed outside and started rioting. The brief and largely bloodless revolution against the Dutch established the Belgian nation. Visiting opera and dance companies often perform at **Cirque Royal** (✉ R. de l'Enseignement 81, ☎ 02/218–2015).

Dance is among the liveliest arts in Belgium. Its seminal figure, Anne Teresa De Keersmaeker, is choreographer-in-residence at the opera house, but her Rosas company also has its own performance space within her **PARTS school** (✉ Av. Van Volxem 164, ☎ 02/344–5598). Alternatively, it performs at the **Lunatheater** (✉ Pl. Sainctelette 20, ☎ 02/201–5959), as do the Royal Flanders Ballet and many other Belgian and international dance troupes. Innovative provincial company Charleroi/Danses opened **La Raffinerie** (✉ R. de Manchester, ☎ 02/410–3341), a new Brussels base, in a splendid old sugar refinery in Molenbeek. The delightful **Chapelle des Brigittines** (✉ R. des Visitandines 1, ☎ 02/506–4300) welcomes cutting-edge productions.

Theater

Nearly all the city's 30-odd theaters stage French-language plays; only a few present plays in Dutch. Talented amateur groups also put on occasional English-language performances, and top British companies, including the Royal Shakespeare Company, are becoming regular visitors. Avant-garde performances are often the most rewarding and show at the **Lunatheater** (☞ Opera and Dance, *above*), **Théâtre Les Tanneurs** (✉ R. des Tanneurs 75, ☎ 02/512–1784), and **Théâtre de Poche** (✉ Chemin du Gymnase 1a, ☎ 02/649–1727). Check what's on at **Rideau de Bruxelles** (✉ Palais des Beaux-Arts, R. Ravenstein 23, ☎ 02/507–8200), **Théâtre Le Public** (✉ R. Braemt 64–70, ☎ 0800/94444), **Théâtre National** (✉ Pl. Rogier, ☎ 02/203–5303), **Théâtre des Martyrs** (✉ Pl. des Martyrs 22, ☎ 02/223–3208), and **Théâtre Varia** (✉ R. du Sceptre 78, ☎ 02/640–8258). The annual Kunsten **FESTIVALdesArts** contemporary arts festival (produced by both Flemish and French-language communities) takes place in May in numerous venues and puts on a cutting-edge selection of theater, music, dance, multimedia, and visual arts from Belgium and abroad.

Nightlife

By 11 PM, most Bruxellois have packed up and gone home. But around midnight, bars and cafés fill up again and roads become congested as the night people take over; many places stay open till dawn. By and large, Belgians provide their own entertainment but, while Brussels's nightclubs are not in the same league as London's or Amsterdam's, the scene has been improving for the past few years.

Bars and Lounges

There's a café on virtually every street corner, most boasting a wide selection of alcoholic drinks. Although the Belgian brewing industry is declining as the giant Interbrew firm muscles smaller companies out of the market, Belgians still consume copious quantities of beer, some of it with a 10% alcohol content. The sidewalk outside **Au Soleil** (✉ 86 R. du Marché-au-Charbon) teems with the hip and would-be hip, enjoying relaxed trip-hop sounds and very competitive prices. Fashionable Flemings, meanwhile, flock to the **Beurs Café** (✉ R. Auguste Orts 20–26), a huge, minimalist hall with a friendly atmosphere next door to the innovative Beursschouwburg cultural center. The nearby **Archiduc** (✉ R. Dansaert 6) attracts a thirtyish fashion crowd in its stylish art deco abode, though it gets smoky up on the balcony. **Chez Moeder Lambic** (✉ R. de Savoie 68, St-Gilles) claims to stock 600 Belgian beers and a few hundred more foreign ones. **De Ultieme Hallucinatie** (✉ R. Royale 316) is an art nouveau masterpiece, with a pricey restaurant as well as a roomy tavern. **Fleur en Papier Doré** (✉ R. des Alexiens 53) was the hangout for Surrealist René Magritte and his artist friends, and their spirit lingers on. At the tiny **Java** (✉ R. de la Grande Ile 22), the bar is shaped like a huge anaconda. On the Grand'Place, **'t Kelderke** (✉ Grand'Place 15) is a bustling, friendly option. In the trendy Place Saint-Géry district, **Zebra** (✉ Pl. St-Géry 35) attracts a comfortably fashionable crowd, while **Mappa Mundo** (✉ R. du Pont de la Carpe 2–6) on the opposite corner packs two floors with an international mix of revelers and poseurs. On warm nights, it's difficult to find a table.

Brussels's sizable French-speaking black population, hailing mostly from the Republic of Congo (the former Zaire), congregates in the area of Ixelles known as Matonge. **Chaussée de Wavre** is the principal street for African shops, bars, and restaurants. The nearby **Ultime Atome** (✉ R. St-Boniface 14, ☎ 02/511–1367) is a fashionable neighborhood bar-restaurant that's busy day and night (and serves food until 1 AM). **L'Amour Fou** (✉ Ch. d'Ixelles 185, ☎ 02/514–2709) has a selection of newspapers for the lone visitor and is popular with the student intellectual crowd.

There are a number of favored Anglo-expat hangouts in Brussels. **Conway's** (✉ Av. de la Toison d'Or ☎ 02/511–2668) is a singles bar where the staff's ice-breaking activities are the stuff of local legend. **Rick's Café Américain** (✉ Av. Louise 344, ☎ 02/648–1451) is flashy and does Sunday brunch.

Like most western European cities, Brussels has a sizable number of "Irish" bars: **The James Joyce** (✉ R. Archimède 34, ☎ 02/230–9894), **Kitty O'Shea's** (✉ Bd. de Charlemagne 42, ☎ 02/230–7875), the heaving **Wild Geese** (✉ Av. Livingstone 2-4, ☎ 02/230–1990), and **O'Reilly's** (✉ Pl. de la Bourse, ☎ 02/552–0481). Among the most popular hotel bars are those in the **Hilton,** the **Amigo,** and the **Métropole** (☞ Dining and Lodging, *above*).

Cabarets

Transvestite shows spark **Chez Flo** (✉ R. au Beurre 25, ☎ 02/512–9496). **La Voix Secrète** (✉ R. du Lombard 1, ☎ 02/511–5679) does food in a gothic atmosphere with costumed waiters and a musical floor show from Wednesday to Sunday. At **Show Point** (✉ Pl. Stephanie 14, ☎ 02/511–5364) the draw is striptease.

Dance Clubs

The dance scene is in perpetual mutation: as fast as a promising new outfit sets up, another falls foul of regulations and shuts down. Look out for posters announcing hot nights—sometimes in obscure venues like the bowels of the Gare Centrale or even the Atomium. Action starts at midnight in most clubs. Salsa addicts can indulge their habit at **Cartagena** (✉ R. du Marché-au-Charbon 70, ☎ 02/502–5908) or the **Montecristo Café** (✉ R. Henri Maus 25, ☎ 02/511–8789). Electronica fans prefer **Fuse** (✉ R. Blaes 208, ☎ 511–9789), a bunker-style techno haven with monthly gay nights. **Mirano Continental** (✉ Chaussée de Louvain 38, ☎ 02/227–3970) remains the glitzy hangout of choice for the self-styled beautiful people, while an affluent set retreat to the **Jeux d'Hiver** (✉ Chemin du Croquet 1, ☎ 02/649–0864), hidden among trees in the Bois de la Cambre. **Tour & Taxi** (✉ R. Picard 6) puts on thumping house and one-off events in the impressive hulk of a former customs depot whose future is decidedly uncertain.

Gay Bars

Brussels is not nearly as advanced as Amsterdam when it comes to gay culture, but several clubs hold regular gay and lesbian nights. La Démence is the monthly gay night at **Fuse** (☞ Dance Clubs, *above*). **Belgica** (✉ R. du Marché-au-Charbon 32) is a trendy meeting point at the heart of what passes for the gay quarter; **Strong** (✉ R. Ste-Christophe 1) is a bar and club from Thursday to Saturday. **Tels Quels** (✉ R. du Marché-aux-Charbon 81, ☎ 02/512–4587) is a social service that publishes a monthly magazine as well as a bar and can offer up-to-date information about the capital's gay scene. For lesbians, the **Café qu'on sert** (✉ Av. Albert 59, ☎ 02/343–0233) or **Le Capricorne** (✉ R. d'Anderlecht 6, ☎ 02/512–1503) are the best bets.

Jazz

After World War II, Belgium was at the forefront of Europe's modern jazz movement: of the great postwar players, harmonica maestro Toots Thielemans and vibes player Sadi are still very much alive and perform in Brussels. Other top Belgian jazz draws include guitarist Philip Catherine and the experimental ethno-jazz trio Aka Moon. Among the best jazz venues are **L'Archiduc** (✉ R. Antoine Dansaert 6, ☎ 02/512–0652), the **New York Café Jazz Club** (✉ Chaussée de Charleroi 5, ☎ 02/534–8509), **Sounds** (✉ R. de la Tulipe 28, ☎ 02/512–9250), and **Travers** (✉ R. Traversière 11, ☎ 02/218–4086).

Mainstream rock acts and big-league French chansonniers stop off at **Forest-National** (✉ Av. du Globe 36, ☎ 02/340–2211). **Ancienne Belgique** (✉ Bd. Anspach 110, ☎ 02/548–2424) hosts a wide range of rock, pop, alternative, and world music, as does **Le Botanique** (✉ R. Royale 236, ☎ 02/218–3732), which has a superb 10-day festival, *Les Nuits Botanique,* in September. Though officially the Galician cultural centre, **La Tentation** (✉ R. de Laeken 28, ☎ 02/223–2275) hosts a broad selection of world music performers in a superb venue, while **Fool Moon Theatre** (✉ Quai de Mariemont 26, ☎ 02/410–1003) headlines artists playing drum'n'bass, trip-hop and other funky sounds, continuing into the night as a dance club. For up-and-coming British and European alternative bands, try **VK** (✉ R. de l'Ecole 76, ☎ 02/414–2907).

OUTDOOR ACTIVITIES AND SPORTS

Participant Sports

Golf

The top clubs in the area are **Keerbergen Golf Club** (✉ Vlieghavenlaan 50, Keerbergen, ☎ 015/234961), **Royal Golf Club de Belgique** (✉ Château de Ravenstein, Tervuren, ☎ 02/767–5801), and **Royal Waterloo Golf Club** (✉ Vieux Chemin de Wavre 50, Ohain, ☎ 02/633–1850). For more information, call the **Royal Belgian Golf Federation** (☎ 02/672–2389).

Health and Fitness

Several hotels have well-equipped fitness centers open to the public. The most luxurious, and the most expensive is **Champneys,** an English import located in the swank Conrad Hotel. A one-day visit costs BF4,500, offering use of the top-notch facilities as well as classes, lunch, and a half-hour massage (✉ Ave. Louise 71B, ☎ 02/542–4666). Other very good and less expensive choices include the **World Class Health Academy** in the Swiss Hôtel (✉ R. du Parnasse 19, ☎ 02/551–5990), **John Harris Fitness** at the Radisson SAS Hotel (✉ R. du Fossé-aux-Loups 47, ☎ 02/219–8254), and **Sheraton** (✉ Pl. Rogier 3, ☎ 02/224–3111). Fees average BF1,000 a session. Prices are considerably lower at independent health clubs, such as **California Club** (✉ R. Lesbroussart 68, ☎ 02/640–9344) and **European Athletic City** (✉ Av. Winston Churchill 25A, ☎ 02/345–3077).

Horseback Riding

For outdoor horseback riding, try **Le Centre Equestre de la Cambre** (✉ Chausée de Waterloo 872, ☎ 02/375–3408), **Musette** (✉ Drève du Caporal 11, ☎ 02/374–2591), or **Royal Etrier Belge** (✉ Champ du Vert Chasseur 19, ☎ 02/374–3870).

Jogging

For in-town jogging, use the **Parc de Bruxelles** (✉ R. de la Loi to the Palace); for more extensive workouts, head for the **Bois de la Cambre** (✉ Southern end of Av. Louise), a natural park that is a favorite among joggers and families with children. The park merges on the south into the beech woods of the 11,000-acre **Forêt de Soignes,** extending as far south as Genval with its lake and restaurants.

Swimming

Hotel swimming pools are few and far between. Among covered public pools, the best are **Calypso** (✉ Av. Wiener 60, ☎ 02/663–0090), **Longchamp** (✉ Sq. de Fré 1, ☎ 02/374–9005), and **Poseidon** (✉ Av. des Vaillants 2, ☎ 02/771–6655).

Tennis

Popular clubs include the **Royal Léopold** (✉ Av. Dupuich 42, ☎ 02/344–3666), **Royal Racing Club** (✉ Av. des Chênes 125, ☎ 02/374–4181), and **Wimbledon** (✉ Waterloosesteenweg 220, Sint-Genesius-Rode, ☎ 02/358–3523).

Spectator Sports

Horse Racing

Going to the races is second in popularity only to soccer, and there are three major racecourses: **Boitsfort** (✉ Chaussée de la Hulpe 53, ☎ 02/675–3015), which has an all-weather flat track; **Groenendael** (✉ Sint-Jansberglaan 4, Hoeilaart, ☎ 02/675–3015), for steeplechasing; and **Sterrebeek** (✉ Du Roy de Blicquylaan 43, Sterrebeek, ☎ 02/675–5293), for trotting and flat racing between February and June. For more information, contact the **Jockey Club de Belgique** (☎ 02/672–7248).

Soccer

Soccer is Belgium's most popular spectator sport, and the leading club, **Anderlecht,** has many fiercely loyal fans—even despite poor showings in recent seasons and the discovery that club bosses bribed referees during a European competition in the early '80s. Their home field is **Parc Astrid** (✉ Av. Theo Verbeeck 2, ☎ 02/522–1539). Major international games are played at the **Stade Roi Baudouin** (✉ Av. du Marathon 135, ☎ 02/479–3654). For information and tickets, contact the **Maison du Football** (✉ Av. Houba de Strooper 145, ☎ 02/477–1211).

SHOPPING

The Belgians started producing high-quality luxury goods in the Middle Ages, and this is what they are skilled at. This is not a country where you pick up amazing bargains. Value added tax (TVA) further inflates prices, but visitors from outside the European Union can obtain refunds.

Shopping Districts

The stylish, upmarket shopping area for clothing and accessories comprises the upper end of **Avenue Louise** and includes **Avenue de la Toison d'Or,** which branches off at a right angle; **Boulevard de Waterloo,** on the other side of the street; **Galerie Louise,** which links the two avenues; and **Galerie de la Toison d'Or,** another gallery two blocks away. The **City 2** mall on Place Rogier and the pedestrian mall, **Rue Neuve,** are fun and inexpensive shopping areas (but not recommended for women alone after dark). There are galleries scattered across Brussels, but low rents have made **Boulevard Barthélémy** the "in" place for avant-garde art. The **Windows** complex (✉ Bd. Barthélémy 13) houses several galleries. On the **Place du Grand-Sablon** and adjoining streets and alleys you'll find antiques dealers and smart art galleries. The **Galeries St-Hubert** is a rather stately shopping arcade lined with upscale shops selling men's and women's clothing, books, and interior design products. In the trendy **Rue Antoine Dansaert** and **Place du Nouveau Marché**

Brussels Shopping

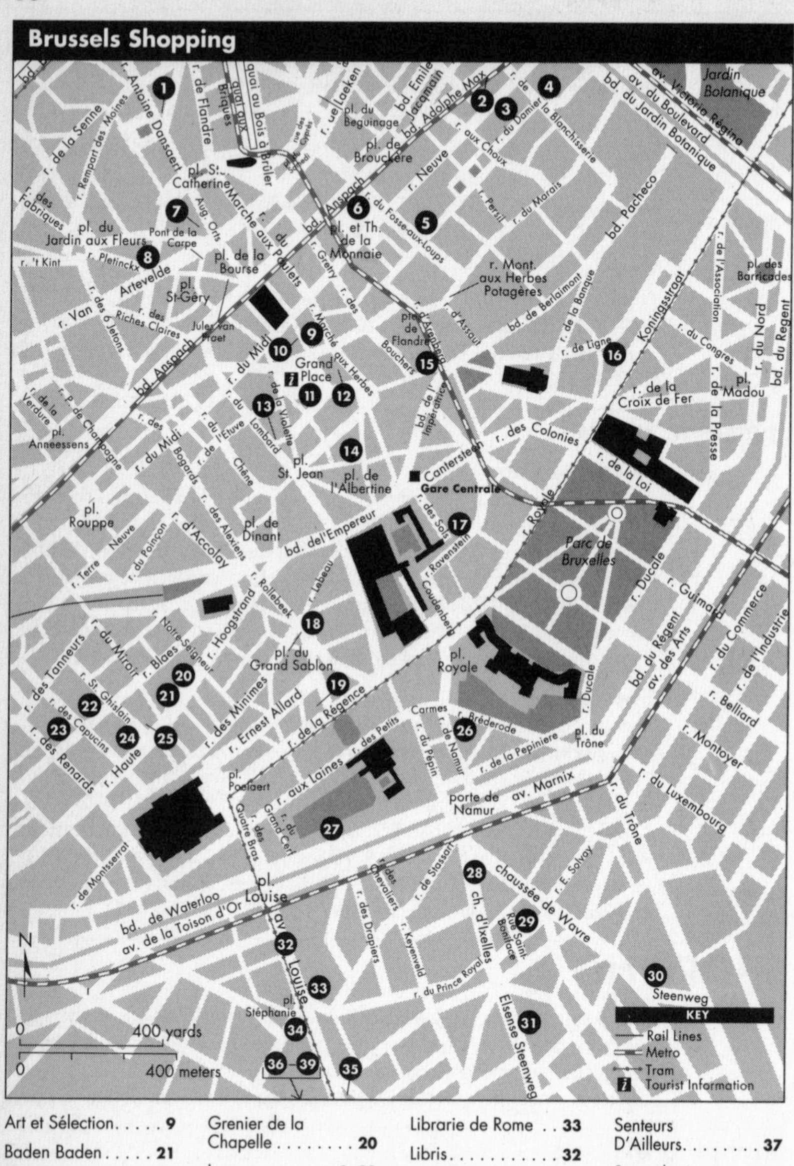

Art et Sélection **9**
Baden Baden **21**
Bonpoint **32**
Chine **8**
Christophe Coppens **1**
Delvaux **27**
Espace 161 . . . . . . **24**
FNAC **4**
400 Bieres Artisinales **30**
Galerie Bortier **14**
Galeries St-Hubert (Delvaux, Kaat Tilley, Librairie des Galeries, Manufacture Belge de Dentelle, Tropismes) **15**
Grenier de la Chapelle **20**
Inno **3, 32**
La Bobine d'Or . . . **23**
La Boite à Musique **17**
La Librarie des Etangs **31**
La Septième Tasse **38**
Le Cheverny **25**
Le Grenier de la Bourse **7**
Lemaire **19**
Leonidas **28**
Le Palais du Gourmet **39**
Librarie de Rome . . **33**
Libris **32**
Maison F. Rubbrecht **11**
Martine Doly **27**
Mary **16**
Natan **36**
Nina Meert **29**
O & Co. **10**
Olivier Strelli **35**
Passage 125 Blaes. **22**
Pierre Marcolini . . . **18**
Pink **27**
Puzzles **1**
Senteurs D'Ailleurs. **37**
Serneels **34**
Sterling **5**
Textilux Center **13**
Tintin Boutique **12**
Vincenti **26**
Virgin Megastore . . . **6**
Waterstone's **2**
Wittamer **18**

aux Grains, near the Bourse, are a number of boutiques carrying fashions by young designers and interior design and art shops. **Place du Chatelaine** and the surrounding streets in Ixelles near Avenue Louise feature a number of upmarket boutiques offering women's and men's clothes, as well as an assortment of other shops, including antiques, housewares, and secondhand clothes.

Department Stores

The best Belgian department store is **Inno** (✉ R. Neuve 111, ☎ 02/211–2111; ✉ Av. Louise 12, ☎ 02/513–8494; ✉ Chaussée de Waterloo 699, ☎ 02/345–3890). Others, such as **C&A** and **Marks & Spencer,** are clustered at the Place de la Monnaie end of Rue Neuve, a tawdry street that is now undergoing a much-needed face-lift.

Street Markets

Bruxellois with an eye for fresh farm produce and low prices do most of their food shopping at the animated open-air markets in almost every borough. Among the best are those in **Boitsfort** in front of the Maison Communal on Sunday morning; on **Place du Châtelain,** Wednesday afternoon; and on **Place Ste-Catherine,** all day, Monday through Saturday. In addition to fruits, vegetables, meat, and fish, most markets include traders with specialized products, such as wide selections of cheese and wild mushrooms. The most exotic market is the Sunday morning **Marché du Midi,** where the large North African community gathers to buy and sell foods, spices, and plants, transforming the area next to the railway station into a vast bazaar.

In the Grand'Place there are a **Flower Market,** daily, except Monday, and a **Bird Market,** Sunday morning. You need to get to the flea market, **Vieux Marché** (✉ Pl. du Jeu de Balle) early. It's open daily 7–2. The **Antiques and Book Market** (✉ Pl. du Grand-Sablon), Saturday 9–6 and Sunday 9–2, is frequented by established dealers.

Specialty Stores

Antiques

For antique bathroom fittings, including deep tubs meant for long soaks and marble washstands go to **Baden Baden** (✉ R. Haute 78–84, ☎ 02/548–9690). **La Bobine D'Or** (✉ R. Blaes 135, ☎ 02/513–4817) is crammed with antique lace, vintage clothes, jewelry, figurines, and just about anything else that can be squeezed in. **Le Cheverny** (✉ R. Haute 126, ☎ 02/511–5495) has a fine selection of art nouveau lamps, as well as some art deco. **Espace 161** (✉ R. Haute 161, ☎ 02/502–3164) offers crystal chandeliers and sumptuous furniture. **Le Grenier de la Bourse** (✉ R. Antoine Dansaert 2, ☎ 02/512–6879) has an eclectic selection of furniture and objects. **Grenier de la Chapelle** (✉ R. Haute 51, ☎ 02/513–2955) offers rustic wood furniture. **Lemaire** (✉ R. de la Régence 34, ☎ 02/511–0513) has an extensive selection of fine porcelain and earthenware. **Passage 125 Blaes** (✉ R. Blaes 121–125, ☎ 02/503–1027) brings together 25 antiques dealers under one roof, with a vast range of goods including chandeliers, bathroom fixtures, art, and furniture in a variety of styles.

Beer

400 bières artisanales (✉ Chaussée de Wavre 175, ☎ 02/511–3742), a little off the beaten track, should be visited by anyone with a serious interest in Belgian beer. The owner is friendly and knowledgeable and his selection of ales is well-judged and continually surprising. Don't forget to buy the glass that goes with your *dubbel* or *tripel.*

Books

The **Galerie Bortier** (✉ R. de la Madeleine–R. St-Jean) is a small, attractive arcade devoted entirely to rare and secondhand books. It was designed by the architect responsible for the Galeries St-Hubert. **Librairie des Galeries** (✉ Galerie du Roi 2, ☎ 02/511–2412) carries an extensive selection of books in both French and English on art, architecture, and photography. This is the place to find books on topics as specialized as 18th- and 19th-century Belgian pottery. **Libris** (✉ Espace Louise, ☎ 02/511–6400) is well stocked with current French-language titles. Shops specializing in comic strip albums include those at Chaussée de Wavre Nos. 167, 179, and 198, and the **Tintin Boutique** (✉ R. de la Colline 13, off Grand'Place). **Tropismes** (✉ Galerie des Princes 11, ☎ 02/512–8852) carries more than 40,000 titles and will help you find out-of-print books.

English-language bookstores include **La Librairie des Etangs** (✉ Chaussée d'Ixelles 319, Ixelles, ☎ 02/646–9786), an international bookseller; **Librairie de Rome** (✉ Av. Louise 50b, ☎ 02/511–7937), which has a large selection of foreign newspapers and magazines; **Sterling** (✉ R. du Fosse-aux-Loups 38, ☎ 02/223–6223), a friendly store run by a team whose enthusiasm for reading is infectious; and the less personal **Waterstone's** (✉ Bd. Adolphe Max 71–75, ☎ 02/219–2708), which carries hardcovers, paperbacks, and periodicals. The *International Herald Tribune* and the *Wall Street Journal* are sold by almost all newsdealers. The Sunday *New York Times* is available at both Librairie de Rome and Waterstone's for a rather princely sum.

Children's Clothes

Bonpoint (✉ Av. Louise 31, ☎ 02/534–1640) is the place to go for those who want to spare no expense dressing the little ones like young royalty. For more practical clothes but with a distinctive style, try **Puzzles** (✉ R. Leon Lepage 1, ☎ 02/512–1172).

Chocolates

Godiva (✉ Grand'Place 22 and other locations) is the best known, with **Neuhaus** (✉ Galerie de la Reine 25–27 and other locations) a close second. **Leonidas** (✉ Chaussée d'Ixelles 5 and other locations) is the budget alternative, but still high quality thanks to Belgium's strict controls on chocolate. The best handmade pralines, the crème de la crème of Belgian chocolates, are made by **Pierre Marcolini** (✉ Pl. du Grand Sablon 39, ☎ 02/514–1206), the boy wonder of the chocolate world; at **Mary** (✉ R. Royale 73, ☎ 02/217–4500); and at **Wittamer** (✉ Pl. du Grand Sablon 12, ☎ 02/512–3742).

Crystal

The Val St-Lambert mark is the only guarantee of handblown, hand-engraved lead crystal vases and other glass. You can buy it in many stores; the specialist is **Art et Sélection** (✉ R. du Marché-aux-Herbes 83, ☎ 02/511–8448).

Lace and Linen

Manufacture Belge de Dentelle (✉ Galerie de la Reine 6–8, ☎ 02/511–4477) and **Maison F. Rubbrecht** (✉ Grand'Place 23, ☎ 02/512–0218) sell local handmade lace. Lace sold in the souvenir shops is likely to come from East Asia. An introductory visit to the **Musée du Costume et de la Dentelle** (✉ R. de la Violette 6, ☎ 02/512–7709) is a good idea if you're planning to shop for lace. For Belgian linen, try **Martine Doly** (✉ Bd. de Waterloo 27, ☎ 02/512–4628).

Tapestries

For tapestries that are evidence of Belgium's long tradition as a high-quality textiles-producing center head for **Textilux Center** (✉ R. du Lombard 41b, ☎ 02/513–5015).

Food

Maison J. Dandoy (✉ R. au Beurre 31, ☎ 02/511–0326) has the best biscuits in Brussels, including the Belgian specialty Speculoos, a spiced cookie available in many shapes and sizes. **Le Palais du Gourmet** (✉ R. du Bailli 106, ☎ 02/537–6653) is a gourmet paradise. The temptations include cheeses, condiments, oils and vinegars, foie gras, caviar, and wine. **O&Co.** (✉ R. au Beurre 28, ☎ 02/502–7511) is stacked to the ceiling with a wide selection of olive oils made by small producers from throughout the Mediterranean, including France, Italy, Spain, Greece, and Israel. **La Septième Tasse** (✉ R. du Bailli 37, ☎ 02/647–1971) sells about 100 different kinds of teas, as well as china teapots and gleaming silver urns. You can enjoy a cup of tea in the shop's cozy café, as well as buy tea to take home.

Hats

Christophe Coppens (✉ R. Léon Lepage 2, ☎ 02/512–7797) is a Flemish milliner designing hats on the cutting edge of fashion. If you're planning a trip to Ascot, this is the place to find that one-of-a-kind creation that will make you stand out in a crowd. **Vincenti** (✉ R. du Namur 30, ☎ 02/512–7902) sells handmade hats, as well as handbags, scarves and jewelry. Hats may also be custom-ordered.

Leather Goods

Delvaux (✉ Galerie de la Reine 31, ☎ 02/512–7198; ✉ Bd. de Waterloo 27, ☎ 02/513–0502) makes outstanding, classic handbags, wallets, belts, and attaché cases. Be prepared to part with a hefty sum, but the Delvaux products last and last.

Men's Clothes

Olivier Strelli (✉ Av. Louise 72, ☎ 02/512–5607) caters to the well-dressed set looking for contemporary, minimalist fashion. If you're looking for shirts, head to **Pink** (✉ Bvd. Waterloo 23., ☎ 02/502–0508). The selection of shirts and ties is vast, and, yes, they come in many colors in addition to pink. There is also a smaller selection of women's shirts.

Music

La Boite à Musique (✉ R. Ravenstein 17–19, ☎ 02/513–0965) is the best place in Brussels for classical music, which is not surprising considering the store's location next to the Palais des Beaux-Arts symphony hall. **FNAC** (✉ City 2, R. Cendres 16, ☎ 02/209–2211) offers a full range of music, from rap to rock to jazz, in a large store that also has a good selection of books, in English as well as French. **Virgin Megastore** (✉ Bd. Anspach 30, ☎ 02/219–9004) is another good site for the full gamut of musical tastes.

Perfume

Senteurs D'Ailleurs (✉ Av. Louise 100, ☎ 02/511–6969) is the Rolls-Royce of perfume shops, with a diverse selection of perfumes, bath products, and candles in scents ranging from floral to thyme and honey from specialized producers.

Toys

Serneels (✉ Av. Louise 69, ☎ 02/538–3066) is a paradise of toys that is as much fun for adults as for children, although the prices tend to be stratospheric. The stuffed animals, many of them virtually life-size and of superb quality, are the stars of the store. But exquisite wooden rocking horses, wooden soldiers, dolls, and model cars, boats, trains, and airplanes add to a setting that's hard to resist.

Women's Clothes

Chine (✉ R. Van Arteveld 2, ☎ 02/503–1499), as the name implies, sells clothes from China, mainly simple silks in softly feminine styles.

Kaat Tilley (✉ Galerie du Roi 4, ☎ 02/514–0763) is a Flemish designer selling fanciful designs in a fairy-like setting. Contemporary jewelry of her own design is also for sale. Flemish designer Edouard Vermeulen, who created the elegantly contemporary wedding gown worn by Belgium's Princess Mathilde at her wedding in 1999 to Crown Prince Philippe, is the genius behind **Natan** (✉ Av. Louise 158, ☎ 02/647–1001). His clothes feature the minimalist, high-fashion look favored by Flemish designers. Natan also has a second location at Rue du Namur 78, as well as a men's shop on Rue Antoine Dansaert. Designer **Nina Meert** (✉ R. St. Boniface 1, ☎ 02/514–2263) comes from a family of painters and opened her house of couture in 1979 in Brussels and Paris. She has dressed the likes of actresses Isabelle Adjani and Meryl Streep and Belgium's Queen Paola.

SIDE TRIPS FROM BRUSSELS

Waterloo

19 km (12 mi) south of Brussels. Waterloo, like Stalingrad or Hiroshima, changed the course of history. There are numerous Waterloos scattered across the world, but this site 19 km (11 mi) south of Brussels is the original. As Brussels spreads south, Waterloo appears to be a prosperous suburb, complete with large, whitewashed villas and smart boutiques, rather than a separate town. Home to two American international schools, it has a cosmopolitan feel to it. More than one fifth of the population is foreign, much of it American, French, and Canadian.

Sights to See

The Duke of Wellington spent the night of June 17, 1815, at an inn in Waterloo, where he established his headquarters. When he slept here again the following night, Napoléon had been defeated. The inn in the center of this pleasant, small town is now the **Musée Wellington** (Wellington Museum). It presents the events of the 100 days leading up to the Battle of Waterloo, maps and models of the battle itself, and military and Wellington memorabilia in well laid-out displays. ✉ *Chaussée de Bruxelles 147,* ☎ *02/354–7806.* 🎫 *BF100/€2.50.* ⊙ *Apr.–Oct., daily 9:30–6:30; Nov.–Mar., daily 10:30–5.*

The actual **Champ de Bataille** (battlefield) is just south of Waterloo (signposted "Butte de Lion"). This is where Wellington's troops received the onslaught of Napoléon's army. A crucial role in the battle was played by some of the ancient, fortified farms, of which there are many in this area. The farm of Hogoumont was fought over all day; 6,000 men, out of total casualties of 48,000, were killed here. Later in the day, fierce fighting raged around the farms of La Sainte Haye and Papelotte. In the afternoon, the French cavalry attacked, in the mistaken belief that the British line was giving way. Napoléon's final attempt was to send in the armored cavalry of the Imperial Guard, but at the same time the Prussian army under Blücher arrived to engage the French from the east, and it was all over. The battlefield is best surveyed from the top of the **Butte de Lion**, a pyramid 226 steps high and crowned by a 28-ton lion, which was erected by the Dutch 10 years later.

The visitor facilities at the battlefield were below par for many years, and some of the tackiness remains, including some overpriced restaurants and a seedy wax museum. The smart **visitor center** is an improvement, offering an audiovisual presentation of the battle, followed by a mood-setting film of the fighting seen through the eyes of children. You can buy souvenirs here, too—from tin soldiers and T-shirts to soft toy lions and model cannons. There are also plenty of books, some highly specialized, about the battle and the men who led the fighting. The adjacent **Battle Panorama Museum,** first unveiled in 1912, contains a vast, circular painting of the charge of the French cavalry, executed with amazing perspective and realism. ✉ *Rte. du Lion 252–254,* ☎ *02/385–1912.* 🎫 *BF300/€7.40, including Butte du Lion and Panorama, BF40 just for Butte du Lion.* ⏲ *Apr.–Sept., daily 9:30–6:30; Oct., daily 9:30–5:30; Nov.–Feb., daily 10:30–4; Mar., daily 10–5.*

From the prevalence of souvenirs and images of Napoléon, you might think that the battle was won by the French. In fact, there were Belgian soldiers fighting on both sides. Napoléon's headquarters during his last days as emperor were in what is now the small **Musée du Caillou** in Genappe, south of the battlefield. It contains the room where he spent the night before the battle, his personal effects, and objects found in the field. ✉ *Chaussée de Bruxelles 66,* ☎ *02/384–2424.* 🎫 *BF60/€1.50.* ⏲ *Apr.–Sept., daily 10:30–6:30; Nov.–Mar., daily 1–5.*

Dining and Lodging

$$$ ✕ **La Maison du Seigneur.** In a peaceful, whitewashed farmhouse with a spacious terrace, Ghislaine de Becker and his son Pilou offer elegant, classical French cuisine. The menu, which changes with the seasons, includes sole with shrimp sauce and veal cooked in Porto and roast cherries. ✉ *Chaussée de Tervuren 389,* ☎ *02/354–0750. AE, DC, MC, V. Closed Mon.–Tues., Feb., and 2nd ½ of Aug.*

$$ ★ ✕ **L'Auberge d'Ohain.** This country inn northeast of Waterloo has an elegant dining room decorated in shades of peach and champagne, and a kitchen capable of great things: tagliatelle with langoustine and salmon, roast pigeon, and langoustine ravioli. The four-course *menu découverte* (tasting menu) is an excellent value. ✉ *Chaussée de Louvain 709,* ☎ *02/653–6497. AE, DC, MC, V. Closed Sun.–Mon. and 2nd ½ of July.*

$ ✕ **L'Amusoir.** Popular with resident Americans, this is an unpretentious steak house in an old white-walled building in the center of town. It serves excellent filet mignon, prepared with a variety of sauces, and hearty Belgian traditional dishes. ✉ *Chaussée de Bruxelles 121,* ☎ *02/353–0336. AE.*

$$ ✕🏨 **Le 1815.** This small hotel is actually on the battlefield. Each room is named for one of the participating generals and decorated with his portrait. The style is art deco, but with details evocative of the period of the battle, and there is even a miniature golf course modeled after the battle. The restaurant is much better than those clustered at the foot of the Butte du Lion. ✉ *Rte. du Lion 367, B1410,* ☎ *02/387–0060,* FAX *02/387–1292. 14 rooms. Restaurant, bar, miniature golf. AE, DC, MC, V.*

Gaasbeek

15 km (9 mi) west of Brussels.

In Gaasbeek you are in Bruegel country, almost as if you had stepped inside one of his paintings of village life. The area is called Pajottenland, and you may be familiar with the landscape from Bruegel's works, many of which were painted here. From the terrace of the **Gaasbeek Château** you have a panoramic view of this landscape. The rulers of Gaasbeek once lorded it over Brussels, and the townspeople took terrible revenge and razed the castle. Restored in the 19th century, it contains outstanding 15th- and 16th-century tapestries. Rubens's will is among the documents in the castle archives. The surrounding park is popular with picnickers. ✉ *Kasteelstraat 40,* ☎ *02/532–4372.*

BF150/€3.70. Apr.–June and Sept.–Oct., Tues.–Thurs. and weekends 10–5; July–Aug., Sat.–Thurs. 10–5.

En Route Beersel is just off the motorway as you head south from Brussels. It is the site of a stark, moat-surrounded, 13th-century fort, the **Kastel van Beersel,** which was part of Brussels's defenses. The interiors are empty except for one room: a well-equipped torture chamber. ✉ *Lotsestraat 65,* ☎ *02/331–0024. BF100/€2.50. Nov. 2–Apr. and July–Aug., Tues.–Thurs. and weekends 10–5.*

BRUSSELS A TO Z

Arriving and Departing

By Bus

Eurolines offers up to three daily express bus services from Amsterdam, Berlin, Frankfurt, Paris, and London. The Eurolines Coach Station is located at CCN Gare du Nord (✉ R. du Progrès 80, ☎ 02/203–0707).

From London, the **City Sprint** bus connects with the Dover–Calais Hovercraft, and the bus then takes you on to Brussels. For reservations and times, call Hoverspeed (☎ 01304/240241).

To **Waterloo,** Bus W from Brussels (Place Rouppe) runs at half-hour intervals.

By Car

Belgium is covered by an extensive network of four-lane highways. Brussels is 204 km (122 mi) from Amsterdam on E19; 222 km (138 mi) from Düsseldorf on E40; 219 km (133 mi) from Luxembourg City on E411; and 308 km (185 mi) from Paris.

If you piggyback on Le Shuttle through the Channel Tunnel, the distance is 213 km (128 mi) from Calais to Brussels; the route from Calais via Oostende is the fastest, even though on the Belgian side the highway stops a few kilometers short of the border. If you take the ferry to Oostende, the distance is 115 km (69 mi) to Brussels on the six-lane E40.

Brussels is surrounded by a beltway, marked RING. Exits to the city are marked CENTER. Among several large underground parking facilities, the one close to the Grand'Place is particularly convenient if you're staying in a downtown hotel.

By Plane

All flights arrive at and depart from **Zaventem** (☎ 02/753–2111), Brussels's National Airport. **American** (☎ 02/548–2122), **Delta** (☎ 02/730–8200), **Sabena** (☎ 02/723–2323), **United** (☎ 02/713–3600), and **City Bird** (☎ 02/752–5252) fly into Brussels from the United States. **Sabena, British Midland** (☎ 02/771–7766), and **British Airways** (☎ 02/548–2122) fly to Brussels from London's Heathrow Airport; **Air UK** from Stansted; and **British Airways** from Gatwick. Several regional centers in the United Kingdom also have direct flights to Brussels, as do all capitals in Europe and a growing number of secondary cities. The no-frills airline **Virgin Express** (☎ 02/752–0505) offers scheduled flights between London and Brussels.

BETWEEN THE AIRPORT AND DOWNTOWN

Courtesy buses serve airport hotels and a few downtown hotels: inquire when making reservations. **Express trains** leave the airport for the Gare du Nord and Gare Centrale stations every 20 minutes (one train an hour continues to the Gare du Midi). The trip takes 20 minutes and costs BF140/€3.45 one way in first class, BF90/€2.25 second class. The trains operate 6 AM to midnight. **Taxis** are plentiful. A taxi to the city center takes about half an hour and costs about BF1,200/€30. You can save 25% on the fare by buying a voucher for the return trip if you use the **Autolux** (☎ 02/411–1221) taxi company. Beware freelance taxi drivers who hawk their services in the arrival hall.

By Train

Eurostar (☎ 0900/10–177) trains from London (Waterloo) use the Channel Tunnel to cut travel time to Brussels (Gare du Midi) to 2 hours, 40 minutes. Trains stop at Ashford (Kent) and Lille (France). At press time there were 11 daily services, and a first-class, one-way ticket cost BF9,500/€235; second-class tickets cost BF6,500/€160 (weekdays) or BF4,250/€105 (weekends). Promotional fares are available but must be booked seven days in advance.

Brussels is linked with Paris, Amsterdam, and Liège by **Thalys** (☎ 0800/95–777) high-speed trains. The TGV links in France and Belgium mean you can go from Brussels to Paris in a stunning 85 minutes. In Holland, until new tracks have been laid (scheduled for 2005), they provide a slower but very comfortable ride of just over 3 hours.

Conventional train services from London connect with the Ramsgate–Oostende ferry, hovercraft, or catamaran, and from Oostende the train takes you to Brussels. The whole journey, using hovercraft or catamaran, takes about 6½ hours; by ferry, about 9 hours. For more information, contact **Connex South-Eastern** (☎ 870/603–0405) or the **British Tourist Authority** (✉ Av. Louise 306, B1050 Brussels, ☎ 02/646–3510). **Belgian National Railways** (SNCB, ☎ 02/555–2525) is the national rail line.

There is frequent commuter train service to **Waterloo.**

Getting Around

By Metro, Tram, and Bus

The metro, trams, and buses operate as part of the same system. All three are clean and efficient, and a single ticket, which can be used on all three, costs BF50/€1.25. The best buy is a 10-trip ticket, which costs BF350/€8.70, or a one-day card costing BF140/€3.45. You need to stamp your ticket in the appropriate machine on the bus or tram; in the metro, your card is stamped as you pass through the automatic barrier. You can purchase these tickets in any metro station or at newsstands. Single tickets can be purchased on the bus or on the tram.

Detailed maps of the Brussels public transportation network are available in most metro stations and at the **Tourist Information Brussels** in the Grand'Place (☎ 02/513–8940). You get a map free with a Tourist Passport (also available at the tourist office), which, for BF300/€7.40, allows you a one-day transport card and reductions at museums.

By Taxi

Call **Taxis Verts** (☎ 02/349–4949) or **Taxis Oranges** (☎ 02/349–4343). You can also catch one at cab stands around town. Distances are not great, and a cab ride costs between BF250/€6.20 and BF500/€12.40. Tips are included in the fare.

Contacts and Resources

Car Rentals

Avis (☎ 02/730–6211). **Budget** (☎ 02/646–5130). **Europcar** (☎ 02/348–9212). **Hertz** (☎ 02/513–2886).

Embassies

U.S. (✉ Bd. du Régent 27, ☎ 02/508–2111). **Canadian** (✉ Av. de Tervuren 2, ☎ 02/741–0611). **British** (✉ R. d'Arlon 85, ☎ 02/287–6211).

Australian (✉ R. Guimard 6, ☎ 02/286–0500). **Irish** (✉ R. Froissart 89, ☎ 02/230–5337). **New Zealand** (✉ Bd. du Régent 47, ☎ 02/512–1040).

Emergencies

Police (☎ 101). **Accident and Ambulance** (☎ 100). **Doctor** (☎ 02/479–1818). **Dentist** (☎ 02/426–1026). One **pharmacy** in each district stays open 24 hours; the roster is posted in all pharmacy windows. In an emergency call ☎ 02/479–1818.

Guided Tours

ARAU (✉ Bd. Adolphe Max 55, ☎ 02/219–3345) organizes thematic city bus and walking tours from March through November, including "Brussels 1900: Art Nouveau" and "Brussels 1930: Art Deco." Tours include visits to some building interiors that are otherwise not open to the public. The cost is BF600/€14.80 for a half-day coach tour and BF300/€7.40 for a half-day walking tour. The original tours run by **Chatterbus** (✉ R. des Thuyas 12, ☎ 02/673–1835; early June–Sept.) either visit the main sights on foot or by minibus (BF600/€14.80), or follow a walking route that includes a visit to a bistro (BF250/€6.20). **De Boeck Sightseeing** (✉ R. de la Colline 8, Grand'Place, ☎ 02/513–7744) operates city tours (BF800/€19.80) with multilingual cassette commentary; they also visit Antwerp, the Ardennes, Brugge, Gent, Ieper, and Waterloo. Passengers are picked up at major hotels or at the tourist office in the town hall. **Pro Velo** (✉ R. de Londres 15, ☎ 02/502–7355) takes visitors on themed cycling tours in and around Brussels. Tours, on themes including "The Heart of Brussels Through the Centuries" and "Comic Strips and Cafès," are available from April through August. Tours in English operate in July and August. The cost is BF300/€7.40, plus BF200/€4.95 for bike rental. Group tours can also be arranged throughout the year at a cost of BF5,000/€124 for up to 20 people for a half-day tour, plus BF200/€4.95 per person for bike rental. Bikes may also be rented for independent use at prices ranging from BF100/€2.50 for one hour to BF2,000/€49.50 for a full week.

Qualified guides are available for individual tours from the **Tourist Information Brussels** (TIB; ☎ 02/513–8940) in the town hall. Three hours costs BF3,200/€79.50, and up to 25 people can share the same guide for a walking tour and up to 50 people for a bus tour.

In Waterloo expert guides, **Les Guides 1815** (✉ Rte. du Lion 250, ☎ 02/385–0625), can be hired to take you around the battlefield for one hour (BF1,400/€34.50) and three hours (BF2,200/€54.50); group tours in English (BF100/€2.50 per person) are weekends at 4, July through August.

Travel Agencies

American Express (✉ Houtweg 24, ☎ 02/245–2250). **Carlson/Wagonlit Travel** (✉ Bd. Clovis, ☎ 02/287–8811).

Visitor Information

Tourist Information Brussels (TIB; ✉ Hôtel de Ville/Grand' Place, ☎ 02/513–8940). **Waterloo Office de Tourisme** (tourist office; ✉ Chaussée de Bruxelles 149, ☎ 02/354–9910).

3 FLANDERS: GENT, BRUGGE, AND THE NORTH SEA COAST

Fairy-tale towns and trenches, belfries and béguinages, winkels and canals—the haunting atmosphere of Flanders beckons. Sleepy Brugge, perhaps the most picturesque town in Europe, is quietly awakening to a new influx of tourists. Thriving Gent contrasts high-tech storefronts with gabled facades and gilded spires. Leafy, lowland villages and sandy North Sea resorts are home to the Fleming, whose ancestors reclaimed their land from the marshes, wove their way to wealth, and endured centuries of battles

By Lea Lane

FLANDERS is something of a mystery. Ask locals to define this region—which covers the northwest corner of Belgium—and you will almost always start a heated argument. Geographically, Flanders is nestled between France to the south and the Netherlands and the North Sea above; politically, however, it's the section of Belgium that lies north and west of Brussels. Many of those who live in the region contend that the capital is Flemish as well, which is historically correct, although it's a point of diplomatic contention. Still, no one can dispute that the two provinces west of Antwerp and Brussels bear the names East and West Flanders.

The Belgae, a Celtic tribe for which Belgium was named, originally occupied this area until they were conquered in 57 BC by Julius Caesar. The Franks replaced the Roman rulers around the 5th century AD, when King Clovis fused the tribes in a mass conversion to Christianity in AD 498. Charlemagne, crowned Holy Roman Emperor in 768, brought Flanders under one political realm. A half-century later, his grandsons divided their kingdom of Francia into three sections: France, Germany, and central Lotharingia, the latter of which honored the powerless emperor Lothair.

Brugge and Gent meanwhile were rising to prominence as cloth trading centers. Fleming textiles, which first gained popularity in the Roman era, were now supplemented by the finest wool from England, Scotland, and Ireland. Weaving guilds were organized as early as AD 1200 in Gent, and the work force rapidly grew as the demand for cloth echoed from all corners of the continent. The guilds were in fact the earliest form of industrialization in Flanders—although they primed the population for communal strife, pitting the interests of the common weavers against those of the patrician traders. Still, merchants and weavers alike grew rich on the profits from the intricate textiles, which provided England with a motive for keeping the French out of Flanders.

In the 11th century, when Flanders was divvied up between France and Britain, the kingdom fell into the hands of French vassals. The Flemish, however, preferred to stay beneath England's wing, and the cultures collided in many a battle over the next 300 years. In 1338, Gent merchant Jan Van Artevelde coaxed the Flemings to side with Britain's King Edward III in a war with France over the wool supply. Viking armies were an added threat to the region, so much so that Baldwin of the Iron Arm, the first Count of Flanders, constructed great forts at Brugge and Gent. And the cities held their own through the centuries, although each yielded to a different fortune. Brugge, once a seaside town, lost its port to erosion and settled into a quiet decline. Gent, however, embraced the industrial revolution and emerged as an important textile center.

The southern cities of Kortrijk and Ieper also have a long, battle-scarred history stemming from Roman times. In the Hundred Years' War, Flemish pikemen unhorsed French cavalry at the Battle of the Golden Spurs in July 1302. In the War of the Spanish Succession, which ran from 1700 to 1713, the Duke of Marlborough confronted Louis XIV on Flemish soil. In World War I, no region suffered more; the unspeakable No-Man's-Land stretched across Flanders Fields. Although Brugge was spared in the latter war, Ieper, only 30 miles away, was destroyed, as were many small villages. Fortunately, during World War II the Germans advanced too swiftly to wreak much physical damage on the freshly scarred land. Today, the North Sea coast is still irresistible to invaders—a more peaceful kind. Tourists come for the region's fresh air, quiet beaches, and quaint, colorful villages.

Pleasures and Pastimes

Art and Architecture

Glorious buildings and art are highlights of a visit to Flanders. Brugge and Gent, the region's textile and artistic centers, are the major places to observe the magnificent flowering of creativity in the late Middle Ages. In the 15th century artists were inspired to create some of the world's greatest treasures, including Hans Memling's St. Ursula Shrine and Jan van Eyck's *Adoration of the Mystic Lamb* altarpiece. Van Eyck, in fact, has been widely credited with inventing oil painting.

Stained glass and religious art including diptychs, triptychs, and polytychs (altarpieces with two or more painted panels) are numerous in this region. Textile merchants showed off their riches by building magnificent houses and by having their portraits painted by famous artists. Similar building materials and local civic spirit add a homogeneous quality to Brugge and Gent, with Kortrijk, Ieper, and the lowland villages following a similar style. All boast chunky churches and town halls, towering belfries, ornate guildhalls, and splendid burgher's homes, many built of sturdy local brick. The majority of buildings destroyed during the First and Second World Wars were rebuilt in their original style; even today, the Flemings build homes that would seem perfectly in place during medieval times.

Beguinages and Belfries

Composer Cole Porter may have popularized the *beguine* (a vigorous dance of Martinique and St. Lucia) in the splendor of the tropics, but here the word refers to a spiritual-minded woman who resides in a peaceful, conventlike garden complex called a beguinage. Today, those who live in the dozen or so beguinages found in the region are most often widows and orphaned daughters. Some also became homes for low-income families. Beguinages were founded during the Crusades by a priest named Lambert le Begue and were throughout Europe until the Reformation. The best beguinages are in Flanders, including in Gent and Brugge—and, increasingly, many are occupied by lady artisans rather than beguines.

Flanders also has numerous belfries, many of which are centrally located civic towers with carillons. The imposing towers once functioned as brick storehouses where medieval merchants protected their goods and kept their records. They were also used as lookout towers to watch for enemy attacks. In current times, citizens still use them as meeting places, and many are landmark tourist sites. Brugge, Gent, Ieper, and many smaller villages have outstanding old belfries, usually situated on large squares.

Biking

Flatter-than-a-Belgian-waffle topography and numerous wooded and dike-lined paths make Flanders a great region for cycling. Bikes can be hired at many hotels, railway stations, and shops. Guided mountain bike tours use back roads to explore countryside that runs through canals, farms, beaches, and battlefields. The tourist boards in Gent and Brugge have special cycling brochures, as well as maps of the best city and rural routes in the region.

Dining

A popular saying goes that Flanders food combines the quality of France with the quantity of Germany (although contrarians may argue vice-versa). The real deal, however, is that local produce is served fresh and presented simply—you won't find painted plates or tiny veggies. Naturally, this is seafood country, with fresh fish shipped in daily to

Brugge; the coastal towns serve authentic North Sea delicacies at terrace restaurants whipped by sand and salt air. Even in landlocked Gent, some 50 km (30 mi) from the coast, locals snack on whelks and *winkles* (sea snails) as if they were popcorn. Flemings are mad about *mosselen* (mussels)—try them steamed, curried, or bathed in a white-wine broth accented with celery, onions, and parsley. Main courses are inevitably accompanied by a mountain of *frites* (french fries), fried twice, making them especially crisp and delicious. For death by fries, buy them piping hot and salty from a stall, as the Belgians do, and dip them in the big dollop of accompanying mayo.

Paling (eels) are one of the region's specialties. The flesh is firm, fatty, and sweet, and served in long cross-sections with a removable backbone. They are served "in green," stewed in a heady mix of sorrel, tarragon, sage, mint, and parsley. Sole and turbot are also popular main courses, served broiled, poached with a light mousseline sauce, or grilled with a rich béarnaise or mustard sauce. Herring is eaten *maatjes* (raw) in the spring. To sound like a local, try repeating these tongue-twisters when you order: *Oostduinkerkse paardevissersoep* (fish soup) and *Dronken rog op Nieuwpoortse wijze* (ray).

When the Flemish aren't eating their fish straight or in a blanket of golden sauce, they consume it in the region's most famous dish, *waterzoi* (a thick broth rich with cream and vegetables). The citizens of Gent have a famous chicken version, as well as *Gentse hutsepot* (a casserole with carrots, onions, potatoes, and meat). For a hearty dish, look for *karbonaden* (beef or pork stew with onions, braised in beer). Horse meat, with its sweet flavor and beefy texture, is considered a delicacy.

For vegetable delights, it's worth arranging your visit to Flanders in springtime. Look for tender, white asparagus, served either in mousseline sauce or with a garnish of chopped hard-boiled egg and melted butter. These pale stalks are sweeter than the familiar green ones and are called "white gold" because the Flemings snap them up as fast as they arrive during their short season. Seek out the rare, expensive *jets de houblon* (delicate shoots of the hops plant) abundant in March and April.

A cheese course is often served before—or in place of—dessert, and there are hundreds of delicious local choices, many runny and pungent. Chocolate and whipped cream are favorite dessert ingredients, and homemade ice cream is enjoyed in warm months. Local pastries include *Gentse mokken* (hard sugar cookies), *lierse vlaaikens* (plum tarts), and *speculaas* (ginger cookies), all of which are often accompanied by coffee. Warm pancakes and Belgian *gaufres* (waffles) topped with fruit or syrup are available everywhere from sidewalk stalls to fancy restaurants. The famous crisp waffles, which have a vanilla flavor, are formed in cast-iron molds with pre-sweetened dough. Dense, rich chocolate candies are carefully crafted for special occasions. Handmade pralines, made with fresh cream, are sold loose in bags or boxes.

Beer—the drink of choice in Flanders—is blended, aged, bottled, and corked like wine. You'll find hundreds of choices, from bitter to sweet, light to strong, and blonde triple to dark double. If you're stuck, try the burgundy-hued Rodenbach, or the fruit-flavored Kriek beers. Amazingly, each type of beer has its own special glass and rules for pouring. A favored lowland liquor is juniper-tinged *geneva* (witteke), which has around 300 distinctive flavorings and is served straight, strong, and fast in tiny glasses.

When you dine out, it's best to make reservations, especially on weekends and holidays. Otherwise, your best strategy for getting a table is to come when the restaurant opens or after the main rush. Note that many restaurants serve meals outdoors, even in winter. A 16% service charge and a 19% VAT are usually included in the tab, so you don't need to leave a tip unless you receive exceptional service.

CATEGORY	COST*
$$$$	over BF3,000/€75
$$$	BF2,000–BF3,000/€50–€75
$$	BF1,000–BF2,000/€25–€50
$	under BF1,000/€25

**per person for a three-course meal, including service, taxes, but not beverages*

Festivals

Year-round dances, concerts, parades, celebrations, markets, fairs, and art exhibits loosen up even the most reserved Flemings. The most famous annual celebration is the Festival of Flanders, a variety of musical events that take place in major cities from April to October. In winter, *Kertsmarkten* (traditional Christmas markets) are held throughout the region. The third week of June brings *Dag van Beiaard* (Day of the Carillon), a celebration of bells and belfries, when chimes echo from city to city. The local tourist boards have calendars of other festive events; check while planning your visit.

Lodging

Accommodations range from luxury city-center hotels to cozy, country bed-and-breakfasts. Brugge is a popular weekend escape, as romantic suites and secluded hideaways abound. You'll find charming, Old Flemish accents at most hotels in the "City of Swans"; many buildings are actually historic landmarks rebuilt in their original styles. Bustling Gent is a modern business town during the week; accommodations here are more sleek and modern. The nearby country houses are what you want for a quiet escape from the city—including the oldest hotel in the world, the St. Jurishof hotel in Gent, said to have been in business since the 13th century.

Many small, quirky, moderately priced hotels are set in historic buildings throughout Flanders. Rates at such places usually include a hearty Belgian breakfast: bread, cereal, cold cuts, cheese, yogurt, eggs, and fruit. For accommodations with meal plans, make arrangements through the Brugge and Gent tourist offices. Although city hotels target weekend and short-term guests, coastal hotels usually offer better prices for longer visits. Many have half-board meal plans; in summer, be sure to book coastal accommodations and hotel meals well in advance. Tax and service are included in the rates.

CATEGORY	COST*
$$$$	over BF7,500/€185
$$$	BF5,500–BF7,500/€135–€185
$$	BF2,500–BF5,500/€60–€135
$	under BF2,500/€60

**for two persons sharing double room, including service and tax*

Nightlife

Sleepy Flemish villages are not exactly party scenes, but coastal towns offer late-night cafés and jazz clubs. A stroll amid the illuminated buildings of Brugge and Gent is a memorable part of the region's nightlife. Enter one of the crowded clubs, cafés, or bars, though, and you'll find the true motto of these two cities: party long, and party hard. Beer is a crucial element of the social scene; make sure to reserve a taxi or walk with others if you've sampled too much.

Shopping

Shops line the streets in tourist areas, and though many display tacky tourist kitsch you'll also find delightful regional crafts. Look for artful displays of fashion items, delicate embroideries, and exquisite candies. Chocolates and lace are traditional items from Flanders, but auctions and open-air markets also offer arts and crafts, antiques, and secondhand bargains. Most shops are open 9–6 Monday to Saturday; markets are usually held on weekend mornings. To reclaim your VAT tax, look for stores that display a "Tax Free for Tourists" logo.

Walks

Flanders beckons walkers with level canal and beach paths, curving lanes that wind between gabled medieval buildings, and country byways that pass forest, farms, and former battlefields. You can feel secure striking out on your own, as petty crime is minimal and Flemings speak enough English to point you in the right direction. One of the great joys of a trip here is strolling in Brugge or Gent in the cool, early morning before the crowds amass, or late in the evening when lighted buildings shimmer like gold along the narrow waterways, and the moon shines silver on cobbled lanes.

Water Sports

With its prevailing breeze and wide, sandy beaches, the Belgian coast, offers splendid opportunities for water sports. Sailing, swimming, windsurfing, and *yachting* (skimming along the beach aboard a wheeled platform equipped with a sail) are all popular options. Even horseback riding is a semi-aquatic sport here, with horses splashing along the water's edge.

Exploring Flanders

The cold North Sea has influenced the wealth and politics of Flanders as well as the region's geography, linking its ports, protecting its people, and providing numerous natural resources. Along the northwest coast, simple settlements are strung between summer resorts and seaside business centers. To the southwest, villages dominated by castles, beguinages, and charming, guild-house-edged market squares remain dependent on canals, agriculture, and age-old artisan skills. However, the battle-scarred relics of the region's wars still remain in the renovated building facades; World War I trenches that cut across from the coast near Nieuwpoort, Diksmuide, and Iper; and the cemeteries that lie in their wake.

Flat land, high-speed trains, narrow canals, and well-marked roads make it easy to get around the leafy lowlands. Brugge and Gent are only 15 minutes apart by rail, and you can even bike between these twin jewels of Flanders. The rest of this compact region is easily accessible as well, with genuine pleasures to be discovered in even the smallest village.

Great Itineraries

IF YOU HAVE 2 DAYS

Get thee to **Brugge** ⑭–㉜ as early as possible on the first day. Must-see spots on the tour list include the Begijnhof near Minnewater, as well as the great buildings around Burg and Markt squares. Don't miss the museums, including the Groeninge, the Memling, and Michelangelo's sculpture in The Church of Our Lady. You might take an afternoon canal ride—or, after dinner, when crowds have thinned, you can wander alongside the water. The second day, head for **Gent** ①–⑪, beginning your tour with a classic view from St. Michael's bridge. Divide the rest of your day between the guild houses of the Graslei district, The Castle of the Counts, and St. Bavo's Cathedral. After a dinner in the lively Patershol area and a walk around the illuminated historic district, catch a late train back to Brugge.

IF YOU HAVE 5 DAYS

Follow the previous itinerary but spend two nights in **Brugge** ⑭–㉜, You could use the second day to explore more of the city's sights and museums, to take a side trip to Damme and other nearby villages, or to explore the battlefields around Ieper. Spend the third and fourth nights in **Gent** ①–⑪, where you'll have extra time to visit the city's attractions and museums or to discover nearby castle towns such as Laarne. Take the last day to explore the rural countryside of western Flanders: Poperinge, Kortrijk, Tyne Cot, and other villages with lovely squares and serene beguinages. Alternately, you could head to one of the North Sea coastal towns, stretching from De Panne to Het Zwin, for sun (sometimes), fun, and fresh seafood.

IF YOU HAVE 7 DAYS

A week is enough for an excellent overview of this crossroads of Europe. Spend the first three nights in **Brugge** ⑭–㉜, taking the days to explore the city and surrounding villages; spend the next two nights in **Gent** ①–⑪, taking the days to savor outstanding Flemish art, architecture, and history; and spend the last night in a rural village or at the coast. When in the towns, make sure to reserve a little time to shop for antiques, lace, and chocolates. You could take your day trips by bicycle, an excellent way to enjoy the region's quiet charms up close.

Numbers in the text correspond to numbers in the margin and on the Gent, Brugge, and the North Sea Coast and the Gent and Brugge maps.

When to Tour Flanders

April to October brings the best weather—and the most tourists—to Flanders. Spring is sunniest, but summer can also be pleasant. Always be prepared for humid heat, driving rain, and cool, cloudy days. Temperatures hover close to freezing in January and February, but you'll have the sights to yourself—note, however, that some restaurants along the coast close during winter. Early spring and late fall are good times to tour Brugge and Gent; the weather is still mild and there are fewer tourists. Remember that museums in Brugge and Oostende are closed Tuesday; museums are closed Monday in the rest of the country.

GENT: MAJESTIC GATEWAY TO FLANDERS

55 km (33 mi) northwest of Brussels, 60 km (36 mi) southwest of Antwerp on E17.

In the 16th century, only Paris was a greater European power than Gent, so it isn't surprising that this governmental seat of East Flanders has more listed monuments than any other Belgian city. Canals, gables, castles, beguinages, medieval lanes, art masterpieces, and settings which recall Breughel paintings beautifully mix with the facades and streetside fashions of the new millennium.

Gent (also called Ghent and Gand) was built around two 7th-century abbeys—Sint-Pieter (St. Peter) and Sint-Baafs (St. Bavo)—and the 9th-century castle of Gravensteen, which dominates the river Leie. Although set far from the coast, the settlement was still open to foreign marauders, such as Viking raiders who maneuvered canoes along the shallow inland rivers to raid the town's treasures. Baldwin of the Iron Arm, the region's first ruler, built a castle to protect his burgeoning kingdom; thus, Gent became the seat of the counts of Flanders. In the 13th century, Gent and Brugge were joined by canal, and 100 years later Gent had attracted more than 5,000 workers in the textile center.

Wealthy burghers were loyal to the counts of Flanders in the early Middle Ages and owed allegiance to the kings of France. However, the weavers were dependent on wool shipments from England, France's enemy in the Hundred Years' War. In 1302, at the crux of the conflict between nations, the weavers took up arms against the French and defeated them in a battle that, to this day, is vividly recalled by Flemish patriots.

In 1448, the people of Gent refused to pay a salt tax imposed by Philip the Good, Duke of Burgundy. For five years their militia stood firm against Philip's troops, and when they were finally overwhelmed, 16,000 townspeople perished. Gent continued to rebel, again and again, against perceived injustices. The emperor himself, Charles V, who was born in Gent, was not immune to their wrath. He responded by razing the St. Bavo Abbey and suppressing the rights of Gent's residents. Religious fervor was added to this volatile mixture when the Calvinist iconoclasts proclaimed the city a republic in 1577, only to be overthrown by Spanish forces seven years later. In the 18th century, French armies marched on Gent on four different occasions. This did little to dampen the conflict between French and Flemish speakers in the city.

Gent was rescued from economic oblivion by a daring young merchant named Lieven Bauwens, who, in 1800, smuggled a spinning jenny out of Britain in a reversal of what had happened hundreds of years earlier, when Flemish weavers emigrated to England. Bauwens's exploit provided the foundation for a cotton textile industry that employed 160,000 workers a century later.

To facilitate textile exports, in 1822 a new canal was built to link Gent's inland port with the North Sea at Terneuzen, and Gent again became a major trade center. Today the canal is still vital to modern industrial development, including the automobile assembly plant that uses the canal to transport huge car carriers. Thus, while the city of Brugge emerged as a tourist center renowned for its cultural sights, Gent transformed its historic center into a commercial area of almost 400,000 residents. Alas, the Leie had been dubbed the Golden River, no longer because of the golden flax processed near its shores, but rather for the color of its chemical pollutants. Things are improving, though: cleanup is ongoing and successful, the historic center is floodlighted, tourism is booming, and Gent today is a proud amalgam of Belgium's past and present.

Exploring Gent

A Good Walk

This is a circle walk, crisscrossing the river for maximum views. Start at **Sint-Michielsbrug** ①, taking in the view of the city's three spires, cross to the east side of the River Leie, on the Kornelei. Stop at the Korenmarkt ②, where you'll find **Sint-Niklaaskerk** ② and go north to the **Graslei** ③, where you can admire the historic buildings. Keep going until you reach Hooiaard, then follow the river along the Vleeshuistragel to the Groenten Markt, then cross into St. Veerleplein and walk up to the medieval **Gravensteen** ④. Take a side trip into J. Breydalstraat and visit the **Museum voor Sierkunst and Vormgeving and Huis der Gekroonde Hoofden** ⑥. From here, head back to Kleine Vismarkt, then turn left onto the narrow Kraanlei street, from where you can step into the **Museum voor Volkskunde** ⑦ and explore the Patershol district. Cross the river via Zuivelbrugstraat, stroll across the Vrijdagmarkt onto Kammerstraat, then turn right down Belfortstraat. Passing the **Stadhuis** ⑧ on your right, head onto the Botermarkt and admire the view from the **Belfort** ⑨, then

Gent, Brugge, and the North Sea Coast

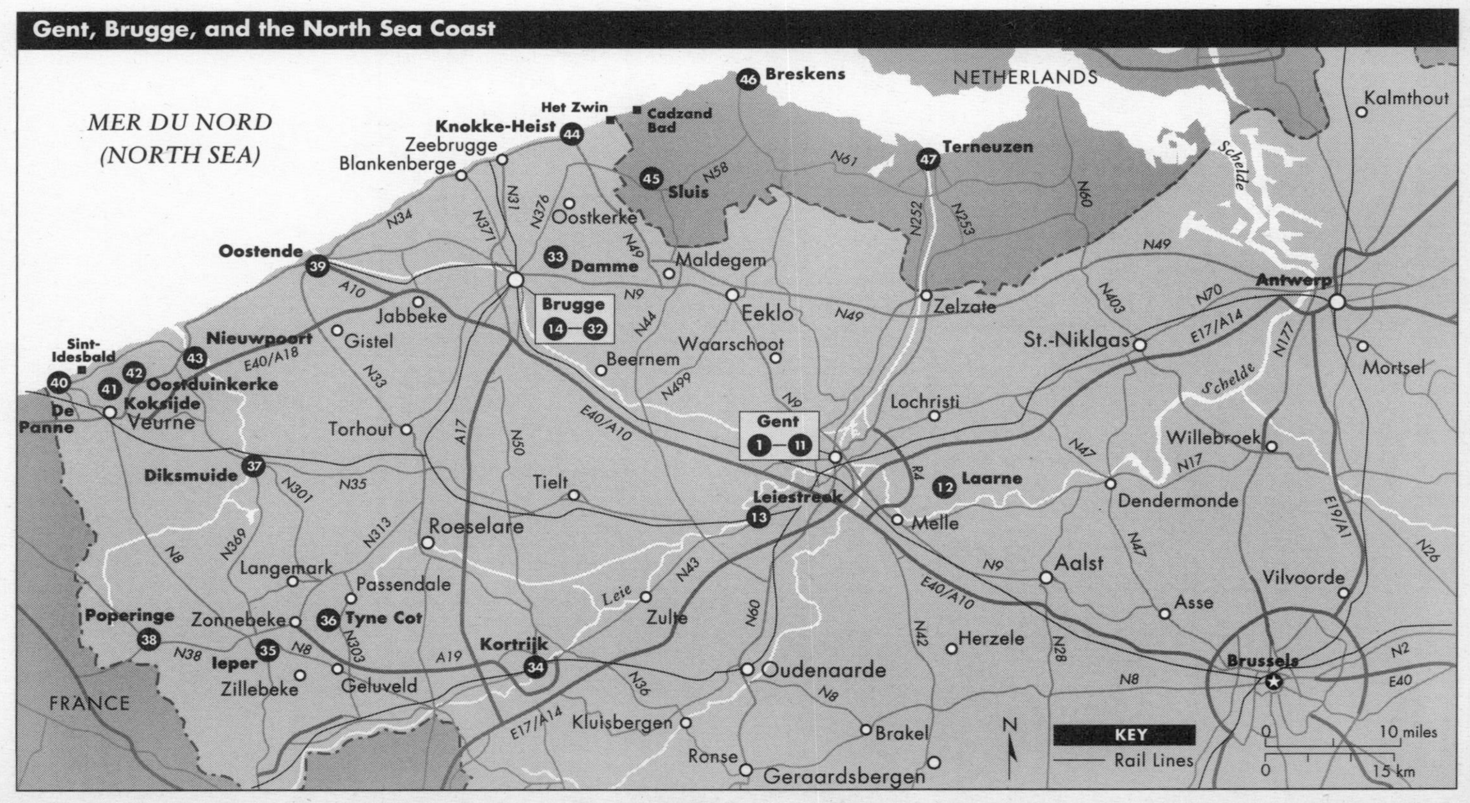

Gent (Ghent, Gand)

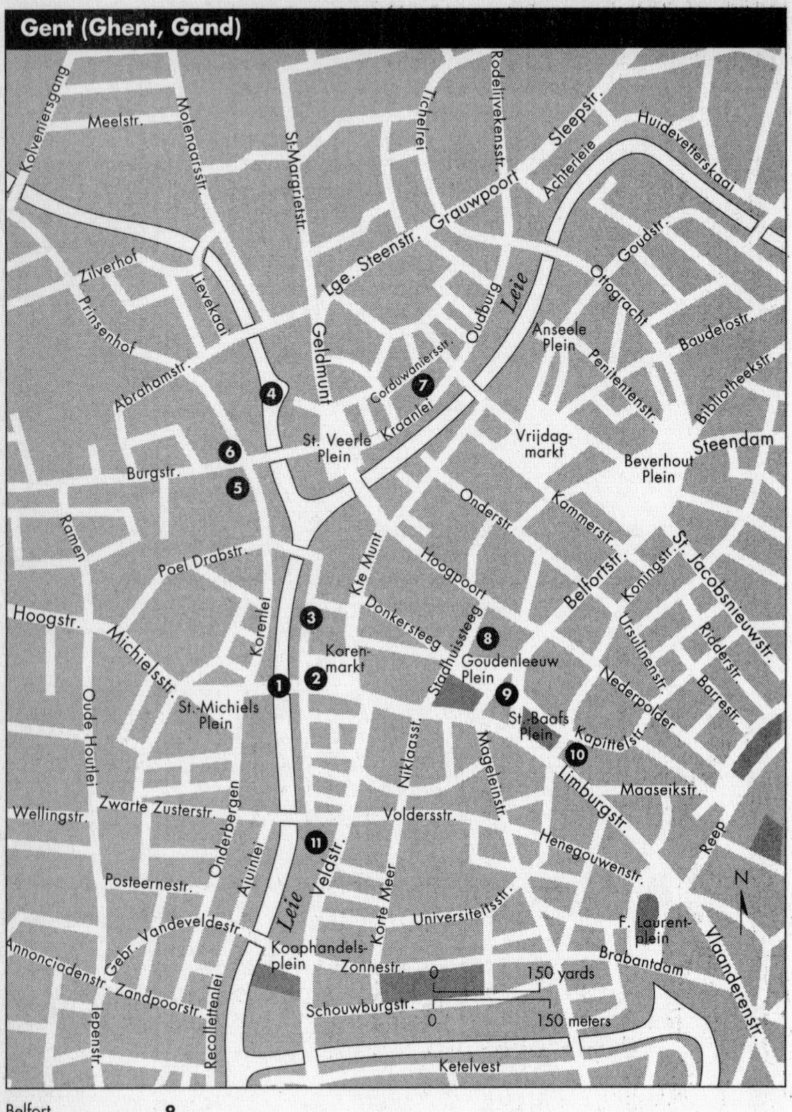

Belfort 9

Graslei 3

Gravensteen 4

Huis der Gekroonde Hoofden 6

Museum A. Vander Haeghen 11

Museum voor Sierkunst en Vormgeving 5

Museum voor Volkskunde 7

Sint-Baafskathedraal . . . 10

Sint-Michielsbrug . . . 1

Sint-Niklaaskerk 2

Stadhuis 8

go to Sint-Baafsplein to see **Sint-Baafskathedraal** ⑩ and Van Eyck's masterpiece. You can reach the **Museum A. Vander Haeghen** ⑪ by returning to Korenmarkt and walking south along the Leie River.

TIMING

Gent sprawls around its scattered historic buildings, but if you get tired you can easily catch one of the north–south trams to St. Pieters, the main train station. Allow a whole morning or afternoon to explore the sights, particularly if you're stopping off to see the *Mystic Lamb*. Although most sites are closed in the evening, many of the prime buildings are illuminated and the view from the bridge at night is stunning—the best view is via a canal-side stroll in the late evening. Note that Gent is cold between December and February, so bundle up for comfort.

Sights to See

❾ **Belfort.** Begun in 1314, the 300-ft Belfry tower symbolizes the power of the guilds. The Belfort actually wasn't completed until 1913, when the spire was added. The structure is crowned with a gilded copper weather vane shaped into a dragon, the city's symbol of freedom. Inside, documents listing the privileges of the city were once kept behind triple-locked doors and guarded by lookouts who toured the battlements hourly to prove they weren't sleeping. When danger approached, bells were rung—until Charles V had them removed. Now a 52-bell carillon, claimed by experts to be the best in the world, is set on the fifth floor; one of the original bells, cast in 1660 and now badly cracked, rests in a garden at the foot of the tower. The view from this landmark is one of the city's highlights. Note that you need a guide to visit the carillon. ✉ *St-Baafsplein,* ☎ *09/233–3954.* *BF100/€2.50, guided visits BF100/€2.50.* ⏲ *Guided visits Apr.–mid-Nov., daily 10–12:30 and 2–5:30; mid-Nov.–Mar., weekdays 10 mins past hr, weekends afternoon only.*

★ ❸ **Graslei.** This magnificent row of guild houses in the original port area is best seen from across the river Leie on the **Korenlei** (Corn Quay). The **Vrije Schippers** (Free Bargemen), at No. 14, is a late Gothic building from 1531, when the guild dominated inland shipping. No. 11 is the **Korenmetershuis** (Grain Measurers' House), a late Baroque building from 1698. Next to it is the narrow Renaissance **Tolhuis** (Toll House), where taxes were levied on grain shipments. It stands side by side with the oldest house of the group, the brooding, Romanesque **Koornstapelhuis** (Granary), which was built in the 12th century and served its original purpose for 600 years; this was where the grain claimed by the tax collectors was stored. The **Eezste Korenmetershuis** (another Grain Measurer's House), representing the grain weighers guild, is next. The guild house of the **Metselaars** (Masons), finally, is a copy of a house from 1527. The original, which stands near the transept of St. Nicholas's Church, has also recently been restored. Every night in season (and Friday and Saturday nights, November through April), the Graslei and all other historic monuments are illuminated from sunset to midnight. ✉ *Graslei.*

NEED A BREAK? If you're wandering around after 7, stop in at **De Tap en de Tepel** (✉ Gewad 7, closed Sun.–Tues. and Aug.), a wine and cheese house filled with flickering candles and lined with shelves of wine bottles.

❹ **Gravensteen.** Surrounded by a moat, the castle of the counts of Flanders resembles an enormous battleship, steaming down the sedate Lieve Canal. From its windswept battlements, there's a splendid view over the rooftops of old Gent. Originally modeled after a Syrian crusader castle, it was rebuilt several times since its inception in 1180—

most recently in the 19th century to reflect what the Victorians thought a medieval castle should look like. Above the entrance is an opening in the shape of a cross, which symbolizes the Count of Flanders's participation in the Crusades, resulting in his death in the Holy Land.

Today's brooding castle has little in common with the original fortress, built by Baldwin of the Iron Arm to discourage marauding Norsemen. Its purpose, too, changed from protection to oppression as the conflict deepened between feudal lords and unruly townspeople. Royalty entertained and feasted here throughout the Middle Ages, and the Council of Flanders met in chambers here for over 500 years. At various times the castle has also been used as a mint, a prison, and a cotton mill. It was here, too, that the country's first spinning mule was installed after being spirited away from England; soon the castle's chambers echoed with the clattering of looms, and Gent became a textile center to rival Manchester.

The castle also houses a torture museum. One of the rooms contains a gruesome display of pain-causing implements, and an *oubliette* (secret dungeon) is located under the building. Spiraling passageways marked by signpost arrows wind through this imposing maze of cold rooms, and the slits in the stones where soldiers launched crossbow arrows and poured boiling oil over unfortunate foes will be of special interest to fans of feudal warfare. If weapons aren't your glass of beer, you can at least enjoy the view from the castle tower. ✉ *St-Veerleplein,* ☎ *09/225–9306.* 🎫 *BF200/€4.95.* ⏲ *Daily 9–6 (Oct.–Mar. until 5).*

Klein Begijnhof. Founded in 1234 by Countess Joanna of Constantinople, the Small Beguinage is the best preserved of Gent's three beguinages. Protected by a wall and portal, the surrounding petite homes with individual yards were built in the 17th and 18th centuries, but are organized in medieval style. Each house features the statue of a saint and a spacious lawn; a few are still occupied by genuine Beguines leading the life stipulated by their founder 750 years ago. Visitors can quietly walk through the main building and peek into the stone chapel—the houses, however, are off-limits. ✉ *Lange Violettenstraat 71.*

Kraanlei. On the narrow, medieval Crane Lane, along this waterfront, two Baroque houses display elaborately decorated facades. The panels of No. 79, which date from 1669 and represent the five senses, are crowned by a figure of a flute player. The panels of No. 77 illustrate six acts of mercy; hospitality to travelers was considered the seventh act of mercy, as the building was once an inn. Further along the street is Gent's version of the *Mannekin Pis,* a cute, pudgy statue relieving himself—locals claim this figure is older than its counterpart in Brussels. ✉ *Kraanlei.*

Lakenhalle. Built as the center for the cloth trade in the 15th century, the Cloth Hall was still unfinished when the trade collapsed. Its vaulted cellar was used as a prison for 150 years; currently it houses a tourist restaurant and serves as the entrance to the Belfort. Be sure to examine the ceiling, which dates from 1741, where a relief depicts an ancient Roman named Cimon who, after being sentenced to starve to death, nurses from his daughter. Locals dub the building *De Mammelokker* (the allurer of maidens). ✉ *St-Baafsplein.*

Museum voor Schone Kunsten. Built in 1902 at the edge of Citadel Park, the neoclassical Fine Arts Museum is one of Belgium's best. Inside are paintings, drawings, engravings, tapestries, and sculptures dating from the Middle Ages to the early 20th century with Rubens, Gericault, Corot, Ensor, and Magritte among the artists represented. The outstanding collection of Flemish primitives includes two fine paintings by Hieronymus Bosch, *Saint Jerome* and *The Bearing of the Cross;* in the latter, Christ is shown surrounded by grotesque faces of unmitigated cruelty. The museum is also strong in Dutch, German, French, English, Italian, and Spanish paintings, and frequent temporary exhibitions augment the permanent collection. If you need a break, check out the comfortable seating areas in the serene ceremonies room, decorated with two outstanding series of tapestries from the 17th and 18th centuries. ✉ *Nicolaas de Liemaeckereplein 3,* ☎ *09/222–1703.* 🎫 *BF100/€2.50.* ⏲ *Tues.–Sun. 9:30–5.*

7 **Museum voor Volkskunde.** The Folklore Museum, the Kraanlei waterfront, and the ancient Patershol district behind it form an enchanting ensemble. The museum includes several settings, including 18 medieval almshouses surrounding a garden, reconstructed to offer an idea of life here 100 years ago. You'll also find a Gent version of Williamsburg, with a grocer's shop, tavern, weaver's workshop, and washroom. The chemist's shop features 17th- to 19th-century pharmacy items, and the pipe and tobacco collection has a large selection of snuff, pouches, and tools. The visitors' route takes you from the houses to the chapel and out through the crypt. Children will especially enjoy the giant pageant figures, board games, and frequent shows in the beamed and brick puppet theater. The star is "Pierke," the traditional Gent puppet. ✉ *Kraanlei 65,* ☎ *09/223–1336.* 🎫 *BF100/€2.50.* ⏲ *Tues.–Sun. 10–12:30 and 1:30–5.*

Oudheidkundie Museum van de Bijloke. Formerly the 13th-century Cistercian abbey of Bijloke, replete with a cloister and abbess's house, the huge and fascinating Archaeological Museum of the Bijloke encompasses 30 rooms, each exhibiting portions of Flanders's history. Gent's development up to the time of the French Revolution is covered in detail, and guild-related items are displayed in the original dormitory. Utensils, clothes, weapons, jewels, paintings, glass, porcelain pieces, and a collection of Chinese art are among the treasures on display in rooms where the old interiors were renovated in authentic fashion. The surviving buildings, constructed between the 14th and 17th centuries, are notable for their Flemish brick exteriors. The portal is through the 17th-century *Groot Begijnhof* (Great Beguinage), which was established here in the 19th century. The abbey medical center later became the Municipal Hospital of Gent. ✉ *North of Citadelpark, at Godshuizenlaan 2,* ☎ *09/225–1106.* 🎫 *BF100/€2.50.* ⏲ *Mon.–Wed. and Fri.–Sat. 10–1 and 2–6.*

Patershol. Close to the Castle of the Counts, this once housed many of the textile workers from the Gravensteen and eventually turned into a badly neglected slum. Its buildings and street pattern are medieval, but the spirit is definitely 21st century. Crammed with smart cafés and restaurants, the district is the in place for young, well-off couples and families who have converted the small houses for their use and pleasures. ✉ *Bounded by Kraanlei, Lange Steenstraat, and Geldmunt.*

NEED A BREAK?

Het Waterhuis aan de Bierkant (✉ Groenmarkt 7), which overlooks the canal and provides a pleasant outside terrace, offers more than 100 beers, each lovingly if eccentrically described on the menu. Simple, inexpensive snacks include a selection of pungent local cheeses.

★ 10 **Sint-Baafskathedraal.** St. Bavo's Cathedral, begun in the 13th century but finished in the 16th in the ornate Brabantine Gothic style, dramatically rises from a low, unimposing entryway. It contains one of the greatest treasures in Christendom: *The Adoration of the Mystic Lamb.* Now in the De Villa Chapel, to the left of the entrance in a glass case where you can see the back as well, this stupendous polyptych by Jan van Eyck and his brother was completed in 1432. Its history is as tumultuous as that of Gent itself: when the iconoclasts smashed St. Bavo's stained-glass windows and other treasures, the painting with its 24 oaken panels was hidden in the tower, and Napoléon later had it carried off to Paris. Joseph II of Austria found the panels of Adam and Eve prurient because theirs were the first naturalistically depicted human bodies in Western art—consequently, they disappeared and remained lost for 100 years. The other side panels were sold and hung in a Berlin museum.

In 1920 the masterpiece was again complete, but 14 years later a thief removed the panels on the lower left side. He returned the St. John the Baptist panel, but apparently died while waiting for a ransom for the panel of the Righteous Judges. Most people believe the panel is hidden somewhere in Gent, possibly even in the cathedral. The whole altarpiece was sent to France for safekeeping during World War II, but the Germans located and stole it. American troops eventually discovered it in an abandoned salt mine in Austria.

Today it is yours to enjoy at leisure, accompanied if you wish by an excellent explanation on audiotape. The central panel is based on the Book of Revelations: "And I looked, and, lo, a Lamb stood on the mount Sion, and with him an hundred forty and four thousand, having his Father's name written in their foreheads." There are not quite that many people in the painting, but it does depict 248 figures and 42 different types of flowers, each botanically correct. But statistics do not even suggest its grandeur. It uses a miniaturist technique to express the universal; realism to portray spirituality; and the blood of the sacrificial lamb mixes with the fountain of life to redeem the world. To the medieval viewer, it was an artistic *Summa Theologica,* a summation of all things revealed about the relationship between God and the world. An old tradition identifies the horseman in the foreground of the panel, to the immediate left, as Hubert van Eyck, Jan's brother, while the fourth figure from the left is believed to be Jan himself. It is now thought by art historians that Hubert, once believed to be co-creator of the luminous oil panels, was merely the carver of the imposing wooden frame of the altarpiece. As for the paintings themselves, Jan used brushes so delicate that the finest consisted of a single boar's bristle. The work was completed on May 6, 1432.

Emperor Charles V was christened here in St. Bavo's, just over 500 years ago. The cathedral was originally dedicated to St. John and it became the site for the veneration of St. Bavo, Gent's own saint, after Charles V had the old Abbey of St. Bavo razed. The Order of the Golden Fleece, instituted in Brugge by Philip the Good in 1430, was convened here in 1559 by Philip II of Spain. It is still in existence, currently presided over by King Juan Carlos of Spain as grand master. The coats of arms of the 51 knights who first belonged to the Order still hang in the south transept. The cathedral's ornate pulpit, made of white Italian marble and black Danish oak, was carved in the 18th century by the sculptor Laurent Delvaux. Angels, cherubs, massive trees, flowing robes, and tresses combine to create a masterwork. A Rubens masterpiece, *Saint Bavo's Entry into the Monastery,* hangs in one of the chapels. Other treasures include a baroque-style organ built in 1623, the largest in the Benelux, and a crypt crammed with tapestries, church paraphernalia, and 15th- and 16th-century frescos. ✉ *St-Baafsplein.* 🎫 *Cathedral free; De Villa Chapel BF100/€2.50.* ⏲ *Cathedral daily 8:30–6; chapel Apr.–Oct., Mon.–Sat. 9:30–5, Sun. 1–6; Nov.–Mar., Mon.–Sat. 10:30–noon and 2:30–4, Sun. 2–5. Closed during services.*

❷ **Sint Niklaaskerk.** St. Nicholas's Church was built in the 11th century in Romanesque style, but was destroyed a century later after two disastrous fires; it was later rebuilt by prosperous merchants. The tower, one of the many soaring landmarks of this city's famed skyline, dates from about 1300 and was the first belfry in Gent. During the French Revolution the church was used as a stable, and its treasures were ransacked. Further restoration began in the 1960s and was completed in 2000, renewing Belgian's best example of Scheldt-Gothic once again. ⊠ *On the Korenmarkt.* *Free.* *Mon. 2–5, Tues.–Sun. 10–5.*

NEED A BREAK? **Poesjkine** (⊠ Jan Breydelstraat 12, ☎ 09/224–2919) is a popular spot for a caffeine fix—or a simple, sinful indulgence. Knowing locals recommend the coffees and the cream and chocolate desserts. Note that it's closed Monday and August 1–15.

❻ **Huis der Gekroonde Hoofden.** Busts of the Counts of Flanders decorate the facade of the Crowned Heads' House, a distinctive Renaissance building which dates from 1559. The lowest row includes the sculpted faces of Maximilian, who inherited Flanders through Mary of Burgundy; his son Philip; his grandson Charles V; and Philip of Spain, Charles's son. Unfortunately, visitors aren't allowed inside. ⊠ *Jan Breydelstraat.*

Korenmarkt. The main Corn Market square is a collection of gabled buildings, cafés, and shops, as well as one of the city's busiest tram stops. Adjoining the square is the Groentemarkt, a former fish market and site of the infamous pillory used in the Middle Ages. ⊠ *Adjacent to St. Niklaaskerk.*

⓫ **Museum A. Vander Haeghen.** Three of Gent's favorite locals are honored in this 18th-century, former governor's home. Nobel Prize–winning playwright and poet Maurice Maeterlinck (1862–1949) kept a library in this elegant, neoclassical building, and it still contains his personal objects, letters, and documents. Painter and theater scenographer Charles Doudelet has a studio and works on exhibit here, as does illustrator and engraver Victor Stuyvaert. Look for the exceptional 18th-century wall decorations in the Chinese salon. ⊠ *Veldstraat 82,* ☎ *09/269–8460.* *Free.* *Weekdays 9:30–noon and 2–4:30.*

❺ **Museum voor Sierkunst en Vormgeving.** Peek into Gent's past in the Museum of Decorative Arts and Design, an 18th-century burgher's house. Furnished interiors show styles from the Renaissance to the 19th century, including an extensive collection of crafts and designs. In the first-floor wooden room, even the chandelier is made of intricately carved wood. One wing is dedicated to such 20th-century themes as art nouveau, art deco, and contemporary designs. ⊠ *St-Jan Breydelstraat 5,* ☎ *09/267–9999.* *BF100/€2.50.* *Tues.–Sun. 9:30–5.*

Schoolmuseum Michel Thiery. Founded in the 7th century, the Michel Thiery School Museum is in a wing of St. Peter's Abbey. During the Middle Ages, it was one of the most important and richest Flemish abbeys; today the building is a cultural center and natural history museum. Here you'll find scientific and nature displays, an Internet station, and a sound-and-light show featuring a large-scale model of 17th-century Gent. Don't miss the abbey, which was rebuilt in the 17th century in baroque style with an octagonal dome. ⊠ *Berouw 55,* ☎ *09/225–0542.* *Free.* *Mon.–Thurs. and Sat. 9–12:15 and 1:30–4:45, Fri. 9–12:15.*

★ ❶ **Sint-Michielsbrug.** The best way to begin a tour of Gent is to view the three medieval towers from St. Michael's Bridge, which leads from the Korenmarkt to the Korenlei and has the most renowned view of Gent.

8 **Stadhuis.** The Town Hall is an early example of what raising taxes can do to a city. In 1516, Antwerp's Domien de Waghemakere and Mechelen's Rombout Keldermans, two prominent architects, were called in to build a town hall that would put all others to shame. However, before the building could be completed, Emperor Charles V imposed new taxes that drained the city's resources. The architecture thus reflects the changing fortunes of Gent: the side built in 1518–60 and facing Hoogpoort is in flamboyant Gothic style; when work resumed in 1580, during the short-lived Protestant Republic, the Botermarkt side was completed in a stricter and more economical Renaissance style; and later additions include baroque and rococo features. The tower on the corner of Hoogpoort and Botermarkt has a balcony specifically built for making announcements and proclamations; lacelike tracery embellishes the exterior. This civic landmark is not usually open to the public, but you can arrange a tour through the Gidsenbond van Gent. Look for the glorious Gothic staircase, the throne room, and the spectacularly decorated halls—the Pacificatiezaal hall is where the Pacification Treaty of Gent between Catholics and Protestants was signed. ✉ *Botermarkt,* ☎ *09/233–0772.*

Stedelijk Museum van Actuele Kunst (SMAK). Housed in a former casino, the Museum of Contemporary Art is one of Belgium's most innovative spaces. Featured are exhibits by CoBrA (Copenhagen, Brussels, and Amsterdam) artists, as well as works by Magritte, Bacon, and Nauman. Performance art is also a highlight. ✉ *Citadelpark,* ☎ *09/221–1703.* 🎫 *BF100/€2.50.* ⏲ *Tues.–Sun. 10–6.*

Dining and Lodging

$$$$ ✕ **Auberge du Pêcheur.** A picturesque, half-hour drive to the charming, riverside village of Sint Martens-Latem brings you to this country inn-style restaurant. For a casual meal, try The Green, a cozy tavern where the menu features such hearty items as dark, meaty spare ribs. The formal Orangerie restaurant turns out six-course meals that might include grilled turbot, pigeon served with sweetbreads, or eel baked in a cream sauce. A daily prix-fixe menu is offered at both establishments. Rooms are available for those who decide to linger in the area. ✉ *Pontstraat 41, 9831,* ☎ *09/282–3144. Reservations essential. AE, DC, MC, V. Closed Mon. No lunch Sat., no dinner Sun.*

$$$$ ★ ✕ **Jan van den Bon.** With room for just 30, this cozy, intimate restaurant serves fine Belgian cuisine and is top-rated by locals. Fresh seafood and seasonal combinations are the specialties. When white asparagus is in season, it's cooked and sauced to perfection—-try eating it like the Gents, with your fingers. ✉ *Koning Leopold II Laan 43,* ☎ *09/221–9085. Reservations essential. AE, DC, MC, V. Closed Sun., Mon., and July 15–Aug. 13. No lunch Sat.*

$$$–$$$$ ✕ **Jan Breydel.** A gardenlike setting along a quaint street in the heart of the historic district delights diners at this popular little bistro. Proprietors Louis and Pat Hellebaut oversee the preparation of each dish, and the food is as fresh as the atmosphere. Regional ingredients are complemented by delicate sauces and seasonings. Try the local specialties of sole, eel, and mussels. ✉ *Jan Breydelstraat 10,* ☎ *09/225–6287. AE, DC, MC, V. Closed Sun. No lunch Mon.*

$$$ ✕ **Café Theatre.** A New York City–style buzz surrounds diners at this restaurant in the shadow of the Gent Royal Opera—it's the city's top place for seeing and being seen. The huge, converted warehouse takes up two levels and is decorated with huge columns, wrought iron, and whimsy (check out the opaque stalls in the loo). Vegetables earn their 15 minutes of fame; if you dine during "Tomato Week," everything from the ravioli to the cappuccino is red. Inventive lobster dishes are a menu

highlight, but you can also create your own grazing menu. ✉ *Schouwburgstraat 5,* ☏ *09/265–0550. AE, DC, V. Closed July 15–Aug. 4.*

$$$ ✕ **De 3 Biggetjes.** The name means "the three little pigs," and you'll definitely be tempted to "pig out" on—or "wolf down"—the wonderful food. The menu includes a fusion of Belgian, Vietnamese, and French items. Seafood dishes are a highlight; ingredients are flown in from all over the world, even the Seychelles. It's a detour from the city center to reach the tiny, step-gabled building in Patershol, but the food makes the trip to the restaurant worth it—even if you have to huff and puff a bit to find it. ✉ *Zeugsteeg 7,* ☏ *09/224–4648. MC, V.*

$$$ ✕ **Graaf van Egmond.** Gaze at the famed spires of Gent from this 13th-century riverside house while you sup on fresh Belgian asparagus and traditional beef stewed in beer. Beautiful beamed ceilings, antique and reproduction pieces, and sparkling chandeliers decorate the interior. Order from the special Charles V menu for the most exquisite choices. ✉ *Sint-Michielslein 21,* ☏ *09/225–0727. AE, DC, MC, V.*

$$$ ✕ **Orangerie.** The Patershol district was named for the solitary monks' caves once found in the area, but this restaurant's airy garden spot is the furthest thing from monastic. Sunshine filters in through a skylight, the sounds of a splashing fountain surround the tables, and greenery accents every corner. The fixed-price menu features French and Belgian classics from starters to desserts, including bouillabaisse and sabayonne. ✉ *Corduwaniersstraat 8,* ☏ *09/224–1008. AE, DC, MC, V. Closed Tues. and Wed.*

$$$ ✕ **Tête á Tête.** Gent residents rave about this small restaurant's fresh seafood. Specialties include fish, eel, and mussels, but scrumptious Flemish and French specialties are served up as well. After your meal, though, don't rave about it in public—locals want to keep this place for themselves. ✉ *Jan Breydelstraat 32–34,* ☏ *09/233–9500. AE, DC, MC, V. Closed Mon. No lunch Tues.*

$$–$$$ ✕ **De Gustibus.** Excellent food and modest prices make this gustatory mecca one of the more gabbed about dining spots in Gent—a city that knows its food and loves to eat lots of it. Recommendations include spicy mussels, crispy vegetables, and chocolate desserts. Fresh, fresh, and more fresh is the motto. ✉ *Bennesteeg 8/10,* ☏ *09/233–7435. MC, V.*

$$–$$$ ✕ **Het Spijker.** Beer is the drink (and the saucing ingredient) of choice in this popular tavern in the heart of the famed waterside district. Strolling amid the historic guild houses to the restaurant's 12th-century, step-gabled facade is a step back in time. Inside, the decor continues the theme, with hand-hewn stone walls, hardwood floors, beamed ceilings, and fortresslike wooden shutters. The stunning dining hall is laid with white linens for dinner, but you'll be treated to hearty portions all day long. ✉ *Graslei 10,* ☏ *09/234–0635. MC, V.*

$$–$$$ ✕ **'t Buikske Vol.** Daring diners might want to sample the *fillet de biche* (doe steak) at this cozy Patershol restaurant suited to special occasions. Unusual flavor combinations make for such pleasantly memorable meals as fillet of Angus beef with onion confit, or rabbit served with crisp sweetbreads. ✉ *Kraanlei 17,* ☏ *09/225–1880. AE, MC, V. Closed Wed. and public holidays. No lunch weekends.*

$$ ✕ **Establissement Max.** Crispy yet soft-centered Belgian waffles are featured here—try one topped with ice cream, whipped cream, and fruit (no guilt allowed). The informal, light-filled faux Art Noveau dining room is always busy, awash in the scent of waffle batter and the aromas of Flemish specialties. Salads and sandwiches are also available if you just want a light meal. ✉ *Gouden Leeuplein 3,* ☏ *09/223–9731. AE, DC, MC, V.*

$$ ✕ **Excelsior Gil De Vriendt.** Set in one of the city's old, comfortable homes, this restaurant serves a selection of brasserie specials. Entrées to savor include goose liver with muscat wine, lamb in thyme sauce, and scampi with Cointreau. The waterzooi is top-class. ✉ *Hoogpoort 29,* ☎ *09/234–2402. Reservations essential. AE, V.*

$$ ✗ **La Petite Provence.** It's a local favorite, in the city center, a modest place with a French twist to the decor. Brick and wicker accents, globe chandeliers, and widely spaced tables make this a comfortable place to linger long after a meal. The seafood and lamb specialties are artistically presented and moderately priced; you may find yourself returning for a meal the next day. ✉ *Donkersteeg 4,* ☎ *09/225–6501. AE, DC, MC, V.*

$ ✗ **Brasserie Keizershof.** When you're looking for a change from the familiar waterzooi, try this inexpensive dining hall. A beamed ceiling and ornate grillwork add style to the simple decor, but you're really here for the food. Light meals and snacks are available all day—toasted sandwiches, spaghetti, and the like—but bring an appetite, because portions are huge. The restaurant's size makes it a favorite of tour groups. ✉ *Vrijdagmarkt 47,* ☎ *09/223–4446. MC, V. Closed Sun. and public holidays.*

$ ✗ **Buddhasbelly.** Tasty vegetarian meals are cooked up at this adorable restaurant. It's a no-frills environment, but the meals are inexpensive and healthy, and served up by philosopher-cum-cooks. Look for light eats, sandwiches, salads, vegetable pies, peanut roasts, and fruit dishes. The interesting combinations will fill *your* belly. ✉ *Hoogpoort 30,* ☎ *09/225–1732. No credit cards. Closed Sun. and 1st 2 wks in Aug.*

$$$–$$$$ ✗🏨 **Sofitel Gent-Belfort.** Located in the heart of the old city, this grand hotel mirrors the elegance of the well-known international chain. Warm beige hues highlight the art nouveau style of the interior, where an ambience of casual elegance emphasizes businesslike comfort rather than old-world romance. Spacious rooms are well-equipped; some are bi-level, with a second TV. The hotel also offers a family deal—up to two children under 16 can stay free in a separate room when adults pay full price. ✉ *Hoogpoort 63, B9000,* ☎ *09/233–3331,* FAX *09/233–1102. 127 rooms, 3 suites. Restaurant, bar, sauna, exercise room, meeting rooms, free parking. AE, DC, MC, V.*

$$$ ✗🏨 **Novotel Gent Centrum.** Scads of white marble and bold colors highlight this modern property. Rooms, which are soundproof, have white laminate furniture, sofa beds, and spacious bathrooms. State your view preference when you book; some windows overlook a landscaped courtyard with a pool, while others have city vistas. The most expensive rooms are sumptuous and have cathedral views. While you're here, check out the only element of the past: a medieval crypt, which now houses a bar and meeting area. ✉ *Gouden Leeuwplein 5,* ☎ *09/224–2230,* FAX *09/224–3295. 117 rooms, 4 suites. Restaurant, bar, pool, sauna. AE, DC, MC, V.*

$$ ✗🏨 **Cour St. Georges St. Jorishof.** One of the oldest hotels in the world, this 1228 step-gabled inn with the Romanesque facade once welcomed Napoléon, Charles V, and Mary of Burgundy. The building was once the guild house of the Crossbowmen, and despite inevitable tinkerings since medieval times, its historical romance and Flemish primitive spirit have been well-preserved. Step into the restored Gothic hall and reception area, with huge chandeliers suspended from the vaulted ceilings, and admire the intricate wrought iron encircling the upstairs balcony. Stained-glass windows color the sunlight that lingers along the dark wall paneling surrounding the enormous main hearth. Rooms are all old-style; however, avoid the annex quarters, which are newer (just 200 years old) but drab. Flemish and fish specialties are served at the restaurant beneath a beamed ceiling; book for the Friday candlelit dinner and Sunday brunch. ✉ *Botermark 2, 9000,* ☎ *09/224–2424,* FAX *09/224–2640. 28 rooms. Restaurant, bar, baby-sitting, meeting rooms, parking (fee). AE, DC, MC, V.*

$$$$ **Alfa Flanders.** A cool white exterior belies the warmth inside this centrally located, midsize hotel. A grand piano dominates a comfortable lounge, paintings by local artists punctuate the walls with color, and a skylight in the breakfast room lets the light pour into the space. All rooms are equipped with desks, sofas, TVs, trouser presses, and hair dryers. Executive rooms have large baths, as well as dining and sitting areas; two suites include fireplaces, CD players, and private terraces. ✉ *Koning Albertlaan 121, 9000,* ☎ *09/222–6065,* FAX *09/220–1605. 49 rooms, 2 suites. Restaurant, breakfast room, piano bar, in-room data ports, in-room safes, minibars, room service, meeting rooms. AE, DC, MC, V.*

$$–$$$ **Astoria.** European charm is evident in this converted brick home with large, shuttered windows. The interior is awash in warm colors, with accents of polished wood and wall sconces. Comfortable rooms feature delicate furnishings that foster romance. The hotel is near the Sint-Pieters tram station and local attractions. ✉ *Achilles Musschestraat 39, 9000,* ☎ *09/222–8413,* FAX *09/220–4787. 14 rooms. Meeting rooms. AE, DC, MC, V.*

$$–$$$ **The Boatel.** Landlubbers will enjoy this opportunity to sleep aboard an authentic Flanders riverboat. Docked on the Leie near the city center, the rebuilt vessel shows off sections of the original woodwork—take note of the restored reception area. Cabins are large and bright, particularly the two master bedrooms above the sea line. The wood floor of the sunny breakfast room can double as the evening gathering spot or even a small meeting room. Pack Dramamine if you tend to get queasy offshore. ✉ *Voorhoutkaai 29 A, 9000,* ☎ *09/267–1030,* FAX *09/267–1039. 7 rooms. Dining room, meeting room. No credit cards.*

$$–$$$ **Charl's Inn.** A wrought-iron arch welcomes you to this country bed-and-breakfast within biking distance of Gent. Cozy public rooms are basic, but the bedrooms are airy (although ask to bypass the cramped "nook" rooms if you're claustrophobic). All rooms have private baths with either tubs or showers. Breakfast is by a brick hearth, and the spacious, groomed grounds and gardens are perfect for strolling and cycling afterward. ✉ *Autoweg Zuid 4, 9051,* ☎ *09/220–3093,* FAX *09/221–2619. 9 rooms. Breakfast room, bar, sauna, baby-sitting, free parking. AE, DC, MC, V.*

$$ **Europa.** Near the Sint-Pieters station, this midsize pension is conveniently close to the waterfront and the *Watersportbaan* and *The Blaarmeersen* suburbs. Large, comfortable rooms have modern features, but you'll want to spend your time participating in the nearby activities: water sports, windsurfing, and tennis. A charming indoor café is the place to snack; in good weather, evening drinks are served on the lawn. ✉ *Zuidstationstraadt 24, 9000,* ☎ *09/222–6071,* FAX *09/220–0609. 34 rooms. Café, baby-sitting, meeting rooms, free parking. AE, DC, MC, V.*

$$ **Gravensteen.** Steps from its namesake Castle of the Counts, this handsome 19th-century mansion emanates an old-world atmosphere. Ornately decorated public rooms feature carved stucco; also look for the marble staircase and cupola. Hallways wind to small rooms decorated in warm hues of orange and teal, and accented with bright fabrics—some even have castle views. Note that bathrooms are small, and some have showers only. ✉ *Jan Breydelstraat 35, B9000,* ☎ *09/225–1150,* FAX *09/225–1850. 37 rooms. Bar, breakfast room, lounge, in-room data ports, minibars, parking (fee). AE, DC, MC, V.*

$$ **Ibis Gent Centrum Kathedraal.** In the shadow of the cathedral and the midst of the historic district, this is another dependable hotel from the popular European chain. The traditional facade shelters standard rooms with modern decor—charm is minimal, but service and comfort are maximum. Aside from requisite amenities, all rooms have desks, and triples are available. ✉ *Limburgstraat 2,* ☎ *09/223–0000,*

FAX *09/233–2000. 120 rooms. Restaurant, bar, meeting rooms, free parking. AE, DC, MC, V.*

$$ **Ibis Gent Centrum Opera.** The distinctive art-deco exterior of this chain hotel in the city center signifies its dedication to modern style. You're just steps away from all the best of Gent's sightseeing, shopping, and nightlife. You can include half-board meals for an additional 650 BEF per person. ✉ *Nederkouter 24–26, 9000,* ☎ *09/225–0707,* FAX *09/223–5907. 134 rooms. Restaurant, bar, meeting rooms, parking (fee). AE, DC, MC, V.*

$–$$ **Eden.** Locals recommend this small hotel to good friends. There are no frills, just comfortable rooms and warm service—as well as a tasty breakfast. Note that, unlike many lodgings in this price group, each room has its own bath. ✉ *Zuidstationstraat 24,* ☎ *09/223–5151,* FAX *09/233–3457. 28 rooms. Bar, free parking. No credit cards.*

$–$$ **Gastenstudios.** Nestled between the city and the marshlands, two Flemish farm cottages are set amid a parklike setting. Inside each you'll find pine furnishings, fireplaces, and kitchenettes that provide a cozy cabin feel. This is a place to stay for a few days, buy your groceries at the local markets, cook up new recipes, and explore the rolling countryside. Cottages, which accommodate 2–4 people, have private entrances and baths. Children will love the pond, play pool, and vast number of birds. ✉ *Meerskant 18, B9270,* ☎ *09/230–4128,* FAX *09/230–4128. 2 cottages. Kitchenettes, minibars, free parking. No credit cards.*

$ ★ **Erasmus.** From the flagstone and wood-beam library-lounge to the stone mantels in the individually decorated bedrooms, every inch of this noble 16th-century town house has been scrubbed, polished, and decked with period ornaments. Even the tiny garden has been carefully manicured. The couple that runs this distinctive hotel near the Korenlei takes care of everything from answering the bell pull at night to serving a delicious breakfast in the parlor. ✉ *Poel 25, B9000,* ☎ *09/224–2195,* FAX *09/233–4241. 11 rooms. Lobby lounge. AE, DC, MC, V. Closed mid-Dec.–mid-Jan.*

Nightlife and the Arts

The Arts

Check the "What's On" and "Other Towns" sections of *The Bulletin* to find schedules of the latest art shows and cultural events. Head for the **Kunstencentrum Vooruit** (✉ St-Pietersnieuwstraat 23, ☎ 09/267–2828), or Vooruit Arts Center, for top-quality dance, theater, and jazz programs; the venue also hosts rock and contemporary classical concerts. **Gele Zaal** (✉ Nonnemeerstraat 26, ☎ 09/235–3702) features avant-garde jazz, classical, and ethnic music performances. **De Vlaamse Opera** (✉ Schouwburgstraat 3, ☎ 09/225–2425), or Flemish Opera House, shares its name—and many productions—with a sister company in Antwerp; if you go, note the splendid ceiling and chandelier.

FESTIVALS

Gent has several marvelous celebrations that you might want to plan around. A town crier rings in activities for the 10-day **Gentse Feesten,** which takes place around the third week of July. Street theater, music, costume balls, banquets, and parades take place around Sint-Jacobs in the inner city. One part of the event is the Tour of the Guild of Ropes, when a barefoot troop dressed in tabards, with ropes around their necks, reenact the penitential trip of 1540. In August, the three-day **Patersholfeesten** offers traditional fun in the historic Het Patershol quarter. Other cultural festivities include **The Flanders Festival for Classical Music,** and the **International Film Festival.** The **Floralien**—which maintains Gent's reputation as "City of Flowers"—is a huge floral exhibition that takes place every five years; the next is scheduled for 2005.

Nightlife

As in most Belgian towns, nightlife in Gent centers around grazing and drinking and talking with friends through the late hours. You'll find a few cabarets and nightclubs, but the Gentenaars really prefer their pubs and cafés. **Backstage** (✉ St-Pietersnieuwstraat 128, ☎ 09/233–3535), a café-restaurant near the Vooruit center, presents occasional classical and jazz concerts. For clubbing, try **Democrazy** (✉ Reynaertstraat 125, ☎ 09/227–5196). **Lazy River Jazz Café** (✉ Stadhuissteeg 5, ☎ 09/223–2301) is a friendly, intimate place beloved by locals and students. **Pakhuis** (✉ Schuurkenstraat 4, ☎ 09/223–5555) is a bustling brasserie/tavern off the Korenmarkt, with trendy modern decor and, incongruously, a giant Greek statue. **De Dulle Griet** (✉ Vrijdagmarkt 50, ☎ 09/224–2455) specializes in the 1.2-liter *Kwak* beer, complete with a collector's stein and stand—however, you must leave one of your shoes as "deposit" when you order.

Outdoor Activities and Sports

Just minutes from the city, the 250-acre **Blaarmeersen** (✉ Zuiderlaan 5, ☎ 09/221–1414) is Gent's recreation center. Here you'll find tennis courts, squash courts, a roller-skating track, jogging and cycling tracks, and facilities for windsurfing, sailing, canoeing, and camping.

Boating is popular along the river and canals. Try a motorboat trip along the river Leie to Deurle and Sint-Martens-Latem.

Shopping

Antiques and paintings on display in the local shops and galleries are evidence of the city's elegant style. **Langemunt** and **Veldstraat** are the major shopping streets, while the smart fashion boutiques are located along **Voldersstraat.** Gent also has several exclusive shopping galleries where such boutiques are surrounded by upscale cafés and restaurants; try the **Bourdon Arcade** (Gouden Leeuwplein) and **Braempoort,** located between Brabantdam and Vlaanderenstraat).

The largest market is the attractive and historic **Vrijdagmarkt,** held Friday 7–1 and Saturday 1–6. This is where leaders have rallied the people of Gent from the Middle Ages to the present day. The huge square is dominated by a turret that was part of the Tanner's Guildhouse, and the statue in the middle is of Jacob van Artevelde, who led a rebellion from here in 1338, defending the neutrality of the city and Flanders during the Hundred Years' War. You can take home a supply of Gentse Mokken, syrup-saturated biscuits available from any pastry shop, or famed Gent mustard. Also visit the flower market on the Kouter, or the poultry market on the Oude Beesten on Sunday mornings.

Laarne

12 *13 km (8 mi) east of Gent.*

Laarne Castle, one of the best-preserved medieval strongholds in the country, was built in the 14th century. The purpose of this moat-surrounded fortress was to protect Gent's eastern approaches, and it was converted to peaceful use in the 17th century. Massive corner towers and pointed rooftops define the exterior; inside are fine examples of Brussels tapestry weaving and an outstanding collection of 15th- to 18th-century silver. Legend has it that a tunnel once linked Laarne with the

Gravensteen castle in the center of Gent. ✉ *R4, Exit 5, Heusden–Laarne,* ☎ *09/230–9155.* 🎫 *BF150/€3.70.* ⏲ *Easter–June and Sept.–Oct., Sun. 2–5; July–Aug., Tues.–Thurs. and weekends 2–5:30.*

Leiestreek

⓭ *Just southwest of Gent.*

Bucolic Leiestreek (Leie Region) has attracted many painters, and it is especially pleasant to discover their work in its original setting. The fact that they are not widely known abroad makes it even more pleasant to discover their work in its original setting. The best way to enjoy the willow-lined banks of the meandering Leie is by rented motorboat or bike. **Sint-Martens-Latem,** with its 15th-century wooden windmill, was home to Gustave van de Woestyne, an early 20th-century artist. After World War I, Constant Permeke and the Expressionists gained popularity. In the village of **Deurle,** the house and studio of the Gent painter Gust De Smet has been turned into the **Museum Dhondt-Dhaenens.** It contains a major collection of Expressionist paintings, including works by Permeke, Van den Berghe, and Albert Servaes. ✉ *Take N466 south from Exit 13 off E40 north from Gent,* ☎ *09/282–5123.* 🎫 *BF70/€1.75.* ⏲ *Feb.–early Dec., Wed.–Fri. 2–6, weekends 10–noon and 2–6.*

In the village of **Deinze,** beside an attractive Gothic church next to the river, you'll find the **Museum van Deinze en Leiestreek,** with works by Luminist pioneer Emile Claus, as well as by the Latem group of painters. Deinze's Sheldt-Gothic Church of Our Lady, built in the 14th century, has a steeple carillon that chimes in major thirds—the world's first. ✉ *Lucien Matthyslaan 3–5,* ☎ *09/381–9670.* 🎫 *BF60/€1.50.* ⏲ *Weekdays except Tues. 2–5:30, weekends 10–noon and 2–5.*

BRUGGE: FAIRYTALE DESTINATION

96 km (58 mi) northwest of Brussels, 45 km (27 mi) west of Gent, 28 km (17 mi) east of Oostende.

Long thought of as a Sleeping Beauty reawakened, Brugge is an ancient village whose heritage has been well preserved. However, the contemporary comparison is sometimes more akin to Beauty and the Beast—particularly in summer, when visitors flock here in overwhelming numbers. Still, in the quiet, colder seasons, the city offers a peaceful refuge, and you can feel the rhythm of life centuries ago.

Although it is often called Bruges, its French name, the city's official name is indeed Brugge (*bruhg*-guh), and you'll score points with the locals by using the Flemish title. The city's history begins some time in the third century, when it was a Gallo-Roman settlement of farmers and merchants who traded with England and Gaul. It remained relatively rural until the 11th century, when its seaside location along the trade path turned it into an international commercial center. Linked with the estuary of the Zwin on the North Sea by a navigable waterway, Brugge was one of the most active members of the Hanseatic League during the 13th century. Top trade items included Flemish cloth, Scandinavian fish, Russian furs, Gasconian wine, and Venetian silk. Italian merchants from Lombardy, Tuscany, and Venice soon set up shop in Brugge, and the town established Europe's first stock exchange.

In 1301, the French queen Jeanne of Navarre was annoyed by the finery flaunted by the women of Brugge. "I thought I alone was queen," she said, "and here I am surrounded by hundreds more." The men of Brugge, in return, were annoyed at being requested to fund a lavish reception for the French royal couple. One fine morning in May 1302, they fell upon and massacred the French garrison, and then joined the men of Gent and Ieper to defeat the French chevaliers in the epic Battle of the Golden Spurs. It must have been a notable battle, for at that time the population of Brugge alone was around 40,000—twice that of the current city center.

Flanders became a Burgundian state in the 15th century, and an era of unprecedented wealth began in Brugge. The famed Flemish style of painting evolved at this time, including oil painting, which is widely believed to have been invented by Jan Van Eyck in the 1420s. This "Flemish Primitive" art style represented a revolution in realism, portraiture, and perspective, bringing the era alive in astonishing detail. For his skills, Jan van Eyck was named court painter to Philip the Good, Duke of Burgundy, who married Isabella of Portugal in a ceremony of incredible luxury in Brugge's Prinsenhof in 1429. It was just one of the lavish celebrations to take place in the city; the last Burgundian feast here was the wedding of Duke Charles the Bold to Margaret of York, sister of England's Edward IV, in 1468.

At the end of the century adversity struck. Flemish weavers had emigrated across the Channel and taught their trade to the English, who became formidable competitors. Even worse, the Zwin began to silt up, and the people of Brugge had neither the will nor the funds to build the canal that might have saved their industry. Instead, trade and fortune and the wool trade switched to Antwerp. The Spaniards conquered Brugge in 1548, and the city fell into poverty.

In the 19th century, British travelers on their way to view the battlefield of Waterloo rediscovered Brugge and spread its fame as a perfectly preserved medieval town. Its look is classic, but much of the city was actually redesigned in the 19th century by British architects keen to spread the Gothic revival. Only two of the original timber medieval houses remain. A novel by Georges Rodenbach, *Bruges-la-Morte* (Brugge, the Dead), brought more visitors but created an image that has been difficult to escape.

Today, Brugge is a city of tangled streets, narrow canals, handsome squares, and old gabled buildings. Its limits now incorporate the port of Zeebrugg, and it is the administrative center of West Flanders. Although strong in politics, proud in history, and centered on soccer, Brugge's principal industry remains tourism. The city has not only awakened from its centuries-old sleep, but it is also bright-eyed with plans for spruced-up shops and services. Declared the Cultural Capital of Europe in 2002, Brugge is a highlight for travelers to the continent. As it becomes ever more popular, the Beast of modern change will undoubtedly grow larger. Happily ever after remains to be seen.

Exploring Brugge

A Good Walk

Begin at the **Markt** ⑭, the old market square. From its southeast corner, follow Breidelstraat to the **Burg** ⑮, the city's main square. In a corner stands the small **Heilig Bloed Basiliek** ⑯, a 12th-century basilica. Also on the Burg is the 14th-century **Stadhuis** ⑰. The Town Hall is linked with the graceful Oude Griffie by a bridge arching over the narrow Blinde Ezelstraat; follow it south across one of the Reien (canals) and turn right on Dijver, moving along the canal to the **Groeninge Museum** ⑱. The canal makes a sharp turn to the left here; you can go across to the **Brangwyn Museum** ⑲ and the adjacent **Gruuthuse Museum** ⑳, the house of a 15th-century nobleman. Continue along Dijver and turn

Brugge (Bruges)

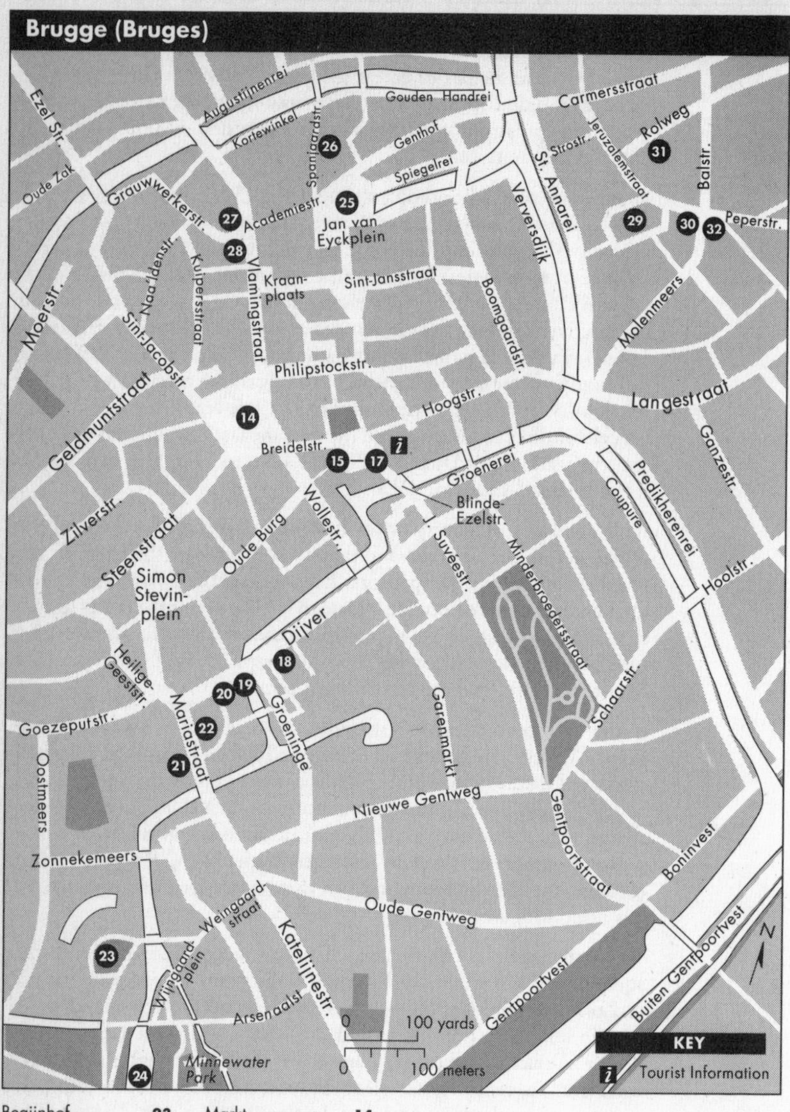

left on Mariastraat to the **Memling Museum** ㉑ on the right. Across the street is the **Onze-Lieve-Vrouwekerk** ㉒. Continue on Mariastraat to Weingaardstraat on the right. Follow it across the canal to the **Begijnhof** ㉓. The canal flows into the **Minnewater** ㉔.

At the other end of the center of the city, north of the Markt, lies **Jan Van Eyckplein** ㉕. Follow **Spanjaardstraat** ㉖ north from the square, turn left at the canal on Kortewinkel and left again on Vlamingstraat. Walk south to the **Huize ter Buerze** ㉗ and the **Saaihalle** ㉘, just across the narrow Grauwwerkerstraat from the Huize ter Buerze. From here, you can follow Academiestraat back through Jan Van Eyckplein to Genthof, across the canal; follow the canal south to Sint-Anna-Kerkstraat and turn left into the **Sint-Anna** ㉙ quarter. Next, follow Jeruzalemstraat to the **Jeruzalemkerk** ㉚. Backtrack on Jeruzalemstraat to Rolweg, and the reconstructed interiors of the **Museum voor Volkskunde** ㉛. Return down Jeruzalemstraat to Peperstraat to see the laces at the **Kantcentrum** ㉜.

TIMING

Brugge is compact, like a small island amid the winding waterways, but the twists and turns may lead you to unexpected pleasures. You'll need at least three hours for this walk, more if you're an art fan or tend to linger at picturesque vistas. The best strategy is to start at dawn with the walkable sights and then to visit the museums as the crowds start to hit the Burg. Alternatively, you could explore the museums first thing and postpone your stroll until the early evening.

Temperatures can be raw in deep winter and hot in summer, so dress in layers and make sure your shoes can cushion the cobblestones. If you need a rest, consider riding high in a carriage behind a clip-clopping steed, or hopping a boat for a swan's-eye view of the canals (although the boats are usually crowded and the pilot's spiels cliched). Brugge is at its most enchanting at night, when lights melt on inky water and bridges become echoing arches. Or in the pink of morning, when bird songs vie with belfry chimes and gliding cygnets seem to play hide-and-seek in the mist. Whenever you walk, bring a camera.

Sights to See

★ ㉓ **Begijnhof.** The 13th-century Beguinage is a serene cluster of small, whitewashed houses, a pigeon tower, and a church surrounding a pleasant green at the edge of a canal. The setting is prettiest in spring, when daffodils are in bloom and dappled sunlight falls in shafts between tall poplars and over the lawns. The Begijnhof was founded in 1245 by Margaret, Countess of Constantinople, to bring together the Beguines, many of whom were widows of Crusaders and girls from all social backgrounds who devoted themselves to charitable work and who were not bound by religious vows. Led by a superintendent known as The Grand Mistress, the congregation flourished for 600 years. The last of the Beguines died about 50 years ago; today the site is occupied by the Benedictine sisters, who still wear the Beguine habit. You may join them, discreetly, for vespers in their small church of St. Elizabeth. Although most of the present-day houses are from the 16th and 17th centuries, they have maintained the architectural style of the houses that preceded them. One house has been set aside as a small museum. Visitors are asked to respect the silence. ✉ *Monasterium de Wijngaard, Oude Begijnhof,* ☎ *050/330011.* 🎫 *Free; house visit, BF60/€1.50.* ⏲ *Apr.–Sept., daily 10–noon and 1:45–5:30; Oct.–Nov. and Mar., daily 10:30–noon and 1:45–5; Dec.–Feb., Wed.–Thurs. and weekends 2:45–4:45, Fri. 1:45–6.*

19 **Brangwyn Museum.** The first floor of this 18th-century **Arentshuis** contains an outstanding collection of bobbins, needlepoint, international lace, and lace-making gadgets, with exhibits focusing on a craft long and lovingly practiced in Brugge. The display includes hundreds of drawings, etchings, and paintings by artist Frank Brangwyn (1867–1956). ✉ *Dijver 16,* ☎ *050/448711.* 🎫 *BF80/€19.90; combination ticket (includes the Gruuthuse, Memling, and Groeninge museums;* ☞ *below) BF450/€11.15.* ⏲ *Apr.–Sept., daily 9:30–5; Oct.–Dec. and Feb.–Mar., Wed.–Mon. 9:30–12:30 and 2–5.*

★ 15 **Burg.** A fine place to meet at the end of the day, this busy square is an enchanting, floodlit scene after dark. Named for the fortress built by Baldwin of the Iron Arm, the Burg was also the former site of the 10th-century Carolingian Cathedral of St. Donaas, which was destroyed by French Republicans in 1799. You can wander through the handsome, 18th-century **Oude Gerechtshof** (Law Court), the **Civiele Griffie** (Town Clerk's Office) with its 15th-century front gable, the **Stadhuis** (Town Hall), and the **Heilig Bloed Basikiek** (Basilica of the Holy Blood). ✉ *Hoogstraat and Breidelstraat.* 🎫 *BF60/€1.50.* ⏲ *Summer: Daily 9:30–noon and 2–6; winter: Thurs.–Tues. 10–noon and 2–4.*

★ 18 **Groeninge Museum.** One of the world's most important art galleries is housed here, with exhibits that include Europe's richest collection of medieval art and a fine display of 15th- to 21st-century Dutch and Belgian works. The first room boasts Jan van Eyck's wonderfully realistic *Madonna with Canon Van der Paele,* in which Van Eyck achieved texture and depth through multiple layers of oil and varnish. Known as one of the original Flemish Primitives, Van Eyck created a technique that has withstood the ravages of more than five centuries. All the Flemish Primitives and their successors—Petrus Christus, Hugo Van der Goes, Hans Memling, Hieronymus Bosch, Rogier Van der Weyden, Gerard David, Pieter Bruegel (both Elder and Younger), Pieter Pourbus—are also represented at the museum. The survey of Belgian art continues through the romantics and realists to Surrealists and contemporary artists. The Groeninge is set back from the street in a diminutive park behind a medieval gate. Although it is blessedly small, its riches warrant a full morning or afternoon. ✉ *Dijver 12,* ☎ *050/448711.* 🎫 *BF200/€4.95; combination ticket (includes the Gruuthuse, Memling, and Brangwyn museums;* ☞ *above and below), BF450/€11.15.* ⏲ *Apr.–Sept., daily 9:30–5; Oct.–Mar., Wed.–Mon. 9:30–12:30 and 2–5.*

NEED A BREAK? The attractive **Taverne Groeninge** (✉ Dijver 13) is decorated with works by Frank Brangwyn.

20 **Gruuthuse Museum.** If you want to understand the daily life of 15th-century Brugge, visit this applied arts museum. The collection is housed in the former home of Lodewijk Van Gruuthuse, a prominent Dutch nobleman who financed Edward IV's campaign to regain the throne of England in 1461. The family made its money from toll rights and from *gruut,* an herb used in brewing beer—a sure way to get rich in Belgium. The home features find displays of furniture, tapestries, lace, ceramics, kitchen equipment, weaponry, and musical instruments. Beamed ceilings, immense fireplaces, and cool stone floors show off the decor of the time. Room 6 has an attractive Gothic interior with a 15th-century mantelpiece and stained-glass windows. Don't miss the 18th-century guillotine—a piece of equipment that most homes of the era fortunately didn't contain. ✉ *Dijver 17,* ☎ *050/448711.* 🎫 *BF80/€2.00; combination ticket (includes the Groeninge, Memling, and Brangwyn museums;* ☞ *above and below) BF450/€11.15.* ⏲ *Apr.–Sept., daily 9:30–5; Oct.–Mar., Wed.–Mon. 9:30–12:30 and 2–5.*

16 **Heilig Bloed Basiliek.** The Lower Chapel of The Basilica of the Holy Blood retains its austere, 12th-century, Romanesque character. The massive pillars supporting a low, vaulted roof, simple interior with bare walls, and three brick aisles combine to make a structure unique in West Flanders. Note the poignant, 14th-century Pieta and the carved statue of Christ in the crypt. The baptismal scene carved on the tympanum is original. An elaborate, external Gothic stairway leads to the Upper Chapel, which was twice destroyed—by Protestant iconoclasts in the 16th century and by French Republicans in the 18th—but both times rebuilt. Behind the iron grill are parts of the original tile flooring, but the original stained-glass windows were replaced in 1845, and then again after an explosion in 1967, when they were restored by the Brugges painter De Loddere. A vial thought to contain a few drops of the blood of Christ was brought from Jerusalem to Brugge in 1149 by Derick of Alsace when he returned from the Second Crusade. It is exposed here every Friday, and on Ascension Day it is carried through the streets in the magnificent Procession of the Holy Blood, a major pageant that combines religious and historical elements. The small **museum** next to the basilica contains the 17th-century reliquary. ✉ *Burg.* 🎫 *BF60/€1.50.* ⏲ *Apr.–Sept., daily 9:30–noon and 2–6; Oct.–Mar., daily 10–noon and 2–4 (closed Wed. PM).*

NEED A BREAK?

Opus 4 is reached through the shopping gallery Ten Steeghere, which starts next to the basilica. Overlooking a pretty stretch of canal, it's a good place for a quiet beer, snack, or cake.

27 **Huize ter Buerze.** Built in 1453 and recently carefully restored, the House of Purses was where money was exchanged and where the burghers and foreign merchants from around Europe who lived in this Hanseatic Quarter talked of fiscal matters. The name of the owners of the house, the Van er Burze, lives on as the modern Beurs, or Bourse, which is now a term synonymous with stock exchange throughout the world. ✉ *Intersection of Academiestraat and Vlamingstraat.*

25 **Jan Van Eyckplein.** This colorful square with a statue of the famed 15th-century painter lies at the center of Hanseatic Brugge. It includes the old **Tolhuis** (Customs House), built in 1477, where vehicles on their way to market had to stop while tolls were levied on goods brought from nearby ports. **Poortersloge**, a late Gothic building with a slender spire, was owned by the guild of porters and used as a meeting place for the burghers. The bear that occupies one niche represents the legendary creature speared by Baldwin of the Iron Arm and later became the symbol of the city. ✉ *Intersection of Spinolarei, Academiestraat, Genthof, Spiegelrei, and Spanjaardstraat.*

30 **Jeruzalemkerk.** The striking, 15th-century Jerusalem Church, with its beautiful stained-glass windows, was built by two pilgrims returning from the Holy Land who copied the city's Church of the Holy Sepulchre. The black marble mausoleum of Genoese pilgrim Anselm Adornes and his wife occupies a central position. Anselm became burgomeister of Brugge, but was murdered in Scotland while he was consul there in 1484. ✉ *Jeruzalemstraat 3.* 🎫 *Free.* ⏲ *Weekdays 10–noon and 2–6, Sat. 10–noon and 2–5.*

32 **Kantencentrum.** The Lace Center maintains the quality and authenticity of the ancient Belgian craft of lace-making. This foundation includes a lace museum in the Jerusalem almshouses in Balstraat, as well as a school where youngsters are taught the intricate art of the bobbins, and a shop to buy all provisions. It is the former home of the Adornes, and adjoins their mausoleum in the Jeruzalemkerk. ✉ *Peperstraat 3,* ☎ *050/*

330072. 🎫 *BF60/€1.50.* ⏲ *Weekdays 10–noon and 2–6, Sat. 10–noon and 2–5.*

⓮ **Markt.** Used as a marketplace since 958, the Market Square has as its focus a statue of the city's medieval heroes, Jan Breydel and Pieter De Coninck, who led the commoners of Flanders to their short-lived victory over the aristocrats of France. The west and north sides are lined with old guild houses, many of them sheltering restaurants that spill out onto the sidewalk. On the east side stand the provincial government house and the post office, an excellent pastiche of Burgundian Gothic. The south side of the Markt is dominated by the medieval **Belfort** (Belfry), rising to a height of 270 ft. Once the valuables of Brugge were kept in the second floor treasury; today the tower commands the city and the surrounding countryside with more presence than grace. The crowning octagonal lantern, added in the 15th century, contains the 47 bells of the remarkable Brugge carillon. If you haven't walked enough, you can climb 366 winding steps to the clock mechanism, and from the carillon enjoy a gorgeous overview. ✉ *Intersection of St-Jacobstraat, St-Amandstraat, Steenstraat, Breidelstraat, Philipstockstraat, Wollestraat, and Vlamingstraat.* 🎫 *BF100/€2.50.* ⏲ *Apr.–Sept., daily 9:30–5; Oct.–Mar., daily 9:30–12:30 and 1:30–5. Carillon concerts: June 15–Sept., Mon., Wed., Sat. 9* PM*–10* PM*, Sun. 2:15–3; Oct.–June 14, Wed. and weekends 2:15–3.*

★ ㉑ **Memling Museum.** The collection contains just six works, but they are of breathtaking quality and among the greatest—and certainly the most spiritual—of Flemish Primitives. Hans Memling (ca.1440–1494) was born in Germany, but spent the greater part of his life in Brugge. In *The Altarpiece of St. John the Baptist and St. John the Evangelist,* two leading personages of the Burgundian court are believed to be portrayed: Mary of Burgundy (buried in the Onze-Lieve-Vrouwekerk; ☞ *below*) as St. Catherine, and Margaret of York as St. Barbara. The "paintings within the painting" give details of the lives of the two saints. The miniature paintings that adorn the St. Ursula Shrine are marvels of fine detail and poignancy; Memling's work gives recognizable iconographic details about cities, such as Brugge, Cologne, Basel, and Rome. The Memling Museum is inside the recently restored **Sint-Janshospitaal,** which was founded in the 12th century and remained in use until the early 20th; it is one of the oldest surviving hospitals in Europe. Furniture, paintings, and hospital-related items are attractively displayed, and the 13th-century middle ward, the oldest of three, was built in Romanesque style. A fascinating 18th-century painting shows patients arriving by sedan chair and being fed and ministered to by sisters and clerics. ✉ *Mariastraat 38,* ☎ *050/448711.* 🎫 *BF140/€3.45; combination ticket (includes Gruuthuse, Groeninge, and Brangwyn museums; ☞ above) BF450/€11.15.* ⏲ *Apr.–Sept., daily 9:30–5; Oct.–Mar., Wed.–Mon. 9:30–12:30 and 2–5.*

㉔ **Minnewater.** Romantically termed "the Lake of Love," this man-made reservoir was created in the 13th century to expand the city harbor, and it often accommodated more than 100 ships. The swans of Minnewater evoke an etymological legend or perhaps an historical truth: in 1488, six years after his wife's death, Maximilian of Austria was imprisoned by the people of Brugge, and his advisor, Pieter Lanchals, was decapitated. Because the name *Lanchals* is very close to the Dutch word for "long neck," when Maximilian was freed, he ordered Brugge to expiate its crime by keeping swans in the canals of the city in perpetuity. Maximilian went on to become emperor; his grandson was Charles V. ✉ *Just south of Begijnhof.*

NEED A BREAK? **Straffe Hendrik,** on the delightful Walplein, is a brewery pub in use since 1856, part of the Henri Maes brewery, which you can tour. "Straffe" means strong, and this beer, at 9% alcohol, certainly lives up to its billing.

31 **Museum voor Volkskunde.** Housed in a row of whitewashed almshouses around a courtyard, the Folklore Museum was originally built for retired shoemakers. The museum now contains various reconstructed interiors: a grocery shop, a living room, a tavern, a cobbler's workshop, a classroom, a pharmacy and a kitchen. You can end your tour at the museum inn, The Black Cat. ✉ *Rolweg 40,* ☎ *050/330044.* 🎫 *BF80/€2.00.* ⏲ *Daily 9:30–5; Oct.–Mar., closed Tues.*

22 **Onze-Lieve-Vrouwekerk.** The towering spire of the plain, Gothic Church of our Lady, begun about 1220, rivals the Belfry as Brugge's symbol. It is 400 ft high, the tallest brick construction in the world. While brick can be built high, it cannot be sculpted like stone; hence the tower's somewhat severe look. The church's most precious treasure is the small *Virgin and Child,* an early work by Michelangelo. The great sculptor sold it to a merchant from Brugge when the original client failed to pay. It was stolen by Napoleon, and during World War II by Nazi leader Herman Goering, and now, carved in white marble, it sits in a black marble niche behind an altar at the end of the south aisle. The choir contains many 13th- and 14th-century polychromed tombs in Renaissance style, as well as two mausoleums: that of Mary of Burgundy, who died in 1482 at the age of 25 after a fall from her horse; and that of her father, Charles the Bold, killed in 1477 while laying siege to Nancy in France. Mary was as well loved in Brugge as her husband, Maximilian of Austria, was loathed. Her finely chiseled effigy captures her beauty. ✉ *Gruuthusestraat.* 🎫 *BF60/€1.50.* ⏲ *Apr.–Sept., daily 10–11:30 and 2:30–5 (Sat. until 4); Oct.–Mar., daily 10–11:30 and 2:30–4:30 (Sat. until 4). Closed Sun.* AM *except to worshipers.*

Oude Griffie. The 16th-century Former Recorder's House, a mixture of Gothic and Flemish Renaissance elements, is still used as part of the law courts and is not open for visitors. Squeezed into the corner next to the Oude Griffie is the tiny **Museum van het Brugse Vrije** (Museum of the Brugge County Council), a remnant of the 15th-century Brugse Vrije county hall. Its principal treasure is the courtroom with its huge oak and black-marble chimneypiece. A large bas-relief depicts a robust, nearly life-size Charles V, carved in dark oak and marble by Lancelot Blondeel while the emperor was still a young man. ✉ *Burg 11a,* ☎ *050/448260.* 🎫 *BF100/€2.50 (joint ticket with Stadhuis;* ☞ *below).* ⏲ *Apr.–Sept., Tues.–Sun. 9:30–12:30 and 1:15–5; Oct.–Mar., 9:30–12:30 and 2–5.*

★ **Reien.** With their old humpbacked stone bridges, the narrow and meandering canals give Brugge its character, opening up perspective and imposing their calm. The view from the **Meebrug** is especially picturesque. Farther along the **Groenereit** and the **Godshuizen De Pelikaan** canals are almshouses dating from the early 18th century. There are several such charitable buildings in the city, tiny houses built by the guilds for the poor, some still serving their original purpose. **Steenhouwersdijk** overlooks the brick rear gables that were part of the original county hall. The Vismarkt (Fish Market) contains 19th-century buildings designed in classical style; fresh seafood from Zeebrugge is sold Tuesday through Saturday. Just beyond is the little **Huidenvettersplein** (Tanners' Square), with its 17th-century guild house. Next to it, from the **Rozenhoedkaai** canal, the view of the heart of the city includes the pinnacles of the town hall, basilica, and belfry—the essence of Brugge.

28 **Saaihalle.** The houses of the Venetian and Florentine merchants have disappeared, but the Genoese Serge Hall trading house still stands. The original crenellated curtain wall, however, has been replaced by a bell-shape gable. ✉ *South corner of Vlamingstraat and Grauwwerkersstraat.*

NEED A BREAK? **Vlissinghe** (✉ Blekersstraat, ☎ 050/343737) is the oldest pub in Brugge; people have been enjoying the beer here since 1552, and it hasn't changed much. You can also relax among the rosebushes in the courtyard.

29 **Sint-Anna.** The neighborhood of Saint Anna's Quarter illustrates how yesteryear's poverty can become today's charm. The small houses that now look so tidy were the homes of the 19th century's truly needy. In contrast, the 17th-century **Sint-Annakerk** (St. Anne's Church) is filled with riches, sculpted wood, copper, and enormous paintings. As in many cases, there is no guarantee of finding the church open except during services; check with the tourist office. ✉ *Sint-Annaplein.* *Free.*

26 **Spanjaardstraat.** The street leads up to the quay where goods from Spain were unloaded. The house at No. 9 was where St. Ignatius of Loyola stayed when he came to Flanders on holidays from his studies in Paris. Directly ahead are the three arches of the **Augustijnenbrug.** Dating from 1391, it's the oldest bridge in Brugge. On the other side of the canal, **Augustijnenrei** is one of the loveliest quays.

17 **Stadhuis.** White sandstone towers with 48 decorated window recesses define the Town Hall, a jewel of Gothic architecture that marked the transition of power from the nobility to the city aldermen. Built at the end of the 14th century, it's the oldest town hall in Belgium and served as the model for the community centers that adorn every Flemish town. The statues that originally embellished the facade were smashed by the French Republicans and have been replaced by modern replicas. From the balcony, the Counts of Flanders used to take their oaths to affirm civic liberties. Inside, a grand staircase ascends to the Gothic Hall, which has a marvelous, double-vaulted timber roof. Its 19th-century frescoes relate a romantic version of the history of Brugge. ✉ *Burg 12,* ☎ *050/448141.* *BF100/€2.50 (includes Museum van het Brugse Vrije;* ☞ *Oude Griffie, above).* *Apr.–Sept., daily 9:30–5; Oct.–Mar., daily 9:30–12:30 and 2–5.*

Dining and Lodging

$$$$ ✕ **Chez Olivier.** Set above a quiet canal, with white swans gliding by as you dine, this French charmer is purely romantic. It's also top-class, with pricey set and à la carte menus, but off-season lunches are a good deal. In the kitchen, Olivier Foucad works up such creative specialties as scallop croquettes with oregano and dill; grilled monkfish on ratatouille, with tomato and basil puree; and red fruit soup with fresh mint. For the best views, request a window seat next to the water. ✉ *Meestraat 9,* ☎ *050/333659. AE, DC, MC, V. Closed Sun. No lunch July and Aug.*

$$$$ ★ ✕ **De Karmeliet.** This stately, 18th-century house with a graceful English garden is a world-renowned culinary landmark. Here you can savor delicacies that include Bresse pigeon in truffle juice or cod carpaccio with asparagus. The wait staff perfectly choreographs each course with a cool professionalism in keeping with the restaurant's formal ambience. An extensive wine cave features a top selection of international labels. ✉ *Langestraat 19,* ☎ *050/338259. Reservations essential. AE, DC, MC, V. No dinner Sun. Closed Mon.*

$$$$ ✕ **De Snippe.** Housed in a lavish 18th-century mansion, this restaurant is well-known for its fine cuisine and first-class service. The spe-

cials are a combination of French and Flemish dishes; the exquisite tastes are well worth the price. Look for fresh game and local seafood—including eel simmered in 14 herbs. ✉ *Nieuwe Gentweg 53,* ☎ *050/337070. Reservations essential. AE, DC, MC, V. Closed Sun and Feb.–Mar. No lunch Mon.*

$$$$ ★ ✕ **De Witte Poorte.** Cross through a courtyard, under low brick vaults and stone arches, to find this formal restaurant that specializes in contemporary French cooking. Thick wood beams and tapestry-covered chairs accent the interior, while the windows look onto a lush little garden. The emphasis is on seafood, including monkfish simmered in white wine and saffron, langoustine waterzooi, and langoustine tails with vinaigrette and truffle juice. You can watch your meal being prepared behind a smoked glass partition. Save room for the goodies on the dessert cart. ✉ *Jan Van Eyckplein 6,* ☎ *050/330883. AE, DC, MC, V. Closed Sun.–Mon.*

$$$$ ✕ **Den Gouden Harynk.** Few culinary artists have the depth and natural flair of chef Philippe Serruys. Guests to his unpretentious, antiques-filled dining room are treated to beautifully presented and imaginatively inspired international cuisine. Try the langoustines brushed with light curry spices, *foie d'oie* (goose liver) on a bed of rhubarb with pink peppercorns. ✉ *Groeninge 25,* ☎ *050/337637. AE, DC, MC, V. Closed Sun.–Mon., Christmas, Easter, and last 2 wks of July.*

$$$–$$$$ ✕ **Spinola.** This multistory canal-house restaurant by the Jan van Eyk statue is a real charmer. From an intimate main dining room, an iron staircase leads to the upper tables; the open kitchen is in back. Here, chef-owners Sam and Vicky Storme cook up rich Burgundian cuisine: fresh game, goose liver, and pigeon with truffles. Dinner by candlelight is the ultimate extravagance, with a choice of some 300 wines. ✉ *Spinolarei 1,* ☎ *050/341785. No credit cards. Closed Sun. No lunch Mon.*

$$$ ✕ **Bistro de Stove.** The cozy, intimate setting and rustic touches here temper the modern decor. Flemish cuisine is a specialty, and meals are creatively prepared with fresh ingredients. If you can't decide, go for one of the terrific lamb or mussel dishes. ✉ *Amandstraat 4,* ☎ *050/337835. MC, V. Closed Wed., Thurs., Jan., and mid-Aug.*

$$$ ★ ✕ **De Waterput.** This small, whitewashed farmhouse in the middle of the polderland hides a superb restaurant. There's no menu—Chef Willy Bataillie makes his daily choices based on what's freshest each morning. Thus, each meal is a delightful surprise, perhaps including smoked salmon, John Dory with chives, wild duck with small onions, or crêpes suzette. The out-of-town detour to this small restaurant is worth the time as much for the scenic drive as for the food. ✉ *Rondsaartstraat 1, Oostkerke, 9 km (5 mi) north of Brugge,* ☎ *050/599256. DC, V. Closed Tues.–Thurs., and mid-Dec.–mid-Jan.*

$$$ ✕ **Grand Café Theatre.** A hip and happening crowd—much like the patrons of its sister café in Gent—make this lively restaurant one of Brugge's busiest. An enormous Belgian flag hangs over the converted warehouse, while the sounds of classic rock and teen pop reverberate between tables. The menu features updated grazing cuisine and glorified bar food, but you can always stop by for the free happy-hour snacks. In warm weather, terrace tables are the perfect place for a breather after seeing the city. ✉ *Kuiperstraat 14,* ☎ *050/334536. AE, DC, MC, V.*

$$$ ✕ **'t Bourgoensche Cruyce.** Although its weathered timbers and sharp-raked roofs were rebuilt at the turn of the 20th century, this restaurant is housed in one of the most medieval-looking buildings in Brugge. It also has one of the city's most romantic, canal-side settings, with the light from the windows shedding kaleidoscope reflections onto the water. The cuisine is as appealing as the setting, with selections including turbot and asparagus *en papillote* (wrapped in paper or aluminum foil) with ginger; roasted lobster with thyme, bay leaf, and sweet garlic; and

pigeon with sautéed spinach and potato *galette* (round, flat cake), tender scallops, and wild mushrooms. ✉ *Wollestraat 41,* ☎ *050/337926. AE, MC, V.*

$$–$$$ ✕ **De Gouden Meermin.** This glass-walled restaurant overlooking the Grote Market offers a prime opportunity for people-watching. Fresh, local ingredients are used in an extensive menu, which includes crêpes, salads, soups, and other light meals, as well as a few inexpensive, heartier selections. ✉ *Wollestraat 35,* ☎ *050/333776. AE, DC, MC, V.*

$$–$$$ ✕ **De Serre-Eetcafé De Vuyst.** The spires of Brugge are dramatically framed within the two-story, glass walls of this trendy, light-filled bistro. You could stop in just to enjoy the views from the garden, or from the cavernous interior; however, it's worth the time to stay for a meal. Dishes are down-to-earth, delightful, and decidedly Belgian. Try the fish soup, mussels, or waterzooi, perfect selections if you're in the mood for a light meal. ✉ *Simon Stevinplein 15,* ☎ *050/342231. AE, DC, MC, V. Closed Tues., mid-Feb., and Nov.*

$$ ✕ **Breydel–De Coninck.** Conveniently located along the route from the Markt to the Burg, this no-frills restaurant is well known among locals. Plain banquettes leave the focus on the fresh seafood for which the establishment is famed. Although eel and steak are available, the restaurant's biggest draw is mussels—there's nothing more basically, and deliciously, Belgian than a huge crock heaped high with shiny, blue-black shells. ✉ *Breidelstraat 24,* ☎ *050/339746. AE, MC, V. Closed Wed. and June.*

$$ ★ ✕ **De Visscherie.** To find this popular restaurant overlooking the Vismarkt, look for the modern sculpture of a fisherman and the large fish hanging from its balcony. Business at the busy, outdoor terrace has been going strong for 25 years, with customers drawn back time and again for the excellent seafood dishes. Try the turbot, prepared in a variety of ways, or the langoustines with foie gras. If you can't decide, order the restaurant's signature dish: codfish tournedos in a polder ham and carrot sauce. ✉ *Vismarkt 8,* ☎ *050/330212. AE, MC, V. Closed Tues. and mid-Nov.–mid-Dec.*

$$ ✕ **'t Dreveken.** For a dining experience drenched in classic European ambience, head for this 1630s building overlooking one of the city's canals. Bright flower beds surround the brick facade, providing a cheery entrance into a timber-beamed dining room accented with lace tablecloths and ever more blossoms. The menu features traditional Flemish dishes and seafood. ✉ *Huidevettersplein 10,* ☎ *050/339506. AE, DC, V.*

$$ ✕ **'t Paardje.** Off the beaten track, this small, family-owned restaurant concentrates on a few meaty specialties. Mussels, eel, and steak are prepared in a variety of sauces, predominantly beer-based. The restaurant's terra-cotta and lace decor is cozy, clean, and unpretentious, and its cooking is dependably good. ✉ *Langestraat 20,* ☎ *050/334009. MC, V. No dinner Mon. or Tues.*

$–$$ ✕ **Brasserie Erasmus.** Enjoy Flemish fare with a twist—usually one that is beer-inspired—while sitting canal-side or in the pretty courtyard. Wicker, woodwork, and copper accents create a comfortable, casual atmosphere. Try the bouillabaisse, cooked with North Sea fish, or the rabbit in beer. More than 200 brews are on the menu as well, making this a popular post-tour stop in the city center. ✉ *Wollestraat 35,* ☎ *050/335781. AE, DC, MC, V. Closed Tues.*

$–$$ ✕ **De Tassche.** Though you may feel removed from the romance of old Brugge, you'll be compensated by the commitment to detail at this restaurant. The building dates from the 17th century, but the mood is contemporary, with pink damask and copper accents. Rabbit is cooked Flemish style, and simple dishes are served well, from steak to crown of lamb to grilled sole. Even the fries are hand-cut, and the chef cruises the dining room like a true gastronome. ✉ *Oude Burg 11,* ☎ *050/330319. MC, V. Closed Tues.*

$–$$ ✕ **Lotus.** A vegetarian menu and hip decor make this popular café tasteful in both senses. Small, cloth-covered tables with fresh flowers line the dining room. Proprietors Ann and Paul Demeon put together a varied veggie menu of the day—and don't miss the desserts. ✉ *Wapenmakersstraat 5,* ☎ *050/331078. No credit cards. Closed Sun.*

$–$$ ✕ **Sint-Joris.** Among the dozen or so competitive brasseries crowded along the Markt, this step-gabled spot across from the Belfry maintains a more civilized profile than its neighbors. Flowers, linens, candles, a roaring fire, and a clutter of ceramics and copper warm the dining room in winter; fine weather opens the terrace for alfresco dining. Regional dishes earn high marks here: try the fish-based waterzooi, the eel in green chervil sauce, or the shrimp croquettes. If you can't decide, go for the succulent mussels. ✉ *Markt 29,* ☎ *050/333062. AE, DC, MC, V. Closed Thurs.*

$ ✕ **Curiosa.** Housed in a cross-vaulted, medieval crypt, this restaurant is a surprisingly comfortable—and atmospheric—hideaway from tourist traffic. It's an ideal place for conversation, a light meal, and one of the myriad local beers. Snacks include omelettes, sandwiches, and *visschotel* (smoked fish plates), as well as pancakes and ice cream for a sweet note. Accompanying music hits some nice notes as well. ✉ *Vlamingstraat 22,* ☎ *050/342334. AE, DC, MC, V. Closed Mon. and July.*

$ ★ ✕ **Staminee De Garre.** Tucked in an alley off the well-worn Breidelstraat, this tiny, two-tier coffeehouse and pub is a brick-and-beam oasis, offering Mozart and magazines along with plunger coffee and over a hundred beers. Cold platters and grilled sandwiches are attractively served, and traditional nibbles of cheese are wonderful with the heartier beers. ✉ *Off Breidelstraat,* ☎ *050/341029. No credit cards.*

$ ✕ **Tom Pouce.** Despite its stuffy, slightly faded air, this friendly, urban tearoom dominates the Burg every afternoon. The decor creates an old world ambience, with heavy velour drapes, splashy carpet, cracked crockery, and a noisy open service bar. Tourists, shoppers, and loyal retirees alike dig into warm apple strudel, freshly made ice cream, and airy waffles. First-timers should order the tour de force: hot *pannekoeken* (light, eggy, vanilla-perfumed pancakes) with a pat of butter and a sprinkle of dark brown sugar. If your appetite dictates a full meal, you'll find lunch plates and stews on the menu as well. ✉ *Burg 17,* ☎ *050/330336. AE, DC, MC, V.*

$$$$ ✕🏨 **De Castillion.** Originally constructed for the Bishop of Brugge, and located just across from the Cathedral, this eclectic and lavishly styled hotel was created from two 17th-century Flemish houses. Cozy rooms have either antique cherry furnishings or modern decor. The restaurant serves such locally inspired combinations as venison filet mignon in Pomerel stock; duck's liver; and monkfish and salmon fricassee. Have your cocktails and cordials in the art-deco salon. ✉ *Heilige Geeststraat 1, 8000,* ☎ *050/343001,* FAX *050/339475. 18 rooms, 2 suites. Restaurant, bar, no-smoking rooms, sauna, exercise room, solarium, meeting rooms, parking (fee). AE, DC, MC, V.*

$$$$ ★ ✕🏨 **Die Swaene.** Deceptively housed behind a painted brick facade along one of the prettiest stretches of canal is this lavish, family-run hotel. Romantics will swoon at the elegant windows done in swagged tulle, the sparkling crystal accents, and the marble antiques. The gilt-ceiling lounge, built in the late 1700s, was once a Guild Hall of the Tailors, and the 15th-century attic still holds meetings for groups of up to 30. One guest room is set in a converted Flemish kitchen with a stone fireplace and a carved four-poster. Carved wooden doors, fireplaces, and sitting areas with antiques and wingback chairs are featured in some suites. The romantic, candlelit French restaurant ($$$$)

overlooking the garden is noted for fish dishes; other specialties include goose liver with caramelized apples, grilled turbot, and lobster-and-spinach lasagna. Breakfast is served in the sun-filled garden room. ✉ *Steenhouwersdijk 1, B8000, ☎ 050/342798, FAX 050/33–6674. 20 rooms, 2 suites. Restaurant, bar, minibars, pool, sauna, meeting rooms, parking (fee). AE, DC, MC, V.*

$$$$ **Crowne Plaza.** Fitting in surprisingly well on the corner of the Burg, this modern brick building stands at attention with all flags flying. Built on the foundation of the former St. Donace Cathedral, it's an archaeological treasure, exhibiting 10th- to 16th-century ramparts, tombs, and other artifacts. The large, bright rooms are cheery, and some are bi-level, with beamed, vaulted ceilings. The attached bar and café are always busy. ✉ *Burg 10, B8000, ☎ 050/345834, FAX 050/345615. 89 rooms, 7 suites. Restaurant, bar, café, pool, sauna, exercise room, convention center, parking (fee). AE, DC, MC, V.*

$$$$ ★ **De Tuileriëen.** Patrician tastes dominate at this 15th-century mansion. The decor is genteel, with antique reproduction furniture and weathered marble complemented by mixed-print fabrics and wall coverings in celadon, slate, and cream. Rooms are romantic, with marble-accented bathrooms, although those with canal views receive traffic noise; courtyard rooms are quieter. The firelit bar is filled with cozy tartan wing chairs, and the neo-Baroque breakfast salon features a coffered ceiling. Breakfast is served on the terrace alongside the canal. ✉ *Dyver 7, B8000, ☎ 050/343691, FAX 050/340400. 18 rooms, 22 suites, 1 penthouse. Bar, indoor pool, hot tub, massage, sauna, bicycles, baby-sitting, laundry service and dry cleaning, parking (fee). AE, DC, MC, V.*

$$$–$$$$ ★ **Oud Huis Amsterdam.** Two noble, 17th-century houses in the elegant Hanseatic district combine the grace of another era with the polish of a modern, first-class property. Parts of this town house date to the 1300s, and owners Philip and Caroline Train have preserved such antique details as tooled Cordoba leather wallpaper, rough-hewn rafters, and Delft tiles. Rooms with canal views overlook the busy street; back rooms with red rooftop views are quieter. Summer concerts are held in the courtyard terrace. ✉ *Spiegelrei 3, B8000, ☎ 050/341810, FAX 050/338891. 34 rooms. Bar, free parking. AE, DC, MC, V.*

$$$ ★ **Anselmus.** Crafted from a 16th-century mansion, this family-run bed-and-breakfast is a find. Rich colors and period accents add romance to otherwise simple, comfortable furnishings, although there are many elegant touches—note the winding staircase in the entryway. Here, European charm comes at a moderate price, with a hearty breakfast included. ✉ *Riddersstraat 15, B8000, ☎ 050/341374, FAX 050/341916. 10 rooms. Bar, breakfast room. AE, MC, V.*

$$$ ★ **Pandhotel.** A member of the Romantik hotel chain, this 18th-century mansion is now an intimate, family-run hotel. Neoclassical public rooms feature restored wood paneling and moldings, rough-hewn flooring, and Oriental rugs. Modern infusions include a skylight in the breakfast room and gleaming copper accents in the open kitchen, where a country breakfast is prepared daily. Individually decorated bedrooms are charming, some with canopy beds and marbleized bathrooms; junior suites feature Ralph Lauren fabrics. Some rooms overlook the Cathedral, others the red roofline. Two- and three-night packages are good deals. ✉ *Pandreitje 16, 8000, ☎ 050/340666, FAX 050/340556. 23 rooms. Bar, breakfast room, meeting rooms. AE, DC, MC, V.*

$$–$$$ **Bryghia.** This restored German–Austrian trade center is a handsome, 15th-century landmark. Outside, the brick walls are lined with paned windows and flower boxes; inside, the hotel is warmed by pastel floral fabrics and beech cabinets. Bedrooms are simple yet comfortable, and the cozy public rooms include small sitting areas and a beamed, slate-floor breakfast salon. ✉ *Oosterlingenplein 4, B8000, ☎ 050/*

338059, FAX *050/341430. 18 rooms. Bar, breakfast room, minibars, parking (fee). AE, DC, V.*

$$–$$$ **Erasmus.** Crisp geometric lines, wood accents, and copper lighting fixtures make this hotel seem more Scandinavian than Belgian. Comfortable guest rooms have desks and modern features. The bar patio is an ideal spot for snacking, sipping a drink, and watching the world go by. Breakfast is included. ✉ *Wollestraat 35, B8000,* ☎ *050/335781,* FAX *050/334727. 9 rooms. Bar, minibars. AE, DC, MC, V.*

$$–$$$ **Wilgenhof.** Halfway between Brugge and Damme and near the canal, this bucolic mansion-on-the-polder is a good base for excursions in either direction and to the coast, which is just 12 km (7 mi) away. Rooms are basic, but the location is ideal for exploring the area. Breakfast is included. ✉ *Polderstraat 151, St. Kruis B8310,* ☎ *050/362744,* FAX *050/362821. 6 rooms. Breakfast room. AE, DC, MC, V.*

$$ ★ **Egmond.** Play Lord of the Manor at this 18th-century house near the Beguinage. Public rooms feature hearths and chimneypieces, beamed ceilings, dark wood moldings, and dormes—just visualize your servants running and fetching for gluttons at the table. Breakfast is served in an oak-beam hall with a Delft-tile fireplace. Each room has a special period feature or two, and all are airy, with garden views. Guests can stroll the perimeter of the Minnewaterpark (the *Lake of Love*) and enjoy tranquil surroundings. The hotel is only 10 minutes' walk from the bustle of central Brugge. ✉ *Minnewater 15, B8000,* ☎ *050/341445,* FAX *050/342940. 8 rooms. Breakfast room, free parking. No credit cards.*

$$ **Europ.** Although this updated 18th-century town house could use some loving care, the coveted property overlooks a canal and is a five-minute walk from the town center. Modern, spartan rooms are beneath low, sloped ceilings with dormers, and beds feature Swiss-flex construction mattresses that ensure a sound night's sleep. A generous Continental buffet breakfast is included. ✉ *Augustijenrei 18, B8000,* ☎ *050/337975,* FAX *050/345266. 28 rooms, 20 with bath. Bar, parking (fee). DC, MC.*

$–$$ **Ter Brughe.** This renovated, 16th-century, step-gabled house is now a slick, efficient hotel. Although the modern decor is generic bamboo and beige, heavy beams, tempera murals, and leaded-glass windows offer glimpses of the building's intriguing former life. The oldest section is the vaulted cellar, originally a warehouse, which now serves as the breakfast room and opens onto the canal. ✉ *Oost-Gistelhof 2, B8000,* ☎ *050/340324,* FAX *050/338873. 24 rooms. Breakfast room, parking (fee). AE, DC, MC, V.*

$ ★ **De Pauw.** From the ivy-covered brick exterior to the fresh flowers and doilies in the breakfast parlor, this is a welcoming little inn. Rooms have names rather than numbers to give them a more homey feel, and needlepoint cushions and old framed prints add to the warmth. Breakfast, which includes cold cuts, cheese, and six kinds of bread, is served on pretty china. ✉ *St-Gilliskerkhof 8, B8000,* ☎ *050/337118,* FAX *050/345140. 8 rooms, 6 with bath. Breakfast room. AE, DC, MC, V.*

$ **Fevery.** This child-friendly hotel is part of a comfortable family home in a quiet corner of Brugge. There's enough clutter to make you feel like you never left your own house, and even a baby monitor so parents can relax with a drink downstairs after putting a child to bed. ✉ *Collaert Mansionstraat 3, B8000,* ☎ *050/331269,* FAX *050/331791. 11 rooms. Bar, baby-sitting, free parking. AE, DC, MC, V.*

$ **Jacobs.** The public rooms are plush and accented with crystal, but this is actually quite a casual place. (Breakfast tables are decorated with plastic waste buckets.) Basic and clean, rooms have a homey flair. ✉ *Baliestraat 1, B8000.* ☎ *050/339831,* FAX *050/335694. 25 rooms. Bar, breakfast room, parking (fee). AE, DC, MC, V.*

Nightlife and the Arts

The Arts

The monthly *Agenda Brugge,* available at the tourist office, gives details of all events in the city. Also check listings in *The Bulletin.*

The **Stadsschouwburg** (City Theater; ✉ Vlamingstraat 38, ☎ 050/443060), which presents classical music, dance, and theater, is a stop-off point for most of the major Flemish companies.

Festivals

More than 2,000 locals take part in **The Procession of the Holy Blood,** which dates back 800 years and is held on Ascension Day. The precious liquid relic is taken from its place in the church of the same name and carried through flag-bedecked streets. The **Cactus Festival** in July is a three-day, open-air music celebration in Minnewater park. The **Festival of the Canals,** held every three years in August (the next is in 2001), features a sound-and-light show with 600 actors, dancers, and musicians. The **Pageant of the Golden Tree** (next in 2005) commemorates the marriage of Charles the Bold and Margaret of York. Other festivals include pre-Lenten **Carnival** and the **May Fair.**

In 2002 Brugge will be honored as the Cultural Capital of Europe, and a new multifunctional concert hall will open. The city will also host the annual **Hanseatic Days,** a four-day event designed to restore the bonds of the former merchant members of the medieval Hansa.

Nightlife

Among the nicest hotel bars are **Academie** (✉ Wijngaardstraat 7–9, ☎ 050/332266), **De Medici** (✉ Potterierei 15, ☎ 050/339833), and **The Meeting** (✉ Spiegelrei 3) at the Oud Huis Amsterdam.

Brugge is not the liveliest city at night, but there are several options. The **Cactus Club** (✉ St-Jakobstraat 36, ☎ 050/332014) is Brugge's major venue for pop, rock, folk, and blues acts. Discos, mostly catering to a clientele not much older than 20, are clustered around Eiermarkt, back of the Markt: **Ambiorix** (✉ Eiermarkt 11 bis, ☎ 050/337400), **Coolcat** (✉ Eiermarkt 11, ☎ 050/340527), and **The Pick** (✉ Eiermarkt 12, ☎ 050/337638). At 't Zand are **Graffiti** (✉ 't Zand 9, ☎ 050/336909) and **Ma Rica Rokk** (✉ 't Zand 8, ☎ 050/338358). **Villa Romana** (✉ Kraanplein 1, ☎ 050/343453) attracts an older crowd.

Outdoor Activities and Sports

Sports Service (✉ Walweinstraat 20, ☎ 050/448322).

Running

The green city wall is pleasant for jogging. For a more extensive workout, try the Tillegembos Provincial Domain in St-Michiels.

Swimming

Enjoy the Olympic-size pool at the new **Provinciaal Olympisch Zwembad** (✉ Olympia Park, Doornstraat, St-Andries, ☎ 050/390200).

Tennis

At the **Bryghia Tennis Club** (✉ Boogschutterslaan 37, St-Kruis, ☎ 050/353406) indoor courts cost BF240/€5.95 per person for one hour, outdoor courts BF200/€4.95 per person per hour.

Shopping

Although there are increasing numbers of tacky stores, Brugge has many trendy boutiques and shops, especially along **Steenstraat** and **Vlamingstraat,** both of which branch off from the Markt. **Ter Steeghere** mall, which links the Burg with Wollestraat, deftly integrates a modern development into the historic center. The largest and most pleasant mall is the **Zilverpand** off Zilverstraat, where 50-odd shops cluster in Flemish gable houses around a courtyard with sidewalk cafés.

Street Markets

The Burg is the setting for the **Wednesday Market** (weekly except July and August) with flowers, vegetables, and fruit. The biggest is the **Saturday Market** on 't Zand. The **Fish Market** is held, appropriately, on the Vismarkt, daily except Sunday and Monday. All three are morning events, from 8 to approximately 12:30. On weekend afternoons (March through October) there's a **Flea Market** along the Dijver.

Specialty Stores

Art and antiques dealers abound. **Guyart** (✉ Fort Lapin 37, ☎ 050/332159) is both an art gallery and a tavern. **Papyrus** (✉ Walplein 41, ☎ 050/336687) specializes in silverware. **'t Leerhuis** (✉ Groeninge 35, ☎ 050/330302) deals in contemporary art.

Brugge has been a center for lace-making since the 15th century. You can find pieces costing a few hundred francs in many souvenir shops. Handmade lace in intricate patterns, however, takes a very long time to produce, and this is reflected in the price. For work of this type, you should be prepared to part with BF10,000/€250 or more. The best shop for the serious lace-lover is in the Sint-Anne Quarter, just behind the church: **'t Apostelientje** (✉ Balstraat 11, ☎ 050/337860).

Damme

7 km (4 mi) north of Brugge.

A quiet agricultural village with a population of about 10,000 Flemings, Damme lies in a peaceful polder landscape of waving fields and far horizons. If you take the miniature paddle steamer *Lamme Goedzak,* which travels along a canal lined with slender poplars, the town is just a half-hour from Brugge. If you're in shape, you could even hike or bike the distance along a common canal path.

Damme owes its place in history to a tidal wave that ravaged the coast in 1134, which opened up an inlet from the Zwin to the environs of Brugge. The little town grew up as a fishing village until a canal was dug to connect Damme to Brugge. The former settlement was soon a key port and snapped up exclusive rights to import such treasured commodities as Bordeaux wine and Swedish herring. The "Maritime Law of Damme" thus became the standard for Hanseatic merchants. Later, when the Zwin channel silted up, Damme's fortunes slowly declined; however, its Burgundian architecture remains well-preserved.

On a clear day you can see as far as the Netherlands from the top of the tower of the **Onze-Lieve-Vrouwekerk** (Church of Our Lady), which rises high above the surrounding farmland as a symbol of Damme's proud past. Poet Jacob van Maerlant, who lived and worked in Damme during the late 13th century, is buried under the main portal below the tower. Charles the Bold and Margaret of York were also married here.

Jacob van Maerlant's statue stands tall and poetic in the center of the charming **Marktplein.** On the facade of the Gothic Stadhuis (Town Hall) you can see Charles, the noble duke, presenting the wedding ring to his fiancée Margaret, plus other stone effigies of Flemish counts set in niches between the high windows. The step-gabled building's interior moldings and clocktower are especially outstanding. Note the **Huyse de Grote Sterre,** a 15th-century patrician's residence that was also home to the Spanish military governor in the 17th century; it's now a tourist office and a literary museum.

The **Boudewijnpark en Dolphinarium** offers dozens of family attractions, including dolphin and ice shows. ✉ *A. De Baeckestraat 12, St-Michiels, 2 km (1 mi) south of Damme,* ☎ *050/383838.* *BF510/€12.65 for all attractions; BF180/€4.45 Dolphinarium only.* *Park: Easter–May, daily noon–6; May–Aug., daily 10–6; Sept., Wed. and weekends noon–6. Dolphinarium: daily, shows at 11 and 4, more during peak season.*

Lodging

$–$$ **Hotel Wilgenhof.** At this renovated farmhouse along the Damme canal you'll eat a real country breakfast and enjoy basic but comfy rooms with modern features. In the sitting room by the fireplace, or in the attractive garden, you can share day's activities around the polderland with other lucky guests. Or, just put your feet up and read a book. ✉ *Polderstraat 151, B8310,* ☎ *050/362744,* FAX *050/362821.. 6 rooms. Restaurant, bar, café, sauna. AE, DC, MC, V.*

$ **Hofstede De Stamper.** For a taste of country Flanders, stay at this 18th-century farmstead whose grounds are home to cattle, sheep, and poultry. Basic rooms and shared facilities are not for everyone, but the real treats are meals prepared with fresh farm products—and, on Sundays, warm, fragrant bread and cakes baked in a wood oven. Available on weekends, and on request during the week, this true farm experience is only 2 km from Damme. ✉ *Zuiddijk 12,* ☎ *050/50500197. 3 rooms. Restaurant. No credit cards.*

OFF THE BEATEN PATH

ZEEBRUGGE – For pleasures on the water, journey to the city's port area, known as the suburban "Brugge on the Sea." Here you'll find a beach, marina, and scenes from a busy fishing trade in an easy day trip. The former fish market has been turned into an attractive sea museum that details the history of the coast, the harbor, and its fishing industry—you can also explore the inside of a Russian submarine and a Belgian lightship. This is also where you can catch a ferry to England.

LISSEWEGE – Surrounded by meadows, this nearby settlement is one of the prettiest and best-preserved of the coastal villages. Whitewashed houses cluster around a 13th-century brick church and line a narrow, flower-bordered canal that runs through the village. The former Cisterian Abbey of Ter Doest includes a perfectly preserved, massive 13th-century barn, still supported by original beams. The train from Brugge to Zeebrugge stops in Lissewege.

En Route The tiny polder villages are a delight to explore by foot, bike, or hand-operated ferry along the canals. **Hoeke,** the Zwin port for German merchants, has a 13th-century church and a 19th-century windmill. Head to **Lapscheure,** on the Dutch border, to explore a major 18th-century dike system. **Moerkerke** is the site of the Battle of the Windmill, which took place late in World War II. **Oostkerke** is a whitewashed little village with a 14th-century castle and a 19th-century mill. **Sijsele** features a unique combination of castle and golf-course green scenery. You'll find neo-Gothic architectural treasures in **Vivenkapelle,** including a 19th-century church, rectory, abbey, and school, designed by the architect Jean de Bethune.

"FLANDERS FIELDS": HISTORIC BATTLEFIELDS

The provinces of West and East Flanders form the original, big-sky "platte land," the flat countryside which haunted singer Jacques Brel's imagination. The historic sites found here are a testimony to the unique spirit of the Belgian people who, centuries ago, took on France, Spain, and Germany. Highways south from Brugge and Gent point to where decisive battles have been waged since the time of Julius Caesar. Here, longbowmen fought cavalry in heraldic colors, and the battles intermittently continued through World War I.

The Flanders Fields evoke both the pastoral peace of a land ready for harvest, dotted with crimson poppies, and the terrible war that shattered it. Indeed, Simon Schama has called it "the blood-polluted source of all our sorrows." Almost a half-million Belgian, British, and British Commonwealth casualties of "The Great War to End All Wars" are buried here, "between the crosses, row on row, That mark our place." These beautiful, horrible words from the famed poem by Canadian colonel John McCrae truly sum up the depth of emotion about these dead, in these fields.

Kortrijk

34 *51 km (31 mi) south of Brugge, 45 km (27 mi) southwest of Gent, 90 km (54 mi) southwest of Brussels.*

Established in ancient Roman times, this town on the river Leie became the flax capital of Europe in the Middle Ages, as well as the uncontested producer of damask during the Renaissance. Today it is a center of carpet and upholstery production, and a university town, with a department of the Catholic University of Leuven. A traffic-free district with shops and restaurants attracts well-to-do customers from throughout the region.

The Battle of the Golden Spurs (which the French call the Battle of Courtrai) was fought immediately outside the city walls, close to the present Groeningelaan. On July 11, 1302, poorly armed weavers and craftsmen from Brugge, Gent, and Ieper took on the French nobility. The battle had actually been going well for the French infantrymen, but they were brushed aside by the mounted knights, who were spoiling for a fight. A hidden canal, the Groeninge, was the Flemings' greatest ally; many of the knights plunged into it, only to be speared by the Flemish pikemen. After the battle, 700 pairs of golden spurs were removed from the bodies and triumphantly hung in the Church of Our Lady in Kortrijk as a votive offering. Eighty years later, however, the French returned, defeated the Flemings, burned the city, and retrieved their spurs. The **Groeningeabdij Museum** depicts the history of Kortrijk and the Battle of the Golden Spurs and has displays of locally produced damask and silver. ✉ *Houtmarkt,* ☎ *056/257892.* 🎫 *Free.* ⏲ *Tues.–Sun. 10–noon and 2–5.*

The **Broeltoren,** on either side of the river Leie, are what remain of the medieval fortifications destroyed by Louis XIV in 1684. A 45-ft-high neo-Gothic monument was erected in 1902 on the spot where the Battle of the Golden Spurs was fought in 1302, and it is commemorated on the weekend closest to July 11 with a parade or a tournament. These are curiously low-key affairs, given the importance of the battle in the annals of Flemish nationalism, although Flanders as a whole is gearing up for a huge celebration of the 700th anniversary in 2002.

The **Begijnhof** (Beguinage), with its cobbled streets and whitewashed houses, has been lovingly restored in Baroque style. It's an oasis of calm, and among the most beautiful beguinages in Europe. The Begijnhof is open to the public from sunrise to sunset, and there's a museum. The adjoining **Onze-Lieve-Vrouwekerk** (✉ Begijnhofstraat and Groeningestraat, ☎ 056/244800; ⏲ Mar.–Sept., 8:30–noon and 2–7; Oct.–Apr. 8:30–noon and 2–4:30), the church where the Golden Spurs once hung, contains an alabaster figure of St. Catherine from 1380, standing in the Chapel of the Counts of Flanders. Art connoisseurs will note that the Van Dyck painting in the north transept, The Raising of the Cross, shows Rubens's influence. ✉ *Begijnhofstraat 8500 Kortrijk,* ☎ *056/244802.* 🎫 *Beguinage: free; museum: BF30/€0.75.* ⏲ *Beguinage: Tues.–Thurs. and weekends 2–5 and by appointment; museum Sat.–Mon. 2–5, Tues.–Thurs. 1–5.*

NEED A BREAK? The elegant **Tea Room D'haene** (✉ Sint-Maartenskerkstraat 4–1) serves tasty pancakes, waffles, and pastries throughout the day, and pleasant light lunches.

The **Nationaal Vlas-, Kant- en Linnenmuseum** (National Flax, Lace, and Linen Museum), in an old farmhouse, tells the story of flax-growing and lace- and linen-making in a series of lifelike tableaux, peopled with wax models of Flemish historical celebrities. The river Leie, which passes through Kortrijk on its way to Gent, was known as the Golden River in the Middle Ages because of the fields of flax along its banks. ✉ *Etienne Sabbelaan 4,* ☎ *056/210138.* 🎫 *Flax wing, BF100/€2.50; linen wing, BF100/€2.50; joint ticket, BF170/€4.20.* ⏲ *Mar.–Nov., Mon. 1:30–6, Tues.–Fri. 9–12:30 and 1:30–6, weekends 2–6; lace and linen sections closed Dec.–Apr.*

OFF THE BEATEN PATH **NATIONAL CYCLE MUSEUM** – Check out this monument to one of the region's most popular pastimes. Displays include bicycle paintings, early designs by Leonardo Da Vinci, and modern bikes *du jour.* ✉ *Polenplein 15,* ☎ *051/268740.* 🎫 *BF100/€2.50.* ⏲ *Jan.–Mar., Tues.–Sat. 2–5.*

Dining and Lodging

$ ✕ **Restaurant Beethoven.** Ludwig may never have devoured the grilled meats at this intimate restaurant, but lots of Flemings do. The chicken with saffron sauce is popular, as are the generous daily specials. ✉ *Onze-Lieve-Vrouwestraat 8,* ☎ *056/225542. No credit cards. No dinner Wed. Closed Mon.*

$$$$ ★ ✕🏨 **Gastronomisch Dorp Eddy Vandekerckhove.** Just south of Kortrijk, Eddy's "gastronomic village" is a surprise. On the menu are such delicacies as new potatoes with langoustines and caviar, lobster and sea scallops with braised chicory and onion marmalade, and thinly sliced venison with *trompettes de la mort* (a kind of black mushroom) and celeriac mousse. The large, luxurious rooms overlook fields on one side and a botanical garden and pond on the other. ✉ *Sint Anna 5, B8500,* ☎ *056/224756,* FAX *056/227170. 7 rooms. Restaurant. AE, DC, MC, V. No dinner Sun. Closed Mon., 2 wks in Nov.*

$$$ ★ 🏨 **Damier.** From its lavish café with florid plasterwork and chandeliers, to its Laura Ashley rooms, to its beeswaxed oak wainscoting and Persian carpets, this is a grand little hotel. It's been impeccably renovated and occupies a superb location. Though the hotel dates from the French Revolution, you'll find no musty corners or creaky halls hiding behind the decor—its comforts are thoroughly modern. ✉ *Grote Markt 41, B8500,* ☎ *056/221547,* FAX *056/228631. 49 rooms. Restaurant, bar, café, sauna. AE, DC, MC, V.*

Ieper

35 *32 km (19 mi) west of Kortrijk, 52 km (31 mi) south of Brugge, 125 km (75 mi) west of Brussels, 91 km (85 mi) northeast of Calais.*

Known as the Ypres of World War I fame and shame, "Wipers" to the Tommies in the trenches, Ieper to the locals, this town was the Hiroshima of The Great War. Founded in the 10th century, as a popular stop on the Brugge–Paris trade route, Ieper's textile industry helped it expand into one of the region's major cities during the Middle Ages. A population of around 100,000 lived here when the city flourished as a mercantile center in the 13th century; however, because it occupied a precarious border with France, the city became a target of political problems and disasters. Epidemics, sieges, repressions, and strife took their toll, and the clothmakers packed their bags in the 16th and 17th centuries. Ieper then became a quiet convent town, the seat of a bishopric, but was drawn into the crossfire of World War I three centuries later. Modern Ieper is a painstaking reconstruction of major medieval buildings rebuilt brick by brick. The city proudly stands as an homage to the spirit of the Flemings, and to the memory of the soldiers who fell in the surrounding fields and who lie at rest in the vast cemeteries spreading over the flat polder plains.

In Flanders Fields Museum, formerly the Ypres Salient Museum, has been transformed into an overwhelmingly powerful interactive display that preserves the memory of those who died in nearby fields. Computer screens, sound effects, scale models, and videos realistically portray the weapons, endless battles, and numerous casualties of the area's wars. Each visitor receives a "smart card" with details of a soldier or civilian and follows that person's fortunes throughout the war. The museum is housed on the second floor of the magnificent Lakenhall (Cloth Hall), a copy of the original 1304 building. If you climb the 264 steps in the square belfry, the view of turrets, towns, and fields seems endless. ✉ *Grote Markt,* ☎ *057/200724.* 🎫 *BF250/€6.20.* ⏲ *Apr.–mid-Sept., daily 10–6; Oct.–Mar., Tues.–Sun. 10–5.*

St. Maartenskathedraal (St. Martin's Cathedral) was rebuilt after the war in the predominant style of 13th-century Ieper. Notable treasures are the 16th-century polyptych near the entrance and the 17th-century alabaster statues above the screen in the baptistry chapel.

St. George's, a small Anglican church built in 1929, contains an abundance of furnishings, decorations, and memorabilia from both World Wars. The adjoining **Pilgrims' Hall** was built for those who visit Ieper looking for a relative's grave. ✉ *Elverdingsestraat 1,* ☎ *057/215685.*

★ East of town, the **Menenpoort** (Menin Gate) is among the most moving of war memorials. After World War I, the British built the vast arch in memory of the 300,000 soldiers who perished nearby. The names of some 55,000 soldiers who died before August 15, 1917, and whose bodies were missing, are enscribed. Since 1928, every night at 8, traffic is stopped at the gate as members of the local fire brigade sound the Last Post on silver bugles, gifts of the British Legion. The practice was interrupted during World War II, but it was resumed the night Polish troops liberated the town, September 6, 1944. ✉ *Menenstraat.*

En Route Hexagonal signs mark the tourist routes 14–18 and lead to military sites and war-related monuments. The **Vladslo German Military Cemetery** confirms that "the other side" also suffered terribly in the trenches of World War I. In nearby Passandale, four more cemeteries are resting places for many thousands of soldiers. Other towns and villages badly damaged by shelling include Veurne, Poperinge, and Diksmuide, with its 2-km (1¼-mi) network of trenches.

Kasteelhof 't Hooge is one of the few places where bomb craters can still be seen. A museum, **Hooge Crater 1914–18**, has been installed in the old chapel. Items on display include bombs, grenades, rifles, and uniforms. At the cemetery here are more than 6,500 graves of British soldiers. ✉ *Meenseweg 467, Zillebeke,* ☎ *057/468446.* 🎫 *BF80/€2.00.* ⏲ *Feb.–mid-Dec. 10–7.*

Follow the signs via Canadalaan and Sanctuary Wood to **Hill 62**, where, in addition to photographs, weapons, and assorted objects salvaged from the field of battle, the owner has preserved some of the original trenches and tunnels on his land. You'll need to wear boots to inspect them. ✉ *Canadalaan, Zillebeke,* ☎ *057/466373.* 🎫 *BF120/€2.95.* ⏲ *Apr.–Sept., daily 9:30–8; Oct.–Mar., daily 9:30–6.*

Municipal Museum. Set in the former St. John church, founded in the 13th century and renovated 300 years later in neo-Gothic and Renaissance style, the history of Ieper unfolds with old maps, paintings, photos, and historical objects. Art collections from the 16th century include paintings, sculptures, and metalwork. Most notable are the pastels and paintings by local artist Louise De Hem (1866–1922). ✉ *Ieperleerstraat 31, Ieper,* ☎ *057/218300.* 🎫 *BF120/€2.95.* ⏲ *Tues.–Sun. 10–12:30 and 2–6.*

Municipal Museum of Education. Ensconced in the former St. Nicolas church, a neo-Byzantine building originally devoted to spiritual matters, the museum presents what seems to be a dull topic—the history of Flanders' education from the Middle Ages to the wired age—but in a charming, informative setting. Especially evocative are the two reconstructed classrooms dating from 1700 and 1930. In the "do" class, kids can scribble with a slate pencil on slate, draw on an old blackboard with chalk, or solve a math problem on an abacus. ✉ *G. de Stuersstraat,* ☎ *057/205836.* 🎫 *BF100/€2.50.* ⏲ *Tues.–Sun 10–12:30 and 2–6.*

The Screaming Eagle ride, stilt walkers from the planet Ciriklis, and the Magic House of Houdini, where you'll lose your sense of direction, may be kid-oriented, but even so, the rides and fantasy of **Bellewaerde Park** may be welcome relief from the grim reality of the fields surrounding it. Other stress-busters include the Niagara, touted as the highest splash ride in Europe; flower castles; and animals and birds including giraffes, lions, tigers, elephants, flamingos, and parrots. ✉ *Meenseweg 597,* ☎ *057/468686.* 🎫 *Varies.* ⏲ *Daily May–Sept.*

Dining and Lodging

$ ✕ **Old Tom.** The name of this traditional restaurant is matter of fact, and the food is too: here you'll find unfussy but appetizing Flemish standards such as beef stew with beer, and chicken waterzooi. ✉ *Grote Markt 8,* ☎ *057/201541. AE, MC, V. Closed Fri.*

$ ✕ **'t Ganzeke.** Giant kebabs and steaks are just a couple of offerings on this menu of hearty meals. The restaurant is a favorite of locals as well as hungry tourists. ✉ *Vandepeereboomplein 5,* ☎ *057/200009. MC, V. Closed Mon.*

$$$ ✕🏨 **Hostellerie Mont Kemmel.** Atop Flanders's highest peak, this luxurious hotel and restaurant offers panoramic views over Flanders Fields from well-appointed rooms. In the elegant restaurant, chef Solange Bentin cooks up such sophisticated specialties as nettle-braised frogs' legs, and squab with a spice crust and port sauce. ✉ *Berg 4, B8958 Kemmel, 7 km/4 mi south of Ieper on N331,* ☎ *057/444145,* FAX *057/444089. 16 rooms. Restaurant, bar, golf privileges, tennis court, meeting rooms. AE, DC, MC, V. No dinner Sun. Closed Mon., mid-Jan.–Feb., 1st wk of July.*

$$ 🏨 **Regina.** In a sturdy neo-Gothic brick building directly on Ieper's Grote Markt, this fresh, comfortable hotel has generous, light-filled spaces and

up-to-date rooms. Just about everything has been upgraded except the windows—alas, the only drawback is the traffic noise. ✉ *Grote Markt 45, B8900,* ☎ *057/219006. 17 rooms. Restaurant, bar. AE, DC, MC, V.*

Festivals

A memorial walking event **Vierdaggse ven de IJzer** occurs in the third week of August—it's literally a moving remembrance of all victims of World War I. The **Festival of the Cats** is one of Europe's most fanciful celebrations, held on the second Sunday in May in even years. A town jester throws hundreds of velvet cats from the town Belfry, a custom originating centuries ago when "Cat Wednesday" marked the final day of the annual market. Until 1817, live cats were tossed, but animal lovers prevailed. The Kattestoet (Cat Parade) came later, and is now a happy tradition, with flags flying, coats-of-arms displayed, and feline giants Cieper and Minneke Poes as special guests.

Tyne Cot

36 *8 km (5 mi) northeast of Ypres.*

Some 44 million shells were fired over this stretch of the Western Front in the two World Wars, and a fair number failed to explode. Flemish farmers still turn up a few every month, and bomb disposal experts often have to be called. **Tyne Cot,** near Passendale, a British cemetery with 12,000 graves, is the best known and largest of more than 170 military cemeteries in the area. Lawns and flowers surround the imposing "Cross of Sacrifice," and a curving wall holds the names of the almost 35,000 soldiers lost after August 1917. The cemetery is awe-inspiring, more austere than many others that dot the countryside. ✉ *From Ieper via Zonnebeke to N303.*

Diksmuide

37 *20 km (12 mi) north of Ieper on N369.*

Here you can visit the so-called **Dodengang** (Death Walk), a network of trenches west of the town, where Belgian troops faced and held off their German adversaries for four years. ✉ *IJzerdijk 65,* ☎ *051/505344.* 🎫 *Free.* ⏲ *Apr.–Sept., daily 10–noon and 1–5:30.*

Like Ieper, Diksmuide has been completely rebuilt in its original style, which you can savor best from the Grote Markt, the spacious square flanked by brick gabled buildings and dominated by the huge, spired St. Niklaaskirk. The nearby **IJzertoren,** a 275-ft tower, was erected in honor of the defenders in the 1950s. It represents the Flemish people's struggle for autonomy, and also provides a splendid view over the hallowed area. A 15-story war museum holds exhibitions about the World Wars, plus changing regional exhibits. ✉ *2 km (1 mi) southwest of Diksmuide.* ☎ *051/500286.* 🎫 *BF200/€4.95.* ⏲ *Daily 10–6; Mar., Oct., Nov., until 5.*

The interactive **Westoria Museum,** opened in 2000, highlights the 10,000-year-old tale of the region's past. Victor the miller and his cat Ceres are your playful guides. Two restored, multistory flour mills provide an imaginative setting. A modern tourist center is also on site. ✉ *Toerismecentrum, Grote Markt,* ☎ *051/519148.* 🎫 *BF240/€5.95.* ⏲ *Daily 9–6.*

The monument in the German war cemetery of **Praetbos-Vlasdo** conveys a touching message. It is a sculpture of two grieving parents by the great German artist Käthe Kollwitz, whose son was among the many young men who fell here. ✉ *4 km (2 ½ mi) northeast of Diksmuide.*

Poperinge

38 *11 km (7 mi) west of Ieper on N38.*

In this town, you'll find one of the rare positive interludes of World War I: the **Talbot House,** founded by an Anglican priest, "Tubby" Clayton. It provided an opportunity for soldiers to get together, just south of the front line, regardless of rank, for mutual support and comradeship. Photographs and art by soldier artists are displayed, and the attic chapel can be visited. Talbot House became known also on the opposite side of the front as a symbol of peace. Today it provides free accommodations for young volunteers who help maintain the war cemeteries. ✉ *Gasthuisstraat 43, Poperinge,* ☎ *057/333228.* 🎫 *BF50/€1.25.* ⏲ *Daily 9–noon and 2–5.*

Poperinge is in the capital of the "Hoppeland" Route, Belgium's main hop-growing region, which provides the yellow meal that gives beer its distinctive flavor. The **Nationaal Hopmuseum** (National Hop Museum) displays tools, audiovisuals, and photos to explain just about anything you want to know about hop-making. ✉ *Gasthuisstraat 71, Poperinge,* ☎ *057/346676.* 🎫 *BF50/€1.25.* ⏲ *Daily 9–noon and 2–5.*

Dining

$$$ ✕ **D'Hommelkeete.** This low-slung, Flemish farmhouse combines rustic and modern decor, and it is—according to experts—the best place to experience the elusive and expensive delicacy called *jets de houblon* (hop shoots). This special treat is only available for three weeks in spring, so call ahead. Braised sea scallops with morel sauce, warm goose liver with Calvados, and venison *noisettes* (nuggets) will ease your disappointment if you arrive at other times. ✉ *Hoge Noenweg 3, Poperinge,* ☎ *057/334365. AE, DC, MC, V. No dinner Sun. and Wed. Closed Mon. and 1st ½ of Aug.*

THE NORTH SEA COAST

Just a century ago, the 65 km (39 mi) stretch from De Panne in the southwest to Knokke (pronounced kuh-nock-kuh) in the northeast was practically unspoiled, with beach dunes connected to the plains beyond by a kilometer or so of moss-covered ground (Ter Streep). The dunes were fortified by dikes as early as the 10th century, but life here remained at the mercy of the sea. Oostende and Nieuwpoort were the only major settlements in 1830, when Belgium achieved independence. Leopold I, Belgium's first king, chose to live here, and royal hangers-on and wannabes followed. Soon a light railway and seawalls appeared, and the coast became safer, more accessible, and even quite fashionable. Today, the resort towns are packed so closely that it's difficult to know where one ends and the next begins. Blocks of housing, campgrounds, villas, and hotels line the waterfronts, united much of the way by promenades. You can walk for miles along the dike, flanked by modern apartment houses that grab much of the view.

Belgians make the most of their wide coastline, especially on summer days when the water warms. Along the coast, children fly kites, teenagers ride pedal cars, horses thunder by along the shore, and lovers walk arm in arm atop the fine, golden sand. Offshore, great yachts with smooth white sails cut through the cold breeze, heading to and from the harbors at Blankenberge, Nieuwpoort, Oostende, and Zeebrugge.

A tram now connects all 13 towns along the coast, so Belgians flock here on weekends year-round. The beach slopes gently to the sea, but for those willing to brave the cold waters, currents can be tricky—swim only at beaches supervised by lifeguards. A green flag means bathing is safe; yellow, bathing is risky but guards are on duty; red, bathing is prohibited. Do not ignore warnings. Many resorts also offer good public outdoor pools, a safer bet. Some prefer this long, wide sea coast best in the off-season, when you can walk quietly along the beach in the pale winter sun and fill your lungs with bracing sea air, then warm up in a cozy tavern with a plate of steaming mussels.

Oostende

 *115 km (69 mi) northwest of Brussels, 28 km (17 mi) west of Brugge, 98 km (59 mi) northeast of Calais.*

A transportation and fishing center and an old-fashioned, slightly raffish resort, Oostende (Ostend in English, Ostende in French) leads a double life. It's the largest town and the oldest settlement on the coast, with a history going back to the 10th century. Long a pirates' hideout, Oostende has hosted many a famous rogue and adventurer, and it was from here that Crusaders also set sail for the Holy Land. In the early 17th century, when villagers backed the Protestant cause, Oostende withstood a Spanish siege for three years.

One of Continental Europe's first railways was built between Oostende and Mechelen in 1838, eventually resulting in regular mail packet services to Dover, England beginning in 1846. (The town remains a favorite day-trip destination for Brits, who ferry across the sea to shop and enjoy the seafood.) Oostende also drew its share of royalty: Leopold II built himself a sumptuous villa on the beach, Belgian Queen Louise-Marie died here in 1850, and Queen Victoria arrived for the sea air. A hundred years ago, the town was at its belle epoque height, with a boom of neoclassical buildings dripping with ornamentation. Elegantly ensembled ladies shaded under parasols strolled along the Promenade on the arms of gents in spats. But during World War II many of the buildings were bombed; times changed, the glamour dimmed.

On the elevated **Albert I Promenade** shops and tearooms compete for attention with the view of the wide beach and the sea, popular here with surfers. At one end stands the **Kursaal** (Casino), which, in addition to gambling facilities, has a vast concert hall and exhibition space. The gaming rooms contain striking murals by Surrealist Paul Delvaux. ✉ *Oosthelling,* ☎ *059/705111; 059/707618 (reservations for shows).* ⏲ *Gaming rooms, 3 PM–dawn.*

Jokingly called "the longest restaurant in Europe," the **Visserskaai** (Fishermen's Wharf) overlooking yachts berthed at Montgomery Dock is a row of fish eateries. Nearby are stalls where women hawk seafood in all its forms. This picturesque area is crossed with narrow streets. ✉ *Albert 1 Promenade, end opposite from Casino.*

NEED A BREAK? **James Café** (✉ James Ensorgalerij, ☎ 059/705245), in a small, refined shopping precinct named after the city's most famous resident, is renowned for its shrimp croquettes.

James Ensorhuis (James Ensor House) is an introduction to the strange and hallucinatory world of the painter James Ensor (1860–1949), who has only lately been recognized as one of the great artists of the early 20th century. Using violent colors to express his frequently macabre or satirical themes, he depicted a fantastic carnival world peopled by masks and skeletons. The displays in this house, which was his home and studio, include many of the objects found in his work, especially the masks, and copies of his major paintings. ✉ *Vlaan-*

derenstraat 27, ☎ *059/805335.* *BF50/€1.25.* ⏲ *June–Sept., Wed.–Mon. 10–noon and 2–5; Oct.–May, weekends 2–5.*

Paintings and drawings by James Ensor, as well as works by Expressionists such as Permeke and Brusselmans, can be seen in the **Museum voor Schone Kunsten** (Fine Arts Museum). ✉ *Wapenplein,* ☎ *059/805335.* *BF50/€1.25.* ⏲ *Wed.–Mon. 10–noon and 2–5.*

Oostende also has a good modern art museum, the **Museum voor Moderne Kunst** (PMMK), with Belgian contemporary artists well represented by Pierre Alechinsky, Roger Raveel, and Paul Van Hoeydonck (whose statuette, *The Fallen Astronaut,* was deposited on the moon by the *Apollo XV* crew), and others. Ceramics, paintings, sculpture, and graphic art are all displayed. The admission fee is increased for special exhibitions. ✉ *Romestraat 11,* ☎ *059/508118.* *BF100–300/€2.50–7.45.* ⏲ *Tues.–Sun. 10–6.*

Mercator, the three-masted training ship of the Belgian merchant marine, which sailed from the 1930s to the 1960s, is now moored close to the city center, ready to sail, if needed. Decks, fittings, and the spartan quarters have been kept intact, and there's a museum of mementoes brought home from the ship's exotic voyages; during one they hauled back mysterious statues from Easter Island. ✉ *Vindictivelaan,* ☎ *059/705654.* *BF100/€2.50.* ⏲ *Apr.–June and Sept., daily 10–1 and 2–6; July–Aug., daily 9–6; Oct.–Mar., weekends 11–1 and 2–5.*

Provinciaal Museum Constant Permeke, the home of Belgium's outstanding Expressionist painter and sculptor (1886–1952), is filled with 150 of Permeke's paintings and virtually all his sculptures. Many of his paintings are somber, in shades of green and brown, drawn from the lives of peasants and fishermen. ✉ *Gistelsesteenweg 341, Jabbeke (between Oostende and Brugge),* ☎ *050/811288.* *BF100/€2.50.* ⏲ *Tues.–Sun. 10–12:30 and 1–6 (until 5 in winter).*

OFF THE BEATEN PATH — **BREDENE** – This town is especially popular with campers for its dunes that slope right onto the beach. Many campers cycle from here along the coast and to Brugge.

Dining and Lodging

$$$ ✕ **Villa Maritza.** Bearing the name of an Austro-Hungarian countess who caught Leopold II's fancy, this 100-year-old villa, furnished in Renaissance Flemish style, serves fine seafood: monkfish roasted with thyme, fennel, and anise; lobster carpaccio with garlic; and duck's liver served sweet-and-sour with sherry. ✉ *Albert I Promenade 76,* ☎ *059/508808. Reservations essential. Jacket and tie. AE, DC, MC, V. Closed Mon. and last 2 wks of June. No dinner Sun. Sept.–June.*

$$ ✕ **Lusitania.** Arguably the best among the several restaurants that crowd the Visserskaai, this one is a little more expensive than its rivals. They all serve variations on the same seafood theme: salad of tiny, sweet shrimp, fish soup, grilled langoustines, and sole prepared many ways, including with béchamel sauce, shrimp, and mussels. ✉ *Visserskaai 35,* ☎ *059/701765. AE, DC, MC, V. Closed Fri.*

$ ✕ **Mosselbeurs.** Mussels are the focus at this cheap and cheery restaurant not far from the station. The mustard-color exterior walls are studded with enormous mock mussel shells, while inside the black-and-white-check floor and tidy decor suggest a maritime theme. Meaty mollusks are served just about any way. ✉ *Dwarsstraat 10,* ☎ *059/807310. AE, DC, MC, V. No lunch Tues. and Wed.*

$$$$ ★ ✕▣ **Oostendse Compagnie/Le Vigneron.** A royal residence still owned by King Albert, this palatial villa is right on the beach, with sea views from the dining room with its splendid terrace and from the large guest

rooms. Tapestries, marble, and modern art set the lush tone, but the friendly, live-in golden retriever adds a family feel—pets are welcome here. A lauded seafood menu with Asian influence offers eels with Chinese cabbage, honey, and dim sum; beef fillet with Perigord truffles and a shallot salad; turbot in fennel cream sauce with caviar; and langoustines with green apple, pasta, and lime. The wine cellar is a superb match. ✉ *Koningstraat 79, B8400,* ☎ *059/704816,* FAX *059/805316. 13 rooms. Restaurant, beach, free parking. AE, DC, MC, V. Closed Mon., 1st 2 wks of Mar., Oct. No dinner Sun.*

$$$$ **Thermae Palace Hotel.** King Leopold II, a dabbling architect, designed this art-deco building, the only grand-dame hotel to survive the pummeling of the World Wars. Tile floors, high ceilings, wide verandas on the sea, and a private beach are some of its charms. As the name suggests, the spa is extensive. Most guest rooms have balconies and are recently refurbished and well equipped. Check out the antique bar for a beer or something harder before or after a meal or a brisk walk. ✉ *Astridlaan 7, B8400,* ☎ *059/806644,* FAX *059/805274. 159 rooms. Restaurant, bar, pool, spa, meeting rooms, free parking. AE, DC, MC, V.*

$$$ **Andromeda.** So close to the Casino that you can practically hear the rolling of the dice, this modern luxury hotel has public rooms in black and white and guest rooms in restful colors that match the sea, making up for the less than splendid facade. Some rooms have balconies overlooking the beach. A sunny terrace restaurant serves North Sea fish and lobster dishes. ✉ *Albert 1 Promenade 60, B8400,* ☎ *059/806611,* FAX *059/806629. 90 rooms. Restaurant, bar, indoor pool, sauna, health club, meeting rooms, free parking. AE, DC, MC, V.*

$–$$ **Old Flanders.** In a handsome brick building opposite the cathedral, this hotel offers family atmosphere, comfortable rooms, and a generous breakfast buffet. ✉ *Jozef II Straat 49, B8400,* ☎ *059/806603,* FAX *059/801695. 15 rooms. Bar, breakfast room. AE, DC, MC, V.*

Nightlife and the Arts

THE ARTS

Check *The Bulletin*'s *What's On* section under "Other Towns" for cultural activities. There are frequent retrospectives at Oostende's museums. Concerts of all kinds, from classical to rock, pop, and jazz, draw crowds from far away to the **Oostende Casino**'s 1,700-seat hall (☎ 059/707618). Flemish singing superstar Helmut Lotti, the best-selling artist in the country's history, is a frequent performer. Blues and jazz clubs are located in and around Kapucijnenstaat, and discos are at Carre beach.

NIGHTLIFE

The closure rate among seasonal nightspots is high; make sure the place you select is still in business. The best bet along the coast is generally the local casino, where gambling underwrites the nightclub entertainment.

The **Bar Baccara** (✉ Oosthelling, ☎ 059/705111), which is run by the Casino, is the classiest nightspot in Oostende (entrance costs BF150/€3.70). Young male visitors from across the Channel who arrive bent on a bender head straight for the dowdy **Langestraat,** where there's a wide choice of snack bars, beer joints, pizza houses, topless bars, and disco-clubs.

Outdoor Activities and Sports

GOLF

There is an 18-hole golf course at **De Haan** (☎ 059/233238), 12 km (7 mi) east of Oostende.

HORSE RACING

In Oostende the **Wellington Hippodrome** (☎ 059/806055) is a top track for flat racing and trotting. Flat racing is July and August, Monday,

Thursday, weekends, and bank holidays; trotting races are May through September, Friday at 6:45 PM.

WINDSURFING

Windsurfing is extremely popular, and special areas have been set aside for it along many beaches. In Oostende, there's a **water sports center** (✉ Vicognedijk 30, ☎ 059/321564 in the afternoon) on the Spuikom waterway (also used for oystering).

De Panne

40 *31 km (19 mi) southwest of Oostende, 55 km (33 mi) southwest of Brugge, 143 km (86 mi) west of Brussels, 63 km (38 mi) northeast of Calais.*

The dunes and the spacious beach may seem peaceful, but history resounds in De Panne: in 1830, local boy King Leopold I first set foot on soil of an independent Belgium. During World War I, King Albert resisted Germans here, as this was one of the few areas not occupied; and in 1940, thousands of failed British forces were evacuated, as in nearby Dunkirk—the British commander, was in fact, stationed in De Panne. A couple of kilometers from the French border, this "wooded valley" is now a family-friendly resort with the widest, whitest beach on the coast. Houses are set among the dunes, south of the beach, and sand yachts looking like sailboats on wheels zip along at up to 120 kph (72 mph). Horseback riding along the beach and on trails through the dunes is also popular.

Two bands of dunes west of the resort make up the 850-acre **Westhoek** nature reserve, which is separated from the sea by trees, shrubs, and a carpet of wild moss and thyme. Here you can roam solo and watch for stoats, martens, short-eared owls, toads, newts and rabbits; guided walks are organized in season. ✉ *Dynastielaan,* ☎ *058/421818.*

The 110 acres of **Calmeynbos** woods were planted in 1903 by Maurice Calmeyn to protect the dunes, and are filled with 25 species of towering trees. Paths from here lead through the dunes to the beach, for a spectacular walk.

Meli Park is a large family attraction with a circus, a playground, action-oriented rides, a nature park with animals and exotic birds, and a dream park where fairy-tale scenes are enacted. Look out for the honeybee mascots. ✉ *De Pannelaan 68, Adinkerke,* ☎ *058/420202.* *BF595/€14.75.* ⏲ *Apr.–1st wk of Sept., daily 10–6 (July and Aug. until 7); rest of Sept., Wed. and weekends 10:30–6.*

Outdoor Activities and Sports

The best places for sand yachting are De Panne and Oostduinkerke (☞ *below*), where the beach is up to 820 ft wide and the facilities are excellent.

Koksijde

★ 41 *5 km (3 mi) southeast of De Panne on N35.*

Koksijde and Sint-Idesbald are small resorts, separated by just a few kilometers, that offer more than beach life. Koksijde has the highest dune on the coast, the **Hoge Blekker,** 108 ft high. Nearby are the ruins of the Cistercian **Duinenabdij** (Abbey of the Dunes), founded in 1107 and destroyed by the iconoclasts in 1566. Traces of the original abbey, the cloisters, and columns from the refectory remain. An archaeological museum shows collections from the digs, as well as interesting examples of regional plants and animals. ✉ *Koninklijke Prinslaan 8,* ☎ *058/511933.* 🎫 *BF100/€2.50.* ⏲ *June 15–Sept. 15, daily 10–6; Sept. 16–Dec. and Feb.–June 14, daily 9–noon and 1:30–5.*

The architecture of the strikingly modern **Onze-Lieve-Vrouw ter Duinenkerk** (Our Lady of Sorrows of the Dunes Church), north of the Abbey, suggests both the dunes and the sea through bold colors, undulating forms and stained glass. The church was built in 1964. A crypt holds the remains of the first abbot of adjacent Dunes Abbey. ✉ *Jaak Van Buggenhoutlaan.*

Many art lovers head for Sint-Idesbald to discover the **Paul Delvaux Museum** in a reconverted Flemish farmhouse. It is dedicated to the painter, famous for his surrealist mix of nudes, skeletons, and trains, who died in 1994 at the age of nearly 100. A pleasant outdoor restaurant is attached to the museum. ✉ *Paul Delvauxlaan 42,* ☎ *058/521229.* 🎫 *BF250/€6.20.* ⏲ *Apr.–June and Sept., Tues.–Sun. 10:30–5:30; July–Aug., daily 10:30–5:30; Oct.–Dec., Fri.–Sun. 10:30–5:30.*

Oostduinkerke

42 *4 km (2 ½ mi) east of Koksijde.*

Beach is the focus here, as in dunes, sand-yachting along the shore, and sand-castle competitions. An unusual beachfront activity—worth a detour—occurs only here: horseback shrimp fishing. The mounted fisherfolk are following a centuries-old tradition when at low tide the sturdy horses, half immersed, trawl heavy nets along the shoreline to catch the tiny crustaceans. If you miss seeing them in action, you can study their unusual approach to fishing in the **Nationaal Visserijmuseum** (National Fisheries Museum), which contains interesting nautical instruments and models of fishing boats over the past millennium. ✉ *Pastoor Schmitzstraat 4,* ☎ *058/512468.* 🎫 *BF80/€2.00.* ⏲ *Apr.–Oct., Tues.–Sun. 10–noon and 2–6; July–Aug., daily 10–noon and 2–6.*

NEED A BREAK?

In De Peerdevisscher (✉ Pastoor Schmitzstraat 6; closed Oct.–Apr.), a traditional *estaminet* (old-style public house) converted into café and snack bar, continues the marine theme of the fisheries museum. You can gobble down those horseback-caught shrimp here, quick boiled.

Nieuwpoort

43 *5 km (3 mi) northeast of Oostduinkerke; Exit 3 from E 40.*

The country's premier yachting center, with some 3,000 leisure craft moored in the estuary, Nieuwpoort was once the home of a sizable fishing fleet. Although the coastal fishing industry has largely been edged out by modern super-trawlers, amateur fishermen can participate in daylong sea fishing trips aboard the *Sportvisser.* There are also a lively fish market and good wharf-side seafood shops and restaurants.

Nieuwpoort isn't new at all, having been founded in the 12th century, and fighting battles for much of the time since. A monument with an equestrian statue of King Albert marks the spot where, in October 1914, the monarch gave the command to open the sluices of the river IJzer, inundating the polder and permanently halting the German advance. Like so many other Belgian towns, Nieuwpoort was ruined in that war, but was restored after 10 years to a semblance of what it had been. The marketplace, ringed with its church, town hall, and commercial buildings is the most historic section of the town.

Dining and Lodging

$$ ✕ **De Braise.** Run by the parents of Le Fox's chef, who ran Le Fox (☞ *below*) when it was a simple tavern, this is the Buyens family's return to their roots: an old-fashioned regional restaurant, offering updated local cooking in a homey setting. Though the menu reads like a thousand others in the region—turbot poached or grilled, sauce hollandaise/dijonnaise, sole meunière—the portions are generous, the preparation superb, and the service sophisticated. ✉ *Bortierplein 1,* ☎ *058/422309. AE, DC, MC, V. Closed Mon., Tues. in off-season, 2nd ½ of Jan., Oct.*

$$$ ★ ✕🏨 **Hostellerie Le Fox.** Chef Stephane Buyens took over his parents' tavern and fashioned a prestigious, welcoming gastronomic retreat. Creating dishes such as Brie, truffles, and roquette salad with honey; and turbot in an aromatic mix of 10 oils, herbs, and beet juice, he has drawn a loyal following. Guests stay in graciously furnished rooms (some have windows angled toward the waterfront) and work as many meals as possible into the weekend. The cozy, casual dining room is an excellent spot to sip a sample from the extensive wine list. ✉ *Walckiersstraat 2, B8620,* ☎ *058/412855. 14 rooms. Restaurant, bar. AE, DC, MC, V. No lunch Tues. Closed Mon., 2nd ½ of Jan., Oct.*

$$ 🏨 **Sparrenhof.** Cut off from the beachfront scene but only 500 ft from the water, this is a self-contained oasis with a pretty pool cloistered in a garden—and many rooms face the greenery. The original building, which has seven guest rooms, dates from the 1950s. The new wing is flashy and modern. The restaurant is open year-round and has a wood-burning fireplace and poolside tables. ✉ *Koninginnelaan 26, B8660,* ☎ *058/411328,* FAX *058/420819. 25 rooms. Restaurant, bar, pool, free parking. AE, DC, MC, V.*

Knokke-Heist

44 *33 km (20 mi) northeast of Oostende, 17 km (10 mi) north of Brugge, 108 km (65 mi) northwest of Brussels.*

Knokke-Heist (which includes five beach resorts—Knokke, Heist, Alberstrand, Het Zoute, and Duinbergen) is an area of dunes and sea, purple wildflowers and groomed golf courses. Heist, Alberstand and Duinbergen are sports- and family-oriented beaches, but to young Belgians of ample means, K-H is the beach to show off designer fashions or a buff new beau. Those who inhabit the old-money villas of Het Zoute, just inland from the beach, wouldn't flaunt their chauffeurs and butlers; you'd assume they were there.

Along the Kustlaan, on the leeward side of the dike, you'll find branches of virtually every fashionable shop in Brussels, all of them open Sunday. The Casino has an enormous 2,000-light Venetian-crystal chandelier in the foyer, perhaps the largest in Europe, and the world's top entertainers come here to perform. Gaming, however, is for members only. In the late 19th century, painters settled in this coastal pleasure zone, and today there are dozens of galleries with works by Belgian and international artists; the Casino displays treasured murals by Rene Magritte, and in front a bronze statue of a poet, cast by Zadkine in 1965.

NEED A BREAK? The Albertplein (Albert Square), widely known as the *Place M'as-tu-vu* (Did-You-See-Me Square), is a gathering place for the chic-at-heart. The most fashionable tearoom-restaurant is **Le Carré** (✉ Albertplein 16, ☎ 050/611222), perfect for people-watching.

★ **Het Zwin** is a remarkable 375-acre nature reserve and bird sanctuary reaching the Netherlands border, preserved thanks to the efforts of naturalist Count Léon Lippens in the early 20th century. The Zwin was once a busy estuary, connecting Brugge with the North Sea. In fact, in 1340 Edward III of England and his Flemish allies sailed here to conquer the French fleet, readying to attack England. But after silting up in the 16th century, the waterway has retreated into quiet marsh and tidal channels, encircled by dunes and dikes—the largest salt marsh in Belgium. Saltwater washes into the soil, making for some unusual flora and fauna. Visit in spring for the bird migrations and from mid-July for the flowers, especially the native *Zwinneblomme,* or sea lavender. Rubber boots are a must, and binoculars can be rented. From the top of the dike there's a splendid view of the dunes and inlets. Storks nest in the aviary, which also holds thousands of aquatic birds and birds of prey, including the red-beaked sheldrake, gray plover, avocet, and sandpiper. A former royal villa, the Châlet du Zwin, is now an attractive restaurant. ✉ *Graaf Léon Lippensstraat 8,* ☎ *050/607086.* 🎫 *BF165/€4.10.* ⏲ *Daily 9–7 (Oct.–Mar. until 5).*

An odd combination, but special fun for children is the **Sincfala Folklore Museum for Polder and Fishery,** set in a 19th-century former school. An old Flanders classroom is recreated completely, from the desks to the wall-hangings. Just outside is the fishing boat, "Jessica." ✉ *Pannenstraat 140,* ☎ *050/630872.* 🎫 *BF100/€2.50.* ⏲ *Daily 2–5.*

A lapidoptrist's fantasy, **The Butterfly Park** is a family attraction where hundreds of brightly colored butterflies flit about in delicate natural display—when the weather is warm enough. ✉ *Bronlaan 14,* ☎ *050/610472.* 🎫 *BF145/€3.60.* ⏲ *Daily 10–5:30 (Mar.–Oct. until 5).*

Dining and Lodging

$$$$ ✕ **Ter Dijken.** Discretion and charm are the bywords at this restaurant, known for its terrace adjoining a magnificent garden. Langoustines with chives au gratin, croquettes of hand-peeled shrimp, and baked potato with caviar are among the favorites here. ✉ *Kalvekeetdijk 137, Knokke,* ☎ *050/608023. Reservations essential. AE, DC, MC, V. Closed Mon.–Tues., Jan.*

$–$$ ✕ **New Alpina.** Despite token efforts at elegance, with pink linens and multiple stemware, this is a seafood diner at heart, where a friendly husband-and-wife team have served North Sea classics since 1970. Fresh skate, turbot, sole, and shrimp are served with simple sauces; the multicourse, fixed-priced "Gourmet Menu" is a seafood feast. It's just off the beach, by the tourist office. ✉ *Lichttorenplein 12, Knokke,* ☎ *050/608985. MC, V. Closed Tues. No dinner Mon.*

$$$$ 🏨 **La Réserve.** This vast hotel, complete with a saltwater treatment center and a man-made lake, evokes a country-club feeling. Flowers and antiques do little to warm the airport-style public spaces, but guest rooms are bright and lovely, decorated in soothing, sponge-painted pastels. You can create anything from a simple package to an extravagant getaway, including simple bed-and-breakfast-style arrangements and a full spa packages. It's across from the Casino, three minutes from the beach. ✉ *Elizabetlaan 158–160, B8300 Albertstrand,* ☎ *050/610606,* FAX *050/603706. 110 rooms, 10 suites. Restaurant, bar, saltwater pool, beauty salon, massage, mineral baths, sauna, 4 tennis courts, windsurfing. AE, DC, MC, V.*

$$$ 🏨 **Katelijne.** The whitewashed brick facade makes this charming 1930s auberge, built in traditional Flemish style, seem out of place amid the boutiques and snaking traffic of the beachfront. It offers an atmospheric retreat, though, with a fireplace, Oriental runners, fringed plush furniture, and darkened timbers. The rooms are equally cozy and dated, though the marble-travertine baths are deluxe. There's a garden and terrace, and a welcoming copper-decked restaurant with an emphasis on fish dishes. ✉ *Kustlaan 166, B8060 Knokke-Le Zoute,* ☎ *050/601216,* FAX *050/615190. 14 rooms. Restaurant, bar. AE, DC, MC, V.*

$$$ **Manoir du Dragon.** Individually decorated rooms with TVs and luxury baths help make this charming manor house overlooking the water a unique choice. Sitting on a chaise in the garden you feel more like a guest than a tourist, and you'll appreciate the bountiful buffet breakfast, too. ⊠ *Albertlaan 73, B8300 Knokke-Heist,* ☎ *050/630580,* FAX *050/630590. 13 rooms with bath. Breakfast room, free parking. AE, DC, MC, V.*

$$ **Rose de Chopin.** This peaceful, whitewashed villa features a romantic garden, comfortable rooms, and big breakfasts. It's a cozy hideaway, shaded by poplars, that offers a taste of Flemish life—and the name alone speaks for its ambience. ⊠ *Elisabethlaan 94, B8300 Knokke-Heist,* ☎ *050/620888,* FAX *050/620413. 7 rooms with bath. Breakfast room, free parking. AE, DC, MC, V.*

Nightlife and the Arts

The **Casino** (⊠ Zeedijk 507, ☎ 050/630500) offers gala nights with international stars, theater, movies, ballet, exhibitions, and two discos, **Number 1** (entrance on Zeedijk) and **Dubbel's** (entrance on Canada Square). Another favorite is the **Gallery Club** (⊠ Canada Square 22, ☎ 050/608133).

Outdoor Activities and Sports

You can bike all or part of a "polder route" from Knokke, past woods, salt marshes, farms, and dikes all the way to Damme and Oosterkerke. This is one of the best bike paths on the coast.

Two 18-hole golf courses are available at Knokke-Heist's **Royal Zoute Golf Club** (⊠ Caddiespad 14, ☎ 050/601227).

Walking is a joy in this coastal area, with promenades along the beach, dunes to climb, and nature preserves to explore. You could start with the **promenade des Fleurs** (Bloemenwandeling), with five signposted miles beside willow-lined avenues, gardens, and mansions. Or walk into the surrounding countryside, a picture-book setting of green fields, and whitewashed farmhouses with red-tiled roofs. Tourist boards offer mapped walking routes ("wandelroutes"), and you can cycle along signed bike paths or ride on horse trails along the routes as well.

Shopping

Aside from the high-end shops, boutiques, and galleries clustered around Het Zoute, the **Centre de Bolle** traditional market near the Heist station is the place to find crafts, clothing, and foodstuffs at fair prices. It's open on Thursdays in July and August.

Dutch Flanders

On the Netherlands side of the border, the Het Zwin nature preserve connects the two countries with a quiet natural environment. Zeeuwsch-Vlaanderen, part of the Dutch province of Zeeland, stretches 60-odd km (about 36 mi) to the mouth of the Scheldt, north of Antwerp. When Belgium declared its independence in 1830, this Protestant province stayed with the Dutch, mostly for religious reasons. The best-known
45 town is **Sluis,** reached from Knokke on N376 (N58 in the Netherlands). This small town shared the wealth of Brugge, for it was on the waterway that linked Brugge with the sea. Many Belgians come here to shop and bank.

The beach proper begins with **Cadzand Bad,** which has several good
46 hotels. From **Breskens,** you can take a car ferry to Vlissingen on Walcheren. Zeeuwsch-Vlaanderen is well suited to a holiday with children precisely because the resorts are uncrowded, with wide, quiet
47 beaches. N252 south, from the port city of **Terneuzen,** links up with

R4 to Gent. There's a second car-ferry service east of Terneuzen, from Kloosterzande on N60 to Kruiningen on Walcheren. Going south on N60 you link up with N49 in Belgium, 26 km (16 mi) from Antwerp.

FLANDERS A TO Z

Arriving and Departing

By Car

Brugge is 5 km (3 mi) north of the E40 motorway, which links Brussels with Gent and Oostende. It is 126 km (76 mi) from the Le Shuttle terminus at Calais.

From Brussels, **Gent** is reached via the E40, which continues to Brugge and the coast. Traffic can be bumper-to-bumper on summer weekends. Gent is 292 km (175 mi) from Paris on the E15/E17.

Kortrijk is reached from Brussels by the E40, branching off on the E17 from Gent (which continues to Lille and Paris), or the A17 from Brugge. The easiest way to reach **Ieper** is via the A19 from Kortrijk, which peters out north of the city; highway N38 continues to Poperinge, where you're close to the French highway linking Lille with Dunkirk and Calais.

The six-lane E40 from Brussels passes both Gent and Brugge en route to **Oostende.** On summer weekends, a better alternative is the N9 from Gent via Brugge; for **Knokke,** you branch off on N49. A back road to the resorts southwest of Oostende is N43 from Gent to Deinze, and then N35 to the coast. From Calais, the E40 has been completed on the French side, but a few kilometers of two-lane road remain before linking up with the rest of the E40 to Oostende and Brussels.

By Train

Two trains leave each hour to **Brugge** from Brussels (50 minutes) and three trains an hour from Gent (25 minutes) and from Oostende (15 minutes). For **train information** in Brugge, call ☏ 050/382382.

Non-stop trains to **Gent** depart on the hour, and 27 minutes past the hour, from Brussels (28 minutes). For **train information** call ☏ 02/203–3640 or 09/221–4444.

Oostende is the terminus of the Cologne–Brussels–Oostende railway line, which connects with ferry service to Ramsgate and the boat train to London. A train departs every hour from Brussels (1 hour, 10 minutes), from Gent (40 minutes), and from Brugge (15 minutes). For **train information** in Oostende, call ☏ 059/701517.

There are local, hourly train service from Gent to **De Panne** (1 hour, 10 minutes), and direct service every hour from Brussels to **Knokke** (1 hour, 15 minutes) via Gent and Brugge.

A train runs every hour from Brussels to **Kortrijk** (1 hour, 10 minutes). There are also several trains a day from Lille (35 minutes), where the *Eurostar* from London stops (change stations from Lille Europe to Lille Flandres). To get to **Ieper** by train you have to change in Kortrijk to an infrequent local service (30 minutes); it also goes to **Poperinge** (40 minutes).

Getting Around

By Bicycle

A bike is perfect for getting around **Brugge** and its environs. Bikes can be rented at the **railway station** (BF150/€3.70 per day with a valid train ticket), at **De Ketting** (✉ Gentpoortstraat 23, ☎ 050/344196; BF150/€3.70 for the day), **Eric Popelier** (✉ Hallestraat 14, around the corner from the Belfry, ☎ 050/343262; BF150/€3.70 for four hours, BF250/€6.20 for the day), or at **Koffiebontje** (✉ Hallestraat 4, ☎ 050/338027; BF150/€3.70 for four hours, BF250/€6.20 for the day). Several hotels provide bikes free of charge for their guests.

In **Gent** you can rent bikes at the train station at a reduced rate. In the **battlefield** region and along the **coast** you can also rent bikes at railway stations.

By Boat

Motorboats for trips around the Gent waterways and/or down the river Leie can be rented from **Minerva** (☎ 09/221–8451), at BF1600/€40.00 for a two-hour cruise. Boats take four to five people and no license is required. The embarkation and landing stage is at Coupure, on the corner of Lindenlei.

By Bus

In **Brugge** the **De Lijn** bus company runs most buses every 20 minutes, including Sunday; minibuses are designed to penetrate the narrow streets.

By Car

Access for cars and coaches into **Brugge**'s old city is severely restricted. There are huge parking lots at the railway station and near the exits from the ring road. To visit the **battlefields,** driving is definitely the best solution, because the various World War I sights are located in different directions from Ieper. The **coastal road,** N34, is very busy in summer. Allow ample time for driving between resorts.

By Taxi

Brugge has large taxi stands at the railway station and at the Markt. In **Gent** there are taxi stands at the railway station and at major squares.

By Tram

If you arrive in **Gent** by train, take Tram 1, 11, or 12 (fare: BF50/€1.25) for the city center.

Along the **coast** there's a tram service—a happily preserved relic of another era—all the way from Knokke to De Panne. The trams are modern, and it's a pleasant ride, but don't expect uninterrupted views of the sea; the tram tracks are on the leeward side of the dike. The service runs every 15 minutes from Easter through September. Tickets cost from BF50/€1.25 depending on distance.

On Foot

The center of **Brugge** is best seen on foot. The winding streets may confuse your sense of direction, but if you look up, there's always the Belfry to guide you back to the Markt. Sturdy footwear is recommended. Key sights are illuminated after sunset, giving the old city an enchanted air.

In **Gent,** as most of the sights are within a radius of half a mile from the Stadhuis, by far the best way to see them is on foot.

Contacts and Resources

Car Rental

For car rental to visit battlefields and the coast from Brugge, try **Europcar** (✉ Spoorwegstraat 106, ☎ 050/385312).

Guided Tours

BY BICYCLE

The **Back Road Bike Co.** (☎ 050/343045) organizes tours covering six villages near Brugge. Mountain bikes are supplied, and the guided four-hour rides take only back roads.

BY BOAT

In **Brugge,** independent motor launches depart from five jetties along the Dijver and Katelijnestraat as soon as they are reasonably full (every 15 minutes or so) daily from March to November and depending on the weather in December and February. The trips take just over half an hour and cost BF175/€4.35.

Sightseeing boats depart from the landing stages at Graslei and Korenlei for 35-minute trips on the **Gent** waterways, Easter through October (BF150/€3.70).

On the coast, **Seastar** (✉ Havengeul 17, Nieuwpoort, ☎ 058/232425) operates regular sailings between Oostende and Nieuwpoort in July and August with departures in both directions. The trip along the coast takes 1½ hours and costs BF450/€11.15.

River excursions on board the ***Jean Bart III*** (☎ 058/232329) on the IJzer, through the polder from Nieuwpoort to Diksmuide and back, are operated daily at 2 PM in July and August; call in the morning at other times. The cost is BF250/€6.20.

BY BUS

Quasimodo (☎ 050/370470) runs all-day minibus tours from Brugge featuring a drive along the coast (Wed. and Fri. in season; BF1300/€3.25) with English-language commentary, or to the "Fields of Flanders" (Sun., Tues., Thurs.; BF1,400/€34.70).

BY CARRIAGE

Horse-drawn carriages wait in Sint-Baafsplein in **Gent.** A half-hour trip for up to four people is BF800/€19.85 and gives you a general idea of the town center. **Brugge** has carriages on the Markt (BF900/€22.30). You may have to wait for more than an hour for a short ride with inadequate commentary and then be asked for "something for the horse." Kids love it, however.

BY TAXI

In Gent you can arrange for a **taxi** with an English-speaking driver (☎ 09/223–2323).

PERSONAL GUIDES

In Brugge you can book an English-speaking guide through the **Toerisme Brugge** (☎ 050/448686). Guides charge a minimum of BF1,500/€37.20 for two hours, BF750/€18.60 per extra hour. In July and August, groups are consolidated at the tourist office every day at 3; the cost per person is BF200/€4.95 (children free).

Your **Gent** experience can be much enhanced by a personal guide. Call **Gidsenbond van Gent** (Association of Gent Guides; ☎ 09/233–0772) weekdays between 9 and 12:30. The charge is BF1,500/€37.20 for the first two hours, BF750/€18.60 per additional hour.

Outdoor Activities and Sports

For information about sports federations throughout the region, contact **BLOSO** (Flemish Sports Association; ✉ R. des Colonies 31, Brussels, ☎ 02/510–3411). For information on water sports, contact **Vlaamse Vereniging voor Watersport** (✉ Beatrijslaan 25, Antwerp, ☎ 03/219–6967).

Visitor Information

For Western Flanders as a whole: **Westtoerisme** (✉ Kasteel Tillegem, Brugge, ☎ 050/380296). **Brugge: Toerisme Brugge** (Brugge Tourist Office; ✉ Burg 11, ☎ 050/448686). City Tourist Information Services (Dienst voor Toerisme): **De Panne** (✉ Zeelaan 21, ☎ 058/421818). **Diksmuide** (✉ Grote Markt 28, ☎ 051/519146). **Gent** (✉ Predikherenlei 2, ☎ 09/225–3641; ✉ Town Hall, under belfry, ☎ 09/266–5232). **Ieper** (✉ Stadhuis, Grote Markt 34, ☎ 057/200724). **Knokke-Heist** (✉ Zeedijk 660, ☎ 050/630380). **Kortrijk** (✉ St-Michielsplein 2, ☎ 056/239371). **Nieuwpoort** (✉ Marktplein 7, ☎ 058/224444). **Oostende** (✉ Monacoplein 2, ☎ 059/701199). **Poperinge** (✉ Stadhuis, Markt 1, ☎ 057/334081).

4 ANTWERP

Antwerp is rich in history and bustling with excitement. It has had myriad identities—as a shipping center (1500s), as a cultural capital (1600s), as a naval base (1800s). Today, the streets are lined with boutiques, cafés, and museums that reflect the different faces of the city. It is ground zero for the international diamond trade, a fashion center the rest of the world takes notes from, and an art treasury where many of the greatest works of its native masters still can be found.

By Leslie Adler and Ursula Fahy

IN ITS HEYDAY, ANTWERP (Antwerpen in Flemish, Anvers in French) played second fiddle only to Paris. Thanks to artists such as Rubens, Van Dyck, and Jordaens, it was one of Europe's leading art centers. Its printing presses produced missals for the farthest reaches of the Spanish empire. It became, and has remained, the diamond capital of the world. Its civic pride was such that the Antwerpen *Sinjoren* (patricians) considered themselves a cut above just about everybody else. They still do.

The Flemish Antwerpen is very close to the word *handwerpen,* which means "hand throwing," and that, according to legend, is exactly what the Roman soldier Silvius Brabo did to the giant Druon Antigon. The giant would collect a toll from boatmen on the river and cut off the hands of those who refused, until Silvius confronted him, cut off the giant's own hand, and flung it into the river Scheldt. That's why there are severed hands on Antwerp's coat of arms.

Great prosperity came to Antwerp during the reign of Holy Roman Emperor Charles V. Born in Gent and raised in Mechelen, he made Antwerp the principal port of his vast domain. It became Europe's most important commercial center in the 16th century, as well as a center of the new craft of printing. The Golden Age came to an end with the abdication of Charles V in 1555. He was succeeded by Philip II of Spain, whose ardent Roman Catholicism brought him into immediate conflict with the Protestants of the Netherlands. In 1566, when Calvinist iconoclasts destroyed paintings and sculptures in churches and monasteries, Philip II responded by sending in Spanish troops. In what became known as the Spanish Fury, they sacked the town and killed thousands of citizens.

The decline of Antwerp had already begun when its most illustrious painters, Peter Paul Rubens, Jacob Jordaens, and Anthony Van Dyck, reached the peak of their fame. The Treaty of Munster in 1648, which concluded the Thirty Years' War, also sealed Antwerp's fate, for the river Scheldt was closed to shipping—it was not to be active again until 1863, when a treaty obliged the Dutch, who controlled the estuary, to reopen it.

The huge and splendid railway station, built at the close of the 19th century, remains a fitting monument to Antwerp's second age of prosperity, during which it hosted universal expositions in 1885 and 1894. In World War I, Antwerp held off German invaders long enough for the Belgian army to regroup south of the IJzer. In World War II, the Germans trained many V-1 flying bombs and V-2 rockets on the city, where Allied troops were debarking for the final push.

Antwerp today is Europe's second-largest port and has much of the zest often associated with a harbor town. The city has traditionally taken pride in being open to influences from abroad and in welcoming newcomers.

Antwerp is known as the City of the Madonnas. On almost every street corner in the old section, you'll see a high niche with a protective statuette of the Virgin. People tend to think that because Belgium is linguistically split it is also religiously divided. This emphatically is not so. In fact, the Roman Catholic faith appears to be stronger and more unquestioning in Flanders than in Wallonia.

Rubens is ever-present in Antwerp, and a genial presence it is. His house, his church, and the homes of his benefactors, friends, and disciples are all over the old city. His wife also seems to be everywhere, for she frequently posed as the model for his portraits of the Virgin Mary. Rubens and fellow Antwerper Van Dyck both dabbled in diplomacy and were knighted by the English monarch. Jordaens, less widely known, stayed close to Antwerp all his life; long regarded as an also-ran, he has only recently been recognized for his artistic genius.

In addition to being home to the Old Masters, Antwerp is also on the cutting edge of contemporary art and fashion. The sharpest designers and avant-garde artists have gravitated here, rather than to the capital, and as a result the galleries and runways have flourished.

Pleasures and Pastimes

Art

Sixteenth-century painter Peter Paul Rubens, arguably Flanders's most famous son, casts a long shadow over Antwerp. His brooding portraits and intense religious depictions are on exhibit throughout the city. They hang not only in Antwerp's art museum and Rubens's own house, but also in churches and other smaller sites. But Rubens was only one among a number of Flemish artists, including painters such as Bruegel and Van Dyck, who captured the region's rich history and its dark, northern atmosphere in paintings that rank among the world's finest. From carefully detailed landscapes that capture the slanting northern light of Flanders to the many religious paintings that reflect the deep influence of the church, Flemish art transports visitors to a period when the region was a power in European affairs.

Architecture

The architectural character of Antwerp was defined during its two great eras of prosperity, in the 16th and 19th centuries. The relative lack of building at other times means that the city is unusually harmonious, with four- and five-story brick buildings mostly undisturbed by skyscrapers and steel-and-glass cubes. Traditional Flemish Gothic architecture pervades Antwerp, from its impressive Grote Markt to the many small, unsung buildings that line the narrow streets of the old town. The style continued to influence construction in the 19th century, but that period also brought the richly ornamented buildings that line Antwerp's main shopping street, as well as the fanciful extravaganzas of the Antwerp zoo. The combination makes a walk through Antwerp an aesthetic delight.

Dining

Antwerp cuisine understandably focuses on fish, presented with few frills in even the finest restaurants, often poached or steamed, and reasonably priced. đFrom the chilled whelks and periwinkles (marine snails) picked out of their shells with pins, to piles of tender little *crevettes grises* (small shrimp), to the steamy white flesh of the mammoth turbot, the scent of salt air and fresh brine is never far from your table. The ubiquitous mussels and eels, showcased in mid-priced restaurants throughout the city center, provide a heavier, heartier version of local fish cuisine. Bought live from wholesalers, the seafood is irreproachably fresh.

CATEGORY	COST*
$$$$	over BF3,000/€75
$$$	BF2,000–BF3,000/€50–€75
$$	BF1,000–BF2,000/€25–€50
$	under BF1,000/€25

**per person for a three-course meal, including service, taxes, but not beverages*

Lodging

Antwerp has a significant traffic in business travelers, and there are numerous hotels, many members of international chains, catering to their needs. If you want something more romantic, you'll find several intimate boutique hotels that fit the bill perfectly. Such places are small by nature, and rooms can book up far in advance, so you're well served to plan ahead.

CATEGORY	COST*
$$$$	over BF7,500/€185
$$$	BF5,500–BF7,500/€135–€185
$$	BF2,500–BF5,500/€60–€135
$	under BF2,500/€60

**for two persons sharing double room, including service and tax*

🖰 following the text of a review is your signal that the property has a Web site, where you will find details and, usually, images; for a link, visit www.fodors.com/urls.

EXPLORING ANTWERP

The area that surrounds Antwerp's magnificent railway station is in the commercial center of the city, but is not representative of its character. Hop on the subway to Groenplaats and walk past the cathedral and then into the Grote Markt. This is where Antwerp begins. Although you can "do" Antwerp in a day, you would do much better with two or three days, allowing time to sample some of the great restaurants and the lively nightlife and to properly explore the rich collections of the Royal Museum of Fine Arts and other museums. Antwerp is also a good base for excursions throughout the province of the same name and neighboring Limburg (☞ Chapter 5). Antwerp can be visited year-round, but avoid coming on a Monday, when the museums are closed, for they are an integral part of the experience. An excursion to the province of Limburg is best made in spring or summer; it is at its very best at apple-blossom time.

Numbers in the text correspond to numbers in the margin and on the Antwerp map.

Great Itineraries

IF YOU HAVE 1 DAY

Head straight for the Grote Markt, the heart of Antwerp's Old Town and a tribute to Flanders's Golden Age with its elaborate Town Hall and guild houses. The nearby Onze-Lieve-Vrouwekathedraal is Antwerp's finest cathedral, remarkable for not only its late Gothic architecture but also its art, including four Rubens altarpieces. Wander the narrow streets of the Old Town, perhaps sampling some local beer along with a lunch of the ubiquitous mussels and french fries. Then head to Rubens Huis to see a faithful and rich re-creation of the famous painter's own house and studio, filled with some of his finest works. Top off the day with a visit to the Plantin-Moretus Museum, the home and printing plant of a publishing dynasty that spanned three centuries. The 16th-century building is a delight for history buffs, art lovers, and bibliophiles alike. The museum overlooks a tranquil square, just the place for a restful café visit at day's end.

IF YOU HAVE THREE DAYS

Explore Antwerp's rich past and lively present in greater depth. Walk along the river Scheldt to appreciate Antwerp's centuries-long tradition as a major European port. Consider a boat tour to see the modern, working harbor. The 9th-century Steen fortress now houses a maritime museum. Take time to visit some of Antwerp's other fine churches, including St. Paul's with its vast art collection, St. Jacob's, where Rubens is buried, and St. Andries, where Rubens and his first wife, Isabella Brant, were married. The Baroque Sint-Carolus Borromeus is another highlight bearing Rubens's mark. Take a break from history with a visit to the Antwerp Zoo, enjoying its Egyptian temple as well as the animals. For peace and quiet, head to the Beginhof, a Beguine convent dating to the 13th century, an almost hidden attraction with many quiet charms. Take advantage of Antwerp's ranking as a key European fashion center, window-shopping along the smaller streets radiating off the Meir. Those who love antiques and rare books should head for the Old Town as well as Oever Straat near the Plantin-Moretus Museum. And along the way, take plenty of time to sample Antwerp's fine cuisine.

The Old Town

The Old Town is where visitors and locals alike go to find the essence of Antwerp. The narrow, winding streets, many of them restricted to pedestrian traffic, are wonderful for strolling, the squares are full of charm, and the museums and churches are the pride of the city.

A Good Walk

From the **Grote Markt** ① walk down Suikerrui toward the river, stopping en route at the **Etnografisch Museum** ②. At the end of the street, turn right to the waterfront fortress, the **Steen** ③. Walk up the block-long Repenstraat to the step-gabled **Vleeshuis** ④. Proceed along Oude Beurs to Schoenmakersstraat, bringing you to the cathedral. Walk down Blauwmoezelstraat in the direction of the Grote Markt, going around the cathedral to its entrance on Handschoenmarkt. The Gothic **Onze-Lieve-Vrouwekathedraal** ⑤ contains some of Rubens's greatest paintings. A few steps to the left from the front of the cathedral, and you're in Koornmarkt. At No. 16 begins the **Vlaeykensgang** ⑥, an old cobblestone lane. It merges into Pelgrimstraat. Turn right, then right again on Reyndersstraat, past the Baroque house of the painter Jacob Jordaens; then left on Hoogstraat and left again on Heilige Geeststraat, and you're at the **Plantin-Moretus Museum** ⑦, the printer's stately home and workshops. Walk along Oever Straat with its many antiques shops to Muntstraat, coming along to **Sint-Andrieskerk** ⑧. Continue on Sleutelstraat, which with a slight jag leads to Oudaan. Follow Oudaan to Korte Gasthuisstraat and turn right. The **Museum Mayer Van den Bergh** ⑨, with its outstanding Bruegels, will be almost immediately on your left. Just a few doors down on Lange Gaasthuisstraat is the **Maagdenhuis** ⑩, a museum displaying artifacts from its days as an orphanage as well as Flemish art. From here you can catch a No. 8 tram to the **Koninklijk Museum voor Schone Kunsten** ⑪, with its stellar collection of Flemish art.

TIMING

Walking this route, with short stops at the museums, will take you two to three hours.

Sights to See

❷ **Etnografisch Museum** (Ethnographic Museum). This fascinating museum explores the art, myths, and rites of the native peoples of Africa, the Americas, Asia, and the South Seas. Among its 30,000 masks, tools, weapons, sculptures, and other objects are several unique pieces, some of them described in *La Musée Imaginaire*, André Malraux's compilation of the world's most important art and artifacts. ✉ *Suikerrui 19,* ☎ *03/220–8600.* 🎟 *BF100/€2.50.* ⏲ *Tues.–Sun. 10–5.*

❶ **Grote Markt.** The heart of the Old Town, the Grote Markt is dominated by a huge fountain splashing water over much of the square. It is crowned by the figure of the legendary Silvius Brabo, who has been about to fling the hand of the giant Druon Antigon into the river Scheldt for the past 100 years. Another famous monster slayer, St. George, is perched on top of a 16th-century guild house at Grote Markt 5, while the dragon appears to be falling off the pediment.

The triangular square is lined on two sides by guild houses and on the third by the Renaissance **Stadhuis** (Town Hall). Antwerp's Town Hall was built in the 1560s during the city's Golden Age, when Paris and Antwerp were the only European cities with more than 100,000 inhabitants. In its facade, the fanciful fretwork of the late Gothic style has given way to the discipline and order of the Renaissance; the public rooms are suitably impressive, though the heavy hand of 19th-century restoration work is much in evidence. ✉ *Grote Markt,* ☎ *03/220–8211.* 🎫 *BF30/€0.75.* ⏲ *Mon.–Wed. and Fri. 8–6, Sat. 8–4; guided tours weekdays 11, 2, and 3, Sat. 2 and 3.*

⓫ **Koninklijk Museum voor Schone Kunsten** (Royal Museum of Fine Arts). A must for the student of Flemish art, the collection here is studded with masterworks from Bruegel to Ensor. Paintings recovered from the French after the fall of Napoléon form the nucleus of a collection of 2,500 works of art. Room H is devoted to Jacob Jordaens; Room J, mostly monumental Rubens; and Room M, Bruegel. The collection of Flemish Primitives includes works by Van Eyck, Memling, Roger van der Weyden, Joachim Patinier, and Quinten Metsys. On the ground floor there's a representative survey of Belgian art of the past 150 years—Emile Claus, Rik Wouters, Permeke, Magritte, Delvaux, and especially James Ensor. ✉ *Leopold de Waelplaats 2,* ☎ *03/238–7809.* 🎫 *BF250/€6.20.* ⏲ *Tues.–Sun. 10–5, Wed. until 9. Take Tram 8.*

⓾ **Maagdenhuis** (Maidens' House). Originally a foundling hospital for children of the poor, the Maagdenhuis opened in 1552 and remained in operation until 1882. A boys' orphanage, the Knechtjeshuis, which had opened nearby in 1558, also closed in 1882 when more modern institutions became available. In a time when it was common for the poor to abandon their babies out of necessity, some buildings—including eight in Belgium—were equipped with special compartments, known as drawers, built into their facades where foundlings could be left. The Maagdenhuis chapel and entrance gateway date from 1564–1568, with the rest of the building dating from 1634–1636, including the somewhat austere but tranquil court, with its Baroque columns and Virgin Mary statuary. Girls at the Maagdenhuis wore uniforms and were raised under strict rules. They were taught both their Dutch mother tongue and French, as well as learning how to sew and make lace. Boys at the Knechtjeshuis orphanage learned a trade, either at the orphanage or with a master in town. The Maagdenhuis Museum houses a collection of objects from the orphanages, including clothes, workbooks, and needlework. The museum also displays paintings and statuary, as well as a collection of rare 16th century Antwerp pottery, including a complete set of porridge basins. Although the collection includes one Rubens, the most important paintings were lent to the Royal Museum of Fine Arts in 1890. In addition to the museum, the building now houses some offices of the Public Centre for Social Welfare. ✉ *Lange Gasthuisstraat 33,* ☎ *03/223–5620.* 🎫 *BF75/€1.85.* ⏲ *Mon., Wed.–Fri. 10–5, weekends 1–5.*

★ ❾ **Museum Mayer Van den Bergh.** Bruegel's arguably greatest and most enigmatic painting, *Dulle Griet,* is the showpiece here. Often referred to in English as "Mad Meg," it portrays an irate woman wearing helmet and breastplate—a sword in one hand, and food and cooking utensils in the other—striding across a field strewn with the ravages and insanity of war. There is no consensus on how to read this painting. Some consider it one of the most powerful antiwar statements ever made. Others claim that it denounces the Inquisition. Either way, nothing could be further from the Bruegelian villages than this nightmare world. In 1894, Mayer van den Bergh bought *Dulle Griet* for BF488. Today it is priceless. There's one more set of Bruegels in the collection, his witty, miniature illustrations of *Twelve Proverbs,* based on popular Flemish sayings.

Mayer van den Bergh was a passionate art connoisseur who amassed a private collection of almost 4,000 works in the 19th century. The collection includes treasures such as a life-size polychrome statue from about 1300 of St. John resting his head on Christ's chest. It is, however, the Bruegels that make this small museum a must. ✉ *Lange Gasthuisstraat 19,* ☎ *03/232–4237.* 🎫 *BF100/€2.50.* ⏲ *Tues.–Sun. 10–5.*

NEED A BREAK? **De Foyer** (✉ Komedieplaats 18) occupies the ornate rotunda of the 150-year-old Bourla Theater. The decor alone is worth a visit, but the café serves buffet lunch and light snacks and is open from noon to midnight. It's popular with locals, especially on Sunday, when the buffet breakfast is booked weeks in advance.

★ ❺ **Onze-Lieve-Vrouwekathedraal** (Cathedral of Our Lady). A miracle of soaring Gothic lightness, the Onze-Lieve-Vrouwekathedraal is topped by its 404-ft-high north spire—now restored to its original gleaming white and serving as a beacon that can be seen from far away. Work began in 1352 and continued in fits and starts until 1584. Despite this, it is a homogeneous monument, thanks to a succession of remarkable architects, including Peter Appelmans, Herman and Domien de Waghemakere, and Rombout Keldermans the Younger. The tower holds a 47-bell carillon (played Friday 11:30 AM–12:30 PM, Sunday 3 PM–4 PM, and Monday in summer 8 PM–9 PM).

The cathedral's art treasures were twice vandalized, first by Calvinists in 1566 and again by the French revolutionary army at the end of the 18th century. The French even broke up the floor so that their horses would not slip on it. The masterpieces were either sold at auction or carried off to Paris. Some, but by no means all, have subsequently been returned. Other works, either donated or purchased, make up an outstanding collection of 17th-century religious art, including four Rubens altarpieces, glowing with his marvelous red, allegedly fortified by pigeon's blood. The panels of *The Descent from the Cross* triptych—Mary's visit to Elizabeth (with the painter's wife as Mary) and the presentation of Jesus in the temple—are among the most delicate and tender biblical scenes ever painted. *The Assumption of the Virgin Mary,* painted for the high altar, shows the Virgin being carried upward by massed ranks of cherubs toward the angel waiting to crown her Queen of the Angels. *The Assumption* is skillfully displayed so that the rays of the sun illuminate it exactly at noon. ✉ *Handschoenmarkt,* ☎ *03/231–3033.* 🎫 *BF70/€1.75.* ⏲ *Weekdays 10–5, Sat. 10–3, Sun. 1–4.*

★ ❼ **Plantin-Moretus Museum.** This was the home and printing plant of an extraordinary publishing dynasty. For three centuries, beginning in 1576, the family printed innumerable bibles, breviaries, and missals; Christophe Plantin's greatest technical achievement was the *Biblia Regia* (in Room 16): eight large volumes containing the Bible in Latin, Greek, Hebrew, Syriac, and Aramaic, complete with notes, glossaries, and grammars.

The first three rooms were the family quarters, furnished in 16th-century luxury and containing several portraits by Rubens. Others remain as they were when occupied by accountants, editors, and proofreaders, while many contain Bibles and religious manuscripts dating back to the 9th century, including one owned by King Wenceslas of Bohemia. The workshops are filled with Plantin's 16 printing presses. Two typefaces designed here, Plantin and Garamond, are still in use. The presses are in working order—you can even purchase a copy of Plantin's sonnet, *Le Bonheur de ce monde (An ode to contentment)*, in any of seven European languages, printed on an original press. ✉ *Vrijdagmarkt 22,* ☎ *03/233–0294.* 🎫 *BF100/€2.50.* ⏲ *Tues.–Sun. 10–5.*

8 **Sint-Andrieskerk** (St. Andrew's Church). This late Gothic building dates to 1514 but reflects substantial Baroque influences from its extension during the 18th century. In addition to the magnificence of its Baroque high altar, stained-glass windows, and columns, the church is notable for its site as the marriage of Rubens and his first wife, Isabella Brant, in 1609. Its most striking feature is the pulpit depicting Peter and his brother Andrew, created by Jan-Baptist Van Hoof and Jan-Frans Van Geel in 1921. ✉ *St. Andriesstraat 5,* ☎ *03/232–0384.* 🎫 *Free.* ⏲ *Closed to visitors during services.*

3 **Steen.** The Steen is more than 1,000 years old and looks it. A 9th-century fortress, it was built to protect the western frontier of the Holy Roman Empire. It was partially rebuilt 700 years later by Emperor Charles V. You can distinguish the darker, medieval masonry extending midway up the walls from the lighter upper level of 16th-century work. The Steen was used as a prison for centuries. Opposite the entrance is a cross where those sentenced to death said their final prayers. It now houses the **National Scheepvaartmuseum** (National Maritime Museum), with a large collection of models, figureheads, instruments, prints, and maps. The adjoining Maritime Park has in it a collection of several dozen ships, including some that you can climb aboard. The park, which also has a small boat-style playground for young children, lets you capture the true feel of the waterside.

The Steen is the only survivor of the original waterfront. Many houses were torn down in the 19th century to make room for the wide, straight quays that today are practically deserted, the port having moved north of the city. The **Noorderterras,** a promenade starting at the Steen, is a popular place for a Sunday stroll along the Scheldt, which here is 550 yards wide. "God gave us the river," say Antwerpers, "and the river gave us all the rest." ✉ *Steenplein,* ☎ *03/232–0850.* 🎫 *BF100/€2.50.* ⏲ *Tues.–Sun. 10–4:45.*

★ 6 **Vlaeykensgang.** A quiet cobblestone lane in the center of Antwerp, the Vlaeykensgang seems untouched by time. The mood and style of the 16th century are perfectly preserved here. There is no better place to linger on a Monday night when the carillon concert is pealing from the cathedral. The alley ends in Pelgrimsstraat, where there is a great view of the cathedral spire. **Jordaenshuis,** nearby, was the home of Jacob Jordaens (1593–1678), the painter many saw as the successor of Rubens. It's a gem adorned with many Baroque touches—and its very attractive courtyard rivals that of the Rubenshuis. ✉ *Reyndersstraat 6,* ☎ *03/233–3033.* 🎫 *Free.* ⏲ *Wed.–Sun. 10–5.*

NEED A BREAK?

De Groote Witte Arend (✉ Reyndersstraat 18), in a secret courtyard near the Jordaens house, is in a former convent. The background music tends to be Vivaldi or Telemann, the atmosphere is genteel without being snobbish, and there's a good selection of draft beers and tasty sandwiches.

Vleeshouwersstraat. The Vleeshuis (☞ *below*) is the most prominent landmark of the residential neighborhood that has arisen in this historic district. Many ancient buildings remain, among them **De Spieghel** (The Mirror) off Oude Beurs at Spanjepandsteeg. Originally built for the archers' guild, it was bought in 1506 by Pieter Gillis, a leading humanist. At the beginning of his most famous work, Sir Thomas More describes a visit to Antwerp. He is walking with Gillis back from Mass in the cathedral when they encounter a traveler, who recounts his adventures on an island named Utopia. Erasmus, another friend of Gillis's, had the first edition of *Utopia* printed in Leuven. ✉ *Bounded by Oude Beurs, Kuipersstraat, Jordaenskaai, Doornikstraat, and Veemarkt.*

4 **Vleeshuis** (Butchers' Hall). This Gothic hall (1501–1504) was once the only place in the city of Antwerp where meat could be sold, and it also contained a chapel and a kitchen. It's now a museum displaying archaeological finds and local historical documents, with Antwerp's most important industries (pottery, glass, art cabinets) featured prominently. The first-floor exhibit displays artifacts including jewelry, weapons, and coins from the period of the separation of the Netherlands between the Fall of Antwerp (1585) and the Peace of Munster (1648). Also, concerts are held here. ✉ *Vleeshouwersstraat 38–40,* ☎ *03/233–6404.* 💳 *BF75/€1.85.* ⏲ *Tues.–Sun. 10–4:45.*

The Center and Diamond District

Here you'll find two of Antwerp's defining elements: Peter Paul Rubens (represented by his home and numerous works found in the surrounding neighborhood), and the Diamond District, world center of the diamond trade. The Centraal Station and adjacent Zoo at the hub of the bustling district are both architectural gems.

A Good Walk

Start at the **Centraalstation** ⑫, with the **Zoo** ⑬ just outside its front door. Cross the Koningen Astrid Plein and turn left on Gemeentestraat, crossing the busy Frankrijklei. Turn right onto Molenbergstraat, then left onto Korte Winkelstraat. Proceed right onto Rodestraat, bringing you to the 13th-century **Begijnhof** ⑭. Retrace your steps to Korte Winkelstraat, crossing Ossen Markt and turning right on Hoboken. Continue to Minderbroederstraat and the museum **Archief en Museum van het Vlaamse Cultuurleven** ⑮. Take a right onto Minderbroedersrui, which becomes St. Paulusstraat, then turn left on Nosestraat, bringing you to **Sint-Pauluskerk** ⑯, with one of Antwerp's finest collections of religious art. Backtrack to Minderbroedersrui and turn right onto Wolstraat to **Sint-Carolus Borromeuskerk** ⑰ on the attractive Hendrik Conscienceplein. Return via Wolstraat to Minderbroedersrui and turn left, then turn right onto Keizerstraat, to **Rockoxhuis** ⑱, the Renaissance home of Rubens's benefactor. Continue along Keizerstraat and turn right on Prinsesstraat, which becomes St. Jacobstraat and leads to **Sint-Jacobskerk** ⑲. St. Jacobstraat becomes Lange Klarenstraat as it crosses Lange Nieuwstraat; proceed along it to Meir, the main shopping street with its many richly ornamented 19th-century buildings, and then make a quick left and right to arrive at Wapper and **Rubenshuis** ⑳, the painter's home. Head west on Meir and its continuations, Leysstraat (where you can check out the **Torture Museum** ㉑ if you have a taste for the macabre) and De Keyserlei. You'll find yourself in the Diamond District—turn right on Appelmansstraat for **Diamondland** ㉒. Just to the south on Lange Herentalsestraat is the **Provinciaal Diamantmuseum** ㉓.

TIMING

Walking this route, with short stops at the museums, will take you two to three hours.

Sights to See

15 **Archief en Museum van het Vlaamse Cultuurleven** (Archive and Museum of Flemish Cultural Life). This museum provides an overview of the past 200 years of art and culture in Flanders, including art objects

Antwerp

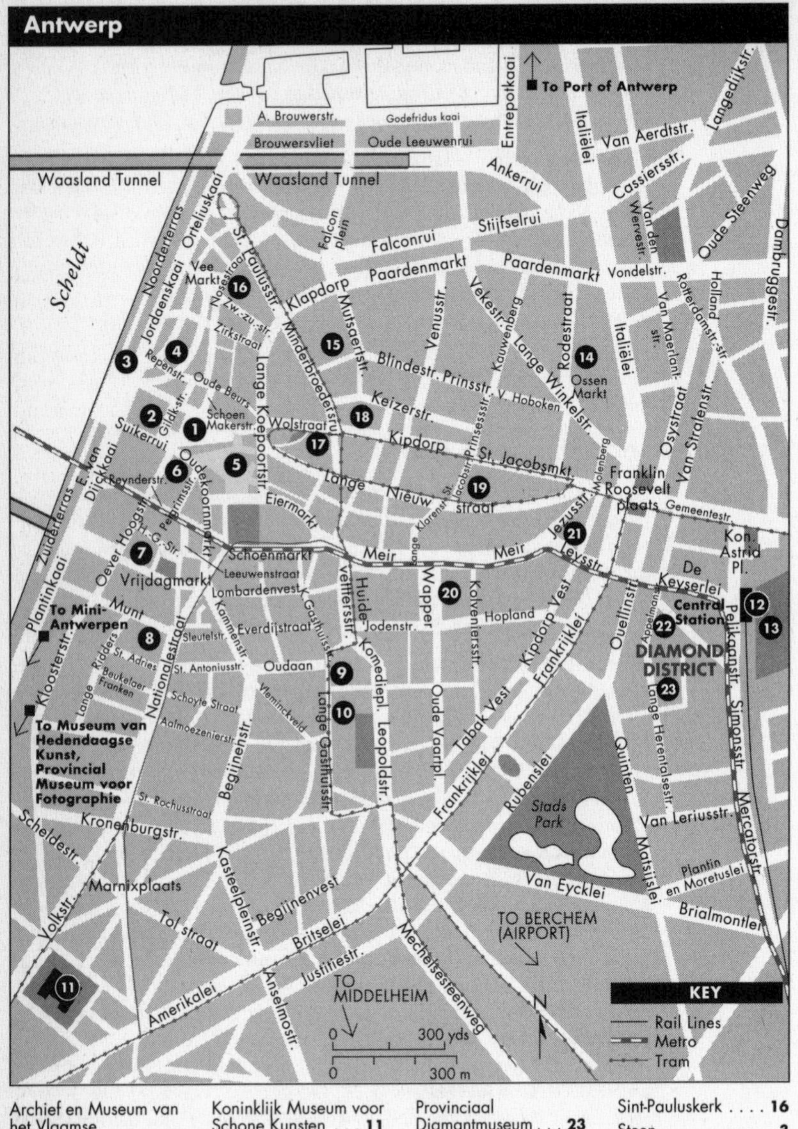

Archief en Museum van het Vlaamse Cultuurleven 15
Begijnhof 14
Centraalstation 12
Diamondland 22
Etnografisch Museum . . 2
Grote Markt 1
Koninklijk Museum voor Schone Kunsten . . . 11
Maagdenhuis 10
Museum Mayer Van den Bergh 9
Onze-Lieve-Vrouwekathedraal 5
Plantin-Moretus Museum 7
Provinciaal Diamantmuseum . . . 23
Rockoxhuis 18
Rubenshuis 20
Sint-Andrieskerk 8
Sint-Carolus Borromeuskerk 17
Sint-Jacobskerk 19
Sint-Pauluskerk 16
Steen 3
Torture Museum . . . 21
Vlaeykensgang 6
Vleeshuis 4
Zoo 13

themselves as well as historical documents. There is an extensive library open to the public. ✉ *Minderbroedersstraat 22,* ☎ *03/232–5580.* 🎫 *BF75/€1.85.* ⏲ *Tues.–Sat. 10–5.*

14 **Begijnhof** (Beguine Convent). The convent dates from the 13th century, but by the 1960s there was only one Beguine nun left. Redbrick buildings surrounding a courtyard garden (which is closed to the public) give a sense of tranquility as you stroll the roughly cobbled walk. Furniture from the convent can be seen in house number 38. ✉ *Rodestraat 39,* 🎫 *Free.* ⏲ *Daily 10–5.*

12 **Centraalstation** (Central Station). The neo-Baroque railway terminal was built at the turn of the 20th century during the reign of Leopold II of Belgium, a monarch not given to understatement. The magnificent exterior and splendid, vaulted ticket-office hall and staircases call out for hissing steam engines, peremptory conductors, scurrying porters, and languid ladies wrapped in boas. Alas, today most departures and arrivals are humble commuter trains. ✉ *Koningin Astridplein.*

Diamond District. The diamond trade has its own quarter in Antwerp, where the skills of cutting and polishing the gems have been handed down for generations by a tightly knit community. Multimillion-dollar deals are agreed upon with a handshake, and the industry has created its own Diamond High Council to establish strict quality control and high standards. Some 70% of the world's uncut diamonds pass through Antwerp. Twenty-five million carats are cut and traded here every year, more than anywhere else in the world. The district occupies a few nondescript city blocks west of Central Station. Shop signs in Hebrew, and the distinctive clothing and ringlets worn by many Hasidic men, are clues that this area is different from the rest of Antwerp. Below the elevated railway tracks, a long row of stalls and shops gleams with jewelry and gems.

Diamond-cutting began in Brugge but moved to Antwerp in the 16th century, along with most other wealth-creating activities. Antwerp's preoccupation with beauty and money helped the diamond trade flourish. Today the industry employs some 18,000 people, divided among 6,000 independent firms. In addition to cutters, grinders, and polishers, there are about 3,000 traders, of whom two-thirds are Jewish and one-fifth Indian, with a heavy sprinkling of Lebanese and Armenians. Nearly all come from long-established diamond families. ✉ *Bounded by De Keyserlei, Pelikaanstraat, Herentalsestraat, and Lange Kievitstraat.*

22 **Diamondland.** A spectacular showroom, Diamondland was created to enable visitors to get a sense of the activity that goes on behind closed doors in the security-conscious Diamond District. Diamondland has three floors of slide shows and films, showcases of rough and polished diamonds, and several diamond cutters at work. ✉ *Appelmansstraat 33A,* ☎ *03/234–3612.* ⏲ *Mon.–Sat. 9–5:30.*

23 **Provinciaal Diamantmuseum** (Provincial Diamond Museum). This museum relates the history of the diamond trade using maps, models, and videos, and there's a complete 19th-century diamond workshop. Exceptional jewelry is displayed in the treasure room. ✉ *Lange Herentalsestraat 31–33,* ☎ *03/202–4890.* 🎫 *Free, except during exhibitions.* ⏲ *Daily 10–5; demonstrations Sat. 2–5.*

NEED A BREAK?

Pakhuis (✉ Vlaamse Kaai 76), a crowded former warehouse, is dominated by a series of shiny vats used to brew the café's three beers; the Antwerp Blond in particular is vastly superior to even Belgium's mass-produced brews. The building's conversion is slightly sterile, but the ales, well-prepared snacks, and professional service can't be faulted.

18 **Rockoxhuis.** This was the splendid Renaissance home of Rubens's friend and patron Nicolaas Rockox, seven times mayor of Antwerp. A humanist and art collector, Rockox moved here in 1603. The art on display includes two of his benefactor's works. One is *Madonna and Child,* a delicate portrait of his first wife, Isabella, and their son, Nicolaas; the other is a sketch for the *Crucifixion.* The collection also includes works by Van Dyck, Frans Snijders, Joachim Patinier, Jordaens, and David Teniers the Younger. The setting is important. Rather than being displayed on museum walls, the paintings are shown in the context of an upper-class Baroque home, furnished in the style of the period. A documentary video describes Antwerp at that time. ⊠ *Keizerstraat 10–12,* ☎ *03/231–4710.* 🎫 *Free.* ⏲ *Tues.–Sun. 10–5.*

★ 20 **Rubenshuis** (Rubens House). A fabulous picture of Rubens as painter and patrician is presented here at his own house. Only the elaborate portico and temple, designed by Rubens in Italian Baroque style, were still standing three centuries after the house was built. Most of what's here is a reconstruction (completed in 1946) from the master's own design. It represents Rubens at the pinnacle of his fame, a period during which he was appointed court painter to Archduke Albrecht and, with his wife, was sent on a diplomatic mission to Madrid, where he also painted some 40 portraits. He conducted delicate peace negotiations in London on behalf of Philip IV of Spain, and while in London he painted the ceiling of the Whitehall Banqueting Hall and was knighted by Charles I of Great Britain. The most evocative room in Rubens House is the huge studio, where drawings by Rubens and his pupils, as well as old prints, help to re-create the original atmosphere. In Rubens's day, visitors could view completed paintings and watch from the mezzanine while Rubens and his students worked. Rubens completed about 2,500 paintings, nearly all characterized by the energy and exuberance that were his hallmark. A few Rubens works hang in the house, including a touching sketch in the studio of the Annunciation and a self-portrait in the dining room. Unfortunately, his young widow promptly sold off some 300 pieces after his death in 1640. ⊠ *Wapper 9,* ☎ *03/232–4747.* 🎫 *BF100/€2.50.* ⏲ *Tues.–Sun. 10–5.*

17 **Sint-Carolus Borromeuskerk** (St. Charles Borromeo Church). Like so much of Antwerp, this Jesuit church bears the imprint of Rubens. The front and tower are generally attributed to him, and his hand can certainly be seen in the clustered cherubim above the entrance. The church's facade suggests a richly decorated high altar, inviting the observer inside. The interior was once magnificent, but most of Rubens's frescoes were destroyed by fire, and other works were carted off to Vienna when the Austrians banned the Jesuits in the 18th century. The square is one of the most attractive in Antwerp, flanked by the harmonious Renaissance buildings of the Jesuit convent, now occupied by the City Library. ⊠ *Hendrik Conscienceplein 12,* ☎ *03/233–8433.* 🎫 *Free.* ⏲ *Mon. 2–4, Wed.–Fri. 10–noon and 2–4, Sat. 10–noon and 3–6:30, Sun. 9:30–12:30.*

NEED A BREAK?

Its name, **Het Elfde Gebod** (⊠ Torfbrug 10), means the 11th Commandment, and it's crammed with plaster saints and angels salvaged from old churches. The food and drink are straightforward but hearty, and you can sit on the terrace.

19 **Sint-Jacobskerk** (St. Jacob's Church). Peter Paul Rubens is buried in this white sandstone Gothic church. A painting depicting him as St. George posed between his two wives, Isabella Brant and Helena Fourment, hangs above his tomb. The elegant, three-aisle church is also home to numerous works of art. ⊠ *Lange Nieuwstraat 73,* ☎ *03/232–1032.* 🎫 *Free.*

16 **Sint-Pauluskerk** (Saint Paul's Church). This late-Gothic church built from 1530 to 1571 is a repository of some of Antwerp's finest art. The more than 50 paintings include three by Rubens, as well as early works by Jordaens and Van Dyck. The church is further enriched by more than 200 17th and 18th century sculptures, including the confessionals attributed to Peeter Verbruggen the Elder. A Baroque altar completed in 1639 towers over the more somber Gothic nave. Sint-Pauluskerk was restored in 1968 after damage from a major fire. There's a series of walking tours and presentations—available in English, French, and Dutch—on the church's history, art, and artifacts. ⊠ *St. Paulusstraat 20,* ☎ *03/232–3267.* 🎟 *Free.* ⏲ *May–Sept., daily 2–5.*

21 **Torture Museum.** For those with a strong stomach, this one-level museum tells the history of torture devices in Western Europe from 1500 to 1800, complete with illustrations and dummies to demonstrate how the devices were used. Be warned, this is not the best place for the young or the squeamish. ⊠ *Leysstraat 27,* ☎ *03/232–8288.* 🎟 *BF100/€2.50.* ⏲ *Daily 10–5.*

13 **Zoo.** The Antwerp Zoo houses its residents in style. Giraffes, ostriches, and African antelopes inhabit an Egyptian temple; a Moorish villa is home to the rhinoceroses; and a thriving okapi family grazes around an Indian temple. In part, this reflects the public's taste when the zoo was created 150 years ago. Today animals are allowed maximum space, and much research is devoted to endangered species. The zoo also has dolphin tanks, an aquarium, and a house for nocturnal animals. ⊠ *Koningin Astridplein 26,* ☎ *03/202–4540.* 🎟 *BF450/€11.15.* ⏲ *Oct.–Mar., daily 9–4:45; Apr.–June and Sept., daily 9–5:45; July–Aug., daily 9–6:15.*

Beyond Central Antwerp

Berchem. In this neighborhood southeast of Antwerp's city center, the 19th-century entrepreneur Baron Edouard Osy and his sister, Josephine Cogels, bought an old castle, demolished it, and built some refreshingly eccentric houses reflecting the eclectic tastes of the era. There are houses in Renaissance, Greek classical, and Venetian styles, but most of all, there are beautiful art nouveau buildings, especially at the southern end of Cogels Osylei and Waterloostraat. Berchem is the first stop on the line to Brussels. This is where international trains stop, rather than going into and backing out of Centraal Station.

Mini-Antwerpen. The name says it all. Most of Antwerp can be found here, replicated on a kid-friendly scale. A tour is available, ending with a miniature sound-and-sights show recounting the history of the city. ⊠ *Hangar 15, Cockerillkaai,* ☎ *03/237–0329.* 🎟 *BF190/€4.70.* ⏲ *Weekdays 10–5, weekends 10–6.*

Museum van Hedendaagse Kunst (MuHKA; Museum of Contemporary Art). Here you'll find contemporary paintings, installations, video art, and experimental architecture, including works by the mysterious Flemish theater director/choreographer/artist Jan Fabre, whose sculptures and installations, often based on or involving insects, have established him as a leading figure in the Belgian art world. The museum is in a renovated grain silo in the trendy Waalse Kaai district. ⊠ *Leuvenstraat 32,* ☎ *03/238–5960.* 🎟 *BF150/€3.70.* ⏲ *Tues.–Sun. 10–5. Bus 23.*

Openluchtmuseum Middelheim (Middelheim Open Air Sculpture Museum). This park is dedicated to the display of sculpture, from Rodin to the present. There are more than 300 pieces on the attractive attractive grounds, including works by Henry Moore, Alexander Calder, and Zadkine. A pavilion houses smaller and more fragile sculptures. Middelheim is just south of the city, above the tunnel for the expressway to Brussels. ✉ *Middelheimlaan 61,* ☎ *03/827–1534.* 🎟 *Free, except for special exhibitions.* ⏲ *Tues.–Sun. 10–sunset.*

Port of Antwerp. Although the Port of Antwerp is 88 km (53 mi) from the sea, it is Europe's second-largest port (after Rotterdam). Giant locks facilitate navigation up the river Scheldt; the largest measures 550 yards by 75 yards. Every year, 100 million tons of goods are shipped here, serving a vast area stretching across half of Europe. Surprisingly, in the midst of all this hustle and bustle is a fishing village, Lillo, nestled among the enormous refineries, the tankers, and the buildings of the chemical industries. In Lillo, life continues as of old. ✉ *Scheldelaan, on the banks of the river 20 km (12 mi) from town.*

Provinciaal Museum voor Fotografie (Provincial Photography Museum). The collection here celebrates the likes of Henri Cartier-Bresson, William Klein, and Man Ray. There's also a display tracing the history of photography, from the "miragioscope" of the early 19th century to a James Bond camera disguised as a gun. This is among the world's leading museums dedicated to photography. ✉ *Waalse Kaai 47,* ☎ *03/242–9300.* 🎟 *Free; temporary shows, BF150/€3.70.* ⏲ *Tues.–Sun. 10–5.*

DINING

$$$$ ★ ✕ **'t Fornuis.** In the heart of old Antwerp, this cozy restaurant, decorated in traditional Flemish style, serves some of the best (and priciest) food in the city. Chef Johan Segers likes to change his French-accented menu at regular intervals, but roasted sweetbreads with a wild truffle sauce are a permanent fixture. ✉ *Reyndersstraat 24,* ☎ *03/233–6270. Reservations essential. Jacket and tie. AE, DC, MC, V. Closed weekends, last 3 wks in Aug., Dec. 25–Jan. 1.*

$$$ **De Manie.** At this comfortable, modern wine cellar, the menu is constantly changing. Come expecting such specialties as seasonal fried liver in honey sauce and fruit, lamb with rosemary and mustard seed, and a variety of parfaits. ✉ *H. Conscienceplein 3,* ☎ *03/232–6438. AE, DC, MC, V. Closed Sun., Wed., last 2 wks in Aug.*

$$$ ✕ **De Matelote.** In a house on a narrow street, this tiny two-level restaurant serves some of the best, most sophisticated fish dishes in the city. Chef Didier Garnich turns out such creations as langoustines in a light curry sauce, sea scallops cooked with a stock of mushrooms and sorrel, and grilled asparagus with fresh morels and poached egg. The crème brûlée is outstanding. ✉ *Haarstraat 9,* ☎ *03/231–3207. Reservations essential. AE, DC, MC, V. Closed Sun., July.*

$$$ ✕ **O'Kontreir.** This stark, minimalist-designed restaurant offers sweet and spicy: great garlic spareribs and spicy shrimp scampi. The menu is seasonal, but steaks are a fixture. ✉ *Isabellalei 145,* ☎ *03/281–3976. Reservations essential. MC, V. Closed Sept.–June, Tues.; July–Aug., Tues., Sun.*

$$ ★ ✕ **Cirque Belge.** A replica of the Atomium, a facsimile of the *Manneken Pis,* portraits of famous Belgians, and paintings of national products from beer to Rizla papers: This is a nation's ironic revenge for decades of Belgian-bashing, a knowingly kitschy extravaganza that extends even to the well-executed, locally inspired cuisine and the huge range of beers. Try fish soup, rabbit in beer, or fried beef in shallots and marvel at this crash course in Belgitude. ✉ *Ernest Van Dijckkaai 13–14,* ☎ *03/232–9439. No credit cards.*

$$ ✕ **Comte Charbons.** A former storage room has been transformed into a warm, inviting restaurant. Highlights of the menu include lamb with an old mustard sauce, fantastic waterzooi, and carpaccio that melts in your mouth. ✉ *Vlaaqmse kaai 6,* ☎ *03/248–4715. Reservations essential. No credit cards. Closed Mon., July.*

Antwerp Dining and Lodging

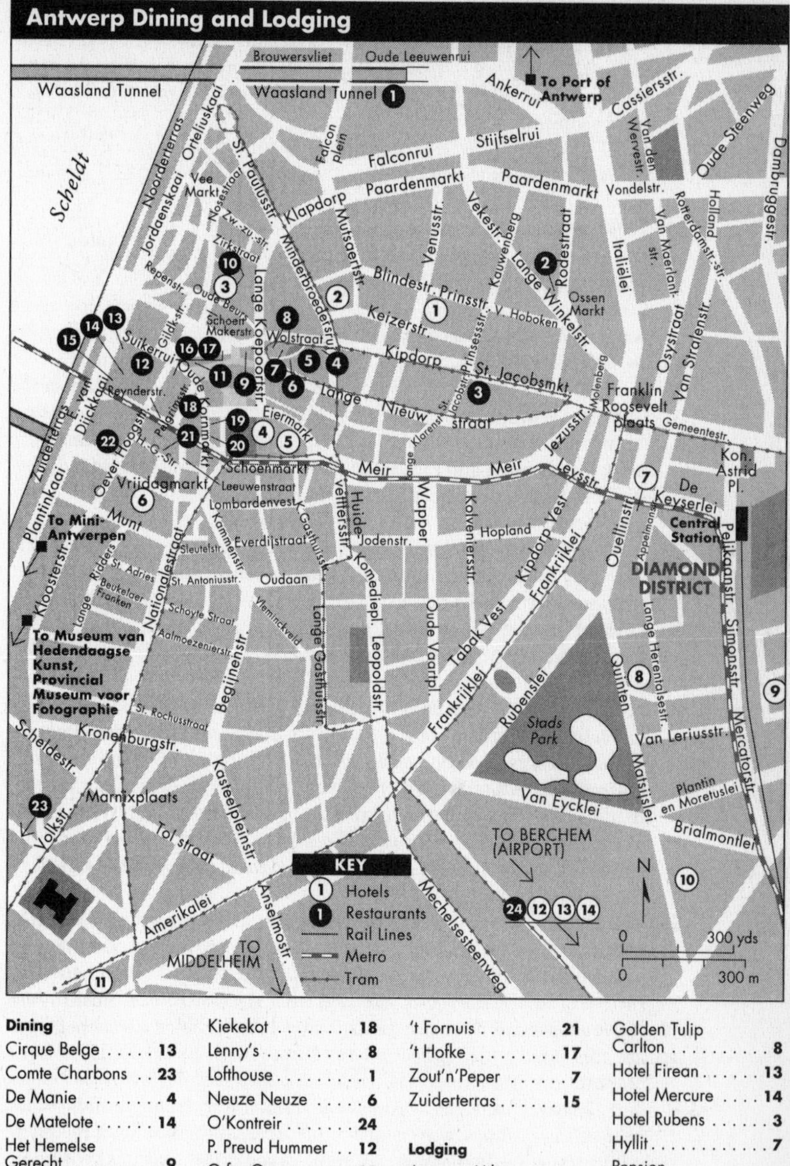

Dining
- Cirque Belge **13**
- Comte Charbons . . **23**
- De Manie **4**
- De Matelote **14**
- Het Hemelse Gerecht **9**
- Het Nieuwe Palinghuis **22**
- Hollywood Witlof . . **10**
- Hungry Henrietta . . . **3**
- In de Schaduw van de Kathedraal **11**
- Kiekekot **18**
- Lenny's **8**
- Lofthouse **1**
- Neuze Neuze **6**
- O'Kontreir **24**
- P. Preud Hummer . . **12**
- Q for Q **19**
- Santatsu Yamayu . . . **2**
- Sir Anthony Van Dijck **16**
- Spaghettiworld **20**
- 't Brantyser **5**
- 't Fornuis **21**
- 't Hofke **17**
- Zout'n'Peper **7**
- Zuiderterras **15**

Lodging
- Antwerp Hilton **4**
- Classic Hotel Villa Mozart **5**
- Crown Plaza Antwerp **12**
- De Witte Lelie. **2**
- Golden Tulip Carlton **8**
- Hotel Firean **13**
- Hotel Mercure **14**
- Hotel Rubens **3**
- Hyllit **7**
- Pension Cammerpoorte **6**
- Plaza Hotel **10**
- Prinse **1**
- Rubenshof **11**
- Scoutel **9**

$$ ✕ **Het Hemelse Gerecht.** In this cozy nook just behind the cathedral, the daily menu is written on a blackboard that seems to be bigger than the restaurant itself. Up on the board you'll find an eclectic mix, from tapas to Ethiopian chicken (in a wildly decorative presentation) to a solid rendition of the classic waterzooi. With just five tables, this is a small gem. You're wise to phone ahead for a table, as hours of operation are sometimes dictated by the reservation book. ✉ *Lijnwaadmarkt 3,* ☎ *03/231–2927. AE, DC, MC, V.*

$$ ✕ **Het Nieuwe Palinghuis.** An Antwerp landmark, it has dark wood, pottery, and a comfortable air. The seafood specialties are well prepared and reasonably priced. The name means The New Eelhouse, and sweet-fleshed eel, prepared in a variety of ways, is the house specialty, along with grilled turbot, grilled scallops, and sole in lobster sauce. ✉ *St-Jansvliet 14,* ☎ *03/231–7445. AE, DC, MC, V. Closed Mon.–Tues., June.*

$$ ✕ **Hollywood Witlof.** Dripping candles and designer furniture set the tone in this cellar dating back to the 16th century. Despite the name, the menu is French-accented, with specialties including escargot with onions and cream and tagliatelle with cold cream and salmon. ✉ *Hofstraat 9,* ☎ *02/233–7331. Reservations essential. AE, MC, V. Closed June–Sept., Mon.–Tues.; Oct.–May, Mon.*

$$ ✕ **Hungry Henrietta.** Father and son run this Antwerp institution next to Sint-Jacobskerk, the church where Rubens is buried. It's a stylish, spacious place, and when weather permits you can dine in the garden. Fillet of salmon with endive, quail salad, and leg of lamb are typical menu selections. ✉ *St-Jacobsstraat 17,* ☎ *03/232–2928. AE, DC, MC, V. Closed weekends, Aug.*

$$ ✕ **In de Schaduw van de Kathedraal.** Cozier and more traditional than the wave of contemporary restaurants dominating the scene, this little place makes good on its name: it has a dining room facing the cathedral square and a terrace where you can take your meal in the cathedral's shadow. Try the nutmeg-perfumed gratin of endive and crevettes grises, or steamed sole with scampi in fresh basil. ✉ *Handschoenmarkt 17,* ☎ *03/232–4014. AE, DC, MC, V. Closed June–Sept., Tues.; Oct.–May, Mon.–Tues.*

$$ ✕ **Lofthouse.** This 300-year-old wine cellar attracts a lively crowd. The menu emphasizes seasonal specials such as asparagus and fresh lobster, and the staff goes out of its way to be helpful. ✉ *Oude Leeuwenrui 7–11,* ☎ *03/226–3840. AE, DC, MC, V. Closed Sun., 2 wks in July.*

$$ ★ ✕ **Neuze Neuze.** Five tiny houses have been cobbled together to create this handsome, split-level restaurant with plenty of nooks and crannies on different levels, whitewashed walls, dark brown beams, and a blazing fireplace. Warm smoked salmon with endive and a white beer sauce, scallops with rhubarb preserve, and goose liver meunière with caramelized pineapple are some of the dishes executed with flair. Service is excellent and the genial patron, Domien Sels, is ever-present. ✉ *Wijngaardstraat 19,* ☎ *03/232–5783. AE, DC, MC, V. Closed Sun., 2 wks in July and 2 wks in Jan. No lunch Sat.*

$$ ✕ **P. Preud Hummer.** In a location that has served as a pastry shop and a gun shop, this exquisite restaurant mixes art nouveau design, antiques, and a 400-year-old Spanish ceiling. The food is on a par with the decor. Chef Dimettri, winner of the esteemed Antwerp Diamond, serves up such delicacies as terrine of goose liver, fried scallops in tomato-basil sauces, and ice cream with hot chocolate. ✉ *Suikerrui 28,* ☎ *03/233–4200. AE, DC, MC, V. Closed Jan.*

$$ ✕ **Q for Q.** Come here for a unique dining concept: a potato and carpaccio shop. Amazingly enough, it works. The secret is the wide selection of dressings. ✉ *Oude Koornmarkt 22,* ☎ *03/233–6155. AE, MC, V.*

$$ ★ ✕ **Sir Anthony Van Dijck.** You used to find well-respected haute cuisine here, but the owner has made the transition to a less pretentious,

more relaxed establishment. Now the monthly-changing menu offers brasserie fare such as salad liègeoise, duck à l'orange, and tuna steak. Under high, massive beams supported by stone pillars, you sit surrounded by flowers and carved wood, at tables overlooking an interior courtyard. There are two seatings a night. ✉ *Vlaeykensgang, Oude Koornmarkt 16,* ☎ *03/231–6170. AE, DC, MC, V. Closed Sun., Aug. 2–30.*

$ ✕ **Kiekekot.** Antwerp students satisfy their craving for spit-roasted chicken and fries at this no-frills "chicken coop," which offers a juicy, golden half-chicken for under BF200/€4.95. As befits the clientele, it's open well into the night. ✉ *Grote Markt 35,* ☎ *03/232–1502. MC, V. Closed Tues. No lunch weekdays.*

$ ✕ **Lenny's.** Great brown-bread sandwiches and fresh, creative salads make this straightforward café a perfect pit stop for lunch. ✉ *47 Wolstraat,* ☎ *03/233–9057. No credit cards. Closed Mon., Tues.*

$ ✕ **Santatsu Yamayu.** Japanese staples—sushi and noodles—are served up at this tiny restaurant in the Ossenmarkt. The extensive lunch menu offers good values. ✉ *19 Ossenmarkt,* ☎ *03/234–0949. AE, DC, MC, V. Closed Mon.*

$ ✕ **Spaghettiworld.** The pasta is good, but the people-watching is even better at this hip joint. The young and the style-conscious fuel up here before a night on the town. ✉ *66 Oude Koornmarket,* ☎ *03/234–3801. No credit cards.*

$ ✕ **'t Brantyser.** This old café, with dark rafters, brick, and stucco, on two open levels, serves more than just drinks and the usual snacks: the tavern fare is supplemented by a range of salads and affordable specials. ✉ *Hendrik Conscienceplein 7,* ☎ *03/233–1833. MC, V.*

$ ✕ **'t Hofke.** It's worth visiting here for the location alone, in the Vlaeykensgang alley, where time seems to have stood still. The cozy dining room has the look and feel of a private home, and the menu includes a large selection of salads and omelettes, as well as more substantial fare. ✉ *Vlaeykensgang, Oude Koornmarkt 16,* ☎ *03/233–8606. AE, MC, V. Closed Mon.*

$ ✕ **Zout'n'Peper.** Among the best of Antwerp's many trendy eateries, Zout'n'Peper has warm, African-influenced decor and jazz and funk music coming from the sound system. The top-value fixed-price menu includes three courses with an aperitif and a generous carafe of wine. Fish soup, grilled salmon, steak diabolo, and desserts are among the high points. ✉ *Wijngaardstraat 5,* ☎ *03/231–7373. MC, V. Closed Wed. No lunch.*

$ ✕ **Zuiderterras.** A stark, glass-and-black-metal construction, this riverside café and restaurant was designed by avant-garde architect bOb (his spelling) Van Reeth during the city's stint as Cultural Capital of Europe in 1993. Here you can have a light meal and enjoy seeing the river traffic on one side and, on the other, a view of the cathedral and the Old Town. ✉ *Ernest Van Dijckkaai 37,* ☎ *03/234–1275. Reservations not accepted. AE, MC, V.*

LODGING

The Antwerp City Tourist Office (☞ Visitor Information *in* Antwerp A to Z, *below*) keeps track of the best hotel prices and can make reservations for you up to a week in advance. Write or fax for a reservation form. It also maintains a list of some 25 recommended bed-and-breakfast accommodations from BF1,200/€29.75 to BF2,000/€49.50.

$$$$ **Antwerp Hilton.** This five-story complex, opened in 1993, incorporates the former fin de siècle Grand Bazaar department store and a gigantic ballroom seating 1,000. Rooms have mahogany doors, three

telephones, safes, and executive desks. Afternoon tea is served in the marble-floored lobby, and lunch and dinner are offered in the Het Vijfde Seizoen restaurant. ✉ *Groenplaats, B2000,* ☎ *03/204–1212,* FAX *03/204–1213. 189 rooms, 18 suites. 2 restaurants, bar, no-smoking floors, sauna, health club, convention center, shops, parking (fee). AE, DC, MC, V.*

$$$$ **Crown Plaza Antwerp.** On the Ring Road outside of the city center, the Crown Plaza is a luxury hotel catering primarily to business travelers; there are 14 banquet halls for conventions and events. Rooms are clean and comfortable, though not long on character, and the staff is first-rate. The Plaza Fitness Club has extensive facilities (including a tanning bed, sauna, and pool), and the hotel bar/brasserie serves quite respectable fare. ✉ *Gerard le Grellelaan 10, B2020,* ☎ *03/237–2900,* FAX *03/216–0296. 262 rooms. Restaurant, bar, pool, sauna, health club, meeting rooms, parking (free). AE, MC, DC, V.*

$$$$ ★ **De Witte Lelie.** Three step-gabled 16th-century houses have been combined to make the "White Lily" Antwerp's most exclusive hotel. Personal service is the watchword in the 10-room hotel, decorated mostly in white, with colorful carpets and modern art on the walls. Sumptuous breakfasts are served on a loggia that opens onto the inner courtyard. ✉ *Keizerstraat 16–18, 2000,* ☎ *03/226–1966,* FAX *03/234–0019. 4 rooms, 6 suites. Breakfast room. AE, DC, MC, V.*

$$$ **Classic Hotel Villa Mozart.** This small, modern hotel, a part of the Best Western chain, is ideally situated in the pedestrian zone next to the cathedral. The rooms, in the European tradition, feel a bit cramped, but they have the business-class features, such as air-conditioning and safes, that you'd expect from an international chain, and many have cathedral views. In fair weather you can take breakfast on the terrace facing the cathedral. ✉ *Handschoenmarkt 3–7, B2000,* ☎ *03/231–3031,* FAX *03/231–5685. 25 rooms. Restaurant, bar, sauna. AE, DC, MC, V.*

$$$ ★ **Hotel Firean.** This Art Deco gem, built in 1929, underwent a major restoration in 1986 that recaptured not only its architectural style but also the grace of a bygone era. It's a welcome contrast to the uniformity of chain hotels. The location, a residential neighborhood south of the center but on the tram line into town, reinforces the tranquility inside, expressed by fresh flowers, rich fabrics, and a tasteful mix of antiques and reproductions. The service is what you'd hope for from a family-owned and -operated establishment. Breakfast eggs come in floral-print cozies, and jazz piano is discreetly piped into public areas. The rooms themselves are quiet sanctuaries. ✉ *Karel Oomsstraat 6, B2018,* ☎ *03/237–0260,* FAX *03/238–1168. 9 rooms, 6 in annex next door. Bar, breakfast room. AE, DC, MC, V. Closed last week of July, 1st ½ of Aug., Dec. 24–1st weekend after Jan. 6.*

$$$ **Hotel Mercure.** The former Antwerp Sofitel is a glass-and-steel structure set in a park 10 minutes south of the city center. The attractive rooms are equipped with the modern conveniences, the service is consistently good, and the restaurant is first-rate. ✉ *Desguinlei 94, B2018,* ☎ *03/244–8211,* FAX *03/216–4712. 221 rooms. Restaurant, sauna, health club, meeting rooms. AE, DC, MC, V.*

$$$ **Hotel Rubens.** There's a romantic air to this small, colorful hotel directly behind the Grote Markt, yet if you're traveling on business you won't feel neglected. The immaculate rooms come with cable television, minibars, and fax machines. Drinks or breakfast under the 16th-century tower and colonnade is a must. ✉ *Oude Beurs 29, B2000,* ☎ *03/222–4848,* FAX *03/225–1940. 36 rooms. Bar, breakfast room, in-room fax, minibars, meeting rooms. AE, DC, MC, V.*

$$$ **Plaza Hotel.** Like its (unrelated) namesake in New York, the Plaza in Antwerp is near Central Park (Stadspark), a brisk walk from the city center. Although it doesn't aspire to the level of elegance of the

New York Plaza, it does have some traditional grace notes, such as cherrywood paneling in the public spaces and a marble entrance. The rooms are good-sized by local standards, with walk-in closets. Ask about special weekend rates. ✉ *Charslottalei 43-49, B2018,* ☎ *03/218–9240,* FAX *03/278–2871. 80 rooms. Bar, breakfast room, in-room safes, minibars, conference room. AE, DC, MC, V.*

$$ **Golden Tulip Carlton.** Facing the Stadspark, this hotel has clean, comfortable rooms and a convenient location, a stone's throw from the Diamond District and within walking distance of all of Antwerp's central sights. Rooms have color televisions, minibars, and hair dryers. The restaurant is respectable, and there's a quaint tearoom. ✉ *Quinten Matsijslei 25, B2018,* ☎ *03/231–1515,* FAX *03/225–3090. 139 rooms. Restaurant, bar, tea shop, in-room safes, minibars, room service, meeting rooms. AE, DC, MC, V.*

$$ **Hyllit.** The Hyllit stands on the corner of De Keyserlaan, a high-end shopping street, with its entrance on Appelmansstraat, the gateway to the Diamond District (reception on second floor). Rooms are decorated in muted colors and equipped with office-style desks; suites have a fax as well. There's a rooftop buffet breakfast room and full room service. ✉ *De Keyserlei 28–30, 2018,* ☎ *03/202–6800,* FAX *03/202–6890. 24 rooms, 56 suites. Breakfast room, room service. AE, DC, MC, V.*

$$ **Prinse.** Set well back from an Old Town street, this 400-year-old landmark with an interior courtyard opened as a hotel in 1990. It was once the home of 16th-century poet Anna Bijns. A member of the Relais du Silence (Quiet Inns) group, the hotel has a modern look, with black leather chairs, soft blue curtains, and tile bathrooms. Exposed beams give top-floor rooms more character. ✉ *Keizerstraat 63, B2000,* ☎ *03/226–4050,* FAX *03/225–1148. 35 rooms. Breakfast room. AE, DC, MC, V.*

$ **Pension Cammerpoorte.** Owned by the managers of the nearby Cammerpoorte Hotel, this small pension is run with considerable enthusiasm by its proprietor. Substantial breakfasts are served in a tidy brick-and-lace café downstairs. The cheerful, sizable rooms—on landings reached by a narrow staircase—are full of bright pastels and offer basic kitchen facilities; some can comfortably accommodate a family of four. ✉ *Steenhouwersvest 55, B2000,* ☎ *03/231–2836,* FAX *03/226–2968. 9 rooms. Breakfast room. AE, DC, MC, V.*

$ **Rubenshof.** Once a cardinal's residence, this hotel shows remnants of its former glory with a mixture of turn-of-the-20th-century styles. The hotel is owned by a friendly Dutch couple, and the location is close to the Fine Arts Museum. ✉ *Amerikalei 115-117, B2000,* ☎ *03/237–0789,* FAX *03/248–2594. 24 rooms, 3 with bath. Breakfast room, free parking. AE, DC, MC, V.*

$ **Scoutel.** This hotel, owned by the Boy Scouts and Girl Guides but open to all ages, is in a modern building five minutes' walk from Central Station. The double and triple rooms are simple but adequate; all have toilets and showers. Rates are lower for people under 25, and most of the guests *are* young people. Breakfast and sheets are included; towels can be rented. Guests are provided with front-door keys. ✉ *Stoomstraat 3, B2000,* ☎ *03/226–4606,* FAX *03/232–6392. 24 rooms with shower. Breakfast room, meeting rooms. No credit cards.*

NIGHTLIFE AND THE ARTS

The Arts

Check *The Bulletin* (☞ Nightlife and the Arts *in* Chapter 2) for details on arts events in Antwerp.

Dance

Antwerp is home to a host of innovative and exciting ballet and dance troupes, and its school is internationally renowned. The major ballet company is the **Koninklijk Ballet van Vlaanderen** (Royal Flanders Ballet; ✉ 't Eilandje, ☎ 03/234–3438), whose productions tour regularly across Belgium. The companies of leading Belgian choreographers, including Anne Teresa De Keersmaeker, Wim Vandekeybus, and Alain Platel, frequently perform at **deSingel** (✉ Desguinlei 25, ☎ 03/248–2424), the city's flagship cultural venue.

Opera and Concerts

Antwerp's opera company is **Koninklijke Vlaamse Opera** (Royal Flanders Opera; ✉ Van Ertboornstraat 8, ☎ 03/233–6685), which has a sister company in Gent. The **Koninklijk Philharmonisch Orkest van Vlaanderen** (Royal Flanders Philharmonic) most frequently performs at **deSingel** (✉ Desguinlei 25, ☎ 03/248–2424). A regular venue for classical music is the **Koningin Elisabethzaal** (✉ Koningin Astridplein 23, ☎ 03/233–8444).

Visiting rock stars perform at the **Sportpaleis** (✉ Schijnpoortweg 113, ☎ 03/326–1010), although Antwerp is inexplicably not on the regular gig circuit.

Theater

The flagship of the more than two dozen theaters in Antwerp is the **Bourla Theater** (✉ Komedieplaats 18, ☎ 03/231–0750), a marvelously restored 150-year-old facility, which is now the home of the **Koninklijke Nederlands Schouwburg** (Royal Dutch-speaking Theater). Theatrical performances regularly occur at the multipurpose **deSingel** (✉ Desguinlei 25, ☎ 03/248–2424). The **Poppenschouwburg Van Campen** (Van Campen Puppet Theater; ✉ Lange Nieuwstraat 3, ☎ 03/237–3716) presents traditional puppet performances in Flemish dialect between September and May.

Nightlife

There are 2,500 taverns in Antwerp—one for every 200 inhabitants—and the city is the club-going capital of Belgium, which means that the centers of nightlife are abuzz till the wee small hours of the morning. The **Grote Markt** area attracts many tourists as well as locals with a range of traditional Belgian alehouses and some small discotheques, especially in the narrow, winding streets around the cathedral. **Leuvenstraat,** particularly around the Museum of Modern Art, teems with cafés and pool halls. Some of the cafés even have small acting troupes that perform nightly. The small, hidden square of **Stadswaag** has a cluster of bars and discos. Along the waterfront at **Vlaamse Kaai and Waalse Kaai** there's a large parking square where you'll find some of Antwerp's biggest clubs (Zillion, Café D'Anvers) as well as a group of smaller pubs. Be advised, though, that they share the area with Antwerp's red-light district.

Bars

Bar Tabac (✉ Waalse Kaai 43, ☎ no phone) is a studiously seedy mock-Gallic truckers' café. **Beveren** (✉ Vlasmarkt 2, ☎ 03/231–2225) is boisterous and old-fashioned. The most famous bar in Antwerp is probably the **Bierhuis Kulminator** (✉ Vleminckveld 32–34, ☎ 03/232–4538), which pours 550 different kinds of beer, including EKU-28, known as the strongest beer on earth; some of the beers are 30 years old. In **Blauwe Steen** (✉ Ernest van Dijckkaai 34, ☎ 03/231–6710), you can listen to street musicians perform while you sip beer. The always-open **Bourla** (✉ Komediplein 7, ☎ 03/231–0750) is a popular meeting place for a nightcap. At the center of the Old City, **Den Engel** (✉ 3 Grote Markt, ☎ 03/233–1223) draws an eclectic clientele. **Kafe Marque** (✉ Grote Pieter Potstraat 3, ☎ 03/233–2428) is a small, bright bar that stocks an impressive range of American and Asian beers and has an unpretentious disco downstairs. African-themed **L'Entrepot du Congo** (✉ 42 Vlaamse Kaai, ☎ 03/238–9232) attracts a refined crowd; music varies, and food is available. The Mediterranean-inspired **Le Routier** (✉ Waalse Kaai 33, ☎ 03/257–1599) is laid-back and friendly. **Pelgrom** (✉ Pelgrimsstraat 15, ☎ 03/234–0809) is in a 16th-century tavern. **Vagant** (✉ Pelgrimsstraat, ☎ 03/236–4676) is a late-night haunt.

Dance Clubs

For mainstream sounds, try **Beach Club Antwerp** (✉ Groenplaats 36, ☎ 03/227—0527). **Café d'Anvers** (✉ Verversrui 15, ☎ 03/226–3870), in the red-light district, is the city's flagship house and techno venue, attracting ravers from across Europe to its friendly dance floors. **Café Local** (✉ Waalse Kaai 25, ☎ 03/238–5004) in the trendy riverfront area south of the center, imaginatively re-creates pre-Castro Cuba, although the music is uninspired chart dance. **Fill Collins Club** (✉ Schipperskapelstraat, ☎ 03/232–4712) was the latest thing as of press time. If you're prepared to venture south of the Waalse Kaai area, **Zillion** (✉ Jan van Gentstraat 4, ☎ 03/248–1516) is the biggest, flashiest nightclub in town.

Gay Bars

Antwerp has a more upfront gay scene than most Belgian cities; Van Schoonhovenstraat, near the Centraal Station, is clustered with gay bars, and there are plenty dotted around the city center. Start at the **Gay and Lesbian Centre** (✉ Dambruggestraat 204, ☎ 03/233–1071), which offers a "gay map" of Antwerp detailing clubs, bars, restaurants, saunas, and clinics. For lesbians, there are **Lady's Pub** (✉ Waalse Kaai 56, ☎ 03/238–5490) and **Shakespeare** (✉ Oude Koornmarkt 24, ☎ 03/231–5058). **'t Catshuis** (✉ Grote Pieter Potstraat 18, ☎ 03/234–0369) is one of the newer hangouts for gay men.

Jazz Clubs

There isn't live music every night in these clubs, so check beforehand. Try **De Hopper** (✉ Leopold De Waelstraat 2, ☎ 03/248–4933), which has music occasionally, in a rather formal environment. **De Muse** (✉ Melmarkt 15, ☎ 03/226–0126) has train-station decor and good jazz sounds. **DeSingel** (✉ Desguinlei 25, ☎ 03/248–2424), one of Antwerp's leading performing-arts venues, sometimes features jazz. **Refrein** (✉ Pelgrimstraat, ☎ 03/231–1689) has a wide variety of live music. **Swingcafé** (✉ Suikerrui 13, ☎ 03/233–1478) is a popular spot that sometimes has jazz and blues performers.

OUTDOOR ACTIVITIES AND SPORTS

Golf

The **Brasschaat Open Golf Club Center** (✉ Miksebaan 248, Brasschaat, ☎ 03/653–1084) is 15 km (9 mi) from the city center.

Skating

The most popular skating rink is **Antarctica** (✉ Moerelei 119, Wilrijk, ☎ 03/828–9928).

Tennis

Beerschot (✉ Stadionstraat, ☎ 03/248–7189) has 10 outdoor and 4 indoor courts. There are eight courts at **Het Rooi** (✉ Berchemstadionstraat 73, ☎ 03/239–6610).

SHOPPING

By Sarah Wolff

That Antwerp is a young, style-conscious city is reflected in it's smart, trendy shops and boutiques. Dedicated followers of fashion regard Antwerp as a trendsetter second only to Milan. Credit for this development goes to the so-called Antwerp Six (students of Linda Loppa from the class of 1981 at Antwerp's Fashion Academy) and in equal measure to the new wave of talent that has more recently stormed the catwalks. Ready-to-wear by stalwarts Ann Demeulemeester, Dirk Bikkembergs, Dries Van Noten, and relative newcomers Raf Simons, AF Vandervorst, and Jurgi Persoons command high prices. However, in the shopping area just south of Groenplaats, prices are less astronomical.

Shopping Streets

The elegant **Meir,** together with its extension to the east, **De Keyserlei,** and at the opposite end, **Huidevettersstraat,** is where you will find high-street standbys and long-established names. Shopping galleries branch off from all three streets—**Century Center** and **Antwerp Tower** from De Keyserlei, **Meir Square** from Meir, and **Nieuwe Gaanderij** from Huidevettersstraat. Relatively new as a shopping hub is the area in and around the glamorous **Horta Complex** in Hopland.

Many boutiques cater to more avant-garde tastes. The best-known area is **De Wilde Zee,** consisting of Groendalstraat, Lombardenstraat, Wiegstraat, and Korte Gasthuisstraat; the nearby Schuttershofstraat, Kammenstraat, and Nationalestraat have also risen to the vogue. Another pedestrian area for general shopping is **Hoogstraat,** between Grote Markt and Sint-Jansvliet, with its appendix, **Grote Pieter Potstraat.** Here you find good secondhand bookshops and all kinds of bric-a-brac.

Street Markets

There's an antiques market on **Lijnwaadmarkt** (Easter–Oct., Sat. 9–5), just north of the cathedral. The **Rubensmarkt** (Rubens Market, Aug. 15 annually) is held on the Grote Markt, with vendors in 17th-century costumes hawking everything under the sun. Public auction sales of furniture and other secondhand goods are held at **Vrijdagmarkt** (Wed., Fri. 9–noon). On Oudervaartplaats (a block south from Rubenshuis on Wapper), there is a general market (Sat. 8–3, Sun. 8–1) selling flowers, plants, fruit, and vegetables. Many locals still refer to it as **Vogelenmarkt** (bird market), in spite of the fact that the sale of live animals at street markets is now banned.

Clothing

Avant-Garde Fashion

The explosive success of the Antwerp Six in the early 1990s put Belgium firmly on the fashion map, and Antwerp in particular is a haven for cutting-edge women's and men's ready-to-wear fashions. **Louis** (⊠ 2 Lombardenstraat, ☎ 03/232–9872) was one of the first places to sell the work of Antwerp's top designers in the late 1980s. Today, it sells the collections of the city's more recent talent—Veronique Branquinho, Jurgi Persoons, AF Vandervorst, Olivier Theyskens, and Raf Simons. Most of the original six now have their own stores. The work of Dries Van Noten is in the splendid renovated **Modepaleis** (⊠ 16 Nationalestraat, ☎ 03/233–9437), a turn-of-the-20th-century men's outfitters. Owned by Walter Van Beirendonck and Dirk Van Saene, **Walter** (⊠ 12 Sint-Antonius-

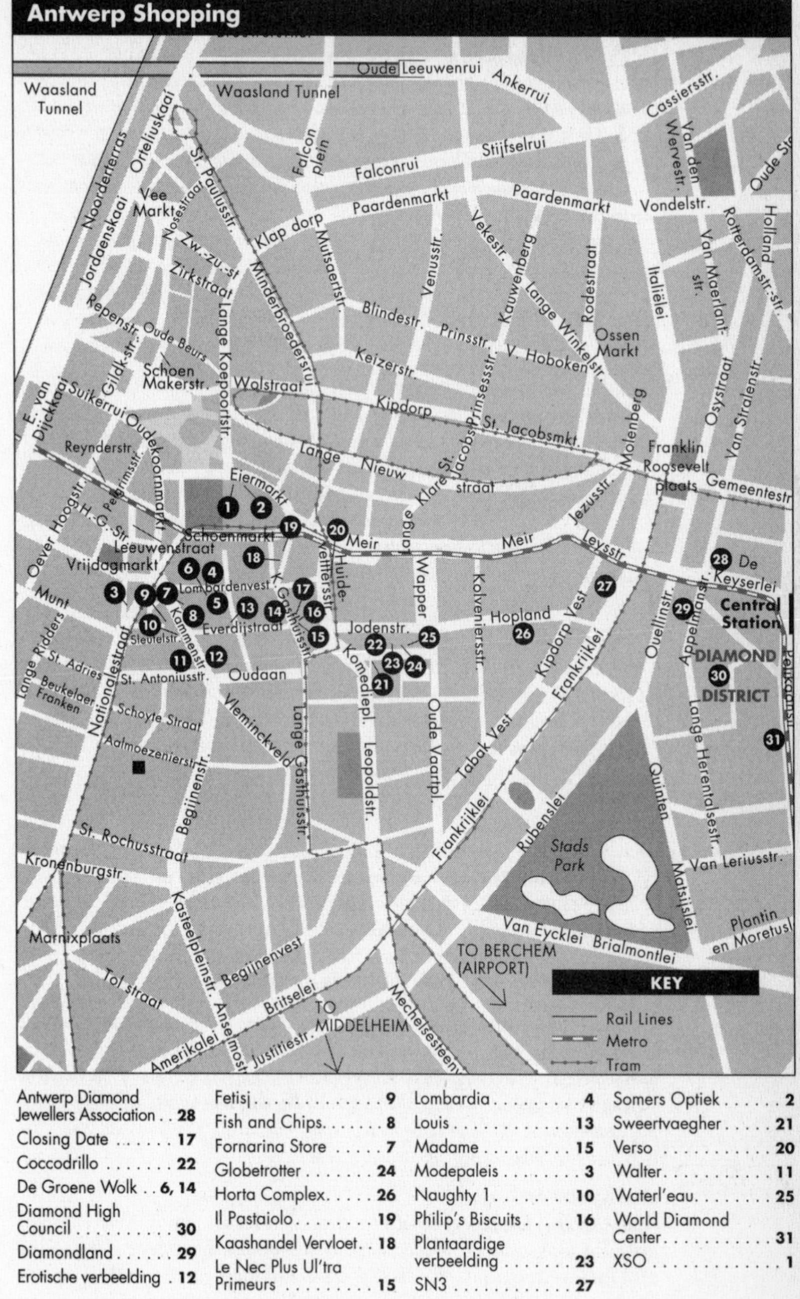

Antwerp Diamond Jewellers Association . . 28
Closing Date 17
Coccodrillo 22
De Groene Wolk . . 6, 14
Diamond High Council 30
Diamondland 29
Erotische verbeelding . 12
Fetisj 9
Fish and Chips 8
Fornarina Store 7
Globetrotter 24
Horta Complex 26
Il Pastaiolo 19
Kaashandel Vervloet . . 18
Le Nec Plus Ul'tra Primeurs 15
Lombardia 4
Louis 13
Madame 15
Modepaleis 3
Naughty 1 10
Philip's Biscuits 16
Plantaardige verbeelding 23
SN3 27
Somers Optiek 2
Sweertvaegher 21
Verso 20
Walter 11
Waterl'eau 25
World Diamond Center 31
XSO 1

Close-Up

ANTWERP À LA MODE

BELGIUM HAS ALWAYS HAD some acclaim for its fashion—designers Olivier Strelli and Gerald Waterlet have dressed Queen Paula and shown in Paris—but in the 1990s its status skyrocketed on the international scene. Credit for the phenomenon goes to the so-called Antwerp Six, and in equal measure to the designer who trained them, Linda Loppa. As the story goes, six graduates of the Antwerp Academy from the years 1980 and 1981 rented a truck and drove to the London fashion week. After taking the show by storm, the members of the group became brand names around the world—literally.

The six are Dries Van Noten, Dirk Bikkembergs, Dirk Van Saene, Ann Demeulemeester, Walter Van Beirendonck, and Marina Yee, and though they shared the same training ground, their styles are distinctly different. (Some contend the label "Antwerp Six" stuck because it was easier for non-Flemings to pronounce than the designers' names.) Van Noten, for example, creates an "East meets West" fusion of classic looks with exotic fabrics; Demeulemeester's styles are feminine and simple; Van Beirendonck's label WLT—Wild and Lethal Trash—is known for bright colors and a futuristic/punk feel.

In the capricious world of fashion, the Antwerp Six have shown notable staying power. Their success has helped to turn Antwerp into a spawning ground for young designers (Stephaan Schneider, Raf Simons, and Kaat Tilley are more recent standouts) and make it a fixture on the fashion map.

traat, ☎ 03/213–2644) sells the best of their collections against a futuristic backdrop. **Ann Demeulemeester** (✉ 38 Verlatstraat, ☎ 03/216–0133) sells her clothes in an elegant corner store close to the Royal Museum of Fine Arts. Shoe shop **Coccodrillo** (✉ 9 Schuttershofstraat, ☎ 03/233–2093) has fashionable footwear for adults and children by the likes of Ann Demeulemeester, Dirk Bikkembergs, and Martin Margiela.

Children from five years old to teens can find the latest attire from Quincy, Max & Lola, Anne Kuris, and Simple Kids at **De Groene Wolk** (✉ 20 Korte Gasthuisstraat, ☎ 03/234–1847). Proving you're never too young to be fashionable, the branch of **De Groene Wolk** at ✉ 66 Lombardenvestraat (☎ 03/226–8161) has Belgium's top kids' fashion labels for the three-months-to-four-years set.

Designer Labels

Antwerp also has plenty to offer the fashion-lover of more conventional tastes. A long-time presence on the designer-clothing scene is **Verso** (✉ 39 Huidevetterstraat, ☎ 03/226–9292), which carries such labels as Prada, Costume National, Dirk Bikkembergs, and Xavier Delcour for men and women. **Closing Date** (✉ 15 Korte Gasthuisstraat, ☎ 03/232–8722) stocks pieces by Vivienne Westwood and Nick Coleman. **XSO** (✉ 13 Eiermarkt, ☎ 03/231–8749) is the place for clothes by Issey Miyake and Kaat Tilley. **SN3** (✉ 46-48 Frankrijklei, ☎ 03/231–0820), in a former cinema, is worth a look for womenswear by Chanel, Prada Sport, Miu Miu, and Sonia Rykiel. For women's lingerie of a high standard—labels include Dior, Ricci lingerie, and Gerbe hosiery—go to **Madame** (✉ 80 Lombardenvest, ☎ 03/232–5062), a tiny boutique that's been around since the 1970s.

Street Scene

Kammenstraat is where it's at for less expensive street fashion, as well as record stores. The best-known clothes shop is **Fish and Chips** (✉ 36–38 Kammenstraat, ☎ 03/227–0824); it has a bargain-basement feel, with vintage '50s to '70s clothes upstairs, as well as a hairdresser and a trendy bar. **Naughty 1** (✉ 65-67 Kammenstraat, ☎ 03/213–3590) is worth checking out for vintage clothing. **Fetisj** (✉ 55 Kammenstraat, ☎ 03/289–3368) has fun fashion for the hip. **Fornarina Store** (✉ 32 Kammenstraat, ☎ 03/213–2023) sells the Italian club-clothes brand of the same name. It's women only at trendy sex shop **Erotische verbeelding** (✉ 10-12 Ijzerenwaag, ☎ 03/226–8950), where the emphasis is on pleasing the wearer (rather than the wearer's partner).

Diamonds

The heart of the city's diamond industry is in and around Appelmansstraat, near the Centraal Station. Here merchants from the world over have dealt in diamonds for 500 years. For advice on buying diamonds at the retail level, you can contact the **Antwerp Diamond Jewelers Association** (✉ 15-17 De Keyserlei, ☎ 03/227–3891), which has a brochure listing the addresses of its members' shops, jewelers who work under the patronage of the city of Antwerp. The largest diamond showroom is **Diamondland** (✉ 33a Appelmansstraat, ☎ 03/234–3612), where tours of polishers, goldsmiths, and setters at work can be arranged before you settle down to business. **The World Diamond Center** (✉ 62 Pelikaanstraat, ☎ 03/233–2529) is a diamond district mainstay with a large retail trade. For certificates of authenticity for polished stones, contact the **Diamond High Council** (✉ 22 Hoveniersstraat, ☎ 03/222–0511), which is in the thick of the wholesale industry.

Food Shops

Upscale takeout and speciality food shops are clustered around the fashionable De Wilde Zee district on Wiegstraat, Schrijnwerkersstraat, and Korte Gasthuisstraat. Fabulous Italian provisioner **Il Pastaiolo** (✉ 18 Wiegstraat, ☎ 03/233–8631) sells ready-to-eat pasta dishes, filled panini, and pizzas to go. **Kaashandel Vervloet** (✉ 28 Wiegstraat, ☎ 03/233–3729) is the best address for regional cheeses. Delicatessen **Le Nec Plus Ul'tra Primeurs** (✉ 5 Korte Gasthuisstraat, ☎ 02/233–3439) is still going strong after 30 years, and it's easy to see why—it stocks an amazing array of olive oils, spices, condiments, fruit, and vegetables. Try juice bar **Lombardia** (✉ 78 Lombardenvest, ☎ 03/233–6819) for wicked fresh-fruit cocktails to drink on site as well as health food products.

If you're after an edible souvenir from Antwerp, head for the old-fashioned biscuit and cake store **Philip's Biscuits** (✉ 11 Korte Gasthuisstraat, ☎ 03/231–2660). *Speculaas, macarons,* and *peperkoek* are best and can be ordered in attractive tins—a good gift alternative to chocolate. If only chocolate will do, try family-run **Sweertvaegher** (✉ 16 Schuttershofstraat, ☎ 03/226–3691), which has been selling the stuff since the 1930s.

Specialty Stores

Backpackers with cash to spare and sporty types should have a look at **Globetrotter** (✉ 29 Schuttershofstraat, ☎ 03/226–5136), where high-performance clothes and equipment by Patagonia and North Face are sold. For some serious pampering, head for **Waterl'eau** (✉ 47 Schuttershofstraat, ☎ 03/226–7586), which in addition to stocking designer bathroom accessories has upmarket beauty products. Top-notch florist **Plantaardige verbeelding** (✉ 12 Schuttershofstraat, ✉ 1 Kelderstraat, ☎ 03/226–1042) is worth a stop even if you are not buying. The bouquets by Helmi Lammers and Charles Breit are to die for at this gorgeous shop. Finally, the visually impaired should pop into **Somers Optiek** (✉ 33 Eiermarkt, ☎ 03/233–4758), where cutting-edge designer frames by Belgian Patrick Hoet are stocked. For attention-grabbing eyewear, this place is a must.

ANTWERP A TO Z

Arriving and Departing

By Car

Antwerp is surrounded by a ring road from which expressways shoot off like spokes in a wheel. The city is 48 km (29 mi) north of Brussels on the E19; 60 km (36 mi) northwest of Gent on the E17; 119 km (71 mi) northwest of Liège on the A13.

By Plane

Deurne Airport (☎ 03/218–1211), 5½ km (3 mi) southeast of the city center, has several flights a day from London. **Brussels National Airport** (Zaventem) is linked with Antwerp by frequent bus service (hourly 7 AM–11 PM). The trip takes 50 minutes.

By Train

Four to five trains an hour link Antwerp with Brussels; the trip takes about 45 minutes. The train ride south from Rotterdam takes an hour. **International Thalys trains** between Paris and Amsterdam stop at Berchem Station south of the city center rather than entering the downtown Centraal Station.

Getting Around

By Bus

De Lijn bus lines mostly begin outside Centraal Station in the Koningin Astridplein. Longer-distance buses start from the Franklin Rooseveltplaats.

By Taxi

There are **taxi stands** in front of Centraal Station and at other principal points. It is often easier to call for one: **Antwerp Taxi** (☎ 03/238–3838). **Metropole Taxi** (☎ 03/231–3131).

By Tram and Subway

You can travel by tram all over central Antwerp. Some operate underground as the pre-Metro system. The **most useful subway line** for visitors links Centraal Station (Metro: Diamant) with the left bank via the Groenplaats (for the cathedral and Grote Markt). A BF40/€1.00 ticket is good for one hour on all forms of public transport; BF105/€2.60 buys unlimited travel for one day. Tickets are available at De Lijn offices, the tourist office, and at the Diamant, Opera/Frankrijklei, and Groenplaats Metro stops.

Contacts and Resources

B&B Reservation Agencies

The **City Tourist Office** (✉ Grote Markt 15, ☎ 03/232–0103, FAX 03/231–1937) has a list of the 20 best bed-and-breakfast accommodations, complete with photographs.

Car Rentals

Avis (✉ Plantin en Moretuslei 62, ☎ 03/218–9496). **Budget** (✉ Ankerrui 20, ☎ 03/232–3500). **Hertz** (✉ Deurne Airport, ☎ 03/233–2992).

Emergencies

Police (☎ 101). **Ambulance** (☎ 100). **Emergency Rooms:** Middelheim (✉ Lindendreef 1, ☎ 03/280–3111); Stuivenberg (✉ Lange Beeldekensstraat 267, ☎ 03/217–7111). The name of the **pharmacy** on night and weekend duty is displayed in all pharmacy windows.

Guided Tours

Flandria (☎ 03/231–3100) operates 90-minute boat trips on the river Scheldt, departing from the Steenplein pontoon, next to the Steen (May–Sept., Tues. and Thurs.–Sun. 1 and 2:30; Oct., weekends 1 and 2:30). The company also offers 2½-hour boat tours of the port, which leave from Quay 13 near Londonstraat (May–Aug., Tues. and Thurs.–Sun. 2:30; 2nd ½ of Apr. and Sept.–Oct., weekends 2:30).

Touristram (☎ 03/480–9388) operates 50-minute tram tours with cassette commentary in the Old Town and old harbor area. Tickets are sold on the tram. Departure is from Groenplaats (⏲ Apr.–Dec., daily, every hour on the hour, 11–5; Feb.–Mar., weekends 11–5).

Qualified **personal guides** are available through the City Tourist Office (☞ Visitor Information, *below*), which requires two days' notice.

Travel Agencies

Huybrechts (✉ Carnotstraat 39–41, ☎ 03/231–9900). **VTB** (✉ St-Jacobsmarkt 45, ☎ 03/220–3232).

Visitor Information

The **Toerisme Stad Antwerpen** (Antwerp City Tourist Office; ✉ Grote Markt 15, ☎ 03/232–0103, FAX 03/231–1937) will assist with hotel reservations. The **Toeristische Federatie Provincie Antwerpen** (Antwerp Provincial Tourist Office; ✉ Karel Oomsstraat 11, ☎ 03/216–2810) will help plan trips throughout the province.

5 NORTHEAST BELGIUM

Far from the beaten path, Belgium's northeast possesses a wealth of history, sites, natural reserves, and untainted charm. From Tongeren, with its Roman past, to Mechelen and its astounding carillons, to the ancient seat of learning at Leuven, you'll find here many hues from Belgium's multicolor past. Quiet and serene, the region offers the depth and scope of larger cities on a smaller and more convivial scale. And there's also a delicious regional cuisine, crowned by the mighty asparagus.

Revised by Eric R. Drosin

THE NORTHEAST QUARTER OF BELGIUM, composed of the provinces of Flemish Brabant, Antwerp, and Limburg, is not frequently visited by travelers from abroad but is much loved by Belgians. It stretches from the sandy moors of Kempen (La Campine to French-speakers) in the north to the fertile plains of Haspengouw (La Hesbaye), with its prosperous-looking farms, orchards, and undulating fields. On the east, it borders the narrow Dutch corridor stretching south to Maastricht.

Within the region you'll find the city of Leuven, its magnificent structures and university faithfully rebuilt following the ravages of both the first and second World Wars. Mechelen too is a town that has held on to its medieval and Renaissance past; it's the residence of the Roman Catholic Primate of Belgium and the Mecca of carillon lovers the world over. Meanwhile, Hasselt prides itself on its ability to challenge Antwerp as the fashion center of Belgium, and on its Japanese Garden, the largest in Europe. The town is also a center of production for the potent, gin-like Belgian beverage *jenever.*

Bokrijk is the largest open-air museum and nature reserve in Europe, and Kalmthout has a vast heath and tree park teeming with wildlife. Lier has canals and a relaxed atmosphere—thereby earning its reputation as a smaller Brugge—while at Sint-Truiden, a wondrous astronomical compensation clock ticks as the apple trees come into bloom. Tongeren contains the richest collection of religious art in Belgium, and the quaint, charming Diest is ringed by a series of forts. The Premonstratensian Abbey of Averbode is a marvelous example of religious architecture.

Pleasures and Pastimes

Architecture

The buildings of the northeast reflect a wide range of architectural styles and influences, from Roman to Renaissance to contemporary. Leuven arguably holds the title of the most flamboyantly Gothic city in the region, while Tongeren merits attention for its simple Roman remains. And notable structures aren't limited to well-known sights; in this part of Belgium, many private homes are architectural gems in their own right.

Dining

By the time you enter Belgium's northeast, you'll likely already have realized that the entire country is a haven for good, hearty food. The same holds true here. Your best bet is to seek out traditional taverns and restaurants, as well as establishments offering more modern twists on the customary cuisine. Strengths of the region include game, fish, and a variety of local specialities. Whether you're sampling Mechelen's asparagus and endive, the syrup-filled biscuits of Lier, or Diest's white beer, dining can always be a high point of the day.

CATEGORY	COST*
$$$$	over BF3,000/€75
$$$	BF2,000–BF3,000/€50–€75
$$	BF1,000–BF2,000/€25–€50
$	under BF1,000/€25

**per person for a three-course meal, including service, taxes, but not beverages*

Lodging

The most distinctive feature of lodging in the northeast is the bargains to be had. Away from the bright lights of the big cities, prices drop considerably, ranging from the astonishingly cheap and clean family-run operations to familiar, comfortable international chains. Your budget for a room with a double bed can start as low as BF1,800/€44.62 a night. And with most hotels enjoying prime locations, the view can be as cheering as the bill.

CATEGORY	COST*
$$$$	over BF7,500/€185
$$$	BF5,500–BF7,500/€135–€185
$$	BF2,500–BF5,500/€60–€135
$	under BF2,500/€60

**for two persons sharing double room, including service and tax*

🖱 following the text of a review is your signal that the property has a Web site, where you will find details and, usually, images; for a link, visit www.fodors.com/urls.

Exploring Northeast Belgium

The northeast region is highly accessible, thanks to a comprehensive highway and train network. With the towns and districts situated so close to one another, you'll have the opportunity to take in all of the region's highlights with a minimum of hassle. And unlike in Brussels, you'll find that the centers of most towns and cities here favor the pedestrian—with Hasselt being a particularly shining example.

Great Itineraries

Numbers in the text correspond to numbers in the margin and on the Northeast Belgium, Leuven, and Mechelen maps.

IF YOU HAVE 1 DAY

Starting from Brussels, make your way by car or train to **Leuven** ①–⑧, where you can spend the morning touring the city center, the sprawling university campus, and the Groot Begijnhof—the largest of this type of traditional Flemish settlement in the country. After lunch at any of the numerous cafés and restaurants, take a tour of the Stella Artois brewery, ground zero for the rightfully famous Belgian beer trade. Devote the rest of your afternoon to nearby **Mechelen** ⑪–㉑, the ecclesiastical center of Belgium. Visit the impressive **Sint-Romboutskathedraal** ⑪ with its unfinished tower and two remarkable 40-ton carillons. It's also worthwhile to make arrangements for a visit to the Royal Tapestry Factory, one of the few places where the art of tapestry weaving is still practiced.

IF YOU HAVE 3 DAYS

Plan to spend an entire day in **Leuven** ①–⑧, taking in the Renaissance and Gothic architecture, religious sights, and wonderful food of this vibrant city. In the late afternoon, head to 🏨 **Tongeren** ㉖ to spend the night. The next morning, take time to admire the Roman underpinnings of one of Belgium's oldest towns, and don't miss its extensive collections of religious art. After lunch, make your way to **Hasselt** ㉔ and spend the afternoon investigating the city's eclectic museums, including the jenever museum, where you can sample Dutch gin. 🏨 **Diest** ⑨, a short jaunt away, is a good spot to spend your evening. On your third morning, tour the forts that surround the city, and visit the Sint-Sulpitiuskerk. After lunch, head off to the glorious Abbey of **Averbode** ⑩; spend the rest of the afternoon on its grounds before making your way back to base.

When to Tour Northeast Belgium

Spring, summer, and fall are all good times to visit the northeast of Belgium. Highlighted by sunshine, the area comes to life, proffering de-

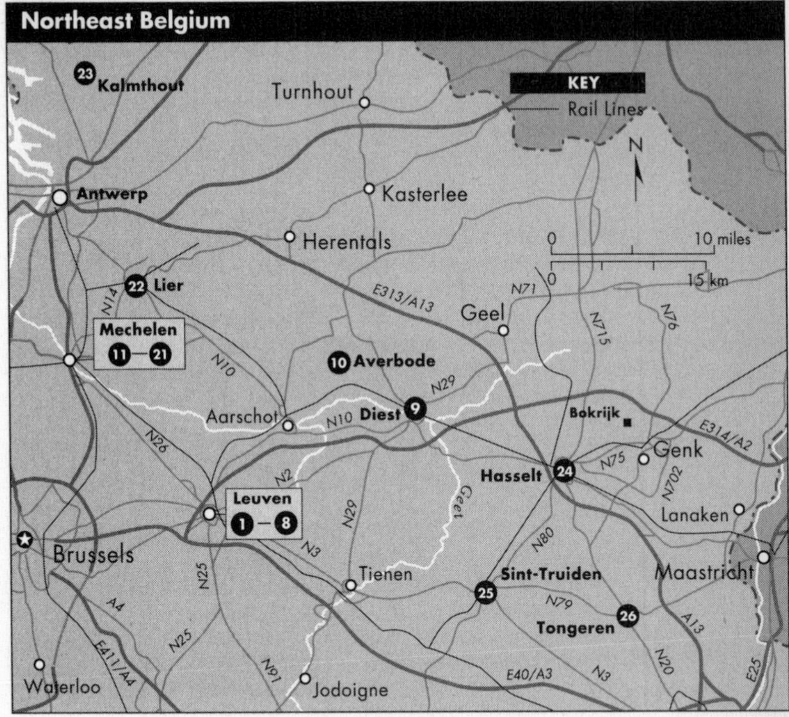

licious vegetables in the spring and summer and game in the autumn. A visit in the off-season will still give you the chance to experience cultural pleasures, but the often-dreary weather can end up hiding the region's beauty.

FLEMISH BRABANT

The central Belgian province of Brabant was divided in two along linguistic lines in 1995, further solidifying the political and cultural divide between Flanders and Wallonia. The capital and social center of Flemish Brabant is Leuven, the home of Belgium's oldest and most esteemed university (though, typically, the French-speaking faction of the school broke off in the 1960s and transplanted itself in Wallonian soil). The city and the province as a whole are steeped in Flemish pride, which at times can carry with it an air of disdain for Brussels, Leuven's centuries-old rival.

Leuven

26 km (16 mi) east of Brussels via the E40 or E314 autoroute.

Leuven (Louvain), like Oxford or Cambridge, is a place where underneath the hubbub of daily life you sense an age-old devotion to learning and scholarship. Its ancient Roman Catholic university, founded in 1425, was one of Europe's great seats of learning during the late Middle Ages. One of its rectors was elected Pope Adrian VI. Erasmus taught here in the 16th century, as did the cartographer Mercator and, in the following century, Cornelius Jansen, whose teachings inspired the anti-Jesuit Jansenist movement. The city was pillaged and burned by the Germans in 1914, with 1,800 buildings, including the university library, destroyed; in 1944 it was bombed again. In the 1960s, se-

Abdij van Park 5
Groot Begijnhof 6
Kruidtuin Hortus 7
Sint-Michielskerk . . 4
Sint-Pieterskerk . . . 2
Stadhuis 1
Stedelijk Museum Vander Kelen-Mertens 3
Stella Artois brewery 8

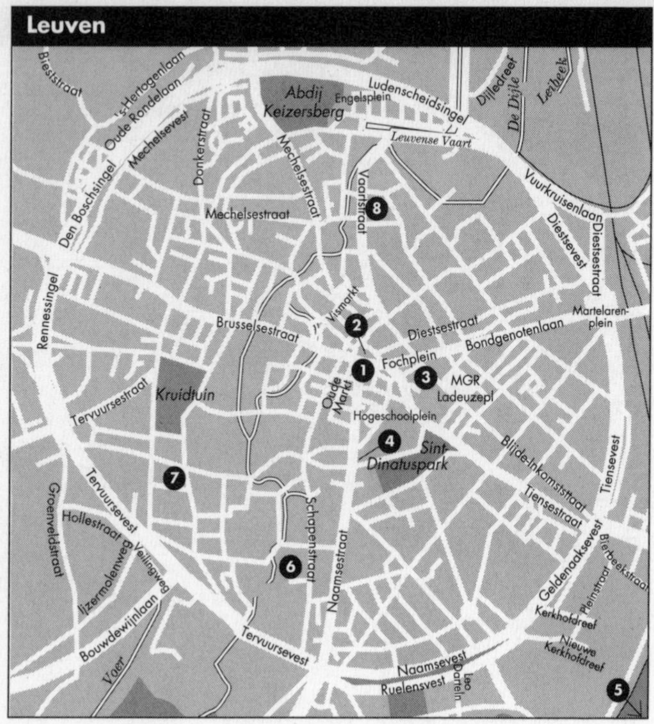

vere intercultural tensions caused the old bilingual university to split into separate French-language and Dutch-language schools. The French speakers moved their university south of the linguistic border to the new town of Louvain-la-Neuve; the Dutch-speakers remained in Leuven. Present-day **Katholieke Universiteit Leuven** has a student body of more than 25,000, including about 1,000 seminarians from many different countries.

★ ❶ Every Flemish town prides itself on its ornate, medieval **Stadhuis** (Town Hall). This one escaped the fires of the invading Germans in 1914 because it was occupied by German staff. It is the work of Leuven's own architectural master of Flamboyant Gothic, Mathieu de Layens, who finished it in 1469 after 21 years' work. In photographs it looks more like a finely chiseled reliquary than a building; it's necessary to stand back from it to appreciate fully the vertical lines in the mass of turrets, pinnacles, pendants, and niches, each with its own statue. The interior contains some fine 16th-century sculpted ceilings. Tours are given in Flemish and English. ✉ *Grote Markt.* 🎫 *BF50/€1.24.* ⏲ *Tours weekdays 11 and 3, weekends 3.*

NEED A BREAK? **Gambrinus,** on the corner of the busy Grote Markt, serves tasty sandwiches either on a terrace with a view of the Stadhuis or inside amid fin de siècle decor. ✉ *Grote Markt 13,* ☎ *016/20–12–38.*

---

❷ **Sint-Pieterskerk** (Collegiate Church of St. Peter) has had a troubled architectural history. A shifting foundation led to the shortening of the tower in the 17th century and to the replacement of the spire with a cupola in the 18th. The interior, however, is remarkable for the purity of the Gothic nave. The ambulatory and choir are closed for restoration, but some treasures usually found there, including *The Last Supper,* by Leuven's 15th-century official painter Dirk Bouts, are on temporary display in the nave. ⊠ *Grote Markt.* *Church and Stedelijk Museum (☞ below), BF200/€4.96.* ⊙ *Tues.–Sat. 10–5, Sun. 2–5; mid-Mar.–mid-Oct., also Mon. 10–5.*

3 The **Stedelijk Museum Vander Kelen-Mertens** (Municipal Museum) gives you an idea of how Leuven's upper crust lived 100 years ago. The building, which dates from the 16th century, was originally a college. It became the mayor's residence in the 19th century. A series of rooms in different styles reflect his taste. The art collection includes works by Albrecht Bouts (died 1549), son of Dirk, and Quentin Metsys (1466–1530), a remarkable portraitist, as well as Brabantine sculptures from the 15th and 16th centuries. ⊠ *Savoyestraat 6,* ☎ *016/22–69–06.* *Museum and St-Pieterskerk (☞ above), BF200/€4.96.* ⊙ *Tues.–Sat. 10–5, Sun. 2–5; mid-Mar.–mid-Oct., also Mon. 10–5.*

4 **Sint-Michielskerk** (Saint Michael's Church), designed by Jesuit architect Willem Hesius and built between 1650 and 1670, has a Baroque facade of great detail and extravagance. The ornate craftsmanship was intended to fill churchgoers with a sense of God's grandeur, and viewers today may feel a similar sense of awe. An exhibit on the church's long history lies inside. ⊠ *Naamsestraat,* ☎ *016/23–12–45.* ⊙ *Apr.–Sept., Tues.–Sun. 10–4.*

5 **Abdij van Park** (Abbey of the Park) is located slightly southeast of Leuven. This 12th-century abbey is surrounded by a water mill, a massive tithe barn—where citizens used to come to donate a tenth of their annual income to the abbey and its residents—and a series of walls and archways. The abbey itself was reconstructed in the 16th and 17th centuries and bears the imprints of various architectural styles, from Romanesque to Gothic to Baroque. Of particular note are the intricate stucco ceilings in the refectory and library, two of just a handful of rooms that are open to the public. But a visit to Abdij van Park is about more than just architecture: there's an air of serenity to the entire complex that may be its greatest pleasure. ⊠ *Abdijdreef 7,* ☎ *016/40–36–40; 016/40–63–29 for group visits.* *BF100/€2.48.* ⊙ *Sun. and public holidays, tour begins at 4; groups by appointment.*

Every Flemish city worth its salt has a *begijnhof,* a city within a city, formerly inhabited by members of a Christian sisterhood dating from the 13th century. The original members were widows of fallen Cru-
6 saders. Leuven's **Groot Begijnhof** is the largest in the country. The quiet retreat numbers 72 tiny, whitewashed houses, with religious statues in small niches, dating mostly from the 17th century, grouped around the early Gothic Church of St. John the Baptist, not far from several university colleges. The carefully restored houses are inhabited by students and university staff. ⊠ *Tervuursevest; from Grote Markt take Naamsestraat to Karmelletenberg and across Schapenstraat.*

7 **Kruidtuin Hortus,** created in 1738, is the oldest botanical garden in Belgium—the name translates simply as "Botanical Garden." It was created to supply medicinal plants to the university, but over time its scope expanded to include rare plants and a host of tree and shrub varieties. The 5½-acre complex includes a vast greenhouse, where you'll find a collection of tropical and subtropical plants. Needless to say, it's best to visit in the spring or summer. ⊠ *Kapucijnenvoer 30,* ☎ *016/29–44–88.* ⊙ *May–Sept., daily 8–8; Oct.–Apr., daily 8–5.*

Leuven is considered the beer capital of Belgium, and Stella Artois the
8 premier institution of Belgian brewing. The **Stella Artois brewery** is a mammoth building with a sleek, modern exterior. Despite the contemporary facilities, beer has been made here since 1366, originally going by the name Den Horen (The Horn). Master brewer Sebastien Artois

took over the operation in 1717, and the barley beer Stella Artois was launched in 1926. Now you can marvel at the sheer enormity of the modern vats as a tour takes you through the entire brewing process. Call ahead to sign up for the tour, which is given in both Flemish and English twice daily during the week, depending on demand. ✉ *Vaartstraat 94-96,* ☎ *016/24–71–11.* *BF120/€2.97 for tour.* ⏲ *By appointment only, weekdays 1:30 and 3.*

Dining and Lodging

$$$ ✕ **Belle Epoque.** This grand town house by the station offers the most lavish dining in Leuven, served with considerable pomp in an art nouveau setting. Try lobster salad with apple, langoustines with caviar, or Bresse pigeon with truffle sauce. There's also a pleasant terrace. ✉ *Bondgenotenlaan 94,* ☎ *016/22–33–89. Reservations essential. AE, DC, MC, V. Closed Sun.–Mon. and 3 wks in July–Aug.*

$$ ✕ **De Blauwe Zon.** This trendy restaurant has a mezzanine and large dining room decorated to resemble a garden. A young crowd dominates the scene; they come for Asian-Continental fusion cuisine, including such dishes as a shrimp tartare with cucumber sauce and eel and shrimp casserole. ✉ *Tiensestraat 28,* ☎ *016/22–68–80. V. Closed Sun., no lunch Sat.*

$ ✕ **De Nachtuil.** Given the name (which translates as "The Night Owl"), it should come as no surprise that this establishment's hours of operation are 6 PM to 6 AM. The menu features fresh, simple, traditional cuisine, with an emphasis on meat dishes. The three dining halls don't score points for their standard brasserie decor, but the varied clientele gives the place a pleasantly relaxed feel. ✉ *Krakenstraat 8,* ☎ *016/22–02–59. No credit cards. No lunch.*

$ ✕ **Domus.** Tucked into a back street off the Grote Markt, this café adjoins the tiny Domus brewery, famous for its honey beer. The ambience is casual, the clientele on the young side, and the decor authentically rustic: craggy old beams, a brick fireplace, a labyrinth of separate rooms, bric-a-brac, and paisley table throws. The Burgundian menu includes traditional dishes such as black-and-white pudding with apples. ✉ *Tiensestraat 8,* ☎ *016/20–14–49. No credit cards.*

$$$ 🏨 **Holiday Inn Garden Court.** The Leuven version of the ubiquitous hotel chain is conveniently located a few minutes' walk from the Grote Markt. The clean, bland accommodations are precisely what you'd expect them to be. ✉ *Alfons Smetsplein 7,* ☎ *016/31–76–00,* FAX *016/31–76–01. 100 rooms. Restaurant, bar, parking. AE, DC, MC, V.*

$$ 🏨 **Jackson's Hotel.** In a modern building opposite the hospital—where you can park for free on the weekends—and a five-minute walk from the town center, Jackson's is pleasant, modest lodging for the budget-minded. You'll find charming owners, a quiet environment, and simple, comfortable rooms (with floral-pattern curtains and bedspreads that may not be to everyone's taste). ✉ *Brusselsestraat 110-112,* ☎ *016/20–24–92,* FAX *016/23–13–29. 14 rooms. Bar. AE, DC, MC, V.*

$ 🏨 **Hotel Professor.** Of the eight immaculate rooms here, three have a terrific view of the Oude Markt, and the price is a bargain for such a prime location. There's a wonderful café on the ground floor of the early 20th-century building. ✉ *Naamsestraat 20 ,* ☎ *016/20–14–14,* FAX *016/29–14–16. 8 rooms. Bar, café. AE, DC, MC, V.*

Nightlife

The intimate **De Blauwe Kater** is one of the only bars in Leuven where you can enjoy free jazz and blues shows. Small bands perform live from October through May, usually on Wednesday and Thursday. When the place isn't swinging, you can sit back and sip a drink by candlelight. And the place doesn't close until the last customer decides to leave. ✉ *Hallengang 1,* ☎ *016/20–80–90. No credit cards.* ⏲ *7–close.*

Diest

9 *30 km (19 mi) northeast of Leuven.*

Outside of the normal tourist circuit, Diest, a town of 22,000, is well worth a visit. It was a fief of the House of Orange in the 15th century, which explains why Queen Beatrix of the Netherlands is the Vrouw van Diest (The Lady of Diest). Fierce battles took place here during Belgium's war of independence in 1830. The town is surrounded by a series of small forts that physically prevent further expansion—thereby helping to keep its traditional charm intact. Beer lovers should make it a point to sample Diest's delicious Gildenbier.

Behind its neoclassical facade, Diest's **Stadhuis** (Town Hall) houses both a tourist information office and a town museum. The museum, in the building's impressive gothic cellars, has a collection of armor, statues of saints, porcelain, various pieces of sculpted furniture, and the well-preserved 15th-century *Judgment Day,* a painting on wood. The presence of a well in the cellars indicates that beer brewing once took place here. ✉ *Grote Markt,* ☎ *013/31–21–21.* 🎫 *BF50/€1.24.* ⏲ *Daily 10–noon and 1–5.*

Built between 1321 and 1354, **Sint-Sulpitiuskerk** (Church of St. Sulpitius) is made of contrasting sandstone and French white stone and designed in Gothic style. It's noteworthy for its bell turret, which contains 43 bells, and its unfinished tower and apse. Inside, the 15th-century choir stalls are carved with illustrations of the seven deadly sins, and the treasury contains several lovely works of gold. ✉ *Grote Markt,* ☎ *013/31–21–21.* 🎫 *BF50/€1.24 for choir and treasury.* ⏲ *May–Aug., daily 2–5.*

Dining and Lodging

$$ ✕ **Bistro In De Zoute Inval.** An aged facade crowned by baroque gables and a soft peach and green interior accented with hanging copper kitchenware give "The Warm Welcome" an agreeable, laid-back ambience. In season, white asparagus, served warm with mousseline sauce or cold with vinaigrette and chopped egg, is a house specialty. The dessert list is highlighted by a sumptuous tarte tatin with vanilla ice cream. ✉ *Grote Markt 6,* ☎ *013/33–60–03. MC, V. Closed Thurs., June, Nov.*

$$ 🏨 **Hotel De Fransche Croon.** This three-star hotel, in an 18th-century former residence, provides fine accommodations at affordable prices. Antiques decorate the public spaces, and the guest rooms are spacious and comfortable. The restaurant serves dependably good Belgian food. ✉ *Leuvensestraat 26-28,* ☎ *013/31–45–40,* FAX *013/33–31–59. 23 rooms. Restaurant, bar. AE, DC, MC, V.*

Averbode

10 *35 km (22 mi) northeast of Leuven.*

★ **Abdij van Averbode** (Abbey of Averbode), founded in 1134 by Count Arnold of Losen, is still run by a small number of priests, clerics, and lay brothers for whom Norbert is the patron saint. The abbey is set near a forest and is highlighted by a baroque church (built in 1672) of majestic dimensions. Of particular note are the famous carved choir chairs, which depict a series of Norbertine saints. ✉ *Abdijstraat 1,* ☎ *013/77–29–01.* 🎫 *BF50/€1.24.* ⏲ *Daily 9–11:30 and 2–5.*

ANTWERP PROVINCE

The northernmost region of Belgium, Antwerp Province lies in the Kempen, a marshy plain that stretches north from the river Demer and east to the Meuse. In addition to the bustling city of Antwerp (☞ Chapter 4), you'll find here several towns that, beneath unassuming surfaces, are rich in culture and history. To the far north is Kalmthoutse Heide, a vast heath popular with hikers and bird-watchers.

Mechelen

28 km (17 mi) north of Brussels, via the E19 autoroute.

Mechelen (Malines in French), north of Brussels, is a small, peaceful gem that has preserved its medieval and Renaissance past but that is never, like Brugge, overrun with tourists. As the residence of the Roman Catholic Primate of Belgium, it's an important ecclesiastical center. It's a center of vegetable production as well; the town and its environs are known for asparagus, whose stalks reach their height of perfection in May, and *witloof,* the Belgian delicacy known elsewhere as chicory or endive.

Mechelen's brief period of grandeur coincided with the reign (1507–30) of Margaret of Austria. She established her devout and cultured court in this city while she served as regent for her nephew, who later became Emperor Charles V. The philosophers Erasmus and Sir Thomas More were among her visitors, as were the painters Albrecht Dürer and Van Orley (whose portrait of Margaret hangs in the Musée d'Art Ancien in Brussels), and Josquin des Prés, the master of polyphony.

★ ⓫ **Sint-Romboutskathedraal** (St. Rombout's Cathedral), completed in the 1520s, represents a magnificent achievement by three generations of the Keldermans family of architects, who were active in cathedral building throughout Flanders. The beautifully proportioned tower, 318 ft high, was intended to be the tallest in the world, but the builders ran out of money before they could reach their goal. Inside are two remarkable 40-ton carillons of 49 bells each; carillon-playing was virtually invented in Mechelen (the Russian word for carillon means "sound of Mechelen"), and student carillonneurs come here from all over the world. The town's carillon school, the oldest in the world, was founded in 1923. The best place to listen to the bells is in the Minderbroedersgang. The interior of the cathedral is spacious and lofty, particularly the white sandstone nave dating from the 13th century. Chief among the art treasures is Van Dyck's *Crucifixion* in the south transept. ✉ *Grote Markt.* ⏲ *Mon.–Sat. 9–4 (until 6 in summer), Sun. 1–5; check tourist office for tower tours; carillon concerts Sat. 11:30 AM, Sun. 3, Mon. 8:30 PM.*

Seldom have two parts of a single building had such vividly contrasting styles as do those of Mechelen's ⓬ **Stadhuis** (Town Hall). To the right is the Gothic, turreted, 14th-century *Lakenhalle* (Cloth Hall). To the left is the flamboyant palace commissioned by Charles V to accommodate the *Grote Raad* (Grand Council) of the Burgundian Netherlands. Work was abandoned in 1547 but resumed and completed in the 20th century in accordance with the original plans of the Keldermans, Mechelen's first family of architects. ✉ *Grote Markt.* ⏲ *Guided tours (from tourist office), Easter–June and Sept., weekends 2; July–Aug., daily 2.*

NEED A BREAK?

The smallest café in Mechelen is the **Borrel Babel** in the charming Sint-Romboutshof, behind the cathedral. Different varieties of jenever (Dutch gin) are the potent specialty.

⓭ By the old **Haverwerf** (Oat Wharf, where oats once were loaded) and near the **Zoutwerf** (Salt Wharf), both on the river Dijle, you'll find three

Haverwerf . . **13**
Het Anker . . **14**
Koninklijke Manufactuur Gaspard De Wit **16**
Museum van Deportatie en Verzet . . . **15**
Oud Paleis van Margareta van Oostenrijk . . **19**
Plancken-dael **21**
Sint-Janskerk . . . **17**
Sint-Pieter en Pauluskerk . . **18**
Sint-Rombouts-kathedraal . . **11**
Speelgoed-museum Mechelen . . **20**
Stadhuis . . . **12**

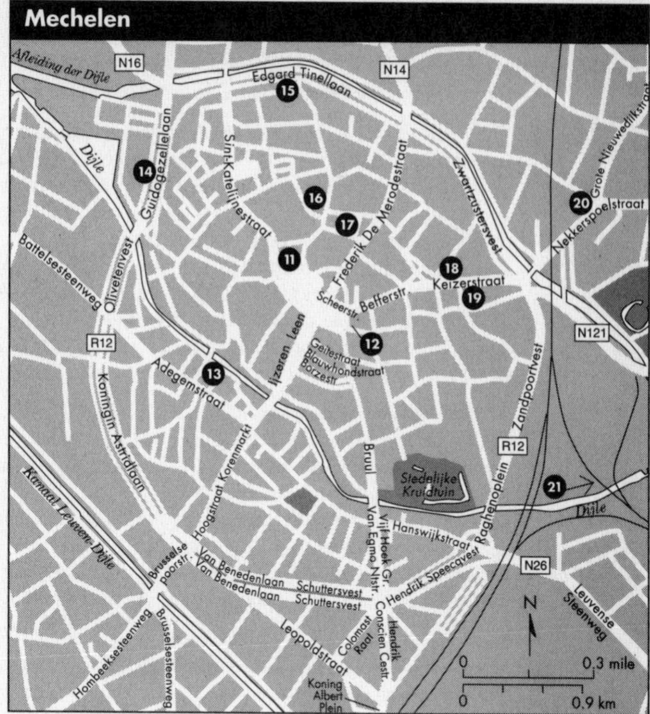

remarkable houses, side by side. The green **Het Paradijs** (Paradise) is Gothic, with a relief showing the banishment of Adam and Eve. Next to it stands the **Duivelsgevel** (Little Devils), with a 15th-century timber facade decorated with carved satyrs. The third of the group is the red **Sint Josef,** a Baroque house from 1669. Also worth note, on the Zoutwerf, is the old **fishmongers' guildhall.** It dates from the 16th century and is embellished by a magnificent golden salmon. ✉ *Haverwerf.*

14 **Het Anker** (The Anchor) is the birthplace of Mechelen's pride and joy, the dark, sweet Gouden Carolus (Golden Charles) beer. Touring this small, intimate brewery, you can witness every stage of the beer-making process. (Tours in English must be arranged in advance.) Devoted beer fans can spend the night—a modest 22-room hotel is part of the brewery complex. ✉ *Guido Gezellelaan 49,* ☎ *015/20–38–80.* 🎫 *BF125/€3.10.* ⏲ *June–Aug., daily 10:30–6, guided tours at 3.*

15 Belgium's Shoah museum, **Museum van Deportatie en Verzet** (The Museum of Deportation and the Resistance), is built in a wing of the former Gen. Dossin de Saint-Georges barracks, used by the Nazis as the starting point for the deportation of some 25,257 prisoners from Mechelen to Auschwitz. The museum's exhibits tell the story of the deportation and extermination of almost half of Belgium's Jewish population during World War II. You'll also find information about the resistance movement, a history of antisemitism, and a chronology of Jewish life in Belgium and Europe. ✉ *Goswin de Stassartstraat 153,* ☎ *015/29–06–60.* ⏲ *Sun.–Thurs. 10–5, Fri. 10–1.*

16 The **Koninklijke Manufactuur Gaspard De Wit** (Royal Tapestry Factory) is a great place to learn about different styles of tapestry weaving, and one of the few places where this ancient and glorious art is still practiced. Tours of the workshops permit you to watch the experts creating new pieces and restoring old ones, and there's a collection of

antique and contemporary tapestries on display. Official opening hours are severely restricted, but see what the Tourist Office can do for you at other times. ✉ *Schoutetstraat 7,* ☎ *015/20–29–05.* 💳 *Guided tours, BF200/€4.96.* ⏲ *Guided tours, Aug.–June, Sat. 10:30.*

17 The 15th-century Gothic **Sint-Janskerk** (Church of Saint John) is a treasure house of religious art. Peter Paul Rubens's tryptich *The Adoration of the Magi,* works by masters such as de Crayer, van der Veken, and Valckx, and the magnificent wood carvings of the pulpit and confessionals merit several hours of your time. Although you'll find art dating from the 16th century through the 20th, the church purchased the majority of its works in the 16th and 17th centuries—a period when it had the benefit of deep coffers. Note that visits are not permitted during church services or on December 25, 26, and 31. ✉ *Sint Jansstraat,* ☎ *015/29–76–55.* ⏲ *Apr.–Oct., daily 1–5; Nov.–Mar., daily noon–4.*

18 The **Sint-Pieter en Pauluskerk** (Church of Saint Peter and Saint Paul) lies on the corner of the *Veemarkt,* or cattle market, its construction completed by the Jesuit order in 1677. This baroque church has an astounding 14 confessionals, artfully crafted oak paneling, and a pulpit made by the sculptor Verbruggen in the early 18th century. You can also enjoy a considerable 17th-century art collection, with works by Coxie and Quellien, among others. Note that visits are not permitted during church services or on Dec. 25, 26, and 31 ✉ *Keizerstraat,* ☎ *015/29–76–55.* ⏲ *Apr.–Oct., daily 1–5; Nov.–Mar., daily noon–4.*

19 The **Oud Paleis van Margareta van Oostenrijk** (Former Palace of Margaret of Austria) was erected in 1507, blending traditional Gothic architecture and early Renaissance design. The gatehouse, for example, designed by French architect Guy de Beaugrant, was one of the first works of the Renaissance style in northwestern Europe. Following its use as a residence by Cardinal Granvelle and as a place of work by the Great Council of the Netherlands, the palace is now the town's justice building, containing a number of courts. You aren't allowed to tour the palace itself, but you can visit the immaculately manicured interior courtyard, with its conical hedges and prim flower beds. ✉ *Keizerstraat,* ☎ *015/29–76–55.* ⏲ *Weekdays 10–5.*

20 **Speelgoedmuseum Mechelen** (Mechelen Toy Museum) is one of the biggest toy museums in the world. It has more than 8,000 tin soldiers standing ready to do battle on a model of Waterloo plus a vast collection of toys and games, both ancient and modern, and a play area for young and old. A regularly rotating series of exhibitions makes this a ceaselessly fascinating place. ✉ *Nekkerspoel 21,* ☎ *015/55–70–75.* 💳 *BF180/€4.46.* ⏲ *Tues.–Sun. 10–5.*

21 At **Planckendael,** more than 1,000 animals lead a life of near-freedom. The vast park has an adventure trail for children, a large playground, and a children's farm. The park can be reached by boat from Mechelen (leaving from the Colomabrug bridge), with departures every 30 minutes starting at 9 in the morning and running through the day. ✉ *Leuvensesteenweg 582, Muizen,* ☎ *015/41–42–49.* 💳 *BF460/€11.40.* ⏲ *Jan., daily 9–4:30; Feb., mid-Oct.–Dec., daily 9–4:45; early Mar., early Oct., daily 9–5:15; late Mar.–June, Sept., daily 9–5:45; July–Aug., daily 9–6:15.*

Dining and Lodging

$$$ ★ ✕ **D'Hoogh.** In a grand gray-stone mansion on the Grote Markt, its second-floor dining room looking over the square, this glamorous landmark presents top-quality *cuisine du marché* (whatever is freshest): smoked-eel terrine with pistachios; poached goose liver in port jelly with caramelized apples; turbot and zucchini spaghetti in vinai-

grette and olive oil; and, in April and May, the most wonderful asparagus imaginable. ✉ *Grote Markt 19,* ☎ *015/21–75–53. Reservations essential. AE, DC, MC, V. Closed Mon. and 1st 3 wks of Aug. No lunch Sat., no dinner Sun.*

$$ ✕ **De Keizeren.** Boasting hearty fare and an even heartier crowd, this tavern-restaurant offers traditional Belgian food at relatively modest prices. The interior decor is uninspired, but the spacious outdoor terrace provides a lovely view of the Grote Markt. On the menu you'll find tasty meat *brochettes* as well as such classics as spaghetti Bolognese and steak béarnaise. ✉ *Bruul 1,* ☎ *015/20–66–41. MC, V.*

$ ✕ **Brasserie Den Beer.** In the pervasively traditional city of Mechelen, Den Beer is an oasis of modernism. The decor is dominated by glass and leather, and the elevated outdoor terrace has the requisite austere gray awning. The food is conventional Continental fare—salad Niçoise, spaghetti Bolognese, and steak with french fries are menu standards. This is a good place to try one (or more) of Mechelen's three speciality beers: Mechelschen Bruyen, Toison d'Or, and Gouden Carolus. The desserts, such as vanilla ice cream covered in a rich raspberry sauce, are particularly recommended. ✉ *Grote Markt 32-33,* ☎ *015/20–97–06. MC, V.*

$ ✕ **'t Korenveld.** This tiny, old-fashioned bistro has been primly restored and decked with pretty floral wallpaper and tile tabletops. Its cuisine is unpretentious, featuring simple fish and steaks at low prices. It adjoins the Alfa Hotel and has some tables in the hotel bar. ✉ *Korenmarkt 20,* ☎ *015/42–14–69. AE, MC, V. Closed Sun.–Mon. and Aug. No dinner Sat.*

$$$ **Hotel Alfa Alba.** Some five minutes' walk from the Grote Markt and right next to the Musée Michiels, the clock and bell museum, this hotel offers a chance to relax in the comfort of a traditional "English library" setting. The rooms are cozy and offer TV, a trouser press, and minisafes. ✉ *Korenmarkt 22-26,* ☎ *015/42–03–03,* FAX *015/42–37–88. 43 rooms. Restaurant, bar, parking (fee). AE, DC, MC, V.*

$$ **Hotel Den Grooten Wolsack.** Located just behind the Sint-Romboutskathedraal, this renovated hotel consists of an original 15th-century building with more recent additions. The clean, adequately large rooms have a neoclassical decor, and the slightly more expensive suites look out onto the peaceful interior courtyard. ✉ *Wollemarkt 16,* ☎ *015/28–55–60,* FAX *015/21–77–81. 14 rooms. Restaurant, bar, parking (fee). AE, DC, MC, V.*

$$ **Hotel Gulden Anker.** Open since 1987, this distinguished hotel prides itself on its terrific restaurant, which blends French and local cuisine, and its comfortable rooms. It's situated a little outside the center of town, near the Vrijbroekpark (Town Park), giving it a calm, bucolic setting. ✉ *Brusselsesteenweg 2,* ☎ *015/42–25–35,* FAX *015/42–34–99. 34 rooms. Restaurant, bar. AE, DC, MC, V.*

Lier

★ 22 *17 km (10 mi) southeast of Antwerp on N10, 45 km (27 mi) northeast of Brussels on E19/N14 via Mechelen.*

The small town of Lier may seem a sleepy riverside settlement, but it has long attracted poets and painters and has even known its moment of glory. It was here in 1496 that Philip the Handsome of Burgundy married Joanna the Mad of Aragon and Castile, daughter of King Ferdinand and Queen Isabella of Spain. From that union sprang Emperor Charles V and his brother and successor as Holy Roman Emperor, the equally remarkable Ferdinand I of Austria.

The **Sint-Gummaruskerk** (St. Gommaire's Church), where Philip and Joanna were wed, is a product of the De Waghemakere–Keldermans architectural partnership that worked so well in building the cathedral in Antwerp. It's notable for its stained-glass windows from the 15th and 16th centuries—those in the choir were the gift of Maximilian of Austria (father of Philip the Handsome), who visited in 1516 and is depicted in one of the windows, along with his wife, Mary of Burgundy. ✉ *Follow Rechtestraat to Kerkstraat.*

The Kleine Nete flows straight through the heart of Lier; the Grote Nete and a canal encircle the center. Along the riverside, willows bend over the water. Across the river stands the **Zimmertoren,** a 14th-century tower renamed for Louis Zimmer, who designed its astronomical clock with 11 faces in 1930. His studio, where 57 dials show the movements of the moon, the tides, the zodiac, and other cosmic phenomena, is inside the tower. ✉ *Zimmerplein 18,* ☎ *03/491–1395.* 🎫 *BF60/€1.49.* ⏲ *Apr.–Oct., daily 9–noon and 1–6; Nov.–Mar., daily 9–noon and 1–5.*

NEED A BREAK?

Van Ouytsels Koffiehoekje (✉ Rechtestraat 27, ☎ 03/480–2917) still roasts its own coffee. Don't pass up the delicious syrup-filled biscuits, *Lierse Vlaaikens,* which are the local specialty.

The **Begijnhof** (Béguinage) differs from most other Beguine communities in that its small houses line narrow streets rather than being grouped around a common. A Renaissance portico stands at the entrance, and on it is a statue of St. Begge, who gave his name to this congregation and who probably derived his own from the fact that he was *un begue* (a stammerer). Beguines were members of ascetic or philanthropic communities of women, not under vows, founded in the Netherlands in the 13th century. ✉ *Begijnhofstraat.*

Stedelijk Museum (Communal Museum), a lovely provincial museum, is home to the extraordinary *Flemish Proverbs,* painted in 1607 by Pieter Bruegel the Younger. In it you can find representations of some 85 Flemish proverbs. Also on display is Jan Steen's splendid *Vechtender Boeren* (Squabbling Peasants), as well as works by such artists as Maurice De Vlaminck and Henri De Braekeleer. ✉ *Florent Van Cauwenberghstraat 14,* ☎ *03/491–1396.* ⏲ *Apr.–Oct., Tues.–Thurs., weekends 10–noon and 1:30–5:30.*

If the weather's nice, and you fancy sitting down while the sights glide past you, then take a 40-minute **cruise on the Nete River** in a traditional Flemish fishing boat. Pickup and drop off are at the Sint-Jansbrug bridge, just behind the Zimmertoren. ☎ *03/480–6640.* 🎫 *BF70/€1.74.* ⏲ *May–Sept., Sun. 2–6.*

Dining and Lodging

$$ ✕ **'t Suyckeren Schip.** Just across from the church, this restaurant offers *cuisine bourgeoise* (French country cooking): steaks with a variety of sauces and five different preparations of sole. The setting has an informal, comfortable, brick-and-beams look. Sunday crowds come after church. ✉ *Rechtestraat 49,* ☎ *03/489–0140. AE, DC, MC, V.*

$–$$ ✕ **De Fortuin.** At this romantic restaurant and tavern, the tavern is less expensive. Shrimp croquettes are a specialty, and the service is friendly. In summer you can eat on the terrace overlooking the river. ✉ *Felix Timmermansplein 7,* ☎ *03/480–2951. AE, DC, MC, V. Closed Mon.*

$$ 🏨 **Hotel Hof Van Aragon.** The only hotel in Lier is situated alongside a small canal. Ask for one of the renovated rooms, which are welcoming and comfortable. ✉ *Mosdijk 4,* ☎ *03/491–0800,* FAX *03/491–0810. 15 rooms. AE, DC, MC, V.*

Kalmthout

23 *18 km (11 mi) north of Antwerp on N11/N122 via Kapellen.*

The **Kalmthoutse Heide** (heath) is a vast area of pines, sand dunes, and ponds, with flourishing bird life. The heath is crossed by marked paths. The Arboretum contains more than 6,000 trees in a 25-acre park, where you can wander freely across the lawns. It's a peaceful oasis with a varied range of colors every season, the presence of wildflowers providing a special accent. ✉ *Heuvel 2,* ☎ *03/666–6741.* 🎫 *BF150/€3.72.* 🕓 *Mar. 15–Nov. 15, daily 10–5.*

LIMBURG PROVINCE

Limburg has the youngest population in Belgium, and it is the province where the rate of development is fastest. Until fairly recently, its economy was linked to its coalfields, but today the explosive growth of small businesses has restored a degree of prosperity. The economy also benefits from the Albert Canal, which leaves the Meuse just north of Liège to follow a course parallel to the river and then veers off across the country to carry the heavy Liège traffic to Antwerp. Thanks to the canal, Genk is a center for the automotive and petrochemical industries. In spite of the presence of industry both light and heavy, this is a green and pleasant land, particularly in the fertile Haspengouw plain south of Hasselt.

Hasselt

24 *77 km (46 mi) southeast of Antwerp, 82 km (49 mi) east of Brussels, 42 km (25 mi) northwest of Liège.*

Limburg's principal town has busy shopping streets, innovative museums, and lively music. Its cathedral has the most striking gargoyles in Belgium.

The **Nationaal Jenevermuseum** perpetuates Hasselt's slightly raffish distinction of having had gin distilling as its major industry. The museum dates from 1803 and includes one of the country's oldest surviving distilleries. Jenever means "gin" in Dutch, and a tour of the installations, which include a computer animation of the production process and changing exhibits such as vintage gin advertising posters, ends at the paneled tasting room. You can sample gin of various ages, flavors, and proofs from two dozen Belgian distilleries. ✉ *Witte Nonnenstraat 19,* ☎ *011/24–11–44.* 🎫 *BF90/€2.23.* 🕓 *Apr.–Oct., Tues.–Sun. 10–5; Nov.–Dec. and Feb.–Mar., Tues.–Fri. 10–5, weekends 1–5.*

The **Stadsmuseum Stellingwerf-Waerdenhof** (Municipal Museum) is a strikingly modern space with white walls, red balconies, and large mirrors, installed in two beautifully converted mansions. Its collection consists of dramatically arranged art nouveau ceramics, church silverware (including the world's oldest monstrance, from 1286), and exhibits illustrating the history of the region. ✉ *Maastrichterstraat 85,* ☎ *011/24–10–70.* 🎫 *BF90/€2.23.* 🕓 *Apr.–Oct., Tues.–Sun. 10–5; Nov.–Dec. and Feb.–Mar., Tues.–Fri. 10–5, weekends 1–5.*

The collection of Hasselt's **Modemuseum** (Fashion Museum), located in a 17th-century hospital building, illustrates the development of fashion trends over the past two centuries. Today's fashion photographers, stylists, and designers of accessories are also represented. ✉ *Gasthuisstraat 11,* ☎ *011/23–96–21.* 🎫 *BF90/€2.23.* 🕓 *Apr.–Oct., Tues.–Sun. 10–5; Nov.–Dec. and Feb.–Mar., Tues.–Fri. 10–5, weekends 1–5.*

NEED A BREAK?

't Stokerijke (✉ Hemelrijk 3), a convivial and attractive bar, is the place to continue your education in Dutch gin—the owner is an expert. It's just behind the cathedral.

The **Japanse Tuin** (Japanese Garden), an exquisite gift from Hasselt's Japanese sister city of Itami, is the largest of its kind in Europe. Six acres are divided into three sections: the first functions as a transition between the western and eastern approaches to gardening; the second is a traditional Japanese garden, including a teahouse; and the third is a small wood with some 250 Japanese cherry trees. ✉ *Gouverneur Verwilghensingel (on the ring),* ☎ *011/23–52–00.* *BF100/€2.48.* ⏲ *Apr.–Oct., Tues.–Fri. 10–5, weekends 2–6.*

★ The **Bokrijk,** outside of Hasselt, is arguably the best and certainly the largest (1,360 acres) open-air museum and nature reserve in Europe. The museum, over 90 acres in size, has more than 100 carefully restored buildings forming four small villages. There's also a small rendition of a 16th-century urban area. The farm buildings have been transplanted from elsewhere in Limburg and from other Flemish provinces. The buildings have their own custodians, many of whom are great sources of local folklore. The interiors are filled with old peasant furniture and utensils. You'll find a chapel, a windmill, a forge, and an inn where you can enjoy traditional fare—spicy sausages, smoked ham, rich cheeses, and red Rodenbach beer. A full complement of artisans work in original costume. There's also a large playground containing a children's village, chutes, pony rides, and other attractions. For more modern-day amusements, a sports center has tennis courts, miniature golf, and a soccer field. The nature reserve shows the unspoiled Kempen country of heather and pine, sand and broom, with marshes and ponds frequented by waterfowl. ✉ *Domein Bokrijk, 6 km (4 mi) northeast of Hasselt, near Genk,* ☎ *011/26–53–00.* *Open-air museum BF250/€6.20 (Apr.–June and Sept., Sun. and holidays; July–Aug., daily), when 33 farmsteads are open and at least 10 craftsmen are on duty; BF200/€4.96 on "green days" (Apr.–June and Sept., Mon.–Sat.), when 22 farmsteads are open and at least 5 craftsmen are on duty; BF100/€2.48 on "blue days" (Oct., daily), when just a few cottages are open. Nature reserve free.* ⏲ *Museum Apr.–Oct., daily 10–sunset; cottages close at 6 (5 in Oct.).*

Dining and Lodging

$ ✕ **Brasserie De Groene Hendrick.** You enter the 18th-century brick building that houses this restaurant through a carriageway that opens onto a paved courtyard. It's a striking setting for enjoying traditional, well-made brasserie fare. The 18-meter-long bar is also an appealing spot for a drink. ✉ *Zuivelmarkt 25,* ☎ *011/24–33–39. AE, DC, MC, V.*

$ ✕ **De Egge.** This charming restaurant offers pretty, tasteful decor, with whitewashed brick and café curtains, and cooking that's imaginative and well executed. Try monkfish on a bed of leeks, or goat cheese brushed with honey and fresh thyme and served hot on a bed of julienne of apple, endive, and *mâche* (lamb's lettuce). ✉ *Walputstraat 23,* ☎ *011/22–49–51. AE, DC, MC, V. Closed Wed.*

$ ✕ **Majestic.** This big tavern on the Grote Markt with leaded glass, high ceilings, and a grand, historic feel draws locals for drinks, cards, snacks, and light meals such as sandwiches, trout, steak, or an inexpensive menu of the day. ✉ *Grote Markt,* ☎ *011/22–33–30. AE, DC, MC, V.*

$$$$ ★ ✕ **Scholteshof.** Owner-chef Roger Souvereyns created a mecca for many a Belgian and foreign gourmet on his 18th-century farm 7 km (4 mi) west of Hasselt. A beautiful fountain graces the interior courtyard, where you can enjoy cocktails. There's also a sculpture-filled English garden and an extensive herb garden. A meal in the candlelit dining

room is a romantic and relaxing experience; the imaginative menu includes pumpkin soup with langoustines, carpaccio with a ball of caviar on green tomato jelly, sweetbreads roasted with rosemary, and grilled turbot with rhubarb mousse. Eating here may be a once-in-a-lifetime experience: the checks are staggeringly high. Rooms are spacious and furnished with magnificent antiques. ✉ *Kermtstraat 130, B3512 Stevoort,* ☎ *011/25–02–02,* FAX *011/2–54–328. 11 rooms, 7 suites. Reservations essential. Jacket and tie. AE, DC, MC, V. Closed Wed.; Tues. during July–Aug.; 2 wks in Jan.*

$$ **Holiday Inn Hasselt.** Completed in 1990, this has become Hasselt's hotel of choice. Centrally located, it's built to the chain's global standards. The design is post–Art Deco and the house color a light oyster gray. ✉ *Kattegatstraat 1, B3500,* ☎ *011/24–22–00,* FAX *011/22–39–35. 107 rooms. Restaurant, bar, pool. AE, DC, MC, V.*

$$ **Hotel Century.** Located just 400 m from Hasselt's Groen Plein, this no-frills hotel is an excellent value. The rooms are tidy, if unimaginatively decorated. The restaurant serves similarly dependable but uninspired Belgian cuisine. ✉ *Leopoldplein 1,* ☎ *011/22–47–99,* FAX *011/23–18–24. 17 rooms. Restaurant, bar. AE, MC, V.*

$$ **Hotel Portmans.** Modern and elegant, this centrally located hotel provides high-quality service and attention to detail that make it worth the slightly higher rates than you pay at other hotels in Hasselt. The restaurant is also worth trying. ✉ *Minderbroedersstraat 12-14,* ☎ *011/26–32–80,* FAX *011/26–32–81. 14 rooms. Restaurant, bar. AE, DC, MC, V.*

Outdoor Activities and Sports

GOLF

There are excellent facilities at the **Vlaams-Japanese Golf & Business Club** (✉ Vissenbroekstraat 15, ☎ 011/26–34–82). Although the 18-hole course is for members only, the nine-hole training course is open to the public.

Sint-Truiden

25 *17 km (10 mi) southwest of Hasselt, 94 km (56 mi) southeast of Antwerp, 63 km (38 mi) east of Brussels, 35 km (21 mi) northwest of Liège.*

All around Sint-Truiden (St-Trond in French, St. Trudo in English) thousands upon thousands of trees are in bloom in the spring, for this is the center of Haspengouw, Flanders's fruit-growing district. The town developed around the abbey founded by St. Trudo in the 7th century. The Begijnhof, dating from 1258, has a well-restored church, from the end of the 13th century. It is now the **Provinciaal Museum voor Religieuze Kunst** (Provincial Museum of Religious Art) and is known for its 38 frescoes, executed over four centuries. ✉ *Begijnhof, off Speelhoflaan,* ☎ *011/69–11–88. Free. Apr.–Oct., Tues.–Fri. 10–12:30 and 1:30–5, weekends 1:30–5.*

At the **Festraets Studio,** also in the Begijnhof, you can see the astronomical compensation clock, constructed by Camille Festraets out of 20,000 mechanical parts. It is more than 6 ft tall and weighs more than 4 tons. ✉ *Begijnhof 24,* ☎ *011/68–87–52. BF60/€1.49. Visits Apr.–Oct., Tues.–Sun. at 1:45, 2:45, 3:45, and 4:45.*

Lace-making has been revived in Sint-Truiden over the past few decades with a great deal of originality. The results can be seen at the **Kantmuseum** (Lace Museum) in the school of the Ursuline Sisters. ✉ *Naamsestraat 5,* ☎ *011/68–23–56. BF30/€0.74. Sun. and holidays 2–5.*

Sint-Gangulfskerk (St. Gangulphe's Church) is three blocks from the Grote Markt and well worth the small detour. One of the few remaining

Romanesque basilicas from the 11th century, it has been carefully restored. ✉ *Diesterstraat.*

The **Sint-Leonarduskerk** (St. Leonard's Church) in Zoutleeuw, west of Sint-Truiden, dates from the 13th century and seems out of proportion to the town's current size. The church's great treasure is a tall paschal candlestick incorporating a Crucifixion scene, made by Renier van Thienen in 1453 and considered one of the finest brass pieces in Belgium. ✉ *12 km (7 mi) northwest of St-Truiden; take N3 and turn right after 8 km (5 mi).* ⏲ *Easter–Sept., Mon.–Sat. 9:30–noon and 1:30–6, Sun. 1:30–5; Oct.–Easter, Sun. 1:30–4.*

Dining

$$$ ✕ **De Fakkels.** This refined French restaurant has a garden, a banquet room, and a 100-seat dining room. The inventive cuisine includes such dishes as truffle ravioli and scallops with a salad of celery and truffle oil. ✉ *Hasseltsesteenweg 61,* ☎ *011/68–76–34. AE, DC, MC, V. Closed Mon., last wk of Jan., 2nd ½ of Aug. No dinner Sun.*

$ ✕ **Century.** A classic old tavern/restaurant on the Grote Markt, with oak, green-velvet banquettes, and great windows framing the market scene, this simple spot is as comfortable for a drink as for a meal. Typical "snacks" include half a roasted chicken with fries and salad, omelets, steaks, sole, and sandwiches. ✉ *Grote Markt 5,* ☎ *011/68–83–41. AE, MC, V.*

Tongeren

26 *20 km (12 mi) east of Sint-Truiden, 20 km (12 mi) southeast of Hasselt, 87 km (52 mi) east of Brussels, 19 km (11 mi) northwest of Liège.*

Tongeren (Tongres in French) started life as a Roman army encampment. It is one of Belgium's two oldest cities (the other being Tournai), and is visibly proud of the fact. This is where Ambiorix scored a famous but short-lived victory over Julius Caesar's legions in 54 BC. The Roman city was considerably larger than the present one; over the centuries, it was repeatedly sacked and burned. By the end of the 13th century, the city had retreated within its present limits and enjoyed the occasionally burdensome protection of the prince bishops of Liège. The Moerenpoort gate and sections of the ramparts remain from that period.

★ The elaborate **Onze-Lieve-Vrouwebasiliek** (Basilica of Our Lady) is one of the most beautiful medieval monuments in the world. The original church was built on Roman foundations in the 4th century and was the first stone cathedral north of the Alps. A siege in 1213 destroyed everything but the 12th-century Romanesque cloister; soon afterward construction of the present-day Basilica began, a project that would take three centuries to complete. The Chapter House contains the Treasury, also known as the **Basilica Museum Tongeren.** This is the richest collection of religious art in the country, including a 6th-century ivory diptych of St. Paul, a Merovingian gold buckle from the same century, and a truly magnificent head of Christ sculpted in wood in the 11th century. The central nave, up to the pulpit, the choir, and the south transept, dates from 1240. The candlesticks and lectern, from 1372, are the work of Jehan de Dinant, one of a number of outstanding metalworkers who flourished in the Meuse valley at that time. The basilica has excellent acoustics and is often used for symphony concerts. ✉ *Grote Markt. Basilica Museum:* ☎ *012/39–02–55.* 🎟 *BF80/€1.98.* ⏲ *May–Sept., Mon. 1:30–5, Tues.–Sun. 10–noon and 1:30–5; Oct.–Apr., by appointment.*

NEED A BREAK? **De Pelgrim** (✉ Brouwerstraat 9) is a charming old-fashioned tavern, open late, that serves light and simple meals such as *omelette paysanne* (country omelet) and cheese croquettes.

Gallo-Romeins Museum (Gallo-Roman Museum) is a breath of fresh air in the museum world, as different from dusty collections of ancient bric-a-brac as you can imagine. Opened in 1994, it displays objects in the same way they were found, allowing visitors to discover them much as they were discovered by archaeologists. The subterranean amphitheater uses visual and sound effects conceived by Stijn Coninx (director of the cult film *Daens*). The symbol of the museum is a 12-facet ball—several such objects have been found, and nobody knows what they represent or were used for. There's also an audiovisual space and a cafeteria. ✉ *Kielenstraat 15,* ☎ *012/23–39–14.* *BF200/€4.96.* ⏲ *Mon. noon–5; Tues.–Fri. 9–5, weekends 10–6.*

Dining and Lodging

$$$$ ★ ✕ **Clos St-Denis.** An enormous 17th-century farmhouse with attached barns is the home of one of Belgium's top restaurants. Chef Christian Denis serves extravagant fare: lobster tartare with chives; gratin of oysters in champagne and caviar; ravioli of *foie d'oie* (goose liver) in truffle cream. There's choucroute with suckling pig and mustard as well. Four dining rooms outdo each other for period luxury—burnished parquet, Persian runners, chinoiserie. ✉ *Grimmertingenstraat 24, Vliermaal-Kortessem,* ☎ *012/23–60–96. Reservations essential. AE, DC, MC, V. Closed Mon., Tues.; 1st ½ Jan., 1st ½ July.*

$$ **Ambiotel.** This cozy hotel in the historic center of Tongeren is right next to the cathedral. The beige-painted rooms are small and functional. Toilets are communal. ✉ *Vleemarkt 2, B3700,* ☎ *012/26–25–90,* FAX *012/26–15–42. 22 rooms with bath or shower. AE, DC, MC, V. Restaurant, bar, meeting room, free parking.*

NORTHEAST BELGIUM A TO Z

Arriving and Departing

By Car

Lier is a short drive from Antwerp on the N10 or from Brussels on the E19/N14 via Mechelen. **Hasselt** is a straight drive, almost as the crow flies, from Antwerp on the A13/E313 motorway (which continues to Liège); from Brussels, take the E40/A2 via Leuven to Exit 26, then the E313 for the last few miles. **Sint-Truiden** is reached from Hasselt on the N80 and **Tongeren** on the N20 (they are linked by the N79); from Brussels take the E40 to Exit 25 for the N3 to Sint-Truiden, to Exit 29 for the N69 to Tongeren. Meanwhile, **Leuven** is a 20-minute drive from Brussels, on the highway to Lige, while **Mechelen** is situated 28 km (17 mi) north of Brussels, on the E19 autoroute which links Brussels to Antwerp. Lastly, **Diest** is a 20-minute trip by car from Leuven on the A2 autoroute.

By Train

There are hourly trains from Antwerp to Lier (15 minutes), Hasselt (1 hour, 5 minutes), and Tongeren (1 hour, 40 minutes). There is also an hourly train from Brussels (Midi, Centrale, and Nord) taking 55 minutes to Sint-Truiden, 1 hour and 10 minutes to Hasselt.

Getting Around

If you're not driving, consider the humble bike. Hasselt, Sint-Truiden, and Tongeren are equidistant from one another, each leg of the triangle about 20 km (12 mi). Local tourist offices can supply maps and information on bicycle trails. Two of the most popular trails are the Trudofietsroute, 54 km (32 mi) long, based on the travels of St. Trudo, and the Tongria route in Tongeren, 45 km (27 mi) long.

Contacts and Resources

Emergencies

Police: ☎ 101. **Ambulance:** ☎ 100. The address of the on-duty **late-night pharmacy** is posted in all pharmacy windows.

Guided Tours

At Lanaken, near the Dutch border east of Hasselt, you can rent a **horse and wagon** through the local tourist office (☎ 089/72–24–67) and set off for a one-day excursion along a route mapped out for you, from May through October.

The Lanaken tourist office also takes bookings for a wide variety of boat trips on the Meuse and the South-Willems and Albert canals. **Stiphout Boat Trips** (☎ 089/72–24–67) runs a candlelight dinner cruise (💷 BF190–BF1,490/€4.71–€36.94; ⏲ Apr.–mid-Sept.).

Outdoor Activities and Sports

For general information on sports facilities and opportunities, contact the **Sportdienst** (✉ Universiteitslaan 1, Hasselt, ☎ 011/23–72–50).

Visitor Information

Provincial Tourist Office, **Limburg** (✉ Universiteitslaan 1, Hasselt, ☎ 011/23–74–50). City Tourist Offices: **Hasselt** (✉ Lombaardstraat 3, ☎ 011/23–95–40); **Leuven** (✉ Leopold Vanderkelenstraat 30, ☎ 016/21–15–39); **Mechelen** (✉ Stadhuis, Grote Markt 21, ☎ 015/29–76–55); **Sint-Truiden** (✉ Grote Markt 68, ☎ 011/70–18–18); **Tongeren** (✉ Stadhuisplein 9, ☎ 012/39–02–55).

6 HAINAUT

Edging along the French border, the western province of Wallonia often stands in the shadows of the country's showpiece northern regions and their celebrated cities. However, Hainaut, too, is a region rich in history and local color. Rather than having two or three treasured settlements, here the wealth has been generously scattered throughout the province, requiring the traveler to seek it out—or, frequently, to stumble across it in serendipitous discovery. And precisely because Hainaut lies off the beaten track, it exudes a genuine feeling of friendliness and authenticity from the smallest village to the largest city—creating an alluring ambience which is itself one of the major attractions of Hainaut.

Revised by Stephen Roth

HAINAUT IS A PROUD OLD REGION that was the nursery of French kings, the rich dowry of dynastic marriages, and for many years the buffer between expansionist France and quarrelsome Flanders. You'll see land scarred by the industrial revolution and ancient, fortified farms turned into centers of highly productive agriculture; cathedrals spared the ravages of war; and parks and châteaux that are reminders of the feudal world that was.

You can explore Hainaut as an excursion from Brussels or as a stopover en route to France. It is also possible to cut across from Bouillon in southwest Luxembourg through France along the scenic, winding road beside the Semois River, and begin the tour of Hainaut in Chimay.

Attention! As you drive south from Brussels through Flemish Brabant, Tournai is signposted as Doornik, Mons as Bergen, and Lille as Rijsel. This changes to Tournai as you cross the linguistic border at Enghien/Edingen.

Pleasures and Pastimes

Art and Architecture

With buildings dating back to the Middle Ages, and having undergone infusions of principally French, Dutch, and Austrian influence, Hainaut exhibits a surprising variety of architectural styles that are often nestled right up against one other. Grandiose cathedrals, fortified castles, and even the houses of ordinary people today carry the imprint of the region's rich, varied history. This variety can be seen, for example, in the train stations of Tournai, Binche, and Charleroi.

The artistic depth of the Hainaut province is, outside of its architecture, found primarily in the numerous museums in Tournai and Mons, and in the ornate cathedrals that dot many settlements. Both provide elaborate shelters for the historic treasures inside: paintings, porcelain, tapestries, and religious relics.

Nature and the Great Outdoors

Nature in southern Belgium is comfortable rather than spectacular. The rolling countryside is laced with navigable canals and rivers, and dotted with parks and gardens. South, toward the French border, the woods become thicker and the hills more pronounced. The province offers a number of ways for the traveler to combine the discovery of culture with the enjoyment of nature. These include narrow hiking trails through the forest as well as commercial amusement parks.

Dining

Given its geography and history, it's logical that Walloon cuisine was strongly influenced by Belgium's renowned neighbor to the southwest. At the same time, there is a wide enough variety of cooking styles to satisfy every budget and taste. The Belgian outlook, however, is to take their cuisine more seriously than they do themselves, which makes dining out both rewarding and fun.

On warm, sunny days and balmy evenings, most restaurants offer alfresco dining on a terrace or patio. If the weather turns unpleasant, most establishments have an upstairs dining room with a cozy, dry view of the city.

CATEGORY	COST*
$$$$	over BF3,000/€75
$$$	BF2,000–BF3,000/€50–€75
$$	BF1,000–BF2,000/€25–€50
$	under BF1,000/€25

**per person for a three-course meal, including service, taxes, but not beverages*

Lodging

Because this area of Belgium is small, when traveling by car it's possible to explore one end of the province and sleep at the other. This can be useful, even necessary at times, because towns here have fewer accommodations options than Brussels or other larger cities.

At the same time, the provinces offer a variety of unique lodging choices, including wayside inns and even rooms in reconverted or functioning farms known as *gîtes ruraux*. For addresses, contact the local tourist bureaus.

CATEGORY	COST*
$$$$	over BF7,500/€185
$$$	BF5,500–BF7,500/€135–€185
$$	BF2,500–BF5,500/€60–€135
$	under BF2,500/€60

**for two persons sharing double room, including service and tax*

Exploring Hainaut

Rail travel between Brussels and the provincial cities is rapid, frequent, and cheap. However, service between these cities is less than ideal.

Hainaut is connected by an efficient network of toll-free highways, which makes crossing the province from end to end a matter of an hour or so. Secondary roads, the ones that take you to the off-the-track sites, are generally sound, though not always clearly signposted. A car is therefore a natural choice for exploring Hainaut.

For those who prefer more contact with the outdoors, the numerous back roads are a biker's dream. You can also combine a driving trip with hikes in the forests and parks or a cruise on one of the rivers that crosses the province.

Note also that many of the châteaux and cathedrals feature concerts and sound and light shows. Stop by the Brussels Office of Tourism behind the Grand'Place to find out if there is something planned during the time you will be in the neighborhood. If so, one or two of these will make good stops on your tour.

Great Itineraries

IF YOU HAVE 1 DAY

Start in Brussels, leaving by car in the early morning for **Tournai** ①–⑬. Break the drive in two with a stop to visit the well-preserved, Louis XV **Château d'Attre.** Visit the ground floor (the upper floor is occupied) and the surrounding gardens. Proceed to Tournai and begin your visit with a walk around the **Grande'Place** ①, taking in the **Beffroi** ④ belfry tower. The medieval **Cathédrale Notre-Dame** ③ will complete your morning. After lunch on the Grand'Place or along the Escaut River, visit the **Musée des Beaux-Arts** ⑨ and the **Musée de la Tapisserie** ⑥. Finish your stay in Tournai with a stroll along the river up to the **Pont des Trous** ⑫. Before leaving, pass by the train station to appreciate its rather astonishing facade and vaulted ceilings. On your return to Brussels, stop off for a visit of the **Château of Beloeil.**

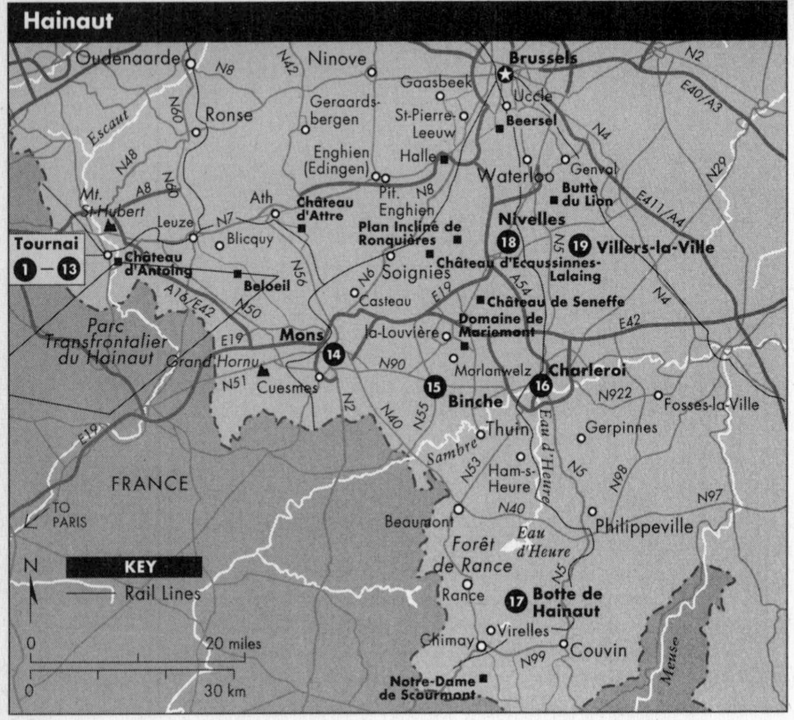

IF YOU HAVE 3 DAYS

The distances are short enough to make your headquarters in Brussels and to make day trips to the rest of the province. However, accommodations will generally be cheaper outside the capital.

Spend the first day as above, but instead of the Château at Beloeil, end your day with a visit of the 12th-century **Château d'Antoing** and its surrounding gardens. If you need fresh air and greenery, the **Parc Naturel Transfrontalier du Hainaut** lies along the Franco–Belgian border just south of Antoing. You can stop off for a hike or just drive through it with your windows down.

In **Mons** ⑭, begin by rubbing with your left hand the head of the monkey set into the facade of the **Hôtel de Ville** in the **Grand'Place.** It's the city's unofficial mascot and is supposed to bring good luck. Visit some of reception halls and the interior courtyard. Nearby is the imposing **Beffroi** (only the grounds are open, as the tower itself is closed until 2005 for restoration, but you can still hear it chime). Around the corner is the 15th-century **Collégiale de St. Waudru** church, the **Musée du Chanoine Puissant** with its heteroclite collections, and the **Musée des Beaux-Arts.** A small detour outside of Mons will bring you to Hornu, the location of the **Grand Hornu,** a former mining complex that included housing for the 450 miners' families.

After a quick visit of **Binche** ⑮ to see the ramparts and visit the **Musée du Carnaval et du Masque,** take the back roads to see the **hydraulic lifts,** elevator locks that actually hoist the boats with their water up nearly 70 m to the higher river. There is an older version, the **ascenseur Nž 3 du Canal du Centre** at Houdeng-Goegnies, which has been classed a historical monument by UNESCO, and two modern versions at nearby Strérpy-Thieu and at Ronquìres. In the same area is the medieval **Château-fort de Ecuassines-Lalaing** and to the east is the 18th century, neoclassical **Château de Seneffe.** Your trip back to Brussels is a great opportunity to visit Waterloo (☞ Side Trips, Chapter 2).

Numbers in the text correspond to numbers in the margin and on the Hainaut and Tournai maps.

When to Tour Hainaut

The same general observations about weather in Belgium are valid for Hainaut and the adjoining regions. Other considerations in planning your trip, though, are the numerous festivities and folklore celebrations in which you might want to participate. Among them are: Binche's **Carnival,** which takes place in February or March; **Ducasse,** which is held in June in Mons; the **Procession of Tournai,** held in September; and the **reconstitution of the Battle of Waterloo,** scheduled in June. Additional shows, concerts, and activities are planned throughout the year; for precise dates and highlights, contact the Office of Tourism in Brussels and in each individual city.

WEST HAINAUT: ART, ARCHITECTURE, AND ARCHAEOLOGY

Western Hainaut—particularly Tournai—was an important center when the Roman legions were marching around these parts. Clovis, the Merovingian king who became the first Christian ruler of France, was born in Tournai in 465. At various times, Tournai has been English, French, and Austrian. Through these vicissitudes the city and the surrounding region have remained a flourishing center of art. The German bombardment in May 1940 destroyed virtually all the priceless old buildings, with the exception of a few Romanesque houses from the 12th century—unique in Western Europe—and a handful of 14th- and 15th-century Gothic buildings.

Tournai

86 km (52 mi) southwest of Brussels, 48 km (29 mi) west of Mons, 28 km (17 mi) east of Lille (France).

❶ The **Grand'Place** is the ideal sight to begin your visit of Tournai—or, indeed, of any city in Belgium. Begin with a leisurely expresso on the *terrasse* of one of the many cafés, followed by a stroll around the triangular perimeter to take in the various 17th-century structures. Although most were destroyed during the conflagration of 1940, they were conscientiously reconstructed according to the ancient styles that had previously graced the Grand'Place. The central statue represents Christine de Lalaing, the wife of the Governor, who is believed to have played an important role in the defense of the city against the Spaniards in 1581.

Although destroyed by fire in 1940 along with many other buildings,
❷ the 14th-century **Eglise Saint-Quéntin,** located on the Grand'Place, was faithfully reconstructed, giving it an eerie look of ancient style combined with modern cleanliness that is rarely seen outside of Disneyland. Visitors may enter during services.

★ ❸ With its five towers, all different, the grand **Cathédrale Notre-Dame** dominates the city today. Built from 1110 to 1170, it's the most original work of religious architecture in Belgium and the beginning of a distinctive style that spread from Tournai down the river Escaut (Scheldt). The best view of the cathedral is from Place Paul-Emile Janson; walk around it to get the full effect of its vast proportions and the massive silhouettes of its five towers. Inside is an overpowering Renaissance screen in polychrome marble, contrasting with the Ro-

Tournai

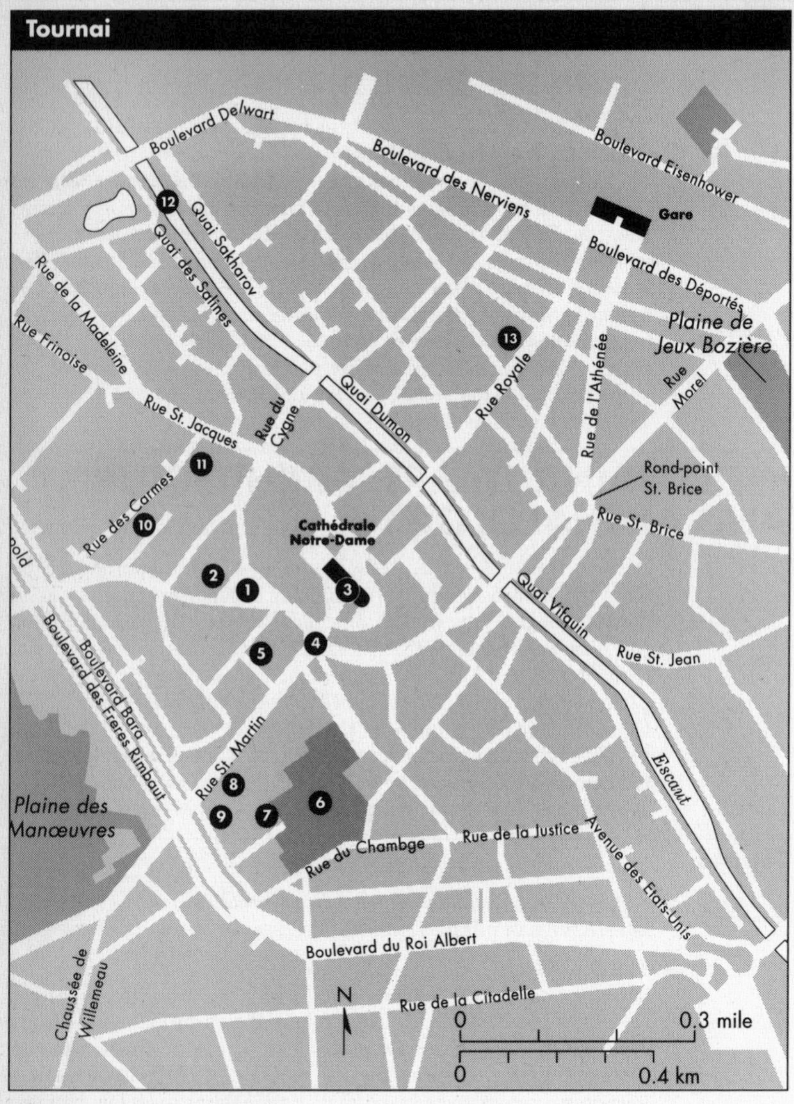

Beffroi 4
Cathédrale Notre-Dame 3
Eglise Saint-Jacques 11
Eglise Saint-Quéntin 2
Grand'Place 1
Musée d'Armes et d'Histoire militaire (Tour Henri VIII) . . .13
Musée de la Tapisserie 6
Musée de l'Archéologie 10
Musée des Arts Décoratifs 8
Musée des Beaux-Arts 9
Musée d'Histoire Naturelle 7
Musée du Folklore 5
Pont des Trous 12

manesque purity of the nave. The transept, almost a cathedral within the cathedral, contains what remains of 12th-century frescoes and well-restored 14th-century windows. In the chapels are paintings by Rubens (the magnificent *Purgatory*), Pourbus the Elder, and Martin de Vos. Foremost among the objects in the treasury are reliquaries in gilded copper and silver by two of the great 13th-century silversmiths and masters of Art Mosan: Nicholas de Verdun and Hugo d'Oignies. ✉ *Pl. Paul-Emile Janson.* ⏲ *Cathedral, daily 9–noon and 2–6; Treasury, Apr.–Oct., Mon.–Sat. 10:15–11:45 and 2–5:45, Sun. and holidays 2–6:45; Nov.–Mar., Mon.–Sat. 10:15–11:45 and 2–3:45, Sun. and holidays 2–3:45.*

4 The 240-ft-high **Beffroi** (Belfry) on the Grand'Place is the oldest in this land of old belfries, dating from 1188. Hanging here are two bells from 1392 and a 15th-century carillon. It cannot be visited as it is undergoing restoration.

5 The **Musée du Folklore** brings to life the trades and crafts that now be-
long to the past: coopering, cobbling, clog making, and many more
that have either ceased to exist or have changed completely over the
years. ✉ *Réduit des Sions 32–36,* ☎ *069/224069.* 🎫 *BF100/€2.50.*
6 ⏲ *Wed.–Mon. 10–noon and 2–5:30.* The **Musée de la Tapisserie**
(Tapestry Museum) vividly illustrates the long and profitable tradition
of tapestry-making in Tournai and displays an outstanding selection
of textiles from the Middle Ages to the present day. In the contemporary section there are demonstrations of tapestry weaving every weekday. ✉ *Pl. Reine Astrid,* ☎ *069/234285.* 🎫 *BF80/€2.00.* ⏲ *Wed.–
Mon. 10–noon and 2–5:30.*

7 The oldest natural history museum in Belgium is the **Musée d'Histoire Naturelle,** which opened in 1828. The neoclassical gallery holds fine specimens of local fauna, as well as exhibits detailing the local environment. ✉ *Cour d'Honneur of the Hôtel de Ville,* ☎ *069/233939.* 🎫 *BF80/€2.00.* ⏲ *Wed.–Mon. 10–noon and 2–5:30.*

8 The **Musée des Arts décoratifs,** next to the Musée d'Histoire Naturelle, contains examples of the porcelain that elevated Tournai to fame between 1752 and 1850. A remarkable collection of silverware and coins are on display, illustrating the skills of the era's versatile craftsmen. ✉ *R. St-Martin 50,* ☎ *069/843795.* 🎫 *BF80/€2.00.* ⏲ *Wed.–Mon. 10–noon and 2–5:30.*

9 The bright, star-shape **Musée des Beaux-Arts** was designed by Victor Horta, the master art nouveau architect, to allow a maximum of natural light. Its exceptional collection of early Flemish art includes copies of works by native son Roger de la Pasture, better known as Rogier Van der Weyden. Look for the Nativity scene and the *Salve Regina* triptych; Impressionist masterpieces such as Manet's *Couple d'Argenteuil;* works by Monet and Seurat; and modern Belgian art, including a witty armadillo sculpted by master ceramist Pierre Caille. ✉ *Enclos St-Martin,* ☎ *069/222043.* 🎫 *BF120/€2.95.* ⏲ *Wed.–Mon. 10–noon and 2–5:30.*

10 A thousand years of history are traced in the **Musée de l'Archéologie.** The displays include exhibits of finds from the Gallo-Roman and the Merovingian eras. ✉ *R. des Carmes 8,* ☎ *069/221672.* 🎫 *BF80/€2.00.* ⏲ *Wed.–Mon. 10–noon and 2–5:30.*

11 The gothic-style **Eglise Saint-Jacques,** a typical representative of Tournaisian architecture, was built in successive stages beginning around 1215 and has justifiably been placed on the list of protected structures in Wallonia. It is small and slightly off the beaten track but worth the detour. Check with the Office of Tourism (☞ Hainaut A to Z, *below*) for service times. ✉ *R. du Palais St Jacques.* ⏲ *During services.*

12 The **Pont des Trous** is a rare example of a 13th-century fortified bridge built to control river access. The bridge was blown up in 1940; it was rebuilt after the war and raised 8 ft to allow river traffic to pass through—exactly what the old bridge was built to prevent. Sightseeing boats leave from the landing stage below the bridge. ✉ *Quai des Salines.*

13 **Musée d'Armes et d'Histoire militaire (Tour Henri VIII).** The Military History and Weapons Museum contains a range of weapons and artifacts from ancient Roman times to the present. ✉ *R. des Remparts,* ☎ *069/223878.* *BF80/€2.00.* *Wed.–Mon. 10–noon and 2–5:30.*

NEED A BREAK? **A l'Bancloque** (✉ R. des Chapeliers 46, ☎ no phone) is a classic Belgian drinking room with high, coffered ceilings and an old stone fireplace.

Tournai Environs

Archeosite is an open-air museum and experimental archaeological center. Featured are prehistoric dwellings with mud walls and thatched roofs reconstructed in accordance with archaeological findings. Activities include basketwork, weaving, pottery, bronze casting, and iron-ore processing. ✉ *R. de l'Abbaye 15, Aubechies,* ☎ *069/671116.* *BF200/€4.95.* *Nov.–Easter, weekdays 9–6; Easter–Oct., weekdays 9–6, weekends 2–7.*

★ **Beloeil** is the magnificent, fairy-tale château of the Prince de Ligne, whose ancestors have lived here since the 14th century. The 17th-century château is partially a reconstruction from the original plans, following a fire in 1900. It contains fine furniture and tapestries, and the heirlooms include gifts from Marie Antoinette and Catherine the Great, friends of the Maréchal de Ligne; his grandson was offered, but refused, the Belgian crown. The elegant park, with a 5-km (3-mi) vista, is patterned after Versailles. ✉ *R. du Château 11, Beloeil,* ☎ *069/689426.* *BF280/€6.95 (tour of castle BF500/€12.40 extra).* *Apr.–Sept., daily 10–6.*

Centre de Loisirs de l'Orient is a family-oriented leisure center with boats, games, barbecues, a swimming pool, and a waterside pub. Note that there's a fee to use the pool and pedal boats. ✉ *Chemin de Mons 8 (Exit 32),* ☎ *069/222635.* *Free.* *Apr.–mid-Sept., daily 10–10.*

Château d'Antoing, located just outside of Tournai, is a Renaissance-style fortress belonging to the Princes of Ligne, whose dungeon dates from the 15th century and its tower from the 16th. It was partially restored in the 19th century and important parts of it can still be visited. ✉ *18, Place Bara, Antoing,* ☎ *069/441729 or 069/442921.* *BF120/€6.20.* *Mid-May–mid-Sept., Sun. and holidays; guided tours at 3, 4, and 5.*

In Attre, near Ath, stands the splendid **Château d'Attre,** built in 1752 and preserved intact. It is still inhabited, and visits are limited to the salons and drawing rooms of the ground floor. Among its treasures are paintings by Franz Snyders and Murillo. The semi-wild park surrounding the château has great charm. ☎ *068/454460.* *BF100/€2.50.* *Mar.–mid-Nov., Tues.–Sun. 10–noon and 2–6; mid-Nov.–Dec. and Feb., Wed. 10–noon and 2–6.*

Le Parc Transfrontalier du Hainaut is a natural park roughly defined by a line connecting Antoing and Beloeil in Belgium and Valenciennes and Douai in France. It's accessible by major roads and crisscrossed by trails open to hikers, equestrians, and cyclists. ☎ *069/779810 Maison du Parc Naturel des Plaines de l'Escaut.*

Mont Saint Aubert is a butte overlooking the Tournaisian plain; from here, you'll find an exceptional view of the region. It's just a half-hour from Tournai—follow the road signs.

Park Paradisio is an ornithologist's dream come true. On a former monastic domain, amid old ruins, bushes, ancient trees, a river, and three lakes, more than 2,500 birds of 400 different species live in semi-liberty. Birds of prey live inside a 50-ft-high cage of 30,000 square ft, which visitors may enter. Special care is taken with endangered species so that their offspring can be returned to the wild. There's also a children's farm, restaurants, and a playground. The park is near Attre. ✉ *Domaine de Cambron, Cambron,* ☎ *068/454653.* *BF395/€9.80.* ⏲ *Daily 10–7.*

Dining and Lodging

$$$ ✕ **Charles Quint.** Right on the Grand'Place and a cobblestone's throw from the Beffroi, this art deco restaurant makes a visible pitch for a clientele who desire a fine meal in tasteful surroundings. Specialties include *foie gras* and seafood. ✉ *Grand'Place, 3,* ☎ *069/221441. AE, DC, MC, V. Closed Thurs., last 3 wks July. No lunch Wed. and Sun.*

$$$ ✕ **Giverny.** Located alongside the Escaut River and away from the press of the main tourist attractions, this tastefully appointed restaurant merits the short walk to find it. Specialties of seafood and game are served with faultless cordiality. ✉ *Quai Marché au Poisson, 6,* ☎ *069/224464. AE, DC, MC, V. Closed last wk July and 1st wk Aug. No dinner Sun. and Mon.*

$$$ ✕ **Le Pressoir.** Tucked away at the end of the Marché-aux-Poteries, between the cathedral and the Beffroi, this elegant but unpretentious restaurant combines historical atmosphere (exposed brick, illuminated oil paintings) with surprising urbanity: The bar draws BCBG (*bon chic–bon genre*) clientele, and the restaurant hosts visiting VIPs. Try the roast farm pigeon with young turnips or saffron-perfumed bouillabaisse of *rouget* (red mullet). ✉ *Marché-aux-Poteries 2,* ☎ *069/223513. AE, DC, MC, V. No dinner Sun.–Thurs. Closed Tues., Carnival wk, last 3 wks of Aug.*

$–$$ ✕ **A la Bonne Franquette.** Perched over the Escaut, this is the provincial restaurant as you imagined it in your trip preparation reveries: unpretentious and friendly, inexpensive but good. If the weather is nice, grab a table outside under an umbrella. The local *lapin à la tournaisienne* (rabbit cooked in beer and prunes) can be had here, but the *anguille au vert* (eel in cream sauce) is the real treat. ✉ *Quai Marché au Poisson, 13,* ☎ *069/840196. MC, V. Closed Mon. and last 2 wks Jan.*

$ ✕ **Bistro de la Cathédrale.** This modernized, brightly lighted storefront restaurant offers reasonable fixed-price menus and large portions of good, simple, well-prepared food: fresh oysters, salads of *crevettes grise* (tiny shrimp), and rabbit with prunes. The ambience is casual, the staff friendly. ✉ *Vieux Marché-aux-Poteries 15,* ☎ *069/210379. AE, DC, MC, V.*

$ ✕ **Ô Pères au Quai.** On the riverside behind the columns of a 17th-century house, this friendly, good-value restaurant consists of one room, where meat is grilled in the large fireplace, and a pleasant garden. Fixed-price menus include an all-you-can-eat buffet of salads and cold meats and a generous supply of wine. ✉ *Quai Notre-Dame 18,* ☎ *069/232922. AE, DC, MC, V. No lunch Sat., no dinner Mon.*

$$$ **Le Panoramique.** As the name indicates, this hotel has sweeping views from its hilltop location a couple of miles from the center of town. Almost all of the modern rooms have been refreshed and one more floor has been added. It's more like a ski lodge than an ordinary hotel—long on comfort, short on charm. ✉ *Pl. de la Trinité 2, B7542 Mont St-Aubert,* ☎ *069/891616,* FAX *069/233323. 46 rooms. Restaurant, meeting rooms. AE, DC, MC, V.*

$$ **Holiday Inn Garden Court.** A fully modernized, chain-style business hotel, it stands at the foot of the cathedral in the center of town. Some rooms look onto the small square. ✉ *Pl. St-Pierre, B7500,* ☎ *069/215077,* FAX *069/215078. 59 rooms. Restaurant, café, meeting rooms. AE, DC, MC, V.*

$ **L'Europe.** On the Grand'Place, with rooms looking out toward the Beffroi and historic architecture, this is a cheerful, comfortable hotel in an old step-gabled house. The rooms, surprisingly quiet at the back given the central location, are cheaply decorated but with a lavish, almost kitschy touch; most have toilets down the hall. The restaurant–tavern downstairs draws crowds of locals for stone-grilled meats. ✉ *Grand'Place 36, B7500,* ☎ *069/224067. 8 rooms. Restaurant. AE, MC.*

Outdoor Activities and Sports

Plaine de Jeux Bozière (✉ Av. Bozière 1B, ☎ 069/223586) has basketball, volleyball, mini-soccer, and tennis.

Mons

14 *48 km (29 mi) east of Tournai, 67 km (40 mi) south of Brussels, 72 km (43 mi) west of Namur.*

The hilly streets of Mons, lined with elegant if grimy 17th- and 18th-century brick houses, have considerable charm. At the highest point stands a remarkable **belfry,** known locally as *le château,* for it stands next to what once was the castle of the counts of Hainaut. Built in the 17th century, it's a Baroque tower, 285 ft high and crowned by an onion dome. The tower is undergoing restoration and cannot be visited, but you can hear the carillon bells ringing the hours. The latter structure contains 49 bells weighing a total of 25,000 kg (54,000 lb), some of which date back to the beginning of the 17th century.

Mons has had its share of misfortunes. Like most of Wallonia's cities, it was repeatedly occupied and lost by the troops of Louis XIV, of the French Revolution, and of Napoléon. It was at Mons in August 1914 that the British Expeditionary Force first battled the Germans. Many of the self-styled Old Contemptibles spoke of a vision of the "Angels of Mons" helping them hold their position longer than seemed possible. Thirty years later, further destruction was wrought by a running battle between advancing American troops and the retreating Germans.

The **Hôtel de Ville** (Town Hall) in the Grand'Place was built in 1456. It is largely the work of Matthieu de Layens, the master of the Town Hall in Leuven, which it vaguely resembles. Next to the door stands a forged-iron statuette of a monkey. If you touch its head with your left hand, it will bring you good luck, as it has done for believers since the Middle Ages. Some rooms are open to visitors if they're not in use. Most impressive is the Salon Gothique, located up a circular stone stairway. In the inner courtyard, the Jardin du Mayeur is a serene little spot where a statue of a young prankster splashes onlookers. Ivy sculptures of Saint Georges and the Dragon sit next to a monolith from the neolithic period.

NEED A BREAK? **La Terrasse** (✉ Grand'Place 6, ☎ no phone) is an attractive café with a yellow facade that serves homemade soups and simple Belgian snacks such as cheese croquettes.

The **Collégiale Ste-Waudru** (Collegiate Church of St. Waudru) is named for the wife of a Merovingian dignitary who, as legend has it, founded a monastery in the 7th century around which the city developed. The church was begun in 1450 by the women of St. Waudru's Noble Chapter of Secular Canonesses. The elaborately decorated *Car d'Or* (Golden

Coach), which carries the reliquary of St. Waudru on an annual procession through the streets on Trinity Sunday (eighth Sunday after Easter), stands in the nave next to doors that are opened only on special occasions. The precious objects in the treasury include what is purported to be St. Waudru's ring. ✉ *Pl. du Chapitre,* ☎ *no phone.* 🎫 *Treasury BF50/€1.25.* ⏲ *Apr.–Oct., Mon.–Sat. 1:30–6, Sun. 1:30–5.*

The **Musée du Chanoine Puissant** contains the unusual and diverse personal collections of the ecclesiastic Canon Puissant, which date from 1880 to 1934. These are housed in the 16th-century Vieux Logis. ✉ *The Vieux Logis, R. Notre-Dame-Débonnaire 22,* ☎ *065/336670.* 🎫 *BF100/€2.50.* ⏲ *Tues.–Sun. noon–6.*

The **Musée du Folklore et de la Vie Montoise,** housed in a former infirmary of a 17th century convent, brings together collections that illustrate various themes of the life and folklore of Mons through the ages. A special place is given to the famous springtime festival, *the Combat of the Lumeçon,* a way to participate in the party even if you cannot be present. ✉ *Maison Jean Lescarts, rue Neuve,* ☎ *065/314357.* 🎫 *BF100/€2.50.* ⏲ *Tues.–Sun. noon–6.*

The **Musée des Arts Décoratifs François Duseberg** has a unique collection of decorative clocks dating from the early 1800s—gilded statuettes, intricate vases and porcelain teapots—all used to tell time decoratively. ✉ *Sq. Franklin Roosevelt 12.* ☎ *065/313684.* 🎫 *BF100/€2.50.* ⏲ *Tues., Thurs., weekends 2–7.*

The town of **Cuesmes** was once home to **Vincent van Gogh.** He came to the Borinage, the depressed area south of Mons, as a preacher in 1878 and stayed with a family of miners, the Decrucqs. It was here that he began drawing the landscape and scenes of the miners' lives, and the house where he lived still stands. The original environment has been reconstructed; there is an exhibition of reproductions of his work and an audiovisual presentation. ✉ *R. du Pavillon 3, Cuesmes,* ☎ *065/355611.* 🎫 *BF100/€2.50.* ⏲ *Tues.–Sun. 10–6.*

★ **Grand-Hornu** is a remarkable example of early industrial architecture seeking to humanize working conditions, in an area dotted with conical slag heaps—reminders of a coal-mining past. The vast, semi-ruined redbrick complex of workshops, offices, and housing, including a library, dance hall, and bathhouse, was built by Henri De Gorge in the early 19th century in neoclassical style, with arcades, pediments, and half-moon windows. It served its purpose for well over a century. Fortunately it was rescued from demolition and is now a multipurpose cultural center, with some offices rented out to companies. Further renovations and an extended cultural program are expected by 2002. ✉ *R. Ste-Louise 82, Hornu, Mons,* ☎ *065/770712.* 🎫 *BF100/€2.50.* ⏲ *Mar.–Sept., Tues.–Sun. 10–6; Oct.–Feb., Tues.–Sun. 10–4.*

Dining and Lodging

$$ ★ ✕ **Alter Ego.** This handsome, stylish brasserie with grape-shape decorations on the ceiling offers regionally inspired cuisine: homemade *confit de canard* (pressed duck), duck fillets cooked in raspberries, and potatoes sautéed in goose fat. ✉ *R. Nimy 6,* ☎ *065/351730. AE, DC, MC, V. Closed Mon., mid-July–mid-Aug. No dinner Sun.*

$ ✕ **La Cervoise.** This picturesque café–restaurant right on the Grand'-Place offers simple but hearty cuisine. Take a table under an umbrella to try one of the nearly 200 beers on offer. If the weather is uninspiring, the upstairs dining room offers a splendid view of the Grand'Place in addition to protection from the elements. ✉ *Grand'Place, 25,* ☎ *065/314606. No credit cards.*

$ ✕ **Le Saint Germain/Saey.** This chic restaurant and tearoom sitting on the Grand'Place offers a wide selection of ice creams, pastries, and *petite cuisine* ("simple fare") that will satisfy any serious appetites or temptations toward self indulgence. ✉ *Grand'Place, 12,* ☎ *065/335448. AE, DC, V.*

$$ ✕ **Casteau Resort Hotel.** The peaceful setting surrounding this modern hotel just northeast of Mons makes it a good base for exploring the region. The standard rooms feature thoughtful amenities, however, including a trouser press. The restaurant serves a selection of unusual but tasty items, including brioche with smoked eel and a poached egg. ✉ *Chaussée de Bruxelles 38, 7061 Casteau,* ☎ *065/320400,* FAX *065/728744. 75 rooms. Restaurant, 2 tennis courts, convention center. AE, DC, MC, V.*

$$ ★ ✕ **Château de la Cense au Bois.** This 19th-century château in a 40-acre park on the outskirts of Mons has luxurious and tasteful rooms and offers gastronomic weekends. Each room is different from the others, but all have large beds, large bathrooms, and a view of the park. There is no obligation to eat in the restaurant, L'Osciètre Gris ($$$; closed Mon., no dinner Sun.), which serves ambitious French, seasonal cuisine. ✉ *Rte. d'Ath 135, B7020 Nimy,* ☎ *065/316000,* FAX *065/361155. 10 rooms. Restaurant, bicycles. AE, DC, MC, V.*

$$ ★ ✕ **Hôtel Saint Georges.** This 19th-century *Hôtel de Maître* is a five-minute walk from the Grand'Place. Eight rooms are larger and have kitchenettes. It's supremely clean and modern, with minimum comforts but at a reasonable price. ✉ *R. des Clercs 15, Mons B7000,* ☎ *065/311629,* FAX *065/318671. 7 rooms, 8 suites. Kitchenettes (some). AE, DC, MC, V.*

Outdoor Activities and Sports

GOLF

Golf du Mont Garni (✉ R. du Mont Garni 3, Baudour, ☎ 065/622719) is an 18-hole, par-74 public golf course west of Mons.

TENNIS

Try the **Waux-Hall** (✉ Av. St-Pierre 17, Mons, ☎ 065/337923) for tennis, boats, and camping.

EAST HAINAUT: RELIGION AND RUINS

This sweeping section of Belgium is steeped in religious history, as shown by the many churches and cathedrals. Small museums highlight the treasures of cities past and present, while monastery ruins are ripe for exploration in the beautiful countryside.

Binche

15 *16 km (10 mi) east of Mons, 62 km (37 mi) south of Brussels.*

Binche is the only remaining walled city in Belgium, and its center, complete with a cobbled, café-fringed square and an onion-dome town hall, is still intact behind 25 towers and 2¼ km (1½ mi) of ramparts. However, its biggest claim to fame is that it is the Carnival capital of Belgium.

The city's festivities begin the Sunday before Ash Wednesday, when hundreds of men dressed as "Mam'zelles" dance in the streets to the music of fiddles, barrel organs, and drums, and 1,500 Binche dancers form a procession. Shrove Tuesday is the big day, when the *Gilles* (dancers) have celebrated the rites of spring since the 14th century. They dance with dignity and gravity, repeating ritual gestures such as ringing cowbells and distributing—throwing, actually—oranges. They assemble at dawn and go from house to house in fantastic costumes emblazoned with red and yellow heraldic lions. In the morning they wear wax-covered masks painted with green glasses, whiskers, and moustaches. In the afternoon, their enormous hats are crowned with huge plumes of ostrich feathers. To the rhythm of drums, the Gilles move through the streets in a slow, shuffling dance. The day ends with fireworks, but the Gilles continue dancing through the night. Traditionally, they drink nothing but champagne.

On your way out of Binche, drop by the train station, which is more reminiscent of a small cathedral than of a way station for the iron horse. The lettering carved into the exterior walls in two languages exemplifies the linguistic and political influences that have governed in this region over the years. That only the French versions are carefully gilded gives an idea of how things stand today.

The **Musée International du Carnaval et du Masque** is installed in the former Augustine college. It contains one of the world's finest collections of masks and costumes, and there's an audiovisual presentation of the local carnival, in case you're in Binche at the wrong time for the real thing. ✉ *R. du St-Moustier 10,* ☏ *064/335741.* 💶 *BF150/€3.70.* ⏲ *Apr.–Oct., Mon.–Thurs. 9–noon and 2–6, Sat. 2–6, Sun. 10–noon and 2–6; Nov.–Mar., Mon.–Thurs. 9–noon and 1–5, weekends 2–6. Closed Carnival, Nov. 1, Dec. 22–Jan. 6.*

The 14th-century **Collégiale Saint Ursmer,** built on the site of a church already 200 years old, was partially destroyed by Henry II's troops in 1554. Restored over the intervening years, it contains a number of minor but surprising wood sculptures, notably the *Notre Dame de Pièta.* ✉ *R. Haute, at the end of the Grand'Place,* ☏ *no phone.* ⏲ *During services.*

★ The **Plan Incliné de Ronquières** is a grandiose engineering feat that did not bring about the hoped-for results. This mile-long inclined plane—one of three similar engineering sites worth visiting in the area—was designed to allow river traffic to enter huge tanks, which were winched up 225 ft to avoid time-consuming locks. Now a new attraction has been added in the tower overlooking the installation. To experience *Un Bateau, une Vie* (A Boat, a Life), visitors are issued infrared helmets that provide an interactive virtual-reality experience. You have the impression of following a boatman down into his barge, living the traditional as well as the modern way of life on the canal, and sharing the confidences of its people. ✉ *N535, Ronquières, halfway between Binche and Brussels,* ☏ *065/360464.* 💶 *Virtual-reality show BF250/€6.20; boat trip BF100/€2.50.* ⏲ *Show: June–Nov., daily 10–7 (last ticket, 5); boats May–Sept., Tues. and Thurs.–Sun. noon, 2:30, 3:30, and 5:30.*

Another gigantic construction meant to remedy the difference of level ★ on the Centre canal is the **boat lifts of Strérpy-Thieu.** Whereas the sloping locks of Ronquières winch a tank full of water with the boat floating in it up a slope, at Strérpy-Thieu it is hoisted vertically—a modern version of the boat lifts at Houdeng-Goegnies. ✉ *E19–E42, Exit 21, Stérpy-Thieu, near La Louvíre, halfway between Mons and Charleroi,* ☏ *064/360464 Hainaut Tourisme in Mons.*

The oldest and perhaps most efficient of the three systems of locks is ★ the **boat lifts of Houdeng-Goegnies.** They date from the beginning of the 1900s and have been classed by UNESCO as World Heritage structures. ✉ *E19–E42, Exit 21, 2 km from La Louvière, Houdeng-Goegnies, halfway between Mons and Charleroi,* ☏ *064/847831.*

The **Domaine de Mariemont** is a 110-acre English-style park, one of the most attractive in Belgium. It is embellished with sculptures by a number of artists, including Auguste Rodin and Constantin Meunier.

Only ruins remain of the château that once stood here, but there is a well-planned museum containing excellent collections of ancient and Chinese art, archaeological finds, and Tournai porcelain. The museum also has a café-restaurant and holds excellent sculpture retrospectives. ✉ *Chaussée de Mariemont, off N59, or Exit 19 from E42, north of Binche, near Morlanwelz,* ☎ *064/212193.* 🎫 *Free.* ⏲ *Tues.–Fri. and most Sat. 10–12:30 and 1:30–6.*

The **Musée des Sciences de Parentville** is a playful, family-oriented science museum with laboratory and interactive displays, plus a playground with scientific games. ✉ *R. de Villers 227, Couillet,* ☎ *071/600300.* 🎫 *BF150/€3.70.* ⏲ *Weekdays 9:30–5:30, Sun. 10–6.*

Dining and Lodging

$ ✕ **L'Industrie.** This is one of the few places serving the Binche specialty, *doubles* (buckwheat pancakes filled with cheese), but you must order by telephone the day before. This gracefully aging restaurant is so discreet that you might miss it. It's on the corner of Grand'Place and Rue de la Hure. Head cheese, *anguilles au vert* (eels with herb sauce), and mussels are standard menu items. ✉ *Grand'Place 4,* ☎ *064/331053. Closed Wed. No dinner Mon. and Tues.*

$$ ✕ **Les Volets Verts.** This small, friendly hotel in the middle of Binche has four comfortable rooms with a shared garden. ✉ *R. de la Triperie 4, 7130,* ☎ *064/333147,* FAX *064/333147. 4 rooms. No credit cards.*

Charleroi

16 *20 km (12 mi) east of Binche.*

Charleroi is much larger than Binche and was former capital of this iron and steel manufacturing region, otherwise known as the "Black Country." However, the town has been hard hit by a recession that has made steel production almost obsolete. Many residents are of Italian origin, some of whom came to work in the mines thanks to a reciprocal, post–World War II labor agreement between Belgium and Italy. Hundreds died in the country's worst mining accident in 1956. Charleroi has a good choice of Italian restaurants, an active contemporary dance scene, and some fascinating museums.

The **Musée de la Photographie,** in an old abbey, tells the story of photography from its infancy to the present day and mounts superb temporary exhibitions. ✉ *Av. Paul Pastur 11,* ☎ *071/435810.* 🎫 *BF150/€3.70.* ⏲ *Tues.–Sun. 10–6.*

The **Musée des Beaux Arts et le Musée Jules Destrée** offers a combination of interesting displays. The former houses a collection of paintings and sculptures from the 19th and 20th centuries, while the latter follows the life of this important man from Charleroi. ✉ *Hôtel de Ville, Place du Manège,* ☎ *071/230294.* 🎫 *BF50/€1.25.* ⏲ *Tues.–Sat. 9–5.*

The **Musée du Verre et le Musée Archéolgique** follows the art, industry, and technique of glassmaking through the centuries. It illustrates the different procedures as they developed over the years and shows related archaeological discoveries in the region. ✉ *Blvd. Defontaine 10,* ☎ *071/310838.* 🎫 *BF50/€1.25.* ⏲ *Tues.–Sat. 9–5.*

★ The **Eglise Saint Christophe** is the result of a post–World War II transformation of an 18th-century structure. The principal attraction is the 200-square-m mosaic in the choir, which was designed by a local artist. As you're admiring it, remember that each one of those tiny glass squares is backed with real gold leaf. ✉ *Pl. Charles II,* ☎ *no phone.* ⏲ *During services.*

★ The **Château de Seneffe** was the Renaissance-style, secondary residence of the Count Julien Depestre, which he built in the 1760s. It now houses a museum of gold- and silversmithing displaying more than 800 articles produced in the 17th and 18th centuries from various centers of production around Europe. ✉ *E19, Exit 20, Seneffe,* ☎ *064/556913.* 🎫 *Château: BF150/€3.70, park and garden: free.* ⏲ *Tues.–Sun. 10–6.*

★ The **Château-fort de Ecaussines-Lalaing** is a 12th-century feudal castle nestled in the countryside. Rooms open to visitors include a chapel, prison, kitchen, and weaponry. A museum houses a furniture collection, blown-glass paintings, porcelain, and old coins. ✉ *Ecaussines, 6 km southeast of Braine-le-Comte,* ☎ *06/442490.* 🎫 *BF200/€4.95.* ⏲ *Apr.–June and Sept.–Nov., weekends and holidays 10–noon and 2–6; July and Aug. Thurs.–Mon. 10–noon and 2–6.*

Botte de Hainaut

17 *50 km (30 mi) south from Charleroi into France.*

The boot-shape Botte de Hainaut region is rich in wooded valleys, villages, châteaux, and lakes. The **Eau-d'Heure** is a lake surrounded by a wild, wooded 4,500-acre park with trails, as well as aquariums, an ecological museum, and a panoramic tower. ✉ *Boussu-lez-Walcourt,* ☎ *071/633534.* 🎫 *BF180.* ⏲ *Easter–Sept., daily 9–6.*

The Tour Salamandre in **Beaumont** is all that remains of a major fortified castle built in the 11th century. The tower has been restored and houses a museum of local and regional history. ✉ *N40 or N53, Beaumont,* ☎ *071/588191.* 🎫 *BF50.* ⏲ *May–Sept., daily 9–7; Oct., Sun. 10–5.*

All the way south is **Chimay,** a small town with vivid memories of the great nation to the south. It was the home of Froissart, the 14th-century historian whose chronicles furnished the background information for many of Shakespeare's plays. Later, Chimay became the home of Madame Tallien, a great beauty who was known to revolutionary France as Notre Dame de Thermidor. She narrowly escaped the guillotine, married her protector, Citizen Tallien, and persuaded him to instigate the overthrow of Robespierre. Eventually she was again married, to François-Joseph Caraman, prince of Chimay, and ended her days in peace and dignity as mistress of the Château de Chimay. The warrant for her arrest, signed by Robespierre, is preserved at the château, along with other French memorabilia, such as the baptismal robe worn by Napoléon's son, the king of Rome. Classical music concerts are held in the castle on the second Saturday of every month. ✉ *R. du Château,* ☎ *060/212823; 060/214444 concerts.* 🎫 *BF200/€4.95.* ⏲ *Guided tours Mar.–Oct., daily 10–noon and 2–6; Nov–Feb. by appointment.*

Notre-Dame de Scourmont is a Trappist monastery whose monks produce some of the best cheese and tastiest, most potent beer in Belgium. Although the monastery is not open to the public, except for retreats, you can purchase Chimay beer and cheese here. ✉ *About 1⅓ km (1 mi) south of Chimay.*

Dining and Lodging

$$ ✕🏨 **Hostellerie du Gahy.** Overlooking a large garden, this small inn has six rooms decorated in traditional style. The ambitious cuisine favors seafood and cakes: try lobster with vanilla flavoring in puff pastry or quails stuffed with foie gras. Half-board is obligatory in summer. ✉ *R. du Gahy 2, B6590 Momignies,* ☎ *060/511093,* FAX *060/512879. 6 rooms. Restaurant. AE, DC, MC, V. Closed Mon. No dinner Sun. and Wed.*

$ ★ **Hostellerie Le Virelles.** Just north of Chimay, in the open greenery around the Etang de Virelles, this old country inn offers simple, regional cooking in a pretty, well-weathered beam-and-copper setting. You can have trout or *escavèche* (spicy, cold marinade of cooked fish), or a more ambitious, multicourse menu based on regional freshwater fish and game. Rooms, named after field flowers, are simple and cozy, some with four-poster beds. The adjacent nature reserve is great for long walks. *R. du Lac 28, B6461 Virelles, 060/212803, FAX 060/512458. 7 rooms. Restaurant. AE, DC, MC, V. Closed Wed. No dinner Tues.*

Outdoor Activities and Sports

ARCHERY

You can practice crossbow shooting in Beaumont at the **Arbaletriers Beaumontois** (Parc de Paridaens, 071/588255).

HORSEBACK RIDING

Horseback riding is popular in many parts of the province, particularly in the less densely populated south. In Chimay you can arrange treks with the **Centre Equestre des Fagnes** (R. de la Fagne 20, 060/411169).

Nivelles

18 *34 km (21 mi) south of Brussels, 13 km (8 mi) west of Villers-la-Ville.*

★ **La Collégiale Ste-Gertrude** (St. Gertrude's Collegiate Church), the pride of Nivelles, is, in fact, a reconstruction. This old town suffered terribly from bombardment in May 1940, when more than 500 buildings were destroyed, including the original church dating from the 7th century when the Merovingian kings ruled the land. Reparations from Germany paid for the rebuilding of the church—Belgium's finest Romanesque building, whose beauty derives from its severe simplicity. The most unusual feature is the two choirs, one symbolizing the power of the Holy Roman Emperor and the other that of the Pope. The church is named for the daughter of Pepin the Old, St. Gertrude, who founded a convent in Nivelles in about 650. The crypt contains the burial vaults of St. Gertrude and her parents. For group guided visits in English, telephone for an appointment. *Grand'Place, 067/882245. BF100/€2.50. Weekdays 9–6 (Oct.–Mar. until 5); guided tours, weekdays 2 and 3:30.*

NEED A BREAK? Locals swear by **Pâtisserie Courtain** (Bd. Fleur de Lys 14, no phone) for the Nivelles specialty, *tarte al djote,* a succulent cheese and vegetable pie, served hot.

Villers-la-Ville

19 *36 km (22 mi) south of Brussels, 15 km (9 mi) southwest of Ottignies/Louvain-la-Neuve, 13 km (8 mi) east of Nivelles.*

★ The **Abbaye de Villers-la-Ville** (Abbey Ruins) dates from 1147. St. Bernard is believed to have laid the foundation stone, and as usual the Cistercians had a knack for building their monasteries in spots of great natural beauty. The abbey became one of Europe's most important and wealthy. It was repeatedly expanded, but it all ended when the French Revolution reached Belgium and the abbey was burned, sacked, and relegated to being a quarry for building material. Cistercian masonry is, however, not easily destroyed, and the walls and vaults of cloister, dormitories, refectory, and chapter hall form an impressive architectural unit. Open-air concerts and drama performances are staged here every summer. *At crossroads north of village, 071/879555.*

BF150/€3.70; guided visits (Sun. 3) BF250/€6.20. ⌚ *Apr.–Oct., Mon.–Tues. noon–6, Wed.–Sun. 10–6; Nov.–Mar., Wed.–Fri. 1–5, weekends 10–5.*

HAINAUT A TO Z

Arriving and Departing

By Car

Roads leading south from Brussels pass through Flemish-speaking Brabant; thus roads are signposted to Bergen (Mons), Doornik (Tournai), and Rijsel (Lille). The E19 motorway from Brussels to Paris passes Mons on the way. The E42 from Liège joins the E19 before Mons and branches off from it between Mons and the border to continue to Tournai and Lille. South of Charleroi, roads are mostly two-lane highways.

By Train

There is one local train an hour from Brussels to Tournai (55 minutes) and one to Mons (45 minutes). Three of the express trains to Paris also stop at Mons. There are two trains an hour to Charleroi (40 minutes).

Getting Around

Tournai, Mons, and Charleroi are linked by rail, with one train an hour taking a half hour between each stop. Excursions to destinations other than these principal cities are best made by car.

Contacts and Resources

Guided Tours

City tours are organized on request by the individual tourist offices in Tournai, Mons, Charleroi, and Binche. For tours of the southern part of the province, contact the tourist office in Beaumont (☞ Visitor Information, *below*).

Visitor Information

Province of Hainaut (✉ R. des Clercs 31, Mons, ☎ 065/360464). **Beaumont** (✉ Grand'Place 10, ☎ 071/588191). **Binche** (✉ Hotel de Ville/Grand'Place, ☎ 064/336727). **Charleroi** (✉ Av. Mascaux 100, Marcinelle, ☎ 071/866152). **Mons** (✉ Grand'Place 22, ☎ 065/335580). **Tournai** (✉ Vieux Marché-aux-Poteries 14, ☎ 069/222045).

7 THE MEUSE AND THE ARDENNES

Rushing streams between steep rocks, high moorland and dense forests, feudal mountaintop castles and hamlets with cottages of rough-hewn stone, Romanesque churches and prosperous fortified farms, rustic inns serving trout from the rivers and wild boar from the woods: this is eastern Wallonia, a rich variety of scenic and historic treasures combined with the pleasures of good food and wine served in atmospheric surroundings.

By Emily Wasserman and Wendy Wasserman

THE MEUSE RIVER VALLEY and the wooded plateau of the Ardennes stretch over Wallonia's three eastern provinces, Namur, Liège, and, to the south, Belgian Luxembourg. The region is a popular travel destination for Belgians and foreign visitors alike; its hilly, even mountainous, terrain is a great draw for nature lovers who enjoy walking, biking, and canoeing.

Natives of the area by and large speak French (though there is a pocket of German-speakers to the east, along the border with Germany). One in three also understands Walloon, a dialect descended from demotic Latin. The linguistic frontier corresponds roughly to the northern boundary of the Roman empire, and "Walas" was the name given to the Romanized Celts of the region. Today, the economy of rust-belt Wallonia has been overtaken by that of high-tech Flanders. The coal mines are a thing of the past, and the steel industry is fighting a tenacious battle to remain competitive. The Walloons are highly conscious of their culture and linguistic heritage and take pride in their separate identity within the framework of the nation.

The Meuse comes rushing into Belgium from France, foaming through narrow ravines. In Dinant it is joined by the Lesse and flows, serene and beautiful, toward Namur, Wallonia's capital city. At Namur comes the confluence with the Sambre, tainted from its exposure to the industries of Charleroi. Here, the river becomes broad and powerful, and gradually the pleasure craft are replaced by an endless procession of tugboats and barges. It passes through Liège, the region's largest city, then up through Holland, where, under a different name, the Maas, it reaches the sea.

From the name of the river is derived the adjective "Mosan," used to describe an indigenous style of metalworking of extraordinary plasticity. It reached its finest flowering during the 12th and 13th centuries with masters such as Renier de Huy, Nicolas de Verdun, and Hugo d'Oignies. They worked with brass, copper, and silver to achieve artistic heights equal to those of the Flemish painters two centuries later.

Liège, the most strongly French-influenced area in Wallonia, is a good jumping-off point for exploration of the Ardennes, a largely wooded region that encompasses the province of Belgian Luxembourg and stretches into the Grand Duchy of Luxembourg to the south. There's a medieval air to the Ardennes; the small towns interspersed among the woods are dominated by centuries-old castles and abbeys and even older Roman ruins. The twisting roads are often a challenge to navigate. Here, as in the Meuse valley and perhaps more so, outdoor activities amid the beautiful scenery are an ever-popular pastime.

To acquire the Wallonia habit, start by leaving the highway, stopping off in a town, or driving around the countryside—and arriving at your final destination a few hours, or a couple of days, late.

Pleasures and Pastimes

Dining

Eating in the Ardennes is one of the most straightforward pleasures Belgium has to offer. The territory is chockablock with atmospheric gray-stone inns. The cuisine is redolent of forest and farm, with ham, sausage, trout, and game to the fore. The region's charcuterie is among the best in central Europe. Ardennes sausage, neat and plump, is made with a blend of veal and pork and is smoked over smoldering oak; its flavor is a wholesome compromise between simple American summer sausage and the milder Italian salamis. The real charcuterie star is *jambon d'Ardennes,* ham that is salt-cured and delicately smoked so that its meat—as succulent as its Parma and Westphalian competitors—slices up thin, moist, and tender, more like a superior roast beef than ham. Restaurants offer generous platters of it, garnished with crisp little gherkins and pickled onions or, if you're lucky, a savory onion marmalade. Trout makes a slightly lighter meal, though once poached in a pool of butter and heaped with toasted almonds, it may be as rich as red-meat alternatives. One pleasant low-fat alternative, though not always available, is *truite au bleu* (blue trout). Plunged freshly killed into a boiling vinegar stock, the trout turns steely blue and retains its delicate flavor.

CATEGORY	COST*
$$$$	over BF3,000/€75
$$$	BF2,000–BF3,000/€50–€75
$$	BF1,000–BF2,000/€25–€50
$	under BF1,000/€25

**per person for a three-course meal, including service, taxes, but not beverages*

Lodging

Hotel rooms in this region tend to be low-priced, even if there's an outstanding restaurant downstairs. They usually fill up on weekends and during high season, June through August. If you prefer to eat somewhere other than in the hotel you've booked, clear it with the management: you're often expected (and sometimes obliged) to eat in their restaurant. Many hotels offer *demi-pension* (half-board) arrangements, as well as "gastronomic weekends," which include two or three lavish meals with two nights' lodging. Also available, and especially popular with families, are a wide variety of farmhouse accommodations and B&Bs.

CATEGORY	COST*
$$$$	over BF7,500/€185
$$$	BF5,500–BF7,500/€135–€185
$$	BF2,500–BF5,500/€60–€135
$	under BF2,500/€60

**for two persons sharing double room, including service and tax*

following the text of a review is your signal that the property has a Web site, where you will find details and, usually, images; for a link, visit www.fodors.com/urls.

The Outdoors

This is one of the great attractions of Wallonia. Hiking on the high moors is an undemanding activity that attracts even the most sedentary. You need to be in somewhat better shape to shoot the rapids in a kayak, but you can pick your river in accordance with skill and the number of watery thrills and spills you think you can handle. Mountain bikes are readily available for hire, and in winter there's generally enough snow for a handful of ski lifts to stay open for a few hopeful weeks. Even from a car, you can discover the real Wallonia along rural routes. You crest a hill, and there's an unexpected vista of miles and miles of woods and lakes and fields; you turn a corner and find yourself in a village where every house has slate walls and roof. You roll down the window and the fresh air is so incredible you have to stop.

Exploring the Meuse and the Ardennes

This part of Belgium is marked by contrasts. The bigger cities of Namur and Liège mix a bit of cosmopolitan bustle with the historical

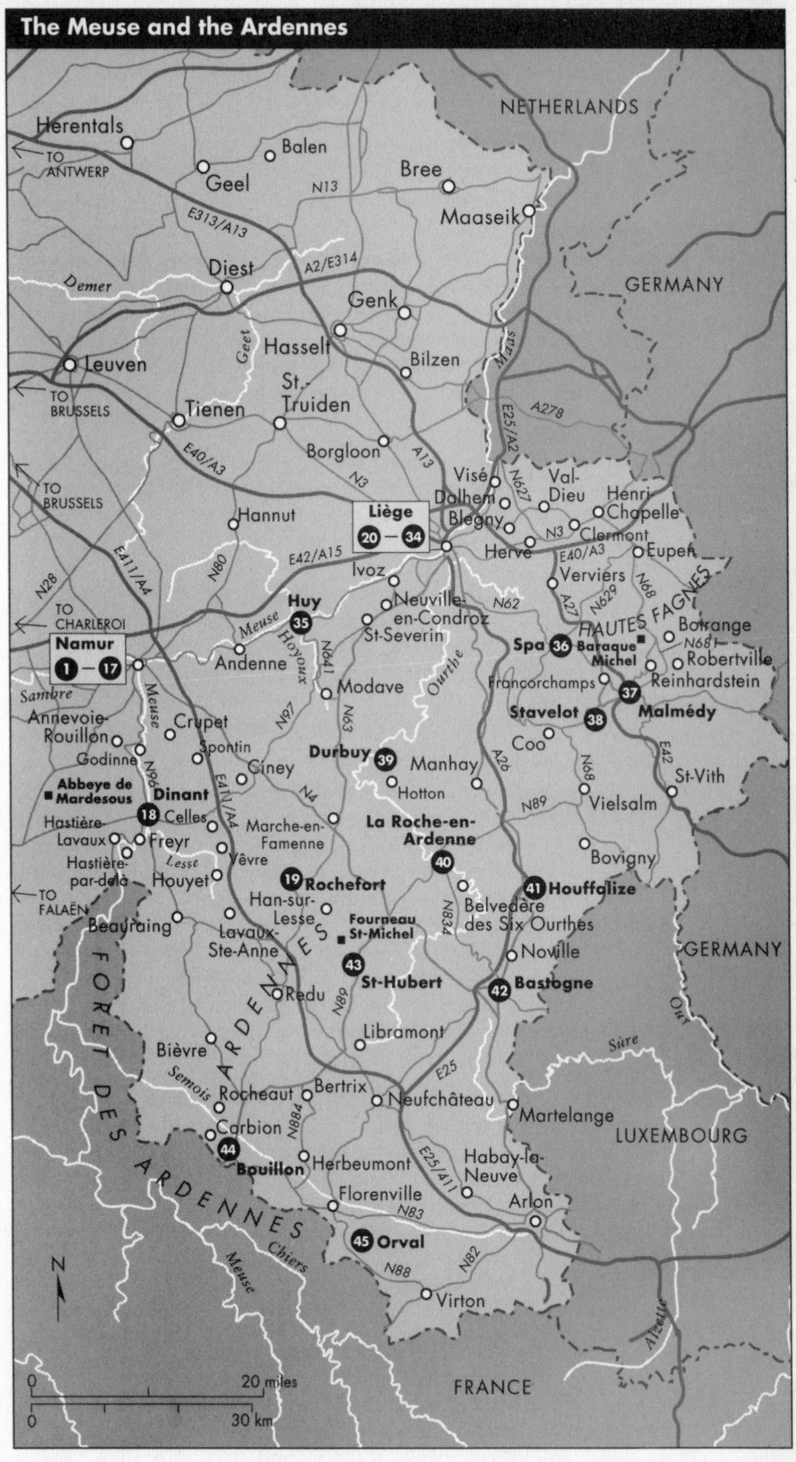
The Meuse and the Ardennes
NETHERLANDS
GERMANY
GERMANY
LUXEMBOURG
FRANCE
Herentals
TO ANTWERP
Balen
Geel
Bree
Maaseik
Diest
Genk
Hasselt
Bilzen
Leuven
TO BRUSSELS
Tienen
St.-Truiden
Borgloon
TO BRUSSELS
Hannut
Liège 20 — 34
Visé
Dalhem
Blegny
Val-Dieu
Henri-Chapelle
Clermont
Herve
Eupen
Verviers
HAUTES FAGNES
Botrange
Ivoz
Huy 35
Neuville-en-Condroz
St-Severin
Spa 36
Baraque Michel
Robertville
Reinhardstein
Francorchamps
37 Malmédy
Stavelot 38
TO CHARLEROI
Namur 1 — 17
Andenne
Modave
Annevoie-Rouillon
Crupet
Spontin
Godinne
Ciney
Durbuy 39
Manhay
Hotton
Coo
St-Vith
Vielsalm
Abbeye de Mardesous
Dinant 18
Celles
Hastière-Lavaux
Freyr
Hastière-par-delà
Vêvre
Houyet
Marche-en-Famenne
La Roche-en-Ardenne 40
Bovigny
TO FALAËN
19 Rochefort
Han-sur-Lesse
Beauraing
Lavaux-Ste-Anne
Fourneau St-Michel
Belvedère des Six Ourthes
41 Houffalize
Noville
43 St-Hubert
42 Bastogne
Redu
Libramont
Bièvre
Rocheaut
Bertrix
Neufchâteau
Martelange
Corbion
44 Bouillon
Herbeumont
Habay-la-Neuve
Florenville
Arlon
45 Orval
Virton
ARDENNES
FORET DES ARDENNES
Demer
Geet
Maas
Meuse
Hoyoux
Ourthe
Sambre
Lesse
Semois
Sûre
Our
Chiers
Alzette
E313/A13
A2/E314
N13
E25/A2
A278
N627
E40/A3
A13
N3
E42/A15
N80
E411/A4
N28
N62
A27
N629
N68
N681
N641
N97
N63
N4
N96
A26
N89
E42
N834
N89
E25
N884
E25/411
N83
N88
N82
N
0 20 miles
0 30 km

appeal of ages-old European towns. In the countryside, major roads lead to tiny hamlets, and rolling hills give way to deep river valleys. There's a lot of territory to cover, and a lot to see and do, whether you're driving along rustic back roads or strolling down city streets.

Great Itineraries

Numbers in the text and in the margin correspond to numbers on the Meuse, Ardennes, Namur, and Liège maps.

IF YOU HAVE 1 DAY

As the regional capital, **Namur** ①–⑰ is the heart of Wallonia. Spend the day meandering through the old city, discovering its charms and treasures—visits to the **Musée Rops** ⑪, the **Musée Groesbeeck de Croix** ⑨, the **Musée Archéologique** ⑫, and the **Eglise St. Aubain** ⑦ are musts. Sunset at the **Citadelle** ⑭–⑰, followed by dinner at L'Essentiel, is a perfect way to end an enchanting day.

IF YOU HAVE 3 DAYS

Spend day one in Namur as described above, and dedicate the morning of the following day to the city as well. Leave Namur heading south toward **Dinant** ⑱, stopping at the **Jardins d'Annevoie**—a horticultural masterpiece—en route. In Dinant you can walk through the quaint town, hike to the fort, or venture out, kayaking along the Meuse or climbing the château ruins in nearby Freyr, taking in the charms of the region as you go. Pick up a *flamiche* or a *croque de Dinant* and stop for a beer at Brasserie du Bocq or the Caracole Brewery. An evening picnic at L'Abbeye de Mardesous is a relaxing way to end the day. The next day, explore the region's famous caves at Grotte de Rochefort and Han-Sur-Lesse near **Rochefort** ⑲.

IF YOU HAVE 7 DAYS

A week will allow you to explore the area's natural beauty and cultural traditions fully. Spend day one in Namur as described above, and devote days two and three to Dinant and Rochefort. Take a long but gorgeous drive to the famous **Abbaye d'Orval** ㊺ and reward yourself with one of its delicious trappist beers or a sample of cheese. Spend the night in or around **Orval**. On day five, meander through the Belgian Ardennes to quaint **La Roche-en-Ardenne** ㊵, where you can lunch on outstanding *jambon d'Ardennes.* **Durbuy** ㊴ is a perfect place to spend the night. Then head back to the city, spending days six and seven in **Liège** ⑳–㉞; try to schedule your visit so that you're there on Sunday for the Batte, the weekly flea market.

When to Tour the Meuse and the Ardennes

The absolutely prime times for touring the Meuse and the Ardennes are April, May, June, September, and October. Note that the Ardennes are very popular with Belgian and Dutch vacationers, especially during the school holiday season.

NAMUR

64 km (38 mi) southeast of Brussels, 61 km (37 mi) southwest of Liège.

In Namur, remnants of the Roman empire stand side by side with the contemporary regional seat of government. The city stands at the confluence of the Meuse and the Sambre rivers, and these strategic waterways neatly divide it into three distinct sections: the partly pedestrian historic center on the banks of the Sambre; the spur of the Citadelle; and the residential Jambes neighborhood across the Meuse. The majority of the city's points of interests lie in the historic center, and the best way to discover them is on foot. However, no visit to Namur is complete without a trip up to the Citadelle. It overlooks Namur's

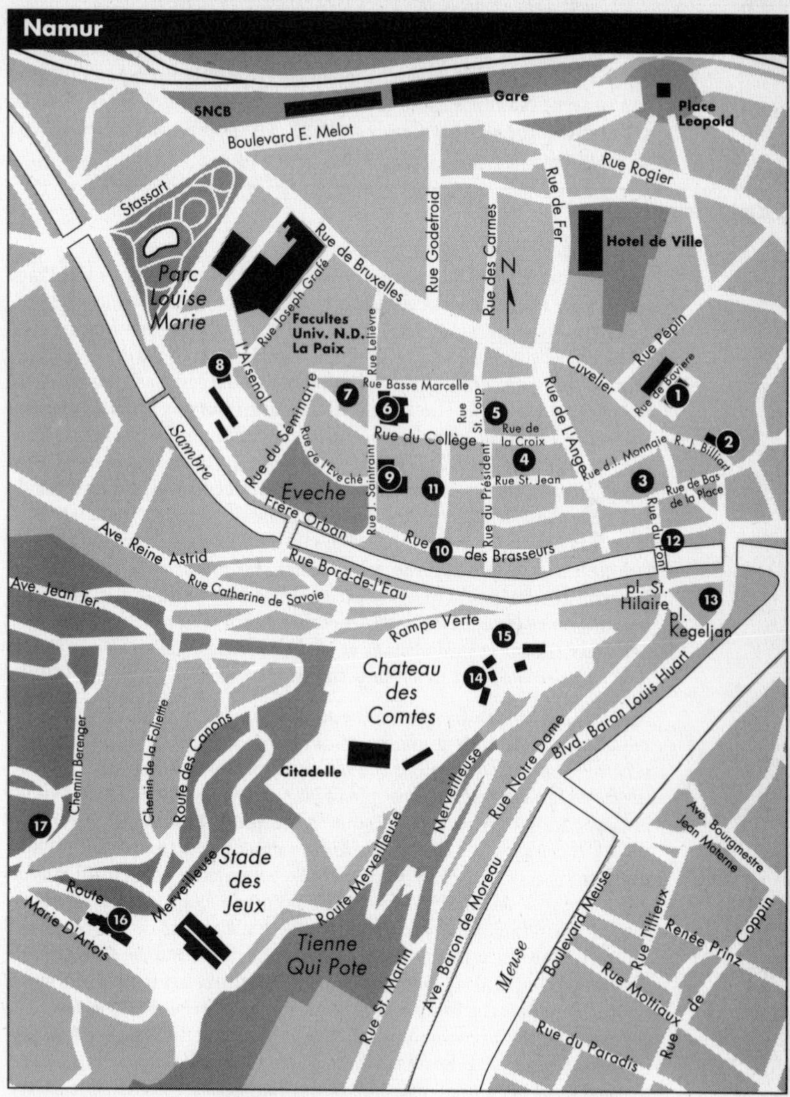

- Count Namur's castle **14**
- Eglise St-Aubain **7**
- Eglise St-Loup **5**
- Institut des Soeurs de Notre-Dame **2**
- L'Arsenal **8**
- Musée Archéologique **12**
- Musée Félicien Rops **11**
- Musée Groesbeeck de Croix **9**
- Musée Parfums Guy Delforge **15**
- Musée Provincial de la Forêt **16**
- Palais Provinçial **6**
- Parc Reine Fabiola **17**
- Place d'Armes **3**
- Place du Marché-aux-Legumes **4**
- Place St-Hilaire **13**
- Rue des Brasseurs . . **10**
- Théâtre Royale de Namur **1**

characteristic 17th-century Mansard rooftops (made from *Pierre de Namur,* a bluish gray stone quarried in the area) and the river valleys beyond. At sunset, the view is magical. From this vantage point you can observe Namur's rapid growth since it was designated the seat of government for all of Wallonia in 1986. The population of 105,000 is now spread among 25 neighboring townships.

Exploring Namur

A Good Walk

Start at the **Théâtre Royale de Namur** ①, which dominates the Place de Théâtre in the heart of the old city. Across the square notice the bust of Nicholas Bosert, a blind 18th-century musician who composed "The Beautiful Bouquet," a Walloon song known to Namur residents of a certain age. Follow rue Julie Billiart to the left past remnants of the original city wall. The street leads to the **Institut des Soeurs de Notre-Dame** ②, which holds what is often referred to as the "seventh treasure of Belgium": the Trésor Hugo d'Oignies, a remarkable collection of religious artifacts from the 12th and 13th centuries. Follow rue de Bas de la Place to the **Place d'Armes** ③, one of Namur's main squares. Rue de la Monnaie, the street of 18th-century money minters, goes across rue de L'Ange, a busy shopping street. From there take rue de la Marché to the city's most popular square, the café-lined **Place du Marché-aux-Légumes** ④, where merchants still sell their produce every Saturday morning in the shadow of the Eglise St. Jean. This is a natural place to stop for lunch or a snack.

Rue St. Loup meanders out of the square toward the **Eglise St-Loup** ⑤, which has been undergoing painstaking renovation for more than 20 years. Pick up rue de Collège and take it to the **Palais Provinçal** ⑥, where the royal family greets the people of Namur. Across the Place St. Aubin is Cathédrale et Musée Diocésoin in the **Eglise St-Aubain** ⑦. Built in the 18th century, it's one of Wallonia's most important churches and holds a relic of the Holy Cross. Duck behind the church on rue de Séminare to **l' Arsenal** ⑧, one of the premiere examples of Sébastien Vauban's architectural prowess. Double back to rue de l'Evêché and on to rue Joseph Saintraint and ring the bell at the **Musée Groesbeeck de Croix** ⑨, an outstanding museum of decorative art from the Namur region. A left on rue Joseph Saintraint will lead to **rue des Brasseurs** ⑩, the heart of the brewing industry in the 18th and 19th centuries. Follow the river to rue Formal where a left turn will lead to the **Musée Félicien Rops** ⑪, a small museum honoring Namur's surrealistic native son. While strolling through these narrow cobblestone streets, look for the animal plaques, once used as address markers, gracing the historic facades. A lion figure, the symbol of Namur, indicates the building was once of city importance. From the Musée Rops, resume walking along the river on the rue des Brasseurs to the rue de Pont. At the base of the bridge is Namur's famous **Musée Archéologique** ⑫, which features some of the archaeological artifacts found throughout the city. To conclude your walk, go over the bridge to **Place St-Hilaire** ⑬. Although at first glance it appears to be a common parking lot and might seem uninteresting, closer inspection reveals an active archaeological dig that continues to yield important historic discoveries. To cap off the day, take a drive up to the **Citadelle** ⑭–⑰ for a grand view of the city.

TIMING

This walk should take four to five hours. Factor in extra time if you plan to linger in any of the museums.

Sights to See

★ ☝ **Citadelle.** Over the past 1,000 years this fortification overlooking Namur has been sieged and occupied more than 20 times. Today you can reach it by the cobblestone, cherry tree–lined Route des Merveilleuse; each curve in the road affords a magnificent view of the city.

One of the complex of buildings that make up the Citadelle is the ruins
14 of the **Count of Namur's castle,** which has been converted into a Namur history museum. Upstairs you'll find a small but amusing exhibit about the area's early history as told through cartoons. Downstairs, the former kitchen has historic artifacts and an exhibit about iron forging (Namur's first industry) where kids can mint their own coins. ⊠ *Rte. Merveilleuse 8,* ☎ *081/22–68–29.* 🎟 *BF240/€5.95.* ⏲ *June–Oct., daily 11–5; Nov.–May, weekends 11–5.*

There are several other decidedly nonmilitary attractions at the Citadelle.
15 The **Musée Parfums Guy Delforge** is in the former officers' mess hall. It's a fragrance factory that allows you to witness the steps of isolating and combining the aromas involved in creating a fine perfume. The shop upstairs exhibits the work of local artists and sells the factory's products. ⊠ *Château de Comtes,* ☎ *081/22–12–19.* 🎟 *BF110/€2.75.* ⏲ *Daily; tours Sat. 3:30 or by prior arrangement.*

16 The **Musée Provincial de la Forêt** (Provincial Forestry Museum), housed in an old hunting lodge, provides an overview of the region's flora and fauna. ⊠ *Rte. Merveilleuse 71,* ☎ *081/74–38–94.* 🎟 *BF50/€1.25.* ⏲ *Apr.–Oct., Sat.–Thurs. 9–noon and 2–5.*

17 The **Parc Reine Fabiola,** on the Citadel grounds, includes a large playground with miniature golf, go-carts, and electric cars. ⊠ *Rond Point Thonar 1,* ☎ *081/73–84–13.* 🎟 *BF100/€2.50.* ⏲ *1st ½ of May and Sept.–mid-Oct., Wed. 1–6, weekends 11–6; mid-May–Aug., Thurs.–Tues. 11–6, Wed. 1–6.*

7 **Eglise St-Aubain.** After floodwaters from the Sambre receded out of Namur in 1751, construction began on this Italian Baroque–style church, made from Belgian marble. Inside, a statue of Notre Dame de la Paix protects the city, and St. Aubain is discreetly represented at the base of the altar, holding his head in his hands. If you're interested in religious relics, take note of the double cross atop the church dome, signifying that a piece of the holy cross is stored on the premises. ⊠ *Place St-Aubain,* ☎ *081/25–10–80.* 🎟 *Free.* ⏲ *Daily 10–5.*

5 **Eglise St-Loup.** Designed by Brother Pierre Huyssens and built in the late 16th century by the Jesuits, this formidable building, now used as a cultural center, is considered part of Wallonia's "Grand Heritage." The marble for the impressive black and red columns was quarried from the Ardennes, and the limestone for the carved ceiling is from Maastricht. The building next door was also built by the Jesuits as a college and is now a state school. ⊠ *Rue du Collège,* ☎ *081/23–07–24.* 🎟 *Free.* ⏲ *Daily 10–5.*

NEED A BREAK? **Café St-Loup** (⊠ Rue de Collège 27), a spacious former auction house, is hidden in a courtyard by the Eglise St. Loup. It's a good spot to pick up a sandwich or light snack.

2 **Institut des Soeurs de Notre-Dame.** Here you'll find the **Trésor Hugo d'Oignies,** a prized collection of crosses, reliquaries, and other religious artifacts made by Brother Hugo d'Oignies for the monastery in nearby Oignies at the beginning of the 13th century. Between the French Revolution and World War II, the collection was protected by the Sisters of Notre Dame. It is considered one of the seven treasures of Belgium.

✉ *R. Billiart 17,* ☎ *081/23–03–42.* 🎫 *BF50/€1.25.* ⏲ *Tues.–Sat. 10–noon and 2–5, Sun. 2–5.*

8 **L'Arsenal.** A long, austere building, the Arsenal has perhaps the prettiest roof in Namur. It's also the best-preserved work of French architect Sébastien Vauban in all of Europe. Originally built under orders from Louis XIV in 1693 as a munitions depot, the building was restored in the early 1980s and now houses a student center for Namur's university. ✉ *Rue de L'Arsenal.*

12 **Musée Archéologique.** Here you'll find Roman and Merovingian antiquities from the Namur region, including a magnificent collection of jewelry from the 1st to the 7th centuries. Some of the artifacts are taken from Namur's archaeological sites and others were found in the Sambre and Meuse rivers. One of the more curious artifacts is a model of the city, fashioned by Louis XV's spies. (The original is at Versailles.) The museum is on the waterfront in the handsome 16th-century Butchers' Hall. ✉ *Rue du Pont,* ☎ *081/23–16–31.* 🎫 *BF80/€2.00.* ⏲ *Tues.–Fri. 10–5, weekends 10:30–5.*

11 **Musée Félicien Rops.** Considered a scandal in his day, Namur native Félicien Rops (1833–1898) is now heralded as an artistic treasure. This museum houses a large collection of his drawings, engravings, and prints, which are by turns surreal, erotic, and whimsical. Although from Namur, Rops spent time in Paris, mingling with the likes of Charles Baudelaire and Stéphane Mallarmé. ✉ *Rue Fumal 12,* ☎ *081/22–01–10.* 🎫 *BF100/€2.50.* ⏲ *Nov.–Easter, Tues.–Sun. 10–5; Easter–June and Sept., Tues.–Sun. 10–6; July–Aug., daily 10–6.*

9 **Musée Groesbeeck de Croix.** Ring the bell to enter this comfortable 18th century house; inside you'll find an extensive collection of Walloon decorative arts. View regional artifacts such as hand-painted Spanish-leather wallpaper, a fine collection of cutlery, an 18th-century handmade parlor board game, and one of the city's first water closets. ✉ *Rue Saintraint 3,* ☎ *081/22–21–39.* 🎫 *BF150/€3.70.* ⏲ *Wed.–Sun. 10–noon and 2–5.*

6 **Palais Provinçal.** This handsome 18th-century manor house was built by Namur's Bishop de Strickland; now the Walloon Parliament meets in what was once the bishop's private chapel. The interior walls of the house are lined with art, including an Italian stucco of the four seasons in the foyer and a Félicien Rops–drawn caricature and a painting by Rops's own teacher, the Flemish-inspired Marinous, in the meeting room. In the receiving room, which was originally the billiard hall, look for the portrait of the handsome man in blue, the bishop himself. ✉ *St-Aubain 2,* ☎ *081/22–70–81,* 🎫 *Free.* ⏲ *Open to groups on request.*

3 **Place d'Armes.** This square has played a part in the economic history of Belgium, for here during the 18th century, when the city was under Austrian rule, the Department of Commerce met and money was minted. It has also felt the brunt of Belgium's position as a European battleground—it was leveled in World War I and again in World War II. The surrounding buildings have been converted into a conference center, and the square itself hosts the annual Christmas Market in early December. Look for the **Beffroi,** a tower that was never a belfry, despite its name. ✉ *Rue de Marchovelette and rue de Monnaie.*

4 **Place du Marché-aux-Légumes.** Originally a Roman graveyard, this is Namur's liveliest square. The statue of an overflowing fruit basket in the middle of the square symbolizes the vendors who have come here for centuries to sell their produce. On Saturday mornings, the tradi-

tion continues. During the annual fall Festival de Wallonie, food, drink, and fun fill the plaza. **Eglise St-Jean,** which fronts the square, was completed in 1890 and took more than 200 years to build. ✉ *Rue St-Jean and rue de President.*

⓭ **Place St-Hilaire.** At the base of the Citadelle (☞ *above*), this spot seems like an unassuming parking lot. In fact it's one of Belgium's most important archaeological sites. In 1992 archaeologists unearthed a corpse dating from 100 BC, and in 2000 a well-preserved body of a 10-year-old boy from the 18th century was found. Peer down into the roped off area of the dig to see remnants of Roman walls, which fuel the theory of many local historians that Julius Caesar himself visited Namur. ✉ *Place St-Hilaire, at base of rue du Pont at rue de Grognon and place Kegeljan.*

❿ **Rue des Brasseurs.** In the 18th and 19th centuries, brewers flocked to this street paralleling the Sambre River for its easy access to water. It quickly became one of Namur's wealthiest strips. Now, old breweries and warehouses have been converted into elegant, fashionable residences.

NEED A BREAK? Relive Namur's brewing legacy at **La Cuvé à Bière** (✉ Rue des Brasseurs 108). This popular tavern is a fine spot to rub elbows with the locals over a game of darts, a quick meal, and a hearty beer.

❶ **Théâtre Royale de Namur.** This regal theater was first built in 1860 and has burned to ground and been rebuilt three times. It was renovated in 1998 to the tune of 500 million Belgian francs and is now home to the Namur Orchestra and Wallonia Orchestra, as well as plays, poetry readings, lectures, and film screenings. To find out what's happening, stop by or look for listings in *La Meuse* or *Vers L'Aenier,* the city's two papers. ✉ *Place du Théâtre,* ☎ *081/22–60–26.*

OFF THE BEATEN PATH **L'ABBEYE DE MARDESOUS** – Take the N92 to Yvoir and go east on N971 to reach this abbey, built in the late 19th century as a cloister for a small order. A school, library, fromagerie, brewery, ceramics studio, and farm were eventually added. Now the sprawling complex dominates the hill, but it remains an idyllic spot for picnics, meditative walks, or evening vespers. In the visitor center you'll find exhibitions about the abbey, a snack bar featuring the abbey's famous beers and cheeses, and a gift shop selling the ceramics and other products that are made by the monks in residence. ✉ *Denee,* ☎ *082/69–82–11.* *Free.* ⏲ *Daily 9–6.*

Dining and Lodging

$$$ ✕ **Biétrumé Picar.** Eating is serious business in this white house in the suburb of Les Plantes, 3 km (2 mi) south of central Namur. (It's difficult to find—call ahead for directions.) Chef Charles Jeandrain focuses his attention on seafood, offering a changing menu that might include oyster soup, salmon wrapped in phyllo, veal ratatouille and crème brûlée made with fresh goat cheese. After your meal, settle in the salon for a cigar or a cognac. ✉ *Tienne Macquet 16, Les Plantes,* ☎ *081/23–07–39. Jacket and tie. AE, DC, MC, V. Closed Mon., 1st wk of Jan., 2 wks late July–early Aug. No dinner Sun.*

$$$ ✕ **Chocolat-Thé.** This restaurant and demonstration room on Namur's main shopping boulevard offers a full menu of dishes made with Galler's artisanal chocolates. The adventurous will be rewarded with surprising and delicious chocolate soup, fish in white chocolate sauce, and foie gras made with wine and dark chocolate. If you prefer your chocolate for dessert, try a praline or a ganache and have the waiter help you pair a coffee or tea with your selection. ✉ *Rue de L'Ange 17,* ☎ *081/22–91–47. MC, V.*

$$$ ★ ✕ **L'Essentiel.** White petals casually strewn over the table settings give you a hint of the artistry and elegance found at this secluded country farmhouse 10 km (6 mi) outside of Namur. It's difficult not to *ooh* and *ahh* as each dish is presented. You could start your meal with Parmesan cheese crème brûlée or white asparagus doppled with caviar, followed by succulent veal with carrots and parsley or a perfectly poached salmon on a bed of shiitake mushrooms. Desserts include a dark chocolate fudge beignet in a ginger-spiced golden biscuit mesh. The surrounding garden is suitably exquisite. ✉ *Rue Roger Clement 32, Temploux,* ☎ *081/56–86–16. Reservations essential. Jacket and tie. AE, MC, V.*

$$$ ★ ✕ **Le Petit Fugue.** Located in an unassuming redbrick house on a quiet street off the Place du Marché-aux-Légumes, this classy restaurant with a delicate musical motif lives up to its name. (In addition to being a musical term, *le petit fugue* also means "the small escape.") The menu, which changes daily, features haute cuisine emphasizing regional ingredients, such as locally caught trout and locally raised lamb; the subtly flavored dishes perfectly match the restaurant's gentle decor. ✉ *Place Chanoine Descamps 5,* ☎ *081/23–13–20. Reservations essential. AE, MC, V.*

$$$ ✕ **La Source Fleurié.** This small, homey restaurant 7 km south of Namur has a glorious garden in the back that sets the atmosphere. You can't go wrong ordering from the tasting menu, which changes daily and might include scampi, barbue (a hearty fish), duck, or crepes. Oddly enough, the wine list features an extensive selection of Austrian wines. ✉ *Avenue General 11, Profondville,* ☎ *081/41–22–28. AE, MC, V.*

$$ ✕ **Brasserie Henry.** Seemingly everyone frequents this spacious, high-ceilinged Namur institution with an extensive menu of well-prepared brasserie fare. Families dig into *moules* (mussels) and *frites* (french fries), young couples dote over escargot and crème brûlée, women sip afternoon tea, and late-night revelers indulge in a fine Belgian beer. ✉ *Pl. St-Aubain 3,* ☎ *081/22–02–04. AE, DC, MC, V.*

$$ ✕ **Le Temps des Cerises.** On a narrow street in old Namur, this cozy, Old Belgium–themed café serves hearty regional food amid cherry red furniture, lace curtains, and lots of antique bric-a-brac. It's a local favorite. ✉ *Rue des Brasseurs 22,* ☎ *081/22–53–26. MC, V. Closed Sun. No lunch Sat.*

$ ★ ✕ **Artisanal Brewery.** The DeBoot family opened this microbrewery across the street from the Namur train station in 1994 and immediately developed a reputation for turning out interesting and unusually flavored beers. (Mustard and apricot-peach are among the regular offerings.) The cozy bar is lined with bottles from some of the specially commissioned beers produced on site. While the beer is the star attraction, the hearty sandwiches and generous fresh salads can't be beat. ✉ *Place de la Station 2,* ☎ *081/23–16–94. No credit cards.*

$–$$$$ ★ ✕🏨 **Les Tanneurs.** This exquisite hotel is the creation of Christian Bouvier, who defied developers prepared to demolish a row of ancient buildings in the heart of Namur. The interiors have been renovated with remarkable taste, using material such as oak and marble, and are decorated with beautiful fabrics and delightful pictures. Each room is different, ranging from simple and inexpensive to a deluxe duplex. There are two restaurants: **L'Espièglerie** ($$$, closed Sun. and mid-July–mid-Aug., no lunch Sat.), serving delicacies such as quail stuffed with sweetbreads and roast duck with figs; and **Grill des Tanneurs** ($), one flight up, which serves a similar menu at a fraction of the cost. ✉ *Rue des Tanneries 13, 5000,* ☎ *081/23–19–99,* FAX *081/26–14–32. 24 rooms. 2 restaurants, bar, sauna. AE, DC, MC, V.*

$$ ✕ Château de Namur. Some of the spacious rooms in this renovated 1930s mansion atop the Citadelle's bluff have balconies and splendid views—both of which more than compensate for the somewhat chilly decor. The restaurant has a handsome brick-vaulted ceiling and a fine French menu. ✉ *Av. de l'Ermitage 1, 5000,* ☎ *081/72–99–00,* FAX *081/72–99–99. 30 rooms. Restaurant, bar, tennis court, convention center. AE, DC, MC, V.*

$$$$ ★ **Villa Gracia.** Proprietors Giselle and Michel Vandenberghen take great pride in their transformation of General Gracia's former mansion on the Meuse into a small, luxurious inn. The immense rococo-style rooms have sitting areas, crystal chandeliers, river views, and enormous marble bathrooms. The beds are lush, right down to the sheets washed in specially softened water. Mornings start on a plant-filled, glass-enclosed terrace overlooking the river, where you're served a breakfast made to order. Right on the bus line to downtown Namur, Villa Gracia is also accessible by car, boat, or helicopter. ✉ *Chaussee de Dinant 1445, B5100, Wépion, 8 km south of Namur,* ☎ *081/41–43–43,* FAX *081/41–12–25. 8 rooms. Meeting rooms, parking. AE, MC, V.*

$$ **Beauregard.** Built into a wing of the Namur Casino, this is a business hotel, with vivid color schemes (lime, salmon, teal) and sleek decor. Rooms with wide views of the river cost slightly more. A breakfast buffet is served in a vast hall overlooking the river. ✉ *Av. Baron de Moreau 1, 5000,* ☎ *081/23–00–28,* FAX *081/24–12–09. 47 rooms. Restaurant, bar, breakfast room, casino. AE, DC, MC, V.*

$$ **Novotel.** This French chain hotel is on the river before you reach Namur coming from Dinant, in the heart of the strawberry-growing region. Worldwide standardization makes rooms, public areas, and restaurant rather impersonal. Still, riverside walks start at the door, and the staff will make all sorts of excursion arrangements. ✉ *Chaussée de Dinant 1149, 5001 Wepion-Namur,* ☎ *081/46–08–11,* FAX *081/46–19–90. 110 rooms. Restaurant, bar, 2 pools, sauna, health club, meeting rooms. AE, DC, MC, V.*

$ **Grande Hôtel de Flandre.** Namur's oldest hotel has been in business for nearly a century, and its grand entrance celebrates its Victorian heritage. Although the spare but adequate rooms could use some renovation, the location (directly across from the train station) puts you in the heart of the city. Rooms in the back tend to be quieter. ✉ *Place de la Station 14, 5000,* ☎ *081/23–18–68,* FAX *081/22-80-60. 30 rooms. MC, V.*

Shopping

The heart of Namur's shopping district is along rue de l'Ange and rue de Fer, which are lined with clothing boutiques, music stores, and other shops catering to a predominantly student crowd. To pick up a gift unique to the Walloon region, head to **La Cave de Wallonie** (✉ Rue de la Halle 6, ☎ 081/22–06–83, closed Mon. morning, Sun.). The small store's shelves are lined with Wallonian food products such as patés, sausages, jams, honey, and liqueurs. Miraculously, there are more than 300 Belgian beers in stock, along with stemware from each of the breweries.

En Route Between Namur and Dinant, the **Château et Jardins d'Annevoie** (Chateau and Gardens of Annevoie) present a happy blend of 18th-century French landscaping and romantic Italian garden design, remarkable for its use of natural waterfalls, fountains, and ponds to animate the gardens with their flower beds, lawns, statues, and grottoes. The water displays function without mechanical aids and have remained in working order for more than two centuries. The château blends perfectly with the gardens; the furniture, paneling, and family portraits all contribute to an ambience of elegant refinement. ✉ *Rte. des Jardins 47,* ☎ *082/61–15–55.* 💳 *BF180/€4.45.* ⏲ *Apr.–Oct., daily 9:30–6:30.*

NAMUR PROVINCE

Roman legions commanded by Julius Caesar marched up the Meuse valley through present-day Namur Province 2,000 years ago and made it one of the principal routes to Cologne. Later, it served a similar purpose for Charlemagne, linking his Frankish and German lands. Little wonder that massive forts were built on the rocks dominating the invasion routes. Even so, the French came through here under Louis XIV and again under Napoléon. The Dutch, who ruled here for little more than a decade after Waterloo, expanded these fortifications. A century later, the Germans broke through here, pushing west and south in World Wars I and II.

This martial past seems altogether out of proportion to the pleasant, peaceful Meuse valley of the present day. South of the city of Namur, the Meuse meanders through the rolling countryside to lovely Dinant, a perfect base for exploring the region by foot, boat, or bicycle. Farther south still, Rochefort and neighboring Han-Sur-Lesse are known for their magical caves. Throughout the province you'll find castles, gardens, abbeys, churches, and charming towns, all of which will reward your attention.

Dinant

18 *29 km (17 mi) south of Namur, 93 km (56 mi) southeast of Brussels, 80 km (48 mi) southwest of Liège.*

Simultaneously hanging off and tucked under spectacular cliffs on the Meuse, Dinant's dramatic setting has been the stage for a turbulent history. The town has been attacked over 200 times in the course of eight centuries. A few of the more notable assaults include when Charles the Bold sacked the town in 1466 and threw 600 men, tied in pairs, into the river; when Henri II took the town in 1554; when Louis XIV stormed through in 1675, and again 17 years later; and most recently when the Germans burned Dinant in World War I and then returned twice during World War II.

The **Rocher Bayard** rock formation on the southern edge of town aptly illustrates how Dinant's natural wonders are linked to its military and folkloric past. Legend has it that the rock got its distinctive needle's-eye-shaped hole when a steed named Bayard—the property of the four Aymon brothers, Charlemagne's foes—split it with his hoof. Allegedly Louis XIV's troops widened the passage when they invaded the city.

Dinant also has a rich industrial past. Between the 12th and 15th centuries, copper production, known as *dinanderie,* boomed. Eventually the metal-working industry gave way to mining and textiles, which governed the local economy up until the beginning of the 20th century. Now Dinant (population 12,500) caterers to the tourists who flock here to discover the city's historic ruins, natural beauty, and culinary pleasures. Music lovers, especially those who fancy jazz, have an additional reason to visit Dinant. Its most famous son is Adolphe Sax, inventor of the saxophone. Belgium honors Sax by using his image on the 200-franc note.

The **Citadelle** is located at the cliff-top, towering directly over the Dinant's city center. You can reach it by cable car or by climbing the 400 steps that were cut into the rock face in the 16th century. The fortress is not as old as you might suspect—the ancient fortification was razed in 1818 by the Dutch, who replaced it with the current structure before being ousted. The view is splendid, and there is an arms museum, where cannon and cannonballs add to the military atmosphere. The **Dinanderie Museum,** also in the Citadelle, has a unique collection of weather vanes and all manner of household utensils, products of the town's metalworking past. ✉ *Le Prieuré 25,* ☎ *082/22–36–70.* 🎫 *BF195/€4.85, including cable car.* ⏲ *Apr.–Oct., daily 10–6; Nov.–Mar., daily 10–4:30.*

The dominant structure in the town of Dinant is the Gothic **Church of Foy Notre-Dame.** It dates from the 13th century; its distinctive blue onion-dome tower was a 17th-century addition. Legend has it that a woodcutter found a statue of the virgin in a nearby tree trunk, and the church has been a pilgrim site ever since. ✉ *Rue du Village 4,* ☎ *082/22–23–35.* 🎫 *Free.* ⏲ *Daily 10–6.*

NEED A BREAK? Dinant's downtown streets along the river are lined with attractive cafés. **Patisserie Laurent** (✉ Grand rue 72) is one of the best places to treat yourself to a *flamiche,* a rich egg and cheese tart that's a local specialty. Try to get one that's hot out of the oven.

Within striking distance of downtown are two cave attractions worth exploring. **Mont-Fat,** 400 ft above Dinant, offers the combination of a guided tour of prehistoric caves and a chairlift ride to an amusement area. ✉ *R. en Rhée 15,* ☎ *082/22–27–83.* 🎫 *BF160/€3.95.* ⏲ *Apr.–Aug., daily 10:30–7; Sept.–Nov. 18, weekends 11–6.*

La Merveilleuse, a cave whose many stalactites are remarkably white, is on Dinant's left bank, about 490 yards from the bridge, on the road toward Philippeville. A visit takes about 50 minutes. ✉ *Rte. de Philippeville 142,* ☎ *082/22–22–10.* 🎫 *BF180/€4.45.* ⏲ *Mar.–May and Sept.–Nov., daily 11–5; June–Aug., daily 10–6.*

If you're interested in Belgium's much-touted beer, you'll find two breweries in the vicinity of Dinant that merit a visit. The Belot family has been brewing at **Brasserie du Bocq** since 1858. Take the informative tour and then visit the small village next door. ✉ *Rue de la Brasserie 4, Purnode,* ☎ *082/61–07–90.* 🎫 *BF120/€2.95.* ⏲ *July–Aug., tours at 2, 4; Sept.–June, tour at 1.*

Brasserie Caracole, in an old mill 7 km south of Dinant, heats its beer in a traditional wood stove and spices it with surprising flavors such as orange peel and coriander. Its signature snail mascot is a whimsical allusion to Namur province's reputation for being slow-paced. Even if you don't drink, the distinctive cavernous tasting room lined with old brewing equipment is worth a visit. ✉ *Cote Marie Thérèse 86, Falmignoul,* ☎ *083/74–40–80.* 🎫 *BF150/€3.70.* ⏲ *July–Aug., tours daily at 2, 3, 4, 5.*

The drive south of Dinant is filled with stunning views from the road of towering rock formations across the river. The town of **Freyr,** on the left bank, is considered the best rock-climbing center in Wallonia. The **Château de Freyr** is an impressive Renaissance building with beautiful interiors decorated with 17th-century woodwork and furniture, including a restored children's coach. Louis XIV visited here during the siege of Dinant in 1675. Its park has been laid out in accordance with the design principles of Le Nôtre, the French landscape architect. ✉ *Domaine de Freyr, Waulsort,* ☎ *082/22–22–00.* 🎫 *BF220/€5.45.* ⏲ *July–Aug., weekends, and holidays 2–6.*

Dining and Lodging

$$$ ✕ **Le Jardin de Fiorine.** The unassuming gray facade belies the elegant interior and pretty garden of this ambitious restaurant. Specialties include lobster and sweetbread salad, sweetbreads with asparagus, fillet of sole with apple and truffle, and roast pigeon with corn cakes. ✉ *Rue Georges Cousot 3,* ☎ *082/22–74–74. AE, DC, MC, V. Closed Wed., 2 wks Feb. and 2 wks July. No dinner Sun.*

$$$ ✕ **Le Vivier d'Oies.** This country inn is in a lovely stone farmhouse with a modern stone-and-glass wing. The ambience is urbane, and the cuisine above reproach: goose liver sautéed with caramelized pears, crayfish with artichoke hearts, and a spring asparagus menu. ✉ *Rue Etat 7, Dorinne, northeast of Dinant, about 3 km (2 mi) east of Yvoir,* ☎ *083/69–95–71. AE, DC, MC, V. Closed Wed., 2 wks June–July, 2 wks Sept.–Oct. No dinner Tues.*

$$ ✕ **Centre Mason.** This grand mansion overlooking the Meuse is now a cooking school where the next generation of Belgian chefs learns the art of fine cuisine. The traditional French food and formal service are of a high standard. Though the dining room is rather plain, it has a beautiful view of the river. ✉ *Ave. Winston Churchill 36,* ☎ *082/21–30–53. Reservations essential. AE, MC, V. Closed weekends. No dinner.*

$$ ✕ **Chez Leon.** Trimmed in yellow, this brightly lit local favorite is part of the Belgian chain famous for its large portions of moules and frites. The kitchen is open late, and its location in the heart of town makes it a convenient place for a quick and satisfying meal. ✉ *Place Astrod 15,* ☎ *082/21–90–40. AE, DC, MC, V.*

$$$ ✕🏨 **Les Cretiás.** The glorious garden and tremendous valley views more than compensate for the smallish rooms, narrow hallways, and somewhat dusty decor of this homestyle inn in the tiny village of Falmignoul. The restaurant serves well-respected traditional French cuisine. Try the risotto St. Jacques with lobster butter, or tongue in phyllo served with mushrooms. The tasting, seasonal, and daily menus also feature an extensive cheese selection. ✉ *Rue des Cretiás 99, 5500 Falmignoul, 7 km (4 mi) south of Dinant,* ☎ *082/74–42–11,* FAX *082/74–40–56. 11 rooms. AE, MC, V. Closed Jan., restaurant closed Mon., Tues.*

$$$ ★ ✕🏨 **Moulin de Lisogne.** The husband-and-wife team of Alan Blondiaux and Martine Legrain have created a sensualist's dream at their romantic inn. The restaurant features goose, veal, and beef raised on the premises, vegetables from the garden, bread baked by M. Blondiaux in the skylighted bakery off the enormous kitchen, and wine from his own vineyard in France. Mme. Legrain has decorated the lodgings with equally elegant flair. Ask to stay in the Tower, which has beautiful oak furniture and an oversize tub sunken into the pale pink marble bathroom. M. Blondiaux doubles as the head of Dinant's tourist office and can help with any questions about the area. ✉ *Rue de la Lisonette, B5501 Lisogne, 7 km (4 mi) northeast of Dinant,* ☎ *082/22–63–80,* FAX *082/22–21–47. 10 rooms. Restaurant. AE, MC, V. Closed mid-Dec.–mid-Feb., restaurant closed Sun., Mon.*

$$ 🏨 **Hôtel de la Couronne.** Seemingly built into the Citadelle's cliffs, this no-frills hotel couldn't be more centrally located. It's been in the same family for four generations and offers many lodging options. Some rooms have bunk beds, some have three beds, some have views, and some have connecting suites. The restaurant serves local fare and there's a lively local bar scene well into the night. ✉ *Rue De Sax 1, 5500,* ☎ *082/22–27–31,* FAX *082/22–70–31. 22 rooms, some with bath. Restaurant. MC, V.*

Outdoor Activities and Sports

Dinant offers opportunities for all sorts of sports enthusiasts. Kayaking or boating on the Meuse is a great way to learn the landscape. Kayaks can be rented from **Les Kayaks Bleus** (✉ Place d'Eglise 2, Anseremme, ☎ 082/22–43–97) or **Ansiaux Kayaks** (✉ Rue du Velodrome 15, ☎ 082/22–23–25). Boats are run by **Bateaux Bayard** (✉ Route de Phillipville, ☎ 082/22–22–10) and **Compaigne des Bateaux** (✉ Rue Daoust 64, ☎ 082/22–23–15). Rail bikes, which run along abandoned railroad tracks in the picturesque valley of Molignee between Falaën and Mardesous, are great fun. Contact **Les Draisines de la Molignee** (✉ Rue de la Gare 82, Falaën, ☎ 082/69–90–79) for information.

En Route **Celles,** southeast of Dinant on N94, is one of the most beautiful villages in Wallonia. Stop in at **Ardennes** for a regional lunch featuring local *jambon d'Ardennes.* (Take a peek in the kitchen, where the hams hang from the ceiling.) After lunch, visit the **Church of St. Hadelin,** a charming spot in this tiny town.

Rochefort

19 *35 km (22 mi) southwest of Dinant, 128 km (79 mi) southwest of Brussels, 55 km (34 mi) southeast of Liège.*

In the 12th century, the Count of Rochefort had the most important feudal estate in the province of Liège. Today, Rochefort is a quiet tourist town sitting on the border of the Namur and Luxembourg provinces. The name Rochefort means "strong rock" and comes from the prominent rock castle, the Château Comtal, that dominats the town center. It's known for its Trappist Rochefort cheese and beer. The town itself has a number of interesting sights, and there are several more in its vicinity, most notably the Grottes de Han (☞ *see below*). The **Rochefort tourist office** (✉ Rue de Behogne 5, ☎ 084/21–25–37) has developed a series of walking tours intended to illustrate town's motto: "On the tracks of a land born from the union of water, earth, and mankind." The office also sells reduced-price package tickets to the region's archaeological sites and caves.

While in Rochefort, be sure to visit the little **Chappelle de Lorette.** Josine de la March, Countess of Rochefort, built the chapel in 1620 in hopes that it would hasten the return of her son—who, so the story goes, had been kidnapped by a monkey, and was returned upon the chapel's completion.

The **Grotte de Rochefort** sits in the center of town. Carved by the Lomme River, the cave maintains a constantly warm temperature. The most remarkable of its many halls is the *Salle de Sabat* (Hall of the Witches' Sabbath), which is more than 250 feet high. ✉ *Dreve de Lorette,* ☎ *084/21–20–80.* 💶 *BF220/€5.45.* ⏲ *Apr.–Nov., daily 10–5.*

Come for the majestic view and explore ruins dating from the 11th through the 19th centuries at the **Château Comtal** (Castle of the Counts), situated on a rise overlooking Rochefort's town center. There is also an active archaeological dig and a small archaeological museum on site. ✉ *Rue Jacquet,* ☎ *084/21–44–09.* 💶 *BF60/€1.50.* ⏲ *Apr., weekends 10–5; May–Sept., daily 10–5.*

Built to incorporate the ruins of a Gallo-Roman villa, the 1,240-acre **Malagne Archeo-Park** has nature trails, regional exhibits, historical reenactments, and an abundance of events specifically for kids. Call ahead for a schedule of events. ✉ *Malagne le Gallo-Romaine,* ☎ *084/22–21–03.* 💶 *BF150/€3.70.* ⏲ *Easter–Oct., daily 10–5.*

★ The magnificent **Grottes de Han** (Han Caves), which had provided refuge for threatened tribes since neolithic times, were rediscovered in the mid-

Close-Up

WHAT IS A TRAPPIST BEER?

IN 1664, Armand-Jean Le Bouthillier, a Benedictine monk on a mission to restore silence, seclusion, and manual labor to the monastic life, found the Abbot of La Trappe monastery in Normandy. This monastery became known as *Trappist* rather than by its full name of "Order of the Reformed Cistercians of Strict Observance." The French Revolution uprooted these monks and forced them into a period of nomadism, with some eventually settling in Belgium. Today Belgium has 12 Trappist monasteries, five of which brew beer: Rochefort in Namur, Orval in Luxembourg, Chimay in Hainaut, Westvleteren in West Flanders, and Westmalle near Antwerp. The *Trappiste* appellation refers exclusively to beers made, following the strictest of Benedictine principles, at these monasteries. Although Trappiste beers may be characterized as yeasty, sweet, fruity, and strong, each of the five monasteries brews a unique product.

St. Arnold, an 11th-century monk and founder of the Abbey of Oudenburg in Brugge (now called the Abbey of Steenbrugge), is Belgium's patron saint of brewing. Legend has it that, during a plague, St. Arnold dipped his crucifix into a brew kettle and encouraged the people to drink boiled beer rather than the contaminated water. Belgium's brewers now pay homage to St. Arnold at an annual church service in Brussels. The Trappist monastery in Rochefort (which is unfortunately not open to the public) has mounted over its brew house a plaque of St. Arnold holding a meshing fork.

19th century. To tour them, board an ancient tram in the center of Han-Sur-Less that carries you to the mouth of the caves. There multilingual guides take over, leading groups on foot through 3 km (2 mi) of dimly lighted chambers. You get occasional glimpses of the underground river Lesse as you pass giant stalagmites and eventually enter the vast cavern called the Dome, 475 ft high, where a single torchbearer dramatically descends the sloping cave wall. The final part of the journey is by boat on the underground river. The trip takes about 90 minutes. ✉ *Rue J.-Lamotte 2, Hans-Sur-Lesse, 6 km (4 mi) southeast of Rochefort,* ☎ *084/37–72–13.* *BF350/€8.70.* ⏲ *Apr. and Sept.–Nov., daily 10–4:30, May–June until 5, July–Aug. until 6.*

The **Réserve d'Animaux Sauvages,** located within the domain of Han, is a 625-acre wildlife reserve filled with animals native to the region, such as wild boars, brown bears, bison, wolves, and lynx. A coach takes you through the park, where you can observe the animals in their natural habitat. The trip takes an hour and 15 minutes. ✉ *Rue J.-Lamotte 2, Hans-Sur-Lesse, 6 km (4 mi) southeast of Rochefort,* ☎ *084/37–72–12.* *BF250/€6.20.* ⏲ *Mar., daily 11:30–1; Apr. and Sept.–Nov., daily 10–4:30; May–June, daily 10–5; July–Aug., daily 10–6.*

Chevetogne Park, 10 km (6 mi) northeast of Rochefort, has glorious gardens, a pool, tennis courts, horseback riding, paddleboats, and miniature golf. In the summer, there are weekend afternoon jazz and classical concerts. ✉ *Chevetogne, 10 km (6 mi) northeast of Rochefort,* ☎ *083/68–72–11.* *BF200/€4.95.* ⏲ *Park: daily; gardens: summer only.*

Dining and Lodging

$$$$ ★ ✕🏨 **Château de Lavaux-Ste-Anne.** The owner decided to plant an herb garden in the courtyard and then proceeded to open a restaurant in this glorious castle. It rapidly became a great success, as the chef progressed from self-taught amateur to virtuoso. The stripped-down decor is offset by a vast hunting painting, and *la patronne* handles the service as if to the manner born. Try rabbit consommé with truffles, pike perch cooked in sauerkraut and wild juniper, or veal kidney in wine served with lamb's lettuce. The smallish rooms (**$$**) are in an annex called Maison Lemonier. ✉ *Rue de château 10, B5580 Lavaux-Ste-Anne, 12 km (7 mi) southwest of Rochefort,* ☎ *084/38–88–83 restaurant, 084/38–72–17 hotel,* FAX *084/38–88–95 restaurant, 084/38–72–20 hotel. 8 rooms. Restaurant, horseback riding. AE, DC, MC, V. Hotel and restaurant closed Mon.–Tues., mid-Dec.–mid-Jan., 1 wk May–June, 1 wk Aug.–Sept.*

$$ 🏨 **La Malle Poste.** This 16th-century building has served as a post office and a Freemason hall. (Note the Freemason emblems on the fireplace and the ceiling in the sitting room.) Conveniently situated in the heart of town, the hotel's current claim to fame is as home base for the American arm-wrestling team, which comes to Rochefort each summer for an international competition. The rooms are cozy, many with exposed beams, stone arches, and garden views. The attached piano bar has live music on weekends and a large selection of Belgian ales. ✉ *Rue de Behogne 46, B5580,* ☎ *084/21–42–73,* FAX *084/22–11–63. 12 rooms. Piano bar. MC, V. Closed Jan.–Mar.*

LIÈGE

61 km (37 mi) northeast of Namur, 97 km (58 mi) east of Brussels, 122 km (73 mi) southwest of Cologne.

The bustling city of Liège—Luik to the Flemish and Dutch, Lüttich to the Germans—sits deep in the Meuse valley at the confluence of the Meuse and Ourthe rivers. After Belgian independence in 1830, Liège was a leader in a countrywide upsurge of industrial activity, and that, for good and bad, has marked its character ever since. The first European locomotive was built in Liège, and the Bessemer steel production method was developed here; it is to the burning furnaces that Liège owes its nickname, *la cité ardente* (the Fiery City). The surrounding hills and rivers were rich in minerals, including potassium, calcium, iron, and sand, and these resources were heavily mined. Drawing on a centuries-old tradition of weapons manufacturing, the Fabrique Nationale started to build precision firearms, and Val St-Lambert began to produce glassware that has gained wide renown. Liège's port, one of the biggest inland waterways in Europe, was busy with barges and other commercial vessels. In August 1914 the forts of Liège kept the German invasion force at bay long enough for the Belgian and French troops to regroup; in 1944–1945, more than a thousand V1 and V2 missiles exploded in the city.

Liège's outskirts are still lined with industrial facilities—some operational, some (notably **Val St-Lambert** and **Blegny**) transformed into innovative museums, and others closed. Although the views may not be beautiful, you shouldn't let this deter you from giving Liège its due. A soot-covered old building may house a historic treasure, a delicious meal, or a glorious flower shop. (Liège has a plethora of talented florists whose windows brighten up the city streets.) An inconspicuous cobblestone alley could be home to busy cafés and architectural gems.

The Liègeois have a reputation for friendliness and are clearly proud of their city. Blue and white plaques are visible on the portals of the many buildings that have been designated Wallonian heritage sights. Walloon can still be heard on the streets and is taught at the local university, where students have been known to say, *"Po brêre on èst chal, po bêure!"* (We are not here to complain, we are here to drink!) Tchantchès, Liège's beloved puppet with his red nose and indefatigable attitude, is the town mascot. Pèkèt, a regional liquor made from juniper berries, is plentiful. And, every Sunday morning, as has happened for centuries, the quai is transformed into **La Batte,** one of Europe's biggest weekly street markets.

In addition to its own merits, Liège is a good urban base from which to explore forests, parks, and other pleasures that lie to its south.

Exploring Liège

The city is roughly divided into three sections. **Le Carré,** bordered by rue de l'Université and boulevard de la Sauvenière, is the city's commercial district. It was originally a small island surrounded by river-fed canals, but the canals were dredged and filled in the 19th century to accommodate street traffic. Now these same streets, some which are limited to pedestrians only and lined with cafés and boutiques, pulsate with shoppers, workers, and tourists. The **Coeur Historique** is chock-full of museums, churches, and cobblestone streets, testament to Liège's rich history. This neighborhood is also being reclaimed as a desirable residential area, with many of the old homes being gentrified. The new development may eventually push out the red-light district that is still operational in a few of the smaller alleys off the quai. **Outremeuse,** across the river, is up and coming. Mostly quiet, it has a few streets lined with ethnic restaurants, bars, and Liège's own unique *cafés chantant* (singing cafés). More establishments are opening regularly. This neighborhood is home to Liège's two most famous sons: Georges Simenon (the writer) and Tchantchès (the puppet).

A Good Walk

This walk will take you through the Coeur Historique and Le Carré, two of Liège's three major neighborhoods.

To get yourself oriented and armed with the latest information, you may want to stop by the Tourist Office at rue St-Georges and Féronstrée, the old ironworkers' street that's now the spine of the Coeur Historique. Take a left on rue St-Georges past the Ilôt St-Georges to the **Musée de l'Art Wallon** ⑳, which showcases centuries of Wallonian artists. Head left onto Sur les Foulons, one of the oldest streets in Liège. Lined with original 16th- and 17th-century houses, the street also boasts a two-tiered 18th-century fountain which provided fresh water to the city's animals and people. Follow rue Hongrée to the quai and go left toward the **Musée d'Armes** ㉑. Farther down the quai is a courtyard leading to the **Musée Curtius** ㉒. Retrace your steps back to Féronstrée and stop at the **Musée d'Ansembourg** ㉓, a decorative arts museum. One block farther down Féronstrée leads to the **Eglise St-Barthélemy** ㉔, a glorious 11th-century cathedral. In the square outside the church the 1992 metal sculpture *Les Principautres* by local artist Mary Andrien playfully celebrates Liège's religious and industrial history. Follow rue des Brasseurs, which at one point was the hub for 32 brewing cooperatives, and cut through to the **Cour St-Antoine** ㉕, a clever example of urban renewal. Leave the square via rue Hors-Château, once Liège's wealthiest corridor, and duck into the **Impasses** ㉖ that angle off of it. Wander back onto rue Hors-Château to the steep steps of **Montagne de Bueren** ㉗. Around the corner is the **Musée d'Art Religieux et d'Art Mosan** ㉘. A nearby cul-de-sac leads to the informative **Musée de la Vie Wallonne** ㉙. Across the rue des Mineurs is the bustling **Place du**

Liège

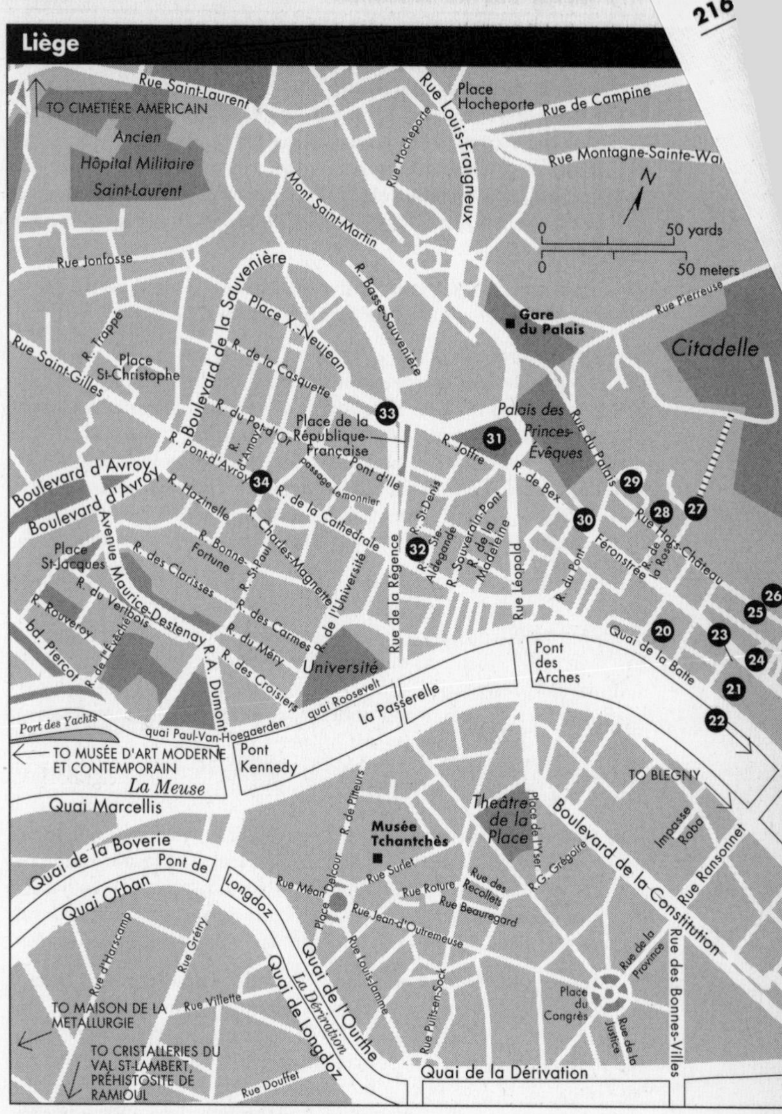

Cour St-Antoine . . . **25**
Eglise St-Barthélemy **24**
Eglise St-Denis . . . **32**
Impasses **26**
Montagne de Bueren **27**
Musée Curtius **22**
Musée d'Ansembourg **23**
Musée d'Armes . . . **21**
Musée d'Art Religieux et d'Art Mosan **28**
Musée l'Art Wallon **20**
Musée de la Vie Wallonne **29**
Place de la Cathédrale **34**
Place du Marché **30**
Place St-Lambert . . . **31**
Theâtre Royal **33**

Marché ㉚. West of that, rue de Bex will lead straight to the **Place St-Lambert** ㉛, the heart of the city. Go south on the pedestrian-only rue Gérardrie to the **Eglise St-Denis** ㉜. Rue de la Régence will lead to the **Théâtre Royal** ㉝, the regal opera house. Head back down rue de l'Université and through Lemmonier, the oldest shopping arcade in Belgium, where you can find everything from soaps to shoes. Finish your day at the **Place de la Cathédrale** ㉞. The gothic Cathédrale St-Paul stands tall over the busy square, which buzzes with cafés and street musicians.

TIMING

The walk itself takes about 90 minutes, but with visits to the museums and shops, plus a stop for lunch, you can fill a day.

Sights to See

Cimetière Américain des Ardennes. This is the final resting place for 5,327 soldiers of the U.S. First Army who fell in the Ardennes, at the Siegfried Line and around Aachen. The memorial, decorated with an immense American eagle, contains a nondenominational chapel. Ceremonies are held here on American Memorial Day in late May. ✉ *Rte. du Condroz 164, Neuville-en-Condroz, southwest of Liège,* ☎ *04/371–4287.* 🎫 *Free.* ⏲ *Apr.–Oct., daily 9–6; Nov.–Mar., daily 9–5.*

Complexe Touristique de Blegny. The highlight of a visit to this complex east of Liège is a trip down the former Blegny Coal Mine, which produced 1,000 tons of coal a day at its peak. The wealth of Liège was based on coal, which was mined from the Middle Ages until 1980. An audiovisual presentation illustrates this history, and former miners lead tours of the surface and underground facilities. A complete visit takes 3½ hours. ✉ *Rue Lambert Marlet 23, Blegny,* ☎ *04/387–4333.* 🎫 *BF290/€7.20.* ⏲ *Early Apr.–mid-Sept., daily 10–4:30; Mar. and mid-Sept.–Nov., weekends 10–4:30.*

25 **Cour St-Antoine.** What was formerly a slum is now a beautifully renovated residential square with a small village feel. The facade of the red house at the north end of the square resembles a church and is connected by a small channel to a pyramid-like structure replicating Tikal, a Mayan ruin in Guatemala. ✉ *Between rue des Brasseurs and rue Hors-Château.*

★ **Cristalleries du Val St-Lambert.** In 1826 the Val St-Lambert factory opened in a renovated 13th-century abbey at Seraing, on the Muese south of Liège, and began producing crystal that became the pride of Belgium and the subject of worldwide acclaim. Eventually production was cut back; now what was once a humming factory is a museum that explores the history of glass manufacturing through clever interactive exhibits and glass-blowing demonstrations. Val St-Lambert crystal is available at the gift shop, which can also mend broken pieces you've brought from home or custom-etch your new treasure. ✉ *Rue du Val 245, Seraing,* ☎ *04/337–0960.* 🎫 *BF200/€4.95.* ⏲ *Tues.–Sun. 9–5.*

★ 24 **Eglise St-Barthélemy.** This church contains Liège's greatest treasure and one of the Seven Religious Wonders of Belgium: the Baptismal Font of Renier de Huy, which dates from between 1107 and 1118. The brass masterpiece of Art Mosan, weighing half a ton, is decorated in high relief with figures of the five biblical baptismal scenes. They're depicted with an extraordinary suppleness, and the font rests on 10 oxen, which are also varied and interesting. During the French Revolution the font was hidden by the faithful, but the cover has disappeared. The church, consecrated in 1015, is one of the rare Romanesque churches to escape transformation into the Gothic style, retaining its austerity. The nave, however, has been retouched in baroque fashion. ✉ *Pl. St-Barthélemy,* ☎ *04/223–4998.* 🎫 *BF80/€2.00.* ⏲ *Mon.–Sat. 10–noon and 2–5 except during services, Sun. 2–5.*

32 **Eglise St-Denis.** This is one of the oldest churches in Liège; its outer walls once formed part of the city's defenses. It has a handsome reredos portraying the suffering of Christ. ✉ *Place St-Denis, rue de la Cathédrale,* ☎ *04/223–5756.* ⏲ *Mon.–Sat. 9–noon and 1:30–5, Sun. 9 AM–10 AM.*

Eglise St-Jacques. The grimy exterior of this minicathedral a few blocks south of Liège's center belies a wonderful interior. Marble, stained glass, and polished wood achieve an outstanding visual harmony. The glory of the church is the Gothic vault, decorated in intricate patterns of vivid blue and gold and containing myriad sculpted figures. ✉ *Pl. St-Jacques,* ☎ *04/222–1441.* ⏲ *Weekdays 8–noon, Sat. 4–6.*

Fort de Battice. This fort brings memories of World War II. It held out against the Germans for 12 days in May 1940, while the German tanks rolled on into France. ✉ *Rte. d'Aubel, Battice, east of Liège,* ☎ *087/67–94–70.* 🎟 *BF100/€2.50.* ⏲ *Guided tours late Mar.–Nov., daily at 1:30.*

Fort de Loncin. Everything here has remained as it was at 5:15 PM on August 16, 1914, when a German shell scored a direct hit, killing most of the garrison. ✉ *Rue des Héros 15 bis, northeast of Liège,* ☎ *04/246–4425.* 🎟 *BF100/€2.50.* ⏲ *Wed.–Sun. 10–4; guided tours Apr.–Sept., 1st and 3rd Sun. of month at 2.*

Henri-Chapelle. Twenty-nine km (18 mi) east of Liège is the burial site of 7,989 American soldiers who fell in the Battle of the Bulge during the last winter of World War II. The crosses and stelae are arranged in arcs converging on the central monument, which also contains a small museum and provides a great view over the plateau of Herve. Ceremonies are held here on American Memorial Day in late May. ✉ *Rte. du Mémorial Américain, Hombourg,* ☎ *087/68–71–73.* 🎟 *Free.* ⏲ *Apr.–Sept., daily 8–6; Oct.–Mar., daily 8–5.*

26 **Impasses.** These narrow mews were where servants had their tiny houses in the days of the prince-bishops. Prominent citizens lived along neighboring En Hors-Château. As late as the 1970s, it was believed that the best approach to urban redevelopment was to tear down these houses. Luckily, common sense prevailed. The **Impasse de l'Ange** and **Impasse de la Couronne** are two fine examples of the six such well-restored impasses in town. Duck under the *àrvô,* the bridge over the alleyway, to discover lush gardens, finely restored Tudor homes, and a number of *potales* (wall chapels), devoted mostly to the Virgin or to St. Roch, who was venerated as the protector against disease epidemics. ✉ *Off En Hors-Château.*

Maison de la Métallurgie. This 19th-century steel mill south of Outremeuse is consecrated to the industrial glory that was Liège's. It's been converted into a museum of industrial archaeology, including a 17th-century Walloon forge. ✉ *Bd. Raymond Poincaré 17,* ☎ *04/342–6563.* 🎟 *BF100/€2.50.* ⏲ *Weekdays 9–5, Sat. 9–noon, Sun. 2–6.*

27 **Montagne de Bueren.** This stairway of 373 steps ascends from Hors-Château toward Liège's citadel. It honors the memory of Vincent van Bueren, a leader of the resistance against Charles the Bold. In 1468 he climbed the hill with 600 men, intending to ambush the duke and kill him. Betrayed by their Liègeois accents, they lost their lives and the city was pillaged and burned. Charles the Bold, a superstitious man, made sure the churches remained untouched while the city was in flames so he wouldn't be sent to hell. At the base of the stairs is a nunnery that has been renovated into a compound for antiques dealers. ✉ *Hors-Château.*

22 **Musée Curtius.** This patrician mansion, built for the arms manufacturer Jean Curtius in the 17th century, contains 100,000 art and ornamental objects. One is a masterpiece, Bishop Notger's *Evangelistery,* an exquisite 10th-century manuscript of the Gospels. On the ornamental cover is an ivory relief, carved in the year 1000, showing the bishop praying to Christ the King. The house, also home to a glass museum, is built in the Mosan style out of *tuffeau,* a soft stone from the local quarries. ☒ *Quai de Maestricht 13,* ☎ *04/221–9404.* 🎟 *BF50/€1.25.* ⏲ *Mon.–Sat. 10–1 and 2–5, Sun. 10–1.*

21 **Musée d'Armes.** Since the Middle Ages, Liège has been famous for its arms manufacturing, and the collection here reflects this with many rare and beautifully executed pieces. The building itself is a handsome 18th-century riverside mansion in the neoclassical style, opulently furnished. Napoléon slept here, at different times, with Josephine and Marie-Louise, and there's a portrait of him as First Consul by Ingres. ☒ *Quai de Maestricht 8,* ☎ *04/221–9416.* 🎟 *BF50/€1.25.* ⏲ *Mon.–Sat. 10–1 and 2–5, Sun. 10–1.*

NEED A BREAK? **A la Bonne Franquette** (☒ En Féronstrée 152) is a no-frills neighborhood eatery where you can enjoy a meal or snack.

23 **Musée d'Ansembourg.** The sculptures, tapestries, marble fireplaces, painted ceilings, and ceramics in this sumptuous mansion evoke the opulent lifestyle of its original owner, 18th-century merchant and banker Michel Willems. It was converted into a decorative and fine arts museum in 1903. ☒ *En Féronstrée 114,* ☎ *04/221–9402.* 🎟 *BF50/€1.25.* ⏲ *Tues.–Sun. 1–6.*

Musée d'Art Moderne et Contemporain. Almost all the big names are represented in this collection of 700-odd French and Belgian paintings dating from the 1850s on. The museum stands in the attractive Parc de la Boverie, much favored by the Liègeois for a stroll far away from the traffic. ☒ *Parc de la Boverie 3,* ☎ *04/343–0403.* 🎟 *BF50/€1.25.* ⏲ *Tues.–Sat. 1–6, Sun. 11–4:30.*

28 **Musée d'Art Religieux et d'Art Mosan.** There are many fine pieces here, including an 11th-century *Sedes Sapientiae* (Seat of Wisdom), a stiff and stern-faced seated Virgin, clearly the product of an austere age. ☒ *Rue Mère Dieu 11,* ☎ *04/221–4225.* 🎟 *BF50/€1.25.* ⏲ *Tues.–Sat. 1–6, Sun. 11–4:30.*

20 **Musée de l'Art Wallon.** Here you'll find works by Walloon artists from the 17th century to the present day, including Surrealists René Magritte and Paul Delvaux. Note next door the **Ilôt St-Georges,** an interesting example of urban archaeology. Twelve dilapidated buildings were taken apart, brick by brick, and put together again to form an appealing architectural whole. ☒ *En Féronstrée 86,* ☎ *04/221–9231.* 🎟 *BF50/€1.25.* ⏲ *Tues.–Sat. 1–6, Sun. 11–4:30.*

29 **Musée de la Vie Wallonne.** In an old Franciscan convent, carefully reconstructed interiors give a vivid and varied idea of life in old Wallonia, from coal mines to farm kitchens to the workshops of many different crafts. The museum even includes a court of law, complete with a guillotine. One gallery is populated by the irreverent marionette Tchantchès and his band, who represent the Liège spirit. ☒ *Cour des Mineurs,* ☎ *04/223–6094.* 🎟 *BF80/€2.00.* ⏲ *Tues.–Sat. 10–5, Sun. 10–4.*

Musée Tchantchès. Discover the mystique and mishaps of Liège's most beloved marionette at this museum in the Outremeuse district. Here you can learn the answers to such burning questions as: How did

Tchantchès meet his girlfriend Nanesse? Why did he have to eat an iron shoe to fight the measles at the age of three? Was he really designed by an Italian puppeteer? See Tchantchès in action at Wednesday and Sunday puppet shows. ✉ *Rue Surlet 56,* ☎ *04/342–7575.* 🎫 *BF40/€1.00.* ⏲ *Puppet shows Wed. 2:30, Sun. 10:30; otherwise open by appointment only.*

★ 34 **Place de la Cathédrale.** Here is Liège's version of a central park. A busy square, it bubbles over with the sounds of families shopping, students gossiping, and other Liègeois just hanging out. Street musicians, mimes, and other performers are common, adding to the mix of sounds and sights. The square is flanked by the north wall of the Gothic **Cathédrale St-Paul.** Inside you'll see handsome statues by Jean Delcour, including one of St. Paul. (Other graceful works by this 18th-century sculptor dot the old city.) The cathedral's most prized possessions are in the Treasury, especially the *Reliquaire de Charles le Téméraire* (Reliquary of Charles the Bold), with gold and enamel figures of St. George and the bold duke himself on his knees; curiously, their faces are identical. This reliquary was presented to Liège by Charles the Bold in 1471 in penance for having had the city razed three years earlier. 🎫 *BF50/€1.25.* ⏲ *Mon.–Sat. 10–11:45 and 2–4 (except during services), Sun. 2–4. Ring bell next to cloister door.*

NEED A BREAK? Grab a freshly baked *gauffre* (Belgian waffle) to go at the popular **Pollux** (✉ Rue de la Cathédrale 2).

30 **Place du Marché.** This square is as old as Liège itself. For centuries it was where the city's commercial and political life was concentrated. The 18th-century Hôtel de Ville is here, with its two entrances: one for the wealthy and one for the common people. A number of the old buildings surrounding it were among the 23,000 destroyed by German bombs. In the center stands the **Perron,** a large fountain sculpted by Jean Delcour, topped with an acorn—the symbol of Liège's liberty. ✉ *Rue du General Jacques, rue des Mineurs, En Feronstree.*

31 **Place St-Lambert.** During the French Revolution the Cathedral of St. Lambert, the largest cathedral in Europe, was destroyed, and the adjoining square fell into a long period of neglect. In 2000, renovation on Place St-Lambert was completed. Now a sculpture honoring both the murdered 8th-century saint and the future of Liège stands proudly at its center. Archaeological evidence indicates that the area may have been populated for as many as 10,000 years; an underground exhibition hall is in the works that will examine this question. The cathedral's chancery is also being renovated. On one side of the square stands the enormous **Palais des Princes-Evêques,** which has been rebuilt at different stages since the days of the first prince-bishops. The present facade dates from 1734. The colonnaded 16th-century courtyard has remained unchanged. Each column is decorated with stone carvings of staggering variety. ✉ *Junction of rue de Bruxelles, rue Léopold, rue Joffre, rue du General Jacques, and rue Souv Pont.*

Préhistosite de Ramioul. The world of early humans is on display at this speculative re-creation of prehistoric dwellings. You can get a sense of your ancestors' technical aptitude while trying your own hand at making pots and polishing stones. The museum is next to the **cave of Ramioul,** where the lighting system brings out the beauty of the rock formations. Guides explain the cave's animal life and its use by humans. ✉ *Rue de la Grotte 128, Ivoz-Ramet, near Seraing, south of Liège,* ☎ *04/275–4975.* 🎫 *BF290/€7.20.* ⏲ *Apr.–Oct., weekdays 2–5, weekends 2–6, one guided visit per day, starting at 2.*

33 **Théâtre Royal** is a handsome 18th-century performing-arts venue in the center of the city. Legend has it that the local composer Grétry had his heart buried underneath the pit. His statue stands outside the building. The well-respected Opéra Royal de Wallonie is based here, and L'Orchestra Philarmonique is often performing. Call for schedule and ticket information. ✉ *Place de la République Française at Boulevard de la Sauvenière and rue Joffre,* ☎ *04/221–4720.*

Wegimont Domaine. This recreation area of 50 acres surrounding a château has sports facilities, fishing, rowing, swimming in a heated outdoor pool, miniature golf, and signposted nature walks. ✉ *Soumagne, east of Liège,* ☎ *04/377–1020.* *BF100/€2.50.* ⏲ *May–Aug., daily 9–8.*

Dining and Lodging

$$$–$$$$ ✕ **Robert Lesenne.** Slick, sleek, and chic, this top-of-the-line restaurant is a place to see and be seen. A design feat, the interior incorporates a 17th-century facade and the bar is dramatically built into a stone courtyard. The fixed-price menu, with a choice of over 30 appetizers, entrées, and desserts, offers a good value. Many are standards given a new twist; sweetbreads are wrapped in crisp bacon, and there is a stew of langoustine and frogs' legs. ✉ *Rue de la Boucherie 9,* ☎ *04/222–0793. Reservations essential. AE, DC, MC, V. Closed Sun., 2nd ½ of July. No lunch Sat.*

$$$ ✕ **As Ouhès.** This stylish spot on the Place du Marché is one of celebrity chef Robert Lesenne's most popular restaurants. Violet walls highlight old black and white photographs of Liège. The menu features large portions of Walloon specialties, including rabbit stewed in beer and succulent *boulets* (traditional meatballs of Liège) served with mounds of frites. Tables are often hard to come by both at lunch and dinner; try for one outside when weather permits. ✉ *Place du Marché 19–21,* ☎ *04/223–3225. AE, MC, V.*

$$$ ★ ✕ **Au Vieux Liège.** The cuisine here is as interesting as the riverside building it's served in: the Maison Havart, a sprawling, ramshackle cross-timbered beauty dating from the 16th century. Duckling prepared with Armagnac and lightly smoked sweetbreads with a spicy rosemary sauce are among the delicacies. Interiors, all creaking parquet and glossy wood beams, have been furnished in Old Master luxury—Delft tiles, brass, pewter, Oriental runners. ✉ *Quai de la Goffe 41,* ☎ *04/223–7748. Reservations essential. Jacket and tie. AE, DC, MC, V. Closed Sun., Easter wk, mid-July–mid-Aug. No dinner Wed.*

$$$ ✕ **Bruit Qui Court.** This regal restaurant is discreetly tucked in a handsome courtyard next to one of Liège's most beautiful flower shops. The interior is draped in African fabric, and the menu offers French-inspired contemporary cuisine. The earlybird special is a great way to begin a night at the opera. ✉ *Blvd. de la Sauveniére,* ☎ *04/232–1818. MC, V.*

$$$ ✕ **Chez Max.** There's never a dull moment at this elegant brasserie run by the charismatic Alain Struvay. Specialties include lobster and langoustines au gratin, turbot in champagne sauce, very tender, lightly smoked salmon—and more than 100 brands of whiskey. There is a spectacular *banc d'écailler* (oyster and seafood display). ✉ *Pl. de la République Française 12,* ☎ *04/223–7748. AE, DC, MC, V. Closed Sun. No lunch Sat.*

$$ ✕ **Au Parc des Moules.** Ask Liège natives about this institution hidden on a pedestrian alley and watch their eyes light up. You won't find a larger or more creative menu of mussels anywhere. Try the *moules flambé* made with cognac, or *moules mexicane* with tequila. ✉ *Rue Tête de Boeuf 19,* ☎ *04/223–71–49. No credit cards.*

$$ ✕ **Le Bistro D'en Face.** The checkered banquettes, large baskets of fresh bread, and tiles with cocks (the symbol of Wallonia) give this bistro a rustic feel. The menu features regional meat specialties such as hot pistachio sausage. ✉ *Rue de la Goeff 8–10,* ☎ *04/223–1584. Reservations essential. AE, MC, V. Closed Mon. No lunch Sat.*

$$ ★ ✕ **Mame Vi Cou.** The name is a Walloon term of endearment for an older woman of ample proportions. So, my *p'tit poyon* (little chicken—another term of endearment), sit back and enjoy traditional Wallonian cuisine here, such as veal in creamy herb mustard or duck in a thick honey sauce. ✉ *Rue de la Wache 9,* ☎ *04/223–7181. AE, DC, MC, V.*

$$ ✕ **La Thème.** You'll always be surprised and seldom disappointed at this whimsical, colorful den where the decor, the menu, and even the type of cuisine served change twice a year. (Call ahead to find out what's currently on the menu.) Hidden on a residential *impasse,* it's very much a part of the vibrant neighborhood. ✉ *Impasse de la Couronne 9,* ☎ *04/222–0202. Reservations essential. MC, V. Closed Sun.*

$–$$ ✕ **La Maison du Pèkèt/A Mon Nanesse.** Playful like the puppet Tchantchès, La Maison du Pèkèt concocts a wide array of cocktails using *pèkèt*—Liège's local liquor—in every way imaginable. When you've had your fill of pèkèts with passionfruit, head next door to the attached restaurant, A Mon Nanesse (reservations essential). Named after Tchantchès's girlfriend, this friendly joint serves hearty Belgian fare made with, of course, pèkèt. ✉ *Rue de l'Epée 4,* ☎ *04/223–6655. No credit cards.*

$ ✕ **Brasserie Florian.** Picture windows over the Meuse grace one wall and a large mural of Liège life graces another. Come here for respectable seafood and the fine view. ✉ *Quai sur Meuse 16,* ☎ *04/232–1880. AE, DC, MC, V. No dinner Sun.*

$ ✕ **Café Lequet.** Known as a Simenon family haunt, this wood-paneled neighborhood stand-by serves unbeatable boulets smothered in Liège's special date and apple syrup and classic moules piled high with the inevitable frites. The place is filled with regulars, young and old. ✉ *Quai sur Meuse 17,* ☎ *04/222–2134. No credit cards. No dinner Sun.*

$ ★ ✕ **Concordia.** A block from the train station, this dinerlike Liège institution has been here for close to 50 years. It serves all day and has a varied menu. Stay for a cup of coffee or a full meal. Watch Madame Somens, the proud proprietor, tempt the neighborhood children with irresistible chocolates as the regulars come and go. ✉ *Rue des Guillemins 114,* ☎ *04/252–2915. AE, MC, V. Closed mid-July–mid-Aug.*

$ ✕ **L'Oeuf Au Plat.** On the quai, this cozy restaurant features—as its name suggests—egg dishes. Try the house specialty, *la fricassette,* an egg-based fondue unique to Liège. The decor includes a handsome wooden cabinet displaying a wide range of culinary objects, all related to the egg. ✉ *Quai de la Batte 30,* ☎ *4/222–4032. AE, MC, V. Closed Tues. No dinner Sun.*

$ ✕ **Vaudree II.** The beer selection is the draw here—there are more than 980 to choose from. The simple menu features sandwiches served with frites. Last call is 1 AM during the week and 3 AM on the weekends. ✉ *Rue St. Gilles 149,* ☎ *04/223–1880. MC, V.*

$ ✕ 🏨 **Simenon.** The owner of this Outremeuse theme hotel meticulously designed each room to reflect one of native son George Simenon's novels. The attached restaurant, the Vine, is modeled after a jail from Simenon. Dine in the dungeon below—order a "bludgeon" (a criminally decadent dessert) and eat with your fingers. ✉ *Bd. de l'Est 16, B4020,* ☎ *04/342–8690,* FAX *04/344–2669. 11 rooms. Restaurant. AE, DC, MC, V.*

$$$ 🏨 **Bedford.** Opened in 1994, this hotel on the banks of the Meuse is just a few blocks from major museums and the old city. The bright, air-conditioned rooms have leather armchairs and marble bathrooms with hair dryers. The brasserie-style restaurant is in the oldest part of the hotel, which dates from the 17th century. The Bedford caters primarily to a business clientele, so you're likely to find discounted rates on weekends. ✉ *Quai St-Léonard 36, B4000,* ☎ *04/228–8111,* FAX *04/227–4575. 149 rooms. Restaurant, bar, meeting rooms. AE, DC, MC, V.*

$$$ **Holiday Inn.** Next to the Palais des Congrès, this is the hotel of choice for European Congress delegates and businesspeople. The lobby and guest rooms are well maintained, and the riverfront location is very pleasant. ✉ *Esplanade de l'Europe 2, B4020,* ☎ *04/342–6020,* FAX *04/343–4810. 219 rooms. Bar, no-smoking rooms, indoor pool, sauna, health club, convention center, parking (fee). AE, DC, MC, V.*

$$$ **Hotel Mercure.** Located in the center of town, this modern, full-service hotel caters to business travelers and families alike. The rooms are comfortable and spacious, done in contemporary style, and the lobby, full of bustle and equipped with comfortable chairs, is a great place for people-watching. The helpful concierge can answer all your Liège-related questions. Ask for weekend rates. ✉ *Boulevard de la Sauvenière, B4000,* ☎ *04/221–7711,* FAX *04/221–7701 105 rooms. Restaurant, bar, meeting rooms, parking. AE, MC, V.*

$$ ★ **Le Cygne D'Argent.** Next door to the British Consulate, this boutique hotel feels like an oasis. Decorated in a gentle pastel pallette, each room is slightly different, but all feature fabric wallpaper, bright bathrooms, and handsome furniture. The front rooms look over Mosan-style residential rooftops, while those in the back have views onto gardens. Breakfast is available but not included with the room. ✉ *Rue Beeckman 49, B4000,* ☎ *04/223–7001,* FAX *04/222–4966. 22 rooms. Lounge, parking. AE, MC, V.*

$–$$ **Passerelle Hotel.** In an animated part of Outremeuse, this modest hotel with threadbare but functional rooms is a favorite with the actors who perform at the theater around the corner. The big windows in the bright, airy breakfast room look onto the bustling street. Breakfast is not included with the room. ✉ *Chausée des Prés, B4020,* ☎ *04/341–2020,* FAX *04/344–3643. 16 rooms. Breakfast room. MC, V.*

$ **Comfort Inn l'Univers.** A cut above most train-station hotels, this landmark has been kept up to date with double windows, sharp room decor (beige and burgundy), and a modernized brasserie-bar downstairs. ✉ *Rue des Guillemins 116, B4000,* ☎ *04/254–5555,* FAX *04/254–5500. 49 rooms. Bar. AE, DC, MC, V.*

Nightlife and the Arts

Check event times at **Infor-Spectacles** (✉ En Féronstrée 92, ☎ 04/222–1111), where you can also buy tickets. For all sorts of events in Liège, look under "Other Towns" in *The Bulletin*'s What's On section.

The Arts

MUSIC AND OPERA

Liège has an excellent opera company, the **Opéra Royal de Wallonie** (✉ Théâtre Royal, rue des Dominicains, ☎ 04/221–4720), considered the country's most innovative. The city's symphony orchestra, **l'Orchestre Philharmonique de Liège,** has recorded prize-winning discs and tours internationally with a largely contemporary repertoire. The **Wallonia Chamber Orchestra** and other ensembles participate in the annual Festival de la Wallonie (in Liège, Sept., ☎ 04/222–1111), with concerts also in Spa and Stavelot. The **Stavelot Music Festival** (☎ 080/86–24–50) is held every August, with concerts in the old abbey.

PUPPET THEATER

On Wednesday at 2:30 and Sunday morning at 10:30 you can see puppet theater featuring the irrepressible Tchantchès at the **Musée Tchantchès**

(✉ Rue Surlet 56, ☎ 04/342–7575) and the theater of the **Musée de la Vie Wallonne** (✉ Cour des Mineurs, ☎ 04/223–6094). The **Théâtre Al Botroule** (✉ Rue Hocheporte 3, ☎ 04/223–0576) has puppet shows for adults (Sat. at 8:30) and for children (Sat. and Wed. at 3).

THEATER

The most interesting theater performances in French or Walloon are generally at the **Théâtre de la Place** (✉ Pl. de l'Yser, ☎ 04/342–0000). It's worth checking out what's on at **Les Chiroux** (✉ Pl. des Carmes, ☎ 04/223–1960). The **Festival du Théâtre de Spa** (☎ 087/77–17–00) is a showcase for young actors and directors. Programs and information about the three-week August season are available starting in early June.

Nightlife

The Liègeois have an amazing ability to stay up until all hours, and nightlife is booming on both sides of the Meuse. The Carré quarter, on the left bank, is favored by students and those who go to a show first and out afterward. In the narrow, cobble-laned Roture quarter in Outremeuse there's hardly a house without a café, club, ethnic restaurant, or jazz hangout.

CAFÉS AND CLUBS

Two cafés chantant, which are very typical of this city, should be tried: **Les Caves de Porto** (✉ En Féronstrée 144, ☎ 04/223–2325; closed Tues. and Thurs.) and **Les Olivettes** (✉ rue Pied-du-Pont des Arches 6, ☎ 04/222–0708). You can finish the evening quietly in an ambience of Liège folklore at the **Café Tchantchès** (✉ rue Grande-Beche, ☎ 04/343–3931), a true Liège institution.

Cirque Divers (✉ En Roture 13, ☎ 04/341–0244) in Outremeuse offers literary happenings, film events, dance, and classical concerts.

Outdoor Activities and Sports

Boating

There's a yacht harbor along Boulevard Frère Orban in Liège, and water sports are popular upstream from the Pont Albert I.

Golf

There are two 18-hole courses in the Liège area: the **International Gomzé Golf Club** (✉ Sur Counachamps 8, Gomzé-Andoumont, ☎ 04/360–9207) and the **Royal Golf Club du Sart Tilman** (✉ Rte. du Condroz 541, Angleur, ☎ 04/336–2021).

Swimming and Skating

The **Palais des Sports de Coronmeuse** (✉ Quai de Wallonie 7, ☎ 04/227–1324) provides facilities for swimming in a heated outdoor pool in summer and skating in winter.

Shopping

In Liège, the **Carré** is almost exclusively a pedestrian area, with boutiques, cafés, and restaurants. The most important shopping arcades are **Galerie du Pont d'Avroy** (✉ off rue du Pont d'Avroy), **Galerie Nagelmackers** (✉ between place de la Cathédrale and rue Tournant St-Paul), and the **Passage Lemonnier** (✉ between Vinâve d'Ile and rue de l'Université).

Glassware from Val St-Lambert can be found in a number of shops and most advantageously at the **Cristalleries du Val St-Lambert** factory shop (✉ rue du Val 245, Seraing, ☎ 04/337–0960). Firearms, an age-old Liège specialty, are still handmade to order by some gun shops, notably **Lebeau-Courally** (✉ R. St-Gilles 386, ☎ 04/252–4843). Keep in mind that only a licensed arms importer may carry arms into the United States.

★ The best, most exciting shopping experience is at **La Batte,** which happens every Sunday morning along the Quai de la Batte. Traffic is diverted for one of Europe's biggest weekly street markets. Vendors and shoppers alike drive for hours from Belgium, France, Germany, and the Netherlands to browse the vast array of goods, which includes everything from antique books, live birds, and spiced sausage to garden plants and contemporary clothing. Plan to spend a few hours here. A word of advice and a word of caution: be prepared to bargain, and be on the lookout for pickpockets.

LIÈGE PROVINCE

The history of Liège Province differs fundamentally from that of the rest of the country. For 8 of its 10 centuries it was an independent principality of the Holy Roman Empire, from the time Bishop Notger transformed his bishopric into a temporal domain at the end of the 10th century. His successors had to devote as much time to the defense of the realm—much larger than the present province—as to pastoral concerns. The power of the autocratic prince-bishops was also hotly contested by the increasingly independent-minded cities. The end was brought about by the French Revolution, which many Liègeois joined with enthusiasm. The ancient Cathedral of St. Lambert in Liège City was razed, and the principality became a French *département* in 1815, after Napoléon.

The natural resources of the region were used during the 19th and 20th centuries to help fuel Belgium's industrial economy, which had one of its centers in Liège City. Much of the area's natural beauty has nonetheless remained intact, and today hiking, biking, canoeing, and kayaking are major draws. Spa—from which all other spas derive their name—is still a popular resort, with regal old buildings and curative waters. And in the easternmost area of the country, where German is spoken, the Haute Fagnes national park possesses an eerie beauty.

Huy

35 *33 km (20 mi) southwest of Liège, 32 km (19 mi) east of Namur, 83 km (50 mi) southeast of Brussels.*

Huy (pronounced "we"), where the Hoyoux joins the Meuse, is a workers' town and the main employer is the power industry. It dates back to 1066, and contains some sights of historical interest. The first stone of the Gothic **Eglise Collégiale de Notre-Dame** (Collegiate Church of Our Lady) was laid in 1311. It has a rose window, the so-called Rondia, 30 ft in diameter. Its treasury contains several magnificent reliquaries, two of them attributed to Godefroid de Huy, who followed in the footsteps of Renier, also a native of Huy and a master of the Mosan style. ✉ *Rue de Cloître.* 🎫 *BF50/€1.25.* ⏲ *Mon.–Thurs. and Sat. 9–noon and 2–5, Sun. 2–5 except during services.*

Huy's **Grand'Place** is dominated by a remarkable fountain, the **Bassinia,** a bronze cistern decorated with saints that dates from 1406. In the 18th century, the Austrians topped it with their double eagle.

From the square you can wander through winding alleys to the old Franciscan monastery, which is now the **Musée Communal,** a mine of local folklore and history with an exceptional Art Mosan oak carving of Christ. ✉ *Rue Vankeerberghen 20,* ☎ *085/23–24–35.* 🎫 *BF100/€2.50.* ⏲ *Apr.–Oct., daily 2–6.*

For a great view of the town and the surrounding countryside, take a mile-long ride on the cable car from the left bank of the Meuse across the river to the cliff-top **Citadelle,** part of the defenses built by the Dutch in the early 19th century. During World War II, the Germans used it as a prison for resistance members and hostages. It now contains a **Musée de la Résistance** with photographs, documents, and scale models. ✉ *Chaussée Napoléon,* ☎ *085/21–53–34.* *BF120/€2.95.* *Apr.–June and Sept., weekdays 10–5, weekends 10–6; July–Aug., daily 10–8; cable car July–Aug., daily.*

Spa

 *38 km (23 mi) southeast of Liège, 18 km (11 mi) north of Stavelot, 139 km (83 mi) southeast of Brussels.*

The Romans came here to take the waters, and they were followed over the centuries by crowned heads, such as Marguerite de Valois, Christina of Sweden, and Peter the Great. Less welcome was Kaiser Wilhelm II, who established his general headquarters in Spa in 1918. By then the town was already past its prime. During the 18th and 19th centuries, it had been the watering place of international high society, and many gracious houses remain from that period. The pleasures of "taking the cure" in beautiful surroundings were heightened in those days by high-stakes gambling, playing *pharaon* or *biribi* for rubles, ducats, piastres, or francs. The **Casino** dates from 1763, making it the oldest in the world. Now, the glamorous gaming rooms support a wide array of cultural activities in addition to gambling. Pick up a casino pass at the Tourist Office, which allows for free admission into the casino.

The casino is only one of the many architectural gems that line the streets of Spa. These glorious buildings, and the rest of the town, are being lovingly restored, and this small city of splendor is once again becoming a destination for people of all ages and interests. Check the well-stocked **Tourist Office** (✉ Place Royale 41, ☎ 087/79–53–53,) for information about walking tours, hikes, sports activities, and special events around town. Spa passes, which grant discounts for admission to Spa's museums and parks, are available free of charge at most hotels and at the Tourist Office.

Of course, people still primarily come for the waters. The two best-known water sources in the center of Spa—locally known as *pouhons*—are the **Pouhon Pierre-le-Grant and Pouhon Prince-de-Condé,** which can be visited by tourists as well as *curistes* (people taking the cure). The price for a glass straight from the source is a modest BF7/€0.15. ✉ *Town center,* ☎ *087/79–53–53.* *Free.* *Baths: Easter–Oct., daily 10–noon and 2–5:30; Nov.–Easter, weekdays 1:30–5, weekends 10–noon and 1:30–5.*

Spa also has a collection of interesting and oddball museums that tell the social and cultural history of the region. At the **Spa Monopole** you can take a tour of the production plant and attached museum dedicated to the famous Spa brand mineral water. ✉ *Rue Auguste 34,* ☎ *087/79–41–11.* *Weekdays 9–11:30, 1–5:30.*

The charming **Laundry Museum** is dedicated to the art and science of keeping clothes clean—not a task to be taken lightly, particularly when royalty and nobility come to town to sweat away their maladies. ✉ *Rue de la Geronstere 10,* ☎ *087/77–14–18.* *BF50/€1.25.* *July–Aug., daily 2–6; Sept.–June, Sun. 2–6.*

The **Spa Museum and Horse Museum** are two institutions in one. The first hosts a permanent exhibit on Spa's waters and fountains, and includes a collection of *jolites,* painted figurines fashioned from local wood. The Horse Museum contains an extensive display of equestrian paraphernalia. ✉ *Avenue Reine 77 B,* ☎ *087/77–4–86.* ⊙ *June 15–Sept. 15, daily 2:30–5:30; Sept. 16–Dec. 24, March. 15–June 14, Weekends 2:30–5:30.*

NEED A BREAK? Settle into a booth at **La Gâterie Tea Room** (✉ Place du Monument 18) for waffles, crepes, homemade ice cream, or a fresh-baked tart.

Elephants, camels, lions, and kangaroos live at **Wild Safari World.** Don't forget to visit the pool, which is home to sea lions and polar bears. The park is easily accessible from downtown Spa by foot, car, or the **Tourist Train,** which tours town daily from June through September. ✉ *Fange de Deigne 3, Aywaille,* ☎ *04/30–90–70.* *BF340/€8.45.* ⊙ *Daily Mar.–Nov.*

Every Tuesday morning, behind the Casino, is Spa's weekly **Farmer's Market.** On Sunday morning, the Parc de Sept-Heures, directly behind the Tourist Office, erupts into a colorful **Flea Market** featuring local artists, craftspeople, and other vendors. Book early if you plan to visit Spa around July 21, Belgium's National Holiday. For six days around that time, the annual **Francofolie Festival** transforms this quiet thermal center into a nonstop bubbling cauldron of French music. A sister festival happens in Quebec City, Canada, at the same time.

Dining and Lodging

$$ ★ ✕ **L'Art de Vivre.** Jean-François Douffet's fresh approach in the kitchen contrasts pleasantly with the old-fashioned gentility of his competitors. Sautéed goose liver accompanied by a potato pancake, pike perch with deep-fried basil leaves, roast pigeon with a balsamic vinegar sauce, and ice cream with figs are among his creations. ✉ *Av. Reine Astrid 53,* ☎ *087/770444. AE, DC, MC, V. Closed Tues., Wed. (except July).*

$$ ★ ✕ **La Brasserie du Grand Maur.** This graceful 200-year-old city mansion houses a lovely restaurant with a loyal clientele. Tartare of salmon, lamb infused with tomato and thyme, and duck's breast with raspberries and red currants are special favorites. The setting is all polished wood, linens, and antiques. ✉ *Rue Xhrouet 41,* ☎ *087/77–36–16. AE, DC, MC, V. Closed Mon.–Tues., 3 wks Dec.–Jan., 2 wks in June.*

$–$$ ✕ **Old Inn.** For more than 22 years, Patrick and Françoise Heuse have been serving hearty portions of pasta, crepes, moules, and meats at this always-packed watering hole. A notch above a tavern, its exposed beams, well-worn wooden booths, green linens, old pictures of Spa, and auto-racing paraphernalia make it a welcoming place to visit afternoon, evening, or late into the night. ✉ *Rue Royale 23–25,* ☎ *087/77–39–43. AE, DC, MC, V. Closed Tues., Wed. (except July and Aug.).*

$ ✕ **Le Clair Obscure.** This informal hangout features a wide selection of salads and delectable desserts. The building itself is an example of how Spa is renovating its architectural gems. Once a discotheque, its brick was restored and the main room brightened up for its transformation into a well-loved eatery. In nice weather, the expansive deck is equally inviting. ✉ *Rue Delhasse 32,* ☎ *087/77–51–38. MC, V. Closed Mon., Tues.*

$$ ✕ **Les Relais.** Although right in the center of town, this small, friendly inn feels simple enough to be in the country. Decorated by horse lovers, the restaurant's curiosity cabinets contain an impressive collection of miniature horses. The menu changes four times a year and always features seasonal treats. The equestrian theme and the gentle yellow of the dining room continue in the guest rooms upstairs. ✉ *Place du Monument 22, 4900,* ☎ *087/77–11–08,* FAX *087/77–25–93. 12 rooms. Restaurant. AE, DC, MC, V. Closed late Nov.–late Dec.*

$$$$ **Hôtel Balmoral.** Up the hill from downtown Spa, this handsome 1905 landmark was where King Leopold II routinely hosted opulent banquets. Its dark wood accents and rich maroon hues are reminiscent of an old-fashion gentleman's club. You can test your skills in the billiards room or linger over the grand piano for a song and a drink. The indoor pool is fed by Spa's own waters. Rooms range from single efficiency units with kitchenettes to sleek executive suites. There's a shuttle to and from town. ✉ *Ave. Leopold 1140, 4900,* ☎ *087/79–21–41,* FAX *087–79–21–15. 88 rooms. Restaurant, pool, hot tub, driving range, tennis courts, billiards. AE, DC, MC, V.*

$$$ ★ **Hôtel Villa des Fleurs.** Fresh flowers abound in this splendid 1880 beaux arts mansion that was once the private home of the director of the Spa Casino. The entry foyer's enormous chandelier and grand staircase set the tone for the rooms' thick draped decor, mammoth beds, and marble bathrooms. Rooms in the back have views of the beautiful garden. ✉ *Rue Albin Body 31, 4900,* ☎ *08/79–50–50,* FAX *087/79–50–60. 12 rooms. AE, DC, MC, V.*

$$ **Cardinal.** Offering a real taste of old Spa, this grand urban resort hotel opened in 1924—and was completely renovated in 1948. Its period decor and interior architecture are completely intact and as fresh as new. Have tea in the muraled salon, hot chocolate in the beautiful all-oak café, or dinner in the swanky chandeliered dining hall. Most rooms have smooth gold oak paneling. ✉ *Pl. Royale 21–27, B4900,* ☎ *087/77–10–64,* FAX *087/77–19–64. 29 rooms. Restaurant, bar, tea shop. AE, MC, V.*

Outdoor Activities and Sports

Motor-sports fans know **Francorchamps** (near Spa) as one of the world's top racing circuits, where Formula 1 drivers zig and zag with astounding speed and precision. The annual Grand Prix race takes place in late August or early September, and there are other events throughout the year. Contact **Intercommunale du Circuit de Spa-Francorchamps** (✉ Rte. du Circuit 55, Francorchamps, ☎ 087/27–51–38) for information.

For those wanting a lift, the **Spa Airfield** (✉ Rue de la Sauveniere, ☎ 087/79–52–60) offers an array of high-flying opportunities, including a parachuting center and gliding.

En Route The road to Malmédy runs through attractive landscape. The shortest route—via Francorchamps—uses, in part, the Grand Prix racing circuit but is not always open. A rewarding detour is through **Coo**; kayak trips down the Amblève River start at the bottom of the waterfalls. Chairlifts take you up to **Telecoo,** a plateau where there's a splendid view of the Amblève River valley, an extensive amusement park, and a 200-acre Ardennes wildlife park (☎ 080/68–42–65).

Twenty-one km (13 mi) northeast of Spa sits **Eupen,** the gateway town ★ for the **Haute Fagnes.** Here, in the heart of the German-speaking part of Belgium, is a splendid 722 square km (279 square mi) ecological expanse of peat bogs, heath, and marshland. This is Belgium's largest area of protected wilderness, and it also happens to be the country's wettest, coldest, and most bizarre terrain. Foggy mists, sometimes dense, make navigating a path through the park's wilderness deceptively difficult. The saturated bogs hide quagmires just waiting to pull down unsuspecting feet—thus, explorations are confined to wooden boardwalks. Don't let the somewhat forebidding circumstances deter you. The Haute Fagnes is one of Belgium's natural wonders, shrouded in mystery and lore. Two 19th century lovers wandered to their death in the shifting landscape; the **Croix des Fiances** near the Baraque Michel Resthouse commemorates their tragic slip into the netherworld. At the à **Botrange** nature center, you can get a professional introduction to the flora and fauna of the park. Parts of the area can only be visited with a guide, particularly the peat bogs and the feeding areas of the *capercaillies* (large and very rare woodland grouse—the park's symbol). You can book an individual guide in advance, and you can also rent boots and bikes. ✉ *Robertville,* ☎ *080/44–57–81.* 🎫 *BF100/€2.50.* ⏲ *Daily 10–6.*

Reinhardstein, the loftiest and possibly the best-preserved medieval fortress in the country, is reached by a mile-long hike through the Hautes Fagnes. It sits on a spur of rock overlooking the river Warche and has been in the hands of such illustrious families as the Metternichs, ancestors of Prince Metternich, the architect of the Congress of Vienna in 1815. The Hall of Knights and the Chapel are gems. ✉ *Robertville,* ☎ *080/44–68–68.* 🎫 *BF200/€4.95.* ⏲ *Tours mid-June–mid-Sept., Sun. at 2:15, 3:15, 4:15, and 5:15; July–Aug., also Tues., Thurs., and Sat. at 3:30.*

Malmédy

37 *57 km (34 mi) southeast of Liège, 156 km (94 mi) southeast of Brussels, 16 km (10 mi) southeast of Spa.*

Malmédy and its neighbor, Stavelot, formed a separate, peaceful principality, ruled by abbots, for 11 centuries before the French Revolution. The Congress of Vienna, redrawing the borders of Europe, handed it to Germany, and it was not reunited with Belgium until 1925. In a scene straight out of *Catch 22,* the center of Malmédy was destroyed by American bombers in 1944 after the town had been liberated. Still, there's enough left of the old town for an interesting walk. And either of the twin towns is an ideal place to stay while exploring the **Haute Fagnes.**

Malmédy's carnival, beginning on the Saturday before Lent, is among the most famous in Belgium. To learn more about it, visit the **Musée du Carnaval.** ✉ *Pl. de Rome 11, 3rd floor (no elevator),* ☎ *080/33–70–58.* 🎫 *BF100/€2.50.* ⏲ *July–Aug., Wed.–Mon. 3–6; Sept.–June, weekends 2:30–5:30.*

NEED A BREAK? **Le Floreal** (✉ Pl. Albert I 8) serves breakfast, lunch, dinner, and snacks, such as the local ham, jambon d'Ardennes.

Dining and Lodging

$$$–$$$$ ✕🏨 **Hostellerie Trôs Marets.** Up the hill on the road toward Eupen, this inn offers a splendid view over the wooded valley. In fall, the fog hangs low over the nearby Haute Fagnes; in winter, cross-country skiing beckons. The main building contains the restaurant and rustic, cozy rooms. A modern annex has suites (furnished in contemporary English style, with fireplaces) and a large indoor pool. The restaurant serves up such specialties as duck's liver with caramelized apples, asparagus in truffle vinaigrette, grilled duckling with honey, and Herve cheese soufflé with Liège liqueur. Half-board is a good value. ✉ *Rte. des Trôs Marets 2, B4960 Bévercé, 3 km (2 mi) north on N68 from Malmédy,* ☎ *080/33–79–17,* FAX *080/33–79–10. 7 rooms, 4 suites. Restaurant, pool. AE, DC, MC, V. Closed mid-Nov.–Dec. 23.*

$$ ★ ✕🏨 **Ferme Libert.** This landmark is beautifully located on the edge of the forest, a few miles north of town on the Eupen road. The architecture is traditional rustic, and the large dining room overlooks the valley. The menu is long on meat of all kinds, including ostrich, bison, and springbok. The ambience is similar to that of an Alpine resort, with skiing in winter (at least for a few weeks) and bracing walks the rest

of the year. Half-board is required on weekends. ✉ *Chaussée de Bévercé–Village 26, B4960 Bévercé,* ☎ *080/33–02–47,* FAX *080/33–98–85. 18 rooms with bath, 22 with shower. Restaurant. AE, MC, V.*

Outdoor Activities and Sports

The **Worriken Sports Center** (✉ Rue Worriken 9, Bütgenbach, ☎ 080/44–69–61) offers horseback riding in the Hautes Fagnes region.

Stavelot

38 *15 km (9 mi) southwest of Malmédy, 59 km (37 mi) southeast of Liège, 158 km (95 mi) southeast of Brussels.*

Although Stavelot is practically a twin town of Malmédy, its traditions differ. Here Carnival is celebrated on the fourth Sunday in Lent and is animated by about 2,000 *Blancs-Moussis* (White Monks), dressed in white with long capes and long bright red noses, who swoop and rush through the streets. The Blancs-Moussis commemorate the monks of Stavelot, who in 1499 were forbidden to participate in Carnival but got around it by celebrating Laetare Sunday (three weeks before Easter). Stavelot was badly damaged in the Battle of the Bulge, but some picturesque old streets survive, particularly rue Haute, off Place St-Remacle.

Stavelot's square is named for St. Remacle, who founded a local abbey in 647. His reliquary, now in the **Eglise St-Sébastien,** is one of the wonders of Art Mosan. Dating from the 13th century, it is 6½ ft long and decorated with statuettes, of the apostles on the sides and of Christ and the Virgin on the ends. ✉ *Rue de l'Eglise 7,* ☎ *080/86–22–84.* *BF50/€1.25.* ⊙ *July–Aug., daily 9–noon and 2–5; rest of yr by appointment.*

Only a Romanesque tower remains of the original buildings that formed the **Ancienne Abbaye** (Old Abbey). Here, ground has been broken for a cultural arts center and three museums. One museum is dedicated to racing cars, another to religious objects, and the third—the only of its kind in the world—features a permanent exhibition devoted to the life and work of the French poet and essayist Guillame Apollinaire. The new complex is scheduled to open in 2001.

Dining and Lodging

$$ ✕ **Hostellerie La Maison de Crouly.** This small, charming spot in the center of town has a Slavic menu that's unique to the area. Relax over blini and caviar or, on a chilly night, warm up with a steaming bowl of hot borscht. The rooms upstairs look over Place St-Remacle. ✉ *Place St. Remacle 19, 4960,* ☎ *080/88–0275,* FAX *080/88–0275. 12 rooms. Restaurant closed Mon., Tues.*

$$$ ★ ✕ **Le Val d'Amblève.** In an unassuming whitewashed main house, guest rooms look out on gorgeous grounds with century-old trees. Inside, the sophisticated restaurant (reservations essential) serves delicacies such as pigeon with a pear and truffle sauce and lobster with celery. Retire to the cozy pink salon for an after-dinner drink. ✉ *Rte. de Malmédy 7, 4970,* ☎ *080/86–23–53,* FAX *080/86–41–21. 13 rooms. Restaurant, tennis courts. AE, DC, MC, V. Closed Mon., 3 wks in Jan. No dinner Thurs.*

$$ ✕ **Hôtel d'Orange.** A former post house, this friendly hotel has been in the same family since 1789. The charming rooms are in Laura Ashley style and there's a range of fixed-price menus, including one for kids. Quail, ever popular in these parts, chicken *à l'estragon* (with tarragon), and lamb are staples on the menu. ✉ *Devant les Capucins 8, 4970,* ☎ *080/86–20–05,* FAX *080/86–42–92. 16 rooms. Restaurant. AE, DC, MC, V. Closed weekends Nov.–Mar.*

Outdoor Activities and Sports

Virtually all the rivers of the Ardennes are great for canoeing, and the meandering Amblève is one of the best. Single or double kayaks can be rented at **Cookayak** (✉ Stavelot, ☎ 080/68–42–65) for a 9-km (5-mi) ride from Coo to Cheneux (about 1½ hrs) or a 23-km (14-mi) ride to Lorcé (about 3½ hrs). Bus service back to the starting point is provided.

BELGIAN LUXEMBOURG

The least populated and largest of the Belgian provinces, Luxembourg's 240,000 citizens inhabit 4,400 square miles of dense forests, rolling hills, and lush river valleys. But Luxembourg's tranquil beauty belies a tumultuous and bloody past, from the first crusade, which was launched at Bouillon, to the Battle of the Bulge, in which, near Bastogne, thousands of soldiers lost their lives. Now you'll find countless scenic back roads that as often as not lead to small stone villages with high-quality, modestly priced restaurants serving the *jambon* (ham) and *fromage* (cheese) for which this region is famous.

Durbuy

★ 39 *40 km (24 mi) southwest of Spa, 51 km (31 mi) south of Liège, 119 km (71 mi) southeast of Brussels.*

Surrounded by deep forests in the Ourthe river valley, an 11th century castle towers over this tiny, picture-perfect town. Ever since John the Blind deemed it a city in 1331, Durbuy has taken pride in promoting itself as "the smallest city in the world." Allegedly, Durbuy derives its name from a pre-Latin dialect in which *duro bodions* translates as "dwellings near the fortress." Durbuy's narrow streets, never more than a stone's throw from the main square, are lined with amazingly well-preserved 16th- and 17th-century architecture. During the summer season they fill with tourists.

For such a small town, Durbuy hosts a surprising number of festivals and markets. In March, chocoholics flock to the **chocolate market.** The last Sunday in August is the **flower market,** where florists carpet the main square in vibrant blossoms. Each Saturday in July there is a classical music concert in the church, and on the second Saturday of the month between April and September an **antiques market** comes to town.

The **Parc des Topiaries** on the bank of the Ourthe offers a lighthearted variation on the concept of a formal European garden. Here, more than 250 box trees have been patiently pruned into a variety of shapes and sizes. Look for the dancing elephant, the sunbathing Pamela Anderson, and the stunning re-creation of Brussels's Mannekin Pis. The café terrace commands an excellent view of the village. ✉ *Rue Haie Himbe 1,* ☎ *086/21–90–75.* 🎫 *BF150/€3.70.* ⊙ *Daily 10–6.*

Discover the region by driving through the lush forests surrounding Durbuy. Take N841 8 km southeast out of town to **Weiris** (designated one of the "most beautiful villages of Wallonia") with its array of half-timber houses and its 11th-century church. Continue south on N841 to 807 East toward **Soy,** home of the **Fantome,** a small artisanal brewery. Farther along the 807 in **Hotton,** climb through caves lined with unusual calcium deposits. Follow N86 to **Barvaux,** a perfect place to swim in the Ourthe River, rent a boat, or play tennis or golf. On the way back to Durbuy, notice the signs for the **Château de Petite Somme,** a renovated 18th-century castle, now home to members of the Hare Krishna.

Dining and Lodging

$$ ✕ **Ferme au Chêne.** Otherwise known as the the "Marckloff," this small artisanal brewery makes 350 liters of beer every 10 days. Brew masters Jacques and Michel Trine calculate that this permits each Durbuy resident one liter of beer during each brew cycle. But there's always some left for visitors to the brewery's restaurant, which specializes in traditional Ardennes sausage and other local cuisine. ✉ *Rue Cte. d'Ursel 36,* ☎ *086/21–10–67. Closed Wed., 1st wk of July.*

$ ✕ **Le Moulin.** In this 13th-century mill the cuisine has a Provençal air, with thyme, garlic, and saffron used liberally. Loin of lamb, duckling breast with honey and sherry, and seafood couscous are among the offerings. ✉ *Place aux Foires 17,* ☎ *086/21–29–70. AE, MC, V.*

$$ ✕🏨 **Du Vieux Pont.** M. and Mme. Stourbes, an affable young couple, have cleverly renovated the attic of this charming 19th-century house (once the residence of the town drawbridge operator) into homey guest rooms. Downstairs, the brasserie's bright yellow walls are adorned with historic photographs of old Durbuy. The menu features fish from the Ourthe and Ardennes ham, and the large outdoor terrace overlooks the main square. ✉ *Place aux Foires 26, 6940,* ☎ *086/21–28–08,* FAX *086/21–82–73. 4 rooms. Restaurant. MC, V. Restaurant closed Wed., hotel closed Jan.*

$$ ✕🏨 **Le Sanglier des Ardennes.** Dominating the center of town, this inn–cum–luxury restaurant has a stone fireplace, beams, and public spaces punctuated by glass cases with perfume, leather, and French scarves for sale. Rooms are classic pastel-modern, and the bathrooms are large. The restaurant (**$$$$**) offers grand French cooking with some regional touches. Back windows overlook the Ourthe River. If there are no rooms available here, ask about one of the other three hotels in town under the same ownership. ✉ *Rue Comte d'Ursel 99, B6940,* ☎ *086/21–32–62,* FAX *086/21–24–65. 41 rooms. Restaurant, bar, outdoor café. AE, DC, MC, V. Closed Thurs., Jan.*

Outdoor Activities and Sports

Durbuy has plenty of opportunities for outdoor activities. **Durbuy Adventure** (✉ Domaine des Cloiseries 62, Barvaux/St-Ourthe, ☎ 086/21–16–15) can arrange kayaking, mountain biking, rafting, and even paint ball. **Durbuy Discovery** (☎ 086/21–44–44) can arrange a variety of outdoor activities.

Shopping

Artisanal products are plentiful in Durbuy. The **Confiture Saint Amour** (✉ Rue St-Amour 13, 2 km [1 mi] from center of town, ☎ 086/21–12–76) has a wide array of homemade lotions, potions, jams, honey, and vinegars. The attached demonstration room allows visitors to discover how fruit from the forest is transformed into delicious jams. At **Diamour** (✉ Rue de la Prevote 50, ☎ 086/21–31–92) a small diamond atelier is attached to a shop where fine jewelry is sold.

La Roche-en-Ardenne

40 *29 km (17 mi) south of Durbuy, 77 km (46 mi) south of Liège, 127 km (76 mi) southeast of Brussels.*

The humble town of La Roche-en-Ardenne (commonly referred to simply as La Roche) is dominated by the medieval château ruins that stand on the hill above it. Cafés, restaurants, and hotels line the street along the river. In summer, they're filled with tourists taking a break from hiking, biking, or kayaking through the picturesque surrounding valley.

The **château** dates from the 9th century. Subsequently it was expanded by a long series of occupants, until the Austrians decided to partially dismantle it in the 18th century. In the summer, the ghost of Berthe, a woman of local legend, appears at sunset. ✉ *Pl. du Marché,* ☎ *061/ 21–27–11.* 🎫 *BF70/€1.75.* ⏲ *Apr.–June and Sept., daily 10–noon and 2–5; July–Aug., daily 10–7; Oct.–Mar., weekends 10–noon and 2–4.*

La Roche suffered badly during World War II's Battle of the Bulge, when 70,000 shells hit the town, leveling everything. After the war, equipment, unexploded ordnance, and other military paraphernalia littered the landscape. A local butcher began collecting this detrius from the woods, and what began as a hobby has ended up as an impressive museum. The **Musée de la Bataille des Ardennes** contains an extensive selection of American, English, and German war relics, including an authentic code-deciphering enigma machine. There are also full-scale dioramas re-creating life in the Ardennes during the war. ✉ *R. Châmont 5,* ☎ *084/41–17–25.* 🎫 *BF180/€4.45.* ⏲ *Daily 10–6.*

La Roche was liberated twice during World War II. An American Pershing M46 tank stands on the Quai de l'Ourthe commemorating the American's efforts during the first liberation on September 10, 1944. In front of the Hôtel de Ville stands an M10 British Achilles tank honoring the role of 55th Division of the Scottish Highlanders (known as the "Black Watch") during the second liberation on January 11, 1945. A moving plaque sits at the intersection of rue de la Gare and rue Ciele, the spot where the Americans and British troops met for the second liberation.

Dining and Lodging

$ ★ ✕ **Maison Bouillon & Fils.** In the heart of town, this charcuterie has been a La Roche institution since 1955. All of the meats are smoked and salted on the premises. House favorites include jambon d'Ardenne, flavored with juniper and laurel; rich *boudin blanc* (white sausage); and delectable *paté de gaume,* a hearty pork pie with white wine and parsley. Eat inside on one of the cheery red-and-white-check gingham tablecloths, or take some *viande* (meats) to go. ✉ *Place du Marche 9,* ☎ *084/41–18–80. No credit cards. Closed Tues.*

$$ ✕🏨 **La Claire Fontaine.** Situated on a gorgeous bluff, this Old World family hotel has a string of cozy parlors lined with eccentric bric-a-brac. The spacious, modern rooms have magnificent views, as does the restaurant, which is seemingly always feeding hungry crowds. ✉ *Route de Hotton 64, 6980,* ☎ *084/41–24–70,* FAX *084/41–21–11. 27 rooms. Restaurant. AE, MC, V.*

$$ ✕🏨 **Les Genets.** At this romantic old mountain inn, the rooms have stenciled wallpaper and a homey mix of plaid, paisley, and chintz. Picture windows take in valley views on two sides. The restaurant offers gastronomic menus with such offerings as trout salad with hazelnut vinaigrette and pigeon in juniper. ✉ *Corniche de Deister 2, B6980,* ☎ *084/41–18–77,* FAX *084/41–18–93. 8 rooms, 7 with bath. Restaurant, bar. AE, DC, MC, V. Closed 3 wks June–July, 1st ½ of Jan.*

$$ ✕🏨 **Hostellerie Linchet.** At the best address in town, this modern hotel has large rooms overlooking the Ourthe valley. The restaurant ($$$) has splendid views and serves traditional cuisine that includes stuffed crayfish, poached trout in Alsatian white wine, and fillet of venison with truffle sauce. There's alfresco dining in season. ✉ *Rte. de Houffalize 11, B6980,* ☎ *084/41–12–23,* FAX *084/41–24–10. 13 rooms. Restaurant. AE, MC, V. Hotel and restaurant closed Mar., 3 wks June–July, Wed.–Thurs.*

$ ✕🏨 **Du Midi.** This tiny old cliff-side hotel is worth a visit for the food, which is the real thing: straightforward regional specialties, simply and stylishly served. In-season wild game such as tenderloin of young boar in old port is superbly cooked and served with *gratin Dauphinois* (scalloped potatoes) and poached pear; there's also air-dried Ardennes ham with candied onions. The hotel is renovated, and the setting is distinctly local—oak, green plush, brass lamps, spinning-wheel chandeliers—though not old. ✉ *Rue Beausaint 6, 6980,* ☎ *084/41–11–38,* FAX *084/41–22–38. 8 rooms. Restaurant. AE, DC, MC, V. Closed 2nd ½ of Jan.*

En Route Follow N834 south and turn left on N843 to **Nisramont,** which has an excellent view. Then cross the river and go left on N860 to Nadrin, and left again on N869 to the **Belvedère des Six Ourthes,** so named because it has six different views of the meandering river. A 120-step climb to the top of the observation tower will reward you with a magnificent view of wooded hills and valleys.

Houffalize

41 *27 km (17 mi) southeast of La Roche-en-Ardennes, 102 km (63 mi) south of Liège, 152 km (94 mi) southeast of Brussels.*

This quaint mountain village is a place for clean air and family fun. There's something here for all ages and all activity levels—from biking and hiking to fishing and boating. The biking terrain is a challenge. Riders in the annual Liège-Bastogne-Liège bike race refer to the mountain as "the first serious hill" in the competition.

Houtopia is a large amusement park for small children, funded in part by UNICEF. Interactive games, multimedia spectacles, and educational programs emphasize the rights and responsibilities of children. ✉ *E25 Liège-Arlon, Exit 25,* ☎ *061/28–92–05,* ⏲ *Feb.–Dec., daily.*

★ The **Brasserie d'Achouffe,** a fast-growing artisanal brewery with a whimsical elf for a mascot, is a family affair. What started as a hobby for Chris Bauweraerts and his brother-in-law, Pierre Goron, has now become an internationally respected brewery featuring unusual, flavorful beers. In 1997, the Beverage Tasting Institute of Chicago selected Achouffe as one of the top 10 breweries of the year. Stop in for a tour and a tasting, or visit their unique gift shop. If hunger strikes, the attached restaurant ($, AE, MC, V) serves fresh trout and unbeatable rabbit stew. ✉ *Achouffe 32,* ☎ *061/28–81–47.* *Tour BF150/€3.70.* ⏲ *Thurs.–Tues., tour 10:30.*

Outdoor Activities and Sports

For kayakers, the territory is fulfilling. **Azimut** (✉ 51 rue de la Roche, ☎ 61/28–86–43) is the local kayak rental shop. **Buitensport AS** (✉ 63 rue de la Roche, ☎ 61/28–83–14) rents kayaks and can recommend several rewarding routes.

Mountain bikers can rent equipment at Azimut (☞ *above*). An alternative choice for bike rental is **Houffa Bike** (✉ 13 rue de Bastogne, ☎ 61/28–93–13).

Bastogne

42 *34 km (20 mi) south of La Roche-en-Ardenne, 88 km (53 mi) south of Liège, 148 km (89 mi) southeast of Brussels.*

Bastogne is where General MacAuliffe delivered World War II's most famous response to a surrender request: "Nuts!" Although a number of Ardennes towns were destroyed during the Battle of the Bulge, Bastogne was the epicenter. The town was surrounded by Germans but held by the American 101st Airborne Division. The weather was miserable, making it impossible for supplies to be flown in to the Americans. On December 22, 1944, the Germans asked the U.S. forces to surrender. They didn't. On December 26 the skies cleared and supplies were flown in, but it took another month before the last German stronghold was destroyed. To this day, a Sherman tank occupies a place of honor in the town square, named after General MacAuliffe himself. The tourist office is also here.

The **Colline du Mardasson** (Mardasson Hill Memorial) honors the Americans lost in the Battle of the Bulge. The names of all U.S. Army units are inscribed on the wall, along with a simple phrase: "The Belgian People Remembers Its American Liberators." Mosaics by Fernand Léger decorate the crypt's Protestant, Catholic, and Jewish chapels. Across the road is **The Woods of Peace,** a forest planted by UNICEF to commemorate the Belgians who lost their lives during the war. The trees are planted in the form of the UNICEF symbol of a mother embracing her child. The **Bastogne Historical Center,** next to the memorial monument, is built in the shape of a five-point star and is filled with uniforms, weapons, and commentary from and about World War II. The script for the introductory film, shown in the amphitheater, was written with help from the Battle of the Bulge's opposing generals, MacAuliffe of the U.S. 101st Airborne Division and Hasso Van Manteufel of the German Fifth Panzer Army. The film, and tours, are available in six languages. ✉ *N84, 3 km (2 mi) east of Bastogne,* ☎ *061/21–14–13.* 🎫 *BF245/€6.05.* ⏲ *Sept.–Apr., daily 10–4; May–June, daily 9:30–5; July–Aug., daily 9–6.*

The American West is alive and well in Wallonia at the **Bison Park.** A local breeder and landowner with a passion for the animals has more than 100 of them grazing on his 250-acre farm. There are also exhibits about various aspects of American Indian culture, including a tepee 7 m (23 ft) tall. ✉ *Recogne, 5 km (3 mi) from Bastogne,* ☎ *061/21–06–40.* 🎫 *BF150/€3.70.* ⏲ *July–Aug., Tues.–Sun. noon–7; mid-Apr.–July and Sept.–Oct., Sun. noon–7.*

Dining and Lodging

$ ✕ **Wagon-Restaurant Léo.** Originally a tiny chrome railroad diner, this local institution has spilled over across the street into the chicly refurbished Bistro Léo. The restaurant serves huge platters of Belgian standards—mussels, trout in riesling, *filet Américain* (steak tartare), frites; in the bistro, cold ham plates, quiche, and homemade lasagna are the fare. ✉ *Rue du Vivier 8,* ☎ *061/21–65–10. MC, V.*

$$ ✕🏨 **Hôtel Collin.** M. Collin, a friendly man never too harried to stop and shake your hand, owns and manages this centrally located inn. The facade is Victorian, but inside the blue and yellow rooms are clean, bright, and contemporary. If you crave open spaces (or if you're traveling with your dog) ask for a room attached to the interior courtyard. M. Collin also owns and operates the attached Café 1900, a local favorite with Victorian-inspired decor. The offerings range from simple afternoon tea to *canard à la framboise* (duck with raspberries). ✉ *Place MacAuliffe 8–9, 6600,* ☎ *061/21–43–58,* FAX *061/21–80–83. 16 rooms. Restaurant. AE, MC, V. Restaurant closed Wed.*

$$ 🏨 **Melba.** A couple of minutes from Place MacAuliffe, this is a modern, somewhat characterless hotel. The rooms here are clean and convenient, but the main attraction is the walking path to the Bastogne Historical Center (☞ *above*), which begins right behind the hotel. ✉ *Av. Mathieu 49–51, B6600,* ☎ *061/21–77–78,* FAX *061/21–55–68. 36 rooms. Breakfast room, meeting rooms. AE, MC, V.* 🚭

St-Hubert

43 *28 km (17 mi) west of Bastogne, 25 km (15 mi) south of La Roche-en-Ardenne, 137 km (82 mi) southeast of Brussels.*

St-Hubert bears the name of the patron saint of hunters. According to legend, Hubert, hunting in these woods on Good Friday in 683, saw his quarry, a stag, turn its head toward him; its antlers held a crucifix. Hubert lowered his bow and went on to become a bishop and a saint. On the first Sunday in September, the old **Basilica** (which houses St. Hubert's tomb) has a special Mass that includes music played with hunting horns, followed by a historical procession; and on November 3, St. Hubert's Feast Day, there's a blessing of the animals in the Basilica. The Basilica is stunningly beautiful, with a late Gothic interior of noble proportions and luminosity. ⊠ *Pl. de l'Abbaye,* ☎ *061/61–23–88.* *BF25/€0.60.* *Daily 9–6.*

Fourneau St-Michel has two interesting museums. One is an **Industrial Museum** that includes a preserved 18th-century ironworks complex and shows ironworking techniques up to the 19th century. The other is an open-air **Museum of Rural Life**, with 25 structures, including thatched cottages, tobacco sheds, a chapel, and a school. ⊠ *Rte. de Nassagne, 7 km (4 mi) north of St-Hubert,* ☎ *084/21–08–90.* *BF100/€2.50 per museum.* *Mar.–Dec. (Rural Life until mid-Nov.), daily 9–5 (July–Aug. until 6).*

The **Euro Space Center** shows off the latest aerospace technology in a futuristic setting, with models (some full-scale) of the *Discovery* space shuttle, *Mir* space station, and *Ariane* satellite launcher. There's an educational program as well. ⊠ *Rue Devant-les-Hêtres 1, Transinne, east of St. Hubert,* ☎ *061/65–64–65.* *BF395/€9.80.* *Apr.–Nov., daily 10:30–6.*

Lodging

$$ **Hôtel de L'Abbaye.** Not much has changed since Ernest Hemingway stayed here for a month in 1944 while covering the war. The hotel's main dining room, with its checkered floors, large stone hearth, historical photographs of the Festival du St-Hubert, and view of the main square, encourages lingering. The guest rooms can be a bit musty and threadbare. ⊠ *Place du Marché 18, 6870,* ☎ *061/61–10–23,* FAX *061/61–34–22. 20 rooms. MC, V. Closed 2 wks in Sept.*

OFF THE BEATEN PATH

REDU – This tiny village 20 km (12 mi) west of St-Hubert is a mecca for bibliophiles. Both the serious and the merely curious book lover will appreciate the numerous book shops, the rows of overstocked book stalls, the array of bookbinding studios, and the small printing museum. (If you come here hoping to pick up something to read, keep in mind that the vast majority of the books are not in English.)

Bouillon

44 *56 km (34 mi) southwest of St-Hubert, 81 km (49 mi) southwest of La Roche-en-Ardenne, 161 km (97 mi) southeast of Brussels.*

In Bouillon, the Semois River curls around a promontory crowned by one of Europe's most impressive castles. This tiny town was capital of a duchy almost equally small, which managed to remain its independent identity from 963 to 1794, though not without many political twists of fate. (Its most famous native son, Godefroid de Bouillon, sold it to the Bishop of Liège in 1095 to improve his cash flow, before departing on the first crusade and becoming Defender of the Holy Sepulchre.) Now the town is annually invaded by tourists. The season officially starts with the **Trout Festival** during the first three weeks of April, continues through the **Medieval Festival** in August, and ends as the spectacular fall foliage begins to fade.

Bouillon's eight centuries of independence were primarily secured by the **Château Fort,** an impressive example of medieval military architecture. Successive modifications have done little to alter the personality of this feudal stronghold, with its towers, drawbridge, guard room, torture chamber, dungeon, and enormous walls. There's an outstanding view from the top of the Tour d'Autriche. Visits by torchlight are organized nightly (except Monday and Thursday) in July and August. ✉ *On hill above city,* ☎ *061/46–62–57.* 🎫 *BF150/€3.70.* ⏲ *Mar.–June and Sept.–Nov., daily 10–5; July–Aug., daily 9:30–7; Dec. and Feb., weekdays 1–5, weekends 10–5.*

The **Musée Ducal** is installed in an 18th-century mansion in front of Bouillon's famous château. Its collections illustrate the history of the Crusades; one section is devoted to the printing press used for the works of Voltaire, Diderot, and other writers when they could not publish in France. ✉ *Rue du Petit 1–3,* ☎ *061/46–69–56.* 🎫 *BF120/€2.95.* ⏲ *Apr.–June and Sept.–Oct., daily 10–6; July–Aug., daily 9:30–6.*

★ The **Archeoscope de Godefroid de Bouillion** opened in 1998 in a former nunnery. The museum's innovative exhibits use interactive technology, video screens, holograms, and music to educate visitors of all ages about the history of the region and the Crusades. There is a re-created cloister from the original nunnery, and a gallery devoted to the Islamic perspective on the Crusades, which characterizes the efforts as an invasion. The gift shop carries a selection of cute and clever Crusade-themed tchotchkes. Museum passes are available here, and at the other museums, for discounted admission. ✉ *Quai des Sauix 14,* ☎ *061/46–83–03.* 🎫 *BF240/€5.95.* ⏲ *Mar.–Apr., daily 10–4; May–June and Sept., daily 10–5; July–Aug., daily 10–6; Oct.–Feb., weekends 10–6.*

Leave time to discover the **Semois valley,** a thickly forested region where unassuming plateaus reveal magnificent hidden castles and ruins. Leave Bouillon on N89 north to N819 west, which will lead you through **Rocheaut,** a small enclave overlooking the valley villages of **Frahan** and **Laviot** and ruins of **Montragut** and **Lyresse.** Continue south on the same road to **Corbion,** the 1520 birthplace of Sebastion de Corbion (also known as Sebastion de Pistolet), the inventor of the pistol. While following N810 back to Bouillon, stop at the **Ramonette Arboretum,** which, in addition to its groves of trees, is known for its collection of medicinal plant species.

Dining and Lodging

$ ✕ **Le Soliel Levant.** Overlooking the Semois, this informal spot offers a simple and reliable menu including salads, hamburgers, and a selection of Belgian beers. ✉ *Grand rue 2,* ☎ *061/46–60–62. AE, MC, V.*

$$$$ ✕🏨 **Auberge du Moulin Hideux.** Nestled in a valley amid leafy woods, this inn is synonymous with gracious living. The fountain is illuminated at night, swans glide in the small pond, and breakfast is served on the flower-bedecked terrace. The cuisine is traditional but updated with a lighter touch; woodcock mousse, black and white *boudins* (blood sausage) with truffles, and fabulous game in season are among the highlights. The rooms have been decorated with great taste by the owner. Interestingly, the name means the "Hideous Mill," a play on words from the fact that there used to be two mills, *il y a deux.* ✉ *Rte. de Dohan 1, B6831 Noirefontaine, 4 km (2½ mi) north of Bouillon,* ☎ *061/46–70–15,* FAX *061/46–72–81. 10 rooms, 3 suites. Restaurant, bar, pool, bicycles. AE, DC, MC, V. Closed Dec.–mid-Mar.*

$$ ★ ✕🏨 **Au Gastronome.** This auberge, once a roadside café, is home to one of Belgium's top restaurants (**$$$$**). The chef produces standards of French haute cuisine with such skill that they seem fresh and original. A local delicacy is suckling pig, roasted in its crisp skin, its juices blending with

the stuffing of green pepper and lime. The setting is a little stuffy, but rooms upstairs are pleasantly old-fashioned, in shades of pink and cream, with floral prints. All overlook the garden. ✉ *Rue de Bouillon 2, B6850 Paliseul, 15 km (9 mi) north of Bouillon,* ☎ *061/53–30–64,* FAX *061/53–38–91. 9 rooms. Restaurant, pool. AE, DC, MC, V. Closed Mon., Jan.–early Feb., last wk June–1st wk July. No dinner Sun.*

$ ✕🏨 **Auberge d'Alsace.** In the center of Bouillon, with the river Semois across the street and the château towering behind, is this ambitious little hotel-restaurant. Having had the interior rebuilt from the ground up, the proprietress has lavished the rooms with flashy materials—brass, lacquer, lace, and the occasional baldachin. Striking a similar balance between store-bought chic and Old Ardennes, the restaurant downstairs offers good cooking: monkfish with kiwi, curried shrimp, home-smoked trout, and *civet de marcassin* (stew of preserved young boar). ✉ *Faubourg de France 1–3, B6830,* ☎ *061/46–65–88,* FAX *061/46–83–21. 36 rooms, 2 suites. Restaurant, café, outdoor café. AE, MC, V.*

$$ 🏨 **De la Poste.** This is the most historic and atmospheric hotel in town, but not consistently the most comfortable. Since Napoléon III, Emile Zola, and Victor Hugo stayed at this 1730 stagecoach stop, its original rooms have been left virtually unchanged, balancing burnished oak and antiques with aged fixtures and small baths. One renovation is an outdoor riverside terrace, and the annex, built in 1990, offers modern comfort. Downstairs, the grandeur remains intact, with a charming mix of Victorian antiques and rustic bric-a-brac. The restaurant stretches along the riverfront; the menu features French classics. ✉ *Pl. St-Arnould 1, B6830,* ☎ *061/46–51–51,* FAX *061/46–51–65. 77 rooms, 68 with private bath. Restaurant, bar, outdoor café. AE, DC, MC, V.*

Shopping

Le Marché de Natalie (✉ Grand rue 22, ☎ 061/46–89–40; closed Wed.) is known throughout the region for its wide array of local culinary products including beers, cheeses, hams, and jams. There is a small artisanal brewery on site.

Orval

45 *29 km (18 mi) southeast of Bouillon, 190 km (118 mi) southeast of Brussels.*

Orval, a few kilometers from Belgium's border with France, is a tiny town hidden in the forest. One major attraction is the draw here: the ★ magnificent abbey. **Abbaye d'Orval** was once one of Europe's richest and most famous monasteries. Founded by Italian Benedictines in 1070, it flourished for 700 years before being twice destroyed by French troops. The grandeur and nobility of the medieval and 18th-century ruins are remarkable. The tomb of Wenceslas, first Duke of Luxembourg, is in the choir of the abbey church, and the gardens contain the spring where Mathilde, Duchess of Lorraine, once dropped her wedding band, only to have it miraculously returned by a trout. (Mathilde's magical fish is the abbey's trademark symbol.) The monastery was reconsecrated as a Trappist abbey in 1948, and now the peaceful gardens and a thoughtful museum are open to visitors. The monks are known not only for their spirituality but also for their excellent bread and potent Trappist beer. ✉ *Villers-devant-Orval,* ☎ *061/31–10–60.* 🎫 *BF100/€2.50.* ⏲ *Mar.–May, daily 9:30–12:30 and 1:30–6; June, daily 9:30–12:30 and 1:30–6:30, Sept.–Feb., daily 10:30–12:30 and 1:30–5:30.*

NEED A BREAK? The summer crowds know that the best spot for an Orval beer or slice of Orval cheese is the **Hostellerie d'Orval** (✉ 14 rue de Orval, Viller-Devant-Orval), about 2 km from the Abbey. It's open all year.

Dining and Lodging

$$$$ ★ ✕🏨 **Château du Pont-d'Oye.** Loll in the lap of luxury at this glorious 17th-century château, which formerly belonged to the infamous Marquise de Pont d'Oye. Each individually named room is decorated with oil paintings, chandeliers, thick drapes, and regal red carpets. There's a wooden chapel on the first floor, and beyond it fragrant rose gardens. The restaurant's daily gastronomique specialties could include foie gras, oysters, lobster, or quail with truffles. This hideaway can fill up quickly, so it's wise to book well in advance. Pension plans are a good deal here. ✉ *Rue du Pont d'Oye 1, B6720 Habay-la-Neuve 25 km* east of Orval, ☎ 063/42–21–48, FAX 063/42–35–88. 18 rooms. Restaurant. AE, DC, MC, V. Closed Mon., 2nd ½ of Feb., last wk in Aug. No dinner Sun.

$$ 🏨 **Hostellerie Sainte Cecille.** A large lyre painted on the outside of this family-run rural inn pays homage to Ste. Cecille, the patron saint of music. The sitting room radiates with the warmth of a woodwind sonata and opens up to the lovely garden, where you can enjoy the sounds of the babbling brook. The cozy, comfortable rooms overlook the fields and gardens. The restaurant serves well-prepared French cuisine. ✉ *Rue Neuve 1, 6820 Ste-Cecille-Sur-Semois, 16 km (10 mi) north of Orval, ☎ 061/31–31–67, FAX 061/31–50–04. 14 rooms. AE, MC, V. Closed mid-Jan.–mid-Mar.*

$$ 🏨 **Hôtel de France.** The grandfather of the family that runs this handsome hotel was friendly with the architect who redesigned, and the bishop who reconsecrated, the Abbaye d'Orval. Hence, the wood-paneled lobby and the dining room are lined with historical photographs of the abbey, and the proprietors are experts on the area. The hotel's range of rooms, decorated with simple wood furniture and exposed wood floors, can accommodate single travelers or large families—they're popular with wild mushroom pickers in the fall season. Rest in the formal French rose garden in back, with its more than 200 bushes. ✉ *Rue des Generaux Cuvelier 26, Florenville, 8 km (5 mi) north of Orval, ☎ 061/31–10–32, FAX 061/32–02–83. 32 rooms. AE, MC, V.*

THE MEUSE AND THE ARDENNES A TO Z

Arriving and Departing

By Car

In the **Meuse valley,** Rochefort is close to the E411 highway, which links Brussels with Luxembourg and runs south and east. Namur is close to the intersection of the E411 with the E42, which links Liège with Charleroi, Mons, and Paris, as well as with Tournai, Lille, and Calais.

Liège is almost halfway to Cologne from Brussels on the E40. The city is also linked with Paris by the E42, which merges with E19 from Brussels near Mons; with Antwerp by the E313; and with Maastricht and the Dutch highway system by E25, which continues south to join the E411 to Luxembourg.

The main arteries to and through the **Belgian Luxembourg** region are the E411 highway from Brussels, which can get very busy during school holidays, and the E25 from Liège, generally less traveled, which joins the E411 not far from the border with the Grand Duchy. When the E411 is busy, the N4 highway from Namur to Bastogne is often a good alternative. The N63 highway from Liège links up with the N4 at Marche-en-Famenne, and the N89 connects La Roche-en-Ardenne with Bouillon via St-Hubert.

By Train

Two trains an hour link Brussels with **Namur** (1 hour from Brussels's Gare du Midi, 50 minutes from the Gare du Nord). They connect with a local service to Dinant (25 minutes). For **train information** in Namur, call ☎ 081/22–36–75.

Two trains run every hour from Brussels to **Liège** (1 hour by express train from Brussels Nord, 1 hour and 10 minutes from Brussels Midi; local trains are 10 minutes slower). Thalys high-speed trains cut 15 minutes off travel time from Brussels Midi. All express trains from Oostende to Cologne stop at Liège, as do international trains from Copenhagen and Hamburg to Paris. Liège's train station is the **Gare des Guillemins** (☎ 04/252–9850).

Local trains from Brussels to Luxembourg stop in **Belgian Luxembourg** at Jemelle (near Rochefort) and Libramont (halfway between St-Hubert and Bouillon). Trains run every hour; the trip to Jemelle takes 1 hour and 5 minutes; to Libramont, 2 hours. The trains connect with local bus services.

Getting Around

By Bus

From train stations in Liège, Verviers, Eupen, and Trois-Ponts there is bus service to other localities. In Liège, a single trip on a bus in the inner city costs BF36/€0.90, and eight-trip cards sell for BF200/€4.95.

By Car

The most convenient way of getting around the Meuse valley, the Liège region, and Belgian Luxembourg is by car. Public transportation services are scant. The E411 highway cuts through the region. Elsewhere, you travel chiefly on pleasant, two-lane roads through lovely scenery. Getting lost on the back roads of Wallonia is a true pleasure.

By Taxi

Taxis are plentiful in Liège. They can be picked up at cab stands in the principal squares or summoned by phone (☎ 04/367–6600).

By Train

Local train services exist from Liège via Verviers to Eupen, and to Trois-Ponts (near Stavelot). The high-speed TGV train runs from points in France and Germany to Liège.

Contacts and Resources

Car Rental

Avis (✉ Bd. d'Avroy 238, Liège, ☎ 04/252–5500; ✉ Av. des Combattants 31, Namur, ☎ 081/735906). **Europcar** (✉ Sq. Léopold 20, Namur, ☎ 081/31–32–56). **Hertz** (✉ Bd. d'Avroy 60, Liège, ☎ 04/222–4273).

Guided Tours

BY BOAT

Boat tours, ranging from short excursions to all-day trips, are available in both Dinant and Namur: **Bateau Ansiaux** (✉ Rue du Vélodrome 15, Dinant, ☎ 082/22–23–25); **Bateau Bayard** (✉ Quai de Meuse 1, Dinant, ☎ 082/22–30–42). With some advance planning, you could probably arrange to sail the entire length of the Meuse from France to the Netherlands by sightseeing boats: **Bateau Val Mosan** (✉ Quai de Namur 1, Huy, ☎ 025/21–29–15).

From Liège, there are **one-day sightseeing boat excursions** to Maastricht in the Netherlands on Friday during July and August. A visit to the Blegny Coal Mine and museum is included. Departures are from the Passerelle on the right bank of the Meuse. For reservations, call ☎ 04/387–4333.

ON FOOT

Guided walks are available April through September in **Mozet** (southeast of Namur; ☎ 085/84–21–55) on the third Sunday of each month, and in **Chardeneux** (✉ off of N63 west of Durbuy; ☎ 086/34–44–07) on the first Sunday of each month. In **Namur,** walking tours of the old city and the Citadelle, plus tours with a theme, such as local painters or gardens in the city, take place every day during July and August, starting at the **Information Center** (✉ Sq. Léopold, ☎ 081/24–64–49). The price, per person, is BF140/€3.45.

You can hire an English-speaking guide from the **Liège City Tourist Office** (☞ Visitor Information, *below*). Rates are BF1,600/€39.65 for two hours, BF2,350/€58.25 for three hours. If your French is up to it, you're welcome to join a guided walking tour with French commentary, starting from the city tourist office, July and August, Wednesday through Sunday, at 2, for BF140/€3.45.

Outdoor Activities and Sports

BIKING

In the **Meuse valley** you can rent mountain bikes at **Bill's Bike Evasion** (✉ Chaussée de Namur 14, Profondeville, ☎ 081/41–41–55), **Kayaks Ansiaux** (✉ Rue du Vélodrome 15, Anseremme-Dinant, ☎ 082/22–23–25), and **Kayaks Lesse & Lhomme** (✉ Le Plan d'Eau, Han-sur-Lesse, ☎ 082/22–43–97).

Biking in **Belgian Luxembourg** requires strong legs. Mountain bikes can be rented from **Ardenne Adventures** and **Ferme de Palogne** (☞ Canoeing, *below*). **Moulin de la Falize** (✉ Bouillon, ☎ 061/46–62–00) is a multisport facility that rents bikes and also has a swimming pool, bowling alleys, a sauna, and a fitness room.

CANOEING, KAYAKING, RAFTING

In the **Meuse valley** region, the Lesse is one of the liveliest tributaries to the Meuse, great for kayaking. You can choose between the upper Lesse, where Lessive is the starting point, and the 21-km (13-mi) ride from Hoyet, through two rapids and past the high cliffs holding Walzin Castle, to Anseremme on the Meuse, just south of Dinant. Most of the kayak-rental companies also have mountain bikes (☞ Biking, *above*); others include **Kayaks Libert** (✉ Quai de Meuse 1, Dinant, ☎ 082/22–61–86) and **Lesse Kayaks** (✉ Pl. de l'Eglise 2, Anseremme, ☎ 082/22–43–97). The season runs from April through October. Rentals start at around BF800/€19.85.

In **Belgian Luxembourg** the rapid rivers of the Ardennes are ideal for all three sports. Equipment can be rented by day or by distance, generally with return transportation to the point of departure. For the river Ourthe, try **Ardenne Adventures** (✉ La Roche-en-Ardenne, ☎ 084/41–19–00; kayaks Apr.–Oct., rafting Nov.–Mar.) or **Ferme de Palogne** (✉ Vieuxville, ☎ 086/21–24–12). For the Semois River, go to **Récréalle** (✉ Alle-sur-Semois, ☎ 061/50–03–81), which also functions as a general sports center with facilities for table tennis, minigolf, bowling, fishing, and volleyball, or **Saty Rapids** (✉ Bouillon, ☎ 061/46–62–00).

FISHING

In the **Meuse valley,** fishing is permitted on several stretches of the Meuse and on some livelier tributaries, where it is mostly of the sitting-on-the-bank kind. Licenses can be purchased at local **post offices** (✉ Rue St-Martin, Dinant; ✉ Av. Bovesse, Namur-Jambes).

HORSEBACK RIDING

In the **Meuse valley** region several stables organize treks with overnight accommodations. Horses can be rented for about BF500/€6.40 per hour. Contact the Provincial Tourist Office (☞ *below*) for a list of more than 20 stables. In Belgian Luxembourg **Centre Equestre de Mont-le-Soie** (✉ Grand-Halleux, Mont-le-Soie, 7km north of Vielsalm, ☎ 080/21–64–43) offers both instruction and guided trail rides.

ROCK CLIMBING

The sheer cliffs along the **Meuse** are excellent. Many hopeful mountaineers learn the skills here for more dramatic exploits. Contact **Club Alpin Belge** (✉ Av. Albert I 129, Namur, ☎ 081/22–40–84).

SAILING

In the **Meuse** region sailing is extremely popular, with yacht harbors at Namur, Profondeville, Dinant, and Waulsort. Contact **Royal Nautique Club de Sambre et Meuse** (✉ Chemin des Pruniers 11, Wepion, ☎ 081/46–11–30).

Visitor Information

For the entire region of Wallonia: **Office de Promotion du Tourisme** (✉ Rue du Marché-aux-Herbes 63, Brussels, ☎ 02/504–0200). Province of Belgian Luxembourg: **Tourist Office** (✉ Quai de l'Ourthe 9, La Roche-en-Ardenne, ☎ 084/41–10–11). Province of Liège: **Tourist Office** (✉ Bd. de la Sauvenière 77, ☎ 04/222–4210). Province of Namur: **Tourist Office** (✉ Parc Industriel, rue Pieds d'Alouette 18, Naninne-Namur, ☎ 081/40–80–10).

City tourist offices: **Arlon** (✉ Rue des Faubourgs 2, ☎ 063/21–63–60); **Bastogne** (✉ Pl. MacAuliffe 24, ☎ 061/21–27–11); **Bouillon** (✉ Bureau du Château-Fort, ☎ 061/46–62–57; during high season, ✉ Porte de France, ☎ 061/46–62–89); **Dinant** (✉ Rue Grande 37, ☎ 082/22–28–70); **Durbuy** (✉ Rue Comte d'Ursel, ☎ 086/21–24–28); **Eupen** (✉ Marktpl. 7, ☎ 087/55–34–50); **Huy** (✉ Quai de Namur 1, ☎ 085/21–29–15); **La Roche-en-Ardenne** (✉ Syndicat d'Initiative, Pl. du Marché 15, ☎ 084/41–13–42); **Liège** (✉ En Féronstrée 92, ☎ 04/221–9221); **Malmédy** (✉ Pl. du Châtelet 10, ☎ 080/33–02–50); **Namur** (✉ Sq. de l'Europe Unie, ☎ 081/24–64–49); **Spa** (✉ Rue Royale 41, ☎ 087/79–53–53); **St-Hubert** (✉ Rue St-Gilles, ☎ 061/61–30–10); **Stavelot** (✉ Ancienne Abbaye, ☎ 080/86–27–06).

8 LUXEMBOURG

Tiny Luxembourg, nestled between Germany, France, and Belgium, has been a pawn of world powers for much of its 1,000 years. Today it looms large as a world financial powerhouse and one of Europe's most scenic countries. Come here for rambles through medieval villages and hilltop castles, strolls along riverbanks and through deep forests, and hearty meals in country inns. From sophisticated Luxembourg City, with its ancient fortifications and modern skyscrapers, to the Ardennes plateau, site of the World War II Battle of the Bulge, to the wineries along the Moselle, Luxembourg is 999 square miles of beauty, history, and good times.

By Michael Schiffer and Wendy Wasserman

THE CAPITAL OF LUXEMBOURG greets visitors with an awe-inspiring view: up and down the length of the Alzette River stretches a panorama of medieval stonework—jutting fortification walls, slit-windowed towers, ancient church spires, massive gates—as detailed and complete as a 17th-century engraving come to life. Then you abruptly enter the 20th century. The boulevard Royal, little more than five blocks long, glitters with glass-and-concrete office buildings, each containing a world-class bank and untold anonymous, well-sheltered fortunes.

Luxembourg, once sovereign to lands that stretched from the Meuse to the Rhine, was reduced over the centuries to being a pawn in the power struggles between its many conquerors. Until recently little more than a cluster of meager farms and failing mines, Luxembourg today enjoys newfound political clout and the highest per capita income in the world.

The Grand Duchy of Luxembourg, one of the smallest countries in the United Nations, measures only 2,597 square km (999 square mi). Smaller than Rhode Island, it has a population of 420,000. It is dwarfed by its neighbors—Germany, Belgium, and France—yet from its history of invasion, occupation, and siege, you would think those square miles were filled with solid gold. In fact, it was Luxembourg's fortresses carved out of bedrock, its very defenses against centuries of attack, that rendered it all the more desirable.

First inhabited more than 3,000 years ago by pre-Celtic tribes, the area now known as Luxembourg was part of the northern region of the Roman Empire. The country's modern history starts in 963, when Charlemagne's descendant Sigefroid, a beneficiary of the disintegration of Central Europe that followed Charlemagne's death, chose a small gooseneck, carved by the Alzette, to develop as a fortress and the capital of his considerable domain. Thanks to his aggressions and the ambitions of his heirs, Luxembourg grew continuously until, by the 14th century, its count, Henry IV, was powerful and important enough to serve as Henry VII, king of the German nations and Holy Roman Emperor. During that epoch, Luxembourg contributed no fewer than five kings and emperors, including Henry VII's son, the flamboyant John the Blind (Jean l'Aveugle), who, despite leading his armies to slaughter in the Battle of Crécy (1346), remains a national hero.

After John the Blind's death, Luxembourg commanded the greatest territory it would ever rule—from the Meuse to Metz and the Moselle—and its rulers, Charles IV, Wenceslas I and II, and Sigismund, carried the name of the House of Luxembourg to European renown. If Luxembourg had a golden age, this was it, but it was short-lived. Plague, the decay of feudalism, marital and financial intrigues among leaders who rarely, if ever, set foot in Luxembourg—all these factors finally left the duchy vulnerable, and Philip the Good, Duke of Burgundy, took it by storm in 1443.

From that point on, Luxembourg lost its significance as a geographical mass and took on importance as a fortress. It was controlled from 1443 to 1506 by Burgundy, from 1506 to 1714 by Spain (with a brief period, 1684–97, under Louis XIV of France), and from 1714 to 1795 by Austria; Napoléon took it from the Habsburgs in 1795. Each, in taking the fortress, had to penetrate miles of outworks whose battlements filled the countryside. After having penetrated the outer defenses, the aggressors then faced a citadel perched on sheer stone cliffs, from which weapons pointed at them and within which the soldiers outnumbered the citizens. To take it by frontal attack was out of the question; the solution, usually, was siege and starvation.

Having been torn and ravaged for 400 years by its conquerors' games of tug-of-war, Luxembourg continued to provoke squabbles well into the 19th century. The Congress of Vienna gave a territorially reduced Luxembourg independence of a sort. The Grand Duke of Luxembourg was also King of Holland when Belgium rebelled against Dutch rule in 1830. Only the presence of a Prussian garrison kept Luxembourg in the Dutch camp. Nine years later, Luxembourg was again partitioned, with the western half becoming a Belgian province. William II became the first and last Dutch Grand Duke to achieve popular acclaim; he created a parliament and laid the foundations for modern Luxembourg. In 1867 Luxembourg was declared an independent and neutral state by the Treaty of London, and its battlements were dismantled, stone by stone. What remains of its walls, while impressive, is only a reminder of what was once one of the great strongholds of Europe.

The grand duchy's neutrality was violated by the Germans in 1914. When World War I ended, the people of Luxembourg gave their confidence, by popular vote, to Grand Duchess Charlotte, who remained a much-loved head of state for 45 years until abdicating in favor of her son, Jean, in 1964. Grand Duke Jean, married to Grand Duchess Joséphine-Charlotte, the daughter of Belgium's King Leopold and his Swedish-born Queen Astrid, abdicated to their son, Henri, in September 2000. The reigning family has remained untouched by the types of scandals that have marred the reputations of other royal houses.

Although more than two-thirds of the country had immigrated to the Americas due to economic hardships in the late 19th century, breakthroughs in both farming and mining technology turned the country around. A new, efficient technique for purifying iron ore created an indispensable by-product, fertilizer, which started a boom that put Luxembourg on 20th-century maps. A steel industry was created and, with it, more jobs than there were local workers. Thousands of workers came from Italy, and later Portugal, to take up residence in Luxembourg. About 20% of the workforce lives outside Luxembourg and crosses the border daily going to and from work. Another 30% are foreigners who reside inside Luxembourg's borders; in the late 1990s they were given the right to vote under EU rules.

Most recently, Luxembourg has become one of the world's top financial centers, with 225 banks from throughout the world established in the grand duchy. The broadcasting and communications satellite industries are also important to the national economy.

Hitler was convinced that Luxembourg was part of the greater Germanic culture. Suppressing *Lëtzebuergsch* (Luxembourgish, the local language) and changing French names into German, he launched a campaign to persuade Luxembourgers to *Heim ins Reich*—come home to the fatherland as ethnic Germans. A visit to any war museum shows that the Luxembourgers were having none of it. As a nation they have yet to forget how the German invasions left Luxembourg hideously scarred, or how thousands of its men were conscripted during the German occupation and sent as so much cannon fodder to the Russian front.

The experiences of two world wars convinced Luxembourg that neutrality does not work. Native son Robert Schuman was one of the founding fathers of the Common Market that eventually became the European Union, with Luxembourg a charter member. The European Court of

Justice and other European institutions are in the Kirchberg section of Luxembourg City.

Soldiers from Luxembourg serve with young men from France, Germany, and Belgium in the European Army. The small force is a powerful symbol of the unity that has replaced old enmities. The men from Luxembourg can communicate with their European brothers readily, because they are fluent in both French and German. French is the official language of the grand duchy, and the teaching of German is mandatory in the schools. Luxembourgers' own language, *Lëtzebuergsch*, descended from the language of the Rhineland Franks, has the added advantage of being understood by virtually no one else. This is the language in which the national motto is expressed: *Mir wölle bleiwe wat mir sin,* "We want to stay what we are." Today that means being a powerful, viable grand duchy in the heart of modern Europe.

Pleasures and Pastimes

Architecture

For architectural buffs, Luxembourg can be very rewarding. In Luxembourg City, walks have been laid out that let you explore the city's 1,000 year history. The Kirchberg Plateau is a sea of contemporary skyscrapers, dominated by the **Grand Duke Jean Museum of Modern Art** designed by I. M. Pei. Around the country, towns such as Esch-sur-Alzette and Grevenmacher feature interesting self-guided architectural tours. Maps are often available at the Hôtel de Ville (town hall).

Castles

There are more than 50 feudal castles in this small country, of all sizes, ages, styles, and states of repair. You come around a bend in a road, or crest a hill, and in front of you looms a feudal stronghold, dominating the surrounding landscape with its squat towers, slender turrets, and massive walls. The government actively encourages towns to renovate their castles into arts centers.

Dining

"French quality, German quantity"—that's an apt and common description of Luxembourg cuisine. Local posted menus tend toward *cuisine bourgeoise*—veal with cream and mushrooms, beef entrecôte with peppercorn sauce, veal *cordon bleu* (stuffed with ham and cheese)—all served in generous portions, with heaps of *frites* (french fries) on the side. Yet this tiny country has its own earthy cuisine, fresh off the farm: *judd mat gardebounen* (smoked pork shoulder with broad beans), *jambon d'Ardennes* (smoked ham served cold with pickled onions), *choucroute* (sauerkraut), batter-fried whiting, and spicy *gromperekichelcher* (fried potato patties). More upscale additions to the national specialties are *écrevisses* (crayfish), cooked with local wine, and all manner of trout.

Luxembourg has more star-studded French *gastronomique* restaurants per capita than any other European country. Many restaurants—including some of the top ones—offer a moderately priced luncheon menu. Ethnic restaurants present less expensive alternatives, and, given the sizable population of people of Italian descent, pasta and pizza have almost acquired the status of a national cuisine. Fast-food eateries are also present in force, especially in the capital.

Lunch takes place mostly between noon and 2. Dinner, except in the fanciest restaurants, tends to be earlier than the European norm, generally between 7 and 9.

CATEGORY	COST*
$$$$	over Flux 3,000/€75
$$$	Flux 1,500–Flux 3,000/€37–€75
$$	Flux 750–Flux 1,500/€18–37
$	under Flux 750/€18

**per person for a three-course meal including service and tax and excluding beverages*

Lodging

Hotels in Luxembourg are tidy and straightforward, rarely reaching the peaks of luxury, but equally rarely representing tremendous bargains. Most hotels in Luxembourg City are relatively modern and vary from the international style, mainly near the airport, to family-run establishments in town. Many of these, often filled with business travelers on weekdays, offer reduced rates on weekends. Outside the capital, hotels are often in picturesque buildings.

The **Office National du Tourisme** (ONT, ✉ B.P. 1001, L1010 Luxembourg, ☎ 4008–0820, FAX 40–47–48) will make hotel reservations free of charge. Such bookings must be confirmed by the traveler. The ONT offices at the airport and railway station will make reservations for travelers arriving without one.

Inexpensive youth hostels are plentiful; many are set in ancient fortresses and castles. Most are linked by marked trails of 10–20 mi. For information, contact **Centrale des Auberges Luxembourgeoises** (✉ 2, R. du Fort Olisy, L2261 Luxembourg, ☎ 22–55–88). The grand duchy is probably the best-organized country in Europe for camping. It has some 120 sites, all with full amenities. Listings are published annually by the National Tourist Office.

CATEGORY	COST*
$$$$	over Flux 8,000/€200
$$$	Flux 5,000–Flux 8,000/€125–€200
$$	Flux 2,500–Flux 5,000/€60–€125
$	under Flux 2,500/€60

**for two persons sharing a double room, including service and tax*

🔗 following the text of a review is your signal that the property has a Web site, where you will find details and, usually, images; for a link, visit www.fodors.com/urls.

Hiking and Biking

Well-marked, well-maintained hiking and biking trails of all levels crisscross Luxembourg, making it easy to hike from town to railway station to village in the north, or from vineyard to vineyard in the Moselle valley. For a small country, the terrain is quite varied. The Ardennes have rolling hills, while more challenging climbs are found in the Petite Suisse, and the Moselle valley and the Redlands are essentially flat. Traffic on the trails tends to be light—you may bump into a few others searching for serenity and solitude, or small groups of Luxembourg kids discovering their own country.

History

You can take a walk through the past in old Luxembourg City, which has been declared a World Heritage Site by UNESCO. Elsewhere in Luxembourg there are sites dating back to the times of the Celts and the Romans. At Dudelange's **Mount St. Jean,** for example, you'll find a 13th-century BC fortification, a 3rd-century AD Roman fort, and the ruins of a 12th-century AD castle. More recently, Luxembourg was the heart of World War II's Battle of the Bulge; just about every town has some historical marker memorializing the event.

Wines and Spirits

Luxembourg doesn't produce a large quantity of wine, and of what it does produce very little is exported, making it an unknown quantity to the outside world. But the soil, sun, and climate of the Moselle valley combine to create a high-quality product. The best of the Luxembourg wines include crisp Riesling and Auxerrois Blanc, a dry Pinot Gris, a rounder Pinot Blanc, and a rare, rosé-like Pinot Noir. In addition, the sparkling white *cremant*—Luxembourg's answer to champagne—is excellent either as an aperitif or with dessert. The day-to-day table wines, often served in pitchers or by the glass, are Rivaner and Elbling. Also popular are the local eaux-de-vie—the fruity *quetsch* (made from a small blue plum), *mirabelle* (from a small, cherrylike yellow plum), kirsch, or—for the hard core—grain, which is best mixed in a mug of strong coffee. Moselle wines can be tasted and purchased in gift packs from most of the wineries, and artisanal distilleries sell their eaux-de-vie along the Moselle highway.

Exploring Luxembourg

The Old Town of Luxembourg is of necessity small; it's contained within the rock walls of a fortress. This makes it eminently walkable, and when you're done there's an elevator to take you down to the level of the surrounding part of town. Short distances make it possible, too, to visit the rest of the country within the space of a few pleasant days.

Outside of Luxembourg City, the country is neatly divided into five sections. The area surrounding the city is known as Le Bon Pays (The Good Country) and is mostly rolling farms and small towns peppered with castle ruins. Les Terres Rouges (The Redlands), Luxembourg's former industrial heartland, is now being revived with museums, hiking trails, and parks. The Moselle valley has charming towns, thermal baths, water sports, and, of course, wine. Le Petit Suisse (Little Switzerland, also called Müllerthal) is an international hiking and caving destination. The rolling forests in the Ardennes—where some of the fiercest fighting during World War II's Battle of the Bulge occurred—has serene villages and numerous impressive castle ruins.

Great Itineraries

Numbers in the text correspond to numbers in the margin and on the Luxembourg and Luxembourg City maps.

IF YOU HAVE 2 DAYS

On the first day, take in the classic sights of **Luxembourg City** ①–㉔, with visits to the French-built Citadelle du Saint-Esprit, the Bock, the maze of underground defense passages known as the Casemates, and the Cathédrale Notre-Dame with its royal crypt. Also worth visits are the interactive Musée de la Ville de Luxembourg, which traces Luxembourg's 1,000-year history; the Palais Grand-Ducal; the art treasures of the Musée National d'Histoire et d'Art; the Grund district along the Alzette; the Vallée de la Petrusse; the banking street, Boulevard Royal; and the main pedestrian shopping street, Grand-Rue.

On the second day, allow ample time for the Wenzel Walk through space and time. It leads from the Bock down into the valley, past ancient gates and ruins, over 18th-century military installations, and along the Alzette, with audiovisual presentations along the way. Use the afternoon to re-enter the 20th century at Kirchberg, a plateau to the east of the old city that is home to European Union institutions, including the European Court of Justice. Here, too, are modern bank palaces of architectural and artistic interest.

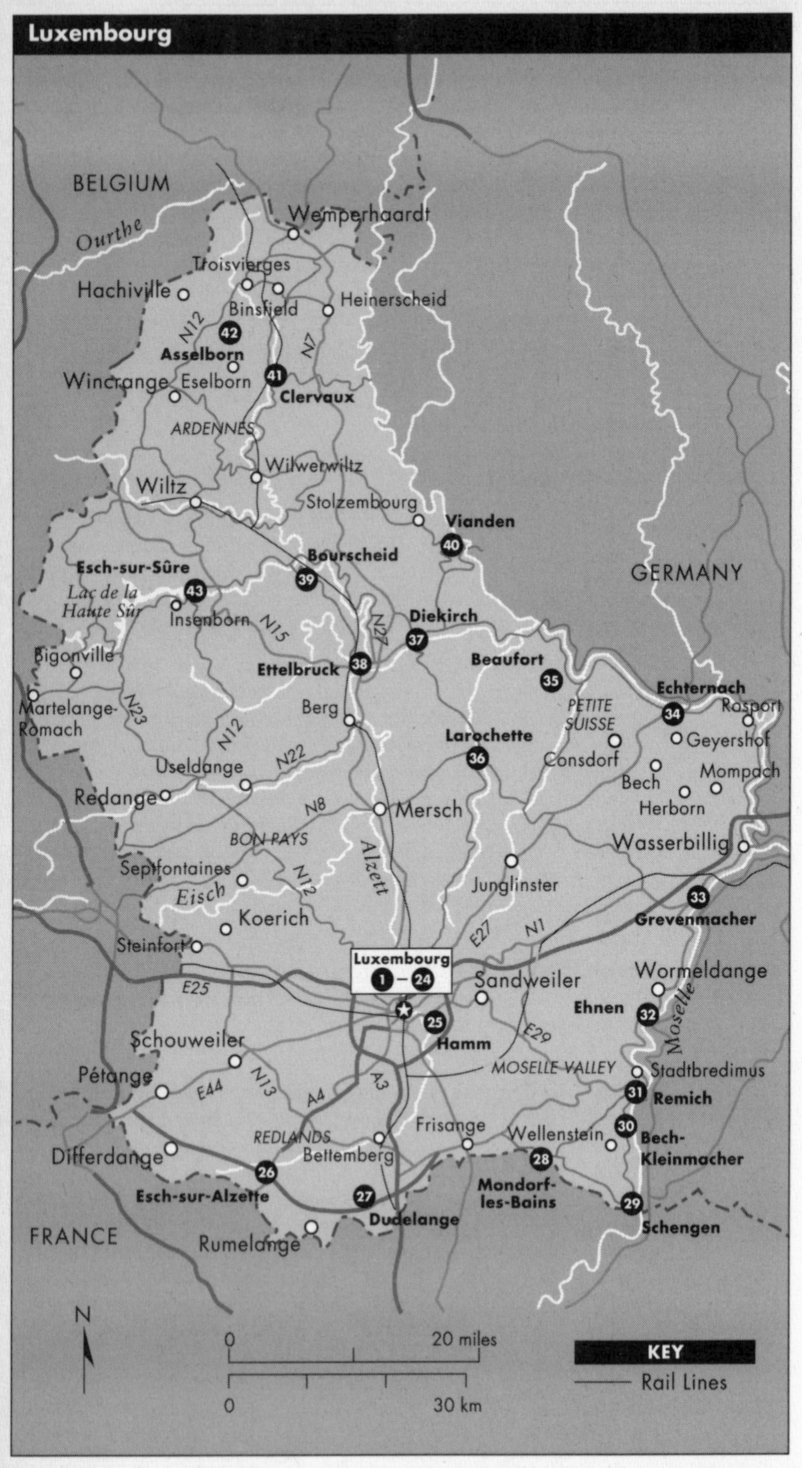
Luxembourg
BELGIUM
GERMANY
FRANCE
Ourthe
Wemperhaardt
Troisvierges
Hachiville
Binsfeld
Heinerscheid
N12
42
N7
Asselborn
41
Wincrange
Eselborn
Clervaux
ARDENNES
Wilwerwiltz
Wiltz
Stolzembourg
Vianden
40
Bourscheid
39
Esch-sur-Sûre
43
Lac de la Haute Sûr
Insenborn
N15
N27
Diekirch
37
Bigonville
Ettelbruck
38
Beaufort
35
Echternach
34
Rosport
Martelange-Romach
N23
Berg
PETITE SUISSE
Geyershof
Larochette
36
Consdorf
N12
N22
Bech
Mompach
Useldange
Redange
N8
Mersch
Herborn
Wasserbillig
BON PAYS
Septfontaines
N12
Alzett
Junglinster
Eisch
33
Koerich
Grevenmacher
E27
N1
Steinfort
Luxembourg
1 – 24
Sandweiler
Wormeldange
E25
Ehnen
32
25
Moselle
Hamm
Schouweiler
E29
MOSELLE VALLEY
Stadtbredimus
Pétange
E44
N13
A3
31
Remich
A4
Frisange
Wellenstein
30
REDLANDS
Bech-Kleinmacher
Bettemberg
Differdange
28
26
Mondorf-les-Bains
Esch-sur-Alzette
27
29
Dudelange
Schengen
Rumelange
N
0
20 miles
0
30 km
KEY
Rail Lines

IF YOU HAVE 3 DAYS

Follow the itinerary above, and on the third day, drive north to the Luxembourg Ardennes via **Diekirch** ㊲, whose Museum of Military History brings alive the Battle of the Bulge, then on to **Vianden** ㊵, home of one of the most spectacular castles you're ever likely to see. Continue north to **Clervaux** ㊶, where there's another sprawling castle, now the permanent home of *The Family of Man* photo exhibition.

Alternatively, you can use the third day to explore the Moselle Valley. Start at Jardins des Papillons in **Grevenmacher** ㉝ and follow the Route de Vins south through its lovely riverside towns, including **Ehnen** ㉜, which is home to Luxembourg's Wine Museum, and the cobblestone streets of **Remich** ㉛. Stop in at any of the vineyards along the way. End the day at the spa waters of **Mondorf-les-Bains** ㉘.

IF YOU HAVE 5 DAYS

Follow the itinerary above and stay overnight in **Clervaux** ㊶. Turning south, stop in tiny **Esch-sur-Sûre** ㊸, circled by the river and dense forests, and continue on to **Bourscheid** ㊴ with its romantic castle ruins overlooking three valleys. Past Diekirch, head for **Larochette** ㊱ and its striking, step-gabled castle. At Reuland, you enter the Müllerthal, the very pretty countryside also known as the Petite Suisse. Stop over at **Echternach** ㉞. On the fifth day, visit this town on the river Sûre, which is the home of the unique and ancient dancing procession at Whitsun (Pentecost). Travel south along the Sûre, which forms the border with Germany until it meets the Moselle. The vineyards have been cultivated since Roman times and cover every slope. Pretty little **Ehnen** ㉜, a well-preserved village, is a good place for a stop to see the wine museum. Heading back toward Luxembourg City from Remich, stop at **Hamm** ㉕ to visit the American Military Cemetery, where General George Patton is buried with 5,000 comrades-at-arms who fell during the liberation of Luxembourg.

When to Tour Luxembourg

April through October is a good time to visit the grand duchy, with spring and early fall being the best. Outside the capital, many museums and other attractions open at Easter and close in October. Landlocked Luxembourg is far enough from the sea so that winters are a bit colder and summers a bit warmer than in neighboring Belgium. Note that a number of the best restaurants are closed most of August.

LUXEMBOURG CITY

391 km (243 mi) southeast of Amsterdam, 219 km (136 mi) southeast of Brussels, 29 km (18 mi) east of Arlon.

The capital, perched on a bluff at the confluence of the Pétrusse and Alzette rivers, goes by the same name as the country—*Lëtzebuerg* in Luxembourgish. When Luxembourgers themselves refer to visiting the capital, they merely say they are going *en ville* (to the city). Ranging from southern European blue-collar workers to international bankers and European civil servants, half of Luxembourg's modest population of 80,000 are foreigners. This has given the city a cosmopolitan sheen and enriched it with a variety of ethnic restaurants, but the Luxembourgers themselves remain essentially homebodies, who go home for lunch if they can and see no point in hanging about in town after dark.

Exploring Luxembourg City

In Luxembourg Ville (Luxembourg City), at leisure, you can explore the fortifications, the old cobbled streets, the parks, the cathedral, and the museums and, after shopping, relax in a shaded terrace café, listening to street musicians or a brass band. The city is small enough to be done in a day if you are pressed for time. But if you have a bit more time, you may find quiet little Luxembourg a romantic base for day trips and a lovely place at night, with its illuminated monuments and walls and its inviting public squares.

A Good Walk

Start at the **Pont Viaduc** ①, spanning the Pétrusse valley, for a view of the ledges on which the city was built. The **Monument National de la Solidarité** ②, at the north end of the bridge, commemorates Luxembourg's World War II victims. East of the monument stands the 17th-century fortress, the **Citadelle du St-Esprit** ③. To the northwest, along the city wall, lies **Place de la Constitution** ④ and the entrance to the **Casemates de la Pétrusse** ⑤, the tunnels carved into the fortifications. A block north of the Place on rue des Capucins and two blocks east on rue Notre-Dame stands the late-Gothic **Cathédrale Notre-Dame** ⑥. East of the cathedral, the outstanding **Musée d'Histoire de la Ville de Luxembourg** ⑦ traces the city's history. The town's three main squares align diagonally from southeast to northwest: first comes elegant **Place Clairefontaine** ⑧, then the market square, **Place Guillaume** ⑨, and finally, the welcoming **Place d'Armes** ⑩. On the southeast corner of the Place d'Armes stands the **Cercle/Palais Municipal** ⑪, the home of the tourist office. The **Maquette de la Forteresse** ⑫, behind the Cercle, is a scale model of the fortifications of the city. Once the residence of the dukes, the **Palais Grand-Ducal** ⑬, east of Place d'Armes, now hosts state occasions. Behind the palace is the square known as **Marché-aux-Poissons** ⑭, the oldest part of town. On the square, inside a row of 16th-century houses, is the collection of the **Musée National d'Histoire et d'Art** ⑮. Northeast of the museum is the **Porte des Trois Tours** ⑯, part of the original battlements. The promontory on which Luxembourg's original castle was built, **Le Bock** ⑰, with an entrance to the casemates, a fascinating museum, and some ruins, looms above the Alzette valley on the eastern side of the city. Return south to Place du St-Esprit, where you can take an elevator down to the **Grund** ⑱ district, in the river valley below the Bock. Here the excellent, interactive **Musée d'Histoire Naturelle** ⑲ explores the secrets of the natural world. North on the riverside rue Munster is the Baroque **Eglise St-Jean Baptiste** ⑳. In the other direction, past the confluence of the Alzette and the Petrusse, the parklands of the **Vallée de la Pétrusse** ㉑ spread westward. Walk up narrow switchbacks from the valley or take the elevator to Place du Saint-Esprit and cut across on Boulevard Roosevelt to **Boulevard Royal** ㉒, Luxembourg's Wall Street. Perpendicular to Royal is **Grand-Rue** ㉓, Luxembourg's pedestrian-only shopping street. Northeast of the center, across the Pont Grande Duchesse Charlotte above the Pfaffenthal district, lies the **Plateau Kirchberg** ㉔, a moonscape of modern architecture housing banks and European Union institutions.

Sights to See

★ ⑰ **Le Bock.** Luxembourg's raison d'être juts dramatically out over the Alzette river valley. This cliff served as the principal approach to the town as far back as Celtic and Roman times, until bridges were constructed. The name comes from the Celtic *büück,* meaning the promontory supporting a castle. Over its farthest point looms the ruined tower of the castle of Sigefroid himself. He founded the fortress Lucilinburhuc in 963; it was expanded, over the centuries, from this dominant point, and finally razed in 1875.

Vertiginous views from here take in the **Plateau du Rham** across the way, on the right, and, before it, the massive towers of **Duke Wences-**

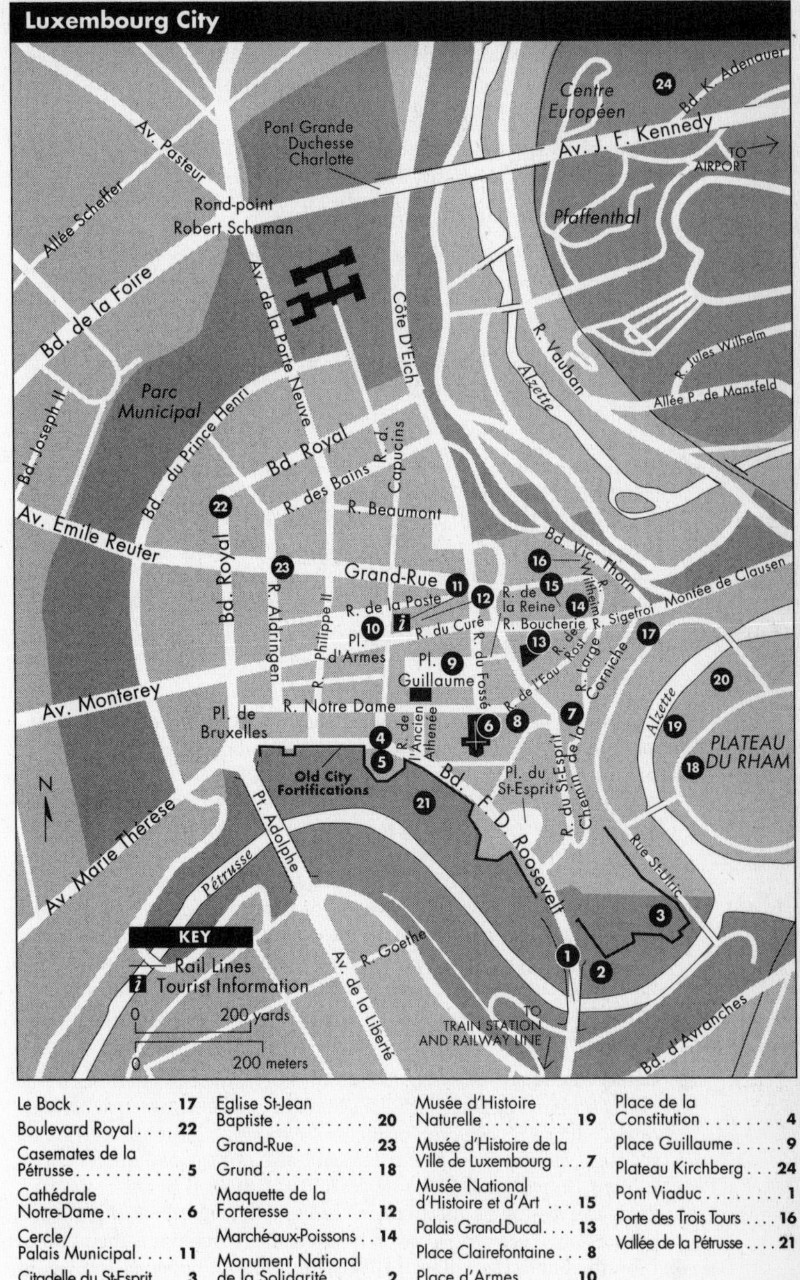

- Le Bock 17
- Boulevard Royal 22
- Casemates de la Pétrusse 5
- Cathédrale Notre-Dame 6
- Cercle/ Palais Municipal 11
- Citadelle du St-Esprit 3
- Eglise St-Jean Baptiste 20
- Grand-Rue 23
- Grund 18
- Maquette de la Forteresse 12
- Marché-aux-Poissons . . 14
- Monument National de la Solidarité 2
- Musée d'Histoire Naturelle 19
- Musée d'Histoire de la Ville de Luxembourg . . . 7
- Musée National d'Histoire et d'Art . . . 15
- Palais Grand-Ducal 13
- Place Clairefontaine . . . 8
- Place d'Armes 10
- Place de la Constitution 4
- Place Guillaume 9
- Plateau Kirchberg . . . 24
- Pont Viaduc 1
- Porte des Trois Tours 16
- Vallée de la Pétrusse 21

las's fortifications, which in 1390 extended the protected area. The block-like casernes (barracks) were built in the 17th century by the French and function today as a hospice for the elderly. Below them, at the bottom of the valley, is the 17th-century **Neumünster Abbey,** which, from 1869 to 1984, served as a prison.

Here also is one access point for the city's underground defensive labyrinth (☞ Casemates de la Pétrusse, *below*), the **Casemates du Bock,** dug into the rock below the city in 1745. At the entrance, the **Archaeological Crypt** provides an excellent introduction, with an audiovisual presentation depicting Luxembourg history from the 10th to the 15th centuries. ✉ *Montée de Clausen.* 🎫 *Crypt and casemates Flux 70/€1.75.* ⏲ *Mar.–Oct., daily 10–5.*

NEED A BREAK? On the Corniche, stop at the shady outdoor tables of the **Breedewée** (✉ Rue Large 9, ☎ 22–26–96) for a drink or a light, French-accented plat du jour.

㉒ **Boulevard Royal.** Luxembourg's mini–Wall Street was once the main moat of the fortress. Lined with as many of the 225 foreign financial institutions as could squeeze onto the five-block street, boulevard Royal is the symbol of a financial center where the securities-trading operation has a higher turnover than that of the New York Stock Exchange. The pinstripe suits can get some relief from their labors by gazing at Niki de St. Phalle's large and brightly colored statue, *La Tempérance,* which adorns their street. ✉ *Between Pl. de Bruxelles and Côte d'Eich.*

❺ **Casemates de la Pétrusse** (military tunnels). At the height of its power and influence, Luxembourg was protected by three rings of defense comprising 53 forts and strongholds. During the many phases of the fortress's construction, the rock itself was hollowed out to form a honeycomb of passages running for nearly 24 km (15 mi) below the town. Ten gates controlled admittance through the walls, and the town was, in effect, 440 acres of solid fort. The Casemates served not only defensive purposes but were also used for storage and as a place of refuge when the city was under attack. Two sections (☞ Casemates du Bock, *above*) of the passages, containing former barracks, cavernous slaughterhouses, bakeries, and a deep well, are open to the public. ✉ *Pl. de la Constitution.* 🎫 *Flux 70/€1.75.* ⏲ *Easter, Whitsun (Pentecost, 7th Sun. after Easter), and July–Sept., daily 11–4.*

❻ **Cathédrale Notre-Dame.** In late-Gothic style, the cathedral has a fine portal sculpted by Daniel Muller of Freiburg and an attractive Baroque organ gallery. During the fortnight of national pilgrimage starting on the third Sunday after Easter, large numbers of Luxembourgers flock to their cathedral. The closing ceremony, attended by the royal family, is an event no politician can afford to miss, regardless of party and persuasion. The crypt, down a broad staircase, contains the tomb of John the Blind, the gallant 14th-century King of Bohemia and Count of Luxembourg, who fell at the Battle of Crécy in France during the Hundred Years' War. Here, too, are the tombs of the grand-ducal dynasty. ✉ *Rue Notre-Dame.* ⏲ *Easter–Oct., weekdays 10–5, Sat. 8–6, Sun. 10–6; Nov.–Easter, weekdays 10–11:30 and 2–5, Sat. 8–11 and 2–5, Sun. 10–5.*

⓫ **Cercle/Palais Municipal** (Municipal Building). With its bas-relief of the Countess Ermesinde granting Luxembourg its charter of freedom in 1244, the municipal building is also the home of the tourist office. ✉ *East end, Pl. d'Armes.*

❸ **Citadelle du St-Esprit** (Citadel of the Holy Spirit). Built by Vauban, the brilliant French military engineer, in the 17th century on the site of a former monastery, the Citadelle has typically wedge-shape fortifications. The "prow" affords wraparound views of the three spires of the cathedral, the curve of the Alzette, and the incongruous white tower of the European Parliament secretariat. ⊠ *Rue du St-Esprit.*

⓴ **Eglise St-Jean Baptiste (Neumünster)** (Church of St. John the Baptist). Once the place of worship of the Benedictines of Neumünster Abbey, who were expelled when the French Revolution hit Luxembourg, the Baroque church contains many treasures. One of its most important is a Black Madonna, whose protection against pestilence was prayed for over many centuries. The church passage along the river provides splendid views of the side of the cliff and the towering fortifications across the Alzette. It leads to a former abbey courtyard, the **Tutesall,** where convicts once worked sewing bags. Today it is a stylish exhibition venue. Another building, the former men's prison, is being converted into a cultural center, scheduled to be completed in 2001. ⊠ *Rue Münster.*

NEED A BREAK? **Scott's Pub** (⊠ Bisserwée 4, ☎ 47–53–52), at the bottom of the valley, is a gathering place for English-speakers, where outdoor tables line the picturesque Alzette. It's the place to have a pint of bitter or sample the Anglo-American cuisine.

㉓ **Grand-Rue.** On Luxembourg's pedestrian-only shopping street the same brands vie for your attention as in New York; but then, investment bankers have pockets here as deep as anywhere else. Pastry shops and sidewalk cafés add the middle-class touch so typical of Luxembourg. There are pooper-scooper automats for the poodles, and the occasional street musician will, as likely as not, be playing a Bach partita. ⊠ *Between bd. Royal and Côte d'Eich.*

★ ⓲ **Grund.** Once considered dank and squalid, this district is now in vogue. You'll find chic restaurants, exclusive clubs, and skylighted, renovated town houses among the tumbledown laborers' homes. ⊠ *Alzette River Valley: R. Munster, R. de Trèves, Bisserwée.*

⓬ **Maquette de la Fortresse** (Scale Model of the Fortress). This relief model is a copy of one (now in Paris) made of the fortress-city for Napoléon in 1804, when the fortified complex was at the peak of its glory. The model shows how the fortress was constructed. ⊠ *Rue du Curé,* ☎ *22–28–09.* 🎫 *Flux 60/€1.50.* ⏲ *Easter–mid-Oct., Mon.–Sat. 10–noon and 2–6.*

⓮ **Marché-aux-Poissons** (Fish Market). In the oldest part of town, the site of the old fish market, you can walk on streets once walked by the ancient Romans. ⊠ *Rues de la Boucherie, du Rost, and Wiltheim.*

❷ **Monument National de la Solidarité** (National Monument of Unity). Commemorating Luxembourg's World War II victims, the stark granite-and-steel monument suggests the prisons and concentration camps where they suffered. The walls of the small chapel, containing a symbolic tombstone, are made entirely of stained glass. It was as a direct result of its war experiences that Luxembourg abandoned traditional neutrality for international cooperation. ⊠ *Bd. F. D. Roosevelt at Citadelle du St-Esprit.*

⓳ **Musée d'Histoire Naturelle** (Museum of Natural History). Housed in a converted women's prison, this museum has thought-provoking interactive exhibits and dioramas. ⊠ *Rue Munster 23,* ☎ *462–2321.* 🎫 *Flux 100/€2.50.* ⏲ *Tues.–Thurs. 2–6, Fri.–Sun. 10–6.*

★ 7 **Musée d'Histoire de la Ville de Luxembourg** (Luxembourg City Historical Museum). Partially underground, this multimedia, interactive museum, opened in 1996, traces the development of the city over 1,000 years. Its lowest five levels show the town's preserved ancient stonework. From a glass-wall elevator, you can enjoy a wonderful view of the ravine from the upper floors. ✉ *Rue du St-Esprit,* ☎ *229–0501.* 🎫 *Flux 200/€4.95.* ⏲ *Tues.–Sun. 10–6, Thurs. 10–8.*

15 **Musée National d'Histoire et d'Art** (National Museum of History and Art). Set in an attractive row of 16th-century houses, the museum has some outstanding paintings by the expressionist Joseph Kutter, probably Luxembourg's greatest artist. The art gallery includes a fine Cranach and two Turner watercolors of the Luxembourg fortress. The museum also hosts the spectacular Bentinck-Thyssen collection of 15th- to 19th-century art, including works by Bruegel, Rembrandt, Canaletto, and other masters. ✉ *Marché-aux-Poissons,* ☎ *479–3301.* 🎫 *Flux 100/€2.50.* ⏲ *Tues.–Sun. 10–5.*

NEED A BREAK?

The **Welle Man** (✉ Rue Wiltheim 12, ☎ 47–17–83), on the street that runs alongside the National Museum, is the quintessential Luxembourgish museum bar. Sit on the tiny terrace and enjoy the magnificent view. Sip a glass of local white Elbling or Rivaner wine, or try a kir, made from black-currant liqueur and white wine.

13 **Palais Grand-Ducal** (Grand-Ducal Palace). The city's finest building dates from the 16th century. Its elaborate facade shows a distinct Spanish-Moorish influence. Formerly home to the Grand Ducal family, it is now used for business and entertaining. Official receptions are held in the festive hall on the second floor, and foreign envoys are received in the Hall of Kings. Its extensive art collection was dispersed during World War II but was returned afterward. ✉ *Rue du Marché-aux-Herbes.* 🎫 *Flux 200/€4.95; tickets sold only at the City Tourist Office (early booking recommended).* ⏲ *July 15–Aug. 29, Mon.–Tues. and Thurs.–Sat.; guided tours only (in English at 4). Opening and tour hours are subject to change; check with City Tourist Office (☞ Visitor Information, below).*

8 **Place Clairefontaine.** This elegant sloping square has a graceful statue of Grand Duchess Charlotte and imposing 18th-century ministerial offices. ✉ *Rues Notre-Dame, du Fosse, de l'Eau, de la Congrégation.*

10 **Place d'Armes.** Once the innermost heart of the fortified city, the square today, lined with symmetrical plane trees and strung with colored lights, is the most welcoming corner of town. In fine weather its cafés and benches are full of both locals and visitors. The bandstand has concerts every summer evening by visiting bands. Every second and fourth Saturday, a *brocante* (antiques/flea) market fills the square. ✉ *Rue de la Poste; av. de la Porte Neuve; rues des Capucins, Génistre, du Curé, de Chimay, and Philippe II; and av. Monterey.*

4 **Place de la Constitution.** This square is marked by the gilt *Gëlle Fra* (Golden Woman), on top of a tall column. This World War I memorial was destroyed by the Nazis in 1940 and rebuilt, with original pieces incorporated, in 1984. ✉ *Bd. F. D. Roosevelt and rue Chimay.*

9 **Place Guillaume.** This square is known locally as the Knuedler, a name derived from the girdle worn by Franciscan monks who once had a monastery on the site. On market days (Wednesday and Saturday mornings) it is a mass of retail fruit and vegetable stands, flower vendors, cheese- and fishmongers, and a few remaining farmers who bring in their personal crops of potatoes, apples, cabbage, and radishes—as

well as homemade jam, sauerkraut, and goat cheese. That's Grand Duke William II on the bronze horse; he reigned from 1840 to 1849, while Luxembourg was flush with new independence. The Hôtel de Ville (Town Hall), its stairs flanked by two bronze lions, was inaugurated in 1844. ⊠ *Off rue du Fossé at rue de la Reine.*

24 **Plateau Kirchberg.** A number of banks, needing more space than that available on boulevard Royal (☞ *above*), have put up huge edifices on Kirchberg, across the Alzette northeast of the center. Gottfried Boehm's glass-and-aluminum **Deutsche Bank** encloses a giant atrium, frequently used for art exhibitions, and Richard Meier's sober **Hypobank** is the perfect foil for an explosively dynamic sculpture by Frank Stella. The banks are cheek to jowl with the modernistic buildings of the European Union institutions, often accompanied by contemporary sculpture—the **European Court of Justice,** with pieces by Henry Moore and Lucien Wercollier; the **Jean Monnet Building,** with a replica of Carl-Fredrik Reuterswärd's *Non-Violence*; the **European Center,** where the Council of Ministers meets; and others, whose presence in Luxembourg are visible reminders of the disproportionately important role played by this tiny country in the politics of the European Union. This is also where the I. M. Pei–designed **Musée d'Art Moderne Grand Duc Jean** is located. ⊠ *Bd. Konrad Adenauer, Niedergrünewald, pl. de l'Europe.*

1 **Pont Viaduc.** From the 200-m-long bridge also known as the Passerelle (footbridge), which spans the Pétrusse valley, you'll have a first glimpse of the rocky ledges—partly natural, partly man-made—on which the city was founded. The Pétrusse, more a brook than a river, is now contained by concrete, but the valley has been made into a singularly beautiful park. ⊠ *Between av. de la Gare and bd. F. D. Roosevelt.*

16 **Porte des Trois Tours** (Gate of the Three Towers). These three turrets, remains of the fortress, are among the city's most romantic sights. The oldest of the towers was built around 1050. During the French Revolution, this was the location of the guillotine. From here you can clearly see the source of Luxembourg's strength as a fortress: the Bock (☞ *above*). ⊠ *Foot of rue Wiltheim at bd. J. Ulveling.*

21 **Vallée de la Pétrusse** (Petrusse Valley). Full of willows, cherry trees, and bluffs, this broad park lies in the canyon of the Pétrusse river. Near the high Viaduc (☞ Pont Viaduc, *above*), you'll see the **Chapelle Saint-Quirin** built into the rocks. The cave is said to have been carved by the Celts; it is known to have housed a chapel since at least the 4th century. ⊠ *Between rue de la Semois and rue St-Quirin.*

Dining

In the capital, as in the rest of the grand duchy, workers drop everything at noon and, jamming the streets, rush home to a leisurely hot meal, then rush back at 2, jamming the streets once more. Most restaurants offer a relatively speedy plat du jour for those who don't commute twice a day. Evening meals at home tend to be a cold supper of ham, sausage, dark bread, and cheese; the occasional meal out is usually a celebration, enjoyed at length. The Sunday noon meal is the most important of the week. Most Luxembourg restaurants are closed on Sunday, but country restaurants—some of the best and most enjoyable in the country, and never very far away—are booked with three-generation families, who spend the afternoon eating and drinking, then take a stroll, after which the men retire to the local pub.

Luxembourg City has a wide variety of restaurants, offering everything from top French cuisine to simple local specialties; you'll also find an assortment of international choices, a plethora of pizzerias, and for some reason, lots of Chinese restaurants. It's easy to find a fixed-price menu or plat du jour by wandering from restaurant to restaurant, but beware: the best places are often booked up at weekday lunchtime; if you know where you want to eat, phone ahead. Dress is casual unless otherwise indicated.

$$$$ ★ ✕ **Clairefontaine.** Airy, bright, and ultrachic, this dining spot on the city's most attractive square attracts government ministers and visiting dignitaries as well as genuine gourmets. Chef-owner Tony Tintinger's inspirations include a showcase of foie gras specialties, innovative fish dishes (soufflé of langoustines flavored with aniseed), and game novelties (tournedos of doe with wild mushrooms). ✉ *Pl. de Clairefontaine 9,* ☎ *46–22–11. Reservations essential. Jacket and tie. AE, DC, MC, V. Closed Sun., 1 wk in May, 2 wks in Aug., 1st wk in Nov. No lunch Sat.*

$$$$ ★ ✕ **Iwwert de Steiler.** Housed in the romantic building that was Luxembourg's first café, this stylish spot overlooks the Alzette and some of the castle ruins. Inside, the three stories of dining rooms are elegantly draped in soothing colors. The food blends together Luxembourg's best—combining fresh fish from the Moselle with French flair, served in German-size portions. The bar downstairs, Ennert de Steiler, is cozy and colorful and offers a simpler menu. ✉ *Rue de La Loge 2,* ☎ *46–08–42. Reservations essential. AE, MC, V. Closed Sun. No lunch Sat.*

$$$ ✕ **Bouzonviller.** The modern, airy dining room is a pleasure in itself with a magnificent view over the Alzette valley. Over the years, Christian Bouzonviller has built up a following among serious gourmets with dishes such as sea scallops in lemon butter, loin of veal with eggplant *pissaladière* (flaky tart filled with onions, anchovies, olives, and eggplant), and unusual desserts, including a chocolate fondant glacé with grapefruit sauce. ✉ *Rue Albert-Unden 138,* ☎ *47–22–59. Reservations essential. Jacket and tie. MC, V. Closed weekends and 3 wks in Aug.*

$$$ ✕ **La Fourchette à Droite.** This spot on the Place d'Armes is as sleek and stylish as they come. The changing menu regularly features seafood, particularly scallop dishes. The glimmering steel furniture, exposed brick walls, and modern art create a fashionable, yet comfortable setting. ✉ *Av. Monterey 5,* ☎ *22–13–60. AE, MC, V. Closed Sun.*

$$$ ✕ **Jan Schneidewind.** Changing art exhibits, chosen by chef-owner Jan Schneidewind, decorate the exposed-brick walls in this cozy but elegant two-story restaurant. The menu focuses on fish and seafood dishes prepared in an ambitious, French-influenced style, such as herb-encrusted king crab in fowl juices, and sole with an asparagus and morel stew. Don't miss the simple but stunning salmon mousse if it's on the seasonally changing menu. ✉ *Rue du Curé 20,* ☎ *22–26–18. AE, DC, MC, V. Closed Mon., 3 wks in Sept. or Feb. No lunch Sat.*

$$$ ✕ **La Lorraine.** Strategically located on the Place d'Armes, this restaurant in landlocked Luxembourg specializes in outstanding seafood. The display of coast-fresh fish and shellfish, in a shop attached to the restaurant, is so attractive it draws photographers. A three-course *menu terroire,* made up of local dishes, can be had in the brick-wall brasserie in back. ✉ *Pl. d'Armes 7,* ☎ *47–14–36. AE, DC, MC, V. Closed Sun. and 2nd ½ of Aug. No lunch Sat.*

$$$ ✕ **Palais de Chine.** There are lots of theories as to why Luxembourg has so many Chinese restaurants, but there's little argument that Palais de Chine is one of the best. The menu, like the decor, has a touch of French flair. Duck, in all of its variations, has a national following. ✉ *Rue de L'Eau 18–20,* ☎ *4–02–83. AE, DC, MC, V.*

$$$ ★ ✕ **Restaurant Bonaparte.** Once the Prussian headquarters during the Napoleonic wars, this romantic restaurant in the Grund takes its name from the small statue of Napoleon that overlooks its cobblestone courtyard. Although the emperor was French, the menu is Italian, with an

Luxembourg City Dining and Lodging

Dining

Bacchus **27**
Bouzonviller **2**
Café Française **15**
Chiggeri **23**
Clairefontaine **28**
Club 5 Remake **5**
Ems **39**
Iwwert de Steiler **25**
Jan Schneidewind . . . **21**
Kamakura **29**
La Fourchette à Droite **14**
La Lorraine **16**
La Table du Pain **13**
Le Jasmin **17**
Mousel's Cantine . . . **24**
Namur **36**
Oberweis **22**
Pad Chi Chi **20**
Palais de Chine **26**
Restaurant Arpège . . **31**
Restaurant Bonaparte **30**
Speltz **18**

Lodging

Auberge le Châtelet **35**
Carlton **37**
Christophe Colomb **32**
Cravat **19**
Domos **12**
Grand Hôtel Mercure Alfa **38**
Hôtel Français **15**
Hôtel Inter-Continental **4**
Italia **33**
Le Royal **8**
Marco Polo **34**
Parc Belair **10**
Parc Belle-Vue **11**
Rix Hôtel **9**
Romantik Hotel/Grunewald **3**
Sheraton Aerogolf . . . **6**
Sieweburen **1**
Sofitel and Novotel . . . **7**

KEY
Rail Lines
Tourist Information
0 200 yards
0 200 meters

emphasis on outstanding homemade pasta. Be sure to save room for desserts such as raspberry-apricot tart with coconut ice cream caged in caramel. In the summer, there is outside seating in the courtyard. As an added bonus, the bar downstairs is modeled after a Ferrari F40 and is the meeting spot for Luxembourg's Ferrari club. ✉ *Bisserwée 7,* ☎ *22–71–66. AE, DC, MC, V. Closed Mon. and Nov.–Mar.*

$$$ ✕ **Speltz.** In the middle of the old city, Speltz's light blue, paneled dining area will transport you to a traditional French sitting room. The menu is simple and refined, offering a range of local meats and seasonal game, followed by an expansive cheese selection. The wine list is equally impressive. ✉ *Rue Chimay 8,* ☎ *47–49–50. Reservations essential. AE, DC, MC, V. Closed Sun., Easter wk. No dinner Sat.*

$$–$$$ ★ ✕ **Chiggeri.** The name means chicory in Luxembourgish, but also loosely translates as "a funny surprise," which is exactly what this restaurant is. The menu features gourmet food with a twist—such as vegetable tempura on a bed of local mushrooms, and lamb shank with pignolis and secret spices. Three floors offer a variety of dining experiences, from the busy, informal bar (which doubles as one of Luxembourg's few Internet cafés) to the lush Moroccan-style *jardin d'hiver* to the Polynesian-themed main dining room. The exceptional wine list has received several awards from *Wine Spectator.* ✉ *Rue du Nord 15,* ☎ *22–82–36 or 22–99–36. AE, MC, V.*

$$ ✕ **Bacchus.** This Italian pizzeria attracts an upscale, downtown set as much for its location in the historic center and its slick peach-and-brass decor as for its food, which is straightforward and reasonably priced. Wood-fired pizza and classic pastas are dependable choices. Reserve a seat in the tranquil courtyard, especially for lunch, when this is a haunt for members of parliament. ✉ *Rue Marché-aux-Herbes 32,* ☎ *47–13–97. AE, DC, MC, V. Closed Sun., Mon.*

$$ ✕ **Café Française.** This Parisian-style café in the heart of the Place d'Armes serves French favorites, from onion soup to paté to pastries. The tuxedoed wait staff is friendly, no matter whether you order an elaborate three-course meal or linger over a cup of coffee. Sit outside and watch the pedestrian parade through the square. ✉ *Place d'Armes,* ☎ *47–45–34. AE, DC, MC, V.*

$$ ✕ **Club 5 Remake.** See and be seen at this chic spot in the Kirchberg. Lines are long for the pizza, pasta, steak, and other simple fare, especially on the weekends when popular movies are playing at the cinema next door. Bistro tables are set up along the mall concourse, which only adds to the buzz. ✉ *Av. J. F. Kennedy 45,* ☎ *42–95–12. AE, MC, V.*

$$ ✕ **Le Jasmin.** Fancy some couscous? This sweet little Middle Eastern oasis offers something different from the standard fare found in the center of the old city. The menu features a range of couscous dishes, and lamb is a specialty. The mint tea is a wonderful way to finish off the meal. ✉ *Rue Louvigny 8,* ☎ *26–20–04. MC, V. Closed Sun.*

$$ ✕ **Kamakura.** If heavy Western cuisine palls, take the elevator down from St-Esprit to the Grund and try this elegant Japanese restaurant. A number of fixed-price menus offer delicate, nouvelle-accented dishes, artfully presented and graciously served. À la carte specialties, considerably more expensive, include impeccably fresh sashimi and light tempura vegetables. ✉ *Rue Munster 2–4,* ☎ *47–06–04. AE, DC, MC, V. Closed Sun. No lunch Sat.*

$$ ✕ **Mousel's Cantine.** Directly adjoining the great Mousel brewery, this comfortable, wood-paneled café serves up heaping platters of local specialties—braised and grilled ham, sausage, broad beans, and fried potatoes—to be washed down with crockery steins of creamy *Gezwickelte Béier* (unfiltered beer). The front café is brighter, but the tiny fluorescent-lighted dining room has windows into the brewery. Although the

equipment is authentic, most of Mousel beer is now brewed at the plant in Diekirch. ✉ *Montée de Clausen 46,* ☎ *47–01–98. MC, V. Closed Sun.*

$$ ✕ **Pad Chi Chi.** Modern, festive, and funky, this local favorite has an ideal location in the center of the old city. Downtown workers flock here, especially for lunch, which might include salmon tartare or an overstuffed *croque monsieur,* both of which come with heaps of outstanding *frites.* Watch for fresh and hearty daily specials posted on the chalkboard outside. ✉ *Place Guillaume 32,* ☎ *22–58–12. Closed Sun.*

$$ ✕ **Restaurant Arpège.** A serene refuge near the busy train station, this quaint neighborhood spot is hidden on an easily missed side street. The menu changes every few months, but always includes fresh seasonal ingredients, including beef, pork, and lamb, all prepared in simple country style. The 20-table dining area is decorated with rattan furniture and soothing original art. ✉ *Rue Ste-Zithe 29,* ☎ *48–88–08. MC, V. Closed Sun.*

$ ✕ **Ems.** Across the street from the train station, this lively establishment with vinyl booths draws a loyal local crowd. Many come for vast portions of mussels in a rich wine-and-garlic broth (available September through March), accompanied by frites and a bottle of sharp, cold, inexpensive Auxerrois or Rivaner. ✉ *Pl. de la Gare 30,* ☎ *48–77–99. AE, DC, MC, V. No lunch Sat.*

$ ✕ **Namur.** A Luxembourg institution since 1863, this classic café (with two locations) attracts elegant older shoppers, teenagers out on dates, and young professionals dodging the office. Both of the charming, regal locations specialize in delicious chocolates, mouthwatering pastries, and flavorful coffee. If you aren't in the mood for something sweet, try a sandwich or a paté. ✉ *Rue des Capucins 27,* ☎ *22–34–08;* ✉ *Ave. de la Liberté 66,* ☎ *49–39–64. MC, V. Closed Sun.*

$ ✕ **Oberweis.** Luxembourg's most famous patisserie is owned by the same extended family that owns Chicago's famous Oberweis. Light lunches are available in the upstairs tearoom—chose your meal at the counter from a selection of quiche Lorraine, spinach pie, and the like, then pick a table and the food will be brought to you. Beer and wine are available. ✉ *Grand'Rue 19–20,* ☎ *47–07–03. Reservations not accepted. AE, DC, MC, V. Closed Sun.*

$ ★ ✕ **La Table du Pain.** This working boulangerie-patisserie is decorated like a French country farmhouse, with pine tables to seat 2 or 20 and rustic sideboards lining the walls. Copious soups, salads, and sandwiches, as well as warm dishes, can be ordered from a waiter. Don't forget to buy a loaf of Luxembourg's best bread or one of the almost-too-pretty-to-eat cakes or pastries. The locally made jams, jellies, and wines on display are also for sale. ✉ *Av. Monterey 19,* ☎ *24–16–08. No credit cards. Closed after 7 PM.*

Lodging

Hotels are clustered in the city center, near the train station, and on the Plateau Kirchberg. Staying in the city center is easier if your plans are to wander around the heart of the old city, but the station area also offers numerous restaurants and shops (as well as easy access to the trains). Most hotels offer weekend rates that can be a significant savings. Always ask if the lower rates are available, even if you will be in Luxembourg City during the week. Also, check at the time of booking whether the room rate includes breakfast.

$$$$ **Hotel Inter-Continental.** Rising above the outskirts of Luxembourg like a 20th-century château-fort, this modern, 19-story deluxe hotel opened in 1985 and competes directly with Le Royal (☞ *below*) downtown. Its rooms are gracious, with large, comfortable beds. The restaurant, Les Continents, attracts locals for its upscale French cooking. ✉

Rue Jean Engling, L1013 Dommeldange, ☎ *43–781,* FAX *43–60–95. 337 rooms. 2 restaurants, bar, café, indoor pool, sauna, health club, convention center, parking (fee). AE, DC, MC, V.*

$$$$ ★ **Le Royal.** This is the most prestigious place to stay in the city, with its glass-and-marble lobby, surmounted by an enormous modern chandelier, and smaller lobbies on each floor. The rooms are comfortable and have the full complement of amenities (though their decor is surprisingly plain after the glitz of the lobby). This is the kind of hotel where cellular phones are not allowed in the restaurants and where the gift shop sells "Les must de Cartier." The piano bar is popular, as is the brasserie–breakfast room Le Jardin, especially when the fountain terrace is open. ✉ *Bd. Royal 12, L2449,* ☎ *241–61–67–56,* FAX *22–59–48. 180 rooms. 2 restaurants, bar, indoor pool, barbershop, beauty salon, sauna, tennis court, exercise room, bicycles, parking (fee). AE, DC, MC, V.*

$$$$ **Sheraton Aerogolf.** Located right next door to the airport—and across the highway from a golf course—the Sheraton Aerogolf serves mostly an international business clientele, and the comfortable, if small, rooms offer all of the deluxe amenities one would expect from such a facility. In addition to the hotel's own business center, some rooms also are equipped with their own fax machines and high-speed internet connections. The hotel offers a shuttle bus into town as well as to the airport terminal. ✉ *Rte. de Trèves, L1019,* ☎ *34–05–71,* FAX *34–02–17. 150 rooms. 2 restaurants, 2 bars, golf, meeting rooms, parking. AE, DC, MC, V.*

$$$$ **Sofitel and Novotel.** Sofitel and Novotel ($$$) are joined properties, both owned by the Accor group, though each is managed separately. The Sofitel, built in 1993, is more spacious than the Novotel, although both share amenities. The Novotel is a good choice if you're doing serious business with the Kirchberg institutions. ✉ *Centre Européen, L2015,* ☎ *43–77–61 Sofitel, 429–8481 Novotel;* FAX *42–50–91 Sofitel, 43–86–58 Novotel. Sofitel: 100 rooms, 4 suites; Novotel: 260 rooms. Restaurant, bar, indoor pool, sauna, conference center. AE, DC, MC, V.*

$$$ ★ **Cravat.** This charming Luxembourg relic—with the understated elegance of an Old World Grand Hotel—overlooks the valley and the Old Town from the best location in the city. The hotel has been in the same family for more than 100 years, and during that time it has hosted numerous dignitaries, including General Omar Bradley during the Battle of the Bulge. The rooms are fresh and welcoming in a variety of tastefully retro styles. The art deco coffee shop and the bar are excellent spots for people watching, and the prime minister and his cabinet can be found in the hotel tavern most Friday afternoons. ✉ *Bd. F. D. Roosevelt 29, L2450,* ☎ *22–19–75,* FAX *22–67–11. 60 rooms. Restaurant, 2 bars. AE, DC, MC, V.*

$$$ **Domus.** The Domus is one hotel with six locations throughout the city, each identically furnished, with all reservations handled by the central office at the city-center location on Avenue Monterey. (The other most central location is near the train station.) The bright primary color scheme and whimsical tiles make the modern and efficient rooms playful. Each room has a built-in kitchen, separate bath, and Murphy bed, and some include sitting rooms as well. ✉ *Ave. Monterey, 37, L2163,* ☎ *46–78–78,* FAX *46–78–79. 40 rooms. Parking, airport shuttle. AE, DC, MC, V.*

$$$ **Grand Hôtel Mercure Alfa.** Conveniently located near the train station, the Mercure Alfa has a striking beaux-arts facade dating from its opening in the 1930s. The rooms have been updated since General Patton stayed here during World War II—they're large, with tasteful modern wood furnishings, hardwood floors, and spacious bathrooms with

marble fixtures. Ask for a room in front, with views of the station and the street life below (and insulated glass windows that keep out the noise). ✉ *Pl. de la Gare, 16, L1616,* ☎ *490–0111,* FAX *49–00–09. 149 rooms. Restaurant, bar, meeting rooms. AE, DC, MC, V.*

$$$ **Parc Belair.** Privately owned and family run, this hotel is a few blocks from the city center. It stands on the edge of the Parc de Merl, next to an attractive playground. Rooms are a warm beige; those facing the park are the quietest. The complex includes a separate restaurant with an outdoor café. A copious buffet breakfast is included. ✉ *Av. du X September 109, L2551,* ☎ *44–23–23,* FAX *44–44–84. 45 rooms. Restaurant, playground, meeting rooms, parking (fee). AE, DC, MC, V.*

$$$ **Parc Belle-Vue.** Steps away from the city center, the Parc Belle-Vue is tucked behind the Pont Adolphe, across from the Parc Ed. Klein, with stunning views of the Pétrusse valley. This renovated dormitory building is owned and operated by the same family that runs the Parc Belair (☞ *above*). The rooms are simple and comfortable, with lots of natural light. The hotel grounds are decorated with stone sculptures and antique statues. In the summer, you can have breakfast on the patio. ✉ *Av. Marie Thérèse 5, L2132,* ☎ *456–1411,* FAX *45–61–41–222. 56 rooms. Restaurant, bar, bowling, parking. AE, DC, MC, V.*

$$$ **Rix Hôtel.** Set back from the boulevard Royal, the family-owned Rix Hôtel may not look like much from the street, but inside it tastefully combines the charm of the old with the comfort of the new. Downstairs, a crystal chandelier hangs over the bar in the timeless parlor, where breakfast is served in the morning. Upstairs, each room is different, but all have contemporary furniture and standard amenities. ✉ *Bd. Royal, 20, L2449,* ☎ *47–16–66,* FAX *22–75–35. 20 rooms. Bar, parking. MC, V.*

$$ ★ **Auberge le Châtelet.** At the edge of a quiet residential area but within easy reach of the train station and the Old Town, this pleasant hotel has stone and terra-cotta floors, double windows, Oriental rugs, and tropical plants. Rooms are freshly furnished in knotty pine with tile baths, and there's a comfortable oak-and-stone bar. The four buildings that make up the hotel surround a central courtyard and patio, where breakfast is served in the summer. ✉ *Bd. de la Pétrusse 2, L2320,* ☎ *40–21–01,* FAX *40–36–66. 40 rooms. Restaurant, bar, sauna, gym, parking. AE, DC, MC, V.*

$$ **Christophe Colomb and Marco Polo.** These simple, straightforward hotels, under the same management and located a few blocks from each other, are two peas in a pod, both providing clean, well-furnished accommodations without a lot of frills. The rooms have comfortable beds, writing desks, ample closet space, and wood-trim decor throughout; bathrooms are small but functional. Each hotel has a small breakfast room and bar. The train station is a short walk away. *Christophe Colomb:* ✉ *rue d'Anvers, 10, L1130,* ☎ *408–4141,* FAX *40–84–08. 24 rooms. www.christophe-colomb.lu. Marco Polo:* ✉ *rue du Fort Neipperg, 27, L2230,* ☎ *406–4141,* FAX *40–48–84. 18 rooms. www.marco-polo.lu. Bar, parking. AE, DC, MC, V.*

$$ ★ **Hôtel Français.** With an exceptional location on the Place d'Armes, this boutique hotel is small, smart, and stylish. Run by the same family for 40 years, it's decorated with Oriental rugs as well as art and sculpture from the family's gallery. The bright lobby is located above the Café Français (☞ *above*), and the second-floor breakfast room features a terrace opening onto the Place d'Armes. Rooms are simple and modern, with contemporary wood furnishings. The ones in the front overlooking the Place d'Armes can get a bit noisy, but it is a small sacrifice to pay for the location. ✉ *Pl. d'Armes, 14, L1136,* ☎ *47–45–34,* FAX *46–42–74. 21 rooms. Restaurant, bar. AE, DC, MC, V.*

$$ ☎ **Italia.** This former private apartment house lost some of its old-world charm in its conversion into a hotel. Nevertheless, the rooms are clean and newly furnished, with private tile bathrooms. Downstairs is one of the city's best Italian restaurants. ✉ *Rue d'Anvers 15–17, L1113,* ☎ *48–66–26,* FAX *48–08–07. 20 rooms. Restaurant, bar. AE, DC, MC, V.*

$$ ☎ **Romantik Hotel/Grunewald.** A member of the Romantik group, the Grunewald, located just outside the city, is at the high end of its price category. The old-fashioned lounge is crammed with wing chairs, knickknacks, and old prints; rooms have Oriental rugs, rich fabrics, and Louis XV–style furniture. Rooms overlooking the attractive garden are worth booking ahead; street-side windows are triple-glazed. There's a terrace for alfresco breakfasts. The pricey restaurant (closed Sun.) serves rich, classic French cuisine. ✉ *Rte. d'Echternach 10–14, L1453 Dommeldange,* ☎ *43–18–82,* FAX *42–06–46. 26 rooms. Restaurant, meeting rooms. AE, DC, MC, V.*

$$ ☎ **Sieweburen.** At the northwestern end of the city is this attractively rustic hotel, opened in 1991; the clean, large rooms have natural-wood beds. There are woods in the back and a playground in front. The brasserie-style tavern, older than the rest of the property, is hugely popular, especially when the terrace is open. ✉ *Rue des Septfontaines 36, L2634,* ☎ *44–23–56,* FAX *44–23–53. 14 rooms. Restaurant, bar, playground, free parking. MC, V.*

$ ☎ **Carlton.** This hotel near the station, built in 1918, has a quiet inner court and is buffered from the Rue de Strasbourg scene by a row of stores. The lobby is plush and inviting, if somewhat faded, and is kept overflowing with fresh flowers year-round. Beveled-glass doors open from the lobby into the warm wood-paneled breakfast room, which starts serving at 5 AM, perfect for someone catching an early train or an insomniac. The rooms are clean, bright, and cheery. The Carlton is in the midst of upgrading its facilities, and some rooms, with private baths, are furnished with sleek modern furniture, while others, which have in-room sinks and shared bath, are decorated with antiques. (Renovations are expected to be completed sometime in 2001, but the date isn't firm.) ✉ *Rue de Strasbourg 9, L2561,* ☎ *48–48–02,* FAX *29–96–64. 8 rooms with private bath, 45 rooms with shared bath. Bar. MC, V.*

Nightlife and the Arts

Luxembourg City hosts a disproportionate number of arts events for its size. Watch for posters on kiosks, and check the City Tourist Office on the Place d'Armes (☞ Visitor Information, *below*), where tickets to many events are sold. Tickets to performances at the **Municipal Theater** (✉ Rond-Point Robert Schuman, ☎ 47–08–95) are sold at its box office. The *Luxembourg News,* an English-language weekly translating local news from the city dailies, offers up-to-date events listings; it is sold at bookstores and magazine stands. *Luxembourg Weekly* and *Rendezvous Lëtzebuerg,* both available at the tourist office, also carry listings, as does the weekly *nightlife.lu,* which can be found all over town.

The Arts

MUSIC

Luxembourg is home to the **Orchestre Philharmonique du Luxembourg,** which performs a series of weekly concerts, usually on Thursday night in the Municipal Theater and Friday night at the new Conservatoire de Musique (✉ Rue Charles Martel 33, ☎ 4796–2950). Watch for posters announcing **Concerts du Midi** (✉ Villa Louvigny, in central municipal park): They may feature Philharmonic Orchestra members as soloists or other professional chamber groups, and they are free.

The city routinely springs to life with music and culture in the warmer months. The **Printemps Musical Festival de Luxembourg** showcases a wide variety of music across the city from March to May. **Summer in the City** presents outside concerts and performances in July and August. **Live at Vauban** schedules music during October and November. And there are daily concerts in the Place d'Armes from April through September.

FILM

The best films in any language usually come to **Cine Utopia** (✉ Av. de la Faiencerie 16, ☎ 47–21–09), where reservations are accepted by phone. The **Cinematheque Municipale** (✉ Pl. Thèâtre 17, ☎ 29–12–59) screens movies from its library of their 10,000 films. At the huge cinema complex **Utopolis** (✉ Av. J. F. Kennedy 45, ☎ 42–95–95), on Plateau Kirchberg, 10 theaters show everything from art-house films to blockbusters, most in the original language. There are no reservations; arrive early on weekends as the theater attracts audiences from France, Germany, and Belgium.

THEATER

Good traveling plays in French and German pass through the municipal theater, the **Théâtre Municipal de la Ville de Luxembourg** (✉ Rond-Point Robert Schuman, ☎ 4796–2710). **Théâtre des Capucins** (✉ Pl. de Thèâtre 9, ☎ 22–06–45), a renovated 17th-century monastery, hosts both local troupes and traveling companies.

VISUAL ARTS

In addition to a number of art galleries, Luxembourg has a permanent space for modern and contemporary art exhibits, the **Casino Luxembourg,** where Liszt played his last public concert; in 1995 it was converted into an exemplary exhibition venue. ✉ *Rue Notre-Dame 41,* ☎ *22–50–45.* *Flux 150/€3.70.* ⏲ *Fri.–Mon. and Wed. 11–6, Thurs. 11–8.*

Nightlife

BARS AND CAFÉS

There's a lively bar scene in each of Luxembourg City's neighborhoods. Wednesday, Friday, and Saturday are considered the big nights out. In the city center, the following are worth checking out: **Chiggeri** (☞ Dining, *above*) draws a sophisticated international crowd. **Bistro de la Presse** (✉ Rue de Marché Aux Herbes 24, ☎ 46–66–69) is a smoke-filled hangout for journalists. **O Bar** (✉ Pl. de Théâtre 13, ☎ 22–83–20) has the hotest buzz in town (at least as this book goes to press). **Ennert de Steiler** (☞ Iwwert de Steiler *in* Dining, *above*) is hip and stylish. In the Grund: **Bonaparte** (✉ Bisserwée 9) has gorgeous outside seating in the summer. **Café des Artistes** (✉ Montée du Grund) is an old, welcoming café with great ambience. **Scott's Pub** (✉ Bisserwée 4) caters to Anglophiles. The prize for the most unusual bar name in all of Luxembourg goes to **Chocolate Elvis** (✉ Rue de Tréves 20), which features lava lamps and leopard prints fit for a King. On the Kirshberg, stop in at **Bistropolis** or **Remake** (both at ✉ Bd. J. F. Kennedy 45) for a drink before or after the movies.

DISCOS

Luxembourg City has a busy club scene, but, like anywhere else, what's hot and what's not changes regularly. Be sure to check out the weekly *nightlife.lu* and ask around for the latest buzz when you're getting ready to go out. That said, some of the city's popular discos include: **Didjeridoo** (✉ R. de Bouillon 41, ☎ 44–00–49) in Hollerich, on the highway to Esch-sur-Alzette, is Luxembourg's largest disco. **Pulp** (✉ Bd. d'Avranches 36, ☎ 49–69–40) is a weekend hot spot. **Conquest** (✉ Rue de Palais de Justice 7, ☎ 22–21–41) is a hopping dance club.

GAY BARS

Popular gay bars include: **Café Big Moon** (☒ Rue Vauban 14, ☏ 43–17–46); **Café du Nord** (☒ Av. Emile Reuter 30, ☏ 45–32–84); and **Chez Gusty** (☒ Côte d'Eich 101, ☏ 43–12–23).

JAZZ CLUBS

Melusina (☒ Rue de la Tour Jacob 145, ☏ 43–59–22) is basically a disco (pop and techno on weekends) but also draws top local musicians and touring guests for occasional jazz concerts.

Outdoor Activities and Sports

Biking

In Luxembourg City, you can rent bicycles for forays throughout the grand duchy from **Vélo en Ville** (☒ Rue Bisserwée 8, ☏ 4796–2383), in the Grund. An extensive map of cycling trails both in the the city and around the countryside is available at the City Tourist Office (☞ Visitor Information *in* Luxembourg A to Z, *below*).

Golf

The **Golf Club Grand-Ducal** (☏ 34090) at Senningerberg, about 7 km (4 mi) east of the city, has narrow fairways surrounded by dense woods; it is open only to members of other private clubs. The **Kikuoka Country Club Chant Val** (☏ 35–61–35) is at Canach, about 10 km (6 mi) east of Luxembourg City. For those who prefer miniature golf, the **Club de Ro'de Le'w** (☒ Valle'e de Pétrusse, ☏ 22–85–30) is open April through September, weather permitting.

Shopping

As Luxembourg has only partially and recently abandoned its rural roots, its citizens are for the most part unsentimental about the traditional blue-and-gray crockery and burnished pewter that once furnished every home; nowadays, they prefer their local Villeroy & Boch vitroporcelain in jazzy, modern designs. All three types can be found in most home-furnishings and gift shops. For souvenirs, there are lovely photography books of Luxembourg's historic sites, as well as reproduced engravings of the city in all its fortified glory. *Taaken,* miniature cast-iron firebacks with bas-relief scenes of Luxembourg, are made by the Fonderie de Mersch and are available in gift and souvenir shops.

Because Luxembourg City is home to a large population of bankers and well-paid Eurocrats, as well as its own newly wealthy, it has an unusually high number of luxury and designer shops for such a city its size. Clerks, however, are not always overwhelmingly friendly.

Shopping Districts

The best of high-end shopping is on the **Grand'Rue** and streets radiating out from it; shops along **Avenue de la Gare** and **Avenue de la Liberté,** both forking north from the train station, offer more affordable goods. The **Plateau Kirchberg** has a wide range of music stores, bookstores, and other mall-type establishments.

Department Stores

C & A (two locations: ☒ Pl. Guillaume; ☒ Rue de la Gare 15) is the continent's answer to Macy's or Marks & Spencer—your basic department store, with added flair. **Centre Brasseur** (☒ Grand'Rue 36–38) and **Centre Neuberg** (☒ Grand'Rue 30) have a mix of independent stores selling housewares, clothing, and specialty foods.

Specialty Shops

CHINA

Villeroy & Boch porcelain has been manufactured in Luxembourg since 1767. The factory outlet (✉ Rue de Rollingergrund 330, Bus 2, ☎ 4682–1278), on the northwest edge of town, offers good reductions on virtually flawless goods, and rock-bottom bargains on pieces with slightly visible flaws, but will not ship your purchases. The glitzy main shop (✉ Rue du Fossé 2, between Grand'Rue and Pl. Guillaume, ☎ 46–33–43) has a wide selection of high-quality, full-price goods and will ship.

CHOCOLATES

Namur (✉ Rue des Capucins 27, ☎ 22–34–08) and **Oberweis** (✉ Grand'Rue 19, ☎ 47–07–03), the city's finest patisseries, both have a successful sideline in *knippercher,* Luxembourg chocolates.

PRINTS

Galerie Kutter (✉ Rue des Bains 17, ☎ 22–35–71) offers good framed prints and stationery taken from the works of Luxembourg watercolorist Sosthène Weiss, who painted Cezanne-like scenes of Luxembourg's Old Town.

Street Markets

An **antiques fair** takes over the Place d'Armes every second and fourth Saturday. The annual **Braderie,** a massive, citywide sidewalk sale, slashes prices on the last weekend in August or the first weekend in September. The main **farmers' market** is held in Place Guillaume every Wednesday and Saturday morning.

Keep your eyes open for **Emiaischen** on Easter Monday behind the Ducal Palace, where you can buy Luxembourg's famous clay whistling birds. The **Schueberfouer,** a folk fair dating from 14th century, takes place on the Glacis, near the Grande-Duchesse Charlotte bridge, at the end of August. At Christmastime, the Place d'Armes is host to a **holiday market.**

Side Trips from Luxembourg City

Valley of the Seven Châteaux

The signposted **Valley of the Seven Châteaux** can be visited on a circle tour west of Mersch, 17 km (10 mi) north of the capital, cutting west to Redange, south to Hollenfels, Marienthal, and Ansembourg (which has an old castle in the heights and a new one in the valley below), then working west to Septfontaines and south to Koerich. The castles, in various stages of repair and representing a broad historical spectrum, have not been restored for visitors, but they loom above forests and over valleys much as they did in Luxembourg's grander days. Follow the road signs marked "Vallée des Sept Châteaux": this rather obscure and never-direct itinerary takes you through farmlands, woods, and—just outside Koerich, at Goeblange—to the foundations of two 4th-century Roman villas, their underground heating and plumbing systems exposed; the rough cobbles leading into the woods are original, too.

Hamm/Sandweiler

25 *5 km (3 mi) east of Luxembourg City.*

At Hamm you'll find the **American Military Cemetery,** where General George Patton chose to be buried with his men. More than 5,000 soldiers of the Third Army were buried here, having died on Luxembourg soil; there are also 117 graves of unknown soldiers. Each grave is marked with either a Star of David or a simple cross, but they are not separated by race, rank, religion, or origin—except for the 22 pairs of brothers, who lie side by side. Only Patton's cross, identical to the others, stands by itself.

From the parking lot of Hamm's American Military Cemetery, a small road, about 1 km (½ mi) long, leads to Sandweiler, and across an intersection to the **German Military Cemetery,** which shelters more than twice as many war dead. Blunt stone crosses identify multiple burial sites, some marked with names and serial numbers, others marked simply *Ein Deutscher Soldat* (a German soldier).

DINING

$$$$ ★ ✕ **Lea Linster.** As the first woman to win France's top culinary award, the Paul Bocuse d'Or, Lea Linster has earned international attention and keeps her modest farmhouse—once her mother's rustic café—full of prominent guests. Have a glass of champagne in the shady garden out back (cows may wander nearby), and then relax in the elegant dining room and enjoy her prize-winning dishes: salmon-stuffed zucchini flowers with cardamom sauce, rack of lamb in a crisp potato crust, and caramelized pears with rosemary-lime ice cream. The wine list is weighted toward the high end, as are the food prices. ✉ *Rte. de Luxembourg 17, Frisange, 12 km (7 mi) south of Luxembourg City,* ☎ *66–84–11. Reservations essential. AE, DC, MC, V. Closed Mon.–Tues.*

$$$ ★ ✕ **A la Table des Guilloux.** Pierrick Guilloux was responsible for the Saint-Michel restaurant in Luxembourg City, in its heyday one of Europe's finest, before "retiring" to the countryside to run this great little restaurant in a converted farmhouse. Here he cooks what he pleases, mostly dishes based on the traditions of his native Brittany. Trust his recommendations; few regret it. ✉ *Rue de la Résistance 17–19, Schouweiler, 13 km (8 mi) southwest of Luxembourg City,* ☎ *37–00–08. No credit cards. Closed Mon.–Tues.*

THE REDLANDS

The southern part of Luxembourg has been a desired destination for over two millennia. Caesar's troops founded a series of villages in the area, and the Celts also settled here. During the Middle Ages, the Redlands was the site of a string of important military fortifications and religious institutions—ruins of which, in many cases, still stand today. By the 19th century, iron and mineral deposits (the region gets its name from the red-tinted, iron-rich soil) were the basis for Luxembourg's strong mining and steel industries. The steel trade crashed in the mid-20th century, prompting a migration from the south into Luxembourg City. Now, however, the migration is going in the other direction—the Redlands has become a desirable place for city workers to commute from. Visitors here find castles to explore, train trips through authentic mines, and parks for kids and families.

Esch-Sur-Alzette

26 *28 km (17 mi) southeast of Luxemburg City.*

Esch-Sur-Alzette, founded in 773, was the heart of the Luxembourg's lucrative mining industry in the 19th century. Now it's becoming a cultural destination, with public art lining pedestrian malls that overflow with café goers in the warmer months. The streets are full of life on market days (Tuesday and Saturday), when vendors sell fresh produce at the Place de la Résistance. The city also has some architectural gems from the past three centuries. A brochure for a self-guided 5-km (3-mi) walk grandly titled "When Facades Relate the Epic of Their City" is available at the National Tourist Office in the Hôtel de Ville.

Luxembourg was deeply scarred by World War II. The **Musée de la Résistance,** which is scheduled to open in spring of 2002, honors Luxembourg's Resistance fighters and is the home of the country's Tomb of the Unknown Soldier. There are plans for sophisticated computer models and exhibitions that focus on the plight of Luxembourg's Jewish population and other communities that were lost during the War. Call before visiting to check on construction schedule. ✉ *Place de la Résistance,* ☎ *547–383–483.*

Dudelange

27 *23 km (14 mi) south of Luxembourg City.*

Once a Roman village, then a monastic retreat, then a stop along the Crusade route, and finally a buzzing mining town, Dudelange has a rich history. It's also known as the most "Mediterranean" town in Luxembourg: over 50% of its 17,000 residents are of Italian heritage and just under 20% are of Portuguese, the descendants of immigrant workers who came here at the height of the mining boom. Dudelange's proximity to the French border lends another influence to the multicultural atmosphere.

Spring and summer are busy with festivals celebrating Dudelange's diversity. Events include the **Celtic festival** in March, the **International Roller Blading and Skateboarding Festival** in May, the **Open Air Music Festival** in June, and the **Third World Market** in July.

With over half of Luxembourg's population being foreign-born, immigration-related issues are central to the country's economic, political, and cultural structure. At the **Centré de Documentation sur les Migrations Humaines** these issues are explored through rotating and permanent exhibitions. In the heart of Dudelange's Little Italy neighborhood in an old railway station, this enlightening museum is considered one of the most important throughout the grand duchy. ✉ *Gare Dudelange-Usines,* ☎ *51–69–85.*

Romans first set up a military camp at the base of what is now **Mount St-Jean** in AD 275. The site was later a stop during the First Crusade, and by the 12th century, the location of a monastery built for the Order of St. Jean of Jerusalem. The current castle ruins—which include the foundation, a small chapel, and a tower—date from the 1550s, and are cared for by the local historical society. Atop Mt. St-Jean, the commanding view goes deep into Luxembourg to the north and France to the south. ⏲ *Daily.*

In a grand mansion once occupied by a wealthy steel baron, the **Musée Municipal** has two distinct missions. On the first level, exhibits focus on archaeological artifacts and historical objects such as fossils and weapons, some of which were excavated from Mt. St-Jean. The gallery upstairs shows contemporary art and has the country's only public art space specifically devoted to contemporary photography. ✉ *Rue Dominique Lang 25,* ☎ *5161–2138.* 🎫 *Free.* ⏲ *Tues.–Sun. 3–5.*

The 240-hectare **Parc L'eh,** which spans the French border, is a product of the area's enthusiasm for green, open spaces. Hiking trails crisscross the border through forests, meadows, and stands of wildflowers. If you're lucky you may spot some of Luxembourg's rare orchids, a testament to the landscape's rich mineral deposits. No matter the season, this is a delightful natural escape. ✉ *Rue de Parc, 1 km outside of town.*

The **Parc Merveilleux** has rides, a petting zoo, a toy train, and miniature golf among its facilities. If you're traveling with kids, this is a great place to let them blow off some steam. ✉ *Rte. de Mondorf, Bettembourg, 4 km (2½ mi) north of Dudelange.* 🎫 *150 Flux/€3.70.* ⏲ *Apr.–Oct. 15, daily 10–8.*

Eglise St-Martin is considered the grand duchy's second most important church, after Notre-Dame in Luxembourg City. The intricate and masterful blue mosaics that grace the ceiling dome were created in the 1920s by the monk Notker Becker, and the dramatic representations of the Stations of the Cross were done by Dominique Lang, one of Luxembourg's most famous painters and a native of Dudelange. ✉ *Rue de L'Eglise.* 🎫 *Free.* ⏲ *Daily 8–6.*

Dining and Lodging

$$$ ✕ **Restaurant Parc L'eh.** A family business for nearly 50 years, this sweet, unassuming restaurant tucked deep in Parc L'eh (☞ *above*) is one of Luxembourg's most scenic eateries. The daily menu features hearty home-style French fare. ✉ *Rue de Parc,* ☎ *51–99–90. AE, MC, V.*

$$ ✕🏨 **Grand Café-Hôtel 1900.** Reviving the belle epoque glory of the turn of the 20th century, this well-situated hotel has a wood-paneled café that's perfect for snacks of all sizes. The renovated rooms are fresh and simple, and the ones in the front have a view of the church. Breakfast is not included in the room rate. ✉ *Rue de Commerce 10, L3450,* ☎ *51–28–48 or 51–29–85,* FAX *51–28–80. 15 rooms. MC, V.*

$ 🏨 **Cottage.** Modern budget hotels are few and far between across the grand duchy. This one offers low prices and easy access to the train station. ✉ *Rue Auguste Liesch, L3474,* ☎ *52–05–91,* FAX *52–05–76. 45 rooms. AE, DC, MC, V.*

THE MOSELLE VALLEY

Legend has it that the rambling vineyards in the fertile Moselle valley were originally developed to satisfy the wine-drinking habits of Roman legions. (Roman antiquities still occasionally surface in the well-cultivated soil.) Today the Moselle river serves as the border between Luxembourg and Germany, and graceful vineyards still line the valley. The **Route Du Vin,** a road and hiking/biking trail, runs up the Luxembourg side of the river from **Schengen** in the south and to **Wasserbillig** in the north. Along the route is a series of villages, many charmingly old-fashioned, and each seemingly with its own microclimate, which accounts for the variety of grapes to be found. The valley produces a spectrum of light, fruity, flavorful white wines as well as *cremant,* a dry sparkling wine similar to champagne.

Mondorf-les-Bains

28 *24 km (15 mi) southwest of Luxembourg City.*

Sitting near the French and German borders, this quaint spa town attracts visitors from hundreds of miles away for its natural spring waters, reputed for centuries to cure whatever ails you. Mondorf's popularity reached its peak at the turn of the 20th century, when it was a premiere destination for Europe's upper classes, with no less than 10 grand hotels catering to their every whim and fancy. At the end of World War II, Mondorf was in the news as a prison camp for high-ranking Nazi party members on their way to the Nuremburg trials. The town then became a more modest draw, catering primarily to Luxembourg's retirees, but in 1988 higher times returned with the opening of Mondorf le Club, an upscale spa and health center. Now the town once again attracts an international crowd of all ages.

Swathed in the scent of eucalyptus, **Mondorf Le Domaine Thermal/Mondorf Le Club** is a state-of-the-art, full-service health and sport facility. You'll find classic spa treatments, including thermal baths, massages, manicures, aromatherapy, and mud baths, as well as health-club features such as a climbing wall and yoga and aerobics classes. Day passes and longer packages are available. Call ahead for special offers. ✉ *Enter through Mondorf Parc Hotel or through the park via Av. Marie Adelaide, L5601,* ☎ *661–2121.* ⏲ *Daily.*

Specifically designed for families, the **Parc Brill** has a public swimming pool, tennis courts, climbing sculptures, miniature golf, and even a fenced in area where young children can safely run wild. ✉ *Av. Marie-Adelaide.* ⏲ *Daily.*

NEED A BREAK? While at the Parc Brill, stop by the **Châlet Parc Brill** for a cold drink or a light snack. There's a kids' menu, too.

Dining and Lodging

$$ **Dolce Vita.** This small, homey spot serves large portions at reasonable prices. The pizzas are made with fresh ingredients and baked in a wood-fire oven. The pastas are flavorful and filling. ✉ *Av. Dr. Klein 4,* ☎ *66–80–73. AE, DC, MC, V.*

$$–$$$ **Hôtel du Grand Chef.** Harkening back to Mondorf's turn-of-the-20th-century splendor, this classic European grand hotel is in its own private park across the street from the spa. Remodeled in 2000, all the amenities have been updated without losing their historic charm. The restaurant is acclaimed throughout the region, offering traditional French cuisine. ✉ *Av. Des Bains 36, L5601,* ☎ *66–80–12,* FAX *66–15–10. 40 rooms. Restaurant, parking. AE, MC, V. Closed mid-Nov.–mid-Mar.*

$$$$ **Mondorf Parc Hôtel.** This deluxe hotel serves guests coming to take the spa waters—the hotel rates include spa fees. The rambling lobby is attached to Mondorf Le Club, allowing you to go from room to spa in your bathrobe. All the rooms, from the lobby areas to the guest rooms, are spacious and soothing. Every guest room has a large bathroom and a balcony overlooking town. There are two restaurants, both serving healthy fare. Rooms in the annex building tend to be less expensive while offering the same features. ✉ *Av. Dr. E. Feltgen, L5601,* ☎ *661–2121,* FAX *66–10–93. 113 rooms. 2 restaurants, pool, parking. AE, DC, MC, V.*

Nightlife

Casino 2000 (✉ Rue Th. Flamang, ☎ 661–0101) has full gaming facilities. Jacket and tie are required to play roulette and blackjack, but not for the slot machines.

Schengen

29 *29 km (18 mi) southeast of Luxembourg City, 11 km (7 mi) south of Remich.*

Located at the point where the Luxembourg, German, and French borders converge, this small town looms large in recent European history. It was here, aboard the boat *Marie-Astrid,* that the final agreement was signed allowing European passport holders to travel freely across the continent. A monument in the middle of town commemorates the event.

The independent vintner **Caves Gloden** is based in Schengen. Because of its small production, on site is one of the few places where you can try its fine white wines. ✉ *29/30 Rte. du Vin,* ☎ *60–098.* ⏲ *Hrs vary; call ahead.*

NEED A BREAK? On the road from Schengen to Remerschen, the stone exterior of the **Caves du Sud** belies the architecturally clever wooden boat in the interior. (The boat itself pays homage to the Romans who sailed the Moselle during harvest time two millennia ago.) Just about every Vinsmoselle wine, liquor, and cremant is available in this shop, and a friendly staff can help find what you're looking for. An adjoining dining room is a perfect place to match Luxembourg's wines with French food for lunch or dinner. Call for dinner reservations. ✉ *Rte. du Vin 32,* ☎ *66–48–26.*

Bech-Kleinmacher

30 *23 km (14 mi) west of Luxembourg City, 1 km (⅔ mi) south of Remich.*

In the small village of Bech-Kleinmacher you'll find the **Musée Folklorique A Possen,** a 17th-century stone wine maker's house. Its extraordinarily atmospheric displays include a "black kitchen," with a ham-smoking chimney, and a cozy bedroom with a four-poster bed and homespun linens; there are museum displays on the wine industry, and a toy collection as well. There's also a **Waistuff** (wine *stube*), where you can taste the local wine and sample dark bread smeared with pungent *kachkeis,* Luxembourg's favorite cheese spread. ✉ *Rue Sandt 16,* ☎ *69–73–53.* *Flux 120/€2.95.* *May–Oct., Tues.–Sun. 2–7; Nov.–Apr., Fri.–Sun. 2–7.*

The **Caves Cooperative Wellenstein** is 2 km (1¼ mi) up the hill from Bech-Kleinmacher, in the tiny village of **Wellenstein.** This is the visitor headquarters for the Vinsmoselle company. A one-hour stop here will allow you to take in a film about Moselle wines, a tour of the facility, and tastings. The caves have been in continual use for over 100 years and are surrounded by 900 hectares of vineyards. ✉ *Rue de Caves 13, Wellenstein,* ☎ *69–98–58.* *Flux 60/€1.50.* *May–Aug., Tues.–Fri. 10–noon and 1–6, weekends 11–6.*

Remich

31 *22 km (14 mi) west of Luxembourg City.*

Once a medieval fortification, Remich is now one of the busier towns along the Moselle, serving as home to the State Viticulture Institute and the National Wine Mark, which oversees, rates, and regulates all the wines produced in Luxembourg. Despite the activity, Remich retains its historic charms. Twisting cobblestone streets, which stretch from the riverbank up to the top of the hill, are lined with art galleries, handsome homes, and lovely gardens. The Esplanade, the park along the river, is a great place to stroll, daydream, and occasionally feed a swan. One of the few bridges linking Luxembourg to Germany across the Moselle is in Remich; if you're heading out of the grand duchy, this is the last place to get gas at Luxembourg prices, which tend to be cheaper than at the German pumps.

St. Nicholas is associated with Christmas elsewhere, but here he's revered as the patron saint of fishermen. Once the formal entrance to Remich, the **St. Nicholas Gate** now stands at the foot of town on the Esplanade, with a rendering of the saint standing over the arch. St. Nicholas is honored in the area every year on December 5.

St-Martin Wine Cellar is a small independent vinter producing white wines, sparkling wines, and grape juices. You can tour the facilities and taste some of the products in the lovely pavilion. ✉ *Rte. de Stadtbredimus,* ☎ *69–97–74.* *Flux 90/€2.25.* *Apr.–Oct., daily 10–noon and 1:30–6.*

NEED A BREAK? Grab a fresh loaf of bread or a sweet pastry from **C. Feltz Salon de Thé and Patisserie** (✉ on the Esplanade). Eat in or, in the warmer weather, treat yourself to a riverside picnic.

Close-Up

WINES OF THE MOSELLE VALLEY

LIKE MUCH ABOUT the small country, Luxembourg's wines are little known outside its borders. Yet the Moselle valley has been producing wine for over 2,000 years—wine good enough to be celebrated in verse by the Roman poet Decimus Magnus Ausonius and to inspire Celtic burial objects with grape and vine motifs.

The Moselle River forms a portion the border between Luxembourg and Germany. The south-facing slopes on Luxembourg's side of the valley have mineral deposits and microclimates ideal for growing a variety of wine grapes, including reisling, pinot gris, pinot blanc, auxerrois, pinot noir, gewürztraminer, rivaner, and elbling. The resulting wines are primarily white and dry (unlike their sweet German counterparts), though many vinters are now experimenting with red and rosewine production. Basic quality standards are established by a 1932 national law and by the *Marque Nationale* certification, created in 1935.

About two-thirds of Luxembourg's wine production is controlled by Les Domaines de Vinsmoselle, a cooperative that dates back to the 1920s. There are also some 50 independent vinters which sell primarily to private clients. Many of the wineries' caves (both Vinmoselle and independent) are open for tastings and as departure points for vineyard tours—just look for signs along the road as you travel the Route du Vin that runs through the valley.

Boating along the Moselle river is a great way to see the valley's varieties of geography. Small cruise boats go along the river, docking at various towns. Remich is often the best place to pick them up. Call ahead for current schedules and fares and to make reservations. **Navitours** (☎ 75–84–89) runs four-hour boat tours both during the day and in the evening. **The Princess Marie-Astrid** (☎ 75–82–75) hosted the signing of the Schengen agreement. Owned by Vinsmoselle, the Princess Marie-Astrid fleet offers entertainment, dancing, and wine on all its trips.

Dining and Lodging

$$ ✕🏨 **Domaine La Forêt.** Located at the top of the hill overlooking town and the river below, this inn is surrounded by a seasonal garden. Although the river view is somewhat obscured, bright windows, handsome furniture, and spacious rooms all create a welcoming environment. The restaurant ($$$–$$$$, reservations required) is known across the country for its fine French cuisine. Pension plans combining room and board are an appealing option. ✉ *Rte. de l'Europe 36, L5531,* ☎ *69–99–99,* FAX *69–98–98. 14 rooms. Restaurant, parking. AE, DC, MC, V.*

$$ ★ ✕🏨 **Hotel St-Nicholas/Lohengrin Restaurant.** Next to the St. Nicholas Gate on the Esplanade, this charming riverside hotel has been in the same family since 1885. As a result, the staff knows the Moselle area and the rest of the grand duchy well and will be happy to help you find the best vineyards, nicest hiking trails, and other prime local spots. The rooms are spacious, and some, like the top-floor suite, have fabulous river views and Jacuzzis. The outstanding Restaurant Lohengrin ($$$, reservations required) specializes in fish and other fresh ingredients and has an extensive international wine list. Half-board plans

are good deals. ✉ *Esplanade 31, L5533,* ☎ *69–88–88,* FAX *69–88–69. 40 rooms. Restaurant, bar, sauna, solarium. AE, DC, MC, V.*

$ ✕🏨 **Hôtel de L'Ecluse.** This family-run hotel specializes in affordable food and lodging. In season, the menu features the valley's regional delight: *friture de la Moselle* (tiny fried fish). Pile your plate high with these taste treats and watch the river flow gently by. The rooms upstairs are quiet and comfortable. ✉ *Rte. du Vin 29, L5450 Stadtbredimus, 4 km (2½ mi) north of Remich,* ☎ *66–95–46,* FAX *69–76–12. 18 rooms. Restaurant, parking. AE, MC, V. Closed Thurs., 2 wks late Dec., 2 wks June.*

NIGHTLIFE

Yachting (✉ Esplanade 37, ☎ 69–79–79) is one of the hippest joints in Remich. The interior is designed to resemble a boat, with sailcloth, weathered wood, and blue lights. The bar features a wide range of local wines and cremants and is open late.

Ehnen

32 *21 km (13 mi) east of Luxembourg City, 12 km (7 mi) north of Remich.*

Ehnen, with its narrow old streets, carved-wood doors, and unusual circular church, is a popular excursion goal for city dwellers who want to contemplate the river and sample the grape. Ehnen is home to a **Musée du Vin** (Wine Museum), set in a typical group of Luxembourgish farm buildings, with pink stucco and cobbled courts. Its rooms are full of tools, equipment, and photographs of the wine-making industry, and a demonstration vineyard is planted with samples of each of the local varietals. There are labels in English. ☎ *76–00–26.* 🎟 *Flux 80/€2.00.* ⏲ *Apr.–Oct., Tues.–Sun. 9:30–11:30 and 2–5; Nov.–Mar. by appointment.*

The remains of the 18th-century **Chapel of St. Nicholas** stand on the road out of town to the north.

Dining and Lodging

$ ★ ✕🏨 **Simmer.** This Moselle institution, built in 1863 and maintained in a welcoming Victorian-rustic style, is the preferred riverfront retreat of the royal family and political luminaries, though its ambience remains comfortable and homey. Incorporating portions of a 1610 house and the founder's butcher shop, it was taken over by the current family in 1955 and built into an elegant hotel-restaurant. The details they added include a 17th-century fireplace in the dining room and carved oak grotesques paneling the salon. Rooms are spacious and solid, with dated glamour (brocade, gilt, crystal) and some antiques; in front there are balconies and in back small suites. Specialties in the restaurant ($$$) include braised *brochet* (pike) in cream and *sandre* (pike perch) in local Auxerrois wine; in summer, you can dine on the full-length, open-front porch. It's next door to the wine museum. ✉ *Rte. du Vin 117, L5416,* ☎ *76–00–30,* FAX *76–03–06. 15 rooms. Restaurant, bar. AE, MC, V. Closed Tues. and Feb.*

En Route In Wormeldange stop at the **Cellars of Pol-Fabaire,** which specializes in cremant (Luxembourg's answer to champagne). In addition to tastings, this winery also offers walking tours through its gracefully sloping vineyards. The café has light fare.

Grevenmacher

33 *32 km (20 mi) east of Luxembourg City, 22 km (14 mi) north of Remich.*

Grevenmacher is one of the largest towns along the Moselle river. Founded in the 7th century, it eventually became a medieval fortress, and a castle tower still dominates the area. Modern-day Gravenmacher is a crossroads between Luxembourg and Germany, and there is often more German spoken in the streets and shops than French or Luxembourgish. The cobblestone alleys are charming and full of historical secrets; a self-guided walking tour starting at the church is available from the Hôtel de Ville.

The **Jardin des Papillons** (Butterfly Garden) seethes with fluttering wildlife, from butterflies to birds to tropical insects, all enclosed in an attractive greenhouse. ✉ *Rte. du Vin,* ☎ *75–85–39.* *Flux 180/€4.45.* *Apr.–mid-Oct., daily 9:30–5.*

The **Caves Bernard-Massard** is an independent vinter specializing in sparkling wines. Its output is tiny, and delicious. Tours, including tastings, are available. ✉ *Rue du Pont 8,* ☎ *750–5451.* *Flux 100/€2.50.* *Apr.–Oct., daily.*

NEED A BREAK? Stop in the **Schumacher Patisserie** (✉ Rue Victor Prost 3) for a sweet treat or a light lunch. Everyone in town comes here at some point during the day.

En Route Luxembourg is a series of microclimates, and nowhere do they change so drastically as at the intersection of the vineyard-strewn Moselle valley and the cliffs and caves of the Müllerthal (Le Petite Suisse). To appreciate this dramatic change, follow the back roads from **Wasserbillig** west to **Larouchette**. (Although the road isn't numbered, it's well marked.) The valley transforms into rolling hills as you pass by the tiny hamlets of **Herborn, Mompach, Bech** (with its charming church and cemetery), and **Consdorf** (with what may be the grand duchy's oddest World War II memorial: a disarmed B-17 bomb mounted in the center of town). Keep going west through **Christnach** to Larouchette, and you'll find yourself in a region thoroughly different from where you started some 30 minutes before.

MÜLLERTHAL/LE PETITE SUISSE

The northeastern quadrant of Luxembourg—a hilly area of dense fir and beech forests, high limestone bluffs, and twisting brooks—goes by two names: Müllerthal and Le Petit Suisse. Müllerthal is the name of the river that wanders through the region. The Petite Suisse appellation comes from the resemblance to Switzerland's rolling mountain valleys. By either name the area is popular with hikers and spelunkers from across Europe. The best place to start exploring the region on foot is the **National Tourist Office** (✉ 7 An Der Laach) in the little town of **Berdorf,** 7 km (4 mi) east of Echternach. It's well stocked with information about hiking trails and cave explorations.

Echternach

34 *58 km (36 mi) southeast of Clervaux, 35 km (22 mi) northeast of Luxembourg City.*

Echternach dates from the 7th century and is the home of the only religious dancing procession remaining in the Western world. You wouldn't guess this at first glance, for modern Echternach has been all but adopted by German visitors from across the Sûre, who fill its hotels, restaurants, and monuments every weekend.

Echternach was founded in 698 by St. Willibrord, who came from Northumberland in England to establish a Benedictine abbey, which thrived until 1795. His remains are enshrined in the crypt of the **Basilica.** The early medieval basilica was destroyed in December 1944 and rebuilt in a modern style. The relics of the saint are contained in a neoclassical marble sarcophagus. Behind the elaborate carvings, you glimpse the simple tooled-stone sarcophagus cut in the 7th century. A few token traces of the original 7th-century chapel, founded by the saint himself, have been left exposed under heavy, modern repairs. On the ground floor of the basilica is a **tourist office**, with information about activities in town and around the region. On a hill just behind the basilica, a church, **Sts. Pierre et Paul,** stands on the remains of a Roman castellum and shows, in its spare architecture, signs of Merovingian, Romanesque, and Gothic influence. Every spring, the two churches host one of Luxembourg's most important arts events: the Echternach Festival of Classical Music.

On Whit Tuesday (eighth Tuesday after Easter), Echternach is transported to the Middle Ages: more than 10,000 pilgrims (most of them young people) from throughout the region come to town to join in—and tourists come to watch—the famous **Springprozession,** a dancing procession down the streets of the town, the marchers bouncing from one foot to the other, to the tune of a polkalike march. Their chanted prayer: "Holy Willibrord, founder of churches, light of the blind, destroyer of idols, pray for us." This unique pilgrimage has been repeated every year since the 15th century.

NEED A BREAK?

Just below the church of Sts. Peter and Paul, you can have coffee and a generous piece of cake at the **Café-Tea Room Zimmer** and pick up something for later in the adjoining bakery-confectionery, perhaps the Echternach specialty, *Macarrons Moux.*

Around the corner from Sts. Peter and Paul is the **Salon de Consommation,** a bustling spot for an afternoon tea treat.

In the Middle Ages, Echternach was known throughout the Western world for the exquisite illuminations (miniature illustrations) that accompanied the hand-copied texts produced by the Benedictine abbey's scriptorium. The original abbey is long gone, but a magnificent quadrant of abbey buildings from the 18th century remains, noble of line and classical in scale. Examples of the artwork produced in the abbey can be viewed in the **Musée de l'Abbaye** (Abbey Museum) in the abbey basement. The books displayed here are painstakingly executed reproductions of the originals, down to their gem-studded covers. The originals are now in various museums abroad. Even so, the exhibition provides an interesting introduction to the art of illumination in the Middle Ages. ✉ *Parvis de la Basilique 11.* 🎫 *Flux 80/€2.00.* ⏲ *Apr.–Oct., daily 10–noon and 2–6; Nov.–Mar., weekends 2–5.*

Echternach's cobbled **Place du Marché,** in the old town center, offers a charming mix of Gothic arcades and restored medieval houses, festooned with wrought-iron signs and sculpted drain spouts; the arched and turreted 13th-century Hôtel de Ville (Town Hall) is its centerpiece.

Dining and Lodging

$$$$ ★ ✕ **La Bergerie.** One of the best restaurants in the country, La Bergerie is in Geyershof, 7 km (4 mi) outside of Echternach, off the road to Luxembourg City. The 19th-century farmhouse nestles in an idyllic setting of forest and fields, with windows and a garden terrace making the most of the expanse of greenery. The graceful, simple dining room features the cooking of owner-chef Claude Phal and his son Thierry, whose specialties include classics (simple foie gras; steamed turbot in champagne sauce) and sophisticated experiments (lobster fricassee with whiskey; scallops with truffles). The strawberry gratin in orange butter uses fruit from the garden; all baked goods are made in the full-

scale pastry kitchen. It's a family effort, with wife, son, and daughter-in-law running the restaurant. ✉ *Geyershof,* ☎ *79–04–64. Reservations essential. AE, DC, MC, V. Closed Mon. and mid-Jan.–Feb. No dinner Sun.*

$$ ✕🏨 **Au Vieux Moulin.** Just outside of town, this family-run inn has simple country decor (yellow wallpaper, wooden furniture, and exposed wood beams) and clean, pleasant rooms. The main attraction, however, is the restaurant ($$$), which serves fine French cuisine emphasizing fresh ingredients; the kitchen is particularly adept with lamb and fish. It is a member of the international *Jeunes Restaurateurs,* which spotlights up-and-coming chefs. ✉ *6 Lauterborn, L6562,* ☎ *72–00–68,* FAX *72–71–25. 6 rooms. MC, V. Restaurant closed Mon.*

$ ✕🏨 **Commerce.** Tucked back from Place du Marché, amid quiet side streets and with an idyllic garden behind it, this simple hotel has been kept in top running order. Although rooms have fixtures of varying vintage, all have fresh decor. The restaurant and café are atmospheric, with oak wainscoting, beams, and pink linens; standard dishes (trout, bouchée à la reine) are moderately priced and well prepared. ✉ *Pl. du Marché 16, L6460,* ☎ *72–03–01,* FAX *72–87–90. 44 rooms. Restaurant, café. AE, MC, V. Closed mid-Nov.–mid-Feb.; weekdays mid-Feb.–Easter.*

$$$$ 🏨 **Hôtel Bel Air.** Perched on a hilltop graciously overlooking expansive gardens, this grand hotel dates back to 1925. The spacious rooms have been updated with new bathrooms and fresh amenities, but they still retain their old world charm. The cozy bar is a great place to relax and chat while lingering over a drink. ✉ *1 Rte. de Berdorf, L6409,* ☎ *72–93–83,* FAX *72–86–94. 40 rooms. Restaurant, bar, sauna, tennis courts, exercise room, meeting rooms. AE, DC, MC, V.*

The Arts

CLASSICAL MUSIC

The **Echternach Festival** of classical music is one of the most important arts events in Luxembourg, bringing in world-class artists and ensembles and showcasing them in the Basilica and the smaller Sts. Peter and Paul's Church. It takes place on weekends for a month during May and June. Tickets sell out quickly; write ahead to Lux-Festival (✉ B.P. 30, L6401, ☎ 72–99–40).

Outdoor Activities and Sports

BICYCLING

You can rent bikes at **Trisport** (✉ 31 Rte. de Luxembourg, ☎ 72–20–86).

En Route On the way from Echternach to Beaufort, you can peer down crevices at **Werschrumsluff** and **Zickzackschluff,** climb to vantage points for vast panoramas at **Perekop** and **Bildscheslay,** and squeeze between the cliffs at the **Gorge du Loup** (Wolf's Throat).

Beaufort

35 *25 km (15 mi) northeast of Luxemburg City.*

At the top of the Ernz Noire valley, a short detour leads to Beaufort. Just west of the village, a splendid ruin, the **Château de Beaufort,** only partially restored to its 15th-century form, rises over green grounds full of sheep and forests laced with walking trails. You can step into guard towers with archers' slits, look down wells, visit the kitchen fireplace, cross a drawbridge, and ogle torture equipment, including a rack, in a dungeon. At the ticket counter, you can buy (drink) samples of the local kirsch and cassis. An easy nature walk is across the street. ✉ *CR128, west of Beaufort,* ☎ *86002.* 🎟 *Flux 60/€1.50.* ⏲ *Late Mar.–Oct., daily 9–6.*

Shopping

At Beaufort, you can pick up a bottle of the locally made kirsch or cassis.

Larochette

★ 36 *22 km (14 mi) southeast of Bourscheid, via Lipperscheid and Diekirch, 23 km (14 mi) northeast of Luxembourg City.*

Larochette has a striking step-gabled **castle** that looks out over the town. The castle is privately owned and occupied, but adjoining ruins from an earlier incarnation (with evocative views over the small houses below) may be visited. An easy footpath, or a nice driving road, leads from town up to the ruins. ✉ *Near N25.* *Flux 50/€1.25.* ⏲ *Easter–Oct., daily 10–6.*

NEED A BREAK? Sip a cup of tea and have a homemade cookie at **Mme. Jacob's Tea Room** (✉ Pl. de Bleech 6), a simple place with wooden booths and tables outside with a view of the castle.

Dining and Lodging

$$ **Auberge Op Der Bleech.** In the heart of Larochette, this simple inn and restaurant takes its inspiration from 19th-century France. The building itself is an architectural time machine, with its brocaded facade. Inside, the rooms are comfortable and clean. The restaurant serves classic French country cuisine. In the warmer seasons you can dine outside in the castle's shadow. ✉ *Pl. de Bleech 4, L7610,* ☎ *87–80–58,* FAX *87–97–25. 9 rooms. Restaurant, solarium. AE, MC, V. Closed mid-Dec.–mid-Jan.*

THE LUXEMBOURG ARDENNES

Vast, rolling green hills and dense fir forests alternate in Luxembourg's northern highlands, the southeast corner of the rocky, wooded Ardennes plateau. Higher and harsher than the duchy's southern Bon Pays (Good Country), with bitter winters and barren soil, it is relatively isolated and inaccessible; indeed, even in the 1940s, no one expected the Germans to attempt an attack across such rough and uneven terrain. They did, of course, twice. The second led to one of the most vicious conflicts in World War II, the Battle of the Ardennes, or the Battle of the Bulge. Throughout its history, the region has been the hunting grounds of kings and emperors, Celts, Romans, and Gauls; shaggy deer and great, bristling wild boar still occasionally charge across a forest road. Castles punctuate its hills and valleys, and rocky rivers and streams pour off its slopes, making this a popular vacation area for northern Europeans seeking wilderness and medieval history.

Diekirch

37 *33 km (20½ mi) north of Luxembourg City.*

Diekirch preserves memories of Roman culture, early Christianity, and the brutalities of World War II. This small, easygoing city, with a pleasant pedestrian shopping area, has several points of interest. In the center of the pedestrian zone, the **Eglise St-Laurent,** a small, ancient Romanesque church, has portions dating from the 5th century. It was first built over the foundations of a Roman temple, the older parts functioning as a cemetery. In 1961, that lower section was uncovered and with it about 30 Merovingian sarcophagi, many of them containing intact skeletons. Since 1978, the cemetery has been restored and open to the public. Some of the ancient foundations of the church can be seen through a grate in the nave; you may enter the crypt by an exterior door on the right of the building. ✉ *Pl. Bech.*

At the Diekirch **Musée Municipal,** in the basement of the primary school, there are two sarcophagi and remains found under the church, along with well-preserved Roman mosaics from the 4th century, found two blocks away. Diekirch is riddled with remains of Roman culture, though most of its treasures were carried away by invading Franks. There is a plan to move the contents of the municipal museum into the basement of the National Museum of Military History (☞ *below*) sometime in 2001. ✉ *Pl. Guillaume.* *Flux 50/€1.25.* ⏲ *Easter–Oct., Fri.–Wed. 10–noon and 2–6.*

In the **Musée National d'Histoire Militaire,** 10 life-size, authentically equipped dioramas depict personal aspects of the hardships of the Battle of the Bulge. Unlike the museum at Bastogne, this thoughtful, neutral effort sidesteps discussions of strategies and fronts; it brings out individual details instead, from yellowed letters and K rations to propaganda flyers—both German and American—scattered to demoralize already homesick soldiers at Christmastime. All paraphernalia are authentic period pieces. The staff often welcomes veterans personally. Other exhibits illustrate Luxembourg military history since the end of the Napoléonic Wars. The museum is scheduled to add the Roman treasures of the Municipal Museum (☞ *above*) in 2001. ✉ *Bamertal 10,* ☎ *80–89–08.* *Flux 200/€4.95.* ⏲ *Easter–Oct., daily 10–6; Nov.–Easter, daily 2–6.*

The **Diewelselter,** an impressive dolmen (stone altar) attributed to the Celts, stands south of Diekirch, overlooking the town. No one is sure who piled the great stones that form this ancient arch—or how they did it.

Dining and Lodging

$$$$ ✕ **Hiertz.** This small hotel-restaurant looks stark and uninviting from the outside, but inside, the dining room is a jewel of a place. Sit in the hotel's pretty terraced garden for summer aperitifs and after-dinner coffee; for dinner, try carpaccio of langoustines with caviar, or turbot flavored with vanilla and raspberry vinegar. The hotel plays second fiddle to the food and is in a lower price category ($$$), but rooms are comfortable; ask for one of the three back rooms facing the garden. ✉ *Rue Clairefontaine 1, L9201,* ☎ *80–35–62,* FAX *80–88–69. 9 rooms. Restaurant. AE, DC, MC, V. Closed Tues., 2nd ½ of Aug., 3 wks over Christmas and New Year's. No dinner Mon.*

Outdoor Activities and Sports

BICYCLING

Bikes can be rented at **Camping de la Sûre** (☎ 80–94–25) and in summer at local train stations.

Ettelbruck

38 *31 km (19 mi) north of Luxembourg City.*

Due north of Luxembourg City, Ettelbruck is a gateway to the Ardennes. Although much of the population commutes to the city daily, the town has a lively pedestrian shopping zone and several spots of particular interest to World War II buffs. The **General Patton Memorial Museum** (✉ 5 Rue Dr. Klein, ☎ 81–03–22) is dedicated to the American general who liberated Ettelbruck on Christmas Day 1944 and is filled with photographs and relics from the World War II era. A lifesize statue of Patton himself, in full combat gear, stands just outside of town.

For a touch of high culture, visit the **Centre des Arts Pluriels,** on the Semois River. Opened in 2000, this performing-arts venue has a concert hall, a music conservatory, and a theater.

Bourscheid

★ 39 *26 km (16 mi) east of Esch-sur-Sûre, 36 km (22 mi) north of Luxembourg City.*

Following the green Sûre valley toward Goebelsmühle—along a quiet, winding road that is one of the most picturesque in the grand duchy—look for signs for Bourscheid Moulin-Plage, where you'll see the romantic ruins of **Bourscheid Castle.** It looms 500 ft above the Sûre River, with commanding views of three valleys. Restorations have made this rambling hodgepodge of towers and walls more accessible; the views are magnificent and there's a snack bar. ☒ *Near N25,* ☎ *90570.* *Flux 80/€2.00.* ⏲ *Apr., daily 11–5; May, June, and Sept., daily 10–6; July–Aug., daily 10–7; Oct., daily 11–4; Nov.–Mar., weekends and holidays 11–4.*

Vianden

★ 40 *11 km (7 mi) northeast of Diekirch, 44 km (27½ mi) north of Luxembourg City.*

In Vianden you come face to face with one of Europe's most dramatic sights: driving around the last bend, you suddenly see a full-length view of its spectacular **castle** rearing up on a hill over the village, replete with conical spires, crenellation, step gables, and massive bulwarks. Its dramatic position enhances the tiny village's medieval air, with its steep, narrow main street and shuttered houses crouched at the feet of the feudal lord. The castle was built on Roman foundations in the 9th century, but its most spectacular portions date from the 11th, 12th, and 15th centuries. Down the hill, by the banks of the river Our, a **chairlift** (Flux 180/€4.45, ⏲ Easter–mid-Oct., daily 10–6) carries visitors up for a remarkable view of the valley. *Castle:* ☎ *84–92–91.* *Flux 180/€4.45.* ⏲ *Mar. and Oct., daily 10–5; Apr.–Sept., daily 10–6; Nov.–Feb., daily 10–4.*

The 13th-century Gothic **Eglise Trinitaire** (☒ Grand'Rue) once functioned as a Trinitarian monastery; its ancient cloisters have been restored to sparkling modernity. Victor Hugo was in Vianden in 1871, and the town will never forget it. The **Musée Victor Hugo,** long closed for renovation, will reopen in 2002 with great fanfare to celebrate the writer's 200th birthday. ☒ *Rue de la Gare 37,* ☎ *84257.* *Flux 45/€1.10.* ⏲ *May–Oct., weekdays 9:30–noon and 2–6; Nov.–Apr. weekdays; phone ahead for exact times.*

NEED A BREAK? Romantically overlooking the Our river, the **Café Dupont** (☒ 1 Grand'Rue) has a range of nibbles to suit any mood.

The **Musée de la Poupée et du Jouet** (Doll and Toy Museum) displays a collection of 500 dolls and toys, including antiques dating from the 16th century. Attached is its sister museum, the **Musée d'Art Rustique,** which features handcrafts from the region. ☒ *Grand'Rue 96,* ☎ *84591.* *Flux 100/€2.50.* ⏲ *Easter–Oct., Tues.–Sun. 11–5.*

Dining and Lodging

$$ **Hôtel Victor Hugo.** At the bottom of the hill and perched on the river, this comfortable hotel pays homage to Vianden's most famous visitor. It's location can't be beat. The rooms behind the German-style facade are small and simple. At the restaurant you'll find Luxem-

bourgish specialities featuring local fish and meat. In the warmer months, linger over a meal or a drink in the lovely terraced garden. ✉ *1 Rue Victor Hugo, L9414,* ☎ *83–41–60,* FAX *84–91–22. 22 rooms. AE, MC, V.*

$$ ★ ✕🏨 **Oranienburg.** In the same family since 1880, this once-traditional lodging has gone deluxe, decorating its rooms and restaurant in lush fabrics and modern, built-in fixtures. Only the café and stairwell retain the old-Vianden atmosphere, with game trophies and burnished oak. The restaurant, Le Châtelain, now contemporary and posh as well, attracts nonguests for its ambitious French cooking and its views toward the village and castle. The hotel café is much more modestly priced. ✉ *Grand'Rue 126, L9411,* ☎ *83–41–53,* FAX *83–43–33. 25 rooms. Restaurant. AE, DC, MC, V. Restaurant closed except for hotel guests Mon. and Tues., 2 wks in Nov.; hotel and restaurant closed Jan.–mid-Mar.*

$ ✕🏨 **Aal Veinen.** Dark, cozy, and casual, this 1683 inn serves simple food—*bouchée à la reine* (chicken à la king) with frites, omelets, cold sausage plates—and a wide selection of grilled meats, cooked in full view of the dining area over a sizzling wood fire. (If you've given up on pork chops, this is the place to get reacquainted.) Rooms upstairs are rustically furnished and tidy, with exposed beams, stucco, and oak armoires. ✉ *Grand'Rue 114, L9401,* ☎ *83–43–68,* FAX *83–40–84. 8 rooms. Restaurant, bar. MC, V.*

$ ✕🏨 **Heintz.** Expanded from its origins as a Trinitarian monastery, this atmospheric hotel has been in the family for four generations. During the war, owner Grandma Hansen worked with the Resistance, hiding hams, cash, and Luxembourgers with equal aplomb. The public spaces are rich with history, from the cross-vaulted oak café to the hallways filled with local antiques; rooms are simple and up-to-date. The oldest rooms, on the first floor, have antique oak furniture and original doors, but baths are down the hall; the best rooms are upstairs, with balconies over the garden and fountain. The restaurant offers French classics—grilled beef with béarnaise sauce, salmon in chives—and authentic German apple strudel with vanilla sauce. ✉ *Grand'Rue 55, L9410,* ☎ *83–41–55,* FAX *83–45–59. 28 rooms, 2 without bath. Restaurant. AE, DC, MC, V. Restaurant closed Wed. (except mid-July–mid-Aug.), hotel and restaurant closed Nov.–Mar.*

En Route The beautiful Our river valley snakes along the border between Luxembourg and Germany. To explore this lovely landscape, follow the unnumbered road north from Vianden through **Stolzembourg** to Rodershuasen. as it hugs the riverbank. From there, take the N10 west to Clervaux.

Clervaux

★ 41 *31 km (19 mi) northwest of Vianden, 62 km (38½ mi) north of Luxembourg City.*

Clervaux, a forest village surrounded by deep-cleft hills, draws vacationers to hike, hunt, listen to Gregorian plainchant, and view *The Family of Man* photo exhibit in the sprawling **castle.** It was from this castle that Philip de Lannoi set forth in 1621 to make his fortune in America; one of his descendants was Franklin Delano Roosevelt (whose middle name is the anglicized version of de Lannoi). The old castle, virtually reduced to rubble in the Battle of the Bulge, has been completely restored. Two floors in the right wing of the castle house the noted exhibition of photo portraits of *The Family of Man*—considered by some to be the greatest photographic exhibition of all time—assembled by the photographer Edward J. Steichen, a Luxembourg native. ✉ *100* *m (110 yds) above center of town,* ☎ *522–4241.* 🎫 *Flux 150/€3.70.* ⏲ *Mar.–Dec., Tues.–Sun. 10–6.*

Clervaux suffered terribly during World War II. The entire town, including the castle, was reduced to rubble, and its people were thrown into poverty. Although the structures have been lovingly rebuilt and the town is now economically healthy, Clervaux still remembers these desperate times. The **World War II Museum,** housed within the castle, is a collection of photographs and artifacts from the war and particularly from the events of the Battle of the Bulge that occurred in and around town. 🎫 *Flux 95/€2.35.* ⏲ *June–Aug., daily 11–6; Mar.–May and Sept.–Dec., Sun. 11–6.*

Discreetly tucked behind the main square on Place Princesse Maria Theresa is a **World War II Memorial.** The humble plaque and surrounding flags honor the 6th Armored Division of the U.S. Army, which liberated the city.

Clervaux is home to the striking **Benedictine Abbey of Sts. Maurice and Maur,** built in 1910 in the style of the Abbey of Cluny, and perched high above town. Mass at 10:30 AM and vespers at 6:30 PM are celebrated with Gregorian plainchant. There's also an exhibition on the monastic life.

Dining and Lodging

$ ★ 🏨 **Hôtel du Parc.** Once the manor house of the Comte de Berlaimont, the Hôtel du Parc sits atop a bluff with wonderful views of the Clervaux valley and the castle. Inside it's regal and warm, without a touch of pretensiousness. The resident cats lounge by the fireplace, and the paneled walls and eclectic furniture enhance the charm. The guest rooms are comfortable and modern. The restaurant ($$) is just as charming. Its French-based menu changes depending on the fresh ingredients of the season. ✉ *2 rue du Parc, L9701,* ☎ *92–06–50,* FAX *92–10–68. 7 rooms. AE, MC, V. Closed Jan., Feb.*

$–$$ 🏨 **Koener/International.** These two hotels, owned by brothers and adjoining a shared indoor pool, offer sleek modern details; rooms on the International side are somewhat more attractive (and more expensive), with dark-green and brass decor. Neither half, aside from some rooms with forest views, has much Ardennes atmosphere, but both offer full comfort. *Koener:* ✉ *Grand'Rue 14, L9701,* ☎ *92–10–02,* FAX *92–08–26. International:* ✉ *Grand'Rue 10, L9701,* ☎ *92–93–91,* FAX *92–04–92. Koener: 53 rooms. International: 41 rooms. Restaurant, café, piano bar, indoor pool, sauna. AE, DC, MC, V. Koener closed mid-Jan.–mid-Mar.*

$ 🏨 **Le Commerce.** Directly below the castle and slightly apart from the hotel-packed center, this spacious hotel has been in the family for two generations and shows their pride: it combines slick, spare modernity—tile, stucco, polished oak—with homey old details (fringed lamps, heavy upholstery), and there's an open fireplace in the restaurant. Some rooms have balconies over the river and hills. ✉ *Rue de Marnach 2, L9709,* ☎ *92–10–32,* FAX *92–91–08. 54 rooms. Restaurant, bar, café. MC, V. Closed mid-Nov.–mid-Mar.*

The Arts

Wiltz, halfway between Clervaux and Esch-sur-Sûre, sponsors a popular **theater and music festival** in July, with performances and concerts in the outdoor amphitheater. Call or write ahead for ticket and schedule information (✉ Syndicat d'Initiative, L9516 Wiltz, ☎ 95–74–41).

Outdoor Activities and Sports

There's an 18-hole golf course (☎ 92–93–95) at **Eselborn,** 3 km (2 mi) northeast of Clervaux. The inexpensive, 10-room **Hôtel du Golf** (☎ 92–93–95) is right by the Eselborn course.

Asselborn

42 *70 km (43 mi) north of Luxembourg City; 8 km (5 mi) northwest of Clervaux.*

The heart of the Ardennes forest is in the northern wedge of the country, where Luxembourg meets Belgium and Germany. Here, quiet and humble agricultural villages are the norm, and often cows and chickens outnumber people. Asselborn is a typical town of this region, with its sparse population and working farms. Here you can hike, bike, and take in the rural beauty around you.

A few kilometers north of Asselborn, the hamlets of **Triosverges, Hachiville,** and **Binsfield** are worth a visit. Troisverges and Hachiville both have small, charming churches featuring Flemish-school paintings. Binsfield is home to the **Musée A Schiewesh,** a collection of antique farming equipment.

Lodging

$$ ★ **Au Vieux Moulin.** Rustic and romantic, this elegantly simple oasis is hidden away on a dirt road, along a bubbling brook on the site of an 11th-century mill. Remnants of the old stone structure have been incorporated into the inn, which opened in 1985. Upstairs, the rooms are warm and inviting, with wood-beam ceilings, and large bathrooms have tiled showers. The downstairs is devoted to a handsome bar and restaurant. The menu offers inventive French-influenced cuisine such as rabbit with sesame seeds, port sauce, and vegetable tempura. Dining on the patio along the stream is a pleasure in warmer months. Between meals, take a long bike ride or hike (trail maps and bicycles are available through the front desk) or visit the on-site exhibit of old mill equipment. ✉ *Maison 158, L9940,* ☎ *99–86–16,* FAX *99–86–17. 15 rooms. Restaurant, bar, bicycles, meeting room. AE, DC, MC, V. Closed 2 wks Jan., 2 wks Nov.*

Esch-sur-Sûre

43 *27 km (17 mi) southwest of Clervaux, 43 km (27 mi) northwest of Luxembourg City.*

Pretty little Esch-sur-Sûre is reached from Clervaux via Wilwerwiltz and Wiltz. Completely circled by densely forested hills, this miniature gooseneck on the river Sûre was once a stronghold, and its ruined **fortress-castle** still towers over the town (unrestored, but open to the public). Legend has it that an Esch Crusader brought home a Turk's head and hung it outside the castle gate and that it reappears to this day to warn of disaster; some claim to have seen it before the German invasion in 1940. The old **textile factory** (✉ Rte. de Lutzhausen, ☎ 899–3311) has been converted into a museum.

Dining and Lodging

$$ ✕ **Beau-Site.** At the edge of the village and overlooking the river, this hotel-restaurant has modern rooms, some with flower boxes and river views. The restaurant offers grilled meats and cream-sauce standards at prices slightly higher than average—but the portions are staggering, and the kitchen cuts no corners. ✉ *Rue de Kaundorf 2, L9650 Esch-sur-Sûre,* ☎ *89–90–21,* FAX *89–90–24. 18 rooms. Restaurant. DC, V. Closed Feb.*

Shopping

In Esch-sur-Sûre, you can buy fine candles at the old *Käerzefabrik* (Candle Factory).

En Route Children who finally tire of pouring imaginary boiling oil and shooting flaming arrows from Ardennes castles and who balk at another uphill forest hike can find adventure swimming or windsurfing at **Lac de la Haute Sûre,** accessible on the south shore at Insenborn and on the north shore below Liefrange.

LUXEMBOURG A TO Z

Arriving and Departing

From North America by Plane

AIRPORTS AND AIRLINES

Most of the main international airlines offer connections—usually with **Luxair** (☎ 4798–5050)—allowing you to fly to London, Amsterdam, or Brussels and then connect into Luxembourg as a final destination at little or no additional cost: **British Airways** (☎ 43–86–47 in Luxembourg; 800/247–9297 in the U.S.), **Delta/Sabena** (☎ 432–4241 in Luxembourg; 800/955–2000 in the U.S.), **Northwest/KLM** (☎ 42–48–42 in Luxembourg; 800/374–7747 in the U.S.). All flights land at **Findel Airport,** 6 km (4 mi) east of the city center.

From the United Kingdom

BY PLANE

Luxair (☎ 4798–4242 reservations in Luxembourg; 4798–5050 information in Luxembourg; 0181/745–4254 in the U.K.), the Luxembourg airline that connects to all major airports in Europe, has regular flights to London Heathrow, London Stansted, and Manchester. **British Airways** (☎ 43–86–47 in Luxembourg; 0141/222–2345 in the U.K.) also has regular flights to and from Luxembourg.

BY CAR AND FERRY

Luxembourg is easily accessible in a day from London and the southeast. Nearly all ferries from Britain to the continent take cars, as does the Channel Tunnel train. Several companies operate sailings direct to the Belgian ports of Oostende and Zeebrugge. Sailings are most frequent from the south coast ports; in summer **Hoverspeed Ltd.** (☎ 0990/59–55–22 or 0990/24–02–41) offers about 5 services daily from Dover to Oostende and up to 12 sailings a day from Dover to Calais. The quickest (but most expensive) ferry crossing is from Dover to Calais via Hoverspeed's Hovercraft link: after a mere 35-minute crossing you continue by car or rail south from Calais to Lille and cut across Belgium, via Mons, Charleroi, and Namur, to reach Luxembourg. If weather and traffic permit, you'll make it from the south coast to Luxembourg in five hours. You also can take a standard ferry from Dover to Calais with **P&O Stena Line** (☎ 0990/98–09–80).

Fares vary considerably according to season, journey time, number of passengers, and length of vehicle. However, the approximate cost of crossing the Channel by ferry on one of the short sea routes in high summer, with an average vehicle of 4¼ m (14 ft) and two adult passengers, works out to about £130 one way. By traveling off-peak, early in the morning or late evening, or in June and September, you can reduce costs.

BY TRAIN

☞ The Channel Tunnel *in* Smart Travel tips A to Z.

Between the Airport and Downtown Luxembourg City

Luxair buses leave the airport hourly from 6 AM to 10 PM, heading non-stop for the train station. Tickets cost Flux 120/€2.95. Luxembourg City Bus 9 leaves the airport at regular intervals for the main bus depot at the train station. Tickets are Flux 40/€1.00. A taxi ride from the airport to the city center costs about Flux 600/€14.85.

Car Rentals

Luxembourg has among the lowest car-rental rates in Europe, as well as easy pickup at the airport and at the train station in Luxembourg City.

Rental agencies: **Avis** (✉ Pl. de la Gare 2, ☎ 48–95–95). **Budget** (✉ Findel Airport, ☎ 43–75–75). **Europcar/InterRent** (✉ Rte. de Thionville 84, ☎ 40–42–28; ✉ Findel Airport, ☎ 43–45–88). **Hertz** (✉ Findel Airport, ☎ 43–46–45). **Rent-a-Car** (✉ Rte. de Longwy 191, ☎ 44–08–61).

Customs and Duties

On Arrival

Americans and other non-EU members are allowed to bring in no more than 200 cigarettes, 50 cigars, 1 liter of spirits, 2 liters of wine or sparkling wine, 50 grams of perfume, and 0.25 liter of toilet water. **EU members** may bring in 800 cigarettes; 200 cigars; 10 liters of spirits; 90 liters of wine, of which 60 liters may be sparkling wine; 50 grams of perfume; and 0.25 liter of toilet water.

On Departure

U.S. citizens may take home $400 worth of foreign merchandise as gifts or for personal use without having to pay duty, provided they have been out of the country for more than 48 hours and provided they have not claimed a similar exemption within the previous 30 days. Every member of a family is entitled to the same exemption, regardless of age, and the exemptions can be pooled. For the next $1,000 worth of goods, inspectors will assess a flat 10% duty, based on the price actually paid, so it is a good idea to keep your receipts. Included in the $400 allowance for travelers over the age of 21 are 1 liter of alcohol, 100 cigars, and 200 cigarettes. Any amount in excess of those limits will be taxed at the port of entry, and it may be additionally taxed in the traveler's home state; be sure to ask, as you may be charged late penalties if you don't pay on arrival. You may not take home meats, fruits, plants, soil, or other agricultural items.

Canadian citizens may take home 50 cigars, 200 cigarettes, and 40 ounces of liquor. Be sure to carry receipts for your purchases abroad, as any totaling more than $300 will be taxed.

British citizens may take home the same quantity of goods they were allowed to carry into Luxembourg (listed above). Because of strict rabies control, no pets or animals may be brought into the United Kingdom.

Guided Tours

General-Interest Tours

See Tour Operators *in* Smart Travel Tips A to Z for tours that cover Belgium and Luxembourg. A sampling of tours and packages that concentrate on Luxembourg is listed below. For additional resources, contact your travel agent or the tourist office of Luxembourg.

FROM THE U.S.

Olson Travelworld (✉ 1145 Clark St., Stevens Point, WI 54481, ☎ 715/345–0505 or 800/421–2255) tailors excursions in Luxembourg for groups.

FROM THE U.K.

Travel Scene (✉ 11–15 St. Anne's Rd., Harrow, Middlesex HA11AS, U.K., ☎ 0181/427–4445) has packages of various lengths and price ranges, by air or rail, to Luxembourg.

In Luxembourg City

Segatos Tourisme (✉ R. Kalchesbrück 7, ☎ 42–22–88 ext. 1) offers two-hour tours (Flux 450/€11.15) in English every afternoon from mid-April through October. Leaving from Platform 5 of the bus station (next to the railway station) or from the war memorial in Place de la Constitution, they visit the historic sights of the center, the area housing various branches of the European Union, and some of the villas on the city outskirts. On weekends from May to September half-day trips take in Vianden and other Ardennes castle towns and the Little Switzerland region.

From March through mid-November, guided **minitrain tours** (☎ 422–2881; 🎫 Flux 230€5.70) of the Old Town and the Pétrusse valley start from Place de la Constitution.

You can rent a **self-guided city walking tour** with headphones and cassette (Flux 190/€4.70) at the bus booth on Place de la Constitution.

The **Vauban Walk** is a self-guided military history tour starting at the Bock that leads through the Pfaffenthal to Les Trois Glands (the Three Acorns), 18th-century Austrian fortifications.

The **Wenzel Walk** allows visitors to experience 1,000 years of history in 100 minutes, though you are well advised to take your time. It is named for Wenceslas II, Duke of Luxembourg and Holy Roman Emperor (no relation to the "good king" of the Christmas carol), who played an important part in fortifying the city. The walk starts at the Bock and leads down into the valley, over medieval bridges, through ancient gates, and past ancient ruins and exact reconstructions (always labeled as such). Two audiovisual presentations are included along the way. The walk also takes in French military architecture of the 17th century and a stroll along the Alzette River, which played an important role in the city's defense system. Good walking shoes and a reasonably sound constitution are required. The walk is signposted, with full explanations at each sight. A descriptive leaflet is available from the City Tourist Office in Place d'Armes, which also can provide a guide (Flux 1,600/€39.60) regardless of the size of the group).

Package Deals for Independent Travelers

The **Centre des Auberges de Jeunesse Luxembourgeoises** (✉ R. du Fort Olisy 2; B.P. 374, L2013 Luxembourg, ☎ 22–55–88), Luxembourg's youth hostel association, offers do-it-yourself city, hiking, and cycling packages (mountain-bike rental included). **Travel Bound** (✉ 599 Broadway, Penthouse, New York, NY 10012, ☎ 212/334–1350 or 800/456–8656) tailors air-hotel-car packages to Luxembourg, through travel agents only.

Language

Luxembourg is a linguistic melting pot. Although its citizens speak Lëtzeburgesch (Luxembourgish), a language descended from an ancient dialect of the Moselle Franks, they are educated in German and French, completing higher studies in French. The younger generation also learns English and is, for the most part, easily conversant. The language used for government documents is French, but many are translated into German as well; a simple church service will often include German, French, Luxembourgish, and a trace of Latin. Within the travel industry, most Luxembourgers you'll meet will speak some English with you, but they'll talk *about* you in Luxembourgish.

Mail

Postal Rates

Airmail postcards and letters weighing less than 20 grams cost Flux 25/€0.60 to the United States. Letters and postcards to the United Kingdom cost Flux 16/€40.

Receiving Mail

Mail can be sent care of **American Express** (✉ Av. de la Porte-Neuve 34, L2227 Luxembourg). This service is free for holders of American Express cards or traveler's checks.

Money Matters

The Luxembourg franc (abbreviated Flux) is equal to the Belgian franc and used interchangeably with it within Luxembourg. Notes come in denominations of 100, 1,000, and 5,000 francs. Coins are issued in denominations of 1, 5, 20, and 50 francs; you will rarely be required to use the 50-centime piece. Be careful not to mix up French 10-franc pieces with Belgian and Luxembourgian 20-franc coins; the French coin is three times as valuable. At press time, rates of exchange averaged Flux 40 to the U.S. dollar, Flux 66 to the pound sterling, and Flux 30 to the Canadian dollar. Rates fluctuate daily, so be sure to check at the time you leave.

Barring any change of plans, the Flux will go into retirement on January 1, 2002, from which time all bank transactions must be made in euros and euro coins and banknotes will replace the coins and notes of the local currency.

Costs

As Luxembourg continues to prosper, the cost of living increases annually, but hotel and restaurant prices tend to rise no more than 5% from year to year. Because of Luxembourg's low VAT (Value Added Tax), perfume, gasoline, cigarettes, and liquor continue to be notably cheaper here than in neighboring countries; you'll find combination gas station/liquor stores clustered at every border crossing. High-octane, unleaded gas costs about Flux 26/€0.65 a liter; in Belgium, you'll pay 8 or 9 francs more.

SAMPLE COSTS

Cup of coffee, Flux 55/€1.35; glass of beer, Flux 45/€1.15; movie ticket, Flux 250/€6.20; taxi ride, 4¾ km (3 mi), Flux 600/€14.85 (10% higher nights, 25% higher Sunday).

Taxes

VAT is 15%, except for hotels and restaurants, where it is 3%. The airport tax (payable with the purchase of your ticket) is Flux 120/€3.00. Purchases of goods for export (to non-EU countries only) may qualify for a refund; ask the shop to fill out a refund form. You must have the form stamped by customs officers on leaving the European Union. A minimum purchase of Flux 3,000/€75.00 is required before you're eligible for a refund.

National Holidays

January 1; Carnival (late February, early March); Easter Monday (April); May Day (May 1); Ascension (late May, early June); Pentecost Monday (late May, early June); National Day (June 23); Assumption (August 15); All Saints' Day (November 1); Christmas (December 25–26). Note: when a holiday falls on a Sunday, the following Monday is automatically a national holiday.

Opening and Closing Times

Banks are generally open weekdays 8:30–4:30, though some close for lunch (noon–2). In Luxembourg City, an automatic exchange machine in the Rue de la Reine accepts banknotes of most foreign currencies. **Museum** opening hours vary, so check individual listings. Most are closed Monday, and in the countryside some also close for lunch (noon–2). **Shops** and department stores are generally open Monday 2–6 and Tuesday–Saturday 9–6. Some close for lunch (noon–2). A few small family businesses are open Sunday 8–noon.

Outdoor Activities and Sports

Biking

Biking is a very popular sport in the grand duchy. Good routes include Ettelbruck–Vianden and Luxembourg City–Echternach. The **Luxembourg National Tourist Office**—as well as those of Luxembourg City, Diekirch, and Mersch—all publish booklets and maps suggesting cycling tours within Luxembourg. Also contact the **Fédération du Sport Cycliste Luxembourgeois** (⊠ B.P. 1074, L1010 Luxembourg, ☎ 29–23–17).

Boating and Water Sports

The Wiltz and the Clerve rivers offer challenging waters for small craft or canoes, but the Our, with its wooded gorges, is the wildest; the Sûre is most rewarding, for its length and for the thrills it offers. For further information, write to the **Fédération Luxembourgeoise de Canoë et de Kayak** (⊠ R. de Pulvermuhle 6, L2356 Luxembourg). People windsurf and sail on Lac de la Haute Sûre.

Camping

Visitors from all over Europe, especially the Netherlands, descend on Luxembourg's campgrounds every summer, making them sociable, crowded places, often near forests and riverbanks. Write for the pamphlet "Camping/Grand-Duché de Luxembourg," available through the national tourist office (☞ Visitor Information, *below*). The **Fédération Luxembourgeoise de Camping et de Caravaning** (☎ 54–48–71) also publishes camping information.

Fishing

If you're in search of trout, grayling, perch, or dace—as well as relaxation—apply for a government fishing permit from the **Administration des Eaux et Forêts** (⊠ B.P. 411, L2014 Luxembourg, ☎ 40–53–10) and a local permit from the owner of the waterfront, which in many cases is your hotel.

Hiking and Walking

Luxembourg is full of well-developed forest trails, often on state lands with parking provided. The book *171 Circuits Auto-pedestres,* which contains maps of walking itineraries, is available in bookshops for Flux 895/€22.00. Trails will be full of strollers late Sunday afternoon, the traditional time for such outings.

Telephoning

Country Code

The country code for Luxembourg is 352.

International Calls

To dial direct internationally, start with the country code (001 for the United States, 0044 for the United Kingdom), and then dial the local number. A **Telekaart,** available with 50 or 150 time units, works in specially equipped booths, usually in post offices, where they are sold. To make an international call without direct access, you must first dial 0010.

The cheapest way to make an international call is to dial direct from a public phone; in a post office, you may be required to make a deposit before the call. To reach an **AT&T** long-distance operator, dial ☎ 0800–0111; for **MCI,** ☎ 0800–0112; for **Sprint,** ☎ 0800–0115.

Local Calls

Public phones aren't always easy to find, especially outside Luxembourg City. The best bet is at post offices and in cafés. A local call costs Flux 10/€0.25. No area codes are necessary within the grand duchy.

Operators and Information

For international **information,** dial 016; for local information, 017.

Tipping

In Luxembourg, service charges of 15% are included in restaurant bills; for a modest meal, most people leave the small change. At a grander restaurant, you will be expected to leave a larger tip—up to 10% extra when a large staff is involved. For porters, a tip of Flux 50/€1.25 per bag is adequate. Cab drivers expect a tip of about 10%.

Transportation: Getting Around

By Bus

The Luxembourg bus system carries passengers to points throughout the grand duchy; most buses leave from the **Luxembourg City train station** (Gare Centrale, ✉ Junction of Av. de la Gare, R. de Strasbourg, Av. de la Liberté, ☎ 49–24–24). You can buy an *horaire* (bus schedule) to plan complex itineraries, or consult the tourist office. The **Oeko-Billjee,** a special day ticket (Flux 180/€4.45), allows you to travel anywhere in the country by bus (including city buses) or rail, from the time you first use it until 8 AM the next day. They're available in Luxembourg City at any train station or at the **Centre Aldringen** (✉ Av. Monterey 8A, at R. Aldringen), the underground bus station in front of the central post office.

Luxembourg City has a highly efficient bus service covering the town and outlying areas. Get tickets and details about services at the information counter of the Centre Aldringen. A 10-ride ticket costs Flux 300/€7.45.

By Car

The best way to see Luxembourg, outside of Luxembourg City, is by car. Castles and attractive villages are scattered around and connected by pleasant, well-maintained country roads. *Priorité à droite* (yield to the right) applies here and should be strictly observed; drivers may shoot out from side streets without glancing to their left. Speed limits are 50 kph (31 mph) in built-up areas, 90 kph (55 mph) on national highways, and 120 kph (75 mph) on expressways.

A car is a liability in small, walkable Luxembourg City. It's best (and least expensive) place to deposit your vehicle in a central parking area, either Parking Glacis, near the Grande-Duchesse Charlotte bridge, or Parking Knuedler, under Place Guillaume.

By Taxi

In Luxembourg City, you can **call for a cab** (☎ 48–22–33 or 48–00–58) or pick one up at stands by the central post office and the train station.

By Train

Train travel within the grand duchy is limited; a north–south line connects Luxembourg City with Clervaux in the north and Bettembourg in the south, and another line carries you to Grevenmacher and Wasserbillig, along the Moselle. For additional information, write or call the **Chemins de Fer Luxembourgeois** (✉ CFL, Pl. de la Gare 9, B.P. 1803, L1018 Luxembourg, ☎ 49–90–1).

Visitor Information

Luxembourg National Tourist Office (✉ Offices at Findel Airport and the railway station, ☎ 40–08–08).

The **Luxembourg City Tourist Office** has pamphlets and brochures and general information about the city. ✉ *Pl. d'Armes,* ☎ *22–28–09.* ⏲ *Apr.–mid-Oct., Mon.–Sat. 9–7, Sun. 10–6; mid-Oct.–Mar., daily 9–6.*

9 PORTRAITS OF BELGIUM AND LUXEMBOURG

Belgium and Luxembourg: A Chronology

Les Moules Sont Arrivées!

Battle Scars from the Bulge

Books and Films

BELGIUM AND LUXEMBOURG: A CHRONOLOGY

55 BC Julius Caesar's legions extend Roman control to the Meuse and Waal rivers.

ca. AD 300 Inundation of the Frisian plain causes Rome to abandon it.

ca. 400 Roman rule retreats before invading Frisians in the north and Franks in the south.

481–511 Under their king, Clovis, the Frankish Merovingians extend their rule north.

800 Charlemagne, king of the Franks, is crowned Emperor of the Romans by the pope. His domains extend from the marches of Denmark to Spain.

843 The Treaty of Verdun divides Charlemagne's empire into three. Luxembourg and the Netherlands are included in the middle kingdom of Lotharingia; Belgium is divided at the Scheldt River between France and Lotharingia. Viking attacks begin along the coast.

862 Baldwin Iron-Arm establishes himself as first count of Flanders, but rule of the Lotharingian lands is constantly disputed.

963 Siegfried, count of Ardennes, purchases an old Roman castle named Lucilinburhuc along the Alzette river. His descendants are named counts of Luxembourg.

1196–1247 Reign of Countess Ermesinde of Luxembourg, who enlarges and unifies the county, grants privileges to its cities, and founds the ruling house of Luxembourg-Limburg.

ca. 1200 With the rise of towns, the collection of duchies and counties that constitutes the Low Countries gains economic power.

1302 The men of Flanders revolt against French attempts at annexation and defeat Philip the Fair's army at the Battle of the Golden Spurs, near Kortrijk. Flanders remains a desirable prize.

1308 Henry VII of Luxembourg is elected Holy Roman Emperor; he grants the rule of the county of Luxembourg to his son, John the Blind (d. 1346).

1354 John's son, Charles, also Holy Roman emperor, raises the status of Luxembourg to a duchy.

1361 Philip the Bold, son of John II of France, establishes the great duchy of Burgundy, which, by Philip's marriage in 1369 to Marguerite, heiress of the count of Flanders, grows to include Flanders, Artois, Limburg, and Brabant.

1419–67 Philip's grandson Philip the Good extends Burgundian rule over Holland, Zeeland, and Hainaut and presides over the golden age of the Flemish Renaissance. Painters include the van Eycks, Hans Memling, and Rogier van der Weyden.

1443 Philip gains Luxembourg.

1464 Philip calls the deputies of the states—nobles, merchants, and churchmen—to meet together, thus beginning the States-General, the Dutch representative assembly.

1477 The death of Philip's son Charles leaves his granddaughter Mary of Burgundy as heiress. Mary marries the Habsburg heir, Maximilian of Austria; their son Philip marries Juana, heiress to the throne of Spain.

1500 Birth in Gent of Charles, son of Philip and Juana, who inherits the collective titles and holdings of Burgundy, Spain, and Austria as Charles V, Holy Roman Emperor.

ca. 1520–40 Protestantism spreads through the Netherlands.

1549 By the Pragmatic Sanction, Charles declares that the 17 provinces constituting the Netherlands will be inherited intact by his son Philip.

1555 Charles V abdicates, dividing his empire between his brother Ferdinand and his son Philip, who inherits Spain and the Netherlands. A devout Catholic, Philip moves to suppress Protestantism in the Netherlands.

1566 Revolt in Antwerp against Spanish rule provokes ruthless suppression by the Spanish governor, the duke of Alva.

1568 Beginning of 80 years of warfare between the 17 provinces and Spain.

1572 The "Sea Beggars" under William of Orange take to the natural Dutch element, water, and harass the Spanish.

1579 The Spanish succeed in dividing the Catholic south from the Protestant north with the Treaty of Arras. The seven Protestant provinces in the north—Holland, Friesland, Gelderland, Groningen, Overijssel, Utrecht, and Zeeland—declare themselves the United Provinces, under the hereditary *stadtholder* (city elder), William the Silent of Orange.

1585 Antwerp falls to the Spanish, and the division of the Netherlands between north and south is effectively completed; the Dutch close the Scheldt to navigation, depriving Antwerp of its egress to the sea and leading to its rapid decline.

1609 The Twelve Years' Truce temporarily ends fighting between the United Provinces and Spain.

1648 By the Treaty of Westphalia, the Spanish finally recognize the independence of the United Provinces. What will become Belgium remains under Spanish control but is a battleground between the ambitions of France and a declining Spain.

1701–17 The War of the Spanish Succession ends with the Treaty of Utrecht, which transfers the Spanish Netherlands (including Luxembourg) to Austria. Depleted of men and money, the Netherlands declines in the 18th century.

1789–90 Inspired by events in France, the Brabançonne revolution succeeds in overthrowing Austrian rule in Belgium, but divisions between conservatives and liberals allow the Austrians to regain their territory.

1795 The French defeat the Austrians and annex the Belgian provinces and Luxembourg.

1806–10 Napoléon establishes the Kingdom of Holland, ruled by his brother Louis Bonaparte, but finally annexes the Netherlands to France.

1815 Napoléon defeated at Waterloo, near Brussels. By the terms of the congress of Vienna, the Netherlands and Belgium are reunited under William I, but the union proves an unhappy one. Luxembourg is divided between William and Prussia.

1830 Again inspired by a revolution in France, the Belgians rise against William I and declare their independence.

1831 With the guarantees of the great powers, the Belgians draw up a constitution and elect as king Leopold of Saxe-Coburg (an uncle to soon-to-be-Queen Victoria of England).

1839 The Netherlands finally recognizes Belgium as an independent, neutral state. Luxembourg is again divided, with 60% going to Belgium while the rest remains a duchy, with William I of the Netherlands as grand duke.

1865 Leopold II succeeds his father as king of the Belgians; begins reign as empire builder in Africa and rebuilder of Brussels at home. By the terms of an international agreement, the Prussian garrisons withdraw and Luxembourg's independence and neutrality are guaranteed.

1885 The establishment of the Congo Free State brings Belgium into the ranks of colonial powers.

1890 King William III of the Netherlands is succeeded by his daughter Wilhelmina; because Luxembourg bars female succession, the grand duchy passes to the house of Nassau-Weilburg.

1903 Birth of Georges Simenon (d. 1989), creator of Inspector Maigret and Belgium's most widely read author.

1908 Congo Free State annexed to Belgium.

1909 Albert succeeds Leopold II of Belgium; leads Belgian resistance from exile during World War I.

1914 In violation of the terms of the 1839 treaty, Germany invades and conquers Belgium at the outset of World War I. Luxembourg is also occupied.

1919 The Franco-Belgian alliance ends Belgian neutrality and signals the dominance of the French-speaking Walloons. Universal male suffrage is granted. In Luxembourg, a plebiscite confirms the continuation of the grand duchy under Grand Duchess Charlotte.

1934 Leopold III succeeds Albert on Belgian throne.

1940 May 10: Nazi Germany launches blitzkrieg attacks on Belgium and Luxembourg as well as the Netherlands. The Dutch army surrenders May 14, the Belgians May 28. Grand Duchess Charlotte and Queen Wilhelmina flee; King Leopold III remains in Belgium, where he is eventually imprisoned. The Nazi occupation leaves lasting imprints on all three countries.

1944 Luxembourg City is liberated.

1947 The Marshall Plan helps rebuild devastated areas. Belgium, Netherlands, and Luxembourg form customs union.

1948 Women gain the vote in Belgium.

1949 Luxembourg joins NATO.

1951 Amid controversy over his wartime role and continued ethnic dissension, King Leopold III of Belgium abdicates in favor of his son, Baudouin.

1957 Belgium, and Luxembourg are charter members of the European Economic Community (EEC).

1960 A 50-year treaty establishes the Benelux Economic Union. The Belgian Congo gains independence.

1964 Grand Duchess Charlotte of Luxembourg abdicates in favor of her son, Jean.

1967 Already the center of the EEC, Brussels becomes host to NATO.

1993 King Baudouin of Belgium dies and is succeeded by his brother, Albert II.

1994 Belgium becomes a confederation with Flanders, Wallonia, and Brussels as semi-autonomous regions.

1995 Jacques Santer, Prime Minister of Luxembourg, is elected President of the European Commission.

— Anita Guerrini

LES MOULES SONT ARRIVÉES!

DAMP AND COLD mist the leaded-glass windows, but inside the café glows a scene worthy of a Flemish Master. The burnished wooden banquettes are Rembrandt's; the lace curtain, Vermeer's. Hals would have painted the diner, a lone bearded man in rumpled black leather and heavy, worn wool, his thick fingers clasping a broad-stemmed bowl of mahogany-brown beer. Before him lies a spread of crockery and mollusks, a still-life in themselves: The two-quart pot is heaped high with blue-black mussels, their shells flecked with bits of onion and celery, the broth beneath them steaming; beside them a bowl piled high with yellow *frites* (french fries), crisp and glistening; in the corner, a saucer of slabs of floury-gold cracked-wheat bread. The man works studiously, absorbed in a timeless ritual: Fish out the shell from the broth with fingers inured to the heat by years of practice. Pluck out the plump flesh with a fork and, while chewing the morsel, chuck the shell aside on a crockery plate. Sometimes he sets down the fork and uses the empty shell as pincers to draw out the meat of the next shell. As the meal progresses, the pile in the pot shrinks and the heap of empty shells grows. As the beer follows the mussels, its strong tonic paints the man's cheeks until two ruby patches radiate above his beard. The painting's caption: "Man eating moules."

It is the central image of the Flemish lowlands—the Netherlands, Flanders, even leaking into landlocked Wallonie and Luxembourg.

But this warmly lit interior scene wouldn't be as striking without its harsh exterior foil: Mussels, like the Dutch and the Flemish, are creatures of the sea; they flourish in cold, inky waters along rock-crusted shores, clustered and stacked like blue-black crystals in muddy tidal pools. They're a product of caustic sea winds and briny, chilly damp, and their bite tastes like salt air itself.

Most of the mussels consumed in the Benelux region come from the North Sea, above all in the Waddenzee, off the northern coast of the Netherlands. Captured by the billions in great nets along the bottom of specially protected, fenced-off nursery beds, they are sorted by weight and auctioned to wholesalers in Zeeland, who return them to shallow tidal waters to recover from the trip, to mature, and to purge themselves of sandy mud. From there, they are harvested en masse and shipped live across Europe.

The cultivation of mussels dates from Roman times, though legend credits an Irish shipwreck victim who settled in La Rochelle, on the west coast of France; he is said to have noticed great colonies of the mollusks clinging to posts he planted to hold fishing nets. By placing posts closer together and arranging branches between them, he was able to create an ideal breeding ground and, in essence, mass-produce the delicacy. (The French, predictably enough, prefer their own, smaller mussels from the coasts of Brittany and Normandy, insisting that North Sea mussels are fleshy, dull, and vulgarly oversized.)

Scrubbed with stiff brushes under running water, soaked with salt to draw out the sand, and often fed flour to plump and purge them, mussels are served throughout the region in dozens of ways. The building block for French or Walloon recipes: simmering them *à la marinière,* in a savory stock of white wine, shallots, parsley, and butter. It's difficult to improve on this classic method, which brings out the best in mussels' musky sea essence—but chefs have been trying for centuries. Another common version is *à la crème,* the marinière stock thickened with flour-based white sauce and a generous portion of heavy cream. Flemish mussels, on the other hand, are nearly always served in a simple, savory vegetable stock, with bits of celery, leek, and onions creeping into the shells. The Dutch have been known to pickle them, or even to fry them in batter. Those who don't want to get their fingers messy may order their mussels *meunière,* removed from the shells in the kitchen and baked in a pool of garlicky butter. Regardless of the preparation, the Belgians and the Dutch wash their mussels down with beer, the Luxembourgers with an icy bottle of one of the coarser Moselle wines—an Elbling or a Rivaner.

Mussels rations are anything but stingy here, and on your first venture you may be appalled by the size of the lidded pot put before you. It's the shells that create the volume, and once you've plucked out the tender flesh, thrown away the shells, and sipped the broth and succulent strays from a colossal soup spoon, you'll soon find yourself at the bottom of the pot. Don't worry: Many restaurants will whisk it away and come back with Round Two—another mountain of the steamy blue creatures, another pool of savory broth. It's called *moules à volonté* (all you can eat), so gird yourself for a feast: The locals have been doing it for 2,000 years.

— Nancy Coons

BATTLE SCARS FROM THE BULGE

THE FIRST THING the sleepy American soldiers noticed was light—pinpoints of light blinking to the east, distinct in the pitch-black of an early midwinter morning. A second, or seconds, later (depending on their distance from the German frontier), there followed the roar of a thousand exploding shells, the pounding percussion of heavy artillery. Rockets and mortars screamed overhead while at five well-spaced points German foot soldiers poured through gaps in the sparsely protected front line, their way lit by searchlights that bounced off the clouds, flooding the land with eerie, artificial "moonlight."

It was 5:30 AM on December 16, 1944, along the eastern border of Belgium and Luxembourg. The Allied armed forces—having landed at Normandy in June and southern France in August and pressed steadily inland; having pushed the German armies back to the old Siegfried line and liberated France, Belgium, and Luxembourg by September; and having fought viciously, died in droves, and been hungry, filthy, and sleepless for weeks at a time—were reveling in the role of heroes in the relatively calm days before Christmas. That morning they were caught with their pants down in one of the most massive and successful surprise attacks in World War II. It was Hitler's last, desperate effort to regain western Europe, and it was one of the greatest failures of Allied intelligence in the war.

In September 1944, when Hitler first announced secret plans for an all-out attack on the western front, his army could scarcely have been in more desperate straits. More than 3½ million German men had died over the preceding five years, and massive Allied bombing raids were leveling German cities day by day. Not only had the enemy driven the Wehrmacht out of France, Belgium, and Luxembourg, but Italy was being lost in bitter fighting as well, and Russia had penetrated west to Warsaw and Bucharest. The Third Reich was in danger of being choked off from all sides, and Hitler—though not his more prudent commanders—saw no option but to strike out offensively. His goal: to take the all-important port at Antwerp, from where the River Schelde flowed from Belgium through the Netherlands and into the North Sea. By closing in on Antwerp, they would not only cut off the most likely source of new supplies, but also surround and capture some 1 million remaining Allied forces. His strategy: to surprise the Allies by attacking through the improbably rough, virtually impassable forest terrain of the Ardennes in southeastern Belgium and northern Luxembourg. He intended to overwhelm them with massive artillery fire, press on to take the strategic bridges of the River Meuse, reinforce with a second wave, and close out defenders with strong flanks at the north and south. Antwerp could be reached in a week, he insisted, and the Allies would be crippled by winter fog, snow, and mud.

For the task of inspiring a bitter, war-weary army to what seemed even then to be a suicidal mission, Hitler named the aristocratic Gerd von Rundstedt commander in chief in the West. And, in a decision that was to set the tone for one of the most vicious and bloody conflicts in the war, in charge of the Sixth Panzer Army he placed Joseph "Sepp" Dietrich, an early Nazi loyalist and SS commander, chief executioner in the 1934 Nazi Party purge (the Night of the Long Knives), notorious for ordering the execution of more than 4,000 prisoners taken over three days at the Russian front. His kindred spirit: SS Lt. Col. Joachim Peiper, in charge of the SS Panzer Division called Leibstandarte Adolf Hitler and also notorious for brutal executions in Russia. It was Dietrich who passed on Hitler's inspirational message that this was "the decisive hour of the German people," that the attacking army was to create a "wave of terror and fright" without "humane inhibitions."

While the Germans were building up staggering quantities of materiel along the Siegfried line—tanks, artillery, rafts, and pontoons—and moving in men from all corners of the shrinking Reich, the Allied command remained remarkably unperceptive. Reconnaissance pilots flew over unwonted activity near Bitburg, Trier, and

Koblenz—trains, truck convoys, heaps of equipment along the roads. Messages were intercepted and deciphered, some asking for increased forces, some for more detailed information on Ardennes and Meuse terrain. Yet Generals Bradley, Eisenhower, Middleton, and Patton continued to misinterpret, anticipating instead a predictable counterattack around Aachen and Cologne, well north of the Ardennes. (Hitler, in fact, counted on this interpretation, strutting a visible buildup of forces in the north while secretly preparing to attack elsewhere.) On December 12, an optimistic Allied intelligence summary described the vulnerability and "deathly weakness" of German forces in the area.

ON THE EVENING of December 15, the German soldiers—until then as unaware of the plan as the Allies—were finally told what morning would bring. The message from von Rundstedt: "We gamble everything . . . to achieve things beyond human possibilities for our Fatherland and our Führer!" Some, convinced the cause was lost, faced the news of further carnage with dismay; others saw a final opportunity to avenge the civilian death toll in German cities. Members of the SS, the greatest believers in the Nazi effort and thus the least restrained by the niceties of the Geneva Convention, welcomed the "holy task" with a blood lust that was to be more than sated in the weeks to come.

That night, across the border in Luxembourg, German-born film star Marlene Dietrich performed for American soldiers and went to bed early.

They attacked at 5:30 AM with a thoroughness and a ruthlessness that impressed soldiers even through their bewilderment. The assault crippled communications, and word moved as slowly as in the era before telegraph. Twenty miles from one prong of the attack, Gen. Omar Bradley had breakfast at the Hotel Alfa in Luxembourg City and, blithely unaware of the change in situation, headed toward Paris for a meeting with Eisenhower, who had just that day been promoted to five-star General of the Army. Neither heard of the conflict until late afternoon; neither believed, at first sketchy report, that it was anything more than a flash in the pan.

It was. From the first wave of "artillery-prepared" assaults—meaning systems stunned by a barrage of shells, followed by a surge of infantry attacks—to the sharp, startled, and for the most part instinctive defense of the Allies, the offensive was to escalate quickly into a battle of staggering scale, the Americans surprising the Germans in their tenacity, the Germans surprising the Americans with their almost maniacal dedication.

Over a month and a half, the two sides bludgeoned each other, struggling through harsh terrain and winter muck, reducing medieval castles to smoking rubble, and razing villages that had been liberated only months before. The ferocious tone of the fight was set early on: On December 17, SS officers of Lieutenant Colonel Peiper ordered the execution of 130 American prisoners outside Malmédy. The victims were left where they fell, periodically kicked for signs of life, and shot again. A few who survived, hiding the steam of their breath, crawled away when night fell and told their story, and the massacre at Malmédy became a rallying point for the bitter Allies. Prisoners of war were murdered on both sides, and at times the gunfights took on a guerrilla aspect, with those in danger of capture, fearing execution, dissolving into the dense forest to go it alone.

And not only soldiers were killed. On December 18, in and near Stavelot, Peiper's SS troops ordered whole families of civilians from their cellars—women, children, elderly men—and shot them methodically; the toll reached 138. On December 24, SS security men assembled all the men of Bande, screened out those over 32, stripped them of watches and rosaries, and executed them one by one. The sole survivor, before he slugged his way free and dashed for the forest, noticed that his would-be executioner was weeping.

And on December 23, Americans wrought their own kind of horror in Malmédy when Army Air Corps Marauders, headed for the German railroad center of Zulpich, mistakenly emptied 86 bombs on the village center, killing as many of its own troops as innocent citizens. As the people dug out from the rubble on December 24, another misguided swarm of American bombers dropped an even more lethal load, leveling what was left of the center. On December 25, four more planes mistook Malmédy for St. Vith and dropped 64 more bombs. Civilian victims—refugees and residents alike—were laid in rows in the school playground.

IT WASN'T A VERY MERRY Christmas anywhere in the Ardennes that year. Sleepless, shell-shocked, often out of touch, soldiers from both sides huddled in icy pillboxes and snowy foxholes. Propaganda flyers fluttered down, carefully phrased in the recipients' mother tongue. For the Americans, the not-so-inspirational message admonished them: "Why are you here? What are you doing, fighting somebody else's war? You will die and your wife, your mother, your daughters will be left alone. Merry Christmas!" For the Germans, the American pamphlets simply assured them they were losing the war, and that they'd long since lost the battle.

That wasn't altogether clear until well into January. By the time the carnage slowed and the tide turned, the Germans had pressed deep into Belgium, the central thrust "bulging" west to within miles of the Meuse and Dinant. Though Hitler grudgingly ordered retreat from the farthest point of the Bulge on January 8, the Germans fought through January 28, as they were driven all the way back to the Siegfried line.

Some 19,000 American soldiers died, and at least as many Germans. Hundreds of Belgian and Luxembourg citizens died as well, and survivors came back to find their villages flattened, their churches gaping shells, their castles—having survived assault for centuries—reduced to heaps of ancient stone. In Luxembourg, the towns of Diekirch, Clervaux, Vianden, and Echternach were prime battle zones, charred and crumbled. In Belgium, St. Vith, Houffalize, and myriad Ardennes resort towns like La Roche were wasted by artillery "preparation" and the gun-and-grenade battles that ensued. And Bastogne, surrounded, besieged, and pounded by artillery for days, lost what was left of its town center in the concentrated bombing Hitler ordered for Christmas Eve.

Today, throughout the Ardennes region, the faces of monuments and main streets are incongruously new and shiny, their resourceful owners having taken charred, roofless, windowless shells and made the best of the worst by installing new plumbing, modern wiring, efficient windows, central heat. Yet there are scars, visible and invisible. Behind the caulked shrapnel holes, which pock foundations and farmhouse walls here and there, lurk bitter memories that weren't altogether appeased at Nuremburg. And the ugliness of the conflict, distorted by a new generation, occasionally rears its head: On the stone memorial at the crossroads outside Malmédy, where the names of the victims of the massacre have been carved, someone has spray-painted a swastika.

The cultural chasm between the two sides of the battle seems embodied in the two military cemeteries outside Luxembourg City. The American plot at Hamm is a blaze of white-marble glory, its 5,000 graves radiating in graceful arcs under open sun, its well-tended grass worn by the shoes of visitors. The German plot, just down the road at Sandweiler, lies apart, heavily shaded and concealed from view, with a few hundred low, dark-stone crosses marking the graves of some 5,000 men. Yet another 5,000, gathered in battle by the U.S. Army Burial Service and dumped unceremoniously in mass graves, were transferred here and buried under one heavy cross, as many as possible identified in fine print crowded on a broad bronze plaque. Those graves are tended today by busloads of German schoolchildren, who visit in the name of a concept long overdue: *Versöhnung über den Gräbern—Arbeit für den Frieden* (Reconciliation over the graves—work for peace).

— Nancy Coons

BOOKS AND FILMS

Belgium

Luc Sante's *Factory of Facts* (Pantheon, 1998) is ostensibly a memoir, but it's foremost a keenly observed examination of Belgian (particularly Wallonian) sensibilities; it's also one of the rare English-language books about Belgium that isn't also about war.

Barbara Tuchman's *A Distant Mirror* (Knopf, 1978), describing 14th-century European affairs, gives valuable insights, illuminated by memorable vignettes, into the conflicts between Flemish towns and the Crown of France. *The Guns of August* (Bantam, 1982) applies Tuchman's narrative technique to the events, largely in Belgium, of the first month of World War I. John Keegan's *The Face of Battle* (Viking Penguin, 1983) includes a brilliant analysis of the Battle of Waterloo. Leon Wolff's *In Flanders Fields* (Greenwood, 1984) is a classic account of the catastrophic campaign of 1917, while John Toland's *No Man's Land* (Ballantine, 1985) covers the events on the Western Front in 1918.

William Wharton's *A Midnight Clear* (Ballantine, 1983) is a fictional account of the Ardennes battle as seen by American GIs. Hugo Claus's *The Sorrow of Belgium* (Pantheon, 1990), an outstanding novel of life during the occupation, has been translated into many languages from the original Dutch.

Two 19th-century novels well worth dipping into are Georges Rodenbach's *Bruges-la-Morte,* (Dufour, 1986) which was contemporaneous with the rediscovery of Brugge, and Charles de Coster's picaresque *La legende d'Ulenspiegel,* which captures the spirit of Belgian defiance of outside authority. Both have been translated into English.

Maurice Maeterlinck, Marguerite Yourcenar, and Georges Simenon were all Belgian writers working in French. So was Jacques Brel, many of whose songs also contain outstanding poetry. Hergé set many of the *Tintin* cartoon adventures in foreign lands, but Tintin himself remained always the quintessential *bon petit Belge.*

Movies that give a sense of aspects of life in Belgium include the award-winning *Ma Vie en Rose* (*My Life in Pink*; 1997), directed by Alain Berliner, which concerns the threats to comfortable bourgeois culture posed by a little boy who truly believes he will turn into a girl. *La Promesse* (*The Promise*; 1996), a thought-provoking film directed by Jean-Pierre Dardenne and Luc Dardenne, examines the lives of a group of immigrants surviving (or not) on the edge of Belgian society and a boy who becomes involved with them. In the blackly comic *Toto the Hero* (1991) director Jaco Van Dormael transforms an old man's recollections into a somewhat suspect universal portrait of modern man.

Luxembourg

The Grand Duchy of Luxembourg: The Evolution of a Nationhood by James Newcomer (University Press of America, Lanham, MD, 1984) is an extensive, fairly readable history of the Grand Duchy's early woes. *A Time for Trumpets* by Charles B. MacDonald (William Morrow and Company, 1985) gives a blow-by-blow account of the Ardennes offensive, as does *The Battle of the Bulge* by Roland Gaul (two volumes, Schiffer Military Books, 1995).

INDEX

C